EB 9/28/70

# HISTORY OF POLITICAL PHILOSOPHY

# HISTORY

# OF

# POLITICAL

# PHILOSOPHY

EDITED BY

## LEO STRAUSS

CLAREMONT MENS COLLEGE

## JOSEPH CROPSEY

THE UNIVERSITY OF CHICAGO

RAND McNALLY & COMPANY • CHICAGO

JA
81
.S75

4/61 Burg. 25

57301

Fifth Printing, 1969

# PREFACE

This book is intended primarily to introduce undergraduate students of political science to political philosophy. The authors and editors have done their best to take political philosophy seriously, assuming throughout that the teachings of the great political philosophers are important not only historically, as phenomena about which we must learn if we wish to understand societies of the present and the past, but also as phenomena from which we must learn if we wish to understand those societies. We believe that the questions raised by the political philosophers of the past are alive in our own society, if only in the way that questions can be alive which, in the main, are tacitly or unwittingly answered. We have written, further, in the belief that in order to understand any society, to analyze it with any depth, the analyst must himself be exposed to these enduring questions and be swayed by them.

This book is addressed to those who for whatever reason believe that students of political science must have some understanding of the philosophic treatment of the abiding questions; to those who do not believe that political science is scientific as chemistry and physics are—subjects from which their own history is excluded. That the great majority of the profession concurs in the view that the history of political philosophy is a proper part of political science we take to be proved by the very common practice of offering courses on this subject matter.

We tender this book to the public in full awareness that it is not a perfect historical study. It is not even a perfect textbook. It is imperfect of its kind, as we freely acknowledge, because for one thing it is not the work of one hand. If the hand could be found that is moved by a single mind with the necessary grasp of the literature, that hand would write, if it found time, a more coherent, more uniform book, certainly a more comprehensive book—and we will ourselves adopt it when it appears. On the other hand, it must be allowed that the reader of a collaborative work is to some extent compensated for these shortcomings by the variety of viewpoints, talents, and backgrounds that inform the parts of the volume.

We are convinced that even the most excellent textbook could serve only a limited purpose. When a student has mastered the very best secondary account of an author's teaching, he possesses an opinion of that teaching, a hearsay rather than knowledge of it. If the hearsay is accurate, then the student has right opinion; otherwise wrong opinion, but in neither case the knowledge that transcends opinion. We would be under the profoundest possible delusion if we saw nothing paradoxical in inculcating opinion about what is meant to transcend opinion. We do not believe that this textbook or any other can be more than a help or a guide to students who, while they read it, are at the same time emphatically directed to the original texts.

We have had to decide to include certain authors and subjects and to omit others. In doing so we have not meant to prejudge the issue as to what part of political philosophy is alive or deserves to be alive. Surely an argument could be made for the inclusion of Dante, Bodin, Thomas More, and Harrington, and for the exclusion of the Muslim and Jewish medievals and of Descartes, for example. The amount of space devoted to each author could also be questioned, as could our abstaining from the practice of mentioning writers' names for the sole purpose of bringing them before the student's eye. We will not bore the reader with a repetition of the anthologist's prayer for the remission of sins. Everyone knows that there cannot be a book like this without decisions and there cannot be a decision without a question as to its rightness. The most we will assert is that we believe we could defend our deeds.

We should like last to record our gratitude to the personnel of Rand McNally & Company, who have done everything possible to lighten our task. Those who ever have served as editors will know immediately the value of the publisher's cordial assistance; others could never imagine it.

L.S.
J.C.

*Note:* At the end of each chapter, a reading suggestion is given, divided into two parts. The part designated as A contains the works or selections that in our opinion are indispensable to the student's understanding, while the list headed B contains important additional material that can be assigned if time permits.

# CONTENTS

# INTRODUCTION

Today "political philosophy" has become almost synonymous with "ideology," not to say "myth." It surely is understood in contradistinction to "political science." The distinction between political philosophy and political science is a consequence of the fundamental distinction between philosophy and science. Even this fundamental distinction is of relatively recent origin. Traditionally, philosophy and science were not distinguished: natural science was one of the most important parts of philosophy. The great intellectual revolution of the seventeenth century which brought to light modern natural science was a revolution of a new philosophy *or* science against traditional (chiefly Aristotelian) philosophy *or* science. But the new philosophy or science was only partly successful. The most successful part of the new philosophy or science was the new natural science. By virtue of its victory, the new natural science became more and more independent of philosophy, at least apparently, and even, as it were, became an authority for philosophy. In this way the distinction between philosophy and science became generally accepted, and eventually also the distinction between political philosophy and political science as a kind of natural science of political things. Traditionally, however, political philosophy and political science were the same.

Political philosophy is not the same as political thought in general. Political thought is coeval with political life. Political philosophy, however, emerged within a particular political life, in Greece, in that past of which we have written records. According to the traditional view, the Athenian Socrates (469–399 B.C.) was the founder of political philosophy. Socrates was the teacher of Plato, who in his turn was the

I

teacher of Aristotle. The political works of Plato and Aristotle are the oldest works devoted to political philosophy which have come down to us. The kind of political philosophy which was originated by Socrates is called classical political philosophy. Classical political philosophy was the predominant political philosophy until the emergence of modern political philosophy in the sixteenth and seventeenth centuries. Modern political philosophy came into being through the conscious break with the principles established by Socrates. By the same token classical political philosophy is not limited to the political teaching of Plato and Aristotle and their schools; it includes also the political teaching of the Stoics as well as the political teachings of the church fathers and the Scholastics, in so far as these teachings are not based exclusively on Divine revelation. The traditional view according to which Socrates was the founder of political philosophy is in need of some qualifications, or rather explanations; yet it is less misleading than any alternative view.

Socrates surely was not the first philosopher. This means that political philosophy was preceded by philosophy. The first philosophers are called by Aristotle "those who discourse on nature"; he distinguishes them from those "who discourse on the gods." The primary theme of philosophy, then, is "nature." What is nature? The first Greek whose work has come down to us, Homer himself, mentions "nature" only a single time; this first mention of "nature" gives us a most important hint as to what the Greek philosophers understood by "nature." In the tenth book of the *Odyssey,* Odysseus tells of what befell him on the island of the sorceress-goddess Circe. Circe had transformed many of his comrades into swine and locked them in sties. On his way to Circe's house to rescue his poor comrades, Odysseus is met by the god Hermes who wishes to preserve him. He promises Odysseus an egregious herb which will make him safe against Circe's evil arts. Hermes "drew a herb from the earth and showed me its *nature.* Black at the root it was, like milk its blossom; and the gods call it moly. Hard is it to dig for mortal men, but the gods can do everything." Yet the gods' ability to dig the herb with ease would be of no avail if they did not know the nature of the herb—its looks and its power—in the first place. The gods are thus omnipotent because they are, not indeed omniscient, but the knowers of the natures of the things—of natures which they have not made. "Nature" means here the character of a thing, or of a kind of thing, the way in which a thing or a kind of thing looks and acts, and the thing, or the kind of thing, is taken not to have been made by gods or men. If we were entitled to take a poetic utterance literally, we could say that the first man we know who spoke of nature was the

Wily Odysseus who had seen the towns of many men and had thus come to know how much the thoughts of men differ from town to town or from tribe to tribe.

It seems that the Greek word for nature (*physis*) means primarily "growth" and therefore also that into which a thing grows, the term of the growth, the character a thing has when its growth is completed, when it can do what only the fully grown thing of the kind in question can do or do well. Things like shoes or chairs do not "grow" but are "made": they are not "by nature" but "by art." On the other hand, there are things which are "by nature" without having "grown" and even without having come into being in any way. They are said to be "by nature" because they have not been made and because they are the "first things," out of which or through which all other natural things have come into being. The atoms to which the philosopher Democritus traced everything are by nature in the last sense.

Nature, however understood, is not known by nature. Nature had to be discovered. The Hebrew Bible, for example, does not have a word for nature. The equivalent in biblical Hebrew of "nature" is something like "way" or "custom." Prior to the discovery of nature, men knew that each thing or kind of thing has its "way" or its "custom"—its form of "regular behavior." There is a way or custom of fire, of dogs, of women, of madmen, of human beings: fire burns, dogs bark and wag their tails, women ovulate, madmen rave, human beings can speak. Yet there are also ways or customs of the various human tribes (Egyptians, Persians, Spartans, Moabites, Amalekites, and so on). Through the discovery of nature the radical difference between these two kinds of "ways" or "customs" came to the center of attention. The discovery of nature led to the splitting up of "way" or "custom" into "nature" (*physis*) on the one hand and "convention" or "law" (*nomos*) on the other. For instance, that human beings can speak is natural, but that this particular tribe uses this particular language is due to convention. The distinction implies that the natural is prior to the conventional. The distinction between nature and convention is fundamental for classical political philosophy and even for most of modern political philosophy, as can be seen most simply from the distinction between natural right and positive right.

Once nature was discovered and understood primarily in contradistinction to law or convention, it became possible and necessary to raise this question: Are the political things natural, and if they are, to what extent? The very question implied that the laws are not natural. But obedience to the laws was generally considered to be justice. Hence one was compelled to wonder whether justice is merely conventional or whether there are things which are by nature just. Are even the laws merely conventional or do they have their roots in nature? Must the laws not be "according to nature," and especially according to the nature of man, if they are to be good? The laws are the foundation or the work of the political community: is the political community by nature? In the attempts to answer these questions it was presupposed that there are things which are by nature good for man as man. The precise question therefore concerns the relation of what is by nature good for man, on the one hand, to justice or right on the other. The simple alternative is this: all right is conventional or there is some natural right. Both opposed answers were given and developed prior to Socrates. For a variety of reasons it is not helpful to present here a summary of what can be known of these pre-Socratic doctrines. We shall get some notion of the conventionalist view (the view that all right is conventional) when we turn to Plato's *Republic,* which contains a summary of that view. As for the opposite view, it must suffice here to say that it was developed by Socrates and classical political philosophy in general much beyond the earlier views.

What then is meant by the assertion that Socrates was the founder of political philosophy? Socrates did not write any books. According to the most ancient reports, he turned away from the study of the divine or natural things and directed his inquiries entirely to the human things, *i.e.,* the just things, the noble things, and the things good for man as man; he always conversed about "what is pious, what is impious, what is noble, what is base, what is just, what is unjust, what is sobriety, what is madness, what is courage, what is cowardice, what is the city, what is the statesman, what is rule over men, what is a man able to rule over men," and similar things.[1] It seems that Socrates was induced to turn away from the study of the divine or natural things by his piety. The gods do not approve of man's trying to seek out what they do not wish to reveal, especially the things in heaven and beneath the earth. A pious man will therefore investigate only the things left to men's investigation, *i.e.,* the human things. Socrates pursued his investigations by means of conversations. This means that he started from generally held opinions. Among the generally held opinions the most authoritative ones are those sanctioned by the city and its laws—by the most solemn convention. But the generally held opinions contradict one another. It therefore becomes necessary to transcend the whole sphere of the generally held opinions, or of opinion as such, in the direction of knowledge. Since even the most authoritative opinions are only opinions, even Socrates was compelled to go the way from convention or law to nature, to ascend from law to nature. But now it appears more clearly than ever before that opinion, convention, or law, contains truth, or is not arbitrary, or is in a sense natural. One may say that the law, the human law, thus proves to point to a divine or natural law as its origin. This implies, however, that the human law, precisely because it is not identical with the divine or natural law, is not unqualifiedly true or just: only natural right, justice itself, the "idea" or "form" of justice, is unqualifiedly just. Nevertheless, the human law, the law of the city, is unqualifiedly obligatory for the men subject to it provided they have the right to emigrate with their property, *i.e.,* provided their subjection to the laws of their city was voluntary.[2]

The precise reason why Socrates became the founder of political philosophy appears when one considers the character of the questions with which he dealt in his conversations. He raised the question "What is . . . ?" regarding everything. This question is meant to bring to light the nature of the kind of thing in question, that is, the form or the character of the thing. Socrates presupposed that knowledge of the whole is, above all, knowledge of the character, the form, the "essential" character of every part of the whole, as distinguished from knowledge of that out of which or through which the whole may have come into being. If the whole consists of essentially different parts, it is at least possible that the political things (or the human things) are essentially different from the nonpolitical things—that the political things form a class by themselves and therefore can be studied by themselves. Socrates, it seems, took the primary meaning of "nature" more seriously than any of his predecessors: he realized that "nature" is primarily "form" or "idea." If this is true, he did not simply turn away from the study of the natural things, but originated a new kind of the study of the natural things—a kind of study in which, for example, the nature or idea of justice, or natural right, and surely the nature of the human soul or man, is more important than, for example, the nature of the sun.

One cannot understand the nature of man if one does not understand the nature of human society. Socrates as well as Plato and Aristotle assumed that the most perfect form of human society is the *polis*. The *polis* is today frequently taken to be the Greek city-state. But for the classical political philosophers it was accidental that the *polis* was more common among Greeks than among non-Greeks. One would then have to say that the theme of classical political philosophy was, not the Greek city-state, but the city-state. This presupposes, however, that the city-state is one particular form of "the state." It presupposes therefore the concept of the state as comprising the city-state among other forms of the state. Yet classical political philosophy lacked the concept of "the state." When people speak today of "the state," they ordinarily understand "state" in contradistinction to "society." This distinction is alien to classical political philosophy. It is not sufficient to say that *polis* (city) comprises both state and society, for the concept "city" antedates the distinction between state and society; therefore one does not understand "the city" by saying the city comprises state and society. The modern equivalent to "the city" on the level of the citizen's understanding is "the country." For when a man says, for example, that "the country is in danger," he also has not yet made a distinction between state and society. The reason why the classical political philosophers were chiefly concerned with the city was not that they were ignorant of other forms of societies in general and of political societies in particular. They knew the tribe (the nation) as well as such structures as the Persian Empire. They were chiefly concerned with the city because they preferred the city to those other forms of political society. The grounds of this preference may be said to have been these: tribes are not capable of a high civilization, and very large societies cannot be free societies. Let us remember that the authors of the *Federalist Papers* were still under a compulsion to prove that it is possible for a large society to be republican or free. Let us also remember that the authors of the *Federalist Papers* signed themselves "Publius": republicanism points back to classical antiquity and therefore also to classical political philosophy.

## NOTES

1. Xenophon *Memorabilia* I. 1. 11–16.
2. Plato *Crito* 51$^{d-e}$.

# PLATO

## 427–347 B.C.

Thirty-five dialogues and thirteen letters have come down to us as Platonic writings, not all of which are now regarded as genuine. Some scholars go so far as to doubt that any of the letters is genuine. In order not to encumber our presentation with polemics, we shall disregard the letters altogether. We must then say that Plato never speaks to us in his own name, for in his dialogues only his characters speak. Strictly, there is then no Platonic teaching; at most there is the teaching of the men who are the chief characters in his dialogues. Why Plato proceeded in this manner is not easy to say. Perhaps he was doubtful whether there can be a philosophic teaching proper. Perhaps he, too, thought like his master Socrates that philosophy is in the last analysis knowledge of ignorance. Socrates is indeed the chief character in most of the Platonic dialogues. One could say that Plato's dialogues as a whole are less the presentation of a teaching than a monument to the life of Socrates— to the core of his life: they all show how Socrates engaged in his most important work, the awakening of his fellow men and the attempting to guide them toward the good life which he himself was living. Still, Socrates is not always the chief character in Plato's dialogues; in a few he does hardly more than listen while others speak, and in one dialogue (the *Laws*) he is not even present. We mention these strange facts because they show how difficult it is to speak of Plato's teaching.

All Platonic dialogues refer more or less directly to the political question. Yet there are only three dialogues which indicate by their very titles that they are devoted to political philosophy: the *Republic,* the *Statesman,* and the *Laws*. The political teaching of Plato is accessible to us chiefly through these three works.

7

## THE REPUBLIC

In the *Republic,* Socrates discusses the nature of justice with a fairly large number of people. The conversation about this general theme takes place, of course, in a particular setting: in a particular place, at a particular time, with men each of whom has his particular age, character, abilities, position in society, and appearance. While the place of the conversation is made quite clear to us, the time, *i.e.,* the year, is not. Hence we lack certain knowledge of the political circumstances in which this conversation about the principles of politics takes place. We may assume, however, that it takes place in an era of political decay of Athens, that at any rate Socrates and the chief interlocutors (the brothers Glaukon and Adeimantos) were greatly concerned with that decay and thinking of the restoration of political health. Certain it is that Socrates makes very radical proposals of "reform" without encountering serious resistance. But there are also a few indications in the *Republic* to the effect that the longed-for reformation is not likely to succeed on the political plane or that the only possible reformation is that of the individual man.

The conversation opens with Socrates' addressing a question to the oldest man present, Kephalos, who is respectable on account of his piety as well as his wealth. Socrates' question is a model of propriety. It gives Kephalos an opportunity to speak of everything good which he possesses, to display his happiness, as it were, and it concerns the only subject about which Socrates could conceivably learn something from him: about how it feels to be very old. In the course of his answer Kephalos comes to speak of injustice and justice. He seems to imply that justice is identical with telling the truth and paying back what one has received from anyone. Socrates shows him that telling the truth and returning another man's property are not always just. At this point Kephalos' son and heir, Polemarchos, rising in defense of his father's opinion, takes the place of his father in the conversation. But the opinion which he defends is not exactly the same as his father's; if we may make use of a joke of Socrates', Polemarchos inherits only half, and perhaps even less than a half, of his father's intellectual property. Polemarchos no longer maintains that telling the truth is essential to justice. Without knowing it, he thus lays down one of the principles of the *Republic.* As appears later in the work, in a well-ordered society it is necessary that one tell untruths of a certain kind to children and even to the adult subjects.[1] This example reveals the character of the discussion which occurs in the first book of the *Republic,* where Socrates refutes a number of false opinions about justice. This negative or destructive work, however, contains within itself the constructive assertions of the bulk of the *Republic*. Let us consider from this point of view the three opinions on justice discussed in the first book.

Kephalos' opinion as taken up by Polemarchos (after his father had left to perform an act of piety) is to the effect that justice consists in returning deposits. More generally stated, Kephalos holds that justice consists in returning, leaving, or giving to everyone what belongs to him. But he also holds that justice is good, *i.e.,* salutary, not only to the giver but also to the receiver. Now it is obvious that in some cases giving to a man what belongs to him is harmful to him. Not all men make a good or wise use of what belongs to them, of their property. If we judge very strictly, we might be driven to say that very few people make a wise use of their property. If justice is to be salutary, we might be compelled to demand that everyone should own only what is "fitting" for him, what is good for him, and for as long as it is good for him. In brief, we might be compelled to demand the abolition of private property or the introduction of communism. To the extent to which there is a connection between private property and the family, we would even be compelled to demand abolition of the family or the introduction of absolute communism, *i.e.,* of communism not only regarding property but regarding women and children as well. Above all, extremely few people will be able to determine wisely which things and which amounts of them are good for the use of each individual— or at any rate for each individual who counts; only men of exceptional wisdom are able to do this. We would then be compelled to demand that society be ruled by simply wise men, by philosophers in the strict sense, wielding absolute power. The refutation of Kephalos' view of justice thus contains the proof of the necessity of absolute communism in the sense defined, as well as of the absolute rule of the philosophers. This proof, it is hardly necessary to say, is based on the disregard of, or the abstraction from, a number of most relevant things; it is "abstract" in the extreme. If we wish to understand the *Republic,* we must find out what these disregarded things are and why they are disregarded. The *Republic* itself, carefully read, supplies the answers to these questions.

Before going any further, we must dispose of a misunderstanding which is at present very common. The theses of the *Republic* summarized in the two preceding paragraphs clearly show that Plato, or at any rate Socrates, was not a liberal democrat. They also suffice to show that Plato was not a Communist in the sense of Marx, or a Fascist: Marxist communism and fascism are incompatible with the rule of philosophers, whereas the scheme of the *Republic* stands or falls by the rule of philosophers. But let us hasten back to the *Republic*.

Whereas the first opinion on justice was only implied by Kephalos and stated by Socrates, the second opinion is stated by Polemarchos, although not without Socrates' assistance. Furthermore, Kephalos' opinion is linked in his mind with the view that injustice is bad because it is punished by the gods after death. This view forms no part of Polemarchos' opinion. He is confronted with the contradiction between the two opinions according to which justice must be salutary to the receiver and justice consists in giving to each what belongs to him. Polemarchos overcomes the contradiction by dropping the second opinion. He also modifies the first. Justice, he says, consists in helping one's friends and harming one's enemies. Justice thus understood would seem to be unqualifiedly good for the giver and for those receivers who are good to the giver. This difficulty, however, arises: If justice is taken to be giving to others what belongs to them, the only thing which the just man must know is what belongs to anyone with whom he has any dealing; this knowledge is supplied by the law, which in principle can be easily known by mere listening. But if the just man must give to his friends what is good for them, he himself must judge; he himself must be able correctly to distinguish friends from enemies; he himself must know what is good for each of his friends. Justice must include knowledge of a high order. To say the least, justice must be an art comparable to medicine, the art which knows and produces what is good for human bodies. Polemarchos is unable to identify the knowledge or the art which goes with justice or which is justice. He is therefore unable to show how justice can be salutary. The discussion points to the view that justice is the art which gives to each man what is good for his soul, *i.e.,* that justice is identical with, or at least inseparable from, philosophy, the medicine of the soul. It points to the view that there cannot be justice among men unless the philosophers rule. But Socrates does not yet state this view. Instead he makes clear to Polemarchos that the just man will help just men rather than his "friends," and he will harm no one. He does not say that the just man will help everyone. Perhaps he means that there are human beings whom he cannot benefit. But he surely also means something more. Polemarchos' thesis may be taken to reflect a most potent opinion regarding justice—the opinion according to which justice means public-spiritedness, full dedication to one's city as a particular society which as such is potentially the enemy of other cities. Justice so understood is patriotism, and consists indeed in helping one's friends, *i.e.,* one's fellow citizens, and harming one's enemies, *i.e.,* foreigners. Justice thus understood cannot be entirely dispensed with in any city however just, for even the most just city is a city, a particular or closed or exclusive society. Therefore Socrates himself demands later in the dialogue that the guardians of the city be by nature friendly to their own people and harsh or nasty to strangers.[2] He also demands that the citizens of the just city cease to regard all human beings as their brothers and limit the feelings and actions of fraternity to their fellow citizens alone.[3] The opinion of Polemarchos properly understood is the only one among the generally known views of justice discussed in the first book of the *Republic* which is entirely preserved in the positive or constructive part of the *Republic*. This opinion, to repeat, is to the effect that justice is full dedication to the common good; it demands that man withhold nothing of his own from his city; it demands therefore by itself—*i.e.*, if we abstract from all other considerations—absolute communism.

The third and last opinion discussed in the first book of the *Republic* is the one maintained by Thrasymachos. He is the only speaker in the work who exhibits anger and behaves discourteously and even savagely. He is highly indignant over the result of Socrates' conversation with Polemarchos. He seems to be particularly shocked by Socrates' contention that it is not good for oneself to harm anyone or that justice is never harmful to anyone. It is most important, both for the understanding of the *Republic* and generally, that we do not behave toward Thrasymachos as Thrasymachos behaves, *i.e.*, angrily, fanatically, or savagely. If we look then at Thrasymachos' indignation without indignation, we must admit that his violent reaction is to some extent a revolt of common sense. Since the city as city is a society which from time to time must wage war, and war is inseparable from harming innocent people,[4] the unqualified condemnation of harming human beings would be tantamount to the condemnation of even the justest city. Apart from this, it seems to be entirely fitting that the most savage man present should maintain a most savage thesis on justice. Thrasymachos contends that justice is the advantage of the stronger. Still, this thesis proves to be only the consequence of an opinion which is not only not manifestly savage but is even highly respectable. According to that opinion, the just is the same as the lawful or legal, *i.e.*, what the customs or laws of the city prescribe. Yet this opinion implies that there is nothing higher to which one can appeal from the man-made laws or conventions. This is the opinion now known by the name of "legal positivism," but in its origin it is not academic; it is the opinion on which all political societies tend to act. If the just is identical with the legal, the source of justice is the will of the legislator. The legislator in each city is the regime—the man or body of men that rules the city: the tyrant, the common people, the men of excellence, and so on. According to Thrasymachos, each regime lays down the laws with a

view to its own preservation and well-being, in a word, to its own
advantage and to nothing else. From this it follows that obedience to
the laws or justice is not necessarily advantageous to the ruled and may
even be bad for them. And as for the rulers, justice simply does not
exist: they lay down the laws with exclusive concern for their own
advantage.

Let us concede for a moment that Thrasymachos' view of law and
of rulers is correct. The rulers surely may make mistakes. They may command actions which are in fact disadvantageous to themselves and
advantageous to the ruled. In that case the just or law-abiding subjects
will in fact do what is disadvantageous to the rulers and advantageous
to the subjects. When this difficulty is pointed out to him by Socrates,
Thrasymachos declares after some hesitation that the rulers are not
rulers if and when they make mistakes: the ruler in the strict sense is
infallible, just as the artisan in the strict sense is infallible. It is this
Thrasymachean notion of "the artisan in the strict sense" which Socrates uses with great felicity against Thrasymachos. For the artisan in
the strict sense proves to be concerned, not with his own advantage,
but with the advantage of the others whom he serves: the shoemaker
makes shoes for others and only accidentally for himself; the physician
prescribes things to his patients with a view to their advantage; hence
if ruling is, as Thrasymachos admitted, something like an art, the
ruler serves the ruled, *i.e.,* rules for the advantage of the ruled. The
artisan in the strict sense is infallible, *i.e.,* does his job well, and he is
only concerned with the well-being of others. This, however, means
that art strictly understood is justice—justice in deed, and not merely
in intention as law-abidingness is. "Art is justice"—this proposition reflects the Socratic assertion that virtue is knowledge. The suggestion
emerging from Socrates' discussion with Thrasymachos leads to the
conclusion that the just city will be an association where everyone is
an artisan in the strict sense, a city of craftsmen or artificers, of men
(and women) each of whom has a single job which he does well and
with full dedication, *i.e.,* without minding his own advantage and only
for the good of others or for the common good. This conclusion
pervades the whole teaching of the *Republic.* The city constructed there
as a model is based on the principle of "one man one job." The soldiers
in it are "artificers" of the freedom of the city; the philosophers in it
are "artificers" of the whole common virtue; there is an "artificer" of
heaven; even God is presented as an artisan—as the artificer even of the
eternal ideas.[5] It is because citizenship in the just city is craftsmanship
of one kind or another, and the seat of craftsmanship or art is in the
soul and not in the body, that the difference between the two sexes

loses its importance, or the equality of the two sexes is established.[6]

Thrasymachos could have avoided his downfall if he had left matters at the common-sense view according to which rulers are of course fallible, or if he had said that all laws are framed by the rulers with a view to their apparent (and not necessarily true) advantage. Since he is not a noble man, we are entitled to suspect that he chose the alternative which proved fatal to him with a view to his own advantage. Thrasymachos was a famous teacher of rhetoric, the art of persuasion. (Hence, incidentally, he is the only man possessing an art who speaks in the *Republic*.) The art of persuasion is necessary for persuading rulers and especially ruling assemblies, at least ostensibly, of their true advantage. Even the rulers themselves need the art of persuasion in order to persuade their subjects that the laws, which are framed with exclusive regard to the benefit of the rulers, serve the benefit of the subjects. Thrasymachos' own art stands or falls by the view that prudence is of the utmost importance for ruling. The clearest expression of this view is the proposition that the ruler who makes mistakes is no longer a ruler at all.

Thrasymachos' downfall is caused not by a stringent refutation of his view of justice nor by an accidental slip on his part but by the conflict between his depreciation of justice or his indifference to justice and the implication of his art: there is some truth in the view that art is justice. One could say—and as a matter of fact Thrasymachos himself says—that Socrates' conclusion, namely, that no ruler or other artisan ever considers his own advantage, is very simple-minded: Socrates seems to be a babe in the woods. As regards the artisans proper, they of course consider the compensation which they receive for their work. It may be true that to the extent to which the physician is concerned with what is characteristically called his honorarium, he does not exercise the art of the physician but the art of money-making; but since what is true of the physician is true of the shoemaker and any other craftsman as well, one would have to say that the only universal art, the art accompanying all arts, the art of arts, is the art of money-making; one must therefore further say that serving others or being just becomes good for the artisan only through his practicing the art of money-making, or that no one is just for the sake of justice, or that no one likes justice as such. But the most devastating argument against Socrates' reasoning is supplied by the arts which are manifestly concerned with the most ruthless and calculating exploitation of the ruled by the rulers. Such an art is the art of the shepherd—the art wisely chosen by Thrasymachos in order to destroy Socrates' argument, especially since kings and other rulers have been compared to shepherds since the oldest times. The shepherd is surely concerned with the well-being of his flock—so that the sheep will supply men with the juiciest lamb chops. As Thrasymachos puts it, the shepherds are exclusively concerned with the good of the owners and of themselves.[7] But there is obviously a difference between the owners and the shepherds: the juiciest lamb chops are for the owner and not for the shepherd, unless the shepherd is dishonest. Now, the position of Thrasymachos or of any man of his kind with regard to both rulers and ruled is precisely that of the shepherd with regard to both the owners and the sheep: Thrasymachos can securely derive benefit from the assistance which he gives to the rulers (regardless of whether they are tyrants, common people, or men of excellence) only if he is loyal to them, if he does his job for them well, if he keeps his part of the bargain, if he is just. Contrary to his assertion, he must grant that a man's justice is salutary, not only to others and especially to the rulers, but also to himself. It is partly because he has become aware of this necessity that he changes his manners so remarkably in the last part of the first book. What is true of the helpers of rulers is true of the rulers themselves and all other human beings (including tyrants and gangsters) who need the help of other men in their enterprises however unjust: no association can last if its members do not practice justice among themselves.[8] This, however, amounts to an admission that justice may be a mere means, if an indispensable means, for injustice—for the exploitation of outsiders. Above all, it does not dispose of the possibility that the city is a community held together by collective selfishness and nothing else, or that there is no fundamental difference between the city and a gang of robbers. These and similar difficulties explain why Socrates regards his refutation of Thrasymachos as insufficient: he says at its conclusion that he has tried to show that justice is good without having made clear what justice is.

The adequate defense or praise of justice presupposes not only knowledge of what justice is, but also an adequate attack on justice. At the beginning of the second book, Glaukon attempts to present such an attack; he claims that he restates Thrasymachos' thesis, in which he does not believe, with greater vigor than Thrasymachos had done. Glaukon also takes it for granted that the just is the same as the legal or conventional, but he attempts to show how convention emerges out of nature. By nature each man is concerned only with his own good and wholly unconcerned with any other man's good to the point that he has no hesitation whatever about harming his fellows. Since everyone acts accordingly, they all bring about a situation which is unbearable for most of them; the majority, i.e., the weaklings, figure out that every one of them would be better off if they agreed among themselves as to what each of them may or may not do. What they agree upon is not stated by Glaukon, but part of it can easily be guessed: they will agree that no one may violate the life and limb, the honor, the liberty, and the property of any of the associates, *i.e.,* the fellow citizens, and that everyone must do his best to protect his associates against outsiders. Both the abstention from such violations and the service of protection are in no way desirable in themselves but only necessary evils, yet lesser evils than universal insecurity. But what is true of the majority is not true of "the real man" who can take care of himself and who is better off if he does not submit to law or convention. Yet even the others do violence to their nature by submitting to law and justice: they submit to it only from fear of the consequences of the failure to submit, *i.e.,* from fear of punishment of one kind or another, not voluntarily and gladly. Therefore every man would prefer injustice to justice if he could be sure of escaping detection: justice is preferable to injustice only with a view to possible detection, to one's becoming known as just to others, *i.e.,* to good repute or other rewards. Therefore since, as Glaukon hopes, justice is choiceworthy for its own sake, he demands from Socrates a proof that the life of the just man is preferable to that of the unjust man even if the just man is thought to be unjust in the extreme and suffers all kinds of punishment or is in the depth of misery, and the unjust man is thought to be of consummate justice and receives all kinds of reward or is at the peak of happiness: the height of injustice, *i.e.,* of the conduct according to nature, is the tacit exploitation of law or convention for one's own benefit alone, the conduct of the supremely shrewd and manly tyrant. In the discussion with Thrasymachos, the issue had become blurred by the suggestion that there is a kinship between justice and art. Glaukon makes the issue manifest by comparing the perfectly unjust man to the perfect artisan, whereas he conceives of the perfectly just man as a simple man who has no quality other than justice. With a view to the teaching of the *Republic* as a whole, one is tempted to say that Glaukon understands pure justice in the light of pure fortitude; his perfectly just man reminds one of the unknown soldier who undergoes the most painful and most humiliating death for no other purpose whatsoever except in order to die bravely and without any prospect of his noble deed ever becoming known to anyone.

Glaukon's demand on Socrates is strongly supported by Adeimantos. It becomes clear from Adeimantos' speech that Glaukon's view according to which justice is choiceworthy entirely for its own sake is altogether novel, for in the traditional view justice was regarded as choiceworthy chiefly, if not exclusively, because of the divine rewards for justice and the divine punishments for injustice, and various other consequences. Adeimantos' long speech differs from Glaukon's because it brings out the fact that if justice is to be choiceworthy for its own sake, it must be easy or pleasant.[9] Glaukon's and Adeimantos' demands establish the standard by which one must judge Socrates' praise of justice; they force one to investigate whether or to what extent Socrates has proved in the *Republic* that justice is choiceworthy for its own sake or pleasant or even by itself sufficient to make a man perfectly happy in the midst of what is ordinarily believed to be the most extreme misery.

In order to defend the cause of justice, Socrates turns to founding, together with Glaukon and Adeimantos, a city in speech. The reason why this procedure is necessary can be stated as follows. Justice is believed to be law-abidingness or the firm will to give to everyone what belongs to him, *i.e.,* what belongs to him according to law; yet justice is also believed to be good or salutary; but obedience to the laws or giving to everyone what belongs to him according to law is not unqualifiedly salutary since the laws may be bad; justice will be simply salutary only when the laws are good, and this requires that the regime from which the laws flow is good: justice will be fully salutary only in a good city. Socrates' procedure implies, furthermore, that he knows of no actual city which is good; this is the reason why he is compelled to found a good city. He justifies his turning to the city by the consideration that justice can be detected more easily in the city than in the human individual because the former is larger than the latter; he thus implies that there is a parallelism between the city and the human individual or, more precisely, between the city and the soul of the human individual. This means that the parallelism between the city and the human individual is based upon a certain abstraction from the human body. To the extent to which there is a parallelism between the city and the human individual or his soul, the city is at least similar to a natural being. Yet that parallelism is not complete. While the city and the individual seem equally to be able to be just, it is not certain that they can be equally happy (cf. the beginning of the fourth book). The distinction between the justice of the individual and his happiness was prepared by Glaukon's demand on Socrates that justice should be praised regardless of whether or not it has any extraneous attractions. It is also prepared by the common opinion according to which justice requires complete dedication of the individual to the common good.

The founding of the good city takes place in three stages: the healthy city or the city of pigs, the purified city or the city of the armed camp, and the City of Beauty or the city ruled by philosophers.

The founding of the city is preceded by the remark that the city has its origin in human need: every human being, just or unjust, is in need of many things, and at least for this reason in need of other human beings. The healthy city satisfies properly the primary needs, the needs of the body. The proper satisfaction requires that each man exercise only one art. This means that everyone does almost all his work for others but also that the others work for him. All will exchange with one another their own products as their own products: there will be private property; by working for the advantage of others everyone works for his own advantage. The reason why everyone will exercise only one art is that men differ from one another by nature, *i.e.,* different men are gifted for different arts. Since everyone will exercise that art for which he is by nature fitted, the burden will be easier on everyone. The healthy city is a happy city: it knows no poverty, no coercion or government, no war and eating of animals. It is happy in such a way that every member of it is happy: it does not need government because there is perfect harmony between everyone's service and his reward; no one encroaches on anyone else. It does not need government because everyone chooses by himself the art for which he is best fitted; there is no disharmony between natural gifts and preferences. There is also no disharmony between what is good for the individual (his choosing the art for which he is best fitted by nature) and what is good for the city: nature has so arranged things that there is no surplus of blacksmiths or deficit of shoemakers. The healthy city is happy because it is just, and it is just because it is happy; in the healthy city, justice is easy or pleasant and free from any tincture of self-sacrifice. It is just without anyone's concerning himself with its justice; it is just by nature. Nevertheless, it is found wanting. It is impossible for the same reason that anarchism in general is impossible. Anarchism would be possible if men could remain innocent, but it is of the essence of innocence that it is easily lost; men can be just only through knowledge, and men cannot acquire knowledge without effort and without antagonism. Differently stated, while the healthy city is just in a sense, it lacks virtue or excellence: such justice as it possesses is not virtue. Virtue is impossible without toil, effort, or repression of the evil in oneself. The healthy city is a city in which evil is only dormant. Death is mentioned only when the transition from the healthy city to the next stage has already begun.[10] The healthy city is called a city of pigs not by Socrates but by Glaukon. Glaukon does not quite know what he says. Literally speaking, the healthy city is a city without pigs.[11]

Before the purified city can emerge or rather be established, the healthy city must have decayed. Its decay is brought about by the emancipation of the desire for unnecessary things, *i.e.,* for things which are not necessary for the well-being or health of the body. Thus the luxurious or feverish city emerges, the city characterized by the striving for the unlimited acquisition of wealth. One can expect that in such a city the individuals will no longer exercise the single art for which each is meant by nature but any art or combination of arts which is most lucrative, or that there will no longer be a strict correspondence between service and reward: hence there will be dissatisfaction and conflicts and therefore need for government which will restore justice; hence there will be need for something else which also was entirely absent from the healthy city, *i.e.,* education at least of the rulers, and more particularly education to justice. There will certainly be need for additional territory and hence there will be war, war of aggression. Building on the principle "one man one art," Socrates demands that the army consist of men who have no art other than that of warriors. It appears that the art of the warriors or of the guardians is by far superior to the other arts. Hitherto it looked as if all arts were of equal rank and the only universal art, or the only art accompanying all arts, was the art of money-making.[12] Now we receive the first glimpse of the true order of arts. That order is hierarchic; the universal art is the highest art, the art directing all other arts, which as such cannot be practiced by the practitioners of arts other than the highest. This art of arts will prove to be philosophy. For the time being we are told only that the warrior must have a nature resembling the nature of that philosophic beast, the dog. For the warriors must be spirited and hence irascible and harsh on the one hand and gentle on the other, since they must be harsh toward strangers and gentle to their fellow citizens. They must have a disinterested liking for their fellow citizens and a disinterested dislike for foreigners. The men possessing such special natures need in addition a special education. With a view to their work they need training in the art of war. But this is not the education with which Socrates is chiefly concerned. They will be by nature the best fighters and the only ones armed and trained in arms: they will inevitably be the sole possessors of political power. Besides, the age of innocence having gone, evil is rampant in the city and therefore also in the warriors. The education which the warriors more than anyone else need is therefore above all education in civic virtue. That education is "music" education, education especially through poetry and music. Not all poetry and music is apt to make men good citizens in general and good warriors or guardians in particular. Therefore the poetry and music not conducive to this moral-political end must be banished from the city. Socrates is very far from demanding that Homer and Sophocles should be replaced by the makers of edifying trash; the poetry which he demands for the good city must be genuinely poetic. He demands particularly that the gods be presented as models of human excellence, *i.e.,* of the kind of human excellence to which the guardians can and must aspire. The rulers will be taken from among the elite of the guardians. Yet the prescribed education, however excellent and effective, is not sufficient if it is not buttressed by the right kind of institutions, *i.e.,* by absolute communism or by the completest possible abolition of privacy: everyone may enter everyone else's dwelling at will. As reward for their service to the craftsmen proper, the guardians do not receive money of any kind but only a sufficient amount of food, and, we may suppose, of the other necessities.

Let us see in what way the good city as hitherto described reveals that justice is good or even attractive for its own sake. That justice, or the observing of the just proportion between service and reward, between working for others and one's own advantage, is necessary was shown in the discussion with Thrasymachos by the example of the gang of robbers. The education of the guardians as agreed upon between Socrates and Adeimantos is not education to justice.[13] It is education to courage and moderation. The music education in particular, as distinguished from the gymnastic education, is education to moderation, and this means to love of the beautiful, *i.e.,* of what is by nature attractive in itself. Justice in the narrow and strict sense may be said to flow from moderation or from the proper combination of moderation and courage. Socrates thus silently makes clear the difference between the gang of robbers and the good city: the essential difference consists in the fact that the armed and ruling part of the good city is animated by love of the beautiful, by the love of everything praiseworthy and graceful. The difference is not to be sought in the fact that the good city is guided in its relations to other cities, Greek or barbarian, by considerations of justice: the size of the territory of the good city is determined by that city's own moderate needs and by nothing else.[14] The difficulty appears perhaps more clearly from what Socrates says when speaking of the rulers. In addition to the other required qualities, the rulers must have the quality of caring for the city or loving the city; but a man is most likely to love that whose interest he believes to be identical with his own interest or whose happiness he believes to be the condition of his own happiness. The love here mentioned is not obviously disinterested in the sense that the ruler loves the city, or his serving the city, for its own sake. This may explain why Socrates demands that the rulers be honored both while they live and after their death.[15] At any rate the highest degree of caring for the city and for one another will not be forthcoming unless everyone is brought to believe in the falsehood that all fellow citizens, and only they, are brothers.[16] To say the least, the harmony between self-interest and the interest of the city, which was lost with the decay of the healthy city, has not yet been restored. No wonder then that at the beginning of the fourth book Adeimantos expresses his dissatisfaction with the condition of the soldiers in the city of the armed camp. Read within the context of the whole argument, Socrates' reply is to this effect: Only as a member of a happy city can a man be happy; only within these limits can a man, or any other part of the city, be happy; complete dedication to the happy city is justice. It remains to be seen whether complete dedication to the happy city is, or can be, happiness of the individual.

After the founding of the good city is in the main completed, Socrates and his friends turn to seeking where in it justice and injustice are, and whether the man who is to be happy must possess justice or injustice.[17] They look first for the three virtues other than justice (wisdom, courage, and moderation). In the city which is founded according to nature, wisdom resides in the rulers and in the rulers alone, for the wise men are by nature the smallest part of any city, and it would not be good for the city if they were not the only ones at its helm. In the good city, courage resides in the warrior class, for political courage, as distinguished from brutish fearlessness, arises only through education in those by nature fitted for it. Moderation on the other hand is to be found in all parts of the good city. In the present context, moderation does not mean exactly what it meant when the education of the warriors was discussed but rather the control of what is by nature worse by that which is by nature better—that control through which the whole is in harmony. In other words, moderation is the agreement of the naturally superior and inferior as to which of the two ought to rule in the city. Since controlling and being controlled differ, one must assume that the moderation of the rulers is not identical with the moderation of the ruled. While Socrates and Glaukon found the three virtues mentioned in the good city with ease, it is difficult to find justice in it because, as Socrates says, justice is so obvious in it. Justice consists in everyone's doing the one thing pertaining to the city for which his nature is best fitted or, simply, in everyone's minding his own business: it is by virtue of justice thus understood that the other three virtues are virtues.[18] More precisely, a city is just if each of its three parts (the money-makers, the warriors, and the rulers) does its own work and only its own work.[19] Justice is then, like moderation and unlike wisdom and courage, not a preserve of a single part but required of every part. Hence justice, like moderation, has a different character in each of the three classes. One must assume, for instance, that the justice of the wise rulers is affected by their wisdom and the justice of the money-makers is affected by their lack of wisdom, for if even the courage of the warriors is only political or civic courage, and not courage pure and simple,[20] it stands to reason that their justice too—to say nothing of the justice of the money-makers—will not be justice pure and simple. In order to discover justice pure and simple, it then becomes necessary to consider justice in the individual man. This consideration would be easiest if justice in the individual were identical with justice in the city; this would require that the individual or rather his soul consist of the same three kinds of "natures" as the city. A very provisional consideration of the soul seems to establish this re-quirement: the soul contains desire, spiritedness or anger,[21] and reason, just as the city consists of the money-makers, the warriors, and the rulers. Hence we may conclude that a man is just if each of these three parts of his soul does its own work and only its own work, *i.e.,* if his soul is in a state of health. But if justice is health of the soul, and con-versely injustice is disease of the soul, it is obvious that justice is good and injustice is bad, regardless of whether or not one is known to be just or unjust.[22] A man is just if the rational part in him is wise and rules,[23] and if the spirited part, being the subject and ally of the rational part, assists it in controlling the multitude of desires which almost inevitably become desires for more and ever more money. This means, however, that only the man in whom wisdom rules the two other parts, *i.e.,* only the wise man, can be truly just.[24] No wonder then that the just man eventually proves to be identical with the philosopher.[25] The money-makers and the warriors are not truly just even in the just city because their justice derives exclusively from habituation of one kind or another as distinguished from philosophy; hence in the deepest re-cesses of their souls they long for tyranny, *i.e.,* for complete injustice.[26] We see then how right Socrates was when he expected to find injustice in the good city.[27] This is not to deny of course that as members of the good city the nonphilosophers will act much more justly than they would as members of inferior cities.

    The justice of those who are not wise appears in a different light when justice in the city is being considered, on the one hand, and justice in the soul on the other. This fact shows that the parallelism between the city and the soul is defective. This parallelism requires that, just as in the city the warriors occupy a higher rank than the money-makers, so in the soul spiritedness occupy a higher rank than desire. It is very plausible that those who uphold the city against

foreign and domestic enemies and who have received a music education deserve higher respect than those who lack public responsibility
as well as a music education. But it is much less plausible that spiritedness as such should deserve higher respect than desire as such. It is true
that "spiritedness" includes a large variety of phenomena ranging
from the most noble indignation about injustice, turpitude, and meanness down to the anger of a spoiled child who resents being deprived
of anything that he desires, however bad. But the same is also true of
"desire": one kind of desire is *eros,* which ranges in its healthy forms
from the longing for immortality via offspring through the longing
for immortality via immortal fame to the longing for immortality via
participation by knowledge in the things which are unchangeable in
every respect. The assertion that spiritedness is higher in rank than
desire as such is then questionable. Let us never forget that while there
is a philosophic *eros,* there is no philosophic spiritedness;[28] or in other
words that Thrasymachos is much more visibly spiritedness incarnate
than desire incarnate. The assertion in question is based on a deliberate
abstraction from *eros*—an abstraction characteristic of the *Republic.*

This abstraction shows itself most strikingly in two facts: when
Socrates mentions the fundamental needs which give rise to human
society, he is silent about the need for procreation, and when he describes the tyrant, Injustice incarnate, he presents him as *Eros* incarnate.[29] In the thematic discussion of the respective rank of spiritedness
and desire, he is silent about *eros.*[30] It seems that there is a tension between *eros* and the city and hence between *eros* and justice: only
through the depreciation of *eros* can the city come into its own. *Eros*
obeys its own laws, not the laws of the city however good; in the good
city, *eros* is simply subjected to what the city requires. The good city
requires that all love of one's own—all spontaneous love of one's own
parents, one's own children, one's own friends and beloved—be sacrificed to the common love of the common. As far as possible, the love
of one's own must be abolished except as it is love of the city as this
particular city, as one's own city. As far as possible, patriotism takes
the place of *eros,* and patriotism has a closer kinship to spiritedness,
eagerness to fight, "waspishness," anger, and indignation than to *eros.*

While it is harmful to one's soul to jump at Plato's throat because
he is not a liberal democrat, it is also bad to blur the difference between Platonism and liberal democracy, for the premises "Plato is
admirable" and "liberal democracy is admirable" do not legitimately
lead to the conclusion that Plato was a liberal democrat. The founding
of the good city started from the fact that men are by nature different,
and this proved to mean that men are by nature of unequal rank.

They are unequal particularly with regard to their ability to acquire virtue. The inequality which is due to nature is increased and deepened by the different kinds of education or habituation and the different ways of life (communistic or noncommunistic) which the different parts of the good city enjoy. As a result, the good city comes to resemble a caste society. A Platonic character who hears an account of the good city of the *Republic* is reminded by it of the caste system established in ancient Egypt, although it is quite clear that in Egypt the rulers were priests and not philosophers.[31] Certainly in the good city of the *Republic,* not descent but in the first place everyone's own natural gifts determine to which class he belongs. But this leads to a difficulty. The members of the upper class, which lives communistically, are not supposed to know who their natural parents are, for they are supposed to regard all men and women belonging to the older generation as their parents. On the other hand, the gifted children of the noncommunist lower class are to be transferred to the upper class (and vice versa); since their superior gifts are not necessarily recognizable at the moment of their birth, they are likely to come to know their natural parents and even to become attached to them; this would seem to unfit them for transfer to the upper class. There are two ways in which this difficulty can be removed. The first is to extend absolute communism to the lower class; and, considering the connection between way of life and education, also to extend music education to that class.[32] According to Aristotle,[33] Socrates has left it undecided whether in the good city absolute communism is limited to the upper class or extends also to the lower class. To leave this question undecided would be in agreement with Socrates' professed low opinion of the importance of the lower class.[34] Still, there can be only little doubt that Socrates wishes to limit both communism and music education to the upper class.[35] Therefore, in order to remove the difficulty mentioned, he can hardly avoid making an individual's membership in the upper or lower class hereditary and thus violating one of the most elementary principles of justice. Apart from this, one may wonder whether a perfectly clear line between those gifted and those not gifted for the profession of warriors can be drawn, hence whether a perfectly just assignment of individuals to the upper or lower class is possible, and hence whether the good city can be perfectly just.[36] But be this as it may, if communism is limited to the upper class, there will be privacy both in the money-making class and among the philosophers as philosophers, for there may very well be only a single philosopher in the city and surely never a herd: the warriors are the only class which is entirely political or public or entirely dedicated to the city; the warriors alone present therefore the clearest case of the just life in one sense of the word "just."

It is necessary to understand the reason why communism is limited to the upper class or what the natural obstacle to communism is. That which is by nature private or a man's own is the body and only the body.[37] The needs or desires of the body induce men to extend the sphere of the private, of what is each man's own, as far as they can. This most powerful striving is countered by music education which brings about moderation, *i.e.,* a most severe training of the soul of which, it seems, only a minority of men is capable. Yet this kind of education does not extirpate the natural desire of each for things or human beings of his own: the warriors will not accept absolute communism if they are not subject to the philosophers. It thus becomes clear that the striving for one's own is countered ultimately only by philosophy, by the quest for the truth which as such cannot be anyone's private possession. Whereas the private par excellence is the body, the common par excellence is the mind, the pure mind rather than the soul in general. The superiority of communism to noncommunism as taught in the *Republic* is intelligible only as a reflection of the superiority of philosophy to nonphilosophy. This clearly contradicts the result of the preceding paragraph. The contradiction can and must be resolved by the distinction between two meanings of justice. This distinction cannot become clear before one has understood the teaching of the *Republic* regarding the relation of philosophy and the city. We must therefore make a new beginning.

At the end of the fourth book, it looks as if Socrates had completed the task which Glaukon and Adeimantos had imposed on him, for he had shown that justice as health of the soul is desirable not only because of its consequences but above all for its own sake. But then, at the beginning of the fifth book, we are suddenly confronted by a new start, by the repetition of a scene which had occurred at the very beginning. Both at the very beginning and at the beginning of the fifth book (and nowhere else), Socrates' companions make a decision, nay, take a vote, and Socrates who had no share in the decision obeys it.[38] Socrates' companions behave in both cases like a city (an assembly of the citizens), if the smallest possible city.[39] But there is this decisive difference between the two scenes: whereas Thrasymachos was absent from the first scene, he has become a member of the city in the second scene. It could seem that the foundation of the good city requires that Thrasymachos be converted into one of its citizens.

At the beginning of the fifth book Socrates' companions force him to take up the subject of communism in regard to women and children. They do not object to the proposal itself in the way in which Adeimantos had objected to the communism regarding property at the beginning of the fourth book, for even Adeimantos is no longer the same man he was at that time. They only wish to know the precise manner in which the communism regarding women and children is to be managed. Socrates replaces that question by these more incisive questions: (1) Is that communism possible? (2) Is it desirable? It appears that the communism regarding women is the consequence or presupposition of the equality of the two sexes concerning the work they must do: the city cannot afford to lose half of its adult population from its working and fighting force, and there is no essential difference between men and women regarding natural gifts for the various arts. The demand for equality of the two sexes requires a complete upheaval of custom, an upheaval which is here presented less as shocking than as laughable; the demand is justified on the ground that only the useful is fair or noble and that only what is bad, *i.e.,* against nature, is laughable: the customary difference of conduct between the two sexes is rejected as being against nature, and the revolutionary change is meant to bring about the order according to nature.[40] For justice requires that every human being should practice the art for which he or she is fitted by nature, regardless of what custom or convention may dictate. Socrates shows first that the equality of the two sexes is possible, *i.e.,* in agreement with the nature of the two sexes as their nature appears when viewed with regard to aptitude for the practice of the various arts, and then he shows that it is desirable. In proving this possibility, he explicitly abstracts from the difference between the two sexes in regard to procreation.[41] This means that the argument of the *Republic* as a whole, according to which the city is a community of male and female artisans, abstracts to the highest degree possible from the highest activity essential to the city which takes place "by nature" and not "by art."

Socrates then turns to the communism regarding women and children and shows that it is desirable because it will make the city more "one," and hence more perfect, than a city consisting of separate families would be: the city should be as similar as possible to a single human being or to a single living body, *i.e.,* to a natural being.[42] At this point we understand somewhat better why Socrates started his discussion of justice by assuming an important parallelism between the city and the individual: he was thinking ahead of the greatest possible unity of the city. The abolition of the family does not mean of course the introduction of license or promiscuity; it means the most severe regulation of sexual intercourse from the point of view of what is useful for the city or what is required for the common good. The consideration of the useful, one might say, supersedes the consideration of the holy or sacred:[43] human males and females are to be coupled with exclusive regard to the production of the best offspring, in the spirit in which the breeders of dogs, birds, and horses proceed; the claims of *eros* are simply silenced. The new order naturally affects the customary prohibitions against incest, the most sacred rules of customary justice.[44] In the new scheme, no one will know any more his natural parents, children, brothers, and sisters, but everyone will *regard* all men of the older generation as his fathers and mothers, of his own generation as his brothers and sisters, and of the younger generation as his children.[45] This means, however, that the city constructed according to nature lives in a most important respect more according to convention than according to nature. For this reason we are disappointed to see that while Socrates takes up the question of whether communism regarding women and children is possible, he drops it immediately.[46] Since the institution under consideration is indispensable for the good city, Socrates thus leaves open the question of the possibility of the good city, *i.e.,* of the just city, as such. And this happens to his listeners and to the readers of the *Republic* after they have made the greatest sacrifices—such as the sacrifice of *eros* as well as of the family—for the sake of the just city.

Socrates is not for long allowed to escape from his awesome duty to answer the question regarding the possibility of the just city. The manly Glaukon compels him to face that question. Perhaps we should say that by apparently escaping to the subject of war—a subject both easier in itself and more attractive to Glaukon than the communism of women and children—yet treating that subject according to the stern demands of justice and thus depriving it of much of its attractiveness, he compels Glaukon to compel him to return to the fundamental question. Be this as it may, the question to which Socrates and Glaukon return is not the same one which they left. The question which they left was whether the good city is possible in the sense that it is in agreement with human nature. The question to which they return is whether the good city is possible in the sense that it can be brought into being by the transformation of an actual city.[47] The latter question might be thought to presuppose the affirmative answer to the first question, but this is not quite correct. As we learn now, our whole effort to discover what justice is (so that we would be enabled to see how it is related to happiness) was a quest for "justice itself" as a "pattern." By seeking for justice itself as a pattern we implied that the just man and the just city will not be perfectly just but will indeed

approximate justice itself with particular closeness;[48] only justice itself
is perfectly just.[49] This implies that not even the characteristic institutions of the just city (absolute communism, equality of the sexes, and
the rule of the philosophers) are simply just. Now justice itself is not
"possible" in the sense that it is capable of coming into being, because it
"is" always without being capable of undergoing any change whatever.
Justice is an "idea" or "form," one of many "ideas." Ideas are the only
things which strictly speaking "are," *i.e.,* are without any admixture
of nonbeing, because they are beyond all becoming, and whatever is
becoming is between being and nonbeing. Since the ideas are the only
things which are beyond all change, they are in a sense the cause of
all change and all changeable things. For example, the idea of justice
is the cause for anything (human beings, cities, laws, commands, actions) becoming just. They are self-subsisting beings which subsist
always. They are of utmost splendor. For instance, the idea of justice
is perfectly just. But their splendor escapes the eyes of the body. The
ideas are "visible" only to the eye of the mind, and the mind as mind
perceives nothing but ideas. Yet, as is indicated by the facts that there
are many ideas and that the mind which perceives the ideas is radically
different from the ideas themselves, there must be something higher
than the ideas: "the good" or "the idea of the good" which is in a
sense the cause of all ideas as well as of the mind perceiving them.[50]
It is only through perception of "the good" on the part of the human
beings who are by nature equipped for perceiving it that the good city
can come into being and subsist for a while.

The doctrine of ideas which Socrates expounds to Glaukon is very
hard to understand; to begin with it is utterly incredible, not to say that
it appears to be fantastic. Hitherto we have been given to understand
that justice is fundamentally a certain character of the human soul, or
of the city, *i.e.,* something which is not self-subsisting. Now we are
asked to believe that it is self-subsisting, being at home as it were in
an entirely different place than human beings and everything else that
participates in justice.[51] No one has ever succeeded in giving a satisfactory or clear account of this doctrine of ideas. It is possible, however,
to define rather precisely the central difficulty. "Idea" means primarily
the looks or shape of a thing; it means then a kind or class of things
which are united by the fact that they all possess the same "looks,"
*i.e.,* the same character and power, or the same "nature"; therewith
it means the class-character or the nature of the things belonging to the
class in question: the "idea" of a thing is that which we mean by trying
to find out the "what" or the "nature" of a thing or a class of things
(see the Introduction). The connection between "idea" and "nature"

appears in the *Republic* from the facts that "the idea of justice" is called "that which is just by nature," and that the ideas in contradistinction to the things which are not ideas or to the sensibly perceived things are said to be "in nature."[52] This does not explain, however, why the ideas are presented as "separated" from the things which are what they are by participating in an idea or, in other words, why "dogness" (the class character of dogs) should be "the true dog." It seems that two kinds of phenomena lend support to Socrates' assertion. In the first place the mathematical things as such can never be found among sensible things: no line drawn on sand or paper is a line as meant by the mathematician. Secondly and above all, what we mean by justice and kindred things is not as such, in its purity or perfection, necessarily found in human beings or societies; it rather seems that what is meant by justice transcends everything which men can ever achieve; precisely the justest men were and are the ones most aware of the shortcomings of their justice. Socrates seems to say that what is patently true of mathematical things and of the virtues is true universally: there is an idea of the bed or the table just as of the circle and of justice. Now while it is obviously reasonable to say that a perfect circle or perfect justice transcends everything which can ever be seen, it is hard to say that the perfect bed is something on which no man can ever rest. However this may be, Glaukon and Adeimantos accept this doctrine of ideas with relative ease, with greater ease than absolute communism. This paradoxical fact does not strike us with sufficient force because we somehow believe that these able young men study philosophy under Professor Socrates and have heard him expound the doctrine of ideas on innumerable occasions, if we do not believe that the *Republic* is a philosophic treatise addressed to readers familiar with more elementary (or "earlier") dialogues. Yet Plato addresses the readers of the *Republic* only through the medium of Socrates' conversation with Glaukon and the other interlocutors in the *Republic*, and Plato as the author of the *Republic* does not suggest that Glaukon—to say nothing of Adeimantos and the rest—has seriously studied the doctrine of ideas.[53] Yet while Glaukon and Adeimantos cannot be credited with a genuine understanding of the doctrine of ideas, they have heard, and in a way they know, that there are gods like *Dike* or Right,[54] and *Nike* or Victory who is not this or that victory or this or that statue of Nike but a self-subsisting being which is the cause of every victory and which is of unbelievable splendor. More generally, they know that there are gods—self-subsisting beings which are the causes of everything good, which are of unbelievable splendor, and which cannot be apprehended by the senses since they never change their "form."[55] This is not to deny that there is a profound difference between the gods as understood in the "theology"[56] of the *Republic* and the ideas, or that in the *Republic* the gods are in a way replaced by the ideas. It is merely to assert that those who accept that theology and draw all conclusions from it are likely to arrive at the doctrine of ideas.

We must now return to the question of the possibility of the just city. We have learned that justice itself is not "possible" in the sense that anything which comes into being can ever be perfectly just. We learn immediately afterward that not only justice itself but also the just city is not "possible" in the sense indicated. This does not mean that the just city as meant and as sketched in the *Republic* is an idea like "justice itself," and still less that it is an "ideal": "ideal" is not a Platonic term. The just city is not a self-subsisting being like the idea of justice, located so to speak in a superheavenly place. Its status is rather like that of a painting of a perfectly beautiful human being, *i.e.,* it is only by virtue of the painter's painting; more precisely, the just city is only "in speech": it "is" only by virtue of having been figured out with a view to justice itself or to what is by nature right on the one hand and the human all-too-human on the other. Although the just city is decidedly of lower rank than justice itself, even the just city as a pattern is not capable of coming into being as it has been blueprinted; only approximations to it can be expected in cities which are in deed and not merely in speech.[57] What this means is not clear. Does it mean that the best feasible solution will be a compromise so that we must become reconciled to a certain degree of private property (*e.g.,* that we must permit every warrior to keep his shoes and the like as long as he lives) and a certain degree of inequality of the sexes (*e.g.,* that certain military and administrative functions will remain the preserve of the male warriors)? There is no reason to suppose that this is what Socrates meant. In the light of the succeeding part of the conversation, the following suggestion would seem to be more plausible. The assertion according to which the just city cannot come into being as blueprinted is provisional, or prepares the assertion that the just city, while capable of coming into being, is very unlikely to come into being. At any rate, immediately after having declared that only an approximation to the good city can reasonably be expected, Socrates raises the question, what feasible change in the actual cities will be the necessary and sufficient condition of their transformation into good cities? His answer is, the "coincidence" of political power and philosophy: the philosophers must rule as kings, or the kings must genuinely and adequately philosophize. As we have shown in our summary of the first book of the *Republic,* this answer is not altogether surprising. If justice is less the giving or leaving to each what the law assigns to him than the giving or leaving to each what is good for his soul, but what is good for his soul is the virtues, it follows that no one can be truly just who does not know "the virtues themselves," or generally the ideas, or who is not a philosopher.

By answering the question of how the good city is possible, Socrates introduces philosophy as a theme of the *Republic*. This means that in the *Republic,* philosophy is not introduced as the end of man, the end for which man should live, but as a means for realizing the just city, the city as armed camp which is characterized by absolute communism and equality of the sexes in the upper class, the class of warriors. Since the rule of philosophers is not introduced as an ingredient of the just city but only as a means for its realization, Aristotle is justified in disregarding this institution in his critical analysis of the *Republic* (*Politics* II). At any rate, Socrates succeeds in reducing the question of the possibility of the just city to the question of the possibility of the coincidence of philosophy and political power. That such a coincidence should be possible is to begin with most incredible: everyone can see that the philosophers are useless if not even harmful in politics. Socrates, who had some experiences of his own with the city of Athens—experiences to be crowned by his capital punishment— regards this accusation of the philosophers as well-founded, although in need of deeper exploration. He traces the antagonism of the cities toward the philosophers primarily to the cities: the present cities, *i.e.,* the cities not ruled by philosophers, are like assemblies of madmen which corrupt most of those fit to become philosophers, and on which those who have succeeded against all odds in becoming philosophers rightly turn their back in disgust. But Socrates is far from absolving the philosophers altogether. Only a radical change on the part of both the cities and the philosophers can bring about that harmony between them for which they seem to be meant by nature. The change consists precisely in this: that the cities cease to be unwilling to be ruled by philosophers and the philosophers cease to be unwilling to rule the cities. This coincidence of philosophy and political power is very difficult to achieve, very improbable, but not impossible. To bring about the needed change on the part of the city, of the nonphilosophers or the multitude, the right kind of persuasion is necessary and sufficient. The right kind of persuasion is supplied by the art of persuasion, the art of Thrasymachos directed by the philosopher and in the service of philosophy. No wonder then that in our context Socrates declares that he and Thrasymachos have just become friends. The multitude of the nonphilosophers is good-natured and therefore persuadable by the philosophers.[58] But if this is so, why did not the philosophers of old, to say nothing of Socrates himself, succeed in persuading the multitude of the supremacy of philosophy and the philosophers and thus bring about the rule of philosophers and therewith the salvation and the happiness of their cities? Strange as it may sound, in this part of the argument it appears to be easier to persuade the multitude to accept the rule of the philosophers than to persuade the philosophers to rule the multitude: the philosophers cannot be persuaded, they can only be compelled to rule the cities.[59] Only the nonphilosophers could compel the philosophers to take care of the cities. But, given the prejudice against the philosophers, this compulsion will not be forthcoming if the philosophers do not in the first place persuade the nonphilosophers to compel the philosophers to rule over them, and this persuasion will not be forthcoming, given the philosophers' unwillingness to rule. We arrive then at the conclusion that the just city is not possible because of the philosophers' unwillingness to rule.

Why are the philosophers unwilling to rule? Being dominated by the desire for knowledge as the one thing needful, or knowing that philosophy is the most pleasant and blessed possession, the philosophers have no leisure for looking down at human affairs, let alone for taking care of them.[60] The philosophers believe that while still alive they are already firmly settled, far away from their cities, in the Isles of the Blessed.[61] Hence only compulsion could induce them to take part in political life in the just city, i.e., in the city which regards the proper upbringing of the philosophers as its most important task. Having perceived the truly grand, the human things appear to the philosophers to be paltry. The very justice of the philosophers—their abstaining from wronging their fellow human beings—flows from contempt for the things for which the nonphilosophers hotly contest.[62] They know that the life not dedicated to philosophy and therefore in particular the political life is like life in a cave, so much so that the city can be identified with the Cave.[63] The cave dwellers (i.e., the nonphilosophers) see only the shadows of artifacts.[64] That is to say, whatever they perceive they understand in the light of their opinions, sanctified by the fiat of legislators, regarding the just and noble things, i.e., of conventional opinions, and they do not know that these their most cherished convictions possess no higher status than that of opinions. For if even the best city stands or falls by a fundamental falsehood, although a noble falsehood, it can be expected that the opinions on which the imperfect cities rest or in which they believe, will not be true. Precisely the best of the nonphilosophers, the good citizens, are passionately attached to these opinions and therefore violently opposed to philosophy,[65] which is the attempt to go beyond opinion toward knowledge: the multitude is not as persuadable by the philosophers as we sanguinely assumed in an earlier round of the argument. This is the true reason why the coincidence of philosophy and political power is, to say the least, extremely improbable: philosophy and the city tend away from one another in opposite directions.

The difficulty of overcoming the natural tension between the city and the philosophers is indicated by Socrates' turning from the question of whether the just city is "possible" in the sense of being conformable to human nature to the question of whether the just city is "possible" in the sense of being capable of being brought to light by the transformation of an actual city. The first question, understood in contradistinction to the second, points to the question whether the just city could not come into being through the settling together of men who had been wholly unassociated before. It is to this question that Socrates tacitly gives a negative answer by turning to the question of whether the just city could be brought into being by the transformation of an actual city. The good city cannot be brought to light out of human beings who have not yet undergone any human discipline, out of "primitives" or "stupid animals" or "savages" gentle or cruel; its potential members must already have acquired the rudiments of civilized life. The long process through which primitive men become civilized men cannot be the work of the founder or legislator of the good city but is presupposed by him.[66] But on the other hand, if the potential good city must be an old city, its citizens will have been thoroughly molded by their city's imperfect laws or customs, hallowed by old age, and will have become passionately attached to them. Socrates is therefore compelled to revise his original suggestion according to which the rule of philosophers is the necessary and sufficient condition of the coming into being of the just city. Whereas he had originally suggested that the good city will come into being if the philosophers become kings, he finally suggests that the good city will come into being if, when the philosophers have become kings, they expel everyone older than ten from the city, i.e., separate the children completely from their parents and their parents' ways and bring them up in the entirely novel ways of the good city.[67] By taking over a city, the philosophers make sure that their subjects will not be savages; by expelling everyone older than ten, they make sure that their subjects will not be enslaved by traditional civility. The solution is elegant. It leaves one wondering, however, how the philosophers can compel everyone older than ten to obey submissively the expulsion decree, since they cannot yet have trained a warrior class absolutely obedient to them. This is not to deny that Socrates could persuade many fine young men, and even some old ones, to believe that the multitude could be, not indeed compelled, but persuaded by the philosophers to leave their city and their children and to live in the fields so that justice will be done.

The part of the *Republic* which deals with philosophy is the most important part of the book. Accordingly, it transmits the answer to the question regarding justice to the extent to which that answer is given in the *Republic*. The explicit answer to the question of what justice is had been rather vague: justice consists in each part of the city or of the soul "doing the work for which it is by nature best fitted" or in a "kind" of doing that work; a part is just if it does its work or minds its own business "in a certain manner." The vagueness is removed if one replaces "in a certain manner" by "in the best manner" or "well": justice consists in each part doing its work well.[68] Hence the just man is the man in whom each part of the soul does its work well. Since the highest part of the soul is reason, and since this part cannot do its work well if the two other parts too do not do their work well, only the philosopher can be truly just. But the work which the philosopher does well is intrinsically attractive and in fact the most pleasant work, wholly regardless of its consequences.[69] Hence only in philosophy do justice and happiness coincide. In other words, the philosopher is the only individual who is just in the sense in which the good city is just: he is self-sufficient, truly free, or his life is as little devoted to the service of other individuals as the life of the city is devoted to the service of other cities. But the philosopher in the good city is just also in the sense that he serves his fellow men, his fellow citizens, his city, or that he obeys the law. That is to say, the philosopher is just also in the sense in which all members of the just city, and in a way all just members of any city, regardless of whether they are philosophers or nonphilosophers, are just. Yet justice in this second sense is not intrinsically attractive or choiceworthy for its own sake, but is good only with a view to its consequences, or is not noble but necessary: the philosopher serves his city, even the good city, not, as he seeks the truth, from natural inclination, from *eros,* but under compulsion.[70] It is hardly necessary to add that compulsion does not cease to be compulsion if it is self-compulsion. According to a notion of justice which is more common than that suggested by Socrates' definition, justice consists in not harming others; justice thus understood proves to be in the highest case merely a concomitant of the philosopher's greatness of soul. But if justice is taken in the larger sense according to which it consists in giving to each what is good for his soul, one must distinguish between the cases in which this giving is intrinsically attractive to the giver (these will be the cases of potential philosophers) and those in which it is merely a duty or compulsory. This distinction, incidentally, under-lies the difference between the voluntary conversations of Socrates (the conversations which he spontaneously seeks) and the compulsory ones (those which he cannot with propriety avoid). This clear distinction between the justice which is choiceworthy for its own sake, wholly regardless of its consequences, and identical with philosophy, and the justice which is merely necessary and identical in the highest case with the political activity of the philosopher is rendered possible by the abstraction from *eros* which is characteristic of the *Republic*. For one might well say that there is no reason why the philosopher should not engage in political activity out of that kind of love of one's own which is patriotism.[71]

By the end of the seventh book justice has come to sight fully. Socrates has in fact performed the duty laid upon him by Glaukon and Adeimantos to show that justice properly understood is choiceworthy for its own sake regardless of its consequences and therefore that justice is unqualifiedly preferable to injustice. Nevertheless the conversation continues, for it seems that our clear grasp of justice does not include a clear grasp of injustice but must be supplemented by a clear grasp of the wholly unjust city and the wholly unjust man: only after we have seen the wholly unjust city and the wholly unjust man with the same clarity with which we have seen the wholly just city and the wholly just man will we be able to judge whether we ought to follow Socrates' friend Thrasymachos, who chooses injustice, or Socrates him-self, who chooses justice.[72] This in its turn requires that the fiction of the possibility of the just city be maintained. As a matter of fact, the *Republic* never abandons the fiction that the just city as a society of human beings, as distinguished from a society of gods or sons of gods, is possible.[73] When Socrates turns to the study of injustice, it even becomes necessary for him to reaffirm this fiction with greater force than ever before. The unjust city will be uglier and more condemnable in proportion as the just city will be more possible. But the possibility of the just city will remain doubtful if the just city was never actual. Accordingly Socrates now asserts that the just city was once actual. More precisely, he makes the Muses assert it or rather imply it. The assertion that the just city was once actual is, as one might say, a mythical assertion which agrees with the mythical premise that the best is the oldest. Socrates asserts then through the mouth of the Muses that the good city was actual in the beginning, prior to the emergence of the inferior kinds of cities;[74] the inferior cities are decayed forms of the good city, soiled fragments of the pure city which was entire; hence the nearer in time a kind of inferior city is to the just city the better it is, or vice versa. It is more proper to speak of the good and inferior regimes than of the good and inferior cities (observe the transition from "cities" to "regimes" in 543$^d$–544$^a$). "Regime" is our translation of the Greek *politeia*. The book which we call *Republic* is in Greek entitled *Politeia*. *Politeia* is commonly translated by "constitution." The term designates the form of government understood as the form of the city, *i.e.,* as that which gives the city its character by determining the end which the city in question pursues or what it looks up to as the highest, and simultaneously the kind of men who rule the city. For instance, oligarchy is the kind of regime in which the rich rule and therefore admiration for wealth and for the acquisition of wealth animates the city as a whole, and democracy is the kind of regime in which all free men rule and therefore freedom is the end which the city pursues. According to Socrates, there are five kinds of regime: (1) kingdom or aristocracy, the rule of the best man or the best men, that is directed toward goodness or virtue, the regime of the just city; (2) timocracy, the rule of lovers of honor or of the ambitious men which is directed toward superiority or victory; (3) oligarchy or the rule of the rich in which wealth is most highly esteemed; (4) democracy, the rule of free men in which freedom is most highly esteemed; (5) tyranny, the rule of the completely unjust man in which unqualified and unashamed injustice holds sway. The descending order of the five kinds of regime is modeled on Hesiod's descending order of the five races of men: the races of gold, of silver, of bronze, the divine race of heroes, the race of iron.[75] We see at once that the Platonic equivalent of Hesiod's divine race of heroes is democracy. We shall soon see the reason for this seemingly strange correspondence.

The *Republic* is based on the assumption that there is a strict parallelism between the city and the soul. Accordingly Socrates asserts that, just as there are five kinds of regime, so there are five kinds of characters of men, the timocratic man, for instance, corresponding to timocracy. The distinction which for a short while was popular in present-day political science between the authoritarian and the democratic "personalities," as corresponding to the distinction between authoritarian and democratic societies, was a dim and crude reflection of Socrates' distinction between the royal or aristocratic, the timocratic, the oligarchic, the democratic, and the tyrannical soul or man, as corresponding to the aristocratic, timocratic, oligarchic, democratic, and tyrannical regimes. In this connection it should be mentioned that in

describing the regimes, Socrates does not speak of "ideologies" belonging
to them; he is concerned with the character of each kind of regime
and with the end which it manifestly and explicitly pursues, as well
as with the political justification of the end in question in contradistinction to any transpolitical justification stemming from cosmology,
theology, metaphysics, philosophy of history, myth, and the like. In his
study of the inferior regimes Socrates examines in each case first the
regime and then the corresponding individual or soul. He presents
both the regime and the corresponding individual as coming into being out of the preceding one. We shall consider here only his account
of democracy, both because this subject is most important to citizens
of a democracy and because of its intrinsic importance. Democracy
arises from oligarchy, which in its turn arises from timocracy, the rule
of the insufficiently musical warriors who are characterized by the
supremacy of spiritedness. Oligarchy is the first regime in which desire
is supreme. In oligarchy the ruling desire is that for wealth or money,
or unlimited acquisitiveness. The oligarchic man is thrifty and industrious, controls all his desires other than the desire for money, lacks
education, and possesses a superficial honesty derivative from the
crudest self-interest. Oligarchy must give to each the unqualified right
to dispose of his property as he sees fit. It thus renders inevitable the
emergence of "drones," *i.e.,* of members of the ruling class who are
either burdened with debt or already bankrupt and hence disfranchised
—of beggars who hanker after their squandered fortune and hope to
restore their fortune and political power through a change of regime
("Catilinarian existences"). Besides, the correct oligarchs themselves,
being both rich and unconcerned with virtue and honor, render themselves and especially their sons fat, spoiled, and soft. They thus become
despised by the lean and tough poor. Democracy comes into being
when the poor, having become aware of their superiority to the rich
and perhaps being led by some drones who act as traitors to their
class and possess the skills which ordinarily only members of a ruling
class possess, make themselves at an opportune moment masters of the
city by defeating the rich, killing and exiling a part of them, and
permitting the rest to live with them in the possession of full citizen
rights. Democracy itself is characterized by freedom, which includes
the right to say and do whatever one wishes: everyone can follow the
way of life which pleases him most. Hence democracy is the regime
which fosters the greatest variety: every way of life, every regime can
be found in it. Hence, we must add, democracy is the only regime other
than the best in which the philosopher can lead his peculiar way of
life without being disturbed: it is for this reason that with some exag-

geration one can compare democracy to Hesiod's age of the divine race
of heroes which comes closer to the golden age than any other. Certainly in a democracy the citizen who is a philosopher is under no
compulsion to participate in political life or to hold office.[76] One is
thus led to wonder why Socrates did not assign to democracy the highest place among the inferior regimes, or rather the highest place simply,
seeing that the best regime is not possible. One could say that he
showed his preference for democracy "by deed": by spending his whole
life in democratic Athens, by fighting for her in her wars, and by dying
in obedience to her laws. However this may be, he surely did not prefer
democracy to all other regimes "in speech." The reason is that, being a
just man, he thought of the well-being not merely of the philosophers
but of the nonphilosophers as well, and he held that democracy is
not designed for inducing the nonphilosophers to attempt to become as
good as they possibly can, for the end of democracy is not virtue but
freedom, *i.e.,* the freedom to live either nobly or basely according to
one's liking. Therefore he assigns to democracy a rank even lower than
to oligarchy, since oligarchy requires some kind of restraint whereas
democracy, as he presents it, abhors every kind of restraint. One could
say that adapting himself to his subject matter, Socrates abandons all
restraint when speaking of the regime which loathes restraint. In a
democracy, he asserts, no one is compelled to rule or to be ruled if he
does not like it; he can live in peace while his city is at war; capital
punishment does not have the slightest consequence for the condemned
man: he is not even jailed; the order of rulers and ruled is completely
reversed: the father behaves as if he were a boy and the son has neither
respect nor fear of the father, the teacher fears his pupils while the
pupils pay no attention to the teacher, and there is complete equality
of the sexes; even horses and donkeys no longer step aside when encountering human beings. Plato writes as if the Athenian democracy
had not carried out Socrates' execution, and Socrates speaks as if the
Athenian democracy had not engaged in an orgy of bloody persecution of guilty and innocent alike when the Hermes statues were
mutilated at the beginning of the Sicilian expedition.[77] Socrates' exaggeration of the licentious mildness of democracy is matched by an almost equally strong exaggeration of the intemperance of democratic
man. He could indeed not avoid the latter exaggeration if he did not
wish to deviate in the case of democracy from the procedure which he
follows in his discussion of the inferior regimes. That procedure consists in understanding the man corresponding to an inferior regime
as the son of a father corresponding to the preceding regime. Hence
democratic man had to be presented as the son of an oligarchic father,

as the degenerate son of a wealthy father who is concerned with nothing but making money: the democratic man is the drone, the fat, soft,
and prodigal playboy, the lotus-eater who, assigning a kind of equality
to equal and unequal things, lives one day in complete surrender to his
lowest desires and the next ascetically, or who, according to Karl
Marx's ideal, "goes hunting in the morning, fishes in the afternoon,
raises cattle in the evening, devotes himself to philosophy after dinner,"
*i.e.,* does at every moment what he happens to like at that moment:
the democratic man is not the lean, tough and thrifty craftsman or
peasant who has a single job.[78] Socrates' deliberately exaggerated blame
of democracy becomes intelligible to some extent once one considers
its immediate addressee, the austere Adeimantos, who is not a friend
of laughter and who had been the addressee of the austere discussion of
poetry in the section on the education of the warriors: by his exaggerated blame of democracy Socrates lends words to Adeimantos' "dream"
of democracy.[79] One must also not forget that the sanguine account of
the multitude which was provisionally required in order to prove the
harmony between the city and philosophy is in need of being redressed;
the exaggerated blame of democracy reminds us with greater force than
was ever before used of the disharmony between philosophy and the
people.[80]

   After Socrates had brought to light the entirely unjust regime and
the entirely unjust man and then compared the life of the entirely unjust
man with that of the perfectly just man, it became clear beyond the
shadow of a doubt that justice is preferable to injustice. Nevertheless
the conversation continues. Socrates suddenly returns to the question
of poetry, to a question which had already been answered at great
length when he discussed the education of the warriors. We must try
to understand this apparently sudden return. In an explicit digression
from the discussion of tyranny, Socrates had noted that the poets praise
tyrants and are honored by tyrants (and also by democracy), whereas
they are not honored by the three better regimes.[81] Tyranny and
democracy are characterized by surrender to the sensual desires, including the most lawless ones. The tyrant is *Eros* incarnate, and the poets
sing the praise of *Eros*. They pay very great attention and homage precisely to that phenomenon from which Socrates abstracts in the *Republic* to the best of his powers. The poets therefore foster injustice.
So does Thrasymachos. But just as Socrates, in spite of this, could be
a friend of Thrasymachos, so there is no reason why he could not be a
friend of the poets and especially of Homer. Perhaps Socrates needs
the poets in order to restore, on another occasion, the dignity of *Eros*:
the *Banquet,* the only Platonic dialogue in which Socrates is shown
to converse with poets, is devoted entirely to *Eros*.

The foundation for the return to poetry was laid at the very beginning of the discussion of the inferior regimes and of the inferior souls. The transition from the best regime to the inferior regimes was explicitly ascribed to the Muses speaking "tragically," and the transition from the best man to the inferior men has in fact a somewhat "comical" touch[82]: poetry takes the lead when the descent from the highest theme—justice understood as philosophy—begins. The return to poetry, which is preceded by the account of the inferior regimes and the inferior souls, is followed by a discussion of "the greatest rewards for virtue," *i.e.*, the rewards not inherent in justice or philosophy itself.[83] The return to poetry constitutes the center of that part of the *Republic* in which the conversation descends from the highest theme. This cannot be surprising, for philosophy as quest for the truth is the highest activity of man, and poetry is not concerned with the truth.

In the first discussion of poetry, which preceded by a long time the introduction of philosophy as a theme, poetry's unconcern with the truth was its chief recommendation, for at that time it was untruth that was needed.[84] The most excellent poets were expelled from the just city, not because they teach untruth, but because they teach the wrong kind of untruth. But in the meantime it has become clear that only the life of the philosophizing man in so far as he philosophizes is the just life, and that that life, so far from needing untruth, utterly rejects it.[85] The progress from the city, even the best city, to the philosopher requires, it seems, a progress from the qualified acceptance of poetry to its unqualified rejection.

In the light of philosophy, poetry reveals itself to be the imitation of imitations of the truth, *i.e.*, of the ideas. The contemplation of the ideas is the activity of the philosopher, the imitation of the ideas is the activity of the ordinary artisan, and the imitation of the works of artisans is the activity of poets and other "imitative" artisans. To begin with, Socrates presents the order of rank in these terms: the maker of the ideas (*e.g.*, of the idea of the bed) is the God, the maker of the imitation (of the bed which can be used) is the artisan, and the maker of the imitation of the imitation (of the painting of a bed) is the imitative artisan. Later on he restates the order of rank in these terms: first the user, then the artisan, and finally the imitative artisan. The idea of the bed originates in the user who determines the "form" of the bed with a view to the end for which it is to be used. The user is then the one who possesses the highest or most authoritative knowledge: the highest knowledge is not that possessed by any artisans as such at all; the poet who stands at the opposite pole from the user does not possess any knowledge, not even right opinion.[86] In order to understand this seemingly outrageous indictment of poetry one must first identify the artisan whose work the poet imitates. The poets' themes are above all the human things referring to virtue and vice; the poets see the human things in the light of virtue, but the virtue toward which they look is an imperfect and even distorted image of virtue.[87] The artisan whom the poet imitates is the nonphilosophic legislator who is an imperfect imitator of virtue itself.[88] In particular, justice as understood by the city is necessarily the work of the legislator, for the just as understood by the city is the legal. No one expressed Socrates' suggestion more clearly than Nietzsche, who said that "the poets were always the valets of some morality. . . ."[89] But according to the French saying, for a valet there is no hero: Are the artists and in particular the poets not aware of the secret weakness of their heroes? This is indeed the case according to Socrates. The poets bring to light, for instance, the full force of the grief which a man feels for the loss of someone dear to him—of a feeling to which a respectable man would not give adequate utterance except when he is alone, because its adequate utterance in the presence of others is not becoming and lawful: the poets bring to light that in our nature which the law forcibly restrains.[90] If this is so, if the poets are perhaps the men who understand best the nature of the passions which the law restrains, they are very far from being merely the servants of the legislators; they are also the men from whom the prudent legislator will learn. The genuine "quarrel between philosophy and poetry"[91] concerns, from the philosopher's point of view, not the worth of poetry as such, but the order of rank of philosophy and poetry. According to Socrates, poetry is legitimate only as ministerial to the "user" par excellence, to the king who is the philosopher, and not as autonomous. For autonomous poetry presents human life as autonomous, *i.e.,* as not directed toward the philosophic life, and therefore it never presents the philosophic life itself except in its comical distortion; hence autonomous poetry is necessarily either tragedy or comedy since the nonphilosophic life understood as autonomous has either no way out of its fundamental difficulty or only an inept one. But ministerial poetry presents the nonphilosophic life as ministerial to the philosophic life and therefore, above all, it presents the philosophic life itself.[92] The greatest example of ministerial poetry is the Platonic dialogue.

The *Republic* concludes with a discussion of the greatest rewards for justice and the greatest punishments for injustice. The discussion consists of three parts: (1) proof of the immortality of the soul; (2) the divine and human rewards and punishments for men while they are alive; (3) the rewards and punishments after death. The central part is silent about the philosophers: rewards for justice and punishments for injustice during life are needed for the nonphilosophers whose justice does not have the intrinsic attractiveness which the justice of the philosophers has. The account of the rewards and punishments after death is given in the form of a myth. The myth is not baseless, since it is based on the proof of the immortality of the souls. The soul cannot be immortal if it is composed of many things unless the composition is most perfect. But the soul as we know it from our experience lacks that perfect harmony. In order to find the truth, one would have to recover by reasoning the original or true nature of the soul.[93] This reasoning is not achieved in the *Republic*. That is to say, Socrates proves the immortality of the soul without having brought to light the nature of the soul. The situation at the end of the *Republic* corresponds precisely to the situation at the end of the first book of the *Republic* where Socrates makes clear that he has proved that justice is salutary without knowing the "what" or nature of justice. The discussion following the first book does bring to light the nature of justice as the right order of the soul, yet how can one know the right order of the soul if one does not know the nature of the soul? Let us remember here also the fact that the parallelism between soul and city, which is the premise of the doctrine of the soul stated in the *Republic,* is evidently questionable and even untenable. The *Republic* cannot bring to light the nature of the soul because it abstracts from *eros* and from the body. If we are genuinely concerned with finding out precisely what justice is, we must take "another longer way around" in our study of the soul than the way which is taken in the *Republic*.[94] This does not mean that what we learn from the *Republic* about justice is not true or is altogether provisional. The teaching of the *Republic* regarding justice, although not complete, can yet be true in so far as the nature of justice depends decisively on the nature of the city—for even the transpolitical cannot be understood as such except if the city is understood—and the city is completely intelligible because its limits can be made perfectly manifest: to see these limits, one need not have answered the question regarding the whole; it is sufficient to have raised the question regarding the whole. The *Republic* then indeed makes clear what justice is. However, as Cicero has observed, the *Republic* does not bring to light the best possible regime but rather the nature of political things—the nature of the city.[95] Socrates makes clear in the *Republic* what character the city would have to have in order to satisfy the highest needs of man. By letting us see that the city constructed in accordance with this requirement is not possible, he lets us see the essential limits, the nature, of the city.

## THE STATESMAN

The *Statesman* is preceded by the *Sophist,* which in its turn is preceded by the *Theaitetos.* The *Theaitetos* presents a conversation between Socrates and the young mathematician Theaitetos which takes place in the presence of the mature and renowned mathematician Theodoros, as well as of Theaitetos' young companion named Socrates, and which is meant to make clear what knowledge or science is. The conversation does not lead to a positive result: Socrates by himself only knows that he does not know, and Theaitetos is not like Glaukon or Adeimantos who can be assisted by Socrates (or can assist him) in bringing forth a positive teaching. On the day following Socrates' conversation with Theaitetos, Socrates again meets with Theodoros, the younger Socrates, and Theaitetos, but this time there is also present a nameless philosopher designated only as a stranger from Elea. Socrates asks the stranger whether his fellows regard the sophist, the statesman, and the philosopher as one and the same or as two or as three. It could seem that the question regarding the identity or nonidentity of the sophist, the statesman, and the philosopher takes the place of the question, or is a more articulate version of the question, What is knowledge? The stranger replies that his fellows regard the sophist, the statesman or king, and the philosopher as different from one another. The fact that the philosopher is not identical with the king was recognized in the central thesis of the *Republic,* according to which the coincidence of philosophy and kingship is the condition for the salvation of cities and indeed of the human race: identical things do not have to coincide. But the *Republic* did not make sufficiently clear the cognitive status of kingship or statesmanship. From the *Republic* we can easily receive the impression that the knowledge required of the philosopher-king consists of two heterogeneous parts: the purely philosophic knowledge of the ideas which culminates in the vision of the idea of the good, on the one hand, and the merely political experience which does not have the status of knowledge at all but which enables one to find one's way in the Cave and to discern the shadows on its walls, on the other. But the indispensable supplement to philosophic knowledge also seemed to be a kind of art or science.[96] The Eleatic stranger seems to take the second and higher view of the nonphilosophic awareness peculiar to the statesman. Yet in the dialogues *Sophist* and *Statesman* he makes clear the nature of the sophist and of the statesman, *i.e.,* the difference between the sophist and the statesman, without making clear the difference between the statesman and the philosopher. We are promised by Theodoros that the Eleatic stranger will also expound (in a sequel to the

*Statesman*) what the philosopher is, but Plato does not keep his Theodoros' promise. Do we then understand what the philosopher is once we have understood what the sophist and the statesman are? Is statesmanship not, as it appeared from the *Republic,* a mere supplement to philosophy, but an ingredient of philosophy? That is to say, is statesmanship, the art or knowledge peculiar to the statesman, far from being merely the awareness necessary for finding one's way in the Cave and far from being itself independent of the vision of the idea of the good, a condition or rather an ingredient of the vision of the idea of the good? If it were so, then "politics" would be much more important according to the *Statesman* than it is according to the *Republic.* Surely the conversation about the king or statesman takes place when Socrates is already accused of a capital crime for the commission of which he was shortly thereafter condemned and executed (see the end of the *Theaitetos*): the city seems to be much more powerfully present in the *Statesman* than in the *Republic,* where the antagonist of Socrates, Thrasymachos, only plays the city. On the other hand, however, whereas in the *Republic* Socrates founds a city, if only in speech, with the help of two brothers who are passionately concerned with justice and the city, in the *Statesman* Socrates listens silently to a nameless stranger (a man lacking political responsibility) bringing to light what the statesman is in the cool atmosphere of mathematics: the concern with finding out what the statesman is seems to be philosophic rather than political.[97] The *Statesman* seems to be much more sober than the *Republic.*

We may say that the *Statesman* is more scientific than the *Republic.* By "science" Plato understands the highest form of knowledge or rather the only kind of awareness which deserves to be called knowledge. He calls that form of knowledge "dialectics." "Dialectics" means primarily the art of conversation and then the highest form of that art, that art as practiced by Socrates, that art of conversation which is meant to bring to light the "what's" of things, or the ideas. Dialectics is then the knowledge of the ideas—a knowledge which makes no use whatever of sense experience: it moves from idea to idea until it has exhausted the whole realm of the ideas, for each idea is a part and therefore points to other ideas.[98] In its completed form dialectics would descend from the highest idea, the idea ruling the realm of ideas, step by step to the lowest ideas. The movement proceeds "step by step," *i.e.,* it follows the articulation, the natural division of the ideas. The *Statesman* as well as the *Sophist* presents an imitation of dialectics thus understood; both are meant to give an inkling of dialectics thus understood; the imitation which they present is playful. Yet the play is not mere play. If the movement from idea to idea without recourse to sense experience should be impossible, if in other words the *Republic* should be utopian not only in what it states about the city at its best but also in what it says about philosophy or dialectics at its best, dialectics at its best, not being possible, will not be serious. The dialectics which is possible will remain dependent on experience.[99] There is a connection between this feature of the *Statesman* and the fact that the ideas as treated in the *Statesman* are classes or comprise all individuals "participating" in the idea in question and therefore do not subsist independently of the individuals or "beyond" them. However this may be, in the *Statesman* the Eleatic stranger tries to bring to light the nature of the statesman by descending from "art" or "knowledge" step by step to the art of the statesman or by dividing "art" step by step until he arrives at the art of the statesman. For a number of reasons we cannot here follow his "methodical" procedure.

Shortly after the beginning of the conversation, the Eleatic stranger makes young Socrates agree to what one may call the abolition of the distinction between the public and the private. He achieves this result in two steps. Since statesmanship or kingship is essentially a kind of knowledge, it is of no importance whether the man possessing that knowledge is clothed in the vestments of high office by virtue of having been elected, for example, or whether he lives in a private station. Second, there is no essential difference between the city and the household and hence between the statesman or king on the one hand and the householder or master (*i.e.*, the master of slaves) on the other. Law and freedom, the characteristically political phenomena, which are inseparable from one another, are disposed of at the very beginning because statesmanship is understood as a kind of knowledge or art, or because abstraction is made from that which distinguishes the political from the arts. The Eleatic stranger abstracts here from the fact that sheer bodily force is a necessary ingredient of the rule of men over men. This abstraction is partly justified by the fact that statesmanship or kingship is a cognitive rather than a manual (or brachial) art. It is, however, not simply cognitive like arithmetic; it is an art which gives commands to human beings. But all arts which give commands do so for the sake of the coming into being of something. Some of these arts give commands for the sake of the coming into being of living beings or animals, *i.e.*, they are concerned with the breeding and nurture of animals. The kingly art is a kind of this genus of art. For the proper understanding of the kingly art it does not suffice to divide the genus "animal" into the species "brutes" and "men." This distinction is as arbitrary as the distinction of the human race into Greeks and barbarians, as distinguished from the distinction into men and women; it is not a natural distinction but a distinction originating in pride.[100] The stranger's training of young Socrates in dialectics or in the art of dividing kinds or ideas or classes goes hand in hand with training in modesty or moderation. According to the stranger's division of the species of animals, man's nearest kin is even lower than it is according to Darwin's doctrine of the origin of the species. But what Darwin meant seriously and literally, the stranger means playfully.[101] Man must learn to see the lowliness of his estate in order to turn from the human to the divine, *i.e.,* in order to be truly human.

The division of "art" leads to the result that the art of the statesman is the art concerned with the breeding and nurture of, or with the caring for, herds of the kind of animal called man. This result is manifestly insufficient, for there are many arts—*e.g.,* medicine and matchmaking—which claim as justly to be concerned with a caring for human herds as does the political art. The error was due to the fact that the human herd was taken to be a herd of the same kind as the herds of other animals. But human herds are a very special kind of herd: the bipartition of "animal" into brutes and men originates not merely in pride. The error is removed by a myth. According to the myth now told in its fullness for the first time, there is once a time (the age of Kronos) when the god guides the whole and then a time (the age of Zeus) when the god lets the whole move by its own motion. In the age of Kronos the god ruled and took care of the animals by assigning the different species of animals to the rule and care of different gods who acted like shepherds and thus secured universal peace and affluence: there were no political societies, no private property, and no families. This does not necessarily mean that men lived happily in the age of Kronos; only if they used the then available peace and affluence for philosophizing can they be said to have lived happily. At any rate, in the present age the god does not take care of man: in the present age there is no divine providence; men must take care of themselves. Bereft of divine care, the world abounds with disorder and injustice; men must establish order and justice as well as they can, with the understanding that in this age of scarcity, communism, and hence also absolute communism, is impossible. The *Statesman* may be said to bring into the open what the *Republic* had left unsaid, namely, the impossibility of the best regime presented in the *Republic*.

The myth of the *Statesman* is meant to explain the error committed by the Eleatic stranger and young Socrates in the initial definition of the *Statesman:* by looking for a single art of caring for human herds they were unwittingly looking toward the age of Kronos or toward divine caring; with the disappearance of divine caring, *i.e.,* of a caring by beings which in the eyes of everyone are superior to men, it became inevitable that every art or every man should believe itself or himself to be as much entitled to rule as every other art or every other man,[102] or that at least many arts should become competitors of the kingly art. The inevitable first consequence of the transition from the age of Kronos to the age of Zeus was the delusion that all arts and all men are equal. The mistake consisted in assuming that the kingly art is devoted to the total caring for human herds (which total caring would include the feeding and mating of the ruled) and not to a partial or limited caring. In other words, the mistake consisted in the disregard of the fact that in the case of all arts of herding other than the human art of herding human beings, the herder belongs to a different species than the members of the herd. We must then divide the whole "caring for herds" into two parts: caring for herds in which the herder belongs to the same species as the members of the herd and caring for herds in which the herder belongs to a different species than the members of the herd (human herders of brutes and divine herders of human beings). We must next divide the first of these two kinds into parts, so that we can discover which partial herding of herds in which the herder belongs to the same species as the members of the herd is the kingly art. Let us assume that the partial caring sought is "ruling cities." Ruling cities is naturally divided into ruling not willed by the ruled (ruling by sheer force) and ruling willed by the ruled; the former is tyrannical, and the latter is kingly. Here we receive the first glimpse of freedom as the specifically political theme. But at the very moment in which the stranger alludes to this difficulty, he turns away from it. He finds the whole previous procedure unsatisfactory.

The method which proves to be helpful, where the division of classes and into classes as well as the myth have failed, is the use of an example. The stranger illustrates the usefulness of examples by an example. The example is meant to illustrate man's situation in regard to knowledge—to the phenomenon which is the guiding theme of the trilogy *Theaitetos-Sophist-Statesman*. The example chosen is children's knowledge of reading. Starting from knowledge of the letters (the "elements"), they proceed step by step to the knowledge of the shortest and easiest syllables (the combination of "elements"), and then to the knowledge of long and difficult ones. Knowledge of the whole is not possible if it is not similar to the art of reading: knowledge of the elements must be available, the elements must be fairly small in number, and not all elements must be combinable.[103] But can we say that we possess knowledge of the "elements" of the whole or that we can ever start from an absolute beginning? Did we in the *Statesman* begin from an

adequate understanding of "art" or "knowledge"? Is it not true that
while we necessarily long for knowledge of the whole, we are condemned to rest satisfied with partial knowledge of parts of the whole
and hence never truly to transcend the sphere of opinion? Is therefore
philosophy, and hence human life, not necessarily Sisyphean? Could
this be the reason why the demand for freedom is not so evidently
sound as many present-day lovers of freedom believe on the basis of very
similar thoughts? (Perhaps this could induce one to consider Dostoyev-
sky's *Grand Inquisitor* in the light of Plato's *Statesman*.) After having
compelled us to raise these and kindred questions, the stranger turns to
his example, which is meant to throw light, not on knowledge in general or on philosophy as such, but on the kingly art. The example chosen
by him is the art of weaving: he illustrates the political art by an emphatically domestic art and not by such "outgoing" arts as herding
and piloting; he illustrates the most virile art by a characteristically
feminine art. In order to find out what weaving is, one must divide
"art," but divide it differently than they divided it at first. The analysis
of the art of weaving which is made on the basis of the new division
enables the stranger to elucidate art in general and the kingly art in
particular before he applies explicitly the result of that analysis to the
kingly art. Perhaps the most important point made in this context is
the distinction between two kinds of the art of measurement: one kind
which considers the greater and less in relation to one another, and
another kind which considers the greater and less (now understood
as excess and defect) in relation to the mean or, say, the fitting, or
something similar. All arts, and especially the kingly art, make their
measurements with a view to the right mean or the fitting, *i.e.,* they
are not mathematical.

By explicitly applying to the kingly art the results of his analysis
of the art of weaving, the stranger is enabled to make clear the relation
of the kingly art to all other arts and especially to those arts which
claim with some show of justice to compete with the kingly art for the
rule of the city. The most successful and clever competitors are those
outstanding sophists who pretend to possess the kingly art, and these
are the rulers of cities, *i.e.,* the rulers lacking the kingly or statesmanly
art, or practically all political rulers that were, are, and will be. Of this
kind of political rule there are three sorts: the rule of one, the rule of
a few, and the rule of many; but each of these three kinds is divided
into two parts with a view to the difference between violence and
voluntariness or between lawfulness and lawlessness; thus monarchy
is distinguished from tyranny, and aristocracy from oligarchy, whereas
the name of democracy is applied to the rule of the multitude regardless

of whether the multitude of the poor rules over the rich with the consent of the rich and in strict obedience to the laws or with violence and
more or less lawlessly. (The distinction of regimes sketched by the
stranger is almost identical with the distinction developed by Aristotle
in the third book of his *Politics;* but consider the difference.) None of
these regimes bases its claim on the knowledge or art of the rulers, *i.e.,*
on the only claim which is unqualifiedly legitimate. It follows that the
claims based on the willingness of the subjects (on consent or freedom)
and on lawfulness are dubious. This judgment is defended with reference to the example of the other arts and especially of medicine. A
physician is a physician whether he cures us with our will or against our
will, whether he cuts us, burns us, or inflicts upon us any other pain,
and whether he acts in accordance with written rules or without them;
he is a physician if his ruling redounds to the benefit of our bodies.
Correspondingly, the only regime which is correct or which is truly a
regime is that in which the possessors of the kingly art rule, regardless
of whether they rule according to laws or without laws and whether
the ruled consent to their rule or not, provided their rule redounds to
the benefit of the body politic; it does not make any difference whether
they achieve this end by killing some or banishing them and thus
reduce the bulk of the city or by bringing in citizens from abroad and
thus increase its bulk.

Young Socrates, who is not shocked by what the stranger says
about killing and banishing, is rather shocked by the suggestion that
rule without laws (absolute rule) can be legitimate. To understand
fully the response of young Socrates, one must pay attention to the
fact that the stranger does not make a distinction between human laws
and natural laws. The stranger turns the incipient indignation of young
Socrates into a desire on the latter's part for discussion. Rule of law is
inferior to the rule of living intelligence because laws, owing to their
generality, cannot determine wisely what is right and proper in all
circumstances given the infinite variety of circumstances: only the
wise man on the spot could correctly decide what is right and proper
in the circumstances. Nevertheless laws are necessary. The few wise
men cannot sit beside each of the many unwise men and tell him exactly what it is becoming for him to do. The few wise men are almost
always absent from the innumerable unwise men. All laws, written or
unwritten, are poor substitutes but indispensable substitutes for the individual rulings by wise men. They are crude rules of thumb which are
sufficient for the large majority of cases: they treat human beings as if
they were members of a herd. The freezing of crude rules of thumb
into sacred, inviolable, unchangeable prescriptions which would be

rejected by everyone as ridiculous if done in the sciences and the arts is a necessity in the ordering of human affairs; this necessity is the proximate cause of the ineradicable difference between the political and the suprapolitical spheres. But the main objection to laws is not that they are not susceptible of being individualized but that they are assumed to be binding on the wise man, on the man possessing the kingly art.[104] Yet even this objection is not entirely valid. As the stranger explains through images,[105] the wise man is subjected to the laws, whose justice and wisdom is inferior to his, because the unwise men cannot help distrusting the wise man, and this distrust is not entirely indefensible given the fact that they cannot understand him. They cannot believe that a wise man who would deserve to rule as a true king without laws would be willing and able to rule over them. The ultimate reason for their unbelief is the fact that no human being has that manifest superiority, in the first place regarding the body and then regarding the soul, which would induce everybody to submit to his rule without any hesitation and without any reserve.[106] The unwise men cannot help making themselves the judges of the wise man. No wonder then that the wise men are unwilling to rule over them. The unwise men must even demand of the wise man that he regard the law as simply authoritative, *i.e.,* that he not even doubt that the established laws are perfectly just and wise; if he fails to do so, he will become guilty of corrupting the young, a capital offense; they must forbid free inquiry regarding the most important subjects. All these implications of the rule of laws must be accepted, since the only feasible alternative is the lawless rule of selfish men. The wise man must bow to the law which is inferior to him in wisdom and justice, not only in deed but in speech as well. (Here we cannot help wondering whether there are no limits to the wise man's subjection to the laws. The Platonic illustrations are these: Socrates obeyed without flinching the law which commanded him to die because of his alleged corruption of the young; yet he would not have obeyed a law formally forbidding him the pursuit of philosophy. Read the *Apology of Socrates* together with the *Crito.*) The rule of law is preferable to the lawless rule of unwise men since laws, however bad, are in one way or another the outcome of some reasoning. This observation permits the ranking of the incorrect regimes, *i.e.,* of all regimes other than the absolute rule of the true king or statesman. Law-abiding democracy is inferior to the law-abiding rule of the few (aristocracy) and to the law-abiding rule of one (monarchy), but lawless democracy is superior to the lawless rule of a few (oligarchy) and to the lawless rule of one (tyranny). "Lawless" does not mean here the complete absence of any laws or customs. It means the habitual disregard of the

laws by the government and especially of those laws which are meant
to restrain the power of the government: a government which can
change every law or is "sovereign" is lawless. From the sequel it appears that, according to the stranger, even in the city ruled by the true
king there will be laws (the true king is the true legislator), but that
the true king, in contradistinction to all other rulers, may justly change
the laws or act against the laws. In the absence of the true king, the
stranger would probably be satisfied if the city were ruled by a code of
laws framed by a wise man, one which can be changed by the unwise
rulers only in extreme cases.

After the true kingly art has been separated from all other arts, it
remains for the stranger to determine the peculiar work of the king.
Here the example of the art of weaving takes on decisive importance.
The king's work resembles a web. According to the popular view all
parts of virtue are simply in harmony with one another. In fact, however, there is a tension between them. Above all, there is a tension between courage or manliness and moderation, gentleness, or concern
with the seemly. This tension explains the tension and even hostility
between the preponderantly manly and the preponderantly gentle
human beings. The true king's task is to weave together these opposite
kinds of human beings, for the people in the city who are completely
unable to become either manly or moderate cannot become citizens at
all. An important part of the kingly weaving together consists in inter-
marrying the children of preponderantly manly families and those of
preponderantly gentle families. The human king must then approximate the divine shepherd by enlarging the art of ruling cities strictly
understood so as to include in it the art of mating or matchmaking. The
matchmaking practiced by the king is akin to the matchmaking practiced by Socrates,[107] which means that it is not identical with the latter.
If we were to succeed in understanding the kinship between the king's
matchmaking and Socrates' matchmaking, we would have made some
progress toward the understanding of the kinship between the king and
the philosopher. This much can be said safely: While it is possible and
even necessary to speak of "the human herd" when trying to define
the king, the philosopher has nothing to do with "herds."

The *Statesman* belongs to a trilogy whose theme is knowledge. For
Plato, knowledge proper or striving for knowledge proper is philosophy.
Philosophy is striving for knowledge of the whole, for contemplation
of the whole. The whole consists of parts; knowledge of the whole is
knowledge of all parts of the whole as parts of the whole. Philosophy
is the highest human activity, and man is an excellent, perhaps the most
excellent, part of the whole. The whole is not a whole without man,

without man's being whole or complete. But man becomes whole not without his own effort, and this effort presupposes knowledge of a particular kind: knowledge which is not contemplative or theoretical but prescriptive or commanding[108] or practical. The *Statesman* presents itself as a theoretical discussion of practical knowledge. In contradistinction to the *Statesman*, the *Republic* leads up from practical or political life to philosophy, to the theoretical life; the *Republic* presents a practical discussion of theory: it shows to men concerned with the solution of the human problem that that solution consists in the theoretical life; the knowledge which the *Republic* sets forth is prescriptive or commanding. The theoretical discussion of the highest practical knowledge (the kingly art) in the *Statesman*, merely by setting forth the character of the kingly art, takes on a commanding character: it sets forth what the ruler ought to do. While the distinction of theoretical and practical knowledge is necessary, their separation is impossible. (Consider from this point of view the description of the theoretical life in the *Theaitetos* 173$^b$–177$^c$.) The kingly art is one of the arts directly concerned with making men whole or entire. The most obvious indication of every human being's incompleteness and at the same time of the manner in which it can be completed is the distinction of the human race into the two sexes: just as the union of men and women, the primary goal of *eros,* makes "man" self-sufficient for the perpetuity, not to say sempiternity, of the human species, all other kinds of incompleteness to be found in men are completed in the species, in the "idea," of man. The whole human race, and not any part of it, is self-sufficient as a part of the whole, and not as the master or conqueror of the whole. It is perhaps for this reason that the *Statesman* ends with a praise of a certain kind of matchmaking.

## The Laws

The *Republic* and the *Statesman* transcend the city in different but kindred ways. They show first how the city would have to transform itself if it wishes to maintain its claim to supremacy in the face of philosophy. They show then that the city is incapable of undergoing this transformation. The *Republic* shows silently that the ordinary city—*i.e.,* the city which is not communistic and which is the association of the fathers rather than of the artisans—is the only city that is possible. The *Statesman* shows explicitly the necessity of the rule of laws. The *Republic* and the *Statesman* reveal, each in its own way, the essential limitation and therewith the essential character of the city. They thus lay the foundation for answering the question of the best political order, the best order of the city compatible with the nature of man. But they do not set forth that best possible order. This task is left for the *Laws*. We may then say that the *Laws* is the only political work proper of Plato. It is the only Platonic dialogue from which Socrates is absent. The characters of the *Laws* are old men of long political experience: a nameless Athenian stranger, the Cretan Kleinias, and the Spartan Megillos. The Athenian stranger occupies the place ordinarily occupied in the Platonic dialogues by Socrates. The conversation takes place far away from Athens, on the island of Crete, while the three old men walk from the city of Knossos to the cave of Zeus.

Our first impression is that the Athenian stranger has gone to Crete in order to discover the truth about those Greek laws which in one respect were the most renowned, for the Cretan laws were believed to have had their origin in Zeus, the highest god. The Cretan laws were akin to the Spartan laws, which were even more renowned than the Cretan laws and were traced to Apollo. At the suggestion of the Athenian, the three men converse about laws and regimes. The Athenian learns from the Cretan that the Cretan legislator has framed all his laws with a view to war: by nature every city is at all times in a state of undeclared war with every other city; victory in war, and hence war, is the condition for all blessings. The Athenian easily convinces the Cretan that the Cretan laws aim at the wrong end: the end is not war but peace. For if victory in war is the condition of all blessings, war is not the end: the blessings themselves belong to peace. Hence the virtue of war, courage, is the lowest part of virtue, inferior to moderation and above all to justice and wisdom. Once we have seen the natural order of the virtues, we know the highest principle of legislation, for that legislation must be concerned with virtue, with the excellence of the human soul, rather than with any other goods is easily granted by the Cretan gentleman Kleinias who is assured by the Athenian that the possession of virtue is necessarily followed by the possession of health, beauty, strength, and wealth.[109] It appears that both the Spartan and the Cretan legislators, convinced as they were that the end of the city is war and not peace, provided well for the education of their subjects or fellows to courage, to self-control regarding pains and fears, by making them taste the greatest pains and fears; but they did not provide at all for education to moderation, to self-control regarding pleasures, by making them taste the greatest pleasures. In fact, if we can trust Megillos, at any rate the Spartan legislator discouraged the enjoyment of pleasure altogether.[110] The Spartan and Cretan legislators surely forbade the pleasures of drinking

—pleasures freely indulged in by the Athenians. The Athenian contends that drinking, even drunkenness, properly practiced is conducive to moderation, the twin virtue of courage. In order to be properly practiced, drinking must be done in common, *i.e.,* in a sense in public so that it can be supervised. Drinking, even drunkenness, will be salutary if the drinkers are ruled by the right kind of man. For a man to be a commander of a ship it is not sufficient that he possess the art or science of sailing; he must also be free from seasickness.[111] Art or knowledge is likewise not sufficient for ruling a banquet. Art is not sufficient for ruling any association and in particular the city. The banquet is a more fitting simile of the city than is the ship ("the ship of state"), for just as the banqueteers are drunk from wine, the citizens are drunk from fears, hopes, desires, and aversions and are therefore in need of being ruled by a man who is sober. Since banquets are illegal in Sparta and Crete but legal in Athens, the Athenian is compelled to justify an Athenian institution. The justification is a long speech, and long speeches were Athenian rather than Spartan and Cretan. The Athenian is then compelled to justify an Athenian institution in an Athenian manner. He is compelled to transform his non-Athenian interlocutors to some extent into Athenians. Only in this way can he correct their erroneous views about laws and therewith eventually their laws themselves. From this we understand better the character of the *Laws* as a whole. In the *Republic*[112] the Spartan and Cretan regimes were used as examples of timocracy, the kind of regime inferior only to the best regime but by far superior to democracy, *i.e.,* the kind of regime which prevailed in Athens during most of Socrates' (and Plato's) lifetime. In the *Laws* the Athenian stranger attempts to correct timocracy, *i.e.,* to change it into the best possible regime which is somehow in between timocracy and the best regime of the *Republic.* That best possible regime will prove to be very similar to "the ancestral regime," the predemocratic regime, of Athens.

The Cretan and Spartan laws were found to be faulty because they did not permit their subjects to taste the greatest pleasures. But can drinking be said to afford the greatest pleasures, even the greatest sensual pleasures? Yet the Athenian had in mind those greatest pleasures which people can enjoy in public and to which they must be exposed in order to learn to control them. The pleasures of banquets are drinking and singing. In order to justify banquets one must therefore discuss also singing, music, and hence education as a whole:[113] the music pleasures are the greatest pleasures which people can enjoy in public and which they must learn to control by being exposed to them. The Spartan and Cretan laws suffer then from the great defect that

they do not at all, or at least not sufficiently, expose their subjects to
the music pleasures.[114] The reason for this is that these two societies are
not towns but armed camps, a kind of herd: in Sparta and Crete even
those youths who are by nature fit to be educated as individuals by
private teachers are brought up merely as members of a herd. In other
words, the Spartans and Cretans know only how to sing in choruses:
they do not know the most beautiful song, the most noble music.[115]
In the *Republic* the city of the armed camp, a greatly improved Sparta,
was transcended by the City of Beauty, the city in which philosophy, the
highest Muse, is duly honored. In the *Laws,* where the best possible
regime is presented, this transcending does not take place. The city
of the *Laws* is, however, not a city of the armed camp in any sense.
Yet it has certain features in common with the city of the armed camp
of the *Republic.* Just as in the *Republic,* music education proves to be
education toward moderation, and such education proves to require the
supervision of musicians and poets by the true statesman or legislator.
Yet while in the *Republic* education to moderation proves to culminate
in the love of the beautiful, in the *Laws* moderation rather takes on
the colors of sense of shame or of reverence. Education is surely education to virtue, to the virtue of the citizen or to the virtue of man.[116]

The virtue of man is primarily the proper posture toward pleasures
and pains or the proper control of pleasures and pains; the proper
control is the control effected by right reasoning. If the result of
reasoning is adopted by the city, that result becomes law; law which
deserves the name is the dictate of right reasoning primarily regarding
pleasures and pains. The kinship but not identity of right reasoning and
good laws corresponds to the kinship but not identity of the good man
and the good citizen. In order to learn to control the ordinary pleasures
and pains, the citizens must be exposed from their childhood to the
pleasures afforded by poetry and the other imitative arts which in turn
must be controlled by good or wise laws, by laws which therefore ought
never to be changed; the desire for innovation so natural to poetry and
the other imitative arts must be suppressed as much as possible; the
means for achieving this is the consecration of the correct after it has
come to light. The perfect legislator will persuade or compel the poets
to teach that justice goes with pleasure and injustice with pain. The
perfect legislator will demand that this manifestly salutary doctrine
be taught even if it were not true.[117] This doctrine takes the place
of the theology of the second book of the *Republic.* In the *Republic*
the salutary teaching regarding the relation of justice and pleasure or
happiness could not be discussed in the context of the education of
the nonphilosophers because the *Republic* did not presuppose, as the

*Laws* does, that the interlocutors of the chief character know what justice is.[118] The whole conversation regarding education and therewith also about the ends or principles of legislation is subsumed by the Athenian stranger under the theme "wine" and even "drunkenness" because the improvement of old laws can safely be entrusted only to well-bred old men who as such are averse to every change and who, in order to become willing to change the old laws, must undergo some rejuvenation like the one produced by the drinking of wine.

Only after having determined the end which political life is meant to serve (education and virtue), does the stranger turn to the beginning of political life or the genesis of the city in order to discover the cause of political change and in particular of the change of regimes. There have been many beginnings of political life because there have been many destructions of almost all men through floods, plagues, and similar calamities bringing with them the destruction of all arts and tools; only a few human beings survived on mountaintops or in other privileged places; it took many generations until they dared to descend to the lowlands, and during those generations the last recollection of the arts vanished. The condition out of which all cities and regimes, all arts and laws, all vice and virtue emerged is men's lack of all these things; the "out of which" something emerges is one kind of cause of the thing in question; the primary lack of what we may call civilization would seem to be the cause of all political change.[119] If man had had a perfect beginning, there would have been no cause for change, and the imperfection of his beginning is bound to have effects in all stages, however perfect, of his civilization. The stranger shows that this is the case by following the changes which human life underwent from the beginnings when men apparently were virtuous because they were, not indeed wise, but simple-minded or innocent yet in fact savage, until the destruction of the original settlement of Sparta and her sister cities Messene and Argos. He only alludes with delicacy to the Spartans' despotic subjugation of the Messenians. He summarizes the result of his inquiry by enumerating the generally accepted and effective titles to rule. It is the contradiction among the titles or the claims to them which explains the change of regimes. It appears that the title to rule based on wisdom, while the highest, is only one among seven. Among the others we find the title or claim of the master to rule over his slaves, of the stronger to rule over the weaker, and of those chosen by lot to rule over those not so chosen.[120] Wisdom is not a sufficient title; a viable regime presupposes a blend of the claim based on wisdom with the claims based on the other kinds of superiority; perhaps the proper or wise blend of some of the other titles can act as a substitute for the title deriving from wisdom. The Athenian stranger does not abstract, as the Eleatic stranger does, from bodily force as a necessary ingredient of the rule of man over man. The viable regime must be mixed. The Spartan regime is mixed. But is it mixed wisely? In order to answer this question one must first see the ingredients of the right mixture in isolation. These are monarchy, of which Persia offers the outstanding example, and democracy, of which Athens offers the most outstanding example.[121] Monarchy by itself stands for the absolute rule of the wise man or of the master; democracy stands for freedom. The right mixture is that of wisdom and freedom, of wisdom and consent, of the rule of wise laws framed by a wise legislator and administered by the best members of the city and of the rule of the common people.

After the end as well as the general character of the best possible regime have been made clear, Kleinias reveals that the present conversation is of direct use to him. The Cretans plan to found a colony, and they have commissioned him together with others to take care of the project and in particular to frame laws for the colony as they see fit; they may even select foreign laws if they appear to them to be superior to the Cretan laws. The people to be settled come from Crete and from the Peloponnesos: they do not come from one and the same city. If they came from the same city, with the same language and the same laws and the same sacred rites and beliefs, they could not easily be persuaded to accept institutions different from those of their home city. On the other hand, heterogeneity of the population of a future city causes dissensions.[122] In the present case the heterogeneity seems to be sufficient to make possible considerable change for the better, *i.e.,* the establishment of the best possible regime, and yet not too great to prevent fusion. We have here the viable alternative to the expulsion of everyone older than ten which would be required for the establishment of the best regime of the *Republic.* The traditions which the various groups of settlers bring with them will be modified rather than eradicated. Thanks to the good fortune which brought about the presence in Crete of the Athenian stranger while the sending out of the colony is in preparation, there is a fair chance that the traditions will be modified wisely. All the greater care must be taken that the new order established under the guidance of the wise man will not be changed afterward by less wise men: it ought to be exposed to change as little as possible, for any change of a wise order seems to be a change for the worse. At any rate without the chance presence of the Athenian stranger in Crete there would be no prospect of wise legislation for the new city. This makes us understand the stranger's assertion that not human beings but chance legislates: most laws are as it were dictated by calamities. Still, some room is left for the legislative art. Or, inversely, the possessor of the legislative art is helpless without good fortune, for which he can only pray. The most favorable circumstance for which the legislator would pray is that the city for which he is to frame laws be ruled by a young tyrant whose nature is in some respects the same as that of the philosopher except that he does not have to be graceful or witty, a lover of the truth, and just; his lack of justice (the fact that he is prompted by desire for his own power and glory alone) does not do harm if he is willing to listen to the wise legislator. Given this condition—given a coincidence of the greatest power with wisdom through the cooperation of the tyrant with the wise legislator—the legislator will effect the quickest and most profound change for the better in the habits of the citizens. But since the city to be founded is to undergo as little change as possible, it is perhaps more important to realize that the regime most difficult to change is oligarchy, the regime which occupies the central place in the order of regimes presented in the *Republic*.[123] Surely, the city to be founded must not be tyrannically ruled. The best regime is that in which a god or demon rules as in the age of Kronos, the golden age. The nearest imitation of divine rule is the rule of laws. But the laws in their turn depend on the man or men who can lay down and enforce the laws, *i.e.,* the regime (monarchy, tyranny, oligarchy, aristocracy, democracy). In the case of each of these regimes a section of the city rules the rest, and therefore it rules the city with a view to a sectional interest, not to the common interest.[124] We know already the solution to this difficulty: the regime must be mixed as it was in a way in Sparta and Crete,[125] and it must adopt a code framed by a wise legislator.

The wise legislator will not limit himself to giving simple commands accompanied by sanctions, *i.e.,* threats of punishment. This is the way for guiding slaves, not free men. He will preface the laws with preambles or preludes setting forth the reasons of the laws. Yet different kinds of reasons are needed for persuading different kinds of men, and the multiplicity of reasons may be confusing and thus endanger the simplicity of obedience. The legislator must then possess the art of saying simultaneously different things to different kinds of citizens in such a way that the legislator's speech will effect in all cases the same simple result: obedience to his laws. In acquiring this art he will be greatly helped by the poets.[126] Laws must be twofold; they must consist of the "unmixed law," the bald statement of what ought to be done or forborne "or else," *i.e.,* the "tyrannical prescription," and the prelude to the law which gently persuades by appealing to reason.[127] The proper mixture of coercion and persuasion, of "tyranny" and "democracy,"[128] of wisdom and consent, proves everywhere to be the character of wise political arrangements.

The laws require a general prelude—an exhortation to honor the various beings which deserve honor in their proper order. Since the rule of laws is an imitation of divine rule, honor must be given first and above everything else to the gods, next to the other superhuman beings, then to the ancestors, then to one's father and mother. Everyone must also honor his soul but next to the gods. The order of rank between honoring one's soul and honoring one's parents is not made entirely clear. Honoring one's soul means acquiring the various virtues without which no one can be a good citizen. The general exhortation culminates in the proof that the virtuous life is more pleasant than the life of vice. Before the founder of the new colony can begin with the legislation proper, he must take two measures of the utmost importance. In the first place he must effect a kind of purge of the potential citizens: only the right kind of settlers must be admitted to the new colony. Second, the land must be distributed among those admitted to citizenship. There will then be no communism. Whatever advantages communism might have, it is not feasible if the legislator does not himself exercise tyrannical rule,[129] whereas in the present case not even the cooperation of the legislator with a tyrant is contemplated. Nevertheless, the land must remain the property of the whole city; no citizen will be the absolute owner of the land allotted to him. The land will be divided into allotments which must never be changed by selling, buying, or in any other way, and this will be achieved if every landowner must leave his entire allotment to a single son; the other sons must try to marry heiresses; to prevent the excess of the male citizen population beyond the number of the originally established allotments, recourse must be had to birth control and in the extreme case to the sending out of colonies. There must not be gold and silver in the city and as little money-making as possible. It is impossible that there should be equality of property, but there ought to be an upper limit to what a citizen can own: the richest citizen must be permitted to own no more than four times what the poorest citizens own, *i.e.,* the allotment of land including house and slaves. It is impossible to disregard the inequality of property in the distribution of political power. The citizen body will be divided into four classes according to the amount of property owned. The land assigned to each citizen must be sufficient to enable him to serve the city in war as a knight or as a hoplite. In other words, citizenship is limited to knights and hoplites. The regime seems to be what Aristotle calls a polity—a democracy limited by a

considerable property qualification. But this is not correct, as appears
particularly from the laws concerning membership in the Council and
election to the Council. The Council is what we would call the executive part of the government; each twelfth of the Council is to govern
for a month. The Council is to consist of four equally large groups,
the first group being chosen from the highest property class, the second
group being chosen from the second highest property class, and so on.
All citizens have the same voting power, but whereas all citizens are
obliged to vote for councillors from the highest property class, only
the citizens of the two highest property classes are obliged to vote for
councillors from the lowest property class. These arrangements are
obviously meant to favor the wealthy; the regime is meant to be a
mean between monarchy and democracy[130] or, more precisely, a mean
more oligarchic or aristocratic than a polity. Similar privileges are
granted to the wealthy also as regards power in the Assembly and the
holding of the most honorable offices. It is, however, not wealth as
wealth which is favored: no craftsman or trader, however wealthy,
can be a citizen. Only those can be citizens who have the leisure to
devote themselves to the practice of citizen virtue.

The most conspicuous part of the legislation proper concerns impiety, which is of course treated within the context of the penal law.
The fundamental impiety is atheism or the denial of the existence of
gods. Since a good law will not merely punish crimes or appeal to
fear but will also appeal to reason, the Athenian stranger is compelled
to demonstrate the existence of gods and, since gods who do not care
for men's justice, who do not reward the just and punish the unjust, are
not sufficient for the city, he must demonstrate divine providence as well.
The *Laws* is the only Platonic work which contains such a demonstration. It is the only Platonic work which begins with "A god." One
might say that it is Plato's most pious work, and that it is for this reason
that he strikes therein at the root of impiety, *i.e.,* at the opinion that
there are no gods. The Athenian stranger takes up the question regarding the gods, although it was not even raised in Crete or in Sparta;
it was, however, raised in Athens.[131] Kleinias strongly favors the demonstration recommended by the Athenian on the ground that it would
constitute the finest and best prelude to the whole code. The Athenian
cannot refute the atheists before he has stated their assertions. It appears
that they assert that body is prior to soul or mind, or that soul or mind
is derivative from body and, consequently, that nothing is by nature
just or unjust, or that all right originates in convention. The refutation
of them consists in the proof that soul is prior to body, which proof
implies that there is natural right. The punishments for impiety differ

according to the different kinds of impiety. It is not clear what punishment, if any, is inflicted on the atheist who is a just man; he is surely less severely punished than, for instance, the man who practices forensic rhetoric for the sake of gain. Even in cases of the other kinds of impiety, capital punishment will be extremely rare. We mention these facts because their insufficient consideration might induce ignorant people to scold Plato for his alleged lack of liberalism. We do not here describe such people as ignorant because they believe that liberalism calls for unqualified toleration of the teaching of all opinions however dangerous or degrading. We call them ignorant because they do not see how extraordinarily liberal Plato is according to their own standards, which cannot possibly be "absolute." The standards generally recognized in Plato's time are best illustrated by the practice of Athens, a city highly renowned for her liberality and gentleness. In Athens Socrates was punished with death because he was held not to believe in the existence of the gods worshipped by the city of Athens—of gods whose existence was known only from hearsay. In the city of the *Laws* the belief in gods is demanded only to the extent to which it is supported by demonstration; and in addition, those who are not convinced by the demonstration but are just men will not be condemned to death.

The stability of the order sketched by the Athenian stranger seems to be guaranteed as far as the stability of any political order can be: it is guaranteed by obedience on the part of the large majority of citizens to wise laws which are as unchangeable as possible, by an obedience that results chiefly from education to virtue, from the formation of character. Still, laws are only second best: no law can be as wise as the decision of a truly wise man on the spot. Provision must therefore be made for, as it were, infinite progress in improving the laws in the interest of increasing improvement of the political order, as well as of counteracting the decay of the laws. Legislation must then be an unending process; at each time there must be living legislators. Laws should be changed only with the utmost caution, only in the case of universally admitted necessity. The later legislators must aim at the same commanding end as the original legislator: the excellence of the souls of the members of the city.[132] To prevent change of laws, intercourse of the citizens with foreigners must be closely supervised. No citizen shall go abroad for a private purpose. But citizens of high reputation and more than fifty years old who desire to see how other men live and especially to converse with outstanding men from whom they can learn something about the improvement of the laws are encouraged to do so.[133] Yet all these and similar measures do not suffice for the salvation of the laws and the regime; the firm foundation is still lacking. That firm foundation can only be supplied by a Nocturnal Council consisting of the most outstanding old citizens and select younger citizens of thirty years and older. The Nocturnal Council is to be for the city what the mind is for the human individual. To perform its function its members must possess above everything else the most adequate knowledge possible of the single end at which all political action directly or indirectly aims. This end is virtue. Virtue is meant to be one, yet it is also many; there are four kinds of virtue, and at least two of them—wisdom and courage (or spiritedness)—are radically different from one another.[134] How then can there be a single end of the city? The Nocturnal Council cannot perform its function if it cannot answer this question, or, more generally and perhaps more precisely stated, the Nocturnal Council must include at least some men who know what the virtues themselves are or who know the ideas of the various virtues as well as what unites them, so that all together can justly be called "virtue" in the singular: is "virtue," the single end of the city, one or a whole or both or something else? They also must know, as far as is humanly possible, the truth about the gods. Solid reverence for the gods arises only from knowledge of the soul as well as of the movements of the stars. Only men who combine this knowledge with the popular or vulgar virtues can be adequate rulers of the city: one ought to hand over the city for rule to the Nocturnal Council if it comes into being. Plato brings the regime of the *Laws* around by degrees to the regime of the *Republic*.[135] Having arrived at the end of the *Laws*, we must return to the beginning of the *Republic*.

## NOTES

1. Plato *Republic* 377 ff., 389$^{b-c}$, 414$^{b}$–415$^{d}$, 459$^{c-d}$.

2. *Ibid.*, 375$^{b}$–376$^{c}$.

3. *Ibid.*, 414$^{d-e}$.

4. *Ibid.*, 471$^{a-b}$.

5. *Ibid.*, 395$^{c}$; 500$^{d}$; 530$^{a}$; 507$^{c}$, 597.

6. *Ibid.*, 454$^{c}$–455$^{a}$; cf. 452$^{a}$.

7. *Ibid.*, 343$^{b}$.

8. *Ibid.*, 351$^{c}$–352$^{a}$.

9. Cf. *ibid.*, 364$^{a, c-d}$, 365$^{c}$ with 357$^{b}$ and 358$^{a}$.

10. *Ibid.*, 372$^{d}$.

11. *Ibid.*, 370$^{d-e}$, 373$^{c}$.

12. *Ibid.*, 342$^{a-b}$, 346$^{c}$.

13. *Ibid.*, 392$^{a-c}$.

14. *Ibid.*, 423$^{b}$; cf. also 398$^{a}$ and 422$^{d}$.

15. *Ibid.*, 414$^{a}$, 465$^{d}$–466$^{c}$; cf. 346$^{e}$ ff.

16. *Ibid.*, 415$^{b}$.

17. *Ibid.*, 427$^{d}$.

18. *Ibid.*, 433$^{a-b}$.

19. *Ibid.*, 434$^{c}$.

20. *Ibid.*, 430$^{c}$; cf. *Phaedo* 82$^{a}$.

21. *Republic* 441$^{a-c}$.

22. *Ibid.*, 444$^{d}$–445$^{b}$.

23. *Ibid.*, 441$^{e}$.

24. Cf. *ibid.*, 442$^{c}$.

25. *Ibid.*, 580$^{d}$–583$^{b}$.

26. *Ibid.*, 619$^{b-d}$.

27. *Ibid.*, 427$^{d}$.

28. Cf. *ibid.*, 366$^c$.
29. *Ibid.*, 573$^{b-e}$, 574$^e$–575$^a$.
30. Cf. *ibid.*, 439$^d$.
31. *Timaeus* 24$^{a-b}$.
32. *Republic* 401$^{b-c}$, 421$^e$–422$^d$, 460$^a$, 543$^a$.
33. *Politics* 1264$^a$ 13–17.
34. *Republic* 421$^a$, 434$^a$.
35. *Ibid.*, 415$^e$, 431$^{b-c}$, 456$^d$.
36. Reconsider *ibid.*, 427$^d$.
37. *Ibid.*, 464$^d$; cf. *Laws* 739$^c$.
38. Cf. *Republic* 449$^b$–450$^a$ with 327$^b$–328$^b$.
39. Cf. *ibid.*, 369$^d$.
40. *Ibid.*, 455$^{d-e}$, 456$^{b-c}$.
41. *Ibid.*, 455$^{c-e}$.
42. *Ibid.*, 462$^{c-d}$, 464$^b$.
43. Cf. *ibid.*, 458$^e$.
44. Cf. *ibid.*, 461$^{b-e}$.
45. *Ibid.*, 463$^c$.
46. *Ibid.*, 466$^d$.
47. *Ibid.*, 473$^{b-c}$.
48. *Ibid.*, 472$^{b-c}$.
49. *Ibid.*, 479$^a$; cf. 538$^c$ ff.
50. *Ibid.*, 517$^c$.
51. Cf. *ibid.*, 509$^b$–510$^a$.
52. *Ibid.*, 501$^b$; 597$^{b-d}$.
53. Cf. *ibid.*, 507$^{a-c}$ with 596$^a$ and 532$^{c-d}$, contrast with *Phaedo* 65$^d$ and 74$^{a-b}$.
54. *Republic* 536$^b$; cf. 487$^a$.
55. Cf. *ibid.*, 379$^{a-b}$ and 380$^d$ ff.
56. *Ibid.*, 379$^a$.
57. *Ibid.*, 472$^c$–473$^a$; cf. 500$^c$–501$^c$ with 484$^{c-d}$ and 592$^b$.
58. *Ibid.*, 498$^c$–502$^a$.
59. *Ibid.*, 499$^{b-c}$, 500$^d$, 520$^{a-d}$, 521$^b$, 539$^e$.
60. *Ibid.*, 485$^a$, 501$^{b-c}$, 517$^c$.
61. *Ibid.*, 519$^c$.
62. *Ibid.*, 486$^{a-b}$.
63. *Ibid.*, 539$^e$.
64. *Ibid.*, 514$^b$–515$^c$.
65. *Ibid.*, 517$^a$.
66. Cf. *ibid.*, 376$^e$.
67. *Ibid.*, 540$^d$–541$^a$; cf. 499$^b$, 501$^{a,e}$.
68. *Ibid.*, 433$^{a-b}$ and 443$^d$; cf. Aristotle *Nicomachean Ethics* 1098$^a$ 7–12.
69. *Republic* 583$^a$.
70. *Ibid.*, 519$^e$–520$^b$; 540$^{b,e}$.

71. Consider *Apology of Socrates* 30$^a$.
72. *Republic* 545$^{a-b}$; cf. 498$^{c-d}$.
73. *Laws* 739$^{b-e}$.
74. Cf. *Republic* 547$^b$.
75. Cf. *ibid.*, 546$^e$–547$^a$ and Hesiod *Works and Days* 106 ff.
76. *Republic* 557$^{d-e}$.
77. See Thucydides VI. 27–29 and 53–61.
78. Cf. *Republic* 564$^c$–565$^a$ and 575$^c$.
79. Cf. *ibid.*, 563$^d$ with 389$^a$.
80. Cf. *ibid.*, 577$^{c-d}$ with 428$^{d-e}$ and 422$^{a,c}$.
81. *Ibid.*, 568$^{a-d}$.
82. *Ibid.*, 545$^{d-e}$, 549$^{c-e}$.
83. *Ibid.*, 608$^c$, 614$^a$.
84. *Ibid.*, 377$^a$.
85. *Ibid.*, 485$^{c-d}$.
86. *Ibid.*, 601$^c$–602$^a$.
87. *Ibid.*, 598$^e$, 599$^{c-e}$, 600$^e$.
88. Cf. *ibid.*, 501$^a$.
89. *The Gay Science*, No. 1.
90. *Republic* 603$^e$–604$^a$, 606$^{a,c}$, 607$^a$.
91. *Ibid.*, 607$^b$.
92. Cf. *ibid.*, 604$^e$.
93. *Ibid.*, 611$^b$–612$^a$.
94. *Ibid.*, 504$^b$, 506$^d$.
95. Cicero *Republic* II.52.
96. Cf. Plato *Republic* 484$^d$ and 539$^e$ with 501$^{a-c}$.
97. Cf. *Statesman* 285$^d$.
98. *Republic* 511$^{a-d}$, 531$^a$–533$^d$, 537$^c$.
99. Cf. *Statesman* 264$^c$.
100. *Ibid.*, 262$^c$–263$^d$, 266$^d$.
101. Cf. *ibid.*, 271$^e$, 272$^{b-c}$.
102. *Ibid.*, 274$^e$–275$^c$.
103. Cf. *Sophist* 252$^{d-e}$.
104. *Statesman* 295$^{b-c}$.
105. *Ibid.*, 297$^a$ ff.
106. *Ibid.*, 301$^{c-e}$.
107. Cf. *Theaitetos* 151$^b$.
108. *Statesman* 260$^{a-b}$.
109. *Laws* 631$^{b-d}$; cf. 829$^{a-b}$.
110. *Ibid.*, 636$^e$.
111. *Ibid.*, 639$^{b-c}$.
112. *Republic* 544$^c$.
113. *Laws* 642$^a$.
114. Cf. *ibid.*, 673$^{a-c}$.
115. *Ibid.*, 666$^e$–667$^b$.

116. *Ibid.,* 643$^c$, 659$^{d-e}$; 653$^{a-b}$.
117. *Ibid.,* 660$^e$–664$^b$.
118. *Republic* 392$^{a-c}$.
119. *Laws* 676$^{a,c}$, 678$^a$.
120. *Ibid.,* 690$^{a-d}$.
121. *Ibid.,* 693$^d$.
122. *Ibid.,* 707$^e$–708$^d$.
123. Cf. *ibid.,* 708$^e$–712$^a$ with *Republic* 487$^a$.
124. *Laws* 713$^c$–715$^b$.
125. *Ibid.,* 712$^{c-e}$.

126. *Ibid.,* 719$^b$–720$^e$.
127. *Ibid.,* 722$^e$–723$^a$; cf. 808$^{d-e}$.
128. Cf. Aristotle *Politics* 1266$^a$ 1–3.
129. *Laws* 739$^a$–740$^a$.
130. *Ibid.,* 756$^{b-e}$.
131. *Ibid.,* 886; cf. 891$^b$.
132. *Ibid.,* 769$^a$–771$^a$, 772$^{a-d}$, 875$^{c-d}$.
133. *Ibid.,* 949$^e$ ff.
134. *Ibid.,* 963$^e$.
135. Aristotle *Politics* 1265$^a$ 1–4.


# READINGS

A.  Plato. *Republic.*
B.  Plato. *Laws.*

# ARISTOTLE

## 384–322 B.C.

Aristotle was born in the seaport town of Stagira in northeastern Thrace. His father was Nicomachus, a court physician to the royal family of Macedon. Aristotle came to Athens in 367 and entered the school of Plato where he remained until the latter's death in 347. He lived in Assos in the Troad (347–344), in Lesbos (344–342), and for about six years at the Macedonian capital of Pella (342–336), during which time his famed association with the young Alexander occurred. In 335 he returned to Athens where he founded his own school, the Lyceum. In the anti-Macedonian reaction that swept Athens and other Greek cities after the death of Alexander in 323, Aristotle was indicted for impiety and fled to Chalcis in Euboea (his mother's birthplace), reportedly saying that "Athens must not sin a second time against philosophy." He died there not long afterwards, in 322.

Aristotle's political philosophy is to be found primarily in two books: the *Nicomachean Ethics* and the *Politics.* An evidently earlier and less definitive work is the *Eudemian Ethics,* the fourth, fifth, and sixth books of which are identical with the fifth, sixth, and seventh books of the *Nicomachean Ethics.* An exhaustive study of Aristotle's political philosophy would include a careful examination of similarities and differences in the two ethical treatises, as well as consideration of a smaller and less scientific work called by the tradition *Magna Moralia.* Finally, we must note the famous 158 constitutions (or regimes) said to have been collected by Aristotle, according to ancient catalogues, and which are referred to in the last paragraph of the *Nicomachean Ethics.* Of these, only one has survived. Fortunately, it is the Athenian constitution or, more accurately, a constitutional history of Athens accompanied by an account of the constitution in Aristotle's time. In this essay we will limit ourselves, in the main, to Aristotle's *Politics,* with such supplementary consideration of the *Nicomachean Ethics* as is necessary to establish the context within which the political treatise (in the narrower sense of the word political) occurs.

The subject of Aristotle's *Politics* is the *polis* or political community. There is no single English word that will translate *polis,* and to understand why is indispensable to any introduction to Aristotle's political philosophy. The *Politics* begins with a definition of the *polis,* and the student who reads this as a definition of the "state," with all the connotations alien to Aristotle in that expression, is apt to be estranged forever from his thought. Our word "politics," although a noun, is the plural form of the adjective "politic." A parallel instance is the word "athletics," formed from the adjective "athletic." Now athletics is what athletes do. The Greek noun *athlētēs*—from which athletic and athletics are derived—survives virtually unaltered in our language. We know what athletics is because we know what an athlete is. The latter is a concrete subject of observation while the former is an abstract general characterization of his activities. But the Greek noun *polis,* which does not survive in our language, is to politics what athlete is to athletics. Politics, the abstract general characterization derived from the Greek survives, but *polis,* the concrete subject, does not.

As we have observed, the usual translation of *polis* is "state." [1] But *polis* and "state" are not even logical equivalents. According to Aristotle, "community" is the genus and "political community" a species. The specifying characteristic of the political community or *polis* is that it is the community that includes all other human communities, while itself being included by none. Because of its all-inclusiveness, the *polis* includes or assimilates within its own end or purpose the end or purpose of every other form of community. The scope of the state is quite different, as we see when we consider the term "state" as it occurs familiarly today in such antinomies as "the individual and the state," "church and state," or "state and society." It is clear that the state, whether separated from or combined with a church, is never understood to include by itself, as an element of its own definition, the function of a church. The purpose of a state, as state, is never understood to be that of providing for the eternal welfare of its citizens or subjects, however much it may assist a church or churches in providing for it. If the functions of church and state happen to be united in the same body, as for example in the Vatican or the British Queen in Parliament, they are still distinct from each other. They are as distinct as, to use an Aristotelian example, the functions of a tragic chorus are distinct from those of a comic chorus, although the human beings who comprise the two choruses may be the same. The decisive consideration is this: the end or function of the state—*e.g.,* to secure the rights to life, liberty, and the pursuit of happiness—when added to the end or function of the church—*e.g.,* to direct men to their eternal welfare—constitute an aggregate of ends or functions different from that of either taken separately. But the concept of the *polis* is such that there is no process of addition by which one could alter, in either a quantitative or a qualitative sense, its end or function.

It is a common error to suppose that, because the *polis* includes all other communities, the end or function of the *polis* is simply the aggregate of the ends of the communities it embraces, with the addition of the end we attribute to the state. This error is expressed in the attempt to explain the comprehensiveness of the *polis* by saying that it "is" simultaneously church and state. In this view, the reason why the end of the *polis* cannot be altered by any process of addition is that it is by definition the sum of the ends it embraces. But the *polis,* while it embraces the ends of all lesser forms of community, is not the sum of them, because it is in no sense an aggregate. Aristotle sometimes conceives of the *polis* upon the analogy of a living organism.[2] Just as the function of the human organism cannot be conceived as the sum of the functions of heart, liver, hand, and brain, so one cannot conceive of the function of the *polis* as the sum of any parts or components. The function of the human organism is not a sum for the same reason that it cannot be divided and allocated among its parts. It is a whole of which heart, liver, hand, and brain are parts. But it is not a mathematical whole. Without all the parts the whole cannot perform its function, or cannot perform it so well; but the function performed by the whole is a function of the whole alone. What we mean by a whole man can never be resolved into his physiological components.

*Polis,* we have said, is logically not the equivalent of "state" because *polis* is the species of community which includes by definition all other (and hence lesser) forms of community. "State" is not the comprehensive form of community, if indeed it can be understood as a species of the genus community at all.[3] The state, and the law of the state, can certainly be better understood as a species of contract. By the *polis* is meant a radically different relationship of the political community to human gregariousness than is meant by these contemporary terms. The *polis* cannot *be* simultaneously church and state because the definition of the *polis* implies a quasi-organic relationship between the subordinate functions of subordinate associations within the *polis* to the superordinate function of the *polis,* a relationship which excludes the very idea of what we understand by either church or state.

As both "church" and "state" are excluded from what Aristotle understands by *polis,* so also are "society" and "individual." The term "society" as used in present-day social science, may be like *polis*—as "state" is not—in that it is frequently taken to refer to the totality of the forms of human association. But it is never conceived to be a unified authoritative whole, as is the *polis.* Sometimes society is conceived simply as an aggregate of all forms of community within a specified locality, sometimes as an organic or quasi-organic unity. But whatever the unity attributed to society, it is not the kind of unity which gives its identity to the *polis.* For the unity of the *polis* is like that of the human organism, in that it is the result of a capacity for deliberate rational purpose. Whatever rationality the eye of the beholder may discover in society, it is never deliberate rational purpose; for the presence of such purpose necessitates government, and the very idea of society was conceived to express the idea of human gregariousness without particular reference to government.

What we mean today by "individual" is logically implied by, and is correlative with, "state," "church," and "society," but is utterly incongruent with *polis.* Modern individualism conceives each human being to have a sphere of privacy wherein are generated activities and ends which the state, as state, can never order or direct to their completion and perfection. Because of this essential incompetence of the state in certain areas, other forms of community, of which the church is the most familiar and convenient, although by no means the sole example, are both possible and necessary. There is a familiar aphorism today, that the state exists for the individual and not the individual for the state. The most common characterization of totalitarianism in the Western world is that it reverses this order and treats the individual as if he exists for the state. One must not, in approaching Aristotle, attempt to characterize his thought in terms of such an aphorism, because it is not possible to substitute *polis* for state. It makes no more sense to say that the *polis* exists for the citizen, or the citizen for the *polis,* than to say that the mind exists for the man or the man for the mind. According to Aristotle man exists ultimately for the sake of the good life, and the good life is the same for one man and for a *polis.* The means-end relationship we predicate of state and individual does not subsist between man and *polis,* and all inferences which assume such a relationship are false.

The *Politics* begins by defining the *polis* as follows:

> Since we see that every *polis* is a community, and that every community
> is established for the sake of some good—since all do everything for the sake
> of what seems to them good—it is clear that as all communities aim at some
> good, the one that does so in the highest degree and aims at the most authori-
> tative of all goods is the community which is the most authoritative of all and
> embraces all others: this is the one called the *polis* or the political community.[4]

What are the elements of this definition? First there is this syllogism:
Every *polis* is a community; every community aims at some good; therefore every *polis* aims at some good. The minor premise is itself the conclusion of an implied syllogism: Every community is constituted by
common action; every action aims at some good; therefore every community aims at some good. To understand the definition of the *polis*
we must then grasp with utmost firmness the meaning and the implications of the proposition that every action aims at or intends some good.

This proposition applies, in Aristotle's whole doctrine (or perhaps
we should say, doctrine of the whole), to all motion in the universe, but
we will consider it only as it refers to voluntary human action. Every
human agent acts voluntarily only as he intends something that, in so
far as it is a motive for him to act, appears to him to be something good.
A hungry man eats because relieving his hunger seems to him to be
good. The man who would eat when he is hungry must work that he
may have food. Work that may itself not otherwise be desired is nonetheless motivated by a seeming good, namely, food. The student studies
that he may learn and learns that he may know. His end is knowledge,
which may be desired for its own sake or for the sake of some work
which it will enable him to do. This work may be desired for its own
sake, or for its consequences (*e.g.,* money or food), or for both. The
thief may steal even as the honest man works, that he may eat. Stealing
may be evil as honest work is good, but the good for the sake of which
the one steals and the other works may nonetheless be the same, namely,
eating. In short, all human action originates in desire for something
which moves to action by its appearance of desirability or goodness.
Desire implies a sense of deficiency in the agent; that which is desired
appears to the agent as capable of overcoming the sense of deficiency. As
such, it appears to him as good, and becomes thereby the motive for
voluntary action.

The question arises, however, as to what is the relationship among
the many things that are desired as good. The answer given in the first
book of the *Nicomachean Ethics,* with an elaborateness and subtlety
which we cannot begin to reproduce, runs somewhat as follows. There

are three kinds of ends. First, those which are purely instrumental, which are desired only for their consequences and never for themselves. Money is the most conspicuous example, medicinal drugs is another. Second, there are those good things which would be desired even if they had no further consequences, but in fact are desired as well because they contribute to the acquisition of other goods. Seeing and hearing are examples of faculties whose activities we delight in for themselves, but which are also means to nearly all the other good things in life, as indeed is health altogether. Honor, pleasure, reason, and every virtue are also things which we would choose, and do choose, for their own sakes, but which are also chosen for their further consequences or advantages. The final class of good is that which is chosen only for its own sake and never for the sake of anything else. Of these three classes it is clear that the merely instrumental, as such, are less valuable than those which are final, meaning thereby the goods which are or can be chosen for their own sakes; and the more final an object of choice is, in comparison with one which is either entirely or partly instrumental, the more inherently valuable it is.

Intrinsic to the distinction between instrumental and final ends and vital to its comprehension is the distinction between ends which are activities and ends which are products. A chair is an end apart from the activity of carpentering which produced it. Singing is both an activity for making music and music itself. In such cases as the carpentering, Aristotle says, it is the nature of the products to be better than the activity. The skill of the carpenter precedes in time the chair which is produced by that skill. But the chair (and other products of carpentering) are desired before carpentering is desired, and the development of the skill of carpentering (in so far as it is a result of deliberate voluntary action) is a consequence of the desire for its products. It is the utility of such products as chairs which is the final cause of carpentering, even as carpentering is the efficient cause of chairs. Because the chairs stand before carpentering in the order of final causality, they enjoy priority in the order of excellence. Now there are many actions, arts, and sciences, and their ends also are many. Sometimes these ends appear unrelated, but sometimes they are evidently related to each other by their relation to a common end. Bridle-making and the other arts of equipping horses fall under the art of riding; but riding falls under the military art, or strategy. The end of strategy is victory in war, and it is the excellence of this end which is the final cause of the excellence of strategy, and of the lesser excellences of the lesser arts which it has, directly or indirectly, called into existence, and which serve it. The same is true of health in relation to medicine and of medicine in relation to the subordinate arts which serve it. And so with buildings in relation to architecture in relation to, *e.g.,* bricklaying and interior decorating.

Now we see that victory, health, and buildings are final in relation to the arts that serve them, and all are worthy of choice for their own sake: victory for the evils of defeat it averts and for the honor it achieves; health for the evils of disease which it averts and for the healthy activity it engenders; buildings for the discomforts they avert and for the comforts they provide. But victory is valuable not only for the foregoing reasons, but far more because of the activities having nothing to do with war which can be pursued only in peace and freedom. The man would be mad who would go to war for the sake of the honor of victory, if peace and freedom were attainable without war. Peace and freedom are ends more final than victory; the intrinsic value of victory derives from peace and freedom no less than the value of weapons derives from the value of victory. And so the question arises, What is the cause of the value of peace and freedom? Or, to put the question in its most comprehensive form, as Aristotle does, Is there not something always desirable for its own sake and never for the sake of something else? If there is then this must be the thing or, if there be more than one such, these must be the things for the sake of which everything else is done.

Now Aristotle maintains that there is one such thing, which stands in the same relation to all the activities of human life as the target stands in relation to the activity of the archer. It is the mark toward which everything we do is ultimately directed, and only as we can see that mark (or as we are directed by those who do see it) can our lives be said to have direction. The ground of Aristotle's opinion is twofold. First, if there were no absolutely final cause of human action, then everything would be desired for the sake of something else and there would be no term or end of human desire. Each human choice, we recall, initiates a movement to overcome some deficiency in the agent, *e.g.,* eating to overcome hunger, learning to overcome ignorance. It is a movement from incompletion toward completion, from imperfection toward perfection. But if each deliberate action were nothing but the way to another action, the notion of progress from lesser to greater finality would be pure illusion. The only actual finality would be an infinite regress, and life would be essentially purposeless and vain. But human action originates in the human soul, the cause of which is nature. Aristotle holds that nature does nothing in vain, and action originating in the soul would be vain if it could not terminate short of infinity. Therefore there must be a final attainable end of all human action. This argument, it will be perceived, depends upon Aristotle's doctrine of nature. But there is another argument as well, namely, that universal opinion testifies to the existence of such an end. And common opinion, to the extent that it is uncontradicted and internally consistent, is always authoritative for Aristotle.[5] All people speak of happiness and all mean by happiness just such a thing as we have specified as a final end: something for the sake of which every good thing can be chosen—including those good things like honor, virtue, and health which can be chosen for their own sakes—but which is never itself chosen for the sake of anything else. To possess happiness means to lack nothing desirable, to be self-sufficient. Self-sufficiency does not imply a solitary condition, but rather whatever a man needs to be happy: parents, children, friends, and fellow citizens. Happiness, unlike other goods, is not to be enumerated *among* good things. To be healthy *and* wealthy *and* wise is better than to be any one or two of these things. But one cannot add wealth or wisdom to happiness to make happiness better, because happiness implies the presence of all other good things in whatever measure is sufficient to define their excellence. Whatever positive measure of goodness can be ascribed to health or wealth or wisdom derives from its ability to contribute to happiness.

We cannot do more here than allude to the substantive meaning of happiness as developed by Aristotle in the ten books of the *Nicomachean Ethics*. The definition given in the first book is that happiness is an activity of soul in accordance with virtue—and if there are many virtues, in accordance with the best and most complete—in a complete life. Virtuous activity is defined as that activity which perfects the specifically human part of the soul, the rational faculty, in the same sense that musical excellence perfects the faculty of music-making in one who has the potentiality to make music. What is crucial in the foregoing for understanding the definition of the *polis* is that the idea of a complete and self-sufficient community, a community that embraces all other communities but is embraced by none, corresponds exactly to the idea of happiness: the human good that embraces and includes within itself as an element of its own definition all other goods, but is itself included in the definition of no other good. Happiness is the term of all human action, and is implicit as the final term of every human action. The *polis* is the term of all human communities, and is the external, organized expression of the unity which governs or ought govern the totality of human actions in all their diversity.

Near the beginning of the *Nicomachean Ethics,* immediately after affirming that there must be one goal for the whole of human life even as there must be a mark for the archer, Aristotle says that of the sciences and faculties the one that would guide us toward this goal or mark would be the most authoritative and the master of all the others. Politics is this supreme discipline, and the language Aristotle uses to describe the relation of politics to all other disciplines corresponds closely to the language used at the beginning of the *Politics* to describe the relation of the *polis* to all other forms of community. Politics determines which of the sciences should be studied in the *polis,* by which of the citizens, and to what degree. Politics alone rules strategy, economics, and rhetoric. For happiness is the end of politics, as victory is of strategy, and wealth of economics. Only the man who understands the requirements of victory can utilize, let us say, a cavalry maneuver, even if he requires a cavalry officer to execute it. And only the one who understands the requirements of happiness can utilize victory, even if he requires a general to secure it. The ultimate end of human life, the good for man, happiness, Aristotle maintains, is one and the same, whether we consider one man or a *polis.* But to attain or preserve it for a *polis* or a nation seems greater or more complete than for one man. The reason why is made clear at the end of the *Nicomachean Ethics,* when the meaning of happiness has been fully elaborated and the transition to the *Politics* is indicated. The conditions of happiness are seldom if ever within the ability of one man to control. Only good men can be happy (although they may not be), but good laws make good men, and good government makes good laws.

Following the definition of the *polis,* the first book of the *Politics* is concerned in the main to establish two things: first, that the unity which constitutes the *polis* is complex rather than simple, that there are several forms of authority within it and not only one; and second, that the *polis* exists by nature and not by law or convention alone, and that the ground of authority in the *polis* is nature and not arbitrary compulsion. Aristotle first attacks "some" (Plato and others) who fail to distinguish between political rule, royal rule, the rule of a household, and the rule of a master, treating them as differing only in the number of those ruling or the number of those ruled. A little later he attacks "others" who maintain that for one man to be master of another is against nature and can be attributed only to unjust force. Those who hold that the distinction between a free man and a slave is altogether artificial maintain as well that all authority is conventional and that there is no nonarbitrary standard by which to distinguish just from unjust compulsion. The Platonic view seems in theory to be the extreme opposite of the conventionalist view, but in practice it appears to have a certain resemblance to it. In the idea of the good, Plato held to an objective standard outside human opinion, and hence outside human convention, which was the ground of all right action, whether by one man or by a *polis*. In the first book of the *Nicomachean Ethics* Aristotle criticizes this doctrine in some detail, the most important result of this criticism, for present purposes, being that such an idea cannot serve as a guide to action. The "good-in-itself" will not serve the weaver, the carpenter, or the doctor, who will not discover from it what is good in cloth, in furniture, or in health. Acting man acts with reference to particulars. The doctor treats not man-in-general, but this man, *e.g.,* Socrates. The doctor must know what health in general is like to treat Socrates, and he does know what such health is like, because he knows what healthy activities of the body are like. But it is these, and not an abstract goodness, that are the tokens of the presence of that good thing, health. The Platonic idea of the good so transcends individual phenomena that it leaves practical life without a guide. Here, we might observe, is also the principle of the criticism of the *Republic* in the second book of the *Politics:* it is an impractical scheme and can no more guide the legislator than the idea of the good can guide the weaver, carpenter, or doctor. The Platonic teaching recognizes an objective standard, but it is impractical; the conventionalists deny that there is an objective standard. Aristotle maintains that we have in nature a standard that is both practical and objective.

Aristotle undertakes to demonstrate both the aforesaid contentions, namely, the differences of the different forms of authority and the naturalness of the *polis,* by tracing the growth of the *polis* from its first beginning and its composition from its elements. Its first beginnings are the coupling together of male and female for the continuation of the species. This clearly is natural and is in accordance with a necessity common to man and all other animals. But the union of male and female for generation is no more intended by nature than the union of ruler and ruled for safety. Foresight of the mind is the basis of ruling the body, as the ability of the body to do what the mind sees is needful is the basis of being ruled. Slave and female are distinct by nature, as the functions of procreation and self-preservation, although intimately connected, are distinct. The right ordering of the family requires recognition of the differences between the two, which the barbarians fail to do by treating women as slaves. The family, arising from natural needs, is a natural community, with a common interest binding its members, male and female, master and slave. Its structuring, in terms of the foregoing distinctions, is not adventitious but is—or should be—rooted in an understanding of nature. The union of several families makes a village, and of several villages a *polis*. When are there enough villages to comprise a *polis?* When the human and nonhuman resources of the several villages, in combination, enable the community to be self-sufficient. What makes a community self-sufficient? When it is able to lead the good life. The distinction between mere life, on the one hand, the consequence of procreation and self-preservation, and the good life, is apparent from the difference between the household and the *polis*.

The union of families into the larger whole is in one sense no less natural than the union of male and female from which the family results. The man who first united villages to form a *polis* was the cause of the greatest goods, says Aristotle, implying that deliberate action, and not the kind of natural necessity that produced the family, is the cause of the political community. But the purpose of the *polis* is no less natural than that of the family, because ultimately they are one and the same. Whether we consider a man, a horse, or a household, the nature of each thing is what it is when it is fully grown and completed. Nature does nothing in vain, and she has endowed man with the faculty of reason and speech. This faculty is not what appears in other animals when they signify pleasure and pain to each other. Nor is the *polis* like the beehive or any other nonhuman community, which carries out the division of tasks by the mechanism of instinct. Reason and speech —not instinct—indicate the useful and the harmful, the just and the unjust. The common burdens and the common advantages must be divided and shared by rules which must themselves be decided upon by the sharers in the common good. What these rules are, and how they are to be applied, is what we mean by the administration of justice in the broadest sense. And it is participation in this which makes a man a citizen, and the partnership in justice is the political community. The family and the village are too narrow for self-sufficiency, and hence too narrow for justice. Hence the *polis,* as the only community adequate for the fulfillment of man's specifically human potentiality, must be *prior* to the family in one of the senses that the oak tree is prior to the acorn. The *polis* is also prior to the family as, in our former analysis, the chair is prior to the carpentering which produces it. That is, it is prior in the order of final causality. The *polis* is also prior to the single human being, as the whole man is prior to the hand or any other organ of the whole. For except as he lives in a *polis* a man cannot live a fully human existence, he cannot function as a man. For man is the rational and political animal.

To comprehend Aristotle's famous discussion of slavery one must remind oneself of the context established by the coincidence of the two contrary theses, Platonic and conventionalist. The latter regards the distinction between master and slave as wholly conventional and as resting upon force. The former, by affirming that there is essentially one science of ruling, and that the variety of forms of rule are differences of degree rather than kind, also affirms by implication that the difference between master and slave, except as an example of the distinction between ruler and ruled, is conventional. Aristotle's crucial thesis, which is itself in agreement with Plato, is that the distinction between ruler and ruled, of which master and slave is an example, is a distinction that we find throughout nature. We find in the cause of the difference between man and the lower animals, and even in inanimate things, as for example in the musical scale, a ruling principle. Above all, we find a principle of rule in the difference between body and soul, and within the soul in the difference between reason and desire. The soul rules the body by a despotic rule, and the reasoning part of the soul rules the passions, by a political or royal rule. By this Aristotle means that the faculties of the body, as such, merely experience pleasure and pain, seeking the one and avoiding the other; but the thinking part of man teaches him that he is sometimes preserved by what is painful (*e.g.*, surgery) and destroyed by what is pleasant (*e.g.*, narcotics). That in man which responds merely to the demands of the body, like a child whom one cannot by any possibility persuade to drink bitter medicine, must simply be ruled or overruled, by deception or force. The passions, unlike the demands of the body, are not the response to mere pleasure and pain. Anger, for example, may lead us to seek revenge, however dangerous or painful the occasion. Here reason rules differently, persuading us to seek revenge only when revenge is justified. The passion of anger is clearly capable of receiving instruction; *i.e.*, one can learn not to feel satisfaction in wrongly indulged anger and to feel satisfaction in a rightly indulged anger. One cannot learn to feel bodily pleasure in the surgeon's knife, or to feel bodily pain in a successful sexual act, however illicit. In the latter case one can simply deny the purely physical impulses, and this is the prototype of despotic rule. In the former case one can discipline one's affections to move of themselves in the directions judged good by reason. Trained obedience, as distinct from brute direction, is the characteristic of being ruled politically or royally.

Perhaps the simplest explanation of what Aristotle means by natural slavery is that it is an example of the relation of body and soul, in which the body of one man is related to the soul of another. If there is a man with a mentality like that of the child, who cannot perceive that it is sometimes good to take bitter medicine, then he must be ruled like a child, for his own good. But such a man cannot have a good of his own, as a normal child can have. That is, the child must be ruled by his father in order that he may eventually become a good man, independent of his father's commands. But the natural slave, being a grown man who must be ruled as a child, can never be a complete human being. Properly speaking, he is not a grown man, although he may have the body of one. He is a part, not a whole, and he may become part of a whole only as he belongs to another, in a sense comparable to that in which any grown man's body is part of him, namely, as an instrument of his intelligence. It is in this sense that a natural slave is property, *i.e.*, he is an instrument for action by a soul able to live a good life. He is properly part of the household, because even as an instrument of action he is capable only of the uncomplicated actions which are directly concerned with the business of the household, the business of providing material conditions for the preservation of life. Noble actions are not possible for one who cannot do noble things for their own sake, and a natural slave is bereft of the higher functions of the soul.

That there are natural slaves, in the aforesaid sense, is the universal experience of mankind. Today we call them mental incompetents, among other things. Aristotle is emphatic that those who are called slaves, but who are in fact competent, are not slaves by nature, but by law and convention only, and the slavery of such men does rest, at bottom, upon force. There is a common interest which unites natural slave with natural master, but this is not true when unjust law and force alone are the ground of the relationship. Who is truly a master, and who is truly a slave, depends then upon the intrinsic characteristics of master and slave. The Platonic thesis is wrong in that it makes one man the ruler of another because the former possesses a certain kind of knowledge. Aristotle admits that there may indeed be a science of ruling slaves, but he denies that it is the possession of this science which, in the first instance, entitles a man to be a master. Rather does such a science profit a master in his use of slaves, just as it may profit him to have his slaves instructed in their duties by those who make a study of such things, even as he might employ someone to train his dogs and horses.

The discussion of the relation of master and slave forms the first part of Aristotle's treatment of the household, and the *polis,* as a compound of communities, is essentially a compound of families or households. To understand the genesis of politics means to understand the functions generated by families but incapable of being carried to perfection within the framework of the family. Families consist of freemen and slaves. The relationships of the free members are those of husband

and wife, father and children. The rule of the husband is a kind of political rule, in that both husband and wife are rational beings, reason being naturally stronger in the man. The husband is like an official permanently in office, and the wife is like a nonofficial citizen (although Aristotle admits that sometimes, contrary to nature, the wife is more rational than the husband). The rule of the father over his children is more royal than political, in that the distance between them is much greater than between husband and wife, but the kind of direction he gives them is entirely different from that which befits slaves, who remain permanently subordinate, while the children eventually become full citizens.

The exact purpose of Aristotle's elaborate discussion of the household in Book I of the *Politics* is the subject of much difference of opinion, and each student can form his own judgment only on the basis of the most detailed consideration. Here we can but set down some guidelines. Clearly, the highest function of the family, like that of the *polis,* is the formation of character. The end of the *Nicomachean Ethics* indicates that the transition from ethics to politics is required by the limitations of the family for the purpose of training. Whether education is public or private, the art of legislating is required for it. That is, not the father as father, but the father who is legislator, can wisely prescribe even to his own son. But in fact it is difficult to have good families in a corrupt *polis,* so for still other reasons legislation is needed. In considering the legislation for the best regime, in Books VII and VIII of the *Politics,* the chief subject is the educational curriculum. But the discussion in Book I is mainly concerned with what we would call economics, or with the provision of the materials by which the bodies of men, rather than their souls, are nourished. Still, the fact that the bodies in question are those of men, and not animals other than man, is the crucial fact when we consider how to provide for their bodies. This may be indicated by considering two texts dealing with the family. In Book VIII of the *Nicomachean Ethics*[6] Aristotle observes that friendship between man and wife seems to exist by nature, since man is more a conjugal than a political animal, and the household prior to and more necessary than the *polis,* as the production of offspring is common to man and the other animals. Yet in the better known passage in the *Politics,* Book I,[7] he says that the *polis* is by nature prior to the household and to each of us. The formal solution of this apparent contradiction is, as we have indicated, in the distinction between what is prior in the order of efficient causality (the household) and what is prior in the order of final causality (the *polis*). However, the question remains as to what are the activities generated by the material requirements of the family, the efficient causes of which are the natural necessities of mere life, necessities consistent with (but not sufficient for) the end of the *polis*.

The analysis consists of two main parts. The basic element of the first part is a comparison of the human family with families of animals other than man. Aristotle had remarked near the beginning of Book I[8] that man in virtue of his rationality was more political than the bee or any other gregarious animal. But the implicit comparison with the beehive was defective in this, that the beehive does not require institution, as does the *polis,* and therefore is in one sense more obviously natural. The comparison of the household with the families of other animals is in one sense more perfect than the comparison of the *polis* with the beehive, since the families of men and of animals other than man are formed in the same way. Deep consideration of similarities and differences of the families of gregarious animals seems to reveal the emergence of the conventional from the natural in the human family by a kind of necessity, and to reveal how nature remains the norm for convention, even as convention replaces nature as the cause of the material conditions of life.

The arts or sciences dealing with the household fall into two classes. First, there are those concerned with household management, which refers to the right use of the goods of the household. Of the goods of the household, there are two kinds: tools or instruments, and materials. A shuttle is an inanimate tool, as a slave is an animate one. Fleece is a material for the weaver, as bronze is for the statuary. Second, there is the art or science of acquisition. Strictly speaking, it is not an art *of* the household, since it is not carried on by the household or in the household, but it provides materials and tools by which the work of the household can be carried on. Of all the goods that must be provided, food of course is the most important. And nature provides not only men, but all animals with food. Some animals are flesh-eating, others grain-eating, and nature points out the proper food to each and provïdes for each the food for which it has adapted them. The natural modes of acquisition for man—corresponding with the grazing or predatory activities of other animals—are those of pastoral nomads, hunters, farmers. The hunters Aristotle divides into brigands or pirates, fishermen, and the hunters of fowl and game. In a summary statement Aristotle lists nomads, farmers, brigands, fishermen, hunters. Brigands are now separated from other hunters; and still later Aristotle includes the art of war as part of the art of hunting—the hunting of human beings for the purpose of reducing to servitude those who are by nature slaves and who resist enslavement. Brigandage as a natural mode of acquisition, and war for the sake of enslavement as part of the art of acquisition, are the striking features of this analysis. The explanation, whatever it may ultimately be, certainly derives from the idea that nature provides man with the necessaries of life even as she provides the other animals. If plants exist for the support of animal life, then the lower animals exist for the higher, and all animals, or such as are serviceable to him, must then exist for man. Since a slave is something less than a full human being, he, too, is a legitimate object of acquisition.

The second part of acquisition, which is in an especial sense wealth-getting, is acquisition by barter and trade. One part of this is natural, namely, acquisition by simple barter, *e.g.,* the exchange of shoes for grain. The second part is acquisition of money, and this branch, although it is originally merely an extension of barter, becomes something very different, and in this difference is not merely not natural, but is contrary to nature.

Money is invented as a convenience, to facilitate such natural exchanges as shoes for grain, because natural goods are difficult to carry about. Money is a common measure for other goods, with only limited intrinsic value itself. Yet as trade continues, the acquisition of money becomes an end in itself, and what is a measure for wealth is identified with wealth. Finally, money is earned, not only from the exchange of goods other than money, but from the exchanging of money, *i.e.,* from usury. This is wholly unnatural and hence bad.

Why does the human faculty of reason lead to such degeneration, proceeding as it does from the extension of natural barter through the use of money to the final corruption of usury? Natural wealth is limited by the needs of the household, for example, the amount of fleece by the amount of cloth needed for clothing, the amount of food by the hunger of a limited number of stomachs. But every art is unlimited with respect to the good at which it aims: medicine does not aim at a certain amount of health, it aims at as much health as possible. Once wealth becomes an end, as it is the end of what we today call economics, it seeks not the amount of wealth needed by the family, but simply wealth. Yet the connection of economics with the family remains in this fact: the family originates in the need to perpetuate life, and economics seeks to accumulate goods that are serviceable for life. That is, it seeks goods that either support mere life or that gratify the appetites necessary for the preservation of life. The drive for accumulation is rooted in the enjoyable excess of those pleasures which are originally the natural concomitants of the preservation of life. Such excess is the natural enemy, we might say, of the perception of the difference between mere life and the good life, and for this reason Aristotle condemns it categorically.

Still, Aristotle admits that the art of acquisition is part of the art of the statesman, and he nowhere excludes the possibility that even usury may be sometimes useful. The *polis* needs the specialized vocations of the arts of acquisition and of medicine, since the families need the benefits of their skills, and the family as family cannot provide them.

If we compare the two branches of acquisition, we must notice that at the center of one is a species of war and that the other is trade, culminating in usury. Neither war nor trade in their developed forms can be carried on by the family. Thus we see that political activity is generated by the requirements of the human family, even though the human family originates in the same necessities as do the families of beasts. To some extent war and trade are alternative modes of acquisition, and Aristotle seems to praise war, or at least just war, while condemning trade, or at least its extreme form. The root of injustice seems to be the abolition of the limits upon the desires of the body of which man, alone among the animals, is capable. Perhaps the extreme of trade, culminating in usury, is more akin to the abolition of those limits than is war. Whether or not this explains Aristotle's judgment, it is clear that nature has established limits for human life, no less than she has done for the other animals, however much she has left it in the hands of men to enforce those limits.

The second book of the *Politics* consists of these main parts: first, critiques of theories or discourses concerning the best regime by men who did not themselves take part in politics (Plato, Phaleas, and Hippodamus); second, critiques of three well-governed actual regimes (Sparta, Crete, and Carthage); and third, a brief discussion of nine famous lawgivers, men who combined theory with practice by either founding regimes or legislating for existing ones. We might then characterize the order of Book II as theoretical, practical, and practical-theoretical.

Book I established the formal definition of the *polis* as the community of communities and affirmed it to be a complex, natural whole. In tracing its genesis from the family, Aristotle traced the genesis within the elements of which the *polis* is compounded to the distinction between mere life and the good life. The full elaboration of this distinction would provide a description of the best of all possible ways of life, it would describe the best *politeia* or regime. This Aristotle actually does in Books VII and VIII, although he has not completed the task when Book VIII breaks off. It is important to realize, however, that for Aristotle the nature of the *polis,* as of everything that exists by nature, is such that its perfection, which is its nature in the most emphatic sense, is to be sought in the first instance in the manner of its generation. And this in turn is due to the way in which Aristotle conceived the relation of theory and practice, speech and deed, essence and existence.

Every actual *polis* presents itself in the form of some regime: it is either a democracy, an aristocracy, an oligarchy, and so on. Similarly, every man whom we see, apart from having a name like Smith or Jones, is either brave or cowardly, just or unjust, wise or foolish. We never *see* a *polis* or a man, we only see individual *poleis* or men, and to be man or *polis* is never identical with being the particular being whom we experience with our senses. Further, Smith may be brave, and Athens may be free, but the quality of being a brave man or a free *polis* is never identical with being Smith or Athens. When we reason out what it is that makes a man brave or a *polis* free, we discover that the quality itself implies more than is or can be perceived in any actual *or possible* Smith or Athens. For Plato, the qualities revealed in speech, the qualities which we contemplate with our minds' eyes, hence the qualities which are the objects of theory, always transcend—thus in some sense differ from or contradict—the things of which we have sensible experience. Reality, for Plato, is thus ineluctably paradoxical. Aristotle denies this. Man (like dogs and horses) is generated by man and the sun. The things discovered in speech are reflections of things themselves or, rather, they are more or less adequate reflections depending upon whether the speech about the things is adequately disciplined by a true method or science of the things. The idea of man is in each man and is ultimately identical with the activity in virtue of which human beings generate human beings and not dogs or horses. There is thus no paradox for Aristotle in the unity of man and the plurality of men. The idea of the *polis* is similarly present in the generating factors of the *polis* (similarly, not identically, because the *polis* requires the assistance of art for its generation in a way that generation which is altogether natural does not). Plato's *Politeia* or *Republic* reveals what Plato regards as the nature of justice, but it transcends every actual or possible *politeia* in the way that speech about every idea reveals tendencies in sensible things that sensible things themselves never fully embody.

In approaching Aristotle's critique of the *Republic,* the dominating topic of Book II, we should consider that Aristotle's demonstration of the impossibility of that regime as a model for political practice (like his demonstration of the impossibility of the idea of the good serving as such a model or guide in Book I of the *Nicomachean Ethics*) is in agreement, rather than disagreement, with Plato. The disagreement lies deeper and concerns whether a model which transcends practice and can never be imitated in practice reveals the nature of practice more truly than a model which lies within the range of what is possible in practice. It is characteristic of the difference between Plato and Aristotle that Plato's quest for the best regime requires a construction in speech (or theory) to which nothing in practice does or can correspond, while Aristotle's quest first takes the form of an inquiry into regimes both of speech and deed, either of which might contain elements of the best regime. As was shown in the chapter on Plato (cf. above, p. 17), the first regime in the *Republic,* the so-called city of pigs, the regime constructed out of the necessities of the bodies of men, revealed nothing of the ultimate demands of justice. For Plato, the generating of living bodies by living bodies does not of itself set in motion the tendencies which culminate in the truly just regime, the regime which can exist only in speech. In Book I of the *Politics* Aristotle contradicts this thesis: the families which result from the generation of the bodies of men evidently require as their complement the *polis.* The justice which makes every *polis* a *polis, i.e.,* the form that justice takes in virtue of which this *polis* is a democracy and not an oligarchy, is a variety of the forms of justice. The unity underlying the plurality of the forms of the *polis* is like the unity underlying the variety of individuals of every species. It results from the nature common to all men, who are all political animals. This nature is *in* all men, not beyond them, and the truth about the *polis* like that about all nature is nonparadoxical because it is constituted, not by the duality of form and matter (to which correspond speech and deed, theory and practice), but by their unity.

The first and dominating topic of Book II, as we have noted, is the consideration of Plato's *Republic.* One must attend with utmost care to the manner of its introduction. The *polis* is a community, a having things in common. It is the community of communities, hence it embraces something common to everyone. Aristotle asks, Is its perfection achieved by making common everything that can possibly be common? Or by making some things common and others not? Or by making nothing common? The last appears to be excluded by definition. If nothing were common it would not be a community. In the *Republic* of Plato, observes Aristotle, Socrates says that children and wives and property are to be shared or made common to all the citizens. Which arrangement is preferable, Aristotle asks, that which now obtains or that in the law set forth in the *Republic?*

To facilitate a concise view of a lengthy argument, it may be well to give Aristotle's answer to the foregoing question at the outset. The present system, of private families and private property, if adorned by good morals and by the right laws, would be much superior. Aristotle does not say flatly that the present system is superior because he does not seem to regard the present system (namely, that of Athens, which is not one of those thought by Aristotle to be well-governed) as good. But the present system can be made good, whereas that of the *Republic* cannot. Why? The fundamental objection to the communism proposed by Socrates is that it aims to produce the greatest amount of unity in the *polis* but mistakes the nature of political unity. To push unity beyond a certain point, says Aristotle, changes the *polis* into a family, and a family (so far as possible) into one man. But in doing this, he says, you do not unify the *polis* but rather destroy it.

Aristotle now demonstrates how the family, whose growth and proliferation require the institution of the *polis,* is structurally part of the perfected *polis,* because the distinctions which give structure to the family—between husband and wife, father and children—are the foundation of morality within the *polis.* To take the broadest ground, the morality which consists in subordination of private interests to public welfare is impossible if the distinction between private and public is abolished. The *polis,* Aristotle holds, is a heterogeneous, not a homogeneous, unity. It is no more unified by abolishing the distinction between private families than by abolishing the distinction between occupations. That is, you do not make the *polis* more a unity by making every man a shoemaker and every man a carpenter; on the contrary, the *polis* requires division of labor, and by reciprocal equality, which means a fair exchange between artisans like the shoemaker and the carpenter, enables all to enjoy better shoes and better houses. In the isolated family the skills of shoemaker and carpenter may be necessary within the same household, but the institution of the *polis,* in which many specialized skills are available to all, is for this very reason self-sufficient in a way the family by itself is not. If two men call the same woman wife, the result is apt to be, not greater friendship, but conflict. In fact, however, Socrates intended all men to call all women their wives, and all the children collectively their children. Each woman was only a fractional wife of each man, and each child only a fractional child of each father. This, says Aristotle, will not strengthen the social bonds but will dilute them. Better for a man to regard a boy as his own nephew than as his and every other man's son. With the

weakening of the strong bonds of private affection and private morality will come a weakening of the moral prohibitions against assaults
and injuries against fathers and kinsmen, not to mention the dissolution
of restraints against incest and homosexuality. To abolish the private
family leads to the abolition of most of the prohibited degrees of sexual
intercourse, and in consequence to the introduction of many forms of
familiarity which lead to immoral intercourse. The claims of morality
cannot thereby be enhanced but are rather dissipated. Aristotle's argument seems to be that the restraints which one learns in the family,
e.g., the respect for authority in the person of the father, and the en-
hancement of an offense of violence if it is against a father, and similarly the horror of incest between parents and children, or between
brother and sister, or of homosexuality between brothers, lays a foundation of restraints upon behavior which is then extended to members
of different families, and finally to civic morality. Civic morality
consists in perfecting the morality whose foundation is the family, at
first by giving it an authority greater than the family can achieve, and
finally by giving it a purpose which transcends the family.

In addition, Aristotle emphasizes the impossibilities of Socrates'
proposal: the resemblances between natural parents and their children
will betray themselves, and attachments will accordingly be formed.
Public property will not be well cared for, some will be slackers in
their work, and quarrels will arise in the distribution of the goods. The
reclassing of children, which Socrates says will go on between the
guardians and the working class, will betray the origins of some, and
even the diluted bonds will be attenuated. Moreover, Socrates leaves
a mass of unsolved difficulties: for example, is communism limited to
the guardian class, or does it include the farmers and artisans? If there
is to be one communist system for them all, so that all are "children"
of the same "parents," how can the two classes be separated into menials
and guardians? And if communism is limited to the upper class, what
will be the political functions and education of the lower class? If they
do have private property, it will be very hard to keep them in a subordinate position.

Private property, Aristotle holds, is rooted in human nature. Selfishness is justly condemned; but this does not mean it is wrong to love
oneself, only that it is wrong to love oneself in excess. Similarly, love of
money is not wrong, but loving it in excess is. The indefeasible roots of
private property are the indefeasibly private pleasures of the body. In
the *Nicomachean Ethics* Aristotle observes that the pleasures of good
food, wine, and sexual intercourse which all men enjoy, pleasures
which are natural and necessary, are not bad.[9] Only their excesses are

bad. Socratic communism in the *Republic* would, by attempting to abolish the occasions of evil, abolish also many of the occasions of virtue. Even if it prevented some evil, it would also prevent much good. The advantages of communism can be gained by making the use of property common, as in Sparta men freely use each other's slaves and horses and dogs and help themselves to the fruits of each other's fields as they travel. But a man cannot practice liberality if he has nothing of his own to give, or show temperance in relation to women if there is not such a thing as another man's wife. The real cause of evil, says Aristotle, is not the absence of communism, but wickedness. What must be made common is not wives and children and property, but a system of education. The *polis* is no more made one by communism than a harmony is made one by converting it into a unison, or a rhythm made one by converting it to a single beat. It is strange, says Aristotle, that one who, like Socrates in the *Republic,* expects to accomplish excellence by education, should at the same time rely on such institutions, instead of relying on customs, philosophy, and laws.

The *Laws,* says Aristotle, was written later, in an attempt to provide a regime nearer to actual *poleis,* although in fact it leads back little by little to the *Republic.* And so most of the same objections made to the *Republic* apply to it. As a proposal for the regime which is next to the first (or best) it is unacceptable, although as a version of polity, or the mean between democracy and oligarchy adaptable to most *poleis,* it might have something to recommend it.

All other regimes are nearer to actual practice than those of Plato. Phaleas of Chalcedon has made a proposal that resembles Plato's in that it attempts to eliminate the causes of division and strife within the *polis* by the regulation of property. Indeed, Aristotle credits Phaleas with being the first to introduce this notion. Phaleas would make the property of the citizens equal at the foundation of a regime, and in those already established would seek to level inequalities by requiring the rich to give but not receive dowries and the poor to receive but not give them. Aristotle comments, first, that such legislation (as also in the case of Plato's *Laws*) will be ineffectual if the total number of children is not limited in proportion to the total amount of property. Secondly, not merely equality and inequality must be considered with respect to men's estates, but their size, which must be neither too large nor too small, tending neither to luxury nor penury. Finally, what is needful is not so much to level men's properties but their desires, and this requires education.

Phaleas, it is true, is consistent in providing the same education for all. But he does not tell us what that education is to be. But, says

Aristotle, dissension is caused not only by inequality of property, but by inequality of honor, the lower classes being concerned primarily with the former, the upper classes with the latter.

According to what Aristotle says here, inequality of property is, relatively speaking, a minor factor in the creation of civil disturbances. This, he maintains, is because it is not so much the avoidance of pain, or the deprivations of the body, which cause trouble as it is the appetites or desires not connected with deprivations. It is not so much to avoid hunger and cold that men steal as to enjoy luxury. That a man's neighbor has a greater estate will not anger him nearly so much as if one he deems his inferior is held in the same honor. There are then three classes of desires which need to be dealt with: those arising from the needs of the body; those arising for the desires of the body in excess of what is necessary; and the desire for pleasures which are not due to pains (*i.e.,* as the pleasure of eating depends upon the pain of hunger). For the first kind of desire, a moderate amount of property accompanied by work is needful; for the second, the virtue of temperance or moderation; for the third, the remedy is philosophy, which alone frees us from dependence upon other men.

Phaleas' scheme is directed only to minor evils and fails to take into account that the greatest crimes are not those connected in any way with property. Men do not become tyrants, observes Aristotle, to avoid hunger and cold, nor does one honor a man for killing a thief as one does for killing a tyrant. Levelling estates is not, then, the place to start in the attack upon political evil. The starting point, says Aristotle, is to train those who are by nature superior not to desire to have more than is right, and to prevent the inferior (while not treating them unjustly) from being able to.

Hippodamus was the first man not engaged in politics to speak of the best regime, even as Plato was first to introduce community of wives and children, and Phaleas first to attack the problem of dissension by the regulation of property. Hippodamus was an eccentric, and Aristotle gives a character sketch of him—the original political scientist—that is without parallel in either the *Ethics* or *Politics*. He had long hair (the Spartan style, considered effeminate in Athens), wore the same cheap clothes summer and winter, but with expensive ornaments, and wished to be learned in the whole of natural science. He was also the man, Aristotle tells us, who invented the division of cities and applied it to Piraeus (the port of Athens). He was, we might add, the father of town planning as well as of political science (in one sense of that term). Perhaps the most revealing brief comment on Hippodamus is one that occurs in Book VII, in the course of Aristotle's the-

matic discussion of his own best regime. The question concerns the
arrangement of streets. The modern fashion introduced by Hippodamus, which is more pleasant and convenient, is for private houses
to be laid out along straight lines. But, says Aristotle, the opposite
arrangement of olden times was much safer, for it was harder for
foreign troops to find their way into the city or make their way through
it. Aristotle's own solution, characteristically, is to combine the two
kinds of plans, designing certain parts of the *polis* for comfort and
beauty and others for security. Hippodamus was, then, a theorist in
the modern sense, *i.e.,* one who approached politics as an abstract
problem in design, without regard for the problems that statesmen as
practical men faced. He was also like certain twentieth-century political scientists in his attempt to assimilate the science of politics to a
mathematically oriented natural science. Hippodamus' scheme has a
certain resemblance to Plato's in that it appears to be an attempt to
impose mathematical harmony upon the *polis.* His best regime had a
population of ten thousand and was divided into artisans, farmers, and
warriors. The land he also divided into three parts: one sacred, one
public, one private. The law, too, he found fell into three categories:
outrage, damage, and homicide. He established one supreme court of
appeal for all cases, to consist of selected elders. He thought that jurors
should not give simple verdicts of guilty or not guilty, according to
the indictment as drawn (the current practice), but should give
qualified verdicts finding guilt on some counts but not others—if this
was the individual juror's belief—and assessing damages according to
the juror's judgment in damage suits. For Hippodamus thought that
the practice of finding a man guilty or not guilty, when the juror
believed him to be guilty of some things but not of others in the indictment, forced the juror to commit perjury. Finally, Hippodamus
proposed a law which would honor anyone who discovered anything
new for the advantage of the *polis,* as well as one that would provide
public support for war orphans. Aristotle dryly observes that Hippodamus apparently thought this last was a new suggestion, but in fact
such a law already exists in Athens and other *poleis.*[10]

The last observation sets the tone of the critique of Hippodamus:
a man who wants to institute systematic search for political novelty
ought to be better acquainted with what already exists. The tripartite
division of the *polis* has an air of simplicity which is specious: all three
classes are to share in the government, but the farmers have no arms,
and the artisans neither arms nor land. The warriors will not tolerate
the political equality of those who are thus much weaker than themselves, and the oppression of the warriors will make the other classes

enemies of the regime. More trenchant still is Aristotle's criticism of the
so-called farming class: on the face of it, no class would seem more
necessary, and yet in fact they farm only for themselves and are politically superfluous. The warriors are to be supported from the public
land, which they must either farm themselves (hindering their ability
to be soldiers), or there will be yet a fourth class to farm it for them,
which in turn will have no political rights. The artisans are self-sup-
porting anyway. Aristotle reveals confusion after confusion beneath the
surface of these proposals.

Again, the proposal to reward those who discover advantageous
novelties is attractive but unsafe. It may cause malicious prosecutions
(either against the innovators or by the innovators) and even revolution. This leads to another, broader question, and it is the fundamental
question raised by Hippodamus: Is politics an art or science like the
other arts or sciences, in which each new discovery is rightly incorporated into the practice of the art or science? Aristotle's reply is that
politics is not like medicine or gymnastics, in which every alteration
from traditional practice, in the light of better knowledge, is rightly
acceptable. Not that tradition as such is a political norm: on the contrary, the most ancient customs are utterly foolish; and in general what
men really seek is not what their fathers had but what is good. The
distinction between the good and the ancestral is as fundamental to
the art or science of politics as to any other. The possibility of improvement in the political order is in fact twofold: first, because of the
progress of general intelligence (including progress in the arts and sciences) from primitive man; and second, because of the necessity of
every law to be framed in general terms, while the actions governed by
law are always particulars. Experience must always reveal ways in
which the laws might be better framed, and therefore how they might
be improved. On the other hand, however, much caution must be
exercised in making these improvements, says Aristotle. Small improvements would not outweigh the harm done by making changes
in the laws, changes which breed distrust in the government. The
example of the other arts is false. Politics is not an art like medicine
and gymnastics, for the law has no power to persuade other than that
derived from custom or habit, and these are formed only over a long
period of time. Changing laws weakens their power, it loosens the
bonds of the community, and this requires the greatest circumspection.
But if changes in the laws are to be made, says Aristotle (and of course
they sometimes must and ought to be made, or why write the
*Politics?*), does this mean that all laws are open to change in every
form of government? To use a modern instance, would we here in

the United States today accept proposals for change in the Bill of Rights in the same spirit as changes in the exemptions in the income tax? And again, Aristotle asks, shall anyone propose changes, or only certain people? For example, does it make no difference whether the changes are proposed by a constitutional convention under the presiding genius of a George Washington, or by anyone anywhere? These things make a difference in politics that they do not make in the practice of the other arts.

After the discussion of the three regimes of speech or theory, we come to the three actual regimes, which exist in deed. Concerning any regime, Aristotle says, there are two questions. First, how does it compare with the best regime? Second, is there anything in its construction contrary to its hypothesis? The meaning of the second question becomes clearer from an explanation, at the beginning of the fourth book, of the different kinds and degrees of political excellence with which the political philosopher must be concerned. The best regime is such as one ought to choose if there were no external impediments, either human or nonhuman, to virtue, or virtuous activity, as the end of life in the *polis*. The hypothesis of the best regime is just this: that virtue is its end and that there are no external impediments to its attainment. In practice, however, there almost always will be impediments, both to the choice of the best end and of the best means. The hypothesis of a regime other than the best is the assumption (or set of assumptions) by which the controlling aim or purpose of the regime is qualified in the light of its impediments, as compared with the best regime.

The analysis of Sparta reveals above all one thing: the inner connection between the quality of the construction of a regime and the quality of its hypothesis. Sparta is defective not merely because conditions are less than perfect, but because the legislator mistook a part of virtue for the whole of virtue, and this intellectual error is the leading cause of the defects Aristotle discovers.

Aristotle's critique of the legislator's purpose comes almost at the end of the discussion of Sparta; but as so often happens, the end is in fact the beginning. The entire ordering of the laws is directed to a part of virtue, the part which contributes to success in war. The Spartans' warrior discipline won them safety in war and an empire. But they had no training in the pursuits of peace and began to go to pieces as soon as they had won their hegemony. They err also in another respect, according to Aristotle, and this error is really at the bottom of the other. They rightly think that the good things won by fighting are the achievements of virtue rather than of vice. But they wrongly suppose that the external rewards of virtue are worth more than virtue. The full meaning

of this observation is given in Book VII in the famous discussion of the
relative merits of the active and the contemplative life, as the ultimate
goal either for a single man or for a *polis*.[11] Sparta is there, too, given
as an example of a *polis* devoted wholly to war, and war is there seen
as the goal of life of those who do not grasp the ultimate supremacy of
thinking over acting, as the basis not only of thought, but of action.

The criticism of Sparta has three main divisions: the last part
centers upon the principle or hypothesis of the regime; the first concerns the defects of Spartan economy (slaves, women, property); the
second concerns political defects in the narrower sense (the ephors,
elders, and kings). We will limit ourselves to the first and last and
their connection. Aristotle begins his criticism of Sparta by observing
that a well-governed *polis* needs leisure, and this can only be provided
by slaves. He says little more on the subject here, other than that the
helots are like an enemy in the Spartans' midst, waiting only for disaster to strike their masters to rise in revolt. Aristotle does not say here
what the remedy for such a situation must be, but the answer has
already been made clear: the art of ruling slaves is a part of household
management, and the Spartans have not cultivated this art. The reason,
too, is clear: household management is an art of peaceful living, and
friendship between master and slave, to the extent it is possible, depends upon a common purpose uniting them in such a way that both
contribute to it according to their natures. War, or success in war, as
an end in itself, means ruling those who are not meant to be ruled
and for a purpose for which men are not meant to be ruled. The
Spartans' defective relation to foreign *poleis,* in virtue of their policy
of conquest, is reflected in their defective internal relation with their
slaves and wives. In cruder terms, in their anxiety to rule those abroad
whom they ought not to rule, they neglect those at home whom they
ought to rule. The same reasoning accounts for the licentiousness of
Spartan women, who by reason of the neglect of the men, preoccupied
with military pursuits, and because of the addiction of soldiers to the
pleasures of love, are self-indulgent and unmanageable. The women
tend to get control of the management of affairs as well. What difference
does it make, asks Aristotle, whether the women rule, or the rulers are
ruled by women? The result is the same. The irony of all this is that
the *polis* that identifies the whole of virtue with the supposedly most
manly of virtues—courage or fighting—is penalized by being dominated
by females. The irony comes full circle when Aristotle points out that,
in neglecting to rule their women properly (along with their slaves),
both because of their absences on military expeditions and because they
had neglected the domestic arts while at home, the Spartans greatly

weakened themselves militarily. For during the Theban invasion, the women of Sparta caused more confusion than the enemy. The subordination of the pursuits of war to those of peace is then a necessary condition of a truly successful military policy.

The defects of the system of property are consequences of the condition of women. It is dishonorable in Sparta to sell a family estate but not to give it or bequeath it. The result is that nearly two-fifths of the land is owned by women. Without regulation of inheritances and with the practice of large dowries, the ban upon alienation of estates has proved inconsequential. As a result of the concentration of ownership, there has been a depopulation of the armed class (who need property to furnish the wealth needed for arms), as well as a social division into extremes of wealthy and of poor. Again, we see the attrition of the regime's military strength as an ultimate consequence of its military nature.

The discussion of Crete, which follows that of Sparta, also has three main parts: first, an account of the relationship of Crete and Sparta; second, an account of analogies in the two systems; and third, an evaluation of similarities and differences. Sparta is held to be an improved imitation (on the whole) of Crete, which is the older regime. This raises some subtle and interesting questions as to the possibilities of political progress, a subject first raised in relation to Hippodamus' proposal to reward political novelties. It also involves the question of the relation of Lycurgus, the Spartan lawgiver, to Minos, the Cretan lawgiver, on the one hand, and to Thales, whose pupil Aristotle says he is reputed to have been. Minos, son of Zeus and Europa, represents the oldest tradition of Greek law as it ascends to the gods; Thales is the traditional founder of philosophy. The Cretan institution which Aristotle praises most highly is that of the common meals, which are paid for from the public lands and are not a private charge as at Sparta. The legislator, he says, has devised many wise means for securing moderation at table. Also, he has segregated the women from the men in order that they might not bear many children and for the same purpose has instituted homosexual relations among the men. Whether this is good or bad, says Aristotle, there will be another opportunity to inquire. There is, however, no further discussion of this question in any surviving text, and we may observe that this perverse institution does offer one solution to a recurring problem in the *Politics:* how to keep the ratio of population to property constant. Another solution, of course, was emigration. Whether Crete is one of the three best-governed actual regimes because of, or in spite of, this one feature remains speculative. The principal explicit criticism of Crete is that it does not have any constitutional means of reconciling the people to the regime (as at Sparta where the people choose the ephors), so that discontented members of the upper classes combine with the people periodically to make what are in effect revolutions.

The discussion of the Carthaginian regime follows the same pattern as that of Crete. First, some general remarks comparing it to the others; second, the principal points of resemblance to Sparta; third, criticism of the principal features of the regime. The most conspicuous feature of the general remarks is the praise of Carthage. Carthage comes closest to Sparta, which has already been praised as better than Crete. The three regimes, says Aristotle, come closer to each other than any of them do to any other regime, and all are greatly superior to any others. The proof of the excellence of Carthage is the fact that the *dēmos* or common people have remained faithful to it, and that neither civil strife nor tyranny worth mentioning has arisen there. Such remarks go quite beyond what Aristotle has said in praise of Sparta and justify classifying Carthage as the best of all actual regimes. Two further points ought to be made here, although they invite the interpretation of Aristotle's silence rather than his words. Carthage is a non-Greek or, in the technical sense, barbarian *polis;* and we are not given any information by Aristotle concerning the legislator or legislators of Carthage, or their relation, if any, to the famous legislators or teachers of legislators concerning whom he says a great deal elsewhere in the *Politics.*

The three points of resemblance to Sparta are: the common messes of the companions (equivalent to the *phiditia*); the office of the one hundred and four (equivalent to the ephorate); and the kings and council of elders (which correspond to the kings and elders at Sparta). In this context Aristotle mentions that the one hundred and four are chosen for merit, not at random, as in Sparta; and the kings are chosen, not from the same families, but from outstanding ones.

As to political criticism, this falls into three categories: features common to Carthage and the other regimes, which Aristotle has sufficiently spoken of in the case of the other two; and those which depart from aristocracy either toward democracy or toward oligarchy. The democratic deviation is the practice of referring to the popular assembly, not only for approval, but for discussion and for ultimate decision, any question upon which kings and elders cannot agree. The oligarchic deviation is in the manner of choosing the magistrates, which is based upon a kind of electoral college system, comprised of "boards of five" which are co-opted and membership in which is clearly restricted to the wealthy classes (although Aristotle does not explicitly say so). But the chief deviation from aristocracy is in an opinion (rather than an institution), and it is one that is shared by the many (as well as the few). For whatever the ruling class holds in honor, Aristotle says in a memorable phrase, the rest of the citizens are certain to follow. This opinion is that rulers should be chosen not only for their virtues but for their wealth. The Carthaginians think that a poor man lacks the leisure for governing well (in which they are of course right), but the legislator errs in not providing from the outset that the best men have sufficient leisure, whether in or out of office.

This leads us to certain observations concerning Aristotle's procedure with these three regimes: the very first question he took up vis-à-vis Sparta concerned the provision of leisure, which he said is not easy to provide. He there speaks of the difficulties that Spartans and Thessalians had with their servile classes (and no solution for the problem of leisure is hinted at which does not require a servile class). The Cretans, we are told, have escaped this problem, mainly because of the fortune of geography. The requirement of leisure is clearly correlated with the "hypothesis" or principle of the regime, and Sparta we saw was severely criticized for mistaking the nature of virtue. In the treatment of Crete, much is made of the advantages they enjoy from geography. They are evidently less warlike than the Spartans, but in this they are weak rather than wiser. Aristotle says remarkably little about the principle or hypothesis of the Cretan regime. With Carthage, he returns somewhat obliquely to the question of the principle of the regime. Carthage is the only regime of the three that he plainly calls aristocratic, although he does so only in pointing out how it deviates from aristocracy. But as Sparta confuses a part of virtue—courage or military valor—with the whole of virtue, so Carthage confuses a condition of virtue—leisure and the wealth required for it—with virtue. In doing so, the legislator has made the whole *polis* avaricious. It is significant how the criticism of Sparta and Carthage, which Aristotle has already said are closest to each other, here coincides: the consequence of Sparta's devotion to war was also to cause a deviation mainly to oligarchy.

We come now to the last of the three main subdivisions of Book II. This section—dealing with lawgivers—is frequently regarded as consisting of "jottings" or "rough notes" either by Aristotle or a later hand. This view fails to consider, however, the way in which this section seems to fulfill a plan in Book II, moving as it does from the "theoretical" to the "practical" to the "practical-theoretical," *i.e.*, from those who took no part in politics but wrote on the best regime, to good regimes of practice, to the views of those who both held opinions concerning the best regime and took part in politics. Moreover, while there are three regimes of "theory" and three of "practice," there are nine legislators mentioned by Aristotle. The central one of these is Onomacritus (whose name means "name-judge"), who was a Locrian who travelled in Crete, where he practiced soothsaying. According to a tradition (in which Aristotle himself places little credence), he was the first man who became skillful in legislation (as Plato was first to introduce community of wives and children, Phaleas first to equalize property, and Hippodamus first, not a politician, to speak of the best regime). Apparently, however, he did not have any pupils, but had as a companion Thales, who in turn had Lycurgus and Zaleucus for pupils. The whole subject of the relation of tradition to the arts (as of Minos to Thales) and the nature of the relation of progress in the one to progress in the other, is certainly involved here, as it is in the great thematic passage on Hippodamus. But only a comprehensive analysis of the admittedly episodic passages in this section, in their relation to similar passages elsewhere in the *Politics,* could establish their meaning.

Book III begins as follows: "To the one inquiring concerning the regime, what each is and of what sort, almost the first inquiry to make is about the *polis,* whatever is the *polis.*"

Aristotle says he must discover "what and what sort" each regime is. There is, then, a variety of regimes. We must try to understand what that variety is by again trying to understand what the *polis* is. But have we not already had the *polis* defined for us? Aristotle carefully says that "almost" the first question is, Whatever is the *polis?* The first question was answered by the definition with which the *Politics* began, a definition elaborated and defended in the remainder of Book I. The opening definition establishes the relation of the *polis* to other species of human community on the one hand, and to the genus "communities of gregarious animals" on the other. In Book I Aristotle established the definition of the *polis* as the community of communities, originating in the need to preserve life, but continuing for the sake of the self-sufficient or good life. The analysis of the household, and the sciences arising from its needs, establishes the necessity of a separate science of the *polis,* as it established the specific differences of *polis* and household. Book II demonstrated the need for a new inquiry into the best regime. Book III supplies us with the science of the *polis* and the leading feature of that science: an adequate inquiry into the principles of regimes, and in particular of the best regime.

In Book I Aristotle controverted two scientific or philosophic doctrines, those of Platonism and conventionalism, to establish the doctrine that the *polis* was a complex natural whole. In doing this, he pursues methods concerning which he makes two remarks near the beginning of Book I. It is his accustomed method, he says, to analyze a compound whole into its simplest, uncompounded elements. What he actually does, however, as he indicates, is rather to trace the genesis of the compound whole from the genesis of the elements of which it is compounded.[12] These two methods are not, of course, exclusive. Both speak of the whole and of the parts, but one begins from the parts and discovers from the parts that they must be compounded into a larger whole to fulfill their function *as* parts. The other begins with the whole, and discovers from the whole that it is resolved into parts whose functioning makes the whole. The parts discussed in Book I, however, are households or families; in Book III, citizens.

Aristotle's point of view in Book I is one of radical detachment from political life. He observes the *polis* as one among the number of forms of community which are the result of the gregarious natures of animals, and he wishes to classify it accurately in relation to the genera and subgenera of which it is a species. In Book II he dissects the various specimens proposed as possessing the perfections upon which the most accurate classification might be based. In Book III, however, when he no longer treats of the opinions of others concerning the regime, but begins to present his own doctrine, he appears not as an external observer but as someone within the *polis*. The conflicts of opinions with which we are immediately confronted are no longer the conflicts between observers of political life, they are the conflicts among participants, among men who differ as to how the burdens and advantages of political life should be divided and shared. What is most significant about Aristotle's method in Book III is not so much that it is analytical in the sense indicated, but that it draws philosophic conclusions from the opinions of men who are neither philosophers nor legislators, but men who are contending for political advantages in political life.

The subdivisions of Book III are not marked in the same manner as those of Book II. This is Aristotle's exposition of his own doctrine and not the critique of other regimes; and there is a continuity in the argument, and a recurrence of themes, which it is not easy to anatomize. Some division of Book III, however provisional, is necessary for an orderly presentation. To begin with, Book III may be divided by the transition from the answer to the opening question, "Whatever is the *polis*?" to the question, "Is there one regime only, or many?[13] It is a matter of speculation whether we should consider the discussion of mon-

archy as a third major subsection, or whether this continues and completes the discussion of regimes.[14] The discussion of monarchy begins by
recalling that it is one of the "correct" regimes, but the form of monarchy which emerges as the most important topic of discussion is *"pam-
basileia."* This is a kind of absolute rule, in which the king is to the *polis*
as the head of the household to the household. It is thus called a kind of
"economic" rule. But, since economic rule is fundamentally different
from political rule, according to the general doctrine of the *Politics,*
it cannot be assumed that this fifth form of monarchy is a form of
regime properly so called. Therefore it is at least doubtful whether the
discussion of monarchy, which culminates in the consideration of *pam-
basileia* or absolute monarchy, forms part of the discussion of the regime,
or is a third major subsection of Book III.

The first subsection may be conveniently (although perhaps not
definitively) divided into three subsections. First, the definition of the
citizen (*politēs*) and therewith the *polis.* Second, the inquiry as to who
is a citizen and what makes the *polis* the same (or different) when the
regime changes because of revolution. Third, the first of the great disputations of Book III, Is the virtue of a good man and of a good citizen
the same or different?

The definition of the citizen is required because it is a matter of
dispute what the *polis* is. Some say that an action is an action of the
*polis,* others that it is an action not of the *polis* but of the oligarchy or
tyrant. Who are they who thus deny that an action is that of the *polis,*
and what is that action? In considering the problem of revolution,[15]
Aristotle makes explicit what is implicit at the beginning of Book III.
When the regime changes from oligarchy or tyranny to democracy, the
people may repudiate the public debt on the ground that the money was
borrowed, not by the *polis,* but by the oligarchic clique or the tyrant.
Hence the denial is a democratic denial of a financial obligation (and the
action is the one of incurring debt). It is well to remember this when we
discover that the first or "absolute" definition of citizenship applies more
particularly to democracies than to other forms.

The absolute or unqualified definition of citizenship is that it is
nothing other than a sharing in the administration of justice and in
office. This means participating in what we would call legislation and
adjudication, with these two "powers" being sufficiently broad to assimilate what we would understand by administration or execution of the
laws. Indeed, Aristotle generalizes from this first definition, saying that
what he really means is participation in "indefinite office." This definition, he then observes, fits democracy particularly well, but not necessarily other regimes. The idea of "indefinite office" fits democracy be-

cause there all free men constitute a body from whom officeholders are drawn, and nearly all free men participate in some offices (particularly those of jurymen, who had a wide variety of functions in ancient democracy, beyond those we assign to jurymen). But such a definition does not fit regimes such as Sparta or Carthage where political participation is narrowly limited and defined, that is, where few people hold any offices, and only some people can hold some offices. Nevertheless, the definition holds if we say that citizenship means participation in the deliberative and judicial functions of the *polis,* and that he is a citizen who can and does so participate. And, finally a *polis* is a collection of citizens numerous enough to lead a self-sufficient life.

Aristotle next considers the phenomenon we call "naturalization," which in turn leads us to the topic of revolution. In practice, he observes, they are called citizens who are born of citizen parents, but this is obviously inadequate, because the first citizens could not have had citizen parents. The question who, in fact, is a citizen is answered differently after a revolution, when different people exercise the powers by which citizen is properly defined. A regime which excludes many who formerly were citizens will regard those excluded as not having been rightly citizens. Conversely, those included by a new regime will regard the regime which formerly excluded them as not a regime, but a rule of force in contravention of law and justice. This, of course, is the view of a democracy which has overthrown a tyranny and repudiates the tyrant's debts. But, says Aristotle, if an action is repudiated on the ground that it is an act of force and not for the common good, then similar acts of democracies can also be repudiated as not truly being acts of the *polis.* The source of authority does not of itself indicate whether actions are impositions of mere force or are actions taken for the common good. In the opening passage of the inquiry as to where the ruling power should be, Aristotle is still more explicit on this point, as we shall see.[16]

When the *polis* changes in the manner just contemplated, what is it that enables us to say that it is the same *polis* or a different one? We have seen that a *polis* is a collection of citizens, but a revolutionary change will result in a different collection constituting the citizen body. Is it then a different *polis* or not? Aristotle first says what does not identify a *polis.* It is not a place, not even a place enclosed with a wall, for a wall around the Peloponnesus would not make those within the wall fellow-citizens. Nor is it population, for the people of a *polis* are always dying and being born, like the water in a river which is ever changing, while the river itself remains the same. The *polis* is a community, a community constituted by a regime (*politeia*), and when the regime changes the *polis* is no longer the same, just as a tragic chorus is not the same as a comic chorus, although the persons of the two choruses may be identical. It is then *chiefly* (although Aristotle is careful not to say solely or exclusively) with respect to the regime that one must say that the *polis* is the same or different. But whether a *polis* which is a democracy should pay the debts of a tyrant whom the democracy has overthrown is not decided by this conclusion, which requires another argument. Aristotle never presents this argument, at least not overtly. We may perhaps infer it from the distinction which he next forces upon our attention: the distinction between a good man and a good citizen. Obligations which men may not have as citizens they may still have as men. If the citizens of a democracy benefited (whether intentionally or not) from the debts contracted by the tyrant, their obligations *as men* would surely be different from what they would be if the debts had been contracted entirely for the purpose of, let us say, unjustly suppressing the democracy.

We come then to a question for which the way has been prepared by the implicit suggestion that, while man as citizen is essentially a member of a regime, man as man may have obligations which do not arise from, and may not coincide with, those of his citizenship. That question is: Is the virtue of a good man and of a good citizen the same, or is it not the same? This third subsection of the first part of Book III is approximately equal in length to the first two together. Complex as the argument is, here, too, there appear to be three well-defined further subsections. First, there is a definition of the virtue of a citizen, which is not, speaking simply or unqualifiedly, the same as that of a good man. Second, there is the inquiry which reaches the conclusion that, while in general the virtue of good man and good citizen are different, they may coincide in the case of a good ruler. Third, there is an inquiry into whether all those admitted to a share of office—who are perforce citizens by the definition previously accepted—can in fact possess the virtue of citizens. To summarize: Aristotle first establishes the general difference between good man and good citizen; next he specifies the case in which a good citizen may be a good man; third, he specifies the cases in which a man *can* be the good citizen who will be a good man. It is most important for the student here to observe how Aristotle, in taking up a new question, enlarges and refines his answer to an old one. For the results of the inquiry in this subsection into the difference between human and civic goodness or virtue establish grounds for distinguishing different kinds of civic excellence that were not before visible. These, in turn, actually transform the definition of citizenship, while preparing as well for the discussion of regimes which follows.

Aristotle employs the familiar "ship of state" metaphor to explain "in outline" what is the virtue of a citizen. Each citizen is a partner, or sharer in a community, like a sailor on a ship. The sailors differ in their functions—one is an oarsman, another a helmsman, another a lookout— yet all share a common purpose, safety in navigation. So do citizens differ. In Book IV Aristotle lists nine different parts of which the *polis* is composed, beginning with the farming and mechanic classes, on through those who fight, who deliberate, and who judge.[17] Different forms of civic virtue would seem to correspond to the different functions of each of these parts of the *polis,* yet the good performance of the work of each part would have one and the same end: the safety of the regime (*politeia*). If, then, there are many forms of regime, there must be many forms of citizen virtue (in addition to the differences internal to each regime arising from the variety of functions therein), yet there can be only one form of excellence or virtue for man as man. Hence the virtue of a good man and of a good citizen cannot be identical.

Aristotle employs yet another argument to establish this conclusion. Not even the best regime could consist entirely of good men, yet if it were in fact the best regime every citizen would have to perform his duties as well as possible. Hence in the best regime it would appear that there would be some good citizens who were not good men. Still a third argument follows. A *polis* is a compound, even as an animal (of soul and body), a soul (or reason and desire), a household (of man and woman), and property (of master and slave). Every compound has a ruling and ruled elements,[18] and the virtue of ruling is evidently different from that of being ruled. Citizenship requires both forms of virtue, but the form of human goodness is one. Hence the virtue of a good man and of a good citizen cannot be the same.

The third argument of the foregoing series leads naturally to the question whether the virtue of a good man and of a good citizen—although they cannot be simply identical, because the virtue of citizenship is twofold—may not nonetheless coincide in a certain case, that of the good ruler. A statesman is a ruler, and hence must be wise in the sense of possessing a form of practical wisdom. (In the *Nicomachean Ethics,* Book VI, Aristotle distinguishes *phronesis,* practical wisdom, of which the virtue of the *politikos* or statesman is a branch, from *sophia,* or philosophic wisdom, which is concerned exclusively with thinking well and not with acting well.) A citizen, simply as citizen, may be a subject, not a ruler, and hence need not have the practical wisdom of a ruler. In the *Nicomachean Ethics* it is affirmed that the moral virtues, in the strict sense, imply the presence of practical wisdom, as the presence

of practical wisdom implies the presence of moral virtue. Hence the
citizen who does not have the practical wisdom of a ruler need not be
even morally good in the highest sense. Nothing sums up this argument
better than Aristotle's own example, given at the end of this discussion
in the *Politics*. While other virtues may be common to ruler and ruled,
practical wisdom (or one form of it) is the ruler's virtue alone. The
subject, the man who is ruled, needs only right opinion. The latter is
like the man who makes flutes, the ruler corresponds to the man who
plays the flute. The virtue of a good man may then coincide with that of
a good citizen in the case of the citizen (*politēs*) who is a statesman
(*politikos*), who is a good ruler (*archon spoudaios*).

Next, Aristotle asks, Can anyone who is called a citizen by our
previous definition—namely, participating in office—be truly a citizen?
To put it slightly differently: Can *any* citizen (so-called by us) be a
good citizen, capable not only of being ruled, but of ruling, and hence
of being a good man? The very intricate discussion of ruling and being
ruled in the previous subsection, of which we have summarized only
the conclusion, indicated that "ruling" and "being ruled" each has different meanings. Being ruled for certain purposes, for purposes which
are in some sense slavish, disqualifies a man for ruling, just as being
ruled in certain other ways is part of the necessary training of a ruler.
In some regimes—*e.g.*, extreme democracies—men whose occupations
are slavish—the mechanic classes—are admitted to citizenship, and
while these men may be good citizens, in the sense that they can perform
their civic duties well enough to preserve the democracy, they cannot be
good men. The conclusion then follows that only under a regime which
admits to citizenship only those men who are capable, by birth and
training, of becoming good men, will it happen that any good citizen
*can* be a good man. The final and strict conclusion of the entire discussion of good man and good citizen is then as follows: He who is capable
of ruling (although he need not be an actual ruler), either alone or in
conjunction with others, in a good regime (*i.e.*, one which admits to
citizenship only those capable of practical wisdom and moral virtue)
is at once a good citizen and a good man.

We come now to the central sequence of topics of Book III. The first
was initiated by the question, Whatever is the *polis?* The second, to
which we now turn, is initiated by the question, Is there one regime or
many? This second main section of Book III is divided as follows. First,
an introduction setting forth the thematic question. Second, an answer
to the twofold question, What is it for which the *polis* is instituted, and
how many forms of rule are there? Third, an answer to the question,
Who (or what) ought to be the ruling authority in the *polis?*[19]

The thematic question may be translated in full thus: Is there one regime, or many, and if many, what are they, how many, and what are the differences between them? There follows a brief definition of regime (*politeia*). It is an ordering (*taxis*) of the *polis* in respect of its offices, and chiefly in respect of the supreme office. The word "office" is, however, a narrow rendering, and the neologism "decision-maker" conveys something important that is lacking from that translation. What Aristotle means is that whoever makes the big and vital decisions for the political community thereby gives the community its structure and form. The "decision-makers" in the true political sense, as Aristotle would understand that term, combine what we normally understand by legal authority with the authority of the "establishment," in the currently fashionable sense of that term. They are, in other words, both legal sovereigns and ruling class in the traditional meaning. In a democracy, says Aristotle, the people are supreme, and in an oligarchy the few. The government (*politeuma*) *is* the regime (*politeia*), meaning that what causes the *polis* to have a certain form *is* the form.

The second subsection is devoted to answering a twofold question. What is it for the sake of which the *polis* is instituted, and how many forms of rule are there of man and of the community? Regimes, we are told, are distinguished in two ways: first, by the distinction between rightly constituted regimes and those which are wrongly constituted or deviant. Second, by the enumeration of the principal varieties of both the rightly and wrongly constituted. It is in establishing the basis for the distinction between rightly and wrongly constituted regimes that Aristotle gives the first elements of his answer to the question of the purpose of the *polis*. That purpose arises from the fact that man is, he repeats from Book I, a political animal. Men are drawn together not only by necessity (the main emphasis in Book I), but by a desire for the company of their fellows, without whom they could not live well. The aim of a common life is not the better supplying of necessities, but the good life. Still, they *do* need each other for the sake of mere life which has a sweetness which makes men cling to it as long as hardships are not unbearable. Next, Aristotle reviews the forms of subpolitical authority—master and slave, father and children, husband and wife—and then forms of nonpolitical authority—those of a trainer and of a pilot. He points out that rule is always either for a common good or for the good of the ruled. In the case of master and slave, the good is primarily that of the master, but they *do* have a common good, because the deterioration of the slave will deteriorate the master's good. At the other extreme, the trainer and pilot consider essentially only the advantage of those under their direction and benefit themselves only incidentally: the trainer as he happens to take exercise himself while exercising his pupil, and the pilot as he happens also to travel on the ship he steers. By nature, a man holding office is like the trainer and pilot, as in looking after the welfare of his fellow citizens, he thereby stands in need of assistance from them in his own private affairs, which he neglects while attending to the common or public concerns. In the present corrupt times, says Aristotle, men seek office avidly, as a means of advancing their private welfare rather than that of the public. Here then we see the nerve of the distinction between rightly and wrongly constituted regimes: it lies in the distinction between regimes in which the rulers, like practitioners of the art of gymnastics or of sailing, rule those in their charge solely for the good of the ruled (and hence require some recompense for their neglect of their private good while thus occupied) or, on the contrary, consider their offices as sources of private profit.[20]

Next Aristotle gives the number and names of the varieties of regimes. To name the regime means to name the government, or ruling group, and this must be either one man, or a few, or the many. When these govern toward the common advantage they are rightly constituted, and when not, they are deviations from the right forms. The usual designation for the rule of one when it is for the common advantage is kingship, that of a few aristocracy, that of the many polity (*politeia*), which is also the generic name for all regimes. Deviations are: tyranny corresponding to kingship, oligarchy to aristocracy, and democracy to polity. In the first, the single ruler considers only his own interest; in the second it is the interest of the rich which governs; and in the third, the interest of the poor. In none of the deviant regimes do the rulers think of a common interest, but only of themselves.

Next Aristotle elaborates upon the foregoing distinctions, with especial reference to the difference between democracy and oligarchy. He introduces this elaboration with the unusual remark—for the *Politics*—that for one who is philosophizing, and not merely looking into a subject with a view to practice, it is proper not to overlook or omit anything, but to set forth the truth. The remark is unusual because of the emphasis, in both the *Ethics* and *Politics,* upon the essentially practical nature of these disciplines.[21] The difference between democracy and oligarchy is then *not* primarily the difference between the rule of the many and of the few, for if there were few poor and many rich the rule of the many would not be democratic nor the rule of the few oligarchic. Democracy is essentially rule of the poor and incidentally rule of the many, and oligarchy is essentially rule of the rich and incidentally rule of the few although, Aristotle observes, the rich are everywhere few, and the many everywhere poor. The particular importance of this theoretical distinction may lie in the peculiar practical importance of democracy and oligarchy as the two regimes which in practice dominate political struggles. And it is also true that it is from the opinions—the erroneous but complementary opinions—of the partisans of democracy and oligarchy that Aristotle compounds the true opinion which is the basis of his own doctrine concerning distributive justice.

We come now to the exposition of oligarchic and democratic justice, or rather to a discourse nominally devoted to this theme, but actually devoted to extracting from the exposition the answer to the broader question of the true purpose of the *polis,* which is the general topic of the entire section. First, Aristotle explains that all men lay hold of a kind of justice. The one kind of partisan says that it is equality, and so it is, *for equals.* The other kind says that it is inequality, and so it is, *for unequals.* Men are bad judges in their own cases. They state the case only to the point it serves their narrow interest, and not as it stands truly. Justice is a relation between things and persons—*e.g.,* positions of honor and trust on the one hand, and men to fill them on the other—and the partisans see very well what is equal or unequal in the division of such places. But they fail to see what it is that makes the men who are to fill them equal or unequal. Those who are freemen think that if they are equal as freemen, they are equal in every respect; those who are rich think that if they are unequal in wealth they are unequal in every respect. But the ruling principle, the truly authoritative consideration they never mention.

Next, Aristotle expounds this ruling or sovereign consideration. It is, of course, that the *polis* exists, not for the sake of life, but for the good life. The fallacy of the partisans is that they confuse the necessary conditions of political life with the sufficient conditions. The oligarchic fallacy would appear to consist in mistaking the *polis* for a kind of joint stock company, in which the man who contributed 99 per cent of the capital is rightly entitled to a larger share, either of principal or profit, than the man who contributed only 1 per cent. On the other hand (and this seems to refer to the democratic partisans), the *polis* is not a military alliance for protection against injury. Mere self-preservation would characterize as well a community of slaves or lower animals. But again, neither is it an association for trade. The Etruscans and Carthaginians have commercial relations, but they are not fellow-citizens. Aristotle cites approvingly the Sophist Lycophron, who said that the law is a pledge or surety of men's just claims against each other.[22] Indeed it is, but abstaining from injustice is not sufficient to make men fellow citizens. Men who abstain from injustice are not for that reason good or just. (The man who practices honesty because it is the best policy is not for that reason honest.) Good government implies a concern with political virtue and vice.

Having pointed out that neither the virtues engendered by trade nor those engendered by war are in and of themselves to be equated with political virtue, Aristotle considers locality. Megara and Corinth would not be one city even if enclosed within the same walls, not even if the citizens of each intermarried, although intermarriage is an important element in making a community. Nor, again, if they lived close together and exchanged goods, as do carpenter, farmer, shoemaker, and in addition were in military alliance, and yet abstained from wrongdoing.

The sufficient conditions of political life will not, of course, be realized without the foregoing necessary conditions—in particular inhabiting the same locality and practicing intermarriage. These conditions are accompanied by the various forms of social life which go beyond mere utility—e.g., fraternal, religious, recreational associations —which, however, arise not from material needs, but from friendship. Friendship—as Aristotle makes clear at great length in Books VIII and IX of the *Nicomachean Ethics*—means active concern for others, a concern with their well-being, which means with their capacity for welldoing. This in turn means a concern with their capacity for virtuous activity, from which happiness results. And so the political community is above all a community for the sake of acting well (or nobly), or for the sake of happiness. Those who contribute most to enabling friends and fellow citizens to become virtuous and live happily have the larger share in the *polis*. They alone are politically superior, be they never so equal or inferior to others in freedom, birth, or wealth.

Next, Aristotle asks, Who (or what) ought to be the supreme ruling authority in the *polis?* This, we might observe, is the supreme political question, for upon the answer to this question every other political question depends. We have been told that oligarchy and democracy are defective regimes, because they mistake contributions to the necessary conditions of the political community's existence for contributions to its true end or purpose; that is, they mistake contributions to the wealth or freedom of the *polis*—things without which there cannot be a *polis,* but which in themselves do not make a *polis*— for contributions to living happily and well. But what weight do we give to the various claims put forward by those who compete for rule? A *polis* is neither a trading community nor a military alliance, but if we reject the claims of the wealthy and the free (those who pay taxes and those who fight), we may not have a *polis* at all. The attempt to realize the higher aims of the *polis* must not be such as to destroy the material conditions which are necessary for the existence of the *polis,* just as the recognition of the material necessities cannot justifiably inhibit the attainment of happiness and a good life.

The subsection we are about to examine is by far the longest of Book III, and in a sense the culminating theoretical analysis of the entire book, and of the entire *Politics.* Let us then describe the topography of this subsection, however provisional the grounds of our distinctions may seem. First, there is an introduction, setting forth the main question, and the other questions into which this main one resolves itself. Second, there is an inquiry into and partial vindication of the claim of the many to rule, as opposed to that of the few best. Thirdly, there is the inquiry into the question into which the opening question is now seen to resolve itself.[23] Justice is the political good, and justice means equality for equals and inequality for unequals, but Equality and Inequality in What?

Turning now to the introductory subsection, we meet the thematic question, What ought to be the ruling authority in the *polis?* The claimants are: the many, the rich, the good, the one best of all, and the tyrant. These correspond to the six regimes enumerated earlier, with the notable difference that "the many" is the numerical and thus ambiguous ground for both democracy and polity. "The many" as such is neither rich nor poor nor, presumably, good nor bad. This is of course only abstractly or theoretically true, and Aristotle characteristically proceeds in a "practical" vernacular. The recognition of the claim to supreme authority by any of these claimants, Aristotle says, appears to have disagreeable consequences. Suppose, for example, the poor divide up the property of the rich. Is this not the extreme of injustice? "By Zeus, it was justly passed by the ruling authority." Thus the response of the partisans of the many, *i.e.,* of the poor and of democracy. It is one of two oaths in the *Politics,* and that it justifies what is characterized as extreme injustice is not without ironical significance. Also, we must recall that the definition of the *polis* called for at the beginning of Book III was required because of the democratic (and possibly unjust) repudiation of the debts of the oligarchy or of the tyrant. That the many identify their authority with their manyness (instead of with their poverty, which is the real reason they seize the wealth of the few) is shown next by the identification of their authority with majority rule. Suppose then, Aristotle asks, the majority again expropriates the minority? Clearly, the principle which justifies expropriation on the ground that the many are the *polis* is a monster which eventually devours even itself. But justice is not a destructive principle, and therefore the rule of the many, as such, cannot be a principle of justice.

Similar considerations rule out the authority of the rich as rich, or of a tyrant.

But what about the claims of the good? Now Aristotle introduces a still greater perplexity. That neither the poor nor the rich have an unfettered right to rule is clear. But this does not mean they have no claims upon authority whatever. Offices are honors, and to be excluded from office is to be excluded from honor. The unqualified rule of the good would seem unjustly to dishonor classes which do contribute to the common good, by contributing to the necessities without which the *polis* cannot be. And the rule of the one best man would seem to carry the foregoing "oligarchical" tendency to a further extreme. But there are those who say that the law should rule. Yet the law itself can be democratic or oligarchic, so that the same difficulty recurs. Here, then, we have the formulation of the problem of this subsection, and the indication as well that there is no solution in terms of any of the regimes mentioned. However, we already noticed that neither democracy nor polity has been explicitly mentioned in the beginning of this introduction, only the many, who are as such the numerical ground for either democracy or polity. In the difficulties presented by the different kinds of claims, we saw the many referred to in the practical terms of their antagonism to the rich. That their claims need not rest upon their poverty, however, and that a regime of the many need not be identical with democracy, it is Aristotle's immediate concern to demonstrate.

In Book IV Aristotle defines polity as a mixture of two "deviant" regimes, democracy and oligarchy.[24] Here, however, he presents the claims of the many as corresponding nevertheless to the claims of virtue. The claims of virtue would appear to be the only intrinsically valid claims, but the recognition of the claims of virtue is not identical with the recognition of the claims of the virtuous. In the first place, the virtuous are somewhat backward in presenting their claims. Aristotle has indicated,[25] in agreement with Socrates in the *Republic,* that the good man will regard office as at best a kind of duty which he must perform in neglect of his own private interests. Another way of putting this is to say that there is a kind of selfishness in the good which causes them to draw back from, if not to turn away from, political competition as insufficiently rewarding. Illustrative of this is the statement in Book V[26] that those who excel in virtue are the ones who might most justly make a revolution (when others with inferior claims are preferred to them), but that they are the ones least likely to do so. To some extent the political problem is one of compounding the simulacra of virtue in the nonvirtuous, as a device rendered necessary by the withdrawal of the virtuous from active contention. To some extent it arises from a different inadequacy of true virtue. First, there are not likely to be enough virtuous men to constitute a *polis*.[27] Next is the fact that virtue is related to the sufficient rather than the necessary conditions of political life. But virtue as productive of sufficient conditions is not necessarily productive of necessary conditions. There is a kind of disproportion between the necessary and sufficient conditions of political life which makes a genuine equation between political honors and political contributions peculiarly difficult, perhaps impossible. *Political virtue,* as we shall see, is a kind of facsimile of true virtue,[28] a facsimile which compounds certain resemblances to virtue in nonvirtue, to give greater dignity to nonvirtue, and which compounds certain resemblances to nonvirtue in virtue, to give greater political effectiveness to virtue. We now witness Aristotle's laborious attempt, in principle, to achieve such a compound. We say "in principle," because it is in Books IV, V, and VI that he does so in any detail. To some extent, the obscurity which surrounds much of the ensuing argument arises from the danger to political life of expounding too openly the indirectness whereby virtue can become politically effective. That is to say, political virtue which is not confused with strict virtue will not be politically effective, and hence will not be political virtue!

The claim of the many to rule in a good regime is recognized as follows: the many, while individually not good men, may be collectively better than those who are superior to each of them separately. Aristotle gives three analogical examples. A feast to which many contribute is better than a feast supplied at one man's cost. The many judge works of music and poetry better, for one man judges one part of a work, another another, and together they judge the whole with superior judgment. The superiority of the painter's art over reality lies in this: he can select the beautiful eyes of this one, some other superior feature from someone else, and so on, so that the painted figure combines the excellences which in nature are scattered among many. The first example corresponds to the refutation of the claims of the rich: the many poor may yet be collectively wealthier than the wealthy few. The second example, involving deliberation and judgment, refutes the claims of the few good. The third example deals with the claims of the one best man: the many may equal or excel him, not individually but collectively. The argument derived from these examples requires the qualification Aristotle promptly adds: it may justify the popular claims to a share in the regime of *some* multitude (or *dēmos*), but not of any and every one. We have already seen the many characterized by the extreme of injustice, as in the passage in which the people swear by Zeus to justify expropriation, believing it right simply because they have decreed it. We must again recall that the question of what the *polis* is arose because of the democratic denial of a debt. Whether this argument (namely, of collective virtue in the many) applies to every people and every multitude, Aristotle says, is unclear, or, rather, he says, "perhaps, by Zeus, concerning every one it is clearly impossible, because the same argument could apply to beasts; and how, so to speak, do some multitudes differ from beasts?" Thus does Aristotle, in the second (and final) oath employed in the *Politics,* balance the emphatic speech of the many in justifying the extreme of injustice with an oath which insists that they are sometimes bestial. At the same time, we are warned of the limitations of an argument which, explicitly deriving from analogies, justifies no more than an analogical virtue.[29]

The argument from collective virtue is next used to decide what offices may, and what may not, be safely entrusted to a *qualified* multitude. They must not participate in the highest offices. By this Aristotle here means those offices for which collective virtue manifestly cannot be a substitute for the virtue of a single man, as would be the case of such modern offices as president, prime minister, cabinet officers, supreme court justices, or speakers and leaders of legislative assemblies. But offices which contribute to collective deliberation and judgment—*e.g.,* voters, members of legislative assemblies, juries petty and grand, and so on—could be filled by and from the many.

Finally, there is a discussion of whether the idea of collective virtue of a lay public does not contradict the experience of the other arts. Aristotle considers the case of medicine, as he had earlier compared politics to the art of the trainer and pilot. The demand for trained intelligence does not, he concludes, rule out the general public, for even in medicine there are qualified nonexperts who can judge the work of experts. The argument from the arts further rules out a brutalized public, but not every public. It leads to Aristotle's final conclusion in this context: the possibility of utilizing collective virtue in a properly circumscribed role demonstrates nothing so much as the need for good laws. For, he implies, the circumscription of the people to their proper functions, and of the higher officials to theirs, as well as the education of both in the requisite virtues, is the work of good laws.

We come now to the third and final subsection of the subsection addressed to the question, Who (or what) ought to be the supreme authority in the *polis?* The problem has been stated, and the claims of the many (under the conditions favorable to those claims) have received their due. Even under favorable conditions, those claims are met without admitting the many to the *supreme* offices. Justice is the political good, and justice is a kind of equality. Common opinion agrees with philosophy in this, that justice is a relation of things and persons, and that to equal persons equal things are due. Offices are honors, and justice demands therefore that for men who are equal there should be equal honors, and for men who are unequal, unequal honors. There is generally no difficulty in discerning whether offices and honors are equal or unequal. But in what is it that men are to be held to be either equal or unequal? This problem, Aristotle says, calls for political philosophy.

In thus defining this supreme political problem, Aristotle twice uses the word "philosophy" as in the foregoing paraphrase. These are the second and third (and last) times the word occurs in Book III. The first time, we recall, was when Aristotle said that for one "philosophizing" (the verb rather than the noun was used) nothing ought to be overlooked or omitted, whether of practical significance or not.[30] What was inquired into then was the essential difference between oligarchy and democracy. That was found to consist in a difference in quality which had no necessary connection with the *numerical* difference between the many and the few. This rejection of a numerical distinction corresponded with Aristotle's opening polemic in Book I against the reduction of the different forms of rule to differences in the *number* of those ruling or ruled. Now, in seeking the thing whose proportions in different men determine the proportions according to which political honors and offices ought to be awarded, we are again concerned with relationships between quantities and qualities.

This becomes more evident when we turn to the thesis which Aristotle now investigates with a view to deciding the matter. "Perhaps someone would say that offices should be distributed unequally according to every excess of a good." According to this thesis, if men are in other respects alike, yet one is taller or has a better complexion, then he should be awarded the office. The fallacy of this thesis, says Aristotle, is evident if we compare the awarding of offices to the awarding of flutes. Among flute-players equally good at playing the flute, we do not give better flutes to the better born. Let us digress, however, and ask whether the idea that a superiority in birth or beauty can contribute to superiority in flute-playing is simply absurd or whether, like many other opinions, it merely requires correction. Good birth is called virtue of race by Aristotle, which also means inherited virtue. Strictly speaking, of course, virtue cannot be inherited, because it is the result of habituation (moral virtue) or teaching (intellectual virtue). Yet there is a kind of virtue[31] which is really an aptitude for

virtue, called by Aristotle natural virtue. No one is, strictly speaking, a
born musician or mathematician, although we call someone a born
musician or mathematician if he becomes one with very little teaching.
Similarly, some are born with an aptitude for courage or temperance
if, with very little moral education, they become brave or self-con-
trolled. Such aptitudes, or natural virtues, can be inherited. Aristotle
says in Book I that nature intends to make the bodies of freemen as
different from those of slaves as the statues of the gods differ from
those of men.[32] In the same way that nature fails to make freemen
visibly different from slaves, she fails to make the sons of good men
good. If nature succeeded, however, the ordering of society would be
relatively simple.[33] As superior bodies and superior minds would go
together, the different kinds of education appropriate to the different
kinds of souls would be indicated by the different shapes of their
bodies. And the different offices would be allocated by the different
virtues resulting from the different kinds of education. Hence good
birth, beauty, and virtue would be found together in the regime which
was thus truly according to nature. Good birth and beauty would not
literally contribute to flute-playing, but aptitude in flute-playing would
very likely be found among those who were well-born and beautiful.
More important, political virtue would certainly be found among the
well-born and beautiful and never among the ill-born and ugly. That
we picture the gods as superior in beauty no less than in wisdom is
itself far from being politically irrelevant.

In this connection we should consider again Aristotle's example
of the painter who collects from many their individual points of perfection—e.g., nose, eyes, foot, hand—to produce a portrait of a perfection surpassing that of any one human being. The painter, in combining these many perfections, achieves what nature intended but failed
to achieve. Art thus perfects nature in one sense, while in another sense
it is nature which perfects art. For in the latter sense it is nature which
enables the artist to achieve perfection by teaching him what he must
do to achieve perfection. The political philosopher might then be
thought of as the artist of the *polis*.

Suppose, Aristotle continues, someone superior in flute-playing, yet
inferior in birth and beauty. Suppose, moreover, that good birth and
beauty surpass flute-playing more than the best flute-player can surpass
all other flute-players. Even so, says Aristotle, we would award the
superior flute to the superior flute-player, be he never so inferior in
birth and beauty. To suppose that any superiority in birth and beauty
could compensate for an inferiority in flute-playing, when it came to a
distribution of flutes, would imply that birth and beauty could in some
way contribute to flute-playing, which they cannot. The argument

Aristotle here controverts implies, he says, the commensurability of every good with every other good. We cannot help being reminded by this observation of the critique of the Platonic idea of the good in Book I of the *Nicomachean Ethics*. According to the Platonic doctrine, as there presented by Aristotle, there is one idea or form of goodness, which is the cause of what is good in every good thing. It would follow from this doctrine that the intrinsic goodness in every good thing is identical with the goodness in every other good thing. From this it would follow that, with respect only to their goodness, they could differ only as more and less, and to such differences numerical values could be assigned.

Why does Aristotle recur to this abstruse metaphysical issue? If the argument from flutes were not sufficient, does not his further example suffice: that athletic prowess is properly rewarded, not by political office, but by athletic prizes? The difficulty here, it seems, lies in the inner inconsistency in the two kinds of opinions upon which Aristotle draws for his conception of distributive justice. On the one hand, opinion says that justice is equality for equals and inequality for unequals. Birth, wealth, and freedom are qualities needed for the existence of the *polis*, hence they and not flute-playing or speed of foot are properly considered with a view to political honors. The same is true of justice and political virtue. The difference between flute-playing and wealth is a difference between nonpolitical and political goods. The difference between wealth and political virtue is a difference between what contributes to the existence and what contributes to the good government of the *polis*. If no amount of a nonpolitical good can equal a political good, can any amount of a necessary good, *e.g.*, wealth, equal any amount of a sufficient good, *e.g.*, virtue? If it cannot, how can the equation of honors or offices with merit be true? In Book V of the *Nicomachean Ethics* we find the formula for distributive justice.[34] It is, says Aristotle, a species of the proportionate, and the proportionate is equality of ratios. In a just distribution, as $A$ is to $B$, so $C$ is to $D$. That is, as the merit of $A$ is to the merit of $B$, so is the honor $C$ (awarded to $A$) to the honor $D$ (awarded to $B$). Now if these are genuine ratios, the terms must be commutable. Thus, not only will $A/B$ equal $C/D$, but $A/C$ will equal $B/D$. Furthermore, $AD$ will equal $CB$. But, and here is the crux of the entire matter, if $AD$ equals $CB$, then *some* multiple of $A$'s excellence equals *some* multiple of $B$'s excellence. But if this is true—as, strictly speaking, it must be— then we are confronted with a dilemma. Either the excellences to be rewarded—namely, $A$'s and $B$'s—must be homogeneous, of one kind, or excellences different in kind are commensurable.

Let us be absolutely clear as to the nature of the foregoing dilemma, for it appears to be the central theoretical problem of the *Politics*. The dilemma stems from the two opinions whose combination yields the formula for distributive justice. One of those opinions is that justice is an equality of ratios. This opinion is itself a philosophic refinement of the nonphilosophic opinions which are the defining characteristics of oligarchic and democratic justice, the former holding that justice is inequality, the latter that it is equality. Combining the two, Aristotle holds that justice is equality for equals, and inequality for unequals, and hence equality of ratios. The other opinion, besides that which holds justice to be equality of ratios, is the one that holds that goods different in kind are incommensurable. But how can one find a set of ratios that will justly relate the claims of wealth and/or freedom, on the one hand, and virtue on the other, unless some amount of wealth and/or freedom will equal some amount of virtue? Or, conversely, how can we deny that some amount of wealth and/or freedom will equal some amount of virtue, unless we deny that justice is an equality of ratios which comprehend the *different* contributions to the common good? We must again recall that the first two books of the *Politics* are pre-eminently devoted to demonstrating that the *polis* is a compound of elements different in kind, to which there correspond virtues or excellences different in kind. In the light of this analysis we can regard the *Republic* of Plato as an attempt to resolve this dilemma by the hypothesis that justice is one and the same in a single man and in a *polis*. The unity sought by Socrates in the *Republic* seemed, however, to reduce the *polis* to a family and the family to one man. This, Aristotle said, does not unify the *polis* but destroys it. Since justice is the preservative, not the destroyer, of political life, this cannot be in accordance with justice. However, we may consider whether Plato took but one horn of the dilemma. If justice demands an equality of ratios, and if such equality cannot be realized unless the different qualities which contribute to the common good are somehow rendered commensurate, then to insist upon the incommensurability of different qualities may also lead to the denial of the possibility of justice.

Aristotle will not sacrifice heterogeneity to homogeneity, nor homogeneity to heterogeneity. His argument seems to turn from the critique of each of these conflicting theses to the critique of the other. And his solution to the problem seems thereby to bear a striking resemblance to the problem itself. We may barely hazard the opinion that the theoretical dilemma which appears to lie at the heart of the analysis of the constituent elements of distributive justice may constitute a ground for rejecting pure theory as a ground for a practical discipline. It may be observed that the doctrine of virtue as the mean, as the right intermediate point between two vicious extremes, in the *Nicomachean Ethics,* is a seemingly mathematical formulation, which proves to be true only in an analogical sense. Virtue is an intermediate point between two extremes, but not a point whose distance from other points can be measured. Something similar is true of Aristotle's solution to the problem of distributive justice, a solution which reflects the theoretical understanding implicit in the grasping of the aforesaid dilemma, but reflects it rather in its negation of the necessity which constitutes the dilemma.

What then is Aristotle's emphatically practical solution? Its principle may be found in the recognition of the claims of the many, which now appears not so much as the recognition of these claims per se as the formula for the commensuration of excellences different in kind. The claims of the many, as they themselves understand those claims, are based upon the freedom of the many. The many think that because they are equal to the rich in freedom they ought to be equal in everything. Aristotle, however, finds a ratio between the claims of the many, on the one hand, and those of the rich and the good, on the other, not by comparing freedom with wealth and virtue, but by comparing the collective wealth and the collective virtue of the many with the collective wealth and virtue of the few. Again, the rich need not only be rich, but may be free and virtuous. And the good may possess not only virtue, but wealth and freedom. In short, each class of claimant can be compared with every other in respect of the claim of the *other,* and in *this* way, heterogeneity can *practically* be homogenized. It may be observed that the class with the intrinsically best claim, that of virtue, is least convincingly collectivized, in respect of the claims of the other classes, and the class with the intrinsically poorest claim, the poor, is most convincingly collectivized. Yet the practical problem is to bring together the extremes, to give the many a claim which will elevate them, and yet restrain them by the very thing that gives them dignity. The many, to repeat, may be lacking in any example of outstanding excellence yet collectively may—in a certain sense—equal or excel in virtue the few, just as they may equal or excel the few in wealth. By teaching the many that the ground of their recognition is not their collective strength, their weight in numbers as freemen, but their collective virtue, a bond is formed between them and the higher classes, in consequence of which the poor gain the respect of the upper classes while gaining as well a motive to earn that respect.

The wealthy, as we also saw, tend to identify political superiority with wealth alone. But as the wealthy see that the poor may collectively make a considerable claim upon the ground of wealth, they will be less inclined to push the argument from wealth, and more inclined to recognize virtue and freedom. Again, the wealthy may also be brought to see that one of their own number may be wealthier than all of the rest of them together. But the wealthy are not likely to wish to be subordinated absolutely to one of their own class either: they are more apt to be inclined to moderate their demands as a class, and rather seek security in a balancing of the different claims of the different classes. The same argument can be applied to the claims of virtue: the advocates of aristocracy do not really wish to yield their claims to virtue alone, when such a claim would result in one man rule; nor, again, would they yield it to the many, if and as the many could prove the superiority of their collective virtue. We can then sum up Aristotle's resolution of the problem of distributive justice as follows. The *polis* is a compound, which requires men who are well-born (of good stock) and hence capable of assuming the responsibilities of free citizens; it requires as well men who are wealthy; it requires also men who are good. It requires all these things, in a certain proportion, a proportion which cannot be decided by abstract reasoning alone, but finally only by perception of the facts in each individual case. Those who are wealthy can rightly demand recognition of their claims, a recognition which will neither overbear, nor be overborne by, the claims of others. Since the wealthy, as wealthy, will not be virtuous, it may be pointed out to them, if they try to absolutize their claims, that the many or the one may be collectively wealthier than they are. Similarly, if the aristocrats absolutize their claims, it can be pointed out to them that either the one or the many may be more virtuous than they. The case of the many differs slightly: the argument from their freedom Aristotle at the end resolves into an argument from good birth (for what distinguishes a freeman from a slave is a good nature), and here again it can be maintained that one or a few may be better born than many. The argument for good birth is at bottom but an attenuated version of the argument for virtue, because a good nature is one with a capacity for virtue. Thus the argument for the many is at bottom an argument for virtue which is fully recognized in the argument for collective virtue. And this, to bring the wheel full circle again, means an argument which, if pushed too far, will justify the claims of the few or the one against the many no less than it will justify the argument for the many. As each rival claimant moderates his claim, in the light of the awareness that it can be turned against him, the idea of a common good in which the rival claims are harmonized emerges. And the idea of the common good necessarily implies both a limitation upon the absolutized claims of each party—including that of virtue—and a priority of the claims of virtue.

Here, then, is Aristotle's resolution of the problem of distributive justice, the just decision of the rival claims to supreme authority in the *polis*.

There is, however, a corollary to the foregoing solution of the problem of distributive justice, and this corollary supplies as well the transition to the subject of monarchy and from monarchy to the other regimes, the regimes which are more important for political practice than those treated in Book III. The quasi-mathematical formula for distributive justice is a means of reconciling the competing claims for political supremacy. In it virtue itself appears as merely one of a number of such claims, although we must recognize a paradox in the play upon different meanings of virtue. Virtue is always directed toward the support of the common good, and yet the common good means a good in which the claims of virtue are moderated to accommodate other claims. What, however, does one do if there is someone whose virtue is so great that no "proportion" is possible between his virtue and the virtue of others?

Let us illustrate the problem by taking wealth, rather than virtue, as the quality to be "proportioned." In so far as wealth is a claim to political office, a rich man who is twice as wealthy as another rich man deserves an office that is twice as important. It would be plausible, for example, to say that the office of Secretary of the Treasury of the United States is twice as important as the office of Undersecretary. But if there is a man who is a thousand, or ten thousand, times as rich as his next richest fellow citizen, then obviously no such plausible proportion can be imagined, for it is not possible to imagine one office that is one ten-thousandth that of another. Any actual allocation of offices will then either overvalue the inferior claimant or undervalue the superior. If we think, however, not of the impossibility of adjusting the claims of two rich men, but of rich and poor, we see that the excessively rich man is, in a sense, the common enemy of both the rich and the poor. The only solution, then, for dealing with someone who is so excessively rich or otherwise powerful is to banish or ostracize him, for he destroys the basis of the reconciliation of competing claims, and hence of the common good. Or, to be more precise, one must either banish him or make him the absolute and sole ruler. In the case of the other claims, ostracism is, Aristotle says, politically just. But in the case of the man who is "excessive" in virtue, which now means excessive in his propensity and ability to serve the common good, a good in which the claims of virtue are moderated in so far as they can *be* moderated, given the qualities present in a community for compounding a common good, this would be a contradiction in terms. In such a case, the only just alternative is to make the man absolute and sole monarch. To repeat: the harmonizing of the claims of the rich and the poor depends upon the poor having sufficient wealth, and the rich having sufficient numbers, so that each can make a claim upon the grounds advanced by the other. But if one man is too rich or too popular, so that this moderation of conflicting claims is rendered impracticable, then it becomes just to ostracize him, as one who makes the common good impracticable. But if one man upsets this balance not by his excess of wealth or other forms of political power, but by his virtue, then it is not just to ostracize him, and he must rather be made king.

This leads us to the final problem of Book III. We have seen that the common good normally leads to a balancing and harmonizing of competing claims, but sometimes demands unfettered and unqualified recognition of the claims of virtue alone. Which is better? The unhampered absolute rule of the one best man, or the rule of the best laws? For the rule of harmonized, competing claims must be a rule of laws. As it is a rule which prescribes that different men take turns in ruling, it therefore prescribes boundaries to the power of men who take up and lay down their offices, as they do so not at their own discretion, but at that of the law. Aristotle's arguments, both pro and con, are substantially the same as those in Plato's *Statesman,* as set forth in the preceding chapter.[35] The decisive reflection is that politics both resembles and yet differs from the other arts, such as medicine. Certainly the doctor ought not to be restrained by written rules, so that he can only choose among treatments set down in a medical handbook, after having similarly chosen among diagnoses. Yet if the patient suspected the physician of being in league with his enemies, he might well prefer inferior medical treatment, and prefer even to doctor himself "by the book" than take a chance that his heirs had made a deal to divide the insurance money with the physician. In the case of politics, we must inevitably suspect of interested motives anyone who puts forward a claim to absolute rule on the ground of superior wisdom and virtue. Still, the intrinsic validity of the claim in the case of *someone*—a someone very unlikely to put the claim forward himself—is not hereby destroyed. Aristotle's final conclusion appears to be that the argument stands as valid, but as the man who could justly make the claim will not do so, the only argument that can and will be validly advanced will be that in favor of the best laws. Still, in the infinite contingencies of political life, a moment might come when, contrary to every normal expectation, the rule of the one best man might have to be advanced in practice as well.

Books IV, V, and VI of the *Politics* are the pre-eminently "practical" books, wherein are applied the principles developed in Books I through III. The opening chapters of Book IV read almost like the beginning of a new treatise. Book III began with a question, Whatever is the *polis?* We were immediately plunged into a controversy, a controversy caused by the repudiation by a victorious democracy of debts contracted by a tyrant. The political philosopher appears in Book III as an arbiter or umpire, finding the element of justice and of injustice in the self-interested assertions and claims of partisans. He alone sees the whole of which the partisans are part. Thus he alone possesses the principle which recognizes the part which each partisan occupies in the whole, and thus can reward him in proportion to the importance of that part. Now the political philosopher appears in a different role, a somewhat less elevated but not less indispensable one. He is likened by Aristotle to the gymnastic or athletic trainer.

A practical program for politics would model itself upon gymnastics. The athletic trainer is not only concerned with the perfect regimen for the perfect physique, but must know how to prescribe for anyone who seeks his assistance. This means knowing what is good for the generality of men no less (in practice, a good deal more) than for the topflight athlete, and not only for the generality but for those with special needs and special handicaps. In like manner, the political teacher must know not only what is the absolutely best regime, but what regime is best for each of the different kinds of political communities. For most, the absolutely best would be as impossible and as undesirable as the training program of an Olympic champion would be for an overweight middle-aged businessman. A political teacher should know of a regime that is not only desirable and possible for most *poleis* but one which they can be easily persuaded to adopt. And for those who cannot adopt this second-best, generally practicable standard, he must have a further range of alternatives: he must know what would be best for each particular community, taking into full account its local peculiarities and shortcomings.

The first requirement for carrying out the foregoing assignment is to have available a full classification of regimes. In Book III Aristotle set out the basic forms of government, the three correct and the three deviant regimes. Now, however, he says that it is as important (perhaps more important in practice) to know the different varieties of each form, *e.g.,* to know the different kinds of democracy and oligarchy, as to know the difference between democracy and oligarchy. For the attempt to establish an aristocracy, let us say, when only a democracy is feasible, may lead to disaster. But the attempt to set up one kind of democracy, when only another kind will work well, may also lead to disaster.

Aristotle now gives as the cause of the variety of regimes the variety of parts from which all *poleis* are compounded. In Book III we saw the variety of regimes as due, in the main, to the different principles by which men justified their claims to supremacy, and in particular wealth, freedom, and virtue. Now we see a still greater variety of regimes due to the variety of functions within the *polis* that must be performed by the rich, the poor, and the good. Aristotle lists these as the parts of the *polis:* farmers, artisans, merchants, unskilled laborers, warriors, judges, councillors, the rich, and magistrates. The many are thus seen to include such different elements as the farmers, the artisans, and the merchants, all of whom may be either rich or poor, as well as common laborers (who may be free or servile). Of crucial significance, however, is this: many of the foregoing can be combined, so that the same men can be farmers and soldiers, or judges and councillors; but the same men cannot be simultaneously rich and poor. And so in an especial sense the *polis* seems to be a compound of rich and poor, and democracy and oligarchy seem to be the two basic regimes, of which all others are variations. In principle, Aristotle denies this view, because the distinction between rightly constituted and wrongly constituted regimes is more fundamental for him. Yet in practice he gives the distinction between democracy and oligarchy the major weight in his approach to the problem of ameliorating political life. His best generally practicable regime is polity (*politeia*), which happens also to be the generic name for all regimes. It is no accident that the specific and the generic name should coincide in the case of the regime which is a compound of democracy and oligarchy. For it coincides in the case of the one regime which balances the two elements which alone cannot be combined. Polity is a kind of virtuous mean between the two vicious extremes constituted by the claims of wealth and poverty.

Democracies will vary as the class of the many comprising the ruling class varies, whether farmers, artisans, merchants, sailors, fishermen, or laborers predominate among them; similarly oligarchies will differ according to the relative weight among their ruling classes of wealth, birth, virtue, and education. The different kinds of democracy vary as the principle of democracy is mitigated by the variety of interests within the *dēmos,* and the inclination to give greater protection to the interests of other classes, first by the rule of law, and second by some representation within the government of interests other than that of the dominant class. Thus the worst form of democracy would be simple, unrestrained majoritarianism, which usually means rule by the worst kind of demagogues. Better forms would, besides restraining the government by laws which circumscribed its power, give some recognition to property, either by property qualifications for the holding of some offices, or by giving some weight to property in the voting in the assembly. In Book VI there is a remarkable passage in which the concept of distributive justice, as developed in Book III, is adapted to the specific problem of tempering democracy.[36] There Aristotle proposes the following voting procedure in the assembly: let rich and poor constitute two voting classes, and let any resolution pass which commands a majority of each. But if the majority in each class is different, let the one whose total property assessment is greater prevail. For example, if on a given proposal, the rich vote 6 to 4 in favor, and the poor vote 15 to 5 against, then the result would be 19 to 11 against, on a purely majoritarian basis. If, however, we assume that each rich man is twice as wealthy as each poor man, and they voted by property assessments, the vote would be 23 to 17 against, i.e., the minority viewpoint would increase its percentage of the vote from 37 per cent to 43 per cent. Aristotle's aim is *not* simply to strengthen the position of the rich by this proposal. Where the poor in a democracy are united in their views, they will prevail. In the foregoing example his proposal strengthens the position of the minority of the poor as well as the majority of the rich. Our numerical values in the examples are unrealistic, in that we supposed, for the sake of convenience, that all the rich would be equally rich and all the poor equally poor, which in practice they would not be. Aristotle's basic aim, of course, is to encourage the combination of the richer of the poor with the poorer of the rich, thus leading the poor from democracy, and the rich from oligarchy, and both into polity.

What, then, is polity, Aristotle's most generally practicable regime, the regime which can solve the fundamental problem of most *poleis?* It is, as has been said, a blend of democracy and oligarchy, and the better the blending, the easier it will be for democrats to confuse it with democracy and oligarchs with oligarchy. Its foundation is the middle class, i.e., the class that is neither very rich nor very poor, and which accordingly has no interest either in equality for unequals or inequality for equals. It does not wish to place property at the mercy of the propertyless, or liberty at the mercy of the propertied. Of the devices for encouraging polity, the one given above must serve as an example of Aristotle's almost limitless resources, resources which manifest themselves not only in the discussion of polity proper, but in the multitudinous ways in which he examines each of the many varieties of democracy, oligarchy, and polity, moderating the two former in the direction of polity, and the last in the direction of aristocracy. Polity, as we have seen, is inherently moderate by the moderation of the interests of the middle class. But this moderation only resembles virtue, it is not virtue itself. It makes men disposed toward virtue, however, and aristocracy can begin to flourish upon the soil of polity.

After demonstrating the variety of regimes, and in particular the varieties of democracy and oligarchy, and how the conflict arising from the irreconcilable antagonism of poor and rich can best be dealt with, Aristotle also points out the appropriateness of one or another regime to one or another people. Although polity is introduced as the generally practicable regime, it depends no less upon fortune than the best regime, in that it depends upon a large middle class, or at least upon a gentle graduation from poor to rich. Yet extremes of wealth or poverty are more the rule. Aristotle recognizes that where such extremes exist only one or another kind of democracy or oligarchy is possible. He lays it down as a principle that the part of the *polis* which wishes the regime to endure must be stronger than the parts which are hostile to it. One must in each case examine the composition of the hostile elements, which must be compounded to produce the regime for the particular *polis*. If the poor have virtuous farmers and degenerate artisans, and if the *polis* must be a democracy, obviously it must be built upon the farming class. If there are degenerate *nouveaux riches,* but there is a public-spirited, educated, old aristocracy, obviously if it is to be an oligarchy it must be constructed around the old families. Where the people are dissolute and the wealthy public-spirited, there one should have an oligarchy, unless the rich are too few and the poor too many, in which case there is no alternative to an inferior democracy. If the people are sober and hard-working and the rich are dissolute, there one should have a democracy, unless the rich are relatively numerous and the poor either relatively few or so situated that they cannot easily combine. These are the kinds of considerations which Aristotle advances for deciding, first, whether a regime should be democratic or oligarchic and, second, what variety of democracy or of oligarchy it should be.

Aristotle concludes Book IV with the first comprehensive account of what we have come to call the three "powers" of government, legislative, executive, and judicial.[37] The concept of a "power" of government is itself, of course, alien to Aristotle, because our use of that expression always implies a delegation of power from a sovereign people to a government which is its instrumentality. For Aristotle, the government (*politeuma*) is the regime (*politeia*), as we cannot too greatly emphasize. The legislative is the deliberating element of the regime, it is not an appointed or elected body deliberating *for* someone else. The idea of representation is nowhere visible in Aristotle's *Politics*, in part because a *polis* so large that it required representation would have seemed to him far too large for political excellence.[38] More important is the fact that what we call the legislative power is only one of a number of elements which in the modern representative democratic state go into the deliberative process. Elections, parties, public opinion polls, and so on, all play a part in this deliberative process. When Aristotle speaks of the deliberative element, he means the element which actually deliberates, not a body to which deliberative functions have been delegated, and which performs these not in its own right, but in virtue of the rights of others.

We cannot say more here of Aristotle's treatment of the three branches of government, other than that it is designed to give the practicing legislator a compendium of all the possible ways in which each of these branches of government can be constructed. The legislator must know not only what are the different regimes, what are their intrinsic merits and demerits, and which kind is suitable for which kind of people. He must know how to construct each regime, and in practice this means knowing how to construct a legislature, a judiciary, and a magistracy suitable to each. This means knowing not only how to construct each of the varieties of the three branches of government, but how to produce each of the varieties of mixtures of each of the branches of government. For example, it means knowing how to add a touch of oligarchy to a democratic legislature, or a touch of aristocracy to an oligarchic judiciary, or a touch of democracy to an oligarchic magistracy (this last being characteristic, for example, of Sparta). Nowhere does the resemblance of the art of the political philosopher and the art of the painter become more patent than in these practical books, wherein the variety of possible forms is seen to be so great that politics becomes as malleable as the forms of nature, when they are reconstructed from the painter's palette. And, yet, in precisely the same sense as the painter imitates nature while perfecting it, so does the political philosopher. The knowledge of nature guides and governs the application of technique at every step.

Of the practical subjects dealt with in Books IV through VI none are more practical than those of Book V, generally known as the book on revolutions. The word revolution has, however, a connotation for us ("drastic change" would be a better translation of *metabolē*) which is quite alien to Aristotle. When we think of the English, American, French, and Russian revolutions, for example, we usually think of a process by which all *anciens régimes,* all regimes based either upon feudal legitimacy or the prescription of ancient customs, are being caused to disappear from the modern world. We think of the replacement of regimes explicitly based upon one or another principle of inequality by regimes all claiming to be based upon equality.[39] We think of a world in which the dynamism of social change culminating in political revolution is rooted in technological change, itself the by-product of a continually progressing body of what we call scientific knowledge. Aristotle's horizon is one in which man's knowledge of nature does not alter the fundamental character of his relations with non-human nature, or his relations with his fellow men. The moral and political alternatives remain basically constant. For Aristotle revolution means primarily the process whereby one regime is replaced by another, as one or another group gains power within the same regime, or as the regime is altered so as no longer to be the same. Aristotle remarks that, in his own time (and he evidently means in Greece), with the growth in the size of the class of the common people, it is hard for any kind of government other than democracy to come into existence.[40] Evidently external conditions may impose sharp limits upon the political choices open at any given time and place. But everything that comes into existence passes out of existence, and although regimes are not strictly speaking mortal, neither are they immortal. External conditions are subject to fortune, and in the fullness of time all possibilities become actualities. Aristotle's horizon envisages as an ultimate possibility the transformation of every regime, through every other regime, into every regime. Book V of the *Politics,* is, then, not a book on revolutions in the sense that Tocqueville's *Democracy in America* is such a book. According to Tocqueville, the progress of the principle of equality, the levelling of all monarchical and aristocratic regimes, is providential and inexorable. The only practical question is whether we adapt ourselves to it in one way or another. For Aristotle there are six principal kinds of regimes, a large number of variants of each, and an almost unlimited number of combinations of variants. The problem of revolution is the problem of knowing what preserves and what destroys each of them.

Book V is the longest of the entire *Politics,* illustrated as it is with a wealth of detail from the political histories of the Greek world that Aristotle had collected. We can do no more here than indicate the scope of the book, and provide an example of how the political philosopher teaches legislators to preserve the regimes he has taught them to construct. The questions Aristotle takes up are these: what are the numbers and kinds of causes of revolutions in general; what causes are peculiar to each kind of regime; out of what into what do regimes usually change; what are the safeguards of regimes in general and of each kind in particular; how are these safeguards put into effect?

The first and most fundamental cause of revolution is identical with the primary cause of the difference of regimes: namely, the different conceptions men have of justice. Those who are equal in one respect think they are equal in all; those who are unequal in one think they are unequal in all. For this reason democrats are the enemies of oligarchs, and oligarchs of democrats, and each will overthrow the other when he can. Yet within democracy and within oligarchy there are those who think they have not got their fair share according to the principle of the regime. And again, there are those who wish to make the democracy more (or less) democratic, or the oligarchy more (or less) oligarchic.

Revolutions originate often in trivial incidents, but these are only the sparks which set the dry tinder aflame. The sense of oppression of the people by the wealthy few, or the sense of dishonor by the few when they are treated as the equals of those they deem their inferiors, this exemplifies the inflammable material. In democracies, for example, the principal cause of revolution—that is, of the rich banding together to overthrow the democracy—is the insolence of demagogues, who court popularity by instituting malicious prosecutions of the rich and stimulating class hatred. In the case of oligarchies, oppression of the poor by the rich corresponds to demagogy. However, it may be the excessive exclusiveness of the oligarchy that drives some of the notables into rebellion against their own class. Again, oligarchies are ruined by riotous living, driving them into oppression and tyranny because of their extravagance, while making themselves contemptible to their rivals, both in their own class and among the people.

As to the things that tend to secure regimes in general, they are the opposite of the things that tend to their destruction. We saw that differences as to what is just are the most fundamental of all causes of dissension. The fundamental cause of security, to be briefer even than Aristotle in this context, is justice. That is, democracies are preserved by refraining from anything that smacks of expropriation, while oligarchies are preserved by the rulers refraining from insolence and oppression. The legislator must know what institutions in a democracy preserve, and what destroy democracy; and what institutions in an oligarchy preserve, and what destroy oligarchy. For example, it is a legitimate aim of oligarchy that superior men not be governed by inferior, and of democracy that freemen have an equal opportunity to share in offices. The two can often be practically reconciled, Aristotle points out, by scrupulous care that no profit is made from public office. If this is achieved, then the poor will relinquish the offices to the rich, since, being poor, they will prefer to devote themselves to their private affairs so long as they think the public funds are not being plundered. And the rich, while not denying offices to the poor, will actually have the offices to themselves. Every *polis* needs both a free multitude and a wealthy minority, and if the poor destroy the rich, or the rich the poor, they will destroy the basis of the common good. The greatest of all means of securing the stability of regimes, Aristotle says, is education. For there is no use in the best possible laws and institutions if the citizens are not trained in their use. But a good education does not mean one that will please oligarchs in an oligarchy, or democrats in a democracy. It means an education that will produce a ruling class that is self-disciplined in respect to its real interests, and not self-indulgent in respect to its pleasures.

Aristotle has a great deal to say about how polities, aristocracies, monarchies, and tyrannies are both destroyed and preserved. Some of the most startling passages in the *Politics* take the form of advice for preserving tyrannies. Tyranny is in one sense no regime, since it is the negation of justice, and regimes are generally understood in terms of their having an element—however incomplete or partial—of justice. But Aristotle takes it for granted that in some cases nothing but tyranny will be possible, and his advice, while calculated to appeal to a tyrant who is rational enough to consider what is in his interest, is also calculated to introduce, however covertly, an element of justice which makes it bearable to consider the tyranny a regime.

In summary, we can describe the spirit and doctrine of the practical books of the *Politics* as follows. Aristotle envisages each kind of regime as being appropriate to a certain set of circumstances. In the case of a people with a wealthy class of ancient lineage, with a tradition of public service and spirit of *noblesse oblige,* an oligarchy, or perhaps an aristocracy, is indicated. In the case of a people whose rich are mostly *nouveaux,* who lack traditions, and who are held in contempt by the common people, aristocracy is out of the question, and oligarchy is doubtful. The same would be true of an ancient ruling class which had grown effete and luxurious. On the other hand, a common people made up largely of sturdy yeoman farmers is much better material for democracy than a *dēmos* of idle artisans, avidly looking for pay from the public treasury as an excuse to leave their work tables. In each situation we must look first for that class which is naturally strongest. If it is the *dēmos,* we must try to build a democracy; if the wealthy, an oligarchy. And if the class that is between rich and poor is sufficiently numerous, we should try to build a polity. But in enfranchising a ruling class, we must always look for those devices which moderate it in the direction of its natural opposite: that is, devices for admitting the poor to office in an oligarchy, devices for honoring the rich in a democracy; and, in a polity, devices for rewarding virtue, or making virtue honored. For polity, although a balance of two bad principles, secures a moderation which permits the recognition of virtue or merit, and this strengthens the foundation of the regime. But the teaching of these books is alive to the mutability of human things, as well as being encyclopedic. Aristotle warns the legislator to be on the lookout for change, not to oppose change per se, but to prevent evils when they are small and still manageable, and constantly to prepare the regime to assimilate changes worked by fortune which are beyond control.

Nothing better illustrates Aristotle's practical teaching than the contrast between the British and continental European ruling classes in the modern centuries. From the days of Henry VIII, or earlier, the general (if not invariable) practice of the British monarchy and aristocracy has been to co-opt the leading members of the newer classes. Britain has always had a ruling class, and it is scarcely less recognizable today than it was four hundred years ago. Feudal overlords have been replaced by merchant princes, by industrialists and financiers, and by leaders of organized labor, by a process in which the old and new have rarely been out of touch and have rarely ceased to share in power and responsibility. The French and Russian monarchies and aristocracies, on the other hand, would not bend and were compelled instead to break. These *anciens régimes* never learned Aristotle's lesson, that a regime must always be constituted by the strongest element in the *polis,* and that the political strength of an element, whether the people, the rich, the well-born, or the good, is a product of its quantity and its quality. This is a nonmathematical product, but the true statesman must nonetheless master this political computation. He must perceive what adjustments must be made in a regime when there is outside the ruling class a quantity so large or a quality so potent that it would ruin if it could not rule. But political computation is not limited to perceiving and judging these invincible products. The introduction of either a new quantity or a new quality into a regime must be done in such wise that the quantity realizes that it becomes a genuine political factor only by its infusion with quality, and quality realizes that it becomes such a factor only as it infuses a quantity. The common good is always a compound of both, and only as there is a common good is there a regime, and a partnership in the good life.

The last two books of the *Politics*—Book VII, and Book VIII as it has come down to us—are the books par excellence on the best regime. As we have seen, the best regime is the implicit subject of every book. In Book I, the understanding of the generation of the *polis* implied an understanding of its perfection—*i.e.,* the best regime—because to understand the generation of anything that exists by nature means to understand the activity of that thing when it has attained its perfection. And the great thesis of Book I, or one form of it, is that the *polis* exists by nature. Book II examined a number of regimes, both of theory and of practice, and they were found wanting. But the principle in virtue of which Aristotle noted those deficiencies was the principle

of the best regime. Book III culminated in the examination of the
principal rival claims to supreme power in the *polis,* the claims of the
poor, the rich, the well-born, and the good. The reconciliation of these
claims, their harmonization into a common good, itself constituted the
principle of the best regime. Books IV, V, and VI demonstrate the
different manners in which this reconciliation or harmonization takes
place when external conditions forbid its full implementation. Or, to
be more precise, the practical books demonstrate the different forms
that justice takes when conditions make the predominant factor in the
product of quantity and quality something other than virtue. For example, pure democracy or pure oligarchy are in a sense not viable
regimes at all. No *polis* can exist without a freeborn and a wealthy
element, and a regime which simply despoiled its rich, or enslaved its
free, would cease to exist as a community. Only the moderation of the
claims of the rich or the poor enables democracy or oligarchy to be
viable, and that moderation is the ground of the intrusion of virtue.
But there is a difference between that intrusion of virtue which enables
a democracy to exist, and a recognition of virtue as the only cause of
that activity for the sake of which every *polis* exists, and which alone
can cause it to be, not only a rich or a free *polis,* but a happy one.

The books on the best regime consist in the main of these two
subjects: first, what it is that is the cause of happiness, in men and in
*poleis;* second, what are the institutions of the best regime. The best
regime is one in which the best men rule. Each regime is *just,* let us
remember, in so far as it is rightly constituted, in so far as it secures
the common good as defined by the greatest product of quality and
quantity that fortune permits a given community to enjoy. Where
fortune permits the qualitative factor to dominate the quantitative factor, that is, where human excellence dominates civic excellence,
there is the best regime. Aristotle turns aside as practically irrelevant
the question of whether that regime is best in which one man so
greatly exceeds all others in virtue that no proportional equality is
possible.[41] For all practical purposes, the best regime appears to be an
aristocracy of a multitude of good men ruled by law. Aristotle discusses the material elements of the best regime, which are its resources
of land, its location, access to the sea, market places, and so on, and
the human stock from which the legislator must raise up citizens.
The formal elements are the classes of farmers, artisans, fighters, the
wealthy, those performing civic functions, and those providing the
services to the gods. Wealth, military service, civic duty, and religious
duty all coincide in a single ruling class. When its members are younger
they are soldiers, when in middle age councillors, magistrates, and
judges, and when in old age priests. The farm laborers are explicitly

servile and the artisans apparently so, although Aristotle does say
that all slaves should have freedom set before them as a prize.

Throughout the *Politics* Aristotle usually speaks of virtue in contradistinction to birth, wealth, freedom, and other conditional claims
to political preference. Yet fundamental to Aristotle's political teaching
is the distinction between the virtue of a citizen and that of a good
man, and there is a constant interplay between these two meanings of
virtue. The virtue of a citizen relates to the regime, and its purpose
will differ from the purpose of true virtue in every regime but the best.
For example, in a democracy happiness will appear to be doing as one
pleases, in an oligarchy it will appear rather as the gratification of
avarice. A happy man *does* do as he pleases, but it pleases him only to
do good. A happy man also possesses wealth, but he will desire not an
unlimited amount of wealth, but only so much as is needed for good
actions. At last, however, we must ask, What limit does the desire of
happiness place upon the need or desire of good actions? Good actions
require only a limited amount both of wealth and freedom. But there
can be no limit upon the desire for good action itself. The final problem of the *Politics* is the problem of establishing clearly that distinction
within true virtue itself which throughout the *Politics* remained almost invisible: the distinction between the virtue of action—moral
virtue plus practical wisdom—and the virtue of thought—theoretical
wisdom. And, corresponding to these two virtues are the two activities,
of the active and of the contemplative life. Political virtue, which in
the best case appears to coincide with human virtue, is practical: that is,
it is concerned with the good things that can be gained, and the bad
things that can be avoided, by wise action and the practice of the moral
virtues. But there is always a limit to the goodness resulting from good
action of this kind. To extend practical activity beyond the bounds of
this limit is to turn it from good to evil. For example, it is good to be
brave and strong, for the weak and cowardly cannot preserve their
freedom, and the unfree cannot live good lives. But those who are
strong and free, and whose strength and freedom are unchallenged,
cannot utilize either their strength or freedom in action. To go into
action to dominate others, merely to exercise one's freedom of action and
one's bravery, is a perversion of virtue; this was the defect of the Spartan regime. Virtuous activity cannot, then, be truly practical, except
as it serves an end which is itself not practical, an activity which is good
solely with reference to itself, an activity to which there are no limits
because its increase does not extend it beyond itself, an activity which
is thus wholly self-contained. This is the activity of thought, the contemplation of the truth, which is the same as the activity of God, or
thought thinking itself. It is the only absolutely self-contained, self-

sufficient activity in the universe, and for this reason unlimited, while being the cause of those limits which prescribe boundaries to every other activity, and in virtue of which every other activity becomes good.[42]

The final cause of excellence, in politics and in human life, as in the universe, is, then, ultimately one and the same. Yet the same man cannot be simply virtuous (which means wise) and politically virtuous, for the same reason that the divine activity is not simultaneously practical and theoretical. The activity of wisdom, pure and simple, is self-regarding and not other-regarding. Yet political rulers must have the spirit and practice of philosophy, which means love of wisdom, as distinct from wisdom itself. The solution of the political problem, in Aristotle no less than in Plato, requires a certain coincidence of philosophy and political power. But for Aristotle, unlike Plato, the activity of wisdom itself issues no commands, although it does always indicate the reason why commands should be issued. There is, then, no such necessary antagonism between philosophy and political life as Plato envisaged. Practical life culminates in the recognition of the activity of wisdom as its final cause.[43]

In the *Nicomachean Ethics* Aristotle expounded the different meanings of virtue, and above all the distinction between the moral and intellectual virtues. In Book X he defended happiness as primarily the activity of theoretical wisdom, and in a secondary sense as the activity of the practical and moral virtues. Finally, he observed that the conditions of happiness, the possibility of the good life, depended upon good laws, and this required the science of politics. At the end of the *Politics* Aristotle considers how the good men who are to make the good laws of the best regime are themselves to be produced. When the eighth book breaks off, either unfinished or lost, he is still engaged in describing the education which will produce the habits of virtue. Fortunately, we already know what these habits are and how they are produced, in principle if not in detail. The end of the *Politics* leads us back to the beginning of the *Nicomachean Ethics*.

## NOTES

1. Frequently this is rendered "city-state," meaning a very small state with an urban center. This, however, only compounds confusion, because it implies that a *polis* is a particular kind of state.

2. One must, however, be careful not to identify Aristotle's use of such analogy with the organismic theories of the nineteenth century, which attribute to the state actual qualities of a real organism.

3. See p. 103 for the Sophist Lycophron's definition of law (Aristotelis *Politica,* ed. W. D. Ross ["Oxford Classical Texts" (Oxford: Oxford University Press, 1957)], 1280ᵇ 10).

4. *Ibid.,* 1252ᵃ 1–6 (trans. H. V. J.).

5. Cf. *Nicomachean Ethics* 1145ᵇ 1 ff.

6. *Ibid.,* 1162ᵃ 16–19.

7. *Politics* 1253ᵃ 19.

8. *Ibid.,* 1253ᵃ 7–9.

9. *Nicomachean Ethics* 1154ᵃ 15 ff.

10. We cannot help being reminded of present-day investigators who pursue elaborate studies with refined mathematical techniques, which end only in the "scientific" demonstration of what everyone always knew.

11. *Politics* 1324ᵃ 5–1325ᵃ 13.

12. *Ibid.,* 1252ᵃ 18; 1252ᵃ 24.

13. *Ibid.,* 1278ᵇ 6.

14. The discussion of monarchy begins at *ibid.,* 1284ᵇ 35.

15. *Ibid.,* 1276ᵃ 9 ff.

16. *Ibid.,* 1281ᵃ 11 ff.

17. *Ibid.,* 1290ᵇ 38 ff.

18. Cf. *ibid.,* Bk I, esp. 1254ᵃ 20 ff., and the remark concerning the musical scale.

19. *Ibid.,* 1278ᵇ 6–15; 1278ᵇ 15–1281ᵃ 10; 1281ᵃ 11–1284ᵇ 34.

20. The student should compare this passage of the *Politics* with the Thrasymachus section of the *Republic* of Plato, Bk I, and in particular 345ᵃ–347ᵉ.

21. Cf. *Nicomachean Ethics* 1094ᵇ 11–27, 1198ᵃ 25, and 1103ᵇ 26.

22. This may be the best single approximation to what is understood by the *state,* as distinct from the *polis.* See above, p. 66.

23. *Politics* 1281ᵃ 11–39; 1281ᵃ 39–1282ᵇ 13; 1282ᵇ 14–1284ᵇ 34.

24. *Ibid.,* 1293ᵇ 29.

25. *Ibid.,* 1279ᵃ 8 ff.

26. *Ibid.,* 1301ᵇ 1.

27. *Ibid.,* 1283ᵇ 10.

28. Cf. *Nicomachean Ethics* 1116ᵃ 17, on the distinction between genuine courage and political.

29. Cf. the resemblance of bestial courage to true courage, *Nicomachean Ethics* 1116ᵇ 10 ff.

30. *Politics* 1279ᵇ 12.

31. Cf. *Nicomachean Ethics* 1144ᵇ 3 ff.

32. *Politics* 1254ᵇ 26 ff.

33. Cf. *ibid.,* Bk VII, 1332ᵇ 17 ff.

34. *Nicomachean Ethics* 1131ᵃ 10–1131ᵇ 24.

35. See pp. 48–50.

36. *Politics* 1318ᵃ 30–38.

37. *Ibid.,* 1297ᵇ 35ff.

38. Cf. the criticism of Plato's *Laws,* in *ibid.,* 1265ᵃ 11 ff. and the size of the best regime, 1326ᵃ 7–1326ᵇ 26.

39. The National Socialist and Fascist regimes, now happily defunct, are only apparent exceptions. Although reviving a kind of primitive tribalism, their use of the plebiscite to establish legitimacy placed them in fundamental opposition to premodern inegalitarians.

40. *Politics* 1286ᵇ 20.

41. *Ibid.,* 1332ᵇ 16–27.

42. Cf. *Metaphysics* 1072ᵇ 13–29, and *Nicomachean Ethics* 1177ᵃ 17–1177ᵇ 26, 1178ᵇ 7–23, with *Politics* 1323ᵇ 23–27, and 1325ᵇ 14–31. Compare also the treatment of self-love in the *Nicomachean Ethics* 1166ᵃ 1 ff.

43. *Nicomachean Ethics* 1144ᵇ 30–1145ᵃ 11.

# READINGS

A. Aristotle. *Politics.*
B. Aristotle. *Nicomachean Ethics.*

# MARCUS TULLIUS CICERO

## 106–43 B.C.

Few of those who have sought to present a systematic account of the development of political philosophy have attached great importance to Cicero's political thought. He has traditionally been regarded as one of that series of less inspired and less inspiring Greek and Roman thinkers who followed in the wake of Plato and Aristotle. Considered a dilettante rather than a serious student of philosophy, his thought has generally been judged eclectic and felt to be characterized neither by any great consistency of doctrine nor depth of understanding. His specifically political works, the *Republic* and the *Laws,* have been regarded as little more than ambitious attempts to justify the ideals and practices of a moribund aristocratic order. His value to later students is thought to lie less in what he himself has to say about the substantive questions of political philosophy than in the detailed account he gives of the doctrines of the several schools of Greek philosophy active in his own day, and of the adaptation of those doctrines to the radically different political and intellectual environment of Rome. His special talent is thought to have rested in the skill with which he synthesized the diverse and often conflicting teachings of these schools, thus making them available in a form congenial to the Roman taste and adequate to satisfy the demands of the practical Roman mind.

Such an assessment contains a measure of truth. It fails, however, to give serious consideration to Cicero's method or to his purpose in treating philosophical materials in the manner in which he did, to say nothing of the substance of his thought. It falls short, therefore, of that understanding essential to an adequate analysis.

A statesman and a serious student of philosophy, Cicero sought in his writings to place his considerable talent and experience as a rhetorician in the service of philosophy, in the service of what he suggested was "the richest, the most bounteous, and the most exalted gift of the immortal gods to humanity." [1] His task, as he conceived it, was to introduce philosophy into Rome. By philosophy he meant not the dogmatic teachings of this or that particular school but a way of life. The task was not simple. Philosophy is always regarded with "suspicion and dislike" by the majority of men, and particularly by those whose taste runs to the practical rather than the speculative.[2] It is particularly suspect if its origins are thought to be foreign. The normal difficulty of introducing that which at all times runs counter to popular taste and thought was thus compounded for Cicero by the fact that the teaching was of Greek origin. The necessity for Cicero to tread lightly on Roman sensibilities and to supply a convincing justification for the existence of philosophy in Rome cannot be ignored if one hopes to appreciate the degree of circumspection with which he felt compelled to approach this task.

Throughout his works Cicero professes to be an Academic Skeptic, a member of that philosophic school whose origins lay in the Platonic Academy but which in his own time stressed as its fundamental thesis the impossibility of absolute knowledge. Man as man, the Skeptics asserted, is limited to opinions of that which is more or less probable. Although man may seek to attain a higher degree of probability by examining, as Socrates did, the relative merits of all opinions, he will never at any point in his inquiry be assured of absolute certainty. He must act, if he chooses to act, with the understanding that the principles which guide his action remain problematic.[3]

While skepticism and the suspension of final judgment which it entails may be philosophically tenable, if such views are taken seriously and developed to their logical extreme by the mass of men, the outcome may well be politically disastrous. The thought, for example, that the commonly accepted standard of what is just and unjust lacks, and must always lack, a fully rational or defensible basis may not unduly disturb the theoretician. It may, however, if clearly impressed upon the mind of the populace, so shake popular confidence in the validity of such a standard that faithful adherence to it, or to any standard resting on such a tenuous and fundamentally arbitrary base, appears foolish. Such an understanding may lead to a widespread questioning of the truth even of those principles which are perhaps essential to the existence of the political order, e.g., that the common good should be preferred by the citizens to their private good.

Cicero was well aware of the potentially unsettling effect skepticism, and perhaps philosophy as such, must have on the city, *i.e.,* the political community. The stark and undiluted truth, the philosophic truth, may shake the very foundations of a given political order. Unlike some of the less perceptive members of his school, Cicero could not view this possibility with equanimity. He was aware of the ultimate dependence of philosophy on the city, and thus of the necessity for philosophy, if it was to survive, to concern itself with the development of a healthy political order. Only within such an order could philosophy exist. The philosopher, if this be true, must be guided by some understanding of the needs of the city and of the practical consequences of his teachings. He must not risk the chaos that might follow a systematic and ruthless public examination of the principles underlying and guiding a particular order, even an order which strikes him as radically defective, without having given some thought to the alternatives. A defective government, a government which falls far short of the best, may be better than no government at all. The philosopher must begin, then, with an understanding of what is possible as well as what is desirable, and direct his efforts, in turn, to the improvement of the health of a given political order, rather than to its destruction.

Cicero's decision to use the dialogue as the vehicle for his teaching springs in part from this reflection on the relation of philosophy to the city and in part from his preference, as a Skeptic and an admirer of Plato ("the wisest and ... most learned man whom Greece has produced" [4]), for the Socratic method. The decision was dictated, he asserts in the *Tusculan Disputations,* by a desire to "conceal his own opinions, to relieve others from error and in every disputation to look for the most probable solution." [5] The dialogue lends itself to the presentation and examination of conflicting opinions. It permits the writer to focus attention on the relative merits of the positions being examined while at the same time suggesting, rather than revealing, the content and direction of his own thought. The form of the dialogue permits the writer to guide the discussion, but places the burden of following the argument to its conclusion upon the reader.

Cicero also saw, as Plato had before him, the possibilities of the dialogue as a work of art, a work so constructed that each element, *e.g.,* the place, the time, and the actions and speeches of the characters, has a part to play in advancing the inquiry.[6] Only careful readers will detect the significance of these additional touches and be led, in turn, to see that the salutary teachings which lie on the surface and are easily grasped by even the casual reader do not exhaust the content of the teaching, that they are at best partial truths. By means of the dialogue, Cicero seeks to emphasize what is politically salutary while at the same time concealing from the eyes of all except serious students those more comprehensive truths which may render political life difficult or impossible for the mass of men. He seeks in this way to fulfill his responsibility both to philosophy and to the political order.

The substance of Cicero's specifically political teaching is contained in two dialogues, the *Republic* and the *Laws*. Each dialogue purports to record an earlier conversation among Romans about political things. In the *Republic,* the conversation allegedly reported by Cicero took place during a Roman holiday in the year 129 B.C., some seventy years prior to the writing of the dialogue. The conversation is one of three days' duration among men belonging to the Scipionic circle, a group whose members combined achievements as Roman statesmen with an interest in philosophy. The *Republic* consists of six books, two devoted to each day's conversation. Cicero appears, and thus speaks in his own name, only as the writer of the preface attached to the first, third, and fifth books. The *Laws* serves to record a much more recent conversation, and one of a single day's duration, among Cicero, his brother Quintus, and Atticus, an Epicurean friend. It is generally thought that the *Laws* also contained, or was to contain, six books, but only the greater part of the first three books remains available to us; the rest of the manuscript has been lost.

Time has been no kinder to the manuscript of the *Republic*. With the exception of the portion devoted to Scipio's dream and a number of quotations scattered through the works of writers familiar with the original, *e.g.,* Augustine, the text of the *Republic* was lost for more than seven centuries. Only fragments, perhaps one-third of the complete work, remained when a copy of the manuscript was discovered in the Vatican Library in 1820. In view of the fragmentary character of the texts of both the *Republic* and the *Laws,* and particularly of the former, any account of Cicero's political thought must remain provisional in important respects.

The fundamental question to which Cicero addresses himself in these two works is that which guided classical political philosophy as a whole: What is the best political order? The *Republic,* the more philosophic of the two dialogues, is directed to answering this question, the *Laws* to sketching the legal and institutional framework of such a regime. The answer to the central question, of course, presupposes some reflection on a number of related questions, although the reflections themselves may not be included in the more popular and consequently less exhaustive works.

One such related question, that of the right life for man, is taken up in the introduction to the first book of the *Republic*. The question is, Which is superior—the active life, *i.e.,* the practical or political life, the life of the statesman; or the contemplative life, *i.e.,* the philosophic life? Cicero's interest in this issue is not simply theoretical, but is stimulated by the growing tendency, encouraged among the Romans by certain philosophers, especially the Epicureans, to denigrate the political sphere and to withdraw from participation in political matters. "We must free ourselves," Epicurus had argued, "from the prison of affairs and politics." Cicero's concern for the fate of the commonwealth dictated that his opening remarks in the *Republic* be directed to the practical end of defending the political life. To this end he examines the common arguments in favor of withdrawal and, while conceding to them a degree of truth, suggests that they can be assigned little weight when viewed in the light of the individual's responsibility both to this city and to his own nature and in the light of the glories to be won within the public sphere. Moreover, he argues, it is absurd to suppose that virtue can exist in a vacuum:

. . . the existence of virtue depends entirely upon its use; and its noblest use is the government of the state, and the realization in fact, not in words, of those very things that the philosophers, in their corners, are continually dinning in our ears.[7]

The man who has both discovered the principles of virtue and compelled others to live in accordance with them, *i.e.,* the statesman, must be deemed far superior, even in wisdom, to those who perhaps speculate about such questions but abstain from any direct participation in political affairs. Cicero's position at this point appears unambiguous: the practical life is to be preferred to the contemplative life. Despite the fervor with which Cicero advances this opinion, however, there are some indications that he does not regard the issue as settled. His praise in the prologue has not been unqualified: the life of the statesman, while "deserving of praise" and "conducive to fame," is neither a completely happy one nor one chosen simply for its own sake. It is soon made clear that necessity and a sense of duty underlie its selection.

The provisional character of this first opinion is emphasized by the fact that the question is immediately reopened as soon as the dialogue proper begins. Asked in the opening scene to give his opinion on the report that a second sun has been observed in the heavens, Scipio, the chief character in the dialogue, expresses a preference for what he calls the Socratic position in regard to such matters, a position which avoids speculative questions on the assumption that they are "either too difficult for the human understanding to fathom or else . . . of no importance whatever to human life."[8] Within a short time, however, Scipio has been led to abandon this position. He concedes not only his

own interest in speculative studies and the immediate relevance, perhaps necessity, of such knowledge for the man of action, but even
admits the utter inadequacy of his earlier emphasis on practical or
earthly considerations:

Who in truth would consider anyone richer than the man who lacks nothing that his nature requires, or more powerful than one who gains all
he strives for, or happier than one who is set free from all perturbation
of mind, or more secure in his wealth than one who possesses only what, as
the saying goes, he can carry away with him out of a shipwreck? What
power, moreover, what office, what kingdom can be preferable to the state
of one who despises all human possessions, considers them inferior to wisdom, and never meditates on any subject that is not eternal and divine?[9]

Both here and in the account of his dream, with which the *Republic*
ends, Scipio seems to leave little doubt of his own preference for the
philosophic rather than the active life as the life of human excellence.
Political life, the dream implies, is a duty to be undertaken by man
while he lives on earth. Power and glory, the earthly rewards which
are showered on the statesman, the rewards of which Cicero spoke
in such glowing terms in the prologue to the first book, are seen to
be both ephemeral and, in the last analysis, meaningless. The true
compensation for the statesman's sacrifices is the heavenly reward, *i.e.,*
the eternal life of happiness and contemplation, granted him after
death.

But there is still another position to be considered. The most
desirable life, Scipio suggests at another point in the *Republic,* is
neither the simply contemplative nor the simply active life but that
which represents a "union of experience in the management of great
affairs with the study and mastery of those other arts," *i.e.,* the life
of a statesman whose horizons have been enlarged by philosophy.[10]
Although Cicero is not without ambiguity on this entire question,
there is reason to doubt that this intermediate position constitutes his
final opinion. He has suggested earlier the potential incompatibility
of the two pursuits. The history of Greece and Rome provides few
examples of those who have in fact combined the two pursuits with
any degree of success. Why, then, does he introduce this third possibility?

Cicero's initial task is the restoration of the primacy of the political
sphere. This restoration is guided, however, by an awareness of the
limitations of the political or active life. He seeks to convey some
sense of these limitations to those among his readers who are potential philosophers, and thus to show them the ultimate supremacy
of the philosophic life. At the same time, he seeks to warn them that

the philosopher, in spite of these limitations, must concern himself, directly or indirectly, with the fate of the commonwealth. What is theoretically higher, he suggests, may have to give way at times to what is necessary, to what is of immediate and urgent concern to most men.

For, in truth, our country has not given us birth and education without expecting to receive some sustenance, as it were, from us in return; nor has it been merely to serve our convenience that she has granted to our leisure a safe refuge and for our moments of repose a calm retreat.[11]

The philosopher must be prepared at certain times to abandon his concern with "eternal and divine" subjects and to place his particular talents at the service of the commonwealth. The third possibility is introduced not only to emphasize this dual responsibility but to offer a model for the many whose talents or inclinations do not lie in the direction of the philosophic life, but who nevertheless will have important political functions. Such men are well advised to seek that life which approximates the best although it necessarily falls short of it, the life of action illuminated by philosophy.

Only after some light has been thrown on the question of the right life for man is Laelius, a participant who believes theoretical knowledge to be impossible or at least irrelevant to the human situation, allowed to introduce the question of the best regime. The subsequent discussion moves along two lines: (1) an attempt to settle the question in speech, *i.e.,* to investigate the nature of political things and thus the nature of the best regime, on a theoretical level; and (2) an attempt to illustrate in deed, by using as an empirical example the Roman republic as it existed some years prior to their own time, what speech, *i.e.,* reason, has been trying to make clear.

The emphasis placed upon this dual approach has occasionally inspired the charge that Cicero's work is little more than a rationalization of an earlier Roman regime. Such an understanding neglects at the very beginning his explicit assertion that the inquiry is directed to the discovery of universally valid political principles, principles designed to "promote the firm foundation of States, the strengthening of cities, and the curing of the ills of peoples." [12] "We are composing laws not for the Roman people in particular," he asserts in the *Laws,* "but for all virtuous and stable nations." [13] The presence or absence of an empirical example does not affect the possibility of such an inquiry.

As for my using our own state as a pattern, I did so, not to help me to define the best constitution (for that could be done without using any pattern at all), but in order to show, by illustrations from the actual history of the greatest state of all, what it was that reason and speech were striving to make clear.[14]

Those who charge Cicero with seeking only to restore the republican constitution of an earlier age also ignore the suggestion, implicit in both the *Republic* and the *Laws,* that even when it was at its peak the Roman republic, the model, fell short of the ideal discovered in speech. The code of laws outlined by Cicero in the *Laws,* the code of that best state discovered in speech, is not identical with that of the Roman republic at any time in its history. The participants in the *Laws,* Quintus emphasizes, are not "simply rehearsing the actual laws of Rome, but restoring old laws which have been lost, or else originating new ones." [15] The specific deviations from what was historically the case are those dictated by reason, the ultimate standard of law and justice. The composite of old and new which results represents his attempt to bridge the gap between the popular or prephilosophic tendency to identify the good with the old, *i.e.,* the ancestral or traditional, and the philosophic identification of the good with the natural, *i.e.,* that which is dictated by reason. By bringing reason to bear on the existing code rather than beginning afresh, Cicero seeks to preserve an essential sense of continuity with the past and thus the sense of respect for the traditional which normally exists in the political community.

There are, of course, certain practical reasons for the use of an empirical model. Cicero's inquiry, which is Greek in both method and conclusions, must be given a Roman character if it is to prove congenial to the Roman palate. His task is thus rendered simpler and his demonstration more convincing if, instead of the "shadowy commonwealth of the imagination" with which Plato is said to have dealt,[16] he can illustrate his understanding of the nature of political things with a concrete example, and not simply any example, but the Roman example.

The inquiry proper begins with Scipio's statement of the essential characteristics of a commonwealth:

A commonwealth is the affair of a people. But a people is not any collection of human beings brought together in any sort of way, but an assemblage of people in large numbers associated in an agreement with respect to justice and a partnership for the common good.[17]

This association ceases to be a commonwealth when it ceases to be guided by the ends—justice and the common good—for which it exists. Scipio asserts that the commonwealth is natural in so far as it is essential to the achievement of a happy and virtuous life. It comes into being not, as some philosophers have suggested, because of any weaknesses of human nature but because of a "certain social spirit which nature has implanted in man." [18] Man is not a "solitary or unsocial creature"; he is driven by his very nature to seek the companionship of his fellows. The government of the commonwealth is no less natural, for without some such arrangement "existence is impossible for a household, a city, a nation, the whole human race, nature and the universe itself." [19] When properly constituted, this government will reflect the hierarchical principle coextensive with the whole of nature, the lower being subordinate in each case to that which is higher.

The character of the commonwealth is ultimately determined by the "arrangements in regard to magistrates," *i.e.,* by the form of government.[20] The three simple forms are kingship, aristocracy, and democracy. The first of these, the rule of one, is characterized by affection: "the name of king seems like that of father to us";[21] the second, the rule of the best, by counsel or wisdom; the third, the rule of all, by liberty. Although kingship is judged the best and democracy the worst of the simple forms, each of the three may offer a decent and even stable government so long as injustice and greed do not destroy the original bond of the association. Unfortunately, each of the simple forms contains within itself not only certain defects but even the seeds of its own destruction:

In kingships the subjects have too small a share in the administration of justice and in deliberation; and in aristocracies the masses can hardly have their share of liberty, since they are entirely excluded from deliberation for the commonweal and from power; and when all the power is in the people's hands, even though they exercise it with justice and moderation, yet the resulting equality itself is inequitable, since it allows no distinctions in rank.[22]

Before each lies its depraved counterpart—tyranny, oligarchy, mob rule —and history serves as a record of the inevitable tendency of each to degenerate into its opposite and the latter in turn to be replaced at some future time by still another form.

Thus the ruling power of the state, like a ball, is snatched from kings by tyrants, from tyrants by aristocrats or the people, and from them again by an oligarchical faction or a tyrant, so that no single form of government ever maintains itself very long.[23]

While it is questionable whether even the enlightened statesman can interrupt this "natural motion and circular course" permanently, there is a way in which he can at least delay the movement. This lies in the creation of a moderate and balanced regime, a regime which incorporates a judicious mixture of the institutions and principles of each of the simple regimes and exhibits in turn an "even balance of rights, duties and functions." [24] Cicero's thought on this point had been anticipated by a number of earlier writers, including Plato and Aristotle, but his immediate guide in the matter of the mixed regime was the Greek historian Polybius (205–123 B.C.). Polybius, seeking an explanation for the extremely rapid, almost unprecedented expansion of Roman power, suggested that the key lay in the mixed character of the Roman constitution, a mixture so successful "that it was impossible even for a native to pronounce with certainty whether the whole system was aristocratic, democratic, or monarchical." [25]

For if one fixed one's eyes on the power of the consuls, the constitution seemed completely monarchical and royal; if on that of the senate it seemed again to be aristocratic; and when one looked at the power of the masses, it seemed clearly to be a democracy.[26]

The mixed constitution made it possible to avoid the defects inherent in each of the simple forms. It prevented an undue concentration of power and provided a system of checks and balances. Within such a framework, Cicero suggested, "the magistrates have enough power, the counsels of the eminent citizens enough influence, and the people enough liberty." [27]

If examined carefully, however, the mixed regime proves to be in the most important respects an aristocracy. The arrangements are designed to ensure that the aristocracy, and thus the element of wisdom or counsel, is assigned the decisive role.[28] While a measure of power is to be vested in the people, it is expected that the actual authority will remain with the Senate, for liberty is to be "granted in such a manner that the people [are] induced by many excellent provisions to yield to the authority of the nobles." [29] The success of this "balanced and harmonious constitution" rests in large measure on the continued existence of an aristocracy possessing the particular qualities described by Cicero in the *Laws*. The aristocracy, he suggests there, must be "free from dishonor" and "a model for the rest of the citizens." [30] The example presented by this order is decisive for the over-all health of the commonwealth:

For it is not so mischievous that men of high position do evil—though that is bad enough in itself—as it is that these men have so many imitators. For, if you will turn your thoughts back to our early history, you will see that the character of our most prominent men has been reproduced in the whole State; whatever change took place in the lives of the prominent men has also taken place in the whole people.[31]

If the quality of the aristocracy is allowed to degenerate, it is extremely unlikely that the regime will manage to survive for any great length of time. It will certainly prove incapable, given such a deterioration, of achieving the end for which it exists, the cultivation of virtue in the citizens.

This exposition of the theoretical principles underlying the mixed regime is followed by Scipio's account of the development and internal composition of the earlier Roman republic—the practical illustration he promised earlier. The scene is set for such a historical treatment by Scipio's reference at the beginning of the discussion to a statement once made by Cato. The latter, a noted Roman statesman of an earlier age, had traced the superiority of the republic to the fact that it was "based upon the genius, not of one man, but of many; . . . founded, not in one generation, but in a long period of several centuries and many ages of men." [32] It rested upon the collective wisdom and experience of many generations of men. Its institutions and practices had demonstrated their merit by passing the severest practical test, the test of time.

Cato's thesis reminds one immediately of that advanced at a much later date by the English statesman Edmund Burke. The superiority of the British Constitution, Burke was to argue, lay in the fact that it was not the product of fabrication or conscious planning. It had not been "formed upon a regular plan or with any unity of design" but had developed "in a great length of time, and by a great variety of accidents"; the parts had "gradually, and almost insensibly, accommodated themselves to each other." [33] Its perfection represents the culmination of a natural process, of a process of slow, continuous, and almost unconscious growth.[34]

Burke's understanding represents a radical departure from the position of the classical thinkers. The latter had taken it for granted that the best regime would be the product of reason and conscious planning. There is evidence that Cicero himself is closer to the classics than to Burke on this point. The basic difference between Cicero and the earlier Greek thinkers does not appear to spring from a disagreement in regard to the principle—the superiority of planning to accident—but from one in regard to the question whether the better plan is more likely to result from the efforts of a single wise man or those of a series of wise men. Cicero did not simply reject the possibility that the best state could be the product of the wisdom of a single founder. He agrees with Polybius as to the accomplishments of Lycurgus, the Spartan lawgiver, and he concludes his account of the contributions of Romulus to the development of the mature Roman order in the following vein:

Do you not perceive, then, that by the wisdom of a single man a new people was not simply brought into being and then left like an infant crying in its cradle, but was left already full-grown and almost in the maturity of manhood?[35]

But such pre-eminently wise men are rare. It is more sensible to plan on the basis of what is more likely to be the case. It is more likely that there will be a series of fairly able men, each of whom can be expected to apply some of the lessons of experience to the task of gradually improving the regime.

The historical account itself deserves careful examination, for it does not appear to be free from irony. History, Cicero assures us in the *Laws,* is distinguished from poetry by its reference to truth rather than fancy. There are a number of suggestions throughout the *Republic* that Scipio's account of the Roman origins falls short of this standard. We are regaled at one point with the tale of the deification of Romulus, and we are assured that the tale must be true for it was accepted as true by the men of Romulus' time—a time, we are told, of culture and learning, a time when men were "quick to mock at and reject with scorn that which could not possibly have happened."[36] To support this last assertion, Cicero presents some examples of the intellectual heights to which the men of this age of culture and learning had risen. But the examples are only of the state of learning in Greece; no examples are given that would allow the reader to make a judgment about the presence or absence of a similar cultivation in Rome. We are left to draw our own conclusions. Shortly thereafter, as if to guide our conclusions, Scipio refers to those allegedly cultured and learned ancestors as simple rustics; and we learn that far from being skeptical about such tales, they were willing to accept the one concerning Romulus on the authority of an "untutored peasant." Moreover, when the matter is raised in a different connection in the *Laws,* Cicero does not hesitate to brand the tale a fable.

Scipio's presentation is not meant to be simple history, but rather is designed to offer an idealized picture of the Roman past, a judicious mixture of fact and fancy. It is designed to demonstrate to the citizens the wisdom and justice of the Roman origins, to show them the firm foundations upon which this Roman example of the best regime rests. The presentation is in its essence a deliberate example of the Platonic "noble lie." While it necessarily falls short of the philosophic truth, such a salutary account of the foundations of the commonwealth may be essential to the cohesion and very existence of the political society. The statesman's task, Cicero would have us understand, rests not in the wholesale destruction of these traditional, if unphilosophic, myths, but in placing the partial truth that they may contain at the service of those policies which reason informs him are conducive to the good of the commonwealth.

Scipio's historical presentation also serves to suggest the provisional sense in which the mixed regime is actually *the* best regime. His account indicates that the Roman decline began in fact with the transformation of kingship into tyranny. The mixed regime is not introduced until some time after this decline has begun. The unqualifiedly best regime for Cicero, as for classical thought generally, is that in which wisdom has an absolute right to rule: the absolute rule of the wise (the true aristocracy) and ultimately the absolute rule of the one man pre-eminent in wisdom and virtue (the true kingship) is the most desirable form of government. The rule of and by wisdom was possible under the early Roman kings, but this was to prove true only so long as the kingship retained its distinctive character. Its character in turn depended on the existence of a succession of good and wise kings, and thus on chance rather than planning. In view of this, kingship proves in practice to be the least stable of the simple regimes, "the first and most certain" to decay;[37] and in fact it required, as Cicero emphasizes, only the excesses of a single king, Tarquinius, to render the very title of king obnoxious to the Roman people.[38]

Scipio's account indicates that the "excellent constitution" established by Romulus and maintained by the Romans for over two hundred years began to wither with this transformation of kingship into tyranny. The subsequent history of Rome is written in terms of a series of more or less successful attempts to control the forces unleashed by this transformation. The mixed regime comes to sight as one such attempt to satisfy the popular thirst for liberty while recapturing, at the same time, a place for the wisdom and virtue characteristic of kingship. Cicero warns us in the *Laws* that the task of the statesman is to "determine not merely what [is] best but also what [is] necessary." [39] One test of his political skill is the extent to which he understands the dictates of necessity and succeeds in operating within the range of possibilities that necessity permits him. Where the absolute rule of the wise is impossible, the mixed regime allows statesmen to attempt to secure popular consent to the rule of wisdom, and thus to achieve that approximation of the best which is conceivable for most societies. The mixed regime incorporates the attributes of what we have come to call the "rule of law." It seeks to embody the precepts of a wise founder in the fundamental laws of the state, and then to insure that the subsequent administration or completion of these laws will be placed in the hands of those least likely to deviate from them and most likely to execute them in accord with the spirit permeating them. The essential elements of this basic code and the attributes of the governing class are sketched in some detail by Cicero in the *Laws*.

The particular strength of such a regime lies in its relative stability; yet, in so far as it seeks to bridge the chasm between wisdom and popular consent, it rests on a precarious foundation. Such a regime is not always easy to achieve and, once achieved, it is hard to maintain for any length of time. Even this second best, this approximation of the simply best may not be possible for all peoples or at all times.

From this analysis of the best regime the discussion shifts to a consideration of the assertion that injustice rather than justice necessarily underlies the successful conduct of the affairs of any state. Although he disclaims any belief in the arguments, Philus, another Academic Skeptic, consents to state the case for injustice as it had been presented by Carneades (214–129 B.C.), an earlier Academic Skeptic. His presentation advances from two main premises: (1) justice is conventional rather than natural; (2) justice is folly.

If justice were natural, he suggests at the beginning of his argument, then, like man's sense of what is hot and cold, it would be the same thing to all men, always and everywhere. In fact, man's conception of what justice entails varies not only from nation to nation but even from one age to another within a single city. Justice is not natural but rather the product of human society, and, more specifically, the product of this or that human society. It rests not on nature but utility; it is not desired for its own sake but only on the basis of calculation. It has no stability; its content depends only on the circumstances. It springs in large measure from man's fear that without such arrangements he, in his weakness, would always be exposed to the depredations of others, particularly of those stronger than himself.

The second and more fundamental strand of the argument presented by Philus begins with the tentative acceptance of the premise earlier denied: there is in fact a common understanding among men regarding the basic dictates of justice. To observe these faithfully, however, is to run counter to human nature, for the dictates of justice are seldom identical with those of wisdom and self-interest.

Wisdom urges us to increase our resources, to multiply our wealth, to extend our boundaries; . . . to rule over as many subjects as possible, to enjoy pleasures, to become rich, to be rulers and masters; justice, on the other hand, instructs us to spare all men, to consider the interests of the whole human race, to give everyone his due, and not to touch sacred or public property, or that which belongs to others.[40]

If this is true, justice cannot be simply natural, for neither man nor the political community can reasonably be expected to select a course of action which, while just, is at the same time the height of folly. Had Rome, Philus asserts, complied with the strict demands of justice in every instance it would not now be an empire but still a poverty-stricken village. Wisdom counsels that it is the appearance rather than the substance of justice which is to be sought, for then one may benefit from the advantages stemming from a reputation for justice while avoiding the misfortunes that may accompany a too strict compliance with its demands.

The case for justice has been entrusted to Laelius, the oldest and most conservative of the group. Unfortunately, only fragments remain of Laelius' statement. The most important of these is that in which he outlines his conception, *i.e.,* the Stoic conception, of natural law.

True law is right reason in agreement with nature; it is of universal application, unchanging and everlasting; it summons to duty by its commands, and averts from wrongdoing by its prohibitions. And it does not lay its commands or prohibitions upon good men in vain, though neither have any effect on the wicked. It is a sin to try to alter this law, nor is it allowable to attempt to repeal any part of it, and it is impossible to abolish it entirely. We cannot be freed from its obligations by senate or people, and we need not look outside ourselves for an expounder or interpreter of it. And there will not be different laws at Rome and at Athens, or different laws now and in the future, but one eternal and unchangeable law will be valid for all nations and all times, and there will be one master and ruler, that is, God, over us all, for he is the author of this law, its promulgator, and its enforcing judge.[41]

While not enforced or strictly enforceable by any human agent, the commands of this law cannot be ignored with impunity. The individual who deviates from them denies what is best in his own nature and suffers in turn the mental torment stemming from self-contempt and conscience. A similar failure upon the part of the commonwealth, Laelius suggests, will eventually result in its destruction. To Philus' contention that the paths of justice and wisdom necessarily diverge, Laelius opposes the assertion that to do what is just will always prove to be the wisest and most rewarding course of action.

Although the position advanced by Laelius is usually thought to be also that of Cicero, there is reason to believe that Cicero regards both the strict moralism of Laelius and what one is tempted to call the Machiavellianism of Philus as fundamentally inadequate. While it is far better in practice that the state seek to be guided by the strict demands of justice rather than by the conception that such standards are arbitrary and ultimately meaningless, it may be impossible for even the best of states to do more than approximate the standard of perfect justice. This is one of the lessons Scipio sought to teach in the course of offering an account of the Roman past in the second book of the *Republic*. Even the past of this regime, the regime which Scipio presents as the best regime, was not free of injustice; even the Romans, "the most just of men" according to Philus, were not above plunder and murder. Cicero's conclusion is fundamentally the same as Plato's: the perfectly just regime probably lies outside the range of human possibilities. Its demands are too severe. The wise statesman, while seeking to be guided in his practice by such standards, will begin with the understanding that there is little likelihood, given the nature of man and the political community, that they can or will be realized fully in any state.

This conception of the limitations intrinsic to political life runs through much of Cicero's thought. It is particularly noticeable in those sections of the *Laws* in which he explores, this time in his own name, the question of justice and the question of the status and character of natural law. The inquiry in the *Laws* is stimulated by the desire to prepare a code suited to the mixed regime, the regime of which he had spoken in the *Republic*. The preparation of the positive law that will go to make up such a code presupposes, however, a much fuller, essentially philosophic, investigation of a number of other questions.

For we must explain the nature of Justice, and this must be sought for in the nature of man; we must also consider the laws by which states ought to be governed; then we must deal with the enactments and decrees of nations which are already formulated and put in writing; and among these the civil law, as it is called, of the Roman people will not fail to find a place.[42]

The first book of the *Laws* is devoted to such an inquiry. The inquiry yields much the same Stoic understanding of man and the universe as that underlying Laelius' position in the *Republic*.[43] Man, the one natural creature possessing a rational soul and sharing the divine faculty of reason with the gods, exists in a rational and ordered universe. By virtue of his unique possession, reason, he may discern and adjust himself to the comprehensive rational order. So far as he achieves this, so far as reason serves as his guiding and ruling element, he fulfills his nature to the highest degree, and he shares both law and justice with the gods. Since reason is the common possession of all men, this highest life, the life "according to nature," is accessible, at least in theory, to all men: "there is no human being of any race who, if he finds a guide, cannot attain to virtue." [44]

Cicero's teaching in the *Laws* thus seems in harmony with the Stoic position developed by Laelius in the *Republic*. Whether this is simply the case, however, remains open to question. Cicero's comments on natural law, for example, are prefaced in the *Laws* by the statement that he is not certain of their truth, although they seem to him "usually and mostly" right.[45] At another point he begs the members of his own school, the Academic Skeptics, not to examine his argument too closely, for if they "should attack what we think we have constructed so beautifully, it would play too great havoc with it." [46] Cicero has good reason to be concerned, for the fundamentally Stoic teaching which he propounds as his own in the *Laws* rests in part on an understanding of divine providence and an anthropocentric teleology which he himself had examined and rejected in two other works—*On the Nature of the Gods* and *On Divination*.

It is reasonable to suggest that this apparent inconsistency has its roots in the fact that the teaching in the *Laws* is addressed not to philosophers but primarily to all decent and honorable men. The immediate task is a practical one: "to promote the firm foundation of states, the strengthening of cities, and the curing of the ills of peoples." [47]

For that reason I want to be especially careful not to lay down first principles that have not been wisely considered and thoroughly investigated. Of course I cannot expect that they will be universally accepted, for that is impossible; but I do look for the approval of all who believe that everything which is right and honourable is to be desired for its own sake, and that nothing whatever is to be counted a good unless it is praiseworthy in itself, or at least that nothing should be considered a great good unless it can rightly be praised for its own sake.[48]

The arguments advanced in support of these principles and to a considerable extent the principles themselves are selected with a view to the appeal that they would have to such men, not simply, or primarily, with a view to theoretical certainty. If Cicero's purpose is kept in mind, then it becomes possible to understand Atticus' unqualified acceptance in the *Laws* of the teachings concerning theology and the primacy of religion in the state.[49] It is perfectly proper for Atticus, in his capacity as a Roman citizen, to assent to these politically salutary teachings, although as an Epicurean philosopher he could not have granted their theoretical soundness. Atticus and Cicero share an understanding of the importance of such teachings to the "firm foundation of states." The Stoic principles, even though inadequate on a theoretical level, are admirably suited to the achievement of this important end.

A further indication of Cicero's own position, and of the severe qualifications with which he adopts that of the Stoics, is reflected in his own treatment of the natural law. Laelius, in arguing the case for justice, had had no difficulty in reconciling the practices of the Roman past with the strict demands of justice embodied in the natural law; moreover, he did not doubt that the precepts of the natural law were fully accessible to everyone. Scipio's historical account leaves little doubt that Cicero did not share this sanguine view of the Roman past; nor, as has been suggested earlier, did he accept the premise essential to such a view, *i.e.,* that the strict demands of justice can be perfectly compatible with those of civil society. Finally, he was not at all certain that everyone is equally equipped to acquire a full understanding of the natural law and equally equipped to be guided by it. While all men may in principle acquire the wisdom and virtue requisite to the life of human excellence, the life according to nature, the life guided by fully developed reason, few in fact do so. Few find that guide of whom he had spoken earlier; most succumb quite easily to "bad habits and false beliefs," to the attractions of pleasure and vice.[50] If this is so, then it is entirely possible that the full demands of natural law are incompatible with the needs and claims of human society as we know it. In the *Republic,* for example, Cicero suggests that the law of the wise, *i.e.,* the unmitigated natural law, would assign property rights simply on the basis of the ability to use the property well.[51] Such a principle would be impossible to implement in civil society as we know it. The lesson is clear: the unmitigated and pure natural law may be inapplicable to the normal human situation. The natural law to which the activities of men and states are normally to be referred must be a diluted version of this true law, one whose standards are necessarily lower.

A similar understanding is present in Cicero's discussion of the rules of personal conduct or action in *De Officiis.* It is soon made clear that the standard being discussed there is that which should govern the conduct of the nonwise rather than the wise man.[52] While adequate to guide the lives of most men, it is inferior to that higher

standard, the standard of nature itself, which guides the actions of
the wise man. The definition of natural law which Cicero propounds
at several points in the *Laws* also possesses this twofold character. In
the second book, for example, he speaks of the natural law in the
following vein:

I find that it has been the opinion of the wisest men that Law is not a
product of human thought, nor is it any enactment of peoples, but something
eternal which rules the whole universe by its wisdom in command and
prohibition. Thus they have been accustomed to say that Law is the primal
and ultimate mind of God, whose reason directs all things either by compulsion or restraint. Wherefore that law which the gods have given to the
human race has been justly praised; for it is the reason and mind of a wise
lawgiver applied to command and prohibition.[53]

The eternal law which rules the universe and exists in the "primal and
ultimate mind of God," the law which both Cicero and Laelius have
referred to elsewhere as "the highest reason inherent in nature," [54] is
not simply or necessarily identical with the second and lower form of
law, "the reason and mind of a wise lawgiver applied to command and
prohibition." The latter is derivative from and based on the former but
reflects an understanding of the lower standards which are a necessary
part of political life. "The essential nature of the commonwealth often
defeats reason." [55] The wise legislator and statesman will thus temper
the demands of pure justice and pure reason, as Cicero does in composing the code suited to his "best" state in the *Laws,* so that they become
compatible with the requirements of civil society. It should be noted, of
course, that this understanding does not force Cicero to embrace the
position advanced by Philus: that justice, because its specific substantive
demands are not always and everywhere the same, is fundamentally
arbitrary, that it is not natural but conventional. The substance of
human justice, although concerned with the particular and dependent
on a variety of contingent circumstances, is not, for Cicero, simply arbitrary. The standards remain, even though their complete realization,
given the nature of man and the nature of political society, is extremely
unlikely. They continue to serve as guides to human action, and one
should always seek to approximate them as nearly as possible.

The *Laws* illuminates the question of the status of the active or
political life with which the inquiry in the *Republic* began. Cicero's
inquiry in these two books is directed to an understanding of the nature
of political things. He has sought, as Plato had done before him, to
pursue this larger inquiry by setting forth the nature of the best political

order. One product of the investigation is the understanding of the limitations intrinsic to political life. Both reason and justice must somehow be diluted to meet the needs of the practical or political life. Those who are in a position to make a choice between the two ways of life, the active and the contemplative, must be aware of this fact.

## NOTES

1. Reprinted by permission of the publishers from "The Loeb Classical Library," Marcus Tullius Cicero, *Laws*, trans. C. W. Keyes (Cambridge, Mass.: Harvard University Press, 1928), I. 58; *Tusculan Disputations*, trans. J. E. King ("Loeb Classical Library" [Cambridge, Mass.: Harvard University Press, 1927]) I. 1–8.

2. *Tusculan Disputations* I. 1–5; II. 4; IV. 5–6.

3. The doctrines of this school are considered in detail in E. Zeller, *The Stoics, Epicureans and Sceptics* (London: Longmans, Green, 1870); and Edwyn Bevan, *Stoics and Sceptics* (Cambridge: W. Heffer and Sons, 1959).

4. *Laws* II. 39.

5. *Tusculan Disputations* V. 11.

6. Paul Friedlander, *Plato; An Introduction* (London: Routledge and Kegan Paul, 1958), pp. 154–70.

7. Reprinted by permission of the publishers from "The Loeb Classical Library," Cicero, *Republic*, trans. C. W. Keyes (Cambridge, Mass.: Harvard University Press, 1928) I. 2.

8. *Ibid.*, I. 15.

9. *Ibid.*, I. 28.

10. *Ibid.*, III. 4–6.

11. *Ibid.*, I. 8.

12. *Laws* I. 37.

13. *Laws* II. 35.

14. *Republic* II. 66.

15. *Laws* III. 37.

16. *Republic* II. 52.

17. *Ibid.*, I. 39.

18. *Ibid.*

19. *Laws* III. 3.

20. *Ibid.*, III. 5.

21. *Republic* I. 54.

22. *Ibid.*, I. 43.

23. *Ibid.*, I. 68.

24. *Ibid.*, I. 69; II. 57, 69.

25. *The Histories*, trans. W. R. Paton ("Loeb Classical Library" [Cambridge, Mass.: Harvard University Press, 1927]), VI. 11.11.

26. *Ibid.*, VI. 11.12.

27. *Republic* II. 57–58.

28. *Laws* II. 30; III. 24–25, 28, **38**.

29. *Ibid.*, III. 25.

30. *Ibid.*, III. 30.

31. *Ibid.*, III. 31.

32. *Republic* II. 2.

33. *The Works of Edmund Burke* (London: "Bohn's Standard Library"), II, 554; V, 253–54.

34. *Ibid.*, II. 307–8.

35. *Republic* II. 21.

36. *Ibid.*, II. 19.

37. *Ibid.*, I. 65.

38. *Ibid.*, II. 52.

39. *Laws* III. 26.

40. *Republic* III. 24.

41. *Ibid.*, III. 33.

42. *Laws* I. 17.

43. For details in regard to the Stoic teaching see E. Vernon Arnold, *Roman Stoicism* (Cambridge: Cambridge University Press, 1911).

44. *Laws* I. 30.

45. *Ibid.*, I. 19.

46. *Ibid.*, I. 39.

47. *Ibid.*, I. 37.

48. *Ibid.*

49. *Ibid.*, II. 15–69.

50. *Ibid.,* I, 29–34, 47.
51. *Republic* I. 27.
52. *De Officiis* I. 7–8; III. 11–17.

53. *Laws* II. 8.
54. *Republic* III. 33; *Laws* I. 18.
55. *Republic* II. 57.

## READINGS

A.  Cicero. *Republic*. Bks I, VI.
    Cicero. *Laws*. Bk I.
B.  Cicero. *Republic*.
    Cicero. *Laws*.
    Cicero. *Offices*. Bks I, III.

# ST. AUGUSTINE

## 354–430

*The City of God,* the great work which contains the political thought of St. Augustine, is not at all a systematic treatise in political philosophy.[1] Acknowledged to be the greatest of the saint's writings (and so acknowledged by Augustine himself), *The City of God* presents a picture of the Christian "world view" that is extremely detailed for all its panoramic character. Begun in 413 and completed only in 426, its composition was directly inspired by the need St. Augustine felt to defend the Christian religion against the charge that it was responsible for the fall of Rome at the hands of Alaric in 410. The defense is divided into two parts: In the first ten books, which make up Part One, St. Augustine is concerned with the polemical task of refuting the pagan charge. Taking note of the curious blindness to the fact that Rome was not protected by the pagan gods during the sack of 410, St. Augustine proceeds in the first ten books to describe the spiritual and moral evils of paganism and to put the pagan theology under some degree of pressure.

The second half of Augustine's work is given over to an altogether original task—that of constructing a Christian philosophy of society. That is to say, matters that belong to the separate philosophical sciences (such as ethics and politics) are given a higher unity by reason of the more universal formality under which they are regarded, namely, Divine Revelation. Because Sacred Science considers things precisely under the formality of being divinely revealed, whatever has been divinely revealed—though it may also be the matter of other disciplines —possesses the one precise formality of the object of Sacred Science. And just as certain human sciences proceed from principles known by the light of a higher science (*e.g.,* the science of perspective proceeds from principles established by geometry and the science of music from principles established by arithmetic), so Sacred Science proceeds from principles established by the light of a higher science, namely, the science of God in Whose Intellect are the principles of this science. And because this is the case, because Sacred Science is established on principles revealed by God, "to this science alone," St. Augustine observes, "belongs that whereby saving faith is begotten, nourished, protected, and strengthened." [2] The fundamental point for understanding *The City of God* is the fact that it is under the formality of Sacred Doctrine that St. Augustine treats of history and politics.

The pertinence of this consideration becomes clear when we inquire how the central idea of St. Augustine's *City of God* is related to the past teaching in political philosophy. If for the moment we take the fundamental point in St. Augustine's political philosophy to be simply that no man owes an unqualified allegiance to any earthly society, then it is clear that this idea was not entirely new to the world. It is to be found in Aristotle's injunction to pursue the life that is more divine than human and in his view that political science is not the highest wisdom, nor man the best thing in the universe.[3] The same idea is to be found in Plato's teaching that there is "a better life than that of politics." [4] The central idea of St. Augustine, on the contrary, emerges only after this very noble and right teaching of the philosophers is subjected to a critique in the light of the higher principles of Sacred Doctrine.

It is the Sacred Scriptures that instruct man concerning the supreme good and the supreme evil, and instruct him unerringly: "Eternal life is the perfection of good, and eternal death the consummation of evil; and the aim of our life must be to avoid the one, and to attain the other. Therefore it is written: 'The just shall live by faith.' " [5]* As for the philosophers,

Their studies seemed wholly to aim at the attainment of beatitude [but] what course, what act can mortal misery perform to the obtaining of true blessedness . . . ? For who can discourse exactly of the miseries of this life? Tully, upon his daughter's death, did what he could. But what could he do? In what person can the first objects of nature be found without alteration? What, have not sorrow and disquiet full power to disturb the pleasure and quiet of the wisest? Even so, strength, beauty, health, vigor, and activity, are all subverted by their contraries. . . . And then the first gifts of nature, whereof sense and reason are the two first, because of the apprehension of truth,

---

*From the book *The City of God* by St. Augustine. John Healey's translation, revised and edited by R. V. G. Tasker. Everyman's Library. Reprinted by permission of E. P. Dutton & Co., Inc.

how easily are they lost! . . . So then far be it from us ever to think that we have attained the true happiness whilst we live here.[6]

Without divine instruction there is indeed neither goal nor path to man's strivings.

Let one look amongst all the multitude of philosophers' writings, and if he find two that tell both one tale in all respects, it may be registered for a rarity. . . . The prophet laughs at them, saying: "The Lord knoweth the thoughts of men" (or, as St. Paul has it, "of the wise") "that they are vain." But the people, state, nation and city of Israel, to whom God's holy laws were left, did not confound with that licentious confusion the false prophets with the true, but all in one consent held and acknowledged the latter for the true authors recording God's testimonies. . . . He that lived after their rules, followed not man, but God, who spake in them. The sacrilege forbidden there, God forbids. The commandment of "Honor thy father and mother" God commands. "Thou shalt not commit adultery, nor murder, nor shalt steal," God's wisdom pronounces this, not the wit of man. For what truth soever the philosophers attained and disputed of amidst their falsehood, as namely, that God framed the world, and governed it most excellently; the honesty of virtue; the love of country; the faith of friendship; just dealing, and all the things belonging to good manners—they knew not to what end the whole was to be referred.[7]

But Israel, the keeper of God's testimonies, knew: "And then it happened as it was prophesized: 'The law shall go forth from Sion, and the word of the Lord from Jerusalem.'" The Church founded by Christ fulfills the ancient prophecies: their witness " 'in Jerusalem, and in all Judea, and in Samaria, and unto the utmost part of the earth.'" [8]

We find in these considerations the essential elements for understanding the four basic concepts of St. Augustine's philosophy of politics: the concepts of Church, State, Heavenly City, and Earthly City. It is the relationship of these concepts that will lead us to St. Augustine's central idea.

The Church, a divinely established society, is the guardian of the Sacred Scriptures, of the Law of the Old and the New Testaments by which men are directed to eternal beatitude in the vision of God, Whom St. Augustine calls the Common Good of the universe. The State is concerned with "just dealing and all the things belonging to good manners": in the measure that men organize for a life of the political virtues as well as the virtues of the mind ("what truth soever the philosophers attained . . .") they compose the political community, the State. The Church and the State are thus recognizable, "visible" societies for the good. But since indeed God alone sounds the heart and plumbs the depths of the mind, there are two invisible "cities": the Heavenly City of the predestined and the Earthly City of the damned.

Those who, availing themselves as far as possible of the grace given through the Church, direct their just dealings and all the things belonging to good manners to final beatitude, are, the world over, members of the Heavenly City. Finally, those who seek no good beyond the present life, or on the other hand, seeking this good contemn the other, that is, "the honesty of virtue; the love of country; the faith of friendship; just dealing and all the things belonging to good manners" are, the world over, members of the Earthly City and destined to eternal death. Indeed, as we shall presently see, the very virtues of those who seek no good beyond the present life are vices; but more often than not such men are without virtue, and their vices are "a harvest of variable impiety." Their fortitude and their patience find expression in suicide; the rule of their prudence is marked by "ambition" and "proud sovereignty."

We are now in a position to see what the central idea of St. Augustine's political philosophy is: "Ambition" and "proud sovereignty" are indeed precisely the wounds of sin inflicted by the Earthly City on the State. The State, whose rule is that of freemen over freemen—embracing "the love of country; the honesty of virtue; the faith of friendship; just dealing, and all the things belonging to good manners"— is required by the very order of nature. The order of nature is not destroyed by sin, but it has been weakened: It is too commonly marked by ambition and proud sovereignty. It is this rule—of masters, as it were, over slaves—to which "guilt and not nature gave origin." But the dominion of freemen over freemen, which is not by domineering but by the service of counsel—this rule is both the prescription of nature itself and the rule established at the moment of creation: "But in the family of the faithful man . . . there the commanders are indeed the servants of those they seem to command; ruling not in ambition, but being bound by careful duty; not in proud sovereignty, but in nourishing pity. Thus has nature's order prescribed, and man by God was thus created." [9] Political authority indeed there is, but its rule is in the service of freedom, and its perfection in proportion to its movement away from mastership, from proud sovereignty, from ambition and the quality of "authoritarianism." It is the members of the Heavenly City who ought to perfect the State, healing its wounded nature and restoring the free character of its rule. If, to be sure, while here on earth the celestial society "increases itself out of all languages, being unconcerned by the different temporal laws that are made," it nonetheless "observes . . . the coherence of men's wills in honest morality . . . not breaking but observing their diversity in divers nations." [10]

For everything that a citizen of the Heavenly City does, he refers both "unto God and his neighbour, because being a citizen, he must not be all for himself, but sociable in his life and actions." Again, if the members of the Heavenly City must refer the "temporal conveniences" of the State to an eternal end, it is indeed nonetheless precisely they alone who may be said to be made happy by these temporal conveniences: "Yet he that has the latter in possession, and applies it all with reference to his hope's firm and faithful object, may not unfitly be called happy already. . . ." [11] For such a man there is nothing false about earthly happiness: it is the very beginning of beatitude. On the other hand, "this present possession without the other hope is a false beatitude" and we must "avouch [such an estate] to be most miserable, were it never so well fraught with temporal conveniences. . . . For herein is no use of the mind's truest good, because there is lacking the true wisdom, which in the prudent discretion, resolute performance, temperate restraint, and just distribution of [these temporal conveniences] should refer his intent in all these unto that end, where God shall be all in all, where eternity shall be firm, and peace most perfect and absolute." [12] For St. Augustine then, social justice should receive its initial movement from the most final of causes, eternal beatitude, the just distribution of temporal goods making us proportionately like God, "the most just Disposer . . . of all the adjuncts of [temporal peace]—the visible light, the breathable air, the potable water, and all the other necessaries of meat, drink, and clothing." [13] This is the root of Christian social justice.

Far from eliminating the State by referring its temporal peace to eternal peace, St. Augustine's thought rather would re-establish the State's integrity both in the mode of its operation (which is free) and in the order to its end (which is the temporal human common good). And if it is to St. Augustine "more than [to] any other individual [that] we owe the characteristically western ideal of the Church as a dynamic social power," [14] it is by this very same ideal that St. Augustine seeks to preserve the State from the inordinateness of that "variable impiety" by which it aims at something more than "the coherence of men's wills in honest morality." For in the Law of the Old and New Testament, by which God instructs man, the Church supplies the doctrinal rectitude concerning man's final end; and in the grace by which God heals human nature, the Church supplies the means for moral rectitude. Here the Church and the Heavenly City do indeed touch and blend.

For we must now note that if the political philosophy of Plato and Aristotle had taught that there is a dimension of life beyond the political which sets limits to political authority, this philosophy had gone

much beyond the common thought of Greece and had gone altogether beyond Greek and Roman practice. The practice had recognized no distinction between secular and religious spheres. Beginning
with Octavius Augustus in 27 B.C., the native cults of Greece and Rome,
fostered for political purposes, yielded to a common religion of empire.
The cult of Isis, brought to Rome from Egypt, and that of Mithra,
brought from Persia, had such great influence on the growing absolutism of the emperor as to transform his rule from something political
and legal into something indeed metaphysical and transcendent. Now
what needs to be most carefully noticed is that in St. Augustine's view
this "ambition" and "proud sovereignty" have their very root in the
natural virtue that does not refer itself to the true God. This very virtue
is a vice. Here the State and the Earthly City do indeed touch and blend.
For if indeed natural justice is "generally found wanting . . . where
God does not govern and men do not obey by sacrificing unto Him
alone," it is also true that even where this justice is found not wanting,
it is rather a vice than a virtue: "No, those things which [the soul]
seems to account virtues . . . if they be not all referred unto God, are
indeed rather vices than virtues. For although some hold them to be
real virtues, when they are desired only for their own account, and
nothing else; yet even so they incur vainglory and so lose their true
goodness." [15] We must try to understand how this is the case.

Desiring the virtues for their own account and not referring them
to God is not "honest morality" because virtue, being a disposition to
choose the mean between two extremes, is taken according to various
circumstances. Nothing hinders something from being extreme (either
by defect or excess) in a particular virtue according to one circumstance
while the same thing is a mean according to other circumstances,
through its conformity with reason. This may be seen in the case of the
virtues of magnanimity and magnificence. If we look at the absolute
quantity of the respective objects of these virtues, we shall call it an
extreme and a maximum; but if we consider the quantity in relation
to other circumstances, then it has the character of a mean, since these
virtues tend to this maximum in accordance with the rule of reason,
*i.e., where* it is right, *when* it is right, and for an *end* that is right.
There will be excess if one tends to this maximum *when* it is not
right, or *where* it is not right, or for an undue *end*. All virtue, then,
St. Augustine is saying, when not referred to God is vice by excess:
being sought on its own account, it is sought as an undue end. As
Augustine puts it, "For as that is not of the flesh, but above the flesh,
that animates the body; so that is not of man, but above man, which
beatifies the mind of man. . . ." [16] It is vainglorious and excessive to

seek virtue without referring it to God, "since" (as Aristotle himself
had put it) "man is not the best thing in the world." Sought on its own
account, all virtue is itself "ambition" and "proud sovereignty," the
beginning of "variable impiety."

It is this precise consideration that leads St. Augustine to remove
"justice" from Cicero's definition of an organized people as "a union
of a number of men associated by the two bonds of common acknowledgment of right (*jus*) and common pursuit of interest." St. Augustine's purpose is not to show that justice is not necessary to a state; it is
to show that the justice by which Cicero defines the *res publica* does
not make a true *res publica* because the circumstance of its not being
referred to God makes it inordinate and therefore not just. And further,
since this precise inordinateness is of the essence of variable impiety, a
good definition of the state must include even those states that are most
impious. As Professor McIlwain well says, this is a *reductio ad ab-
surdum,* but it is not so much the absurdity of Cicero's definition as it
is of heathenism.[17] The inordinateness of seeking virtue on its own
account is of the essence of variable impiety because the frustration of
man's final end (eternal beatitude) leads to an insane search for a
substitute infinity—as in emperor worship—and destroys the proper
forms by which human life is well lived on this earth.

For St. Augustine wishes us to see that it is only the well-instructed
pursuit of the Heavenly City that makes it possible for man to hold in
their proper order the temporal conveniences of earthly peace. "In contemplation one may not seek for idleness, but for truth; . . . and not to
grudge to impart it unto others"; and in the civil life, the life of action,
"one may not aim at power or honor . . . but unto the benefit of the
subject." [18] Asking why God punishes the good as well as the evil in
this life, St. Augustine answers by saying that the good, while indeed
turning away from the conduct of the wicked, are blameworthy in
"keeping aloof, [forbearing] to give [the wicked] due instructions,
admonitions, or reprehensions . . . [eschewing] their hate for [their
own] greater temporal preferment, [winking] at their . . . exorbitances
because they fear to lose by them their own vain temporalities. . . ." [19]
If the citizens of the Heavenly City neglect the duty laid upon them
in this world by its temporal exigencies they are not without fault:
"wholly abhorring the course of the wicked, [they] yet spare to tax
others' sins . . . because they fear to . . . be hurt in their possession of
those things whose use is lawful . . . desiring temporalities . . . far more
greedily than is fit. . . ." For it should be carefully understood that if
indeed it is only the saints who, having temporal conveniences in possession, "may not unfitly be called happy already," by the same token

"the saints in their loss of things temporal lose not anything at all." [20] The fall of Rome is a very small matter. The large matter is the Heavenly City's continuing task of "laying up . . . a good foundation against the time to come" by "the honesty of virtue; the love of country; the faith of friendship; just dealing, and all the things belonging to good manners."

Thus it becomes saints—as it becomes no others—to effect the good of earthly peace itself. This is the central idea, the chief significance for politics and political philosophy of *The City of God*. "They that follow the Lord's counsel . . .: 'Lay not up treasures for yourselves upon the earth where the moth and rust corrupt, or where thieves dig through and steal, but lay up treasures for yourselves in heaven, where neither rust nor moth corrupt, nor thieves dig through and steal' "— they alone know how to make a just distribution of temporal conveniences in imitation of "the most just Disposer of all the adjuncts of temporal peace." They have the needed mandate and the only mandate: " 'Charge them that are rich in this world that they be not high-minded, and that they trust not in their uncertain wealth, but in the living God, who giveth us plentifully all things to enjoy: that they do good and be rich in good works, ready to distribute and communicate: laying up in store for themselves a good foundation against the time to come, that they may obtain the true life.' " [21]

# NOTES

1. The Latin text, *De Civitate Dei*, edited by the Benedictines of St. Maur, will be found in *Patrologia Latina* XLI, 11–804. An acceptable text, with notes in English, is S. Aurelii Augustini, *De Civitate Dei contra Paganos*, ed. J. E. C. Welldon (2 vols.; London: Macmillan, 1924). In the present study all references are to the English version by J. Healey (London, 1610), St. Augustine, *The City of God*, ed. R. V. G. Tasker, with an introduction by Sir Ernest Barker (2 vols.; "Everyman's Library" [New York: Dutton, 1947]).

2. 14 *de Trinitate* (c.l.a.).

3. *Ethics* 1177[b] 26–35; 1141[a] 20.

4. *Republic* VII. 514–21.

5. *The City of God*, XIX. iv (vol. II, p. 237).

6. *Ibid.*, XVIII. xli (II, 214); XIX. iv (II, 237–38).

7. *Ibid.*, XVIII. xli (II, 215).

8. *Ibid.*, l (II, 224).

9. *Ibid.*, XIX. xiv–xv (II, 252–53).

10. *Ibid.*, xvii (II, 255).

11. *Ibid.*, xx (II, 257).

12. *Ibid.*

13. *Ibid.*, xiii (II, 251).

14. Christopher Dawson, "St. Augustine and His Age," in M. C. D'Arcy and others, *A Monument to St. Augustine* (New York: Meridian Books, 1957), p. 76.

15. *The City of God*, XIX. xxv (II, 265).

16. *Ibid.*

17. Charles Howard McIlwain, *The Growth of Political Thought in the*

*West* (New York: Macmillan, 1932), p. 157.

18. *The City of God,* XIX. xix (II, 256–57).

19. *Ibid.,* I. viii (I, 10–11).

20. *Ibid.,* ix (I, 12).

21. I Timothy 6:17–19; cited in *The City of God,* I. ix (I, 13).

## READINGS

A.  St. Augustine. *The City of God.* Ed. R. V. G. Tasker, with an introduction by Sir Ernest Barker. 2 vols. "Everyman's Library," New York: Dutton, 1947. Bks I, XIX.

B.  St. Augustine. *The City of God.* Bks XI–XVIII.

# ALFARABI

*circa* 870–950

Alfarabi (al-Fārābī) was the first philosopher who sought to confront, to relate, and as far as possible to harmonize classical political philosophy with Islam—a religion that was revealed through a prophet-legislator (Muhammad) in the form of a divine law, that organizes its followers into a political community, and that provides for their beliefs as well as for the principles and detailed rules of their conduct. Unlike Cicero he had to face and solve the problem of introducing classical political philosophy into a radically different cultural atmosphere; unlike Augustine he did not have a relatively free sphere of this-worldly life in the organization of which classical political philosophy could apply unchallenged, but had to face and solve the problem of the conflicting claims of political philosophy and religion over the whole of man's life.

The importance of Alfarabi's place in the history of political philosophy consists in his recovery of the classical tradition and in making it intelligible within the new context provided by the revealed religions. His best-known writings are political works concerned with the political regimes and the attainment of happiness through political life. They present the problem of the harmony between philosophy and Islam in a new perspective—that of the relation between the best regime, in particular as Plato had understood it, and the divine law of Islam. His position in Islamic philosophy corresponds to that of Socrates or Plato in Greek philosophy in so far as their chief concern may be said to be the relation between philosophy and the city. He was the founder of a tradition that looked to him, and through him to Plato and Aristotle, for a philosophic approach to the study and understanding of political and religious phenomena. His works inspired men like Avicenna, Averroes, and Maimonides. They admired him as their "second teacher" after Aristotle, and he was the only postclassical thinker whose authority commanded their respect alongside that of the ancients.

## DIVINE AND POLITICAL SCIENCE

There are a number of striking resemblances between many of the fundamental features of Islam and the good regime envisaged by classical political philosophy in general, and by Plato in the *Laws* in particular. Both begin with a god as the ultimate cause of legislation and consider correct beliefs about divine beings and the world of nature as essential for the constitution of a good political regime. In both, these beliefs should reflect an adequate image of the cosmos, make accessible to the citizens at large (and in a form they can grasp) the truth about divine things and about the highest principles of the world, be conducive to virtuous action, and form part of the equipment necessary for the attainment of ultimate happiness. Both consider the functions of the founder and legislator, and after him of his successors in the leadership of the community, of absolutely central importance for its organization and preservation. Both are concerned with the giving and the preserving of divine laws. Both are opposed to the view that mind or soul is derivative from body or is itself bodily—a view that undermines human virtue and communal life—and to the timorous piety that condemns man to despair of the possibility of ever understanding the rational meaning of the beliefs he is called upon to accept or of the activities he is called upon to perform. Both direct the eyes of the citizens to a happiness beyond their worldly concerns. Finally, both relegate the art of the jurist and that of the apologetic theologian to the secondary position of preserving the intention of the founder and of his law, and of erecting a shield against attacks.[1]

Alfarabi's important political works (*The Virtuous City, The Virtuous Religion,* and *The Political Regime*) are a meeting ground between Islam and classical political philosophy where these affinities, and not possible differences or conflicts, occupy the foreground. By laying the stress on such affinities, and by encouraging or even forcing both Islam and philosophy each to take a step in the direction of the other, he intends to make visible the common elements in both and to encourage and guide his Muslim reader to understand the characteristic features of classical political philosophy. This is revealed first of all in the very style of these works and in the way in which they are composed. Stylistically, they bear as much resemblance to legal codes as to philo-

sophic treatises. They consist mainly of positive statements about the
attributes of God, the order of the world, the place of man within it,
and how a good society is to be organized and led. Following a pattern
common to Plato's *Laws* and the Koran, many of these statements are
preceded by preludes preparing the way to the promulgation of sound
laws for regulating the conduct of rulers and prescribing the beliefs
and the actions of the citizens. Although not philosophic or political
treatises or specific legal promulgation, in the strict sense, these works
contain the results of philosophic and political investigations presented
in a practically useful way—as a basis for formulating a plan to order
a good political regime. They are works whose form and intention
could be readily understood by a Muslim reader committed to the
acceptance of a true view of the world at large and to obedience to laws
that promote virtue and lead to ultimate happiness. But they also conform to the intention of classical political philosophy in that they aim
at presenting a rational and persuasive account of the world, couched
in terms understandable to the citizens. They perform an important
practical task in so far as they indicate by their appearance the possibility of a rational understanding that does not destroy, but preserves
and explains, the beliefs and actions prescribed by the revealed law;
and they achieve a preparatory task inasmuch as they indicate the direction in which such a rational understanding can be sought.

Alfarabi's political works form a new genre of writing in Islamic
political literature. With habitual caution, he discreetly abstains from
directly quoting, expounding, or even referring to the Koran, Muhammad, or specifically Islamic religious issues. Yet the first impressions
that Alfarabi's works leave on his readers are unmistakable: the author
intends to enable his coreligionists, and indeed all communicants of
revealed religions, to see the wide area of harmony that exists between
their divine law and the practical intention of classical political philosophy. These readers could now see in their divine law a practical fulfillment of the doctrines of the most prominent wise men of antiquity.
They could turn to the study of these philosophers, not merely for the
limited purpose of defending their own beliefs and practices, or the
negative purpose of assuring themselves that rational understanding is
powerless before the higher authority of revelation and the divine law,
but for rising above the slavish state of blind believers and for penetrating into the secret intentions of revelation and the divine law—to
enlighten themselves, through the understanding of the most respectable
tradition of human wisdom, about the wisdom of their religion. Alfarabi gives them in these works the possibility of gaining a new attitude
toward the study of the works of Plato and Aristotle. He encourages

them to cease considering these philosophers as the originators of a foreign tradition that might undermine their beliefs and social virtues, a tradition that they ought to study with a view to refuting and combating it. He makes them see that this tradition belongs to them no less than to the Greeks, and that they must make it their own because it is concerned with matters closest to their minds and hearts. They are made to hope for a fuller understanding of their highest political and religious concern—the things that constitute the essence of their religion and their way of life, distinguish them from their heathen ancestors, and give them their unique claim to superiority over other communities.

## The Virtuous Regime

The central theme of Alfarabi's political writings is the virtuous regime, the political order whose guiding principle is the realization of human excellence or virtue. He conceives of human or political science as the inquiry into man in so far as he is distinguished from other natural beings and from divine beings, seeking to understand his specific nature, what constitutes his perfection, and the way through which he can attain it. Unlike other animals man is not rendered perfect merely through the natural principles present in him, and unlike divine beings he is not eternally perfect but needs to achieve his perfection through the activity proceeding from rational understanding, deliberation, and choosing among the various alternatives suggested to him by reason. The initial presence of the power of rational knowledge, and of the choice connected with it, is man's first or natural perfection, the perfection he is born with and does not choose. Beyond this, reason and choice are present in man to use for realizing his end or the ultimate perfection possible for his nature. This ultimate perfection is identical with the supreme happiness available to him. "Happiness is the good desired for itself, it is never desired to achieve by it something else, and there is nothing greater beyond it that man can achieve." [2]

Yet happiness cannot be achieved without being first known, and without performing certain orderly (bodily and intellectual) activities useful or leading to the achievement of perfection. These are the noble activities. The distinction between noble and base activities is thus guided by the distinction between what is useful for, and what obstructs, perfection and happiness. To perform an activity well, with ease, and in an orderly fashion requires the formation of character and the development of habits that make such activities possible. "The forms and states of character from which these [noble] activities emanate are the virtues; they are not goods for their own sake but goods only for the sake of happiness." [3] The distinction between virtue and vice presupposes knowledge of what human perfection or happiness is as well as the distinction between noble and base activities.

The virtuous regime can be defined as the regime in which men come together and cooperate with the aim of becoming virtuous, performing noble activities, and attaining happiness. It is distinguished by the presence in it of knowledge of man's ultimate perfection, the distinction between the noble and the base and between the virtues and the vices, and the concerted effort of the rulers and the citizens to teach and learn these things, and to develop the virtuous forms or states of character from which emerge the noble activities useful for achieving happiness.

The attainment of happiness means the perfection of that power of the human soul that is specific to man, of his reason. This in turn requires disciplining the lower desires to cooperate with and aid reason to perform its proper activity and also acquiring the highest arts and sciences. Such discipline and learning can be accomplished only by the rare few who possess the best natural endowments and who are also fortunate to live under conditions in which the requisite virtues can be developed and noble activities performed. The rest of men can only attain some degree of this perfection; and the extent to which they can attain that degree of perfection of which they are capable is decisively influenced by the kind of political regime in which they live and the education they receive. Nevertheless, all the citizens of the virtuous regime must have some common notions about the world, man, and political life. But they will differ with regard to the character of this knowledge, and hence with regard to their share of perfection or happiness. They can be divided broadly into the following three classes: (1) The wise or the philosophers who know the nature of things by means of demonstrative proofs and by their own insights. (2) The followers of these who know the nature of things by means of the demonstrations presented by the philosophers, and who trust the insight and accept the judgment of the philosophers. (3) The rest of the citizens, the many, who know things by means of similitudes, some more and others less adequate, depending on their rank as citizens. These classes or ranks must be ordered by the ruler who should also organize the education of the citizens, assign to them their specialized duties, give their laws, and command them in war. He is to seek, by persuasion and compulsion, to develop in everyone the virtues of which he is capable and to order the citizens hierarchically so that each class can attain the perfection of which it is capable and yet serve the class above it. It is in this manner that the city becomes a whole similar to the cosmos, and its members cooperate toward attaining happiness.

The virtuous regime is a nonhereditary monarchical or an aristo-cratic regime in which the best rule, with the rest of the citizens divided into groups that (depending on their rank) are ruled and in turn rule—until one arrives at the lowest group that is ruled only. The sole criterion for the rank of a citizen is the character of the virtue of which he is capable and that he is able to develop through his participation in the regime and obedience to its laws. Like the regime itself, its citizens are virtuous, first, because they possess, or follow those who possess, correct similitudes of the knowledge of divine and natural beings, human per-fection or happiness, and the principles of the regime designed to help man attain this happiness; and, second, because they act in accordance with this knowledge in that their character is formed with a view to performing the activities conducive to happiness.

Once the main features of the virtuous regime are clarified, the understanding of the main features and the classification of all other regimes become relatively simple. Alfarabi divides them into three broad types. (1) The regimes whose citizens have had no occasion to acquire any knowledge at all about divine and natural beings or about perfection and happiness. These are the *ignorant* regimes. Their citi-zens pursue lower ends, good or bad, in complete oblivion of true happiness. (2) The regimes whose citizens possess the knowledge of these things but do not act according to their requirements. These are the *wicked* or *immoral* regimes. Their citizens have the same views as those of the virtuous regime; yet their desires do not serve the rational part in them but turn them away to pursue the lower ends pursued in ignorant regimes. (3) The regimes whose citizens have acquired certain opinions about these things, but false or cor-rupt opinions, that is, opinions that claim to be about divine and natural beings and about true happiness, while in fact they are not. The similitudes presented to such citizens are, consequently, false and cor-rupt, and so also are the activities prescribed for them. These are the regimes that have been led astray or the *erring* regimes. The citizens of such regimes do not possess true knowledge or correct similitudes, and they, too, pursue the lower ends of the ignorant regimes. The regimes in error may have been founded as such. This is the case with the regimes "whose supreme ruler was one who was under an illusion that he was receiving revelation without having done so, and with regard to which he had employed misrepresentations, deceptions, and delu-sions." [4] But they may also have been originally virtuous regimes that had been changed through the introduction of false or corrupt views and practices.

All these types of regimes are opposed to the virtuous regime be-cause they lack its guiding principle, which is true knowledge and virtue or the formation of character leading to activities conducive to true happiness. Instead, the character of the citizens is formed with a view to attaining one or more of the lower ends. These ends are given by Alfarabi as six, and each of the general types mentioned above can be subdivided according to the end that dominates in it. (1) The regime of *necessity* (or the *indispensable* regime) in which the aim of the citizens is confined to the bare necessities of life. (2) The *vile* regime (oligarchy) in which the ultimate aim of the citizens is wealth and prosperity for their own sakes. (3) The *base* regime the purpose of whose citizens is the enjoyment of sensory or imaginary pleasures. (4) The regime of *honor* (timocracy) whose citizens aim at being honored, praised, and glorified by others. (5) The regime of *domination* (tyranny) whose citizens aim at overpowering and subjecting others. (6) The regime of *corporate association* (democracy) the main purpose of whose citizens is being free to do what they wish.

### The Philosopher-King and the Prophet-Legislator

To combine divine and political science is to emphasize the political importance of sound beliefs about divine beings and about the principles of the world. We saw that both Islam and classical political philosophy are in agreement concerning this issue. Muslims believed that the primary justification of their existence as a distinct community was the revelation of the truth about divine things to Muhammad, and that, had he not come to them with his message, they would have continued to live in misery and uncertainty about their well-being in this world and the next. It was also because of such considerations that Plato thought that kings must become philosophers or philosophers kings. Once the quest for the best regime arrives at the necessity of combining divine and political science, it becomes necessary that the ruler should combine the craft of ruling with that of prophecy or of philosophy. The ruler-prophet or the ruler-philosopher is the human being who offers the solution to the question of the realization of the best regime, and the functions of the ruler-prophet and of the ruler-philosopher appear in this respect to be identical.

Alfarabi begins his discussion of the supreme ruler with the emphasis on the common function of the ruler-philosopher and the ruler-prophet as rulers who are the link between the divine beings above and the citizens who do not have direct access to knowledge of these beings. He is the teacher and guide "who makes known" to the citizens what happiness is, who "arouses in them the determination" to do the things necessary for attaining it, and "who does not need to be ruled by a man in anything at all." [5] He must possess knowledge, not need any other man to guide him, have excellent comprehension of everything that must be done, be excellent in guiding all others in what he knows, have the ability to make others perform the functions for which they are fit, and have the ability to determine and define the work to be done by others and to direct such work toward happiness. These qualities evidently require the best natural endowments, but also the fullest development of the rational faculty. (According to Aristotelian psychology as Alfarabi presents it in his political works, the perfection of the rational faculty consists of its correspondence to, or "union" with, the Active Intellect.) The supreme ruler must be a man who actualizes his rational faculty or who is in union with the Active Intellect.

This man is the true prince according to the ancients; he is the one of whom it ought to be said that he receives revelation. For man receives revelation only when he attains this rank—that is, when there is no longer an intermediary between him and the Active Intellect. . . . Now because the Active Intellect emanates from the being of the First Cause [God], it can for this reason be said that it is the First Cause that brings about the revelation to this man through the mediation of the Active Intellect. The rule of this man is the supreme rule; all other human rulerships are inferior to it and are derived from it.[6]

This supreme ruler is the source of all power and knowledge in the regime, and it is through him that the citizens learn what they ought to know and to do. As God or the First Cause of the world directs everything else, and as everything else is directed toward Him, "the case ought to be the same in the virtuous city: in an orderly fashion, all of its parts ought to follow in their activities in the footsteps of the purpose of its supreme ruler." [7] He possesses unlimited powers and cannot be subjected to any human being or political regime or laws. He has the power to confirm or abrogate previous divine laws, to enact new ones, and "to change a law he had legislated at one time for another if he deems it better to do so." [8] He alone has the power to order the classes of people in the regime and assign to them their ranks. And it is he who offers them what they need to know.

For most people, this knowledge has to take the form of an imaginative representation of the truth rather than a rational conception of it. This is because most people are not endowed, or cannot be trained to know divine things in themselves, but can only understand their imitations, which should be made to fit their power of understanding and their special conditions and experience as members of a particular regime. Religion is such a set of imaginative representations in the form of a divine law, legislated for a particular group of men, and necessitated by the incapacity of most men to conceive things rationally and their need to believe in the imitations of divine beings, and of happiness and perfection, as presented to them by the founder of their regime. The founder must then not only present a rational or conceptual account of happiness and the divine principles to the few, but also adequately represent or imitate these same things for the many. All the citizens are to accept and preserve that with which he entrusts them: "the ones who follow after happiness as they cognize it and accept the [divine] principles as they cognize them are the *wise men;* and the ones in whose souls these things are found in the form of images, and who accept them and follow after them as such, are the *believers."* [9]

Thus far Alfarabi identifies the ruler-prophet and the ruler-philosopher. They are both supreme rulers absolutely, and both have absolute authority with regard to legislating beliefs and actions. Both acquire this authority in virtue of the perfection of their rational faculty, and both receive revelation from God through the agency of the Active Intellect. Wherein, then, does the ruler-prophet differ from the ruler-philosopher?

The first and primary qualification that the ruler of the virtuous regime must possess is a special kind of knowledge of divine and human things. Now, man possesses three faculties for knowledge: sensation, imagination, and reason (both theoretical and practical), and these develop in him in that order. Imagination has three functions: (1) It acts as a reservoir of sensible impressions after the disappearance of the objects of sensation. (2) It combines sensible impressions to form a complex sensible image. (3) It produces *imitations.* It has the capacity to imitate all nonsensible things (human desires, temperament, passions) through sensible impressions or certain combinations of them. When later the rational faculty develops, and man begins to grasp the character, essence, or form of natural and divine beings, the faculty of imagination receives and imitates these rational forms also, that is, it *represents* them in the form of sensible impressions. In this respect, imagination is subordinate to the rational faculty and depends on it for the "originals" that it imitates; it has no direct access to the essence of natural and divine beings. Further, the limitations that it fabricates are not all good copies: some may be more true and nearer to the originals, others defective in some respects, and still others extremely false or misleading copies. Finally, only the rational faculty that grasps the originals themselves can judge the degree of the truth of these copies and of their likeness to the originals. The rational faculty is the only faculty that has access to the knowledge of divine or spiritual beings, and it must exercise strict control to insure that the copies offered by the imaginative faculty are good or fair imitations. It may happen in rare cases that this imaginative faculty is so powerful and perfect that it overwhelms all the other faculties, and proceeds directly to receive or form images of divine beings. This rare case is the case of prophecy:

It is not impossible that man, when his imaginative power reaches utmost perfection, should receive in his waking hours from the Active Intellect . . . the *imitations* of separate [immaterial] intelligibles and all other noble [sacred] beings, and to view them. By virtue of the intelligibles he had received, he will thus have [the power of] prophecy about divine things. This, then, is the most perfect stage reached by the power of imagination and the most perfect stage at which man arrives by virtue of his imaginative power.[10]

The description of the nature of prophecy thus leads to the distinction between the faculty of imagination and the rational faculty. It explains the possibility of prophecy as the perfection of the faculty of imagination, and that imagination can almost dispense with the rational faculty and receive the images of divine beings directly and without the latter's mediation. There are two powers by means of which man can communicate with the Active Intellect: his imagination and his rational faculty or his intellect. When he communicates with it by means of his imagination, he is "a prophet who warns about what will happen and who informs about what is taking place now"; while when he communicates with it by means of his rational faculty he is "a wise man, a philosopher, and has complete intelligence." [11]

It would appear then that the ruler-prophet and the ruler-philosopher both can be said to possess the qualification of knowledge required for being the supreme ruler of the virtuous city; or that two kinds of equally virtuous regimes are possible, one ruled by a prophet without philosophy and the other ruled by the philosopher without prophecy. Yet in his political writings Alfarabi does not even consider the possibility of a virtuous regime ruled by a prophet who does not possess a developed rational faculty. The distinction between prophecy and philosophy is a psychological distinction, and it is useful for understanding the nature of prophecy and philosophy respectively. But in discussing the quality of knowledge required by the supreme ruler, Alfarabi is explicit in demanding the perfection of both faculties: the supreme ruler is not called a perfect prophet or a perfect philosopher, but a "perfect human being." To begin with the philosopher, even his philos-

ophy or the wisdom he is seeking remains incomplete so long as he
does not possess perfect mastery in imitating the rational or theoretical
knowledge in his possession in order to teach it to the young or to present it to the multitude. This lack becomes an essential defect when he
is faced with the task of governing a city and educating it. His very
quality as philosopher (that is, as one who devotes himself to theoretical
knowledge irrespective of its use in, or relation to, the city) disqualifies
him as a ruler. He cannot be a *ruler*-philosopher without the power of
imagination of which the prophet is the most accomplished representative.

As to the prophet, while his imaginative power seems to make him
particularly fit for ruling, the workings of his imagination do not enjoy
the benefit of rational control: he lacks the constant check of the degree
of truthfulness or verisimilitude of the imitations produced by his powerful imagination, a function that only the rational faculty can perform.
The best ruler for the virtuous city must therefore be a ruler-philosopher-
prophet. Alfarabi does not say whether Muhammad the prophet was
also a philosopher, but he requires the combination of prophecy and
philosophy, or the exercise of the imaginative and the rational powers,
in the supreme ruler of the virtuous city. Philosophy or wisdom is indispensable for ruling a virtuous city. "If it should happen at any time
that wisdom has no share in ruling, and [the ruling authority] fulfilled
all other conditions, the virtuous city remains without a prince, the ruler
who takes care of the business of this city will not be a prince, and the
city will be exposed to perdition. Thus if it does not happen that there
should exist a wise man to associate with him, then after a time the city
will surely perish." [12]

## LAW AND LIVING WISDOM

Wisdom or philosophy is an indispensable condition for the founding
and survival of the virtuous city. Prophecy, on the other hand, is indispensable for founding a virtuous city but not for its survival. In enumerating the qualities of the supreme ruler or the founder of the virtuous city, Alfarabi stipulates the coincidence of excellent rational and
prophetic faculties. This requirement is imposed by the composition of
the virtuous city as a political community, that is, the fact that it must
be made up of two broad groups: (1) the few who are philosophers or
can be addressed through philosophy, and who can be taught the
theoretical sciences and hence the true character of divine and natural
beings as they are; (2) the many who (because they lack the necessary
natural endowments or have no time for sufficient training) are not

philosophers, who live by opinion and persuasion, and for whom the ruler must imitate these beings by means of similitudes and symbols.

While the few can be made to grasp rationally the meaning of human happiness and perfection and the rational basis or justification of the virtuous activities that lead to man's ultimate end, the many are incapable of such understanding and have to be taught to perform these activities by persuasion and compulsion, that is, by explanations that could be understood by all the citizens regardless of their rational capacity, and by prescribed rewards and punishments of an immediate tangible kind. The supreme ruler teaches the few in his capacity as philosopher, and he presents similitudes and prescribes rewards and punishments for the many in his capacity as prophet. To be believed and practiced by the many, these similitudes and prescriptions should be formulated by the prophet, and accepted by the citizens, as true, fixed, and permanent; that is, the citizens should expect definite rewards and punishments for belief and unbelief, and for obedience and disobedience. The prophetic faculty culminates, then, in laying down laws concerning both the beliefs and the practices of the many, and the prophet who assumes this function becomes a prophet-legislator. The rational faculty, in contrast, culminates in teaching the theoretical sciences to the few. In his summary of Plato's *Laws,* Alfarabi also understood Plato to say that these virtuous few "have no need for fixed practices and laws at all; nevertheless they are very happy. Laws and fixed practices are needed only for those who are morally crooked." [13]

It is only as viewed by the subjects that laws are fixed and are of unquestionable divine authority. We saw that the supreme ruler of the virtuous regime is the master and not the servant of the law. Not only is he not ruled by any man, he is also not ruled by the law. He is the cause of the law, he creates it, and he abrogates and changes it as he sees fit. He possesses this authority because of his wisdom and his capacity to decide what is best for the common good under given conditions; and conditions can arise under which the changing of the law is not only salutary but indispensable for the survival of the virtuous regime. In so doing he must be extremely cautious not to disturb the faith of the citizens in their laws, and should consider the adverse effect that change has on attachment to the law. He must make a careful appraisal of the advantage of changing the law as against the disadvantage of change as such. Thus he must possess, not only the authority to change laws whenever necessary, but also the craft of minimizing the danger of change to the well-being of the regime. But once he sees that changing the law is necessary and takes the proper precautions, there is no question as to his authority to change the law. Therefore, so long as he lives, the rational faculty rules supreme and laws are preserved or changed in the light of his judgment as philosopher.

It is this coincidence of philosophy and prophecy in the person of the ruler that insures the survival of the virtuous regime. As long as rulers who possess these qualities succeed each other without interruption, the same situation obtains.

The successor will be the one who will decide about what was left undecided by his predecessor. And not this alone. He may change a great deal of what his predecessor had legislated and make a different decision about it when he knows this to be best in his own time—not because his predecessor had committed a mistake but because his predecessor decided upon it according to what was best in his own time, and the successor decides according to what is best for a later time. Were his predecessor to observe [the new conditions] he would have changed [his own law] also.[14]

The coincidence of philosophy and prophecy is extremely rare, and chance may not always favor the virtuous regime with the availability of a man who possesses all the necessary natural endowments and whose training proves successful. Thus the question arises as to whether the virtuous city can survive in the absence of a man with all the qualifications required in the supreme ruler, and particularly those of philosophy and prophecy. Granting that the best possible arrangement demands the existence of all these qualifications in one man who must rule, can the regime originated by such a ruler survive at all in his absence? The only qualification that Alfarabi is willing to drop in *The Virtuous City* is prophecy, and then only if provisions are made for the presence of proper substitutes for prophetic legislation. These substitutes consist of (1) the body of laws and customs established by the "true princes," and (2) a combination of new qualities in the ruler that make him proficient in the "art of jurisprudence," that is, knowledge of the laws and customs of his predecessors, willingness on his part to follow these laws and customs rather than change them, the capacity to apply them to new conditions by the "deduction" of new decisions from, or the "discovery" of new applications for, established laws and customs, and the capacity to meet every new situation (for which no specific decisions are available) through understanding the *intention* of previous legislators rather than by the legislation of new laws or by any formal change of old ones. So far as the law is concerned, this new ruler is a jurist-legislator rather than a prophet-legislator. He must, however, possess all the other qualities, including wisdom or philosophy, that enable him to discern and promote the common good of his regime at the particular period during which he rules.

In the event that no single human being should exist who possesses all these qualifications, then Alfarabi suggests a third possibility: a philosopher and one other man (who possesses the rest of the qualities, except philosophy) should rule jointly. Were even this to prove unobtainable, he suggests finally a joint rule of a number of men possessing these qualifications severally. This joint rule does not, however, affect the presence of the required qualifications but only their presence in the *same* man. Thus the only qualification whose very presence may be dispensed with is prophecy. The substitutes for prophecy are the preservation of old laws and the capacity to discover new applications for old laws. To promote the common good and preserve the regime under new conditions as these emerge, neither the coincidence of philosophy and prophecy in the same man, nor the coincidence of philosophy and jurisprudence, proves to be an indispensable condition. It is sufficient to have philosophy in the person of a philosopher who rules jointly with another man or a group of men who possess, among other things, the capacity to put old laws to new uses. Unlike prophecy, philosophy cannot be dispensed with, and nothing can take its place. Unlike the absence of prophecy, the absence of philosophy is fatal to the existence of the virtuous regime. There is no substitute for living wisdom.

## War and the Limitations of Law

In addition to philosophy and prophecy (or else proficiency in the art of jurisprudence), there is a third and indispensable qualification that must be present in the ruler of the virtuous regime or in one of the group that rule it jointly: that is, daring and warlike virtue. This qualification is required for carrying out the ruler's responsibility as the supreme educator of all the citizens, that is, to form and improve their moral character. Since not all men can be convinced, or aroused to perform virtuous activities, by means of persuasive and passionate speeches, the method of persuasion or consent is not sufficient. As the father does with his children and the schoolteacher with the young, so the ruler has to use force and compulsion with those who, out of nature or habit, cannot be educated or persuaded to obey the law spontaneously. Hence the ruler needs to employ two groups of educators: a group that educates the citizens by persuasion and by means of arguments; and a warlike group to compel the lazy, the wicked, and the incorrigible to obey the laws by force. The supreme ruler, or the rulers, should lead, direct, and supervise the activities of both groups. To command the second group, he or they should possess a daring nature and excel in the art of war.

The nature and the extent of the compulsion and force to be applied within a certain regime depend on the character of the citizens: the more virtuous they are, the less need there is to apply force. But there are cases where the ruler may have to conquer a whole city and force it to accept his virtuous or divine law, or where the use of force would considerably shorten the time required to establish his law while the issue of persuasion is too uncertain and its prospects too remote. Compulsion is legitimate inside the regime with regard to those citizens who are of intractable natures or bad habits, and with respect to a whole city as a prelude to the establishment of a new divine law where it is lacking. Physical force, overpowering, or war is a "fundamental element" of the law and one of the basic "preludes" for establishing it. Alfarabi seems to favor not only defensive war but offensive war also; and he speaks of the war conducted by the ruler of the virtuous regime as a just war and of his warlike purpose as a virtuous purpose.

Further, while like Plato and Aristotle, Alfarabi considers the "city" the first or smallest unit that constitutes a political whole and in which man can attain his political perfection, unlike them he does not seem to consider the city also the largest possible unit in which a virtuous regime can be expected to flourish. Instead, he speaks of three "perfect" human associations: the largest in size is the association of all men in the entire inhabited world; the intermediate is the association of a nation in a portion of the inhabited world; and the smallest is the association of the inhabitants of a city in a portion of the land inhabited by a nation. If we combine his teaching about just or virtuous war and conquest with the idea of a perfect human association extending over the entire inhabited world, we can be led to the conclusion that Alfarabi deliberately modified the teachings of Plato and Aristotle on an important issue with the intention of supplying a rational justification for the Islamic concept of holy war whose aim was to propagate the divine law everywhere on earth;[15] that he favored a war of civilization whereby a more advanced nation justifies the conquest of more backward nations; or that he preached the idea of a universal or a world state. These conclusions must now be examined in the light of Alfarabi's views on war and the character of the law.

He mentions two extreme views regarding war. The first is the view that to overpower and dominate others is the natural state of man and that war is therefore the only universally just course of conduct. The second is that the natural state of man is universal peace and peaceful coexistence is therefore the only just course of conduct. This latter view can in turn have the corollary that only in defensive war, war forced upon one by the unnatural conduct of a warlike enemy, is there

a just cause for taking up arms. These are according to him the views
of the inhabitants of the "ignorant and erring cities" that are opposed
to the virtuous regime.[16] They give rise to two types of regimes, "tyrannies" and "peace-loving regimes." The latter are not considered sufficiently important; and their view, though mistaken, is evidently not
dangerous. At any rate, he does not list them as a main subdivision of
the regimes opposing the virtuous regime which is partly due to the fact
that, unlike war, peace is not one of the main "ends" pursued by men
but a means to other ends, such as pleasure or gain.

War, conquest, the overpowering and enslaving of others, and
tyranny over them, is, in contrast, one of the supreme ends pursued by
men. It gives rise to the "tyrannical regime" in which men associate with
each other, practice warlike activities, frame their laws, and order their
regime with the main purpose of enslaving each other or other regimes.
They do not enslave and kill to attain other ends, but to satisfy a
supreme end common to all of them, "the love of tyranny." Indeed, the
bad regimes pursuing other ends, such as wealth, honor, or pleasure, are
in many cases transformed into tyrannies when these other ends are
attained. The satisfaction of these desires seems to free the citizens of
bad regimes to pursue the highest evil of "ignorant and erring" regimes,
that is, the view that "tyranny is the good." War as an end in itself is
for Alfarabi the supreme vice that can have no place in the regime
whose end is the supreme virtue.

Having made use of the advantages of war and compulsion to
establish his divine law and to suppress the wicked and the incorrigible,
the ruler of the virtuous regime must return to promote friendship
among the citizens and to the peaceful work of persuasion and free
consent. To persuade the majority of citizens, he has to produce similitudes of divine and natural beings, and of virtue and happiness, that
are adequate in respect of their proximity to the original forms of these
things, but that are also adequate with respect to those who are to be
persuaded by them. The similitudes should bear some relation to the
nature, past experience, and habits of the citizens. Unlike the business
of war, peaceful persuasion requires the legislator to make concessions
to the character of the ruled, the degree of their preparation for virtuous
laws, differences among them, and the extent to which the citizens can
be improved. These are prelegal conditions that he does not create but
must presuppose and that he cannot change except to a limited extent
and then only gradually.

Further, the legislator cannot produce similitudes and utilize persuasive methods designed to meet the peculiar nature and habits of each
individual citizen; the law cannot treat each man as a case by himself.

General beliefs and practices must be prescribed for all the citizens and must correspond to their distinctive character as a group. Now, what is adequate for one group and hence just with regard to them may be inadequate for another group and hence unjust with regard to them. To legislate for all men with respect to "human nature" or what they all have in common will mean being unjust to most if not to all men. Therefore, if it is the case that the inhabited world is divided into nations and cities, and this division is based not on arbitrary but on natural distinctions or distinctions that are somehow related to nature, such distinctions could form the limits within which general beliefs and practices that are both effective and just could be prescribed.

Alfarabi qualifies his statement about the three perfect associations (the city, the nation, and the association of all men in the entire inhabited world) with the observation that the association of all men in the entire inhabited world is divided into nations. "Nations are distinguished from each other by two natural things—natural make-up and natural character—and by something that is composite (it is conventional but has a basis in natural things), namely, language." [17] These distinctions are the product of geographical differences among the various parts of the earth (temperature, foodstuff, and so on) that in turn influence the temperament of their inhabitants. But although they constitute the nation as a natural unit, these natural national similarities are not a sufficient political bond for the sake of which the members of a nation should like each other or dislike other nations. The proper objects of like and dislike are the perfections or the virtues, and these are not given by nature but by the Active Intellect, by science, and by legislation. The nation is in turn divided into cities or city-states that are distinguished by their regimes and laws.

Only the city is likened by Alfarabi to the perfect living body. The organs of the living body do not simply cooperate toward a common end; they have different ranks, each of which is perfect when it performs its proper function (be that a subordinate or a superior one), and all of which are ruled by the most perfect organ. Applied to the nation and the association of all men in the entire inhabited world, this similitude would require the subordination of cities to each other, and of nations to each other, according to their degree of perfection. Yet Alfarabi never speaks of such subordination as being legitimate except within a single city; and the cities opposed to the virtuous city are not investigated with a view to being subordinated to a virtuous city but to being transformed into such a city. A virtuous nation is not a group of cities ruled by a virtuous or perfect city, but the nation "*all* of whose cities *cooperate* regarding the things by which happiness is attained"; and the association of all men in the entire inhabited world is virtuous "only when the nations in it *cooperate* to achieve happiness." [18] The virtuous community of all men presupposes virtuous nations, and the virtuous nation in turn presupposes virtuous cities.

The consideration of the specific character and function of the prophetic faculty and of the divine law points to the conclusion that religion should be particularly sensitive to the limitations imposed by the natural and conventional differences among nations and cities. If a religion or divine law is not spurious, obscurantist, or fanatic, it does not promote but suppresses and transcends the ends pursued in ignorant regimes (including tyranny), and substitutes for them the end that can be pursued only through the belief in adequate or salutary similitudes of divine and natural beings, and through commands and prohibitions that promote virtue and happiness among a particular group ready for its message. It must therefore abandon the end of the tyrannical regime whose aim is absolute and universal tyranny and restrict the use of force to the extent to which it is necessary to establish a new regime and suppress the wicked and the incorrigible inside that regime. Otherwise, it will be forced to legislate beliefs and practices that can be accepted and performed by all men, that is, to lower its standards to conform to the natural capacity of the overwhelming majority of men rather than uphold the ones that help a relatively good city or nation to achieve true virtue or happiness. The alternative aim of promoting virtue or happiness among the best or the elect in every city and nation is ruled out because this is not the proper function of religion but of philosophy. We recall Alfarabi's distinction between the functions of prophecy and philosophy in the virtuous regime. The few who are endowed with rare natures and are given proper training are offered, not similitudes, but theoretical knowledge of the divine and natural beings themselves, and of virtue and happiness, while the beliefs and practices legislated in the divine law aim at the many.

Now, the natural and quasi-natural distinctions among cities and nations need not form a barrier against the transmission of theoretical knowledge. Such knowledge presupposes the presence of a tradition of theoretical inquiry and of rare individuals; but once these conditions are fulfilled, it can be freely transplanted from one city to another and from one nation to another. The universal community of the superior men of every city and nation or of the uncrowned kings of humanity is not a community of believers in a particular set of dogmas. It is the community of lovers of the one and true wisdom. By its very nature, according to Alfarabi, a religion cannot provide the basis for such a community. Religion arises because of the incapacity of the many to understand the true character of beings and of human happiness. It remedies this situation by presenting them with similitudes that take

into account the limitations of their understanding and their natural
and conventional characteristics as a distinct group. Also, because the
true principles of nature and true political principles are invariable, they
are inflexible and cannot themselves be adjusted to the degree of understanding and the particular character of a distinctive political group.
Similitudes, in contrast, may be adjusted for this purpose because they
can be nearer to, or remote from, reality. In addition, there can be a
number of good similitudes of the same reality. These similitudes are
all good or virtuous if they succeed in making the members of the particular political groups for which they are designed good or virtuous.
"Consequently, there may be a number of virtuous nations and a number of virtuous cities whose religions are different." [19] Alfarabi's approach to religion leads to a philosophic science of divine laws. By presenting divine laws, jurisprudence, and theology as parts of political
science, he points to the possibility of a neutral discussion of all religions
or "sects" [20] and of the features common to them all.

### DEMOCRACY AND THE VIRTUOUS REGIME

Of the six regimes opposed to the virtuous regime, the first and the last,
that is, the regimes of necessity and democracy, occupy the privileged
position of supplying the most solid and the best starting point for the
establishment of the virtuous regime and for the rule of virtuous men.
The regime of necessity (as the counterpart of the city of the pigs in
Plato's *Republic*) offers the opportunity for introducing a virtuous
regime among citizens who are not as yet corrupted by the love of
money or honor, by indulgence in pleasures, or by the desire for glory.
But since all of these exist in democracy, it is not clear at first sight what
contribution democracy could make to the virtuous regime.

Following Plato's description (*Republic* VIII), Alfarabi sets down
the first principle of democracy (that is, of pure democracy, or of
extreme democracy, as Aristotle calls it) as freedom, and he calls the
democratic regime also the "free" regime. Freedom means the ability
of everyone to pursue anything he desires, and that he should be left
alone to do anything he chooses in the pursuit of his desires. The second
principle is equality, which means that no man is superior to another
in anything at all. These two principles define the basis of authority,
the relation between the ruler and the ruled, and the attitude of the citizens to each other. Authority is justified only on the basis of the
preservation and promotion of freedom and equality. Whatever the
accomplishments of the ruler, he rules only by the will of the citizens,
however unaccomplished he or they may be: he must follow their
wishes and cater to their whims. The citizens honor only those who

lead them to freedom and to the achievement of whatever makes possible the enjoyment of their desires, and those who preserve that freedom and make it possible for them to enjoy their different and conflicting desires, and who defend them against external enemies. If such men can perform these functions and still remain themselves content with the bare necessities of life, then they are considered virtuous and are obeyed. The rest of the rulers are functionaries who perform services for which they receive adequate honors or financial remunerations; and the citizens who pay them for these services consider themselves, because of this, superior to these rulers whom they support. Such also is the case of those whom the public lets rule either because it takes a fancy to them or because it wants to reward them for a service rendered by their ancestors. Despite these differences, a close investigation of the democratic regime shows that, ultimately, there are really no rulers and ruled; there is one supreme will, which is that of the citizens; and the rulers are instruments serving the desires and wishes of the citizens.

Unlike the other five regimes, there is no single or dominating end desired or wished for by the citizens of the democratic regime. They form innumerable groups, similar and dissimilar, with a variety of characters, interests, aims, and desires. So far as ends are concerned, democracy is a composite regime: various groups, aiming at the ends characterizing the other regimes, exist side by side and pursue different ways of life; they form a conglomeration in which the different parts are interwoven with each other; and they are free to fulfill their distinct aims independently or in cooperation with others.

Because the democratic regime makes possible, preserves, protects, and promotes every kind of desire, all kinds of men come to admire it and consider it as the happy way of life. They come to love democracy and to love to live in it. A great number migrate to it from different nations, and residents and foreigners meet, mix, and intermarry. The result is the greatest possible diversity of natural character, upbringing, education, and ways of life; yet every type of man is encouraged, or allowed, to achieve what he desires as far as his capacity admits. A fully developed democratic regime presents a colorful spectacle of infinite diversity and luxury.

But this means that, of all the regimes opposed to the virtuous regime, the democratic regime contains the greatest amount and variety of good and evil things; and the more it expands and becomes perfect, the more the goodness and the evil it contains. It will therefore also contain a number of the parts of the virtuous city. Alfarabi mentions in particular the possibility of the rise of virtuous men, and of the presence of wise men, rhetoricians, and poets (that is, men who deal with demonstrative science, persuasion, and imitation) in all kinds of things. If the regime of necessity contributes citizens uncorrupted by unessential desires and pleasures, the democratic regime, most of whose citizens are corrupted by luxury, offers the highly developed sciences and arts essential for the establishment of the virtuous regime. And in the absence of the virtuous regime in which these sciences and arts have the best opportunity to develop in the right direction, the democratic regime is the only regime that provides ample opportunity for their development and allows the philosopher to pursue his desire with relative freedom.

## NOTES

All of the citations in these notes refer to the Arabic texts. Some of the works referred to have been translated into English. The translations, which reproduce the pagination of the Arabic texts, are given in the list of Readings at the end of this chapter. Translations of quotations within the chapter have been made by the author.

1. Alfarabi, *The Enumeration of the Sciences,* ed. Osman Amine (2nd ed.; Cairo: Dār al-Fikr al-'Arabī, 1949), v; *The Virtuous Religion,* MS, Leiden, Cod. Or. No. 1002, fols. 53*v*–54*v*.

2. *The Virtuous City,* ed. Fr. Dieterici (Leiden: Brill, 1895), p. 46; cf. *The Political Regime* (Hyderabad: Dā'irat al-Ma'ārif al-'Uthmāniyyah, 1345 A. H.), pp. 42–45, 48.

3. *Virtuous City,* p. 46; cf. *Political Regime,* pp. 43–44.

4. *Virtuous City,* p. 63; cf. *Political Regime,* p. 74.

5. *Political Regime,* pp. 48–49.

6. *Ibid.,* pp. 49–50.

7. *Virtuous City,* pp. 56–57; cf. *Po-* *litical Regime,* pp. 53–54.

8. *Political Regime,* pp. 50–51.

9. *Ibid.,* p. 56.

10. *Virtuous City,* p. 52.

11. *Ibid.,* pp. 58–59.

12. *Ibid.,* p. 61.

13. *Plato's Laws,* ed. Franciscus Gabrieli (London: Warburg Institute, 1952), p. 41.

14. *Virtuous Religion,* fol. 54*r*.

15. See below, pp. 240ff.

16. *Virtuous City,* pp. 75–80.

17. *Political Regime,* p. 40.

18. *Virtuous City,* p. 54.

19. *Political Regime,* p. 56; *Virtuous City,* p. 70.

20. See below, p. 229.

## READINGS

A. Alfarabi. *The Political Regime,* in *Medieval Political Philosophy.* Ed. Ralph Lerner and Muhsin Mahdi. New York: The Free Press, 1963. Selection 2, pp. 39–76.
   Alfarabi. *The Enumeration of the Sciences,* in *ibid.,* Selection 1, chap. v.
B. Alfarabi. *Plato's Laws,* in *ibid.,* Selection 4. Introduction and Discourses I–II.
   Alfarabi. *The Attainment of Happiness,* in *Alfarabi's Philosophy of Plato and Aristotle.* Trans. Muhsin Mahdi. New York: The Free Press, 1962. Part I.
   Alfarabi. *The Philosophy of Plato,* in *ibid.,* part II.

# MOSES MAIMONIDES

## 1135–1204

A discussion of medieval Jewish political philosophy might appear to suffer from a serious, perhaps hopeless, difficulty. Is there any reason to assume that the subject matter exists? Little in the present-day historical literature suggests that it does. When the medieval Jewish philosophers appear at all in current histories, they do so mainly for their antiquarian interest, as links in a chain of the transmission of ideas. This neglect is even more pronounced in the histories of political thought; medieval Jewish writers appear to be regarded as irrelevant. It would not be difficult to find some plausible reason for this neglect: a people that for more than a millennium lacked the least appearance of autonomous political life and that for the most part was firmly excluded from governance and administration is not a likely source of independent political reflection. Yet for all its plausibility, this assumption is false; the fact remains that problems that we can recognize as falling within the province of political philosophy *are* discussed in the writings of medieval Jews. Speculation about political things has never been a preserve open only to statesmen and full citizens.

We can go further in trying to understand why medieval Jews concerned themselves with political philosophy. To begin with, the Diaspora, or dispersion of the Jews, was regarded by the Jews themselves as an abnormal situation at least as early as the time of Philo (d. A.D. 54). In traditional, nonpolitical terms, exile was seen as a divinely ordained punishment for the people's iniquity. Just as certainly as sinfulness had led to the destruction of the Jewish commonwealth, so would repentance lead to its restoration. *When* this abnormal situation might come to an end, no one could ascertain, but *that* it would cease was not to be doubted. To this extent, at least, reflection on political things was not regarded as an utterly arid exercise. A more powerful impetus to speculation of this sort was to be found in the concern of Jewish scholars with the Torah and the Talmud. Unlike Christian scholasticism, medieval Jewish political philosophy developed in the context of a divine revelation that assumed the form of law rather than dogma or faith. That law, as any reader of the Pentateuch can observe, aims at prescribing and regulating, down to the smallest detail, the conduct and beliefs of an entire community. The crucial consideration is not merely that political matters figure large in both Torah and Talmud; even more significant as a stimulus to political inquiry and as a partial determinant of the manner in which that inquiry was carried on is the *legal* character of those writings. At least for these reasons, men were led to consider political things at a time when there was little in everyday life to suggest the utility or propriety of such speculation.

Another, and no less perplexing, difficulty arises when we turn to the writings of the medieval Jewish scholars, however. They do not appear to have written political treatises as such, and there is not even much in the way of sustained thematic treatment of political matters. Typically, medieval Jewish political philosophy emerges from a discussion of some other subject: the interpretation of the Bible, the principal features of the divine law, the meanings of certain biblical terms, the systematic restatement of talmudic legislation, the defense of Judaism. The reason for this has already been indicated: the very circumstances we have mentioned, which, among others, led certain Jewish scholars to political philosophy, also affected the manner in which they philosophized or in which they presented their teachings. The nonthematic presentation of their political philosophy stems in part from the necessity for Jewish philosophers (like their Muslim counterparts) to justify their philosophic activity before the tribunal of the revealed law. None would have dared to begin a work with the question that opens the *Summa Theologica:* "Whether, besides the philosophical disciplines, any further doctrine is required?"

In Judaism, even more than in Islam, the case for philosophy had to be made and won before one could philosophize in public. Stated differently, that which commonly is said to be the principal concern of medieval political philosophy—demonstrating the harmony between the revealed teaching and the Aristotelian teaching—presupposes the legitimacy of philosophizing. As is clear from the chapter on Alfarabi, establishing the legitimacy of philosophic pursuits requires arguments that derive from neither the revealed teaching nor the Aristotelian teaching. The first necessity was to understand the revealed law in a way that allowed for—even required—philosophy. As far as Judaism is concerned, the decisive work in this task was done by Moses ben Maimon (Maimonides). His predominance in medieval Jewish philosophy is such that one can, without gross injustice to the others, view his teaching as the core and take note of other Jewish thinkers where they elaborate upon, or deviate from, his political teaching in some significant way. In considering his political teaching, it is well to remind oneself that philosophy by no means forms the core of the Jewish religion. Philosophy appeared rather late in Judaism and, as has been indicated, never achieved a status that made it unqualifiedly acceptable. However, in accord with the plan of this work, the present discussion will limit itself to political philosophy proper.

If one is to discuss the objects and character of law, one must proceed from an understanding of the beings for whose sake a law is made. Maimonides proceeds accordingly; in his philosophic treatise, the *Guide of the Perplexed,* he examines the need for law before presenting those chapters that may be said to be devoted to the theme of law. Of all the species, it is man and man alone who is strictly speaking a political animal. There are indeed animals that we justly call social, but none of the animals other than man requires reflection or foresight in order to survive. If man were left to lead the life of the beasts, he would perish immediately; by themselves, his animal faculties would fall far short of what is required for his survival. It is only through his rational faculty, by means of which he exercises thought and foresight, that man can accomplish what is needed for self-preservation. Food, shelter, clothing —all require the application of some art to the raw materials of nature in order to make them fit for use by man. Since the arts, in turn, presuppose the use of tools and the existence of men skilled in their use, it follows that man's survival depends upon the division of labor and upon an orderly social arrangement under which each individual can devote himself to some particular occupation, secure in the knowledge that his contribution to the preservation of his fellows is requited by their contributions toward his preservation.[1]

Men's need to live in an organized society is increased further by the uniquely great variety prevailing among them, for the range of differences in conduct is so extreme that two individual men might appear to belong to two different species. In the face of such variety, men would not be able to live together without the supervision and control of someone who restrains and moderates individual excesses. Just as society appears to be required by man's nature, so does the perfection of that society require a ruler "who gauges the actions of the individuals, perfecting that which is deficient and reducing that which is excessive, and who prescribes actions and moral habits for all of them to practice always in the same way, until the natural diversity is hidden by the many points of conventional accord, and so the society becomes well-ordered." The means by which this natural variety is made to vanish is law. This law, said by Maimonides to "have a basis in what is natural" although not being natural, must be examined in greater detail.[2]

The very circumstances that call forth law necessitate its concern with both actions and opinions. But there is a multiplicity of laws, human and divine, and this fact alone—saying nothing of their mutually exclusive character—requires that we be able to distinguish the one kind of law from the other. Considering the possible objects of legislation, Maimonides finds that they correspond to the twofold perfectibility of human beings: perfection of the body and perfection of the soul. A law might be concerned solely with establishing good order within the city. It would seek to prevent wrongdoing on the part of the citizens by restraining and directing their actions; it would seek to abolish injustice and to secure public tranquillity; it would seek to inculcate certain moral qualities in the population—qualities that facilitate peaceful social life; it would seek to enable men to attain happiness or, more precisely, to attain what the lawgiver imagines to be happiness. The sole object of such a law is the well-being of the body. Its complete preoccupation with the good order of the city is matched by its utter indifference to the kind of opinions prevailing in that city (as long as these are compatible with peaceful civil life). Maimonides calls such a law a *nomos*.[3]

In contrast, a law might seek to promote both perfections of man: like the *nomos* it would prescribe the measures required for a decent social life, thereby enabling men not only to preserve themselves, but to live in the very best bodily state. Going beyond this, it would seek to promote a corresponding perfection of the soul by inculcating correct opinions in everyone according to his individual capacity. This concern with the welfare of the soul (as well as that of the body), this effort to develop each man's understanding of everything that exists as far as is humanly possible, is the distinguishing feature of a divinely revealed law.[4]

Summarily stated, Maimonides distinguishes between a *nomos* whose object is imaginary happiness and a divine law whose object is true happiness. But the very possibility of securing this nobler aim—that is, perfecting men's souls by helping them to acquire correct opinions—is contingent upon the attainment of the well-being of the body.

Inferior though they may be in dignity, the needs of the body (and, by extension, the decent ordering of society, which makes it possible for those needs to be met), have priority in time. Political welfare is the indispensable precondition of man's ultimate perfection.[5]

For Maimonides, the ultimate perfection of man is far removed from any concern with the body. Those subjects that figure so large in any legislative code—human actions and moral qualities—form no part of it. Man's perfection consists rather in his obtaining correct opinions, opinions to which he is led by speculation and that he establishes as true by means of the theoretical sciences. Law occupies a position of crucial importance, for its prescriptions order men's lives in a way that permits them to pursue their ultimate perfection. Once social life is made possible, men can turn to that private activity through which alone they can reach their proper end. In a sense it is true that the law or the study of the law is "a small thing." But in another sense it is "the great good" that the deity has caused to overflow onto the world. All the actions prescribed by the divine law, be they acts of worship or useful moral habits, are intended to regulate men's social relations. Maimonides notes repeatedly that prescriptions of this sort do not partake of the dignity of the highest end of man, but are merely preparations, albeit necessary ones, for the attainment of that end.[6]

The importance of law is in no way diminished by this view. Indeed one could say that for Maimonides the highest form of revelation is highest in virtue of its legal character. God had made His will manifest to men both before and after Moses, but the prophecies of the other men differed radically from that of Moses. The difference is so great, the one was so far superior to the others, that Maimonides declares that the term "prophet" cannot be applied with the same meaning to both. The detailed discussion of the superiority of Moses' prophecy is reserved for Maimonides' legal works, the *Commentary on the Mishnah* and the *Code;* it is only alluded to in the *Guide.*[7]

Nevertheless, the purpose of that philosophic work does lead Maimonides on at least two occasions further to distinguish Moses' prophecy from that of the other prophets. The earlier prophets, for example Abraham or Noah, were addressed by God with sole regard to their private affairs; the end in view was the perfection of themselves and of their descendants. While Abraham did in fact address other men as well, his call to them was composed of eloquent speeches and speculative proofs by which he hoped to instruct men in the truth he had grasped. In short, what Abraham received from God did not have the form of law; his efforts at persuasion lacked the means of compulsion. The essentially private character of all prophecy before Moses meant that

there was no explicit attempt on the part of those prophets to fashion
or to improve a social and political order. The fundamental distinction
between the Mosaic and pre-Mosaic prophecies is precisely this: what
was given to Moses had the form of law. No one of his known predecessors ever came before the people and said, "God has sent me to you
and has commanded me to say to you such and such things; He has
forbidden you to do this and has commanded you to do that." While
the prophets prior to Moses instructed the people, their call to the people
did not take the form of divine legislation; the prophets who followed
Moses were concerned principally with inducing the people to observe
his law. Moses' distinction and the mark of his superiority to the
prophets who preceded and succeeded him consist in his being the only
legislating prophet.[8]

From this it follows that the Mosaic law is the only divine law or
at any rate the only perfect divine law, although some men may continue to prophesy and to apprehend truths concerning God and the
angels. Similarly it follows for Maimonides that this divine law of
Moses is unchanging and unchangeable. In its character as law, it pays
no heed to the isolated or rare case; it cannot concern itself with the
unique human being who suffers because of the generality of the law.
Indeed, as we have already noted, it is a part of the purpose of law to
obscure the natural diversity of men by imposing a kind of conventional
harmony that makes for civic peace. Law ought to be absolute and
universal in its prescriptions and prohibitions, even though what the
law requires is fitting only in the majority of cases and even though
times and circumstances change. To deny this principle and to attempt
to pattern legislation after medicine, where due account is taken of the
particular traits of the individual, would entail the corruption of the
whole fabric of the law.

Unlike Alfarabi, whom he regarded as second only to Aristotle
among the philosophers, Maimonides does not explicitly discuss the
possibility of the rule of living wisdom in the place of fixed written laws.
Where circumstances require it, precautionary regulations may be laid
down by the Great Court of Law, embodying the judgment of the men
of knowledge of a given period; such regulations take the form of permanent additions to the divine law. In the extreme case, prescriptions
or prohibitions of the divine law may be suspended temporarily by the
Great Court of Law. But aside from these exceptions, no one can effect
any change in the divine law; that law remains intact and unalterable,
the unique and perfect example of its kind.[9]

This conclusion of Maimonides is explicitly denied by Joseph Albo
(d. 1444). In his *Book of Roots,* in which he distinguishes the various

types of law and examines the principles of divine law, Albo notes that there have been a number of divine laws. He cites as examples the laws of Adam, Noah, Abraham, and Moses, with the clear implication that this list may not be exhaustive. For much the same reason that one *nomos* would not be appropriate for all men in the world, one divine law would similarly be unsuitable for all men everywhere. Human temperaments differ radically due to heredity and habitat, and these differences, in turn, entail different customs and conventions. Upon analysis, the divine laws will disclose certain fundamental principles shared by all of them—indicative of the unity of the giver of those laws —and, at the same time, great differences in their detailed prescriptions —reflecting the heterogeneity of the recipients of those laws. Divinely revealed laws may coexist at any given moment, although differing in the scope and rigor of their regulations. The law of Noah and the law of Moses, for example, are equally divine; they both lead to human happiness, albeit to different degrees. The fact that one divine law is superseded by another divine law for a particular people argues no defect or change in the giver and is in no way evidence that true opinions change. What has changed is the character of the recipients. Like a physician or teacher who knows that what is proper at one moment will not suffice forever, God gives a divine law only with a view to preparing men for a more difficult regimen. The succession of divine laws in the world has effected great changes in what is permitted to men and what is forbidden them; these changes have been made to accord with the changing times and with changing human character.[10]

Albo sees no reason for thinking that this alteration in the divine law may not occur again, permitting some things that now are forbidden. Not only does he deny that there is any evidence for Maimonides' contention that immutability is a root of the Mosaic law, but he denies that there is any evidence or any necessity for regarding divine law in general or the Mosaic law in particular as fundamentally beyond change or repeal. It is safe to leave it at saying that belief in the genuineness of Moses' mission implies the belief that the Mosaic law will not be altered or superseded by another divine law brought by another prophet.[11]

Jewish political philosophy, like that of Islam, attached very great importance to prophecy. Unlike Thomas Aquinas, whose discussions of prophecy make no mention of legislation,[12] Maimonides, like Alfarabi, regards the prophet as performing the decisive political function. Belief in the divine law unconditionally presupposes belief in prophecy, "for if there is no prophet, there can be no divine law." This may be

stated in another manner: since human survival depends on the existence of society, and since society rests on a harmony that must be
imposed upon contrary human temperaments, divine wisdom has endowed certain human individuals with the faculty of ruling. Included
in this order of men who have the capacity of governing others are
certain ranks of the prophets. In its more perfect manifestations, the
prophet's inspiration serves a public or political, rather than a private,
purpose. Tentatively, that purpose may be said to be the improvement
of a social order.[13] After reviewing Maimonides' definition of prophecy,
we shall return to examine the relation between the objects of the
divine law and the object of the highest form of prophecy.

Maimonides' teaching concerning prophecy is identical with that
of the Islamic philosophers in almost all major respects. He himself
distinguishes three opinions with regard to prophecy that are held by
those who admit the existence of the deity. The first is that held by the
vulgar, be they pagans or Jews: God chooses whomever He wishes and
transforms him into a prophet. According to this view, the only preconditions of prophecy are a certain goodness and sound morality. The
second opinion is identified by Maimonides as being that of the philosophers: prophecy is the natural outcome of an individual's realizing in
himself the highest perfection that is potential in the entire human
species. If a superior man has attained perfection in his rational and
moral qualities and in his imaginative faculty, and if he has undergone
the proper preparation, he necessarily must become a prophet. The third
is "the opinion of our Law": like the second opinion, it asserts that "the
natural thing is that everyone who is fit by his natural disposition and
who trains himself in his education and study will become a prophet."
According to Maimonides, natural equipment and training are the
necessary, but not—as they are according to the philosophers—the sufficient, condition for prophecy: a man may be fit and prepared for
prophecy and yet *miraculously* not become a prophet.

Prophecy is defined as an overflow from God toward a man's rational faculty and thereafter toward his imaginative faculty. To receive
this divine emanation, a man must have attained the ultimate perfection possible for the human species of reason, morals, and imagination.
His intellect is perfected through study of the speculative sciences; his
imagination must be perfect in its original natural disposition—a natural defect here cannot be remedied; his morals are perfected through
a conscious and habitual preoccupation with noble and divine things
and through freeing his thoughts from any desire for bodily pleasures
and for domination over others. One who has attained these perfections
is the highest kind of man. No greater perfection can exist in the human
species; a prophet, as such, is superior to the wisest philosopher.[14]

Before proceeding with Maimonides' discussion of prophecy, it is necessary to trace the relation between this threefold perfection and the prophet's function. The belief in the divine law presupposes the belief in prophecy because the revelation of that law occurs through the instrumentality of the prophet. The divine law, as we have seen, aims at securing two great ends: the well-being of the body and the well-being of the soul or, in other words, the decent ordering of society and the acquisition of correct opinions and true knowledge through speculation. The divine law is addressed to a large number of men, but they are unequal in their capacities to understand and to be perfected; the divine law must somehow speak to a great variety of human types and must somehow be appropriate for a great variety of human conditions.

These difficulties are resolved through the characteristics of the divine messenger or prophet who brings the divine law to men. Because of the perfection of his intellect, the prophet has direct knowledge of speculative truths. Unlike the philosophers, he need have no recourse to premises and inferences in order to comprehend. More than this, the prophet is able to comprehend directly and immediately what non-prophetic men cannot attain fully or at all. Man as man is limited to direct knowledge of the sensible world about him. Thus, for example, while Aristotle's teaching concerning this sublunar world is correct in all respects, his teaching concerning the upper world, the world beyond the lunar sphere, the world of God and the angels, is not perfectly correct. Here only the prophet has direct knowledge. The prophet, then, is superior to the philosopher in the very point in which the philosopher is superior to all nonphilosophic men.[15]

Moral perfection, which Maimonides lists as another precondition of prophecy, is connected most directly to the prophet's intellectual superiority; for while the desire for speculative knowledge and its attainment up to a point are not dependent upon moral perfection, the preoccupation with sensual pleasures distracts a man's thoughts from the upper world. The prophet distinguishes himself from other men by his complete preoccupation with divine things. "Interested only in the knowledge of the deity and in reflection on His works and on what ought to be believed with regard to that," a perfect man of this sort "will see only God and His angels." [16] More than any other man, the prophet is completely concerned with understanding everything that exists.

By virtue of the perfection of his intellect, the prophet is the teacher of all men. But all men cannot be taught in the same way; they are not equally capable of receiving from the prophet those speculative truths that he has apprehended with regard to God and the angels. Indeed, the overwhelming knowledge that the prophet has achieved would confuse and bewilder all but the most perfect intellects. That knowledge, or at least its general conclusions, must somehow be presented to men, particularly to nonphilosophic men, in a form that they can grasp. By means of his perfect imagination, which, through his intellect, has received a divine emanation, the prophet is able to represent these speculative truths metaphorically. This metaphoric presentation of theoretical knowledge might be said to represent the prophet's practical understanding.

Maimonides interprets the verse of Proverbs, "A word fitly spoken is like apples of gold in settings of silver," in the light of this analysis of prophecy. He explains the verse as follows: a saying uttered with a view to two meanings is like an apple of gold overlaid with silver filigree work having very small holes. Its external meaning ought to be as beautiful as silver, while its internal meaning ought to be still more beautiful, being in comparison to the exterior as gold is to silver. Its external meaning ought to give some indication of what is to be found within, though the inattentive observer will mistake it for "an apple of silver." If one considers the parables with which the speeches of the prophets abound, they are seen to have both an external meaning and an internal meaning. "The external meaning contains wisdom that is useful in many respects, among which is the welfare of human societies. . . . Their internal meaning contains wisdom that is useful for beliefs concerned with the truth as it is." That intellectual perfection which qualifies a prophet to be a teacher of all men finds correspondence in that perfection of his imagination which qualifies him to be a leader of men. The prophet is a man with perfect theoretical and practical understanding.[17]

This doctrine may be restated as follows: as a result of his perfect intellect and perfect imagination, the prophet unites in himself the traits of men who have attained perfection in only one or the other faculty. The divine emanation affects only the rational faculty in the case of the men of science who are engaged in speculation. It affects only the imaginative faculty in the case of the class of men who govern political communities—legislators, soothsayers, and the like. As the former class embodies theoretical understanding, so the latter may be said to represent practical understanding. In receiving a divine overflow that affects both his perfect intellect and his perfect imagination, the prophet becomes at one and the same time a philosopher and a statesman and a legislator and a soothsayer. More precisely, the union of both perfections enables the prophet to surpass any one of these nonprophetic men. As the bringer of the divine law, the prophet becomes *the* teacher of men, hence of philosophers as well; he becomes *the* leader of men, hence of the rulers of political communities as well.

It is with a particular view to this political function of prophecy that Maimonides speaks of the prophet's need to have highly developed faculties of courage and divination. His "ascent" to knowledge of divine things is followed by a "descent with whatever decree the prophet has been informed of—with a view to governing and teaching the people of the earth." By virtue of his superiority, the prophet is obliged to prophesy—that is, to instruct men in practical affairs or in speculative matters. Unable to resist the divine overflow that moves them, the prophets find themselves exposed to grave dangers from the unjust and disobedient people to whom they address their call. Courage, therefore, is an indispensable prerequisite for all prophets. When present in its most highly developed form, "the lone individual, having only his staff, went boldly to the great king in order to save a religious community from the burden of slavery, and had no fear or dread because it was said to him: 'I will be with thee.' " [18] We have already mentioned Maimonides' discussion of man as a political animal. That which requires society likewise requires law to govern that society. That certain human individuals possess the faculty of ruling is a token of divine wisdom in perpetuating the species. In the first rank of those whom Maimonides mentions as possessing this faculty is the prophet or bringer of the *nomos*. These men proclaim the law; the enforcement of the proclaimed law is the province of the king. It is thus that the prophet emerges not only as divine messenger, but as lawgiver and founder of a political society.[19] To explore further this role of the prophet, we must turn to Maimonides' discussion of the law given by that "lone individual," Moses.

In a statement on political science occurring in his *Treatise on the Art of Logic,* Maimonides, after noting that the philosophers have written many books on political science, says: "In these times, all this—I mean the regimes and the *nomoi*—has been dispensed with, and men are governed by divine commands." In saying this, he suggests that the practical teaching of the philosophers in matters having to do with politics is now superfluous; he makes no such inference with respect to the philosophers' works on ethics and political philosophy. The change that has rendered the philosophers' practical political teaching superfluous "in these times" is the predominance of revealed religion. His statement suggests the decisive political importance of divine law. Maimonides' discussion of the Mosaic law in the *Guide of the Perplexed* supports this interpretation. The divine law seeks to secure the welfare of both body and soul. In aiming at these objectives, the Mosaic law treats of political matters—of matters having to do with the governance of men—extensively, precisely, and in detail; but of speculative matters, the Torah speaks in a summary fashion. In other words, since the Torah is the repository of all necessary information having to do with the governance of the household and the governance of the city, there is no need to turn to the works of the philosophers for guidance here. It is only as the Torah treats summarily those correct opinions through which men may attain their ultimate perfection, that individuals who are equipped to do so need direct their attention to the theoretical sciences.[20] The decisive point is that Maimonides regards the law given by the highest prophet as absolutely superior to the philosopher's law. The city founded by the philosophers and governed by their law is inferior to the city founded by a prophet and governed by his law, for the philosopher-legislator is inferior to the prophet-legislator.

Earlier, when discussing the relation between the objects of revelation and the object of prophecy, we tentatively concluded that the prophet's purpose was to improve a social order. That statement may now be seen to be insufficient. The divine law aims to lead men to correct opinions about God and the angels, but it does this in the main by presenting conclusions. Its principal effort is directed at establishing a certain kind of political community. If one reflects on the actions of the Patriarchs and of Moses, it becomes clear that "the end of their efforts during their life was to bring about a religious community that would know and worship God." The object of revelation, "the great good" that God causes to come forth upon the sublunar world, is the founding of a perfect religious community. This object can be attained only if the minds and actions of all men can be reached by that revelation. If the divine purpose is to be realized, the revelation must take the form of law—a perfect law that serves as the constitution, so to speak, of the perfect nation. Moreover, the revelation must be presented in a manner that all people—including the young and women—can understand. That is why "the Torah speaks in accordance with the language of the children of man." That is why a man of the utmost perfection of intellect and imagination is needed to proclaim the perfect law. The highest form of prophecy is legislative, and Moses is the greatest prophet because his prophecy is the only genuine legislative prophecy. The greatest prophet is the founder and lawgiver of the perfect city.[21]

It is typical of Maimonides' teaching that it places greater emphasis upon political considerations than upon miraculous explanations. This tendency is evident not only in his teaching concerning prophecy, but also in his discussions of two related themes—kingship and the Messianic age—in his legal *Code*. The *Code's* Hebrew title, *Mishneh Torah* (Repetition of the Torah), is the phrase by which tradition has designated the fifth book of the Bible. The book of Deuteronomy restates, and adds to, the legislation of the preceding three books; it concerns itself with the needs of a people no longer wandering in the desert and shielded and cared for by extraordinary divine providence, but rather inhabiting their own land and faced with problems arising out of agriculture, domestic strife, and foreign aggression. Maimonides' *Code* has a similar character; in it he restates the laws of the Torah and of the Talmud without limiting himself to those laws that are applicable to life in the Diaspora. Maimonides' *Mishneh Torah,* like Moses', is concerned with the practical needs of an actual state, that is, the Jewish state prior to the Diaspora and after the coming of the Messiah.

Kingship in Israel is obligatory; it is a necessity sanctioned, indeed commanded, by the divine law. According to Maimonides, the principal reason for appointing a king is that he "execute judgment and wage war." War is intimately connected with kingship; of the twenty-three commandments discussed in the section of the *Code* entitled "Laws concerning Kings and their Wars," all but five deal with some aspect of military law, while the chapters devoted to the remaining five commandments, governing the choice and mode of life of the king, all allude to war more or less openly. After subduing those nations against whom the Bible makes war obligatory, the king is free to wage "permissive war . . . against the other nations in order to enlarge the boundary of Israel and to increase his greatness and fame." The king also has a sweeping power of judgment, unlike the courts of law, which are hedged in by procedural safeguards in capital cases. Where an extreme situation requires it, he may put to death many offenders in a single day, then hang them for display for as long as he pleases, "to lay down fear."

Notwithstanding these prerogatives of office, the king remains subordinate to the law and therewith subordinate to the lawgiver and to the interpreters of that law. His function is ancillary to that of the prophet or lawgiver; the king compels people to observe the divine law or *nomos* established by these men. The fear and awe that he inspires and the deterrents that he has at his command are in the service of the judges. In a number of ways, Maimonides suggests very strongly that the king is not in fact the first man of the commonwealth. He explicitly states that the king is subject to the law and hence to the courts of law. He draws attention to the king's subservience to the spoken word of God, to God's command as spoken by the prophet. Indeed, even the greatest kings—those who, like David and Solomon, were inspired to speak of governmental and divine matters—even they have reached only the stepping-stones leading to prophecy. The greatest kings are below the prophets.[22]

Maimonides' analysis of kingship as a political and military institution is considerably qualified by Isaac Abravanel (1437–1508). Similarly, he rejects Maimonides' view of the prophet as philosopher-statesman. Drawing upon Seneca's *Ninetieth Epistle,* Abravanel builds his argument upon fundamentally antipolitical premises. For him, political society as such is an artificiality. The founding of cities, the institution of private property, the subdivision of the human race into nations—all are products of rebellion against the natural and divine order. In the beginning, men lived in a state of innocence in the fields; all enjoyed nature's goods in common; men lived in a state of liberty and equality. Abravanel sees a parallel to this natural state in the life of the Children of Israel during their wanderings in the desert—that is to say, in a life marked by a continual miraculous protection by God. Political life represents a revolt against God. Not surprisingly, Abravanel, almost alone among the medieval Jewish commentators, denies that the Bible (in Deut. 17:14 f.) made kingship mandatory in Israel. He maintains that kingship is a transgression, that in the very act of investing a man with a royal title the people "were abandoning the rule of the Lord"; "the sin lay in their rejection of the divine kingdom and in choosing the human kingdom." The best that can be said for kingship is that the divine law permitted it, recognizing it as an act of the evil urge in man and making allowance for this human weakness.

Despite his adverse judgment on the utility and propriety of monarchy, Abravanel holds that the proper government of the Jewish nation culminates in monarchic rule. He views that government as having been composed of what in Christian doctrine is known as the two swords, temporal and spiritual; each of these governments in turn contained democratic, aristocratic, and monarchic elements. At the head of the temporal mixed regime stands a man like Moses; "Moses . . . was the first king to reign over Israel." At the head of the spiritual government stands a prophet. The predominant elements of the Jewish state, in Abravanel's account, are the priests and the prophets. Though the prophet is a ruler, he is not, properly speaking, political. The greatest prophet, Moses, had to be taught by a Gentile who was not a prophet (Jethro) how to organize the administration of justice. This suggests that for Abravanel the rule of the prophet is not properly a consideration of political philosophy, as it is for Maimonides. For Abravanel prophecy, being a divine gift, is supernatural; the prophet is superpolitical. By borrowing heavily from the Christian scholastic writers, and particularly from those of extreme papalist views, Abravanel comes to conclusions that are radically at odds with those of Maimonides concerning the ideal form of government. In place of a leader who embodies the traits of both a philosopher and a king, Abravanel considers the ideal ruler to be a priest-king.[23]

The sobriety of Maimonides' teaching regarding the Messiah stands in striking contrast both to the legendary themes with which the preceding Jewish tradition had occupied itself and to the passionate speculation about the miracles to be wrought that characterizes Abravanel's Messianic writings. It is noteworthy that the thematic discussion of the Messiah is located in the concluding chapters of the fourteenth and final section of the *Code,* which deals with laws concerning kings and their wars. Maimonides' fundamental thesis is that the Messianic age is distinguished from the present only by the change in the political status of the Jewish people. "Let it not be imagined that in the days of the Messiah any thing in the world will change its way or there will be any innovation in creation. The world will go on in its accustomed way. . . ." The nonmiraculous character of Messianic times is emphasized by Maimonides in several ways. In this part of the *Code,* the Messiah appears to be first and foremost a king; not once is he here referred to as "prophet." Speaking of Bar Kokhba, the leader of the Jewish revolt against the Romans in A.D. 132, Maimonides calls him "the king" who was regarded as "the King Messiah." Only when Bar Kokhba was killed did the Jewish sages realize that they had erred in so regarding him. Maimonides makes no mention here of any claim Bar Kokhba might have on the grounds of ability to prophesy, and he explicitly denies that any miraculous deeds are required to authenticate the Messiah. The question rather is reduced to one of political and military success: Maimonides' Messiah is a warlike liberator whose primary task is to break Israel's shackles and to restore the ancient political order.

The tendency of Maimonides' teaching is to oppose the traditional notion of the Messiah as a miracle-working prophet and the more fantastic speculations concerning the Messianic age. How far Maimonides went in giving a political interpretation of the future and past fate of the Jewish people can be seen in his letter to the rabbis of southern France showing the cause of the Jews' loss of their kingdom and their subsequent dispersion. According to the traditional view, exile is a divinely inflicted punishment of a sin. That sin was understood to be idolatry or, in its common manifestation, astrology. The Jews, at the time of their kingdom, were preoccupied with astrology. "They erred and were drawn after [such subjects,] imagining them to be celebrated science and to be of great utility. They did not busy themselves with the art of war or with the conquest of lands, but imagined that those studies would help them. Therefore the prophets called them fools and dolts. And truly fools they were, for they walked after confused things that do not profit." Maimonides does not here teach that astrology is a transgression of the divine law to be punished by direct intervention of God. He rather suggests that folly brings its own punishment. By devoting their time and energies to useless confusion, the ancient Jews prepared their own downfall. Maimonides' account of the future restoration of the Jewish state is informed by this analysis of its downfall. The warlike liberator who receives the title "King Messiah" is known by his acts—political and military acts—and confirmed by his successes —political and military victories. In brief, the Messiah is a successful Bar Kokhba or, more precisely, a son of David: a general rather than a prophet.

Political success, however, is not an end in itself; it is in the service of something higher. In proportion as Maimonides regards the means to the higher end as being natural or within human power, he attaches importance to reason and politics. The evils that beset this life flow from men's "purposes, desires, opinions, and beliefs," and all of these derive from some fundamental ignorance. The vision of universal peace in Isaiah 11 is contingent upon a true knowledge of God: "For through cognition of the truth, enmity and hatred are removed. . . ." The "days of the Messiah" will differ from the present in that the Jews will return to their ancestral homeland with the aid of a successful military leader, and men will cease injuring one another out of ignorance. These two changes are related, for one of the tasks of the conquering Messiah is to "prepare the whole world to serve the Lord with one accord." The Messiah shows the world the true way, but not by means of miracles; he fights the battles of the Lord—and wins. Messianic times are indeed an object of hope, yet the goal that will then have been achieved is not the highest end of man, but rather the establishment of certain political preconditions of that end; political action in general is in the service of "the world to come." The restoration of political rule to Israel means that those laws intimately tied to the life of the people in Palestine can once again be observed; free from tyrannical oppression, the Jews can devote themselves to the undisturbed study of the Torah and its wisdom. As a result, the way is prepared for the total final reward, "the ultimate good": life in "the world to come." Maimonides here connects "the world to come" with the immortality of the soul that follows as a matter of course from a life devoted to learning and piety. The possibility of attaining the ultimate good appears as a consequence of political success.[24]

It is noteworthy that medieval Jewish political philosophy speaks little, if at all, about natural law. But the problem that is indicated by the term "natural law" is dealt with, generally in the form of the question, Are there rational laws, as distinguished from revealed laws? The

Jewish *locus classicus* of this distinction is in the *Book of Doctrines and Beliefs* by Saadya Gaon (892–928). Saadya speaks at first of a class of divine commandments whose necessity is dictated by reason. Such rational divine laws may be classified as enjoining divine worship, prohibiting idolatry, and forbidding acts of injustice. The approval and disapproval of the specific actions that are the objects of these laws are implanted in our reason; thus speculation provides independent confirmation of their necessity. The categorical dictates of the revealed laws, on the other hand, have no such independent verification. Apparently repeating his discussion, Saadya then speaks of rational laws that are suggested by wisdom. This second discussion presents a simplified account of the social utility of the rational laws. These laws are now said to be the prevention of homicide, the prohibition of adultery, the prohibition of theft, and the injunction to speak the truth. Reason is neutral or silent about such matters as religious festivals or the prohibition against eating certain foods or of marriage within certain degrees of kinship. However, most of the revealed laws have some evident practical usefulness. According to Saadya, prophetic revelation is needed to establish both classes of law, rational as well as revealed. While reason by itself is sufficient to formulate the rational commandments, it is unable to establish all the concrete details of legislation. Thus, for example, "reason deems it right that every crime be punished according to its measure, but does not define its measure." Revelation is needed to settle such details; without it men would never agree on anything beyond the general principles.[25]

In his discussion of this problem, Maimonides not only takes a stand against Saadya's teaching or a part of it, but also to a degree separates himself from the traditional orthodox view. In the letter referred to above, Maimonides states that in the *Guide* he has given clear reasons for all the biblical commandments. He silently rejects the orthodox view that it is a good thing that the Bible does not state the reasons underlying its commandments; full obedience, according to traditional religion, requires the acceptance of a commandment without knowing or seeking the reason for it. Yet in suggesting that every commandment has its reason and that its reason is within the grasp of the human intellect, Maimonides still is very far from admitting the possibility of rational commandments. He notes that the prohibitions against action that is generally regarded as evil, such as bloodshed, theft, ingratitude, and contempt for parents, are called "commandments" by the Jewish sages. "Some of our later sages"—he has Saadya, among others, in mind—"who suffered from the disease of the Mutakallimūn [Muslim dialectical theologians] called them rational commandments."

What then is the status of the moral principles? In his *Treatise on the Art of Logic,* Maimonides describes as merely conventional or generally accepted the assertions that uncovering the private parts is base and that generously compensating a benefactor is noble. In the *Guide of the Perplexed,* he asserts that only the first two commandments of the Decalogue—those proclaiming the existence and the unity of God—are knowable by human speculation alone. The remaining commandments have no rational basis; they belong to the class of generally accepted opinions and those adopted in virtue of tradition. At one point Maimonides says that what is innate in man prescribes good actions and condemns bad ones; man is rewarded or punished accordingly, quite irrespective of the specific commands of a prophet. But this is not to say that such prescriptions and prohibitions are rational. By virtue of his intellect, man knows only the distinction between truth and falsehood. The distinction between the noble and the base—that is to say, moral principle—belongs to the class of things that are generally accepted as known, but not to the class of things cognized by the intellect. It is only the latter that remain immutably true. The principles of morality, on the other hand, are at best only probable; Maimonides suggests that the status of the moral virtues is derived from their importance in maintaining the peace of the world. Moral virtue also is required for man's ultimate perfection, that is, theoretical understanding, since a preoccupation with the pleasures of the senses or a desire for domination over others would be a barrier to such perfection. But it is primarily with a view to their political function that Maimonides understands the moral virtues. His stigmatization as "diseased" of those who affirmed the existence of rational commandments, and his studied efforts to point to the political function and conventional character of moral principle constitute a tacit denial that natural law is, strictly speaking, rational.[26]

Yehudah Halevi (1085–1141), is, among Jewish writers, perhaps the most outstanding critic of the philosophers. His positive teaching is based entirely on revelation; here, however, discussion is limited solely to what he says about the philosophers. In his dialogue, the *Kuzari,* he affirms the existence of rational *nomoi,* but the end result of his argument is something considerably different from the natural law of, say, Thomas Aquinas. Halevi designates by the one term, "rational *nomoi,*" both the human codes of the pagans (as, for example, Plato's *Laws*), and the indispensable framework of any code—manmade or divine. More precisely, he identifies that part of the philosopher's code which governs the philosopher's social conduct toward nonphilosophers, on the one hand, with that body of rules which prescribes the minimal morality needed for even the lowest form of communal life, on the other; and he calls both rational *nomoi*. By means of this identification of the two, Halevi suggests that the governmental parts of the philosopher's code are but means to the higher end of speculation and accordingly are not to be understood as categorical rules, but rather as prudent rules of conduct that are valid for the most part. Similarly, he suggests that the indispensable framework of every code (or, as one might say, natural law), lacks absolute validity and universality. He further suggests in this manner that a natural law or moral code that applies equally to philosophers living in political society and to a band of robbers is neither absolutely binding upon men nor truly rational.[27]

Halevi's and Maimonides' rejection of the notion of a rational natural law is presented with greater forthrightness by Joseph Albo. Although Albo speaks explicitly of a natural law, his description of it is closer to that of Hobbes than to that of Aquinas. In content, Albo's natural law resembles Saadya's second formulation of the rational laws: it embodies that minimum of social control without which men would be unable to live together. Albo's natural law is concerned with a rudimentary justice that keeps men from theft, robbery, and murder. It is a law unconcerned with what is noble and silent about divine worship. Albo's natural law corresponds crudely to the second Table of the Decalogue if one disregards the tenth commandment. Like Halevi's rational *nomoi*, it may be said to be directed solely toward the perfection of the body. Albo suggests that this natural law is not absolutely necessary for man because it is not absolutely necessary for man to live in political society; moreover, he suggests that the validity of this natural law depends upon its establishment by some human individual. By pointing to the possibility of life outside the city, Albo casts some doubt on the obligatory character of natural law. By further distinguishing the purpose of this natural law from the perfection that is proper to man, Albo in effect denies that natural law is, strictly speaking, natural.[28] This point, on which the Muslim and Jewish medieval political philosophers agreed, was restated for the Christian world by Marsilius of Padua.

# NOTES

1. Moses Maimonides, *Guide of the Perplexed*, I 72; III 27.

2. *Ibid.*, II 40.

3. *Ibid.*, II 40; III 27.

4. *Ibid.*, II 39–40; III 27.

5. *Ibid.*, III 27.

6. *Ibid.*, III 27–28, 54; *Code, Yesodei ha-Torah*, iv.13.

7. *Guide*, II 35. (Cf. *Commentary on the Mishnah, Sanhedrin* X, Introduction, article 7, and *Code, Yesodei ha-Torah*, vii.6.)

8. *Guide,* I 63; II 39; *Code, De'oth,* i.7.

9. *Guide,* II 39–40; III 34, 41, 46.

10. Joseph Albo, *Book of Roots,* I 4, 25; III 13–14.

11. *Roots,* III 14–16 (cf. 19).

12. Cf., *e.g., Summa contra Gentiles,* iii.154.

13. *Guide,* II 37, 40; III 45.

14. *Ibid.,* II 32, 36 (cf. 23).

15. *Ibid.,* II 22, 38 (cf. I Introduction).

16. *Ibid.,* II 36.

17. *Ibid.,* I Introduction; III 28.

18. *Ibid.,* I 15; II 37–38, 45.

19. *Ibid.,* II 40.

20. *Ibid.,* III 27–28, 51, 54; *Treatise on the Art of Logic,* xiv.

21. *Guide,* I 33; III 51; *Code, Yesodei ha-Torah,* iv.13.

22. *Guide,* II 40, 45; III 41; *Code, Melakhim,* i.1, 8; iii.1–7, 10; iv.10; v.1.

23. Commentary on Gen. 11:1 ff., Exod. 18:13 ff., Deut. 17:14 f., I Sam. 8:6 ff., I Kings 1 and 3.

24. *Guide,* III 11; *Code, Teshubah,* ix; *Melakhim,* xi.1, 3–4; xii.1, 4; *Letter on Astrology.*

25. Saadya Gaon, *Book of Doctrines and Beliefs,* III 2–3.

26. *Guide,* I 2; II 33, 36; III 17; *Logic,* viii; *Eight Chapters,* iv, vi. (Cf. *Guide,* II 40; III 27–28, 46.)

27. *Kuzari,* II 48; III 7; IV 19.

28. *Roots,* I 5, 7; III 7, 26.

# READINGS

A. Maimonides, Moses. *Guide of the Perplexed,* in *Medieval Political Philosophy.* Ed. Ralph Lerner and Muhsin Mahdi. New York: The Free Press, 1963. Selection 12. Part I, chap. 71; Part II, chaps. 32, 36–40, 45; Part III, chaps. 27–28, 34.

B. Maimonides, Moses. *Treatise on the Art of Logic,* in *ibid.* Selection 11. Chap. xiv.

Maimonides, Moses. *Letter on Astrology,* in *ibid.* Selection 13.

Albo, Joseph. *Book of Roots,* in *ibid.* Selection 14. Bk. I, chaps. 5–10.

Abravanel, Isaac. *Commentary on the Bible,* in *ibid.* Selection 15. Gen. 11:1–9; Exod. 18:13–27; Deut. 17:14–15; I Sam. 8:4–7; I Kings 3:10–12.

# ST. THOMAS AQUINAS

## 1225–1274

The political philosophy of St. Thomas Aquinas is not found in any single treatise but is scattered throughout the *Summa Theologica,* the *Summa Contra Gentiles,* the authentic parts of the *De Regimine Principum,* and the great *Commentaries* on Aristotle's *Ethics* and *Politics.* Although St. Thomas substantially adopts the political doctrine of Aristotle, that doctrine is greatly in debt to the extraordinarily profound and thorough explication made of it by St. Thomas, particularly in the *Commentary* on the *Ethics* and that portion of the *Commentary* on the *Politics* of which St. Thomas was the author.[1] In two areas, however, St. Thomas' thought extends beyond Aristotle's treatment of political questions. One of these areas lay entirely beyond possible consideration by Aristotle—the question of the relation of Church and State. But St. Thomas' thought on this matter is greatly shaped by Aristotle's treatment of what he considered to be the ultimate political question—the question of human happiness, of the last end of human life. The second matter on which St. Thomas' thought, while remaining faithful to Aristotle's principles, goes beyond the letter of his master's thought, is the purely political question of the nature of constitutional government.

### The Question of Church and State

Professor Sabine says that "the rise of the Christian church, as a distinct institution entitled to govern the spiritual concerns of mankind in independence of the state, may not unreasonably be described as the most revolutionary event in the history of western Europe, in respect both to politics and political philosophy." [2] The reason he implies for this view is precisely that before the rise of the Christian Church the State was considered to have an important role in these matters. Aristotle had declared politics to be "the master art . . . for it is this that ordains which of the sciences should be studied in a state and which each class of citizens should learn and up to what point they should learn them." [3] And of all the forms of knowledge "wisdom must plainly be the most finished. . . ." [4] Wisdom is knowledge of the "highest objects," and life according to this wisdom is "divine" rather than "human": "But we must not follow those who advise us, being men, to think of human things, and, being mortal, of mortal things, but must, so far as we can, make ourselves immortal, and strain every nerve to live in accordance with the best thing in us; for even if it be small in bulk, much more does it in power and worth surpass everything." [5]

Although the State is the highest society that Aristotle knows, the political life is explicitly declared to be less good than the contemplative life: that is to say, there is a common good knowable by man (the extrinsic common good of the universe, the principle upon which "depend the heavens and the world of nature" [6]) that is better than the political common good. For although Aristotle had indeed called this latter good more "divine" than the good that perfects a man in relation only to himself, he had done so because its likeness to God is a greater one by way of "proportion," that is, the common good of men is more "divine" than a private good of the same order because it is a more perfect imitation of the ultimate essential good which draws all things to itself. The whole good of the practical intellect is "divine" only by way of "proportion." "But the likeness of the speculative intellect to God is one of union and informing; which is a much greater likeness." [7] If then the State is the highest society, and politics the master art, the highest care of this art is the cultivation of wisdom in its citizens.

We must next observe more closely the nature of the State's authoritative role in the task of cultivating wisdom in its citizens. Because Aristotle had established political science as a practical science, its authoritative role can extend to all other sciences only in so far as these deal with things that are operable by man—in so far as they are practical. And therefore the text of Aristotle on this matter establishes a difference in the exercise of the authoritative role of politics for theoretical and for practical sciences. In directing matters of practical science (concerned with things operable by man) the art of politics is authoritative to the extent of determining the work itself that is done. But in fulfilling its role as the promoter and guardian of truth (which is the good of the speculative intellect and the object of theoretic science) the State may not interfere with its free determination.[8]

As St. Thomas puts it in commenting on this doctrine of Aristotle, the State ordains that some should teach geometry, but it does not prescribe for geometry what should be the conclusion concerning the triangle.[9] The reason for this is that such matters are not subject to the human will: in theoretic knowledge the intelligence is measured by its object, not the other way around. And therefore when it is said that the State may not interfere with the free determination of truth, it should be carefully noticed that the freedom here asserted is primarily in behalf of truth itself and only consequently in behalf of man. It is truth, then, that is sovereignly free, and man becomes free in proportion as he knows the truth and the highest truth. For indeed, by this good of the speculative intellect "if [it] be perfect, the whole man is perfected and made good thereby." [10]

Hence politics serves this good and "is not *supreme* over philosophic wisdom . . . anymore than the art of medicine is over health; for it does not use it but provides for its coming into being; it issues orders, then, for its sake, but not to it. Further, to maintain its supremacy would be like saying that the art of politics rules the gods because it issues orders about all the affairs of the state." [11] And so St. Thomas remarks, "And [thus] political prudence does not *use* philosophic wisdom, telling it how it ought to judge concerning divine things, but prescribes for it, ordaining how men can come to wisdom." [12] In providing for its communication the State professes the wisdom of its wise men, and the State makes this profession by respecting the freedom of truth—that is, by not entering into the interior truth of the speculative sciences but, by a prudential judgment, prescribing for wisdom precisely under the aspect of the good of the speculative intellect, a good which the political community seeks from its wise men, and which, as such, political prudence is competent to prescribe for.

We must next notice that however solicitous the State may be both for the attainment of truth and its freedom, the likelihood of reaching the highest truths is not very great. For human nature "is in many ways in bondage," so that "the possession of [wisdom] might be justly regarded as beyond human power." [13] If perfect happiness consists, as Aristotle avers, in the operation of the speculative intellect according to its highest virtue (wisdom) such a life is nevertheless declared to be "too high for man"; he must "strain every nerve to live in accordance with it." [14] The truths about the highest objects are not to be had by many and are had by the few with the admixture, often, of many errors and with much uncertainty. The State then, even when it most rigorously protects freedom of inquiry, is seriously handicapped in its highest care by the very condition of human nature.

Now this fact suggests that the knowledge about God acquired by demonstration and held by natural wisdom cannot be the perfect happiness that all men seek. Not denying that happiness consists in the operation of the speculative intellect according to its highest virtue, St. Thomas is saying, in accordance with the teaching laid down in the second book of the *Physics* (as well as the first book of the *Ethics*), that since things belonging to a species attain for the most part to the end of that species (because nature achieves its purpose always or for the most part and fails in only a few instances because of some corruption), the happiness that all men naturally seek as their final perfection cannot consist in that which is attained only by a very few.[15] But further, even if all or most men were to attain wisdom, this wisdom is itself insufficient for constituting the perfect happiness that men seek. Again without abandoning the view that happiness consists in the operation of the speculative intellect according to its highest virtue, St. Thomas points out that in the present life the operation of the speculative intellect is very unsatisfactory—it is neither continuous nor one, but multiplied and discontinuous.[16] If indeed, as Aristotle says, "we can contemplate truth more continuously than we can *do* anything," it is nonetheless the case that—as he also says—"the future is obscure to us, while happiness, we claim, is an end and something in every way final." [17] And "if so," he concludes, we may call men happy but only as men—that is, as falling short of possessing perfect happiness.

But we must observe that this imperfect happiness, although the best that can reasonably be looked for in this life, does not remove the fact that man's natural desire is not at rest in this life: it is only at rest with respect to what is *possible in this life*. It is for this reason that St. Thomas draws our attention to the fact that Aristotle's explanation does not remove Aristotle's own arguments to the effect that man seeks a happiness "in every way final" and that "nature does nothing in vain." Pursuing this point, St. Thomas observes that although man is below the "separate substances" (in whom, according to Aristotle's doctrine, the intellectual nature is perfect), he is above irrational creatures, and so

he attains his ultimate end in a more perfect way than they. Now these attain their last end so perfectly that they seek nothing further. Thus . . . when an animal enjoys sensible pleasure, its natural desire is at rest. Much more, therefore, when man has obtained his last end, must his natural desire be at rest. But this cannot happen in this life. Therefore in this life man does not obtain happiness considered as his proper end, . . . . Therefore he must obtain it after this life.

Again, natural desire cannot be empty, since "nature does nothing in vain." (Aristotle *De Caelo* II, XI, 291$^b$ 13) But nature's desire would be empty if it could never be fulfilled. Therefore man's natural desire can be fulfilled. But not in this life. Therefore man's ultimate happiness is after this life.[18]

Final happiness can consist in nothing else than the vision of God in His Essence, a vision which surpasses altogether the grasp of man's natural reason. The Sacred Scriptures contain the revealed word of God in Whose Intellect are the principles of that Sacred Science whereby "saving faith is begotten." These instruct us concerning our final end: " 'The eye hath not seen, besides thee, O God, what things thou hast prepared for them that wait for Thee.' "[19] The final aim of social life is, then,

not merely to live in virtue, but rather through virtuous life to attain to the enjoyment of God. If indeed it were possible to attain this object by natural human virtue, it would, in consequence, be the duty of kings to guide men to this end. . . . But the enjoyment of God is an aim which cannot be attained by human virtue alone, but only through divine grace. . . . Only a divine rule, then, and not human government, can lead us to this end. Such government belongs only to that King who is both man, and also God: that is to Jesus Christ, our Lord, Who, making men to be Sons of God has led them to the glory of heaven.

This, then, is the government entrusted to Him: a dominion which shall never pass away, and in virtue of which He is called in the Holy Scriptures, not only a priest, but a king: as Jeremias says (XXIII, 5): 'A king shall reign and shall be wise'. It is from Him that the royal priesthood derives; and, what is more, all the Faithful of Christ, being members of Him, become thus, priests and kings. The ministry of this kingdom is entrusted not to the rulers of this earth but to priests, so that temporal affairs may remain distinct from those spiritual: and, in particular, it is delegated to the High Priest, the successor of Peter and Vicar of Christ, the Roman Pontiff: to whom all kings in Christendom should be subject, as to the Lord Jesus Christ Himself. For those who are concerned with the subordinate ends of life must be subject to him who is concerned with the supreme end and be directed by his command.[20]

The community that has found this supreme end has found the way to the true life. This life is in se superior to the political. The roles of State and Church vis-à-vis each other are determined by this hierarchy. The function of the State with respect to wisdom is tutelary, that is, the State has the obligation to protect and encourage the wisdom of its wise men. By providing effectively for its communication, the State fulfills its obligation of professing this wisdom without violating the proscription against the State's determining the truth in these matters: it provides for "its coming into being, [issuing] orders for its sake, but not to it." Vis-à-vis the State, the role of the Church, as guardian of the Law of the Old and New Testaments whereby man is directed to the ultimate end of eternal beatitude, is to keep "the business of [the State] what we believe [it] is, supreme direction of temporal affairs." [21] For indeed, the "Divine law which is the law of grace, does not do away with human law which is the law of natural reason," and therefore it is necessary "in strictly civil matters to obey the secular rather than the spiritual authority." [22]

But to keep "the business of [the State] what we believe [it] is" implies the right of the Church in certain circumstances to intervene in temporal affairs. For although temporal authority "preceded the distinction of faithful from unbelievers" so that this distinction, "considered in itself," does not do away with the authority of human law, this authority—which, indeed, it is necessary "in strictly civil matters to obey"—may be "justly done away with by the sentence or ordination of the Church who has the authority of God. . . ." [23] What circumstances, then, account for the possibility of this extraordinary exception, of the pope's doing away with the authority of human law? The civil authority, which in strictly civil matters is supreme, may be done away with by the pope where the civil power exceeds its jurisdiction, which is over the matter of the practical sciences, i.e., the sciences concerned with human affairs. [24]

To understand the force here of the phrase "human affairs," we may advert to the classical definition given by Aristotle to political justice: "Of political justice part is natural, part legal—natural, that which everywhere has the same force and does not exist by people's thinking this or that; legal, that which is originally indifferent, but when it has been laid down is not indifferent. . . ." [25] It is part of the limited or constitutional character of government that it may not legislate contrary to the ends appointed by the natural law: the natural part of political justice belongs to the divine-natural law and is not a "strictly civil" matter. It is not a "human affair," for it "does not exist by people's thinking this or that." The legal part of political justice prescribes "that which is originally indifferent"; it is of "strictly civil matters." This means that the civil law may not prescribe what is of itself contrary to natural justice, for this is not a matter of indifference.

Aristotle had given an excellent example of this latter kind of thing in speaking of the practice of abortion. While recommending abortion in certain circumstances, he insists that it should be ". . . procured before life and sense have begun," and adds: "what may or may not be lawfully done in these cases depends on the question of life and sensation."[26] What may or may not be "lawfully done" in these cases is not a matter of indifference: it is prescribed by the natural law which is the divine law as it appears in man as measured and ruled by the Divine government. This natural law is prior to any civil jurisdiction and its general principles must be observed by every civil authority in its proper enactments: it may issue orders for its sake, but not to it. The Church, as the guardian of the divine law, claims the right to decide such cases in the light indeed of theological science served by all the theoretic sciences.

The second class of cases in which the Church may touch the civil law at the point where the civil law itself touches matters that are not "indifferent" has to do with all matters that concern the Faith and the law of the Church itself. The deposition of heretical rulers was a lively question in the Middle Ages. In asking whether a ruler forfeits his authority over his subjects on account of apostasy from the Faith, St. Thomas answers as follows:

As stated above, unbelief, in itself, is not inconsistent with dominion, since dominion is a device of the law of nations which is a human law: whereas the distinction between believers and unbelievers is of Divine right, which does not annul human right. Nevertheless a man who sins by unbelief may be sentenced to the loss of his right of dominion, as also, sometimes, on account of other sins.

Now it is not within the competency of the Church to punish unbelief in those who have never received the Faith. . . . She can, however, pass sentence of punishment on the unbelief of those who have received the Faith: and it is fitting that they should be punished by being deprived of the allegiance of their subjects: for this same allegiance might conduce to great corruption of the Faith. . . . Consequently, as soon as sentence of excommunication is passed on a man on account of apostasy from the Faith, his subjects are *ipso facto* absolved from his authority and from the oath of allegiance whereby they were bound to him.[27]

In virtue of the same principle, the Church may ask the aid of the State in curbing heresy. St. Thomas expresses the view that persons who at some time have accepted the Faith should be compelled to "fulfill what they promised"—on the ground that if the acceptance of the Faith is indeed a matter of freedom of conscience its retention is a matter of contract, which should be enforced.[28] On the other hand, "those who have never received the Faith . . . are by no means to be compelled to the Faith . . . because to believe depends on the will." Further, the rites of unbelievers who are neither formal heretics nor apostates ought to be tolerated by the State, for human government is derived from the Divine government and should imitate it in permitting things that are "quite inferior" and indeed in permitting things that are evil; lest by preventing them "greater good might be forfeited or greater evils ensue." [29]

For indeed, as we have seen, "dominion and authority are institutions of human law [and] the Divine law which is the law of grace, does not do away with human law which is the law of natural reason." And since law "as a measure and rule of human acts . . . should be homogeneous with that which it measures . . . laws imposed on men should . . . be in keeping with their condition, for . . . law should be possible both according to nature, and according to the customs of the country." As we shall presently see when we consider St. Thomas' theory of constitutional government, "consent" and "possibility" are intrinsic determinants of the power of human law. The law, while aiming always at the good and avoiding evil, must consider the interior habits of a people, which in turn depend on their internal natural liberty. For the appetitive part of the soul obeys the reason not instantaneously, but with a certain natural right of opposition; and for this reason both Aristotle and St. Thomas say that the reason commands the appetitive part by a *political* rule, whereby a man rules over subjects that are free, having a certain right of opposition. And thus the factors of consent and possibility are present both in the attainment of the perfection of man's liberty—in the discovery of wisdom—and in the attainment of something "quite inferior." This doctrine of tolerance has its root in St. Thomas' jurisprudence and naturally leads to an inquiry into his theory of constitutional government.

## THE THEORY OF CONSTITUTIONAL GOVERNMENT

In the course of the second book of the *Physics* Aristotle demonstrated in many ways that nature acts for an end. In the light of this demonstration St. Thomas defines nature as "a reason put into things by the divine art so that they be moved to a determinate end." [30] This inclination inhering in things by virtue of their ordination by the Divine Practical Intellect is precisely the Natural Law, for "law is something ordained to an end." [31] As wholly measured by the Divine Intellect, the natural universe stands in relation to God as subject to ruler. But nature inclines to things in different ways, the reason for which is that there are specifically different natures to which being is attached in different ways:

> This is evident to anyone who studies the nature of things. For if he will consider carefully he will find that the diversity of things is made up of degrees, since above inanimate bodies he will find plants, and above these, irrational animals, above these intelligent substances, and in each one of these he will find diversity according as some are more perfect than others; so much so that the highest members of a lower genus appear to be close to the higher genus, and conversely, *e.g.* animals that cannot move are like plants. . . .[32]

Now the rule and measure of the Divine Intellect is found in the rational nature not as determining it without awareness, but in the form of knowledge: there is in man an inclination of the natural law toward the human good ("to its proper act and end") known by the reason. Unlike natures which do not share in an intellectual and rational manner in the law governing them, man has in himself a principle of self-government. As St. Thomas points out, man is a free nature because "the form understood, through which the intellectual substance acts, proceeds from the intellect itself as a thing conceived, and in a way contrived by it; as we see in the case of the artistic form, which the artificer conceives and contrives, and through which he performs his works. Intellectual substances, then, move themselves to act, as having mastery of their own actions." [33] But although man is thus set apart by intellect and will,

we must not be abrupt in separating [him] from nature even with respect to these specific faculties. For intellect and will are also founded upon nature, and all activity is reducible to a principle which is natural "as that which belongs to a prior cause is participated in by what is subsequent" ("*sicut quod est prioris causae participetur a posteriori*"). In the very faculties which are at the root of his freedom we can distinguish an orientation that is physical, determined, necessitated, and even blind in as much as it is indeliberate and not waiting upon choice. This is manifest as regards the intellect which forms its first principles naturally (*naturaliter*). But it is no less true of the will. While its proper privilege is to be master of its own act, its first motion in pursuit of its object, the good (*bonum*), is from nature and not within its own power.[34]

> This inclination of the will toward the human good as apprehended by the reason is the natural law as it exists in man. And this law extends to all other faculties in so far as they come under the direction of the will.

Since . . . good has the nature of an end, and evil, the nature of the contrary, hence it is that all those things to which man has a natural inclination are
naturally apprehended by reason as being good, and consequently the objects
of pursuit, and their contraries as evil, and objects of avoidance. Therefore,
the order of the precepts of the natural law is according to the order of natural
inclinations. For there is in man, first of all, an inclination to good in accordance with the nature which he has in common with all substances, inasmuch,
namely, as every substance seeks the preservation of its own being, according
to its nature; and by reason of this inclination, whatever is a means of preserving human life, and of warding off its obstacles, belongs to the natural
law. Secondly, there is in man an inclination to things that pertain to him
more specially, according to that nature which he has in common with other
animals; and in virtue of this inclination, those things are said to belong to the
natural law *which nature has taught to all animals,* such as sexual intercourse,
the education of offspring and so forth. Thirdly, there is in man an inclination
to good according to the nature of his reason, which nature is proper to him.
Thus man has a natural inclination to know the truth about God, and to live
in society; and in this respect, whatever pertains to this inclination belongs to
the natural law: *e.g.* to shun ignorance, to avoid offending those among
whom one has to live, and other such things regarding the above inclination.[35]

The judgments regulating these basic inclinations are precepts of the
natural law in its strictest sense—that is, these precepts derive not from
individual insight and discursive reasoning, but spontaneously and with
necessity from the "natural reason." They are not *products* of practical
reason but rather first principles directing practical reason. Both Aristotle and St. Thomas compare them with the first principles of demonstration in the theoretic sciences.[36]

But we must now observe that "from these principles one may proceed in various ways to judge of various matters." [37] For if these principles indeed

are conceived as radiating from the center of nature, we can see how in
proportion to their distance from the hard core, the centripetal force of nature
trails off and the inclinations become less and less imperious. Other forces
arise to block or divert them. . . . Hence there is an inevitable ambiguity in
the expression natural law due to the existence of a borderline where nature
begins to yield to other forces and manifest its contingency. We cannot draw
the exact line of natural law.[38]

There is indeed a difference in degree of imperiousness even in the
things that are known naturally, a degree of difference that constitutes
one of the ways in which the distinction between primary and secondary
precepts of natural law is made. Actions that are naturally known as
bearing an "absolute natural commensuration" with man's being are

among the things that belong to the primary precepts of natural law.[39] The ends of the moral virtues, appointed by the natural reason, are precepts in this way. But there are certain things, also naturally known, which bear only a "relative natural commensuration" with man's being: things without which the principal ends of human life cannot be attained except with the greatest difficulty: the political community is said to be natural to man in this second way.

## THE POLITICAL COMMUNITY: THE LAW OF THE CONSTITUTION

". . . Since man is a part of the home and state, he must needs consider what is good for him by being prudent about the good of the many." [40] A social life cannot exist among a number of people unless under a government to look after the common good: "Hence the Philosopher says, in the beginning of the *Politics,* that wherever many things are directed to one, we shall always find one at the head directing them." [41] Just as the inclination inhering in all the species of natural things is toward the common good of the universe, so man in his self-government must imitate the rule of the universe by appointing an authority to administer the community.

Now in nature there is to be found both a universal and a particular form of government. The universal is that by which all things find their place under the direction of God, who, by His providence, governs the universe. The particular is very similar to this divine control, and is found within man himself; who, for this reason, is called a microcosm, because he provides an example of universal government . . . so in a certain sense, reason is to man what God is to the universe.[42]

The political community is, then, one of self-governing men. Since law as a measure and rule must be homogeneous with what it measures, the homogeneity of human law with the community whose acts it rules is found initially in the derivation itself of the first human law—the constitution—from the community of freemen: For freemen, who are equal in having the disposal of themselves, are of such nature as to make it impossible that any one of them should have an absolute natural right to rule over the others and to make it unreasonable that any rule be imposed without all being taken into counsel in some fashion. At the same time, because the individual good is impossible without the common good of all, this good is an end that belongs to all, and therefore it is within the competence of the whole multitude to make the very first law—that of the constitution by which the government (whatever its form) is set up. And if any one or group of persons should presume to found a state, this action is justifiable only on the grounds of their representing in some fashion the will of the whole people. As St. Thomas puts it:

A law properly speaking, regards first and foremost the order to the common good. Now to order anything to the common good belongs either to the whole people or to someone who is the vicegerent of the whole people . . . for in all other matters the direction of anything to the end concerns him to whom the end belongs.[43]

Two elements of constitutional government thus emerge: The first is the element of consent, based on man's moral freedom. The second is the principle of rule to which consent is given:

In whatever things are constituted of many parts there is found a ruling and a subject element. But a multitude of men is constituted from a number of individuals; and therefore among men it is natural that one should rule and another be subject. . . . He [Aristotle] says therefore . . . that whatever things are constituted from many in such a way that from this many a community results, whether the parts are continuous, as are the members of the body which are joined in the constitution of the whole, or whether they are discrete, as from many soldiers one army is constituted, in all of these there is found a ruling and a subject element. And this is both natural and expedient, as will be apparent from any example.[44]

In a natural composite the ruling and subject parts are brought in by nature itself, and the commensuration of one with respect to the other is natural by an "absolute" commensuration. Thus, St. Thomas says, the intellect is by its very nature, considered absolutely, commensurate with the sense appetites to regulate them; and the male by its very nature is commensurate with the female to beget offspring by her, and the parent with the child to nourish it. But in a community where ordering to the common good is among persons in whom there is found no absolute commensuration of one as ruler with the other as subject, this relation is introduced by the natural reason in imitation of what nature elsewhere brings in.

There is, finally, a third element of constitutionalism: the element of possibility, which corresponds to man's physical freedom. Comparing the art of gymnastic with that of politics, Aristotle had observed that a man may not desire the best habit of body even though this be physically possible to him; and a man for whom there is a physical impediment to acquiring the best habit of body may desire what the circumstances permit, or he may desire something even less than the circumstances permit. "The same principle equally holds in medicine and ship-building, and the making of clothes, and in the arts generally." [45] On the basis of that comparison, Aristotle had argued that political science "has to consider what government is best and of what sort it must be, to be most in accordance with our aspirations, if there were no external impediment, and also what kind of government is adapted to particular states." [46]

Thus political science will deal even with states that are "neither . . . the best under the circumstances, but of an inferior type," much as medicine is concerned to know to what degree a person can in fact attain health. And since the moral sciences bear on the contraries of good and evil only in the sense that they pursue the one and avoid the other, a constitutional government cannot be one that is simply bad, though it may be neither the best absolutely, nor best as what is best suited to the majority of states, nor even best in the circumstances. But it cannot be simply bad, for the "rule of law" that Aristotle had required of all good government requires a *right* consent: "The tyranny that is the counterpart of perfect monarchy . . . no freeman, if he can escape from it, will endure." [47] The element of possibility allows for the choice of a government that may indeed be "quite inferior" and less good even than the circumstances permit; but it does not extend to permitting what of itself would be contrary to natural law—the tyranny that no freeman, if he can escape from it, will endure.

The incompetence of a primitive people is analogous to the incompetence of a corrupt people, and, as St. Thomas points out, where a people are thoroughly corrupt and entrust the government to scoundrels and criminals, "the right of appointing their public officials is rightly forfeit to such a people and the choice devolves upon a few good men." [48] Such a people do not, then, have a constitutional government that is properly political, for they are not competent to share in government. Politically immature or corrupt, they may be likened to brute natures, for like nonrational nature they need to be directed to their proper end by an intelligence extrinsic to them. But the seeds of political life are there: they have the kind of government that their nature and condition require for growth in political maturity. As St. Thomas says, different things are expedient to different men because of the difference of their condition. If then, a people originally incompetent by reason either of corruption or immaturity come to "have a sense of moderation and responsibility and are most careful guardians of the common welfare, it is right to enact a law allowing such people to choose their own magistrates for the government of the commonweal." [49] And indeed,

along with growing maturity in political virtue there is advancement
in the science of government:

. . . it seems natural to human reason to advance gradually from the imperfect to the perfect. Hence in the speculative sciences, we see that the
teaching of the early philosophers was imperfect, and that it was afterwards
perfected by those who succeeded them. So also in practical matters, for those
who first endeavored to discover something useful for the human community, not being able themselves to take everything into consideration,
set up certain institutions which were deficient in many ways; and these
were changed by subsequent lawgivers who made institutions that might
prove less frequently deficient in relation to the common welfare.[50]

### THE BEST FORM OF GOVERNMENT

The problem of the best constitution is that of combining the elements
of consent and possibility with the perfection of the governing principle
—the unity, effectiveness, and stability of the form of government.
Aristotle had found each of the simple forms of good government defective in relation to the common welfare on the score either of inadequate allowance for the elements of consent and possibility or of
inadequate provision for effectiveness in the governmental structure—
the two aspects of constitutional government. The simple form of
monarchy—which Aristotle considered to be, absolutely speaking, the
best form because it best imitates the perfection of the governing principle of the rational soul over the "free" appetites—has the curious disadvantage that there are no citizens in such a state; neither the ruler
nor the subjects are true citizens, "for the virtue of a citizen includes
ruling and obeying." [51]

Despite its acknowledged primacy from the point of view of the
perfection of the governing principle, this form, if it be transferred to
a community where the ideal prerequisites for it are lacking, loses its
advantage of unity of rule, St. Thomas points out, by a lack of interest
in the common welfare on the part of the members of the community,
who do not share in the government.[52] On the other hand, democracy,
the simple "political" form, in which citizens rule and are ruled in turn,
has for Aristotle the more serious disadvantage that by dividing political
authority among equals it tends to ostracize the better element and to
seek equality in everything.

To retain the democratic principle of ruling and being ruled in
turn—without, however, retaining the democratic principle of absolute
equality and the social instability that it entails—Aristotle had suggested a substitute for absolute kingship modeled on the substitute that

the continent man employs for true virtue. The kind of consent to true rule and the possibility of it that are found in the average (continent) man were made to serve as the model for the average political community. The unity of rule that is exemplified in the virtuous man's government of himself is imitated in the continent man by a somewhat precarious combination of the two extremes that lie outside the intermediate of true virtue. The man who is overindulgent by nature moves toward the opposite extreme of total abstention, and thus by a combination of the two extremes imitates the intermediate condition of true temperance. In similar fashion the extremes of freedom and equality (on the one hand) and wealth (on the other) are brought together in a large middle class by a wide distribution of property; and this large middle class is capable of a unity of action that imitates the unity of absolute kingship. For just as the continent man does not live by virtue precisely, but by something less, so the middle-class polity lives by the steadying effects of property values.

St. Thomas does not disagree with this diagnosis and prescription. Speaking of the various kinds of law that are distinguished in reference to the various kinds of government, he observes that the best form of government is made up of all the good forms together with the forms of government that are not altogether corrupt—of monarchy, aristocracy, democracy, and oligarchy.[53] He shows himself sensitive, too, to the importance of property distribution in creating a stable and enduring society:

As the Philosopher says, the regulation of possessions conduces much to the preservation of a state or nation. Consequently, as he himself observes, it was forbidden by the law in some of the pagan states that anyone should sell his possessions, except to avoid manifest loss. For if possessions were to be sold indiscriminately, they might happen to come into the hands of a few, so that it might become necessary for a state . . . to become void of inhabitants.[54]

We must note, however, that Aristotle's solution to the problem of combining consent and possibility with unity of rule achieves the latter in regard to the stability of unified rule but not in regard to effectiveness of legislative prudence (what we today would call policy-making authority). For if the stability that is lacking in the simple democratic principle of freedom and equality is achieved through the middle-class character of the government, the democratic principle of rule by turns retains the need for a fixed order both of succession and of power of legislation. Where the citizen at times rules and at other times is ruled, the government is carried out "*in eodem modo*"—that is, in conformity with restrictions upon the policy-making authority.[55] Thus the purely "political" principle, though "corrected" in the direction of stability, retains the weakness of constricting legislative prudence. Instead of the full capacity to proceed in the manner of genuine government, there is a restriction that tends to convert the government into a mere administrator of the *status quo*. Stability is indeed a peculiar and special need for the "art" of politics, but it must not exclude the need for change in law—a need which springs, as we have noticed, partly from men's changed condition and partly from advance in the science of government.

St. Thomas' task was to devise on the basis of Aristotle's principles a form of government that would combine stability of middle-class government with the need for change in law. St. Thomas was well aware of the paralyzing effect of concretizing political prudence in existing property relations: the feudal system of the Middle Ages stood as eloquent testimony to this consequence. Indeed, as Mrs. Ewart Lewis says, "feudalism tended to dissolve governmental functions themselves into forms of property," and "in the context of the medieval problem, one of the most important strands of thought was that which supported and clarified . . . the gradual emancipation of an effective public authority from the bonds of feudal traditions." [56] St. Thomas' theory of constitutional government represents this most important strand of thought.

To the device of middle-class government (which for Aristotle combines the elements of consent and possibility—the "political" elements of constitutional government—with stability—one of the two elements of "royal" rule) St. Thomas adds the second element of "royal" rule, namely, effective leadership. And he does this by restoring the exercise of government to the one best-qualified man conceived now, by the tying of the instruments of his power, as representative of the people. It is this latter conception that introduces the "political" element into the concept of royal rule itself.[57]

St. Thomas' theory of the "mixed monarchy" has been the subject of a good deal of misunderstanding. The key to the theory is to be found in his concept of the people sharing in rule without dividing the government, of introducing the "political" element through the concept of representation. If we suppose—as for example Professor McIlwain does—that a genuinely "mixed monarchy" cannot be had without the existence of two independent and competing organs of government, then we would be justified in declaring St. Thomas' mixed monarchy no different from pure monarchy.[58] But if we consider the possibility of pure monarchy being "tempered" [59] by "tying the instruments it was to act by," [60] then this monarchy, while retaining the purity of the form (for the authority is not divided), is "mixed" with the political element; it is in this way distinguished from the "pure monarchy" which signifies simply the form as such of monarchical government untempered. This latter was called simply "royal," while the former was called "royal and political." St. Thomas' "mixed monarchy" is not, then, identical with pure monarchy, although it does indeed retain the *form* of pure monarchy; it is not, as is pure monarchy, "suprapolitical."

The English monarchy of the late Middle Ages amply illustrates these principles of constitutionalism. Sir John Fortescue, Chief Justice of the Court of King's Bench under Henry VI (1422–61), was the author probably most relied upon in the constitutional struggles of the seventeenth century. He was among the greatest of the medieval English writers on law and politics. In the *De Natura Legis Naturae,* in the *De Laudibus Legum Angliae,* and in *The Governance of England,* Fortescue speaks of two kinds of regime—a *dominium regale* (royal rule) and a *dominium politicum et regale* (royal and political rule). In support of this distinction he calls upon the authority of St. Thomas Aquinas. The editor of *The Governance of England,* Mr. Charles Plummer,[61] equates Fortescue's *dominium regale* with "absolute monarchy," and the *dominium politicum et regale* with "constitutional monarchy." Fortescue describes *dominium regale* as a government in which the king "mey rule his peple bi suche lawes as he makyth hymself"; and a *dominium politicum et regale* as a government in which the king "may not rule his peple bi other lawes than such as thai assenten unto." [62] In the *De Natura Legis Naturae* Fortescue clarifies the nature of the limits put on the exercise of the king's authority in the *dominium politicum et regale* by saying that the king rules *"secundum leges quas cives instituerunt"* (according to laws which the citizens have instituted).[63] The past tense of *instituerunt* suggests, as Professor McIlwain rightly avers, that the laws according to which the king rules are constitutional laws—laws tying the instruments by which the king acts.

We shall examine briefly the philosophical roots of this doctrine of the mixed monarchy. We should recall that Aristotle had himself described the virtuous man's rule over himself as "royal *and* political." This he did by way of indicating the relatively "free" nature of the sense appetites that are ruled by the reason. But the "justice" that may be said to be established by the virtuous man's rule over himself is merely "metaphorical": Justice, properly speaking, because it implies some equality and independence, denotes the relation of one thing to another and must needs be between beings capable of action.[64] Hence justice properly speaking is only in one man toward another. Now free-men—as distinguished, in Aristotle's doctrine, from the so-called natural slave—are not instruments of another but are fitted by nature to have the disposal of themselves; and so there can be justice between them not merely as men but as freemen, that is to say, as belonging to the political community; for the freeman, as a subject, is not the instru-ment of the ruler.[65] Because they have the disposal of themselves, the rule that they introduce among themselves is—as we have seen—not accomplished without their taking counsel among themselves and is not continued without their being taken into counsel by the govern-ment that they establish. A slave, to be sure, is not capable of being taken into counsel in so far as he is a slave (for thus he is the instrument of his master), but a freeman must be taken into counsel because as a sub-ject he is not the instrument of the ruler.

Thus the free subject by virtue of the free nature which gives him disposal of himself shares in the prudence of the *ruler as such* by being taken into counsel in the formulating of law, in the determining of policy: he is "re-presented" by the ruler as the slave is not by the mas-ter. We distinguish, as both St. Thomas and Aristotle do, between "common political prudence," which is in all subjects and enables them to govern themselves in their own individual acts in accordance with the governance of the ruler, and "legislative" or "regnative" prudence, which is the virtue proper to the ruler.[66] St. Thomas' teaching is that more than common political prudence is required of the free subject, for as a freeman having the disposal of himself he shares in the legis-lative prudence of the ruler by being taken into counsel in the for-mulating of law. Indeed, a free people, St. Thomas tells us, are capable of legislating for themselves, but—for reasons that we have observed—the purely democratic or political form is defective in legislative pru-dence; it is perfected in the degree to which it is made to share in "king-ly" government.[67] Thus it is that St. Thomas concludes:

Two points are to be observed concerning the right ordering of rulers in a state or nation. One is that all should take some share in the govern-ment. . . . The other point is to be observed in respect of the kinds of govern-ment, or the different ways in which the constitutions are established. For whereas these differ in kind, as the Philosopher states, nevertheless, the first place is held by a *kingdom,* where the power of government is vested in one, and *aristocracy,* which signifies government by the best, where the power of government is vested in a few. Accordingly, the best form of govern-ment is in a state or kingdom, wherein one is given the power to preside over all, while under him are others having governing powers. And yet a government of this kind is shared by all, both because all are eligible to govern, and because the rulers are chosen by all. For this is the best form of polity, being partly kingdom, since there is one at the head of all; partly aristocracy, in so far as a number of persons are set in authority; partly democracy, *i.e.* government by the people, in so far as the rulers can be chosen from the people, and the people have the right to choose their rulers.[68]

In this passage St. Thomas speaks of tempering the rule of the one best-qualified man first by making him responsible to the people through the elective process, and second by setting up a political body having governing powers under the one who "presides over all." And in another passage he specifies this second means: the ruler is to be responsible to the people through the ratifying process—"of law sanctioned by the Lords and Commons," which, he says, is the law proper to "the best form of government." [69]

## Consent and Possibility: Intrinsic Limits on Positive Law

"We must notice finally that the canon of consent, based on man's moral freedom, and the canon of possibility, based on his physical freedom, carry intrinsic limitations on positive law. Aristotle had defined positive law as the "legal part" of political justice, of which the other part is natural—"having the same force everywhere and . . . not such by people thinking this or that." [70] Positive law does indeed, as part of its function, declare natural right, but it does not establish it.[71] Its main function is to declare the "legal just," that "which is originally indifferent, but when it has been laid down is not indifferent, *e.g.* that a prisoner's ransom shall be a mina, or that a goat and not two sheep shall be sacrificed. . . ." [72] For positive law derives from the natural law not in the way of conclusions from its first principles, but by way of determination of these common notions.[73] It derives from the natural law in such fashion simply that what it prescribes may not of itself be contrary to natural right. In its function of establishing the legal just, human law is a *product* of the practical reason, and its dependence on natural law is only one of the properties that its structure must take account of. Human law falls short of the natural law's participation in the objective order of essences that is the eternal law,[74] for it is applied to very refractory material, to the common condition of men. As we have seen, law as a measure and rule must be homogeneous with what it measures, and human law as a work of the practical reason ought to be imposed on men according to their condition:

Now human law is framed for the multitude of human beings, the majority of whom are not perfect in virtue. Therefore human laws do not

forbid all vices, from which the virtuous abstain, but only the more grievous
vices, from which it is possible for the majority to abstain; and chiefly those
that are injurious to others, without the prohibition of which human society
could not be maintained. Thus human law prohibits murder, theft, and the
like.[75]

The purpose of human law is to lead men to virtue, not suddenly, but
gradually. Therefore it does not lay upon the multitude of imperfect men
the burdens of those who are already virtuous, *viz.,* that they should abstain
from all evil. Otherwise these imperfect ones, being unable to bear such
precepts, would break out into yet greater evil.[76]

There is, then, for St. Thomas a distinction between the juridical
order and the moral order. The purpose of law is indeed, as he says,
"to make men good," but the good which the law can achieve is the
human good of a multitude of persons the majority of whom are not
perfect in virtue.[77] It is enough, then, for the common good of the state
"that the citizens (other than the rulers) be so far virtuous that they obey
the commands of their rulers." [78] It is enough—that is, *more does not
come under the precept of the law.* But it is not the end at which the
law aims, for the virtuous performance of virtuous acts "is the end at
which every lawgiver aims." [79] St. Thomas is not saying then, that the
common good is subordinate to the private good of the individual, as if
one's private good consisted in the virtuous performance of acts of virtue. On the contrary, he is saying that the end which the law seeks is a
common good predicated not on force and fear of the law but on a free
advancing to the perfection of the virtues directed to the common good
of each and all. What law accomplishes is an extrinsic and remote disposing of the citizen for inward growth in the virtues; force and fear
only supply motives for regulating the passions and developing true
virtue. The ultimate aim of the law is accomplished only through one's
interior freedom. That a whole people have "a sense of moderation and
responsibility" [80] depends essentially on a free commitment to the ends
appointed by the natural law.
But we have seen that beyond the first common principles of natural
law, certainty in the mind's grasp of its precepts cannot be depended
upon. And the common principles themselves, as applied to particular
action, can be blotted out of the conscience.[81] If then, as we have been
saying, it is part of the very structure of human law, in its declaring of
natural law principles, to fall short of the natural law's participation in
the objective order of essences that is the eternal law, and if the natural
law itself is uncertain as regards the mind's grasp of those precepts that
are not naturally known though objectively certain, it follows that

neither the positive law nor the natural law are effective norms for liberty. The end of a political community, the end at which "every law-giver aims" (but which does not come under the precept of human law), can be adequately assured only with the help of a law which does not suffer the deficiencies of human and natural law—the divine positive law. Hence St. Thomas:

Besides the natural and the human law it was necessary for the directing of human conduct to have a divine law. . . . because by reason of the uncertainty of human judgment . . . different people from different judgments on human acts. . . . In order, therefore, that man may know without any doubt what he ought to do and what he ought to avoid, it was necessary for man to be directed in his proper acts by a law given by God, for it is certain that such a law cannot err.

[Again] because man can make laws in those matters of which he is competent to judge. But man is not competent to judge of interior movements, that are hidden, but only of exterior acts which are observable; and yet for the perfection of virtue it is necessary for man to conduct himself rightly in both kinds of acts. Consequently, human law could not sufficiently curb and direct interior acts, and it was necessary for this purpose that a divine law should supervene.

[Again] because as Augustine says, human law cannot punish or forbid all evil deeds, since, while aiming at doing away with all evils, it would do away with many good things, and would hinder the advance of the common good, which is necessary for human living. In order, therefore, that no evil might remain unforbidden and unpunished, it was necessary for the divine law to supervene, whereby all sins are forbidden.[82]

These considerations of the role of divine positive law in preserving the structure of constitutional rule by supplying the deficiencies of both natural and human law as norms for liberty, bring us, as it were, full circle in the appreciation of the significance that St. Thomas attributes to Christianity in politics and political philosophy. The analysis of constitutional liberty showed that the civil law may not force the highest virtues on men or force men to perform virtuously the acts which it prescribes. The perfection of liberty must come through a law that, by reaching the interior movements of the soul, forbids and prescribes, rewards and punishes without compelling. And this perfection of freedom is the end at which every lawgiver aims. Fortunate then, St. Thomas says, is the community that comes by this wisdom. It will "issue orders . . . for its sake, but not to it," determining nothing and compelling no one.

Indeed, Aristotle had called the political life "god-like" and had done so by reason of the measure in which it imitates the Divine freedom which freely causes the goodness of order in the whole universe and which draws all things to itself, the ultimate essential goodness. Now it is this goodness of order (which defines the common good) that the divine positive law alone can bring to perfection; for the good to which this law directs man is that "supereminent principle of wisdom" by which "the whole man is perfected and made good." It alone reaches the individual in that which is most determinate and proper, most profound and obscure in him—the interior movements of the soul. Unlike civil law which, finding the common denominator, extends indifferently to all (*"communiter proponitur"*)[83] and unlike the natural law, which reflects an objective order of essences, the divine positive law brings the perfect order of the common good by extending to individuals in their very diversity, in their being not all alike. In St. Thomas' doctrine, the divine law, by providing the ultimate safeguard against mere conformity and conventionality, makes possible the ultimate verification of the meaning of constitutional liberty.

## NOTES

1. St. Thomas Aquinas was the author of the *Commentary on the Politics of Aristotle* as far as III. vi. The remainder was the work of St. Thomas' pupil, Peter of Auvergne.

2. George H. Sabine, *A History of Political Theory* (rev. ed.; New York; Holt, 1950), p. 180.

3. *Nicomachean Ethics* 1094a 27–1094b 3.

4. *Ibid.*, 1141a 20.

5. *Ibid.*, 1177b 27–1178a.

6. *Metaphysics* 1072b 13.

7. *The Summa Theologica of St. Thomas Aquinas,* trans. by the Fathers of the English Dominican Province (New York; Benziger, 1917), I–II, Q. 3, Art. 5 ad 1.

8. *Ethics* 1094a 28–1094b 7. See St. Thomas Aquinas *In I Ethics* I, Lectio ii, n. 26, n. 27.

9. *In I Ethics* I, Lectio ii, n. 27.

10. *Summa Theologica* I–II, Q. 3, Art. 5 ad 2.

11. *Ethics* 1145a 7–12.

12. *In VI Ethics* XIII, Lectio xi, n.

1290 (trans. C. M.).

13. *Metaphysics* 982b 28.

14. *Ethics* X, vii, 1177b 26–35.

15. *The Summa Contra Gentiles of St. Thomas Aquinas,* trans. by the Fathers of the English Dominican Province (London: Burns & Oates, 1928), III. xxxix. Cf. Aristotle *Ethics* 1099b 15–20.

16. *Summa Theologica* I–II, Q. 3, Art. 2 ad 4. Cf. Aristotle *Ethics* 1177a 23–24.

17. *Ethics* 1101a 18; 1177a 23.

18. *Contra Gentiles* III. xlviii.

19. Citing Isaias 64:4. I, Q. 1, Art. 1; also I–II Q. 3, Art. 8.

20. *On Princely Government,* xiv, in *Aquinas' Selected Political Writings,* ed. A. P. D'Entreves, trans. J. G. Dawson (New York: Macmillan, 1949), pp. 75–77.

21. *Ibid.*, p. 75.

22. *Summa Theologica* II–II, Q. 10, Art. 10 C; *Sentences of Peter Lombard,* Bk II, Dist. 44, Q. 3, cited in D'Entreves, *op. cit.*, p. 187.

23. *Summa Theologica* II-II, Q. 10, Art. 10 C.

24. Cf. *In I Ethics* I, Lectio i, No. 31.

25. *Ethics* 1134$^b$, 18–20.

26. *Politics* 1335$^b$ 24–26.

27. *Summa Theologica* II-II, Q. 12, Art. 2 C.

28. *Ibid.*, Q. 10, Art. 8 C.

29. *Ibid.*, Art. 11.

30. *In II Physics* VIII, Lectio xiv, n. 8 (trans. C. M.).

31. *Summa Theologica* I-II, Q. 95, Art. 3 C.

32. *Contra Gentiles* III. xcvii.

33. *Ibid.*, II. xlvii.

34. Joseph V. Dolan, S. J., *Natural Law and Modern Jurisprudence* (Quebec; Librairie Philosophique M. Doyon, 1958), pp. 68–69. Reproduced by permission of the Committee on Philosophy of the Graduate School of Laval University.

35. *Summa Theologica* I-II, Q. 94, Art. 2 C.

36. Aristotle *Physics* 200$^a$ 21; St. Thomas *Summa Theologica* I, Q. 82, Art. 1 C.

37. *Summa Theologica* I-II, Q. 100, Art. 1 C.

38. Dolan, *op. cit.*, p. 71. See *Summa Theologica* I-II, Q. 94, Arts 4, 5, 6.

39. *Summa Theologica* II-II, Q. 57, Art. 3; also III (Supplement), Q. 65, Art. 1. I say "among the things that belong to the primary precepts" because there are other primary precepts of natural law which, however, are known through discursive reason. As St. Thomas says, ". . . some matters connected with human actions are so evident that after very little consideration one is able at once to approve or disapprove of them by means of these common first principles; while other matters cannot be the subject of judgment without much consideration of the various circumstances. Not all are able to do this carefully, but only those who are wise; just as it is not possible for all to consider the particular con-

clusions of the sciences. . . ." I-II, Q. 100, Art. 1 C.

40. *Ibid.*, II-II, Q. 47, Art. 10 ad 2.

41. *Ibid.*, I, Q. 96, Art. 7 C.

42. *On Princely Government*, xii, in D'Entreves *op. cit.*, p. 67.

43. *Summa Theologica* I-II, Q. 90, Art. 3 C.

44. *In I Politics* Lectio iii (trans. C. M.).

45. *Politics* 1288$^b$ 19–20.

46. *Ibid.*

47. *Ibid.* 1295$^a$ 24.

48. *Summa Theologica* I-II, Q. 97, Art. 2 C.

49. *Ibid.*

50. *Ibid.*

51. In the *Commentary on the Politics* St. Thomas explains the consistency of Aristotle's absolute preference for this form of government. "Nor is there validity to the objection that such a ruler is not a citizen: for what is true is that just as he who rules by reason of exceeding all others in virtue is not a citizen but above citizenship, so in the same way we recognize the excellence of any citizen by the way he relates himself to the law (for he who obeys virtuously is a good man and above being merely a good citizen); but the assumption that only a citizen may rule does not hold for the royal polity, which is that which is best simply speaking." *In III Politics* Lectio xii (trans. C. M.).

52. *On Princely Government*, iv, in D'Entreves, *op. cit.*, p. 21. Further, of course, where there is no one man whose virtue ("heroic," "godlike") exceeds that of the whole people, it would be contrary to simple justice "that [he] should be lord of all." *Politics* 1288$^a$ 1–3.

53. *Summa Theologica* I-II, Q. 95, Art. 4 C.

54. *Ibid.*, Q. 105, Art. 2 ad 3.

55. Discussing the difference between this "political" principle and the "royal" principle, St. Thomas writes: "But

the state can be ruled by a two-fold government: namely, political and royal. The regime is royal indeed when he who is head of the state has a plenitude of power. But the government is political when he who is the ruler has power which is constricted by certain laws of the state. . . .

"For when one man rules simply and with respect to everything, the regime is royal. But when, according to the principles of this science, he rules only over certain things—that is, according to laws laid down according to the science of politics—the regime is political; for he rules in part —with respect to those matters which fall under his authority; and in part he is subject—with respect to the things concerning which he himself is under the law." *In I Politics* Lectio i (trans. C. M.); see *In III Politics* Lectio xv.

56. *Medieval Political Ideas* (New York: Knopf, 1954), I, 88; "The Contribution of Medieval Thought to the American Political Tradition," *American Political Science Review*, L, No. 2 (June, 1956), 463.

57. *Summa Theologica* I-II, Q. 90, Art. 2 C. Aristotle's "royal rule" was indeed, as we have seen St. Thomas call it, "supra-political." See above, n. 51.

58. "On the whole," says Professor McIlwain, "it is pure monarchy, whether elective or not, which seems to me to be St. Thomas' mature choice as the general form of royal government best adapted to the needs of Europe in the Thirteenth Century." *The Growth of Political Thought in the West* (New York: Macmillan, 1932), p. 331, n. 1; p. 332.

59. *On Princely Government,* I. vi, in D'Entreves, *op. cit.,* pp. 28–29.

60. Sir Roger Twysden, *Certayne Considerations upon the Government of England* (Camden Society), p. 111. Cited in McIlwain, *op. cit.,* p. 366.

61. (Oxford: Clarendon, 1885), p. 83.

62. *Ibid.,* p. 109. Cited in McIlwain, *op. cit.,* p. 358.

63. *The Works of Sir John Fortescue, Knight,* ed. Thomas (Fortescue) Lord Clermont (London, 1869), I. xvi (I, 77).

64. *Summa Theologica* II-II, Q. 58, Art. 2 C.

65. See *ibid.,* I, Q. 96, Art. 4; II-II, Q. 57, Art. 4 ad 1, ad 2.

66. "Of wisdom concerned with the city, the practical wisdom which plays a controlling part is legislative wisdom, while that which is related to this as particulars to their universal is known by the general name 'political wisdom'; this has to do with action and deliberation, for a decree is a thing to be carried out in the form of an individual act." Aristotle *Ethics* 1141$^b$ 24–26. Cf. *Politics* 1277$^b$ 28 and St. Thomas *In III Politics* Lectio iii.

67. *Summa Theologica* II-II, Q. 50, Art. 1 C; ad 2, ad 3.

68. *Ibid.,* I-II, Q. 105, Art. 1 C.

69. *Ibid.,* Q. 95, Art. 4 C. We have alluded to the uncertainty that Professor McIlwain experiences with the notion of the "mixed regime" of St. Thomas. In one place McIlwain says that "the political" element in mixed monarchy only substituted "the directive force of law for the king's unbridled will" (*op. cit.,* p. 362), while in another place he admits that the limitations on the king's will in medieval monarchy "were considered to be, and actually were in some degree legal and practical and not merely 'moral', truly coercive and not simply a 'bridle'" (*ibid.,* pp. 365–66). Professor McIlwain's uncertainty here comes from an original failure to see that in the virtuous man's "royal and political" rule over himself, the independence of the "free" appetites in relation to the governing reason comes precisely from

the fact that the power and operation of the sense appetites do not derive from the governing (rational) principle but from the law of man's nature as *rational animal,* from the way he is constituted by nature. Similarly, the right of freemen to share in the government is not derived from the government: it derives from the constitution of a community of freemen, whose participation in "legislative prudence" is incorporated in the positive law of the constitution. Nor does this sharing divide the exercise of governmental authority: the king, in the mixed monarchy (as in the unmixed) is *legibus solutus* with respect to the civil law; but in the mixed monarchy he is under not merely the natural moral law but under the positive law of the constitution which fixes the mode of exercise of his authority by establishing the participation of the citizens in formulating the civil law.

70. *Ethics* 1134$^b$ 18.

71. ". . . a thing becomes just in two ways: first by the very nature of the case, and this is called *natural right,* secondly by some agreement between men, and this is called *positive right.* Now laws are written for the purpose of manifesting both these rights, but in different ways. For the written law does indeed contain natural right, but it does not establish it, for the latter derives its force, not from the law but from nature: whereas the written law both contains positive right, and establishes it by giving it force of authority." *Summa Theologica* II-II, Q. 60, Art. 5 C.

72. Aristotle *Ethics* 1134$^b$ 22.

73. "But it must be noted that something may be derived from the natural law in two ways: first, as a conclusion from principles; secondly, by way of a determination of certain common notions. The first way is like to that by which, in the sciences, demonstrated

conclusions are drawn from the principles; while the second is likened to that whereby, in the arts, common forms are determined to some particular. Thus, the craftsman needs to determine the common form of a house to the shape of this or that particular house. . . ." *Summa Theologica* I-II, Q. 95, Art. 2 C.

74. *Ibid.,* Q. 96, Art. 2 ad 3.

75. *Ibid.,* Art. 2 C.

76. *Ibid.,* ad 2.

77. "Human law aims at one part of the moral order, the good of justice, whereby is furthered the good of political society. It is through man's social nature that law connects with the moral order, regulating him with respect to other individuals and the common good. His own moral integrity is of no *immediate* interest to the law except as it touches on justice. The law will not bother him be he ever so concupiscent until he upsets the common life. The legislator does not seek an individual's moral virtue as the good of that individual in the way a parent seeks the moral good of his child. If the law aims to make Socrates temperate and brave, it is not with a view to his own everlasting crown. It is so that he will not become publicly drunk or panic in battle. All the virtues admit some connection with legal justice and the law wants them not as goods for Socrates (which they are) but for the common good in which Socrates shares." Dolan, *op. cit.,* p. 232. Italics supplied.

78. *Summa Theologica* I-II, Q. 92, Art. 1 ad 3.

79. *Ibid.,* Q. 96, Art. 3 ad 2. Indeed, of the ruler true virtue is required. See *ibid.,* Q. 92, Art. 1 ad 3.

80. *Ibid.,* Q. 97, Art. 1 C.

81. *Ibid.,* Q. 94, Art. 6 C.

82. *Ibid.,* Q. 91, Art. 4 C.

83. *In X Ethics* Lectio xiv, n. 2154.

## READINGS

A. Aquinas, St. Thomas. *Summa Theologica. Treatise on Law* I-II, Qq. 90–97;
Q. 105, Art.1; *Treatise on Prudence and Justice* II-II, Q. 47; Q. 50; Q. 57;
Q. 58.

*The Pocket Aquinas.* Ed. Vernon J. Bourke. New York: Washington Square
Press, 1960. Chaps v–vi, pp. 132–33.

B. Aquinas, St. Thomas. *Summa Theologica. Treatise on Unbelief and Heresy*
II-II, Q. 10, Art. 8, Art. 10; Q. 11, Art. 3; Q. 12, Art. 2. *Treatise on the
Last End* I-II, Qq. 1–6.

Aquinas, St. Thomas. *Summa Contra Gentiles.* Vol. III, chaps xxxix, xlviii.

*Aquinas' Selected Political Writings.* Ed. A. P. D'Entreves. New York: Macmillan, 1949.

# MARSILIUS OF PADUA

## *circa* 1275–1342

Marsilius, whose chief work is entitled *Defender of the Peace* (1324), was a Christian Aristotelian. But both his Christianity and his Aristotelianism differ profoundly from the beliefs of the most celebrated Christian Aristotelian, Thomas Aquinas. Marsilius lives as it were in another world than Thomas. In the whole *Defender* he refers to Thomas only once, but even then, when he claims to quote Thomas, he in fact quotes only the statement of another authoritative Christian writer which Thomas had inserted with that writer's name[1] in a compilation he had made. Thomas had accepted the traditional ecclesiastical polity of the Roman Church. Marsilius admits that the Christian priesthood is divinely established as distinct from the Christian laity, both being part of the Christian order; but he denies that the ecclesiastical hierarchy is divinely established. According to him all Christian priests are essentially equal in all respects as far as divine right is concerned. He also denies that any priest, even if he be bishop or pope, has by divine right any of the following powers: the power to command or to coerce; the power to decide whether and how coercion is to be exercised against apostates and heretics, be they subjects or princes; and the power to determine in a legally binding way what is orthodox and what is heretical. But we cannot go into Marsilius' doctrine of the Church although it was of the greatest political importance, especially during the Reformation, for that doctrine belongs to political theology rather than to political philosophy. By following this distinction, we do not distort Marsilius' teaching, for he himself distinguishes throughout his work the political teaching which is "demonstrated" by "human demonstration" from the political teaching which is revealed by God immediately or mediately and is therefore accepted by simple faith as distinguished from reason.[2] This is not to deny that the principle of his doctrine regarding the Christian priesthood supplies the key to almost all the difficulties in which his work abounds, for that principle explains his only explicit deviation from the teaching of Aristotle.

As regards the principles of political philosophy, Marsilius presents himself as a strict follower of Aristotle, "the divine philosopher" or "the pagan sage." [3] He explicitly agrees with Aristotle regarding the purpose of the commonwealth: the commonwealth exists for the sake of the good life, and the good life consists in being engaged in the activity becoming a free man, *i.e.*, in the exercise of the virtues of the practical as well as of the speculative soul. While practical or civic felicity "seems to be" the end of human acts, in fact the activity of the metaphysician is more perfect than the activity of the prince who is the active or political man par excellence.[4] Marsilius explicitly agrees with Aristotle in regarding the purpose of the commonwealth as the ground for the other kinds of causes (material, formal, and moving) of the commonwealth and of its parts. He explicitly agrees with him in very many other points. He has only one reservation against Aristotle: Aristotle did not know one very grave disease of civil society, an "evil thing, the common enemy of the human race" which must be eradicated. This ignorance does not derogate from Aristotle's supreme wisdom. Aristotle did not know the "pestilence" in question because he could not know it, for it was the accidental consequence of a miracle and it could have been even less foreseen by the wisest man than the miracle itself. The miracle was the Christian revelation, and the grave disease arose from the claims, in no way supported by Scripture, of the Christian hierarchy—claims which culminate in the notion of papal plenitude of power. Marsilius declares that this is the only political disease with which he will deal, since the others have been properly dealt with by Aristotle.[5] One ought therefore not even to expect to find a complete presentation of political philosophy in the *Defender*. The work comes to sight as a kind of appendix to that part of Aristotle's *Politics* which may be said to deal with the diseases of civil society.

Yet Aristotle's unawareness of a single, if unusually grave, disease of civil society is only the reverse side of his fundamental error: he was a pagan. That error affects his political philosophy immediately only in one point, however, in the teaching regarding the priesthood. He did not know the true Christian priesthood but only the false pagan priesthoods. This does not mean that his teaching regarding the priesthood is entirely wrong. On the contrary, within political philosophy that teaching is in the main correct. He saw clearly that the priesthood forms a necessary part of the commonwealth, even a noble part, but cannot be the ruling part: priests cannot have the power to rule or to judge. He also saw clearly that it cannot be left entirely to the individuals whether they become priests or not; the number as well as the qualifications of the priests, and in particular the admission of foreigners to priesthood in the commonwealth, is subject to the decision of the government of the commonwealth. The Christian revelation does not contradict this demonstrated teaching,[6] since revelation is indeed above reason but not against reason. Nor is this all. Aristotle did not indeed know the true ground of the priesthood which can only be divine revelation. But if not Aristotle, at any rate other philosophers (who, as philosophers, did not believe in another life) devised or accepted allegedly divine laws accompanied with sanctions in another life, because they held that such sanctions would induce the nonphilosophers to avoid the vices and to cultivate the virtues in this life. Christianity is a truly divine law and the Christian faith in punishments and rewards after death is the true faith; on the basis of the Christian faith one may then indeed say that the commonwealth is directed toward both this-worldly felicity and otherworldly bliss. But since the otherworldly end cannot be known or demonstrated, political philosophy must conceive of that end as a postulated means for promoting the this-worldly end. Besides, while Christianity is exclusively or chiefly concerned with the other life, it too makes men's fate in the other world dependent on how they lived in this world, and it too contends that the belief in punishments and rewards after death is also politically salutary.[7] The reasoning of the pagan philosophers is then true, and therefore may be said to form a part of the demonstrated political teaching. At any rate, that reasoning leads to the philosophic concept, accepted by Marsilius, of the "sect" as a society constituted by belief in a peculiar divine law or by a peculiar religion; that concept embraces equally all allegedly and all truly divine laws, for the truth of the true religion escapes philosophy as philosophy. This religiously neutral concept of the sect is an essential part of Marsilian political science, just as it had been of Alfarabi's political science.[8] It leads to the rational concept of the priesthood according to which the priests are essentially teachers and not rulers or judges: the essential function of the priests in any divine law is to teach a salutary doctrine concerning the afterlife or, more generally, to teach the divine law in which their society happens to believe. The priests are the only teachers who as teachers form a part of the commonwealth.[9] According to Aristotle's *Politics,* the priests form indeed one of the six parts of the commonwealth, but their function does not consist in teaching. Marsilius' deviation from Aristotle to this point is, however, not based on a misunderstanding; he deviates from the letter rather than from the spirit of his master. By asserting that the priesthood is the only part of the commonwealth which is essentially dedicated to teaching, Marsilius draws our attention to the most important fact that, according to Aristotle, the philosophers, so far from being the ruling part of the best commonwealth, as they are according to Plato, are not even as such a part of any commonwealth, for the end of the commonwealth as commonwealth is not speculative perfection: cities and nations do not philosophize.

The fact that the pagan philosophers in general and Aristotle in particular elaborated the rational teaching regarding the priesthood does not mean that Aristotle's whole teaching on this subject is true. According to Aristotle, the action of the priest is less noble or perfect than the action of the ruler, but in "the law of the Christians," and only in that law, the action of the priest is the most perfect of all. According to Aristotle, only old men of the upper class ought to be priests, another point which is denied by Christianity. Finally, according to Aristotle, the priests are simply citizens, but, since the Christian priests ought to imitate Christ and hence to live in Evangelical poverty and humility, it would appear that they must not have anything to do with the things that are Caesar's.[10]

The diseases of the commonwealth which Aristotle had discussed endanger this or that kind of government or render good government impossible. But in Marsilius' opinion the disease with which the *Defender* is concerned renders any government impossible, for it destroys the unity of the government and of the legal order, or it brings about permanent anarchy since it consists in the belief that the Christian is subject in this world to two governments (the spiritual and the temporal) which are bound to conflict. That disease endangers not only the good life or the fruits of peace, for the sake of which the commonwealth exists, but mere life or mere peace which is merely the condition—although the necessary condition—for the realization of the true end of the commonwealth. From this we see how appropriate the title of Marsilius' work is: the work is a defender, not of faith, but of peace, and of nothing but peace—not, to repeat, because peace is the highest good or the only political good but because, being a tract for the time, the work is chiefly concerned with the disease of the time. This is the reason why Marsilius apparently lowers his sights. Thus he abstracts from the question concerning the best regime without in any way denying its importance: any regime is better than anarchy. Thus he is more concerned with mere law, with law as law, than with good laws or the best laws, and with mere government than with the best government.

Thus he is satisfied with mere consent as the criterion of legitimacy as distinguished from the level of consent. Aristotle had as it were provided against Marsilius' predicament. When Marsilius in effect says that the law as law need not be good or just whereas the perfect law must be just, he is in entire agreement with Aristotle's remark that a ruler is no less a ruler because he rules unjustly, or with the usage of Aristotle and indeed of common sense which entitles us to speak of bad or unjust laws; to say nothing of the fact that when Aristotle opposes slavery by nature to slavery by law, he certainly does not mean by law a just law. When Marsilius frequently or mostly abstracts from the fact that the commonwealth is ordered toward virtue, he acts in entire agreement with Aristotle's observation that almost all cities are not concerned with virtue—an observation which does not prevent Aristotle from calling those bad cities "cities." [11]

Marsilius' sole reservation against Aristotle was the immediate consequence of the fact that Aristotle was a pagan. It concerned political philosophy or the rational political teaching only accidentally. Still, according to Aristotle, the best polity is the rule of gentlemen who rule their city, a fairly small society, and are enabled to do so because they are men of wealth. How can such men be thought to be rulers in a Christian society where they would have to rule Christian priests and hence the Church? For in a Christian society the activity of the priest is more noble than that of the ruler. Furthermore, the Church is universal. Finally, the best men in Christendom, *i.e.,* the best Christians, must live in Evangelical poverty. This was the problem which Marsilius believed he had to solve and that he had solved.

The problem of how to reconcile the Aristotelian principle (the men dedicated to the most noble practical activity ought to rule in their own right) with the Christian principle (the activity of the priest is more noble than that of the gentleman) could seem to have been solved in the clearest and simplest manner by the doctrine of papal plenitude of power. Marsilius avoids that conclusion within the confines of political philosophy by teaching that in every commonwealth, the fundamental political authority is not the government or the ruling part but the human legislator, and that the human legislator is the people, the whole body of the citizens. To express this in the language of Rousseau, Marsilius asserts that the only legitimate sovereign is the people but that the sovereign is to be distinguished from the government. He thus succeeds in subordinating the Christian priests to the Christian laity, the Christian aristocracy to the Christian *populus* or *demos*. But in taking these steps he seems to deviate flagrantly from the teaching of his revered master who may be said to have identified the sovereign with the government and, above all, to have preferred the sovereignty or government of the gentlemen (aristocracy) to the sovereignty or government of the people (democracy).

Marsilius does not dispose of the difficulty by accepting Aristotle's assertions according to which democracy or the rule of the vulgar is a bad regime, and the farmers, artisans and money-makers, who constitute the vulgar, are not in the strictest sense parts of the commonwealth. He rather increases the difficulty by ascribing to Aristotle himself the following teaching: the legislative power must be entirely in the hands of the whole citizen body; the government ought to be elected by the whole citizen body and ought to be responsible to it; the government must rule in strict adherence to the laws and if it transgresses a law it is liable to punishment by the whole citizen body. This teaching ascribed to Aristotle is much more democratic than Aristotle's authentic teaching: in the whole body of the citizens, as Marsilius understands it, the vulgar must play a very great, not to say a decisive role. The reasoning in favor of the vulgar by which Marsilius supports his teaching is indeed almost identical with the argument in favor of democracy which Aristotle had reported and considered in the course of his ascent from the defective regimes to aristocracy (or kingship). And Marsilius does not tire of explicitly quoting Aristotle in this context, although not without strange misinterpretations. Still stranger is his complete silence in this context about Aristotle's antidemocratic argument. He reports the antidemocratic argument but omits any reference to Aristotle. He quotes only one authority for the antipopulist position: the saying of the wise king Solomon according to which "the number of the fools is infinite." Marsilius had not quoted any biblical passage in his populist reasoning; he thus perplexes us for a moment by making us think that the Bible, or at any rate Solomon, might favor aristocracy. Yet he disposes of this possibility by suggesting that the sage meant perhaps by the fools the infidels who, however wise in the worldly sciences, are nevertheless absolutely foolish, since, according to Paul, the wisdom of this world is foolishness with God. For from this it follows that the faithful man, and hence all the more the faithful multitude, is truly wise and hence perfectly competent to make laws and to elect kings or magistrates.

There is at least one other remark of Marsilius which shows that his belief in the competence of the people at large originated in his concern, not with authority as such, but with authority in Christendom. He says in effect that the necessity of giving the multitude power to legislate and to elect officials is less evident than the necessity of entrusting the multitude with the power to elect priests and remove them from their priestly offices; for error in the election of a priest can lead to eternal

death and to very great harm in this life. That harm consists in the
seduction of women during the secret conversations in the course of
which they confess their sins to a priest. It is obvious that the simplest
citizen, and surely therefore the faithful multitude, is as able to judge
the trustworthiness of any individual priest in such matters as the most
learned men could be; and the simple multitude might even be better
informed in such respects than the learned. Marsilius also suggests that
the whole body of all the faithful which is guided in its deliberations by
the Holy Spirit, as distinguished from the whole body of citizens as
mere citizens, is infallible.[12] By far the most important argument for
popular government, however, is supplied by the example of the Church
in its purest form, in which there were not yet Christian princes, and
the Church consisted exclusively of priests and a multitude of such laymen as were subjects. Precisely in that epoch "Church" meant only the
whole body of the faithful, and thus all Christians were ecclesiastics.
Hence the traditional distinction between the people and the clergy
must be radically revised in favor of the people. In accordance with the
practice of the early Church, the election to all priestly offices belongs
to the whole multitude of the faithful. This reasoning is not weakened
but strengthened by the fact that in the very early Church the multitude
was uncivilized and inexperienced: if even then the bishops were frequently elected by the multitude, this procedure is all the more appropriate after the faith has taken root in both subjects and princes.[13]

Let us return to the confines of political philosophy and consider
Marsilius' doctrine of the human legislator somewhat more closely.
He devotes two whole chapters out of fifty-two to the statement, the
proofs, and the defense of that doctrine. He advances three proofs to
which he adds a fourth, but that fourth proof is, as he says, hardly more
than a summary of the first three. (1) The legislative power ought to
belong to those from whom alone the best laws can emerge, but this is
the whole citizen body; one reason is that no one harms himself knowingly and hence, we may add, when each thinks of his interest, no one's
interest will be neglected or the interest of all will be duly provided for.
(2) The legislative power ought to belong only to those who can best
guarantee that the laws made will be observed, but this is the whole
citizen body, for each citizen observes better a law, even if it is not good,
"which he seems to have imposed on himself"; the reason for this is
that every citizen not only is a free man, *i.e.,* not subject to a master, but
desires to be a free man. We may note that this argument causes a difficulty which Marsilius never discussed regarding the God-given and
hence not even apparently self-imposed law. (3) What can benefit and
harm each, and hence all, ought to be known and heard by all so that

all and each can attain the benefit and repel the harm. The defense of
the doctrine is stated in three arguments which are in the main taken
from the populist reasoning reported by Aristotle. In the second of the
latter group of arguments, Marsilius illustrates the danger of entrusting
legislative power to a few or to one by referring to the oligarchic or
tyrannical character of the canon law.[14] Marsilius' populist thesis thus
appears to be derived from his anticlericalism.

Marsilius ascribes the fundamental political power, the power of
the human legislator, not simply to the whole citizen body but to "the
whole citizen body or its stronger or superior part." By the stronger or
superior part he certainly does not mean the unqualified majority. The
stronger or superior part, which as it were replaces the whole citizen
body, must be understood in terms of both number and quality, so that
the vulgar may not be entirely at the mercy of the better people nor the
latter entirely at the mercy of the former. The arrangement sketched by
Marsilius might be called a "polity"—a mean between oligarchy and
democracy—were it not for the fact that "polity" is a form of government, while Marsilius speaks of the sovereign as distinguished from the
government. Furthermore, whereas in a democracy, in Aristotle's sense,
the common people participate fully in deliberation and jurisdiction,
Marsilius reserves these functions for the government or the ruling part
as distinguished from the whole citizen body or its stronger or superior
part.[15] Above all, as Marsilius already discloses in the chapters explicitly
devoted to the definition of the human legislator, the human legislator
may delegate his legislative power to one or to several men. Marsilius
thus allows the sovereignty of the people to remain entirely dormant.
In the same breath in which he proclaims the transcendent virtue of
everyone's actually participating in legislation, he dismisses that participation as irrelevant. One must go further and say that he retracts the
very principle of popular sovereignty. He compares the position of the
ruling part in the body politic to that of the heart in the human body:
it is that part which molds the other parts of the body politic. But if this
is so, the ruling part is not derivative from a pre-existing sovereign, the
human legislator, or the people, *i.e.,* the whole which consists of all
parts of the body politic in their proper proportion, but is rather the
cause of the alleged sovereign. In accordance with this Marsilius compares the position of the ruling part in the commonwealth to that of the
prime mover in the universe, *i.e.,* of the Aristotelian God who surely is
not subject to laws made by the other parts of the universe. In a word,
Marsilius returns to the Aristotelian view according to which the human legislator (the sovereign) is identical with the ruling part (the
government) or according to which the stronger or superior part is iden-

tical with the ruling part; for in every stable political order, the ruling part, whether it consists of one man or a few or the many, is as a matter of course the stronger or superior part. Marsilius even explicitly identifies the ruler with the legislator, *e.g.,* by calling the Roman emperors legislators. He does not leave it at saying that the human legislator can give the ruler "plenitude of power." He goes so far as to say that the ruler owes his position to "the human legislator or any other human will": the ruler may owe his position to his own will.[16]

If the ruling part is the legislator it cannot be simply subject to the law. Even in a republic, where no individual is the legislator and hence somehow above the law, it is sometimes necessary for an individual magistrate to act illegally in order to save the republic, as Cicero did when quenching the Catilinian conspiracy. When Marsilius suggests that the ruler is subject only to the divine law, we must not forget that according to him the divine law is not as such knowable to human reason nor does it as such have coercive power in this world. Furthermore, if the ruling part (the government) is the legislator (the sovereign), the government is not subject to punishment in case of misconduct for the same reason for which the sovereign people in the populist hypothesis is not subject to punishment.[17] To sum up, in spite of its dogmatic tone, Marsilius' populist teaching proves to be, if in a different way, as provisional or as tentative as the democratic argument in Aristotle's *Politics*.


The characteristic of the *Defender of the Peace* viewed as a treatise of political philosophy is that it very emphatically sets forth and literally at the same time retracts the doctrine of popular sovereignty. What is the meaning of this striking contradiction concerning the very foundation of political society? What is the meaning of Marsilius' vacillation between populism and what one may call monarchic absolutism? One could say that he takes the side of the people when the people is understood in contradistinction to the clergy and to nothing else, and that he takes the side of the Roman emperors, ancient or medieval, against the popes. In other words, the contradiction disappears once one assumes, as some scholars have done, that the *Defender* is inspired by nothing but anticlericalism. He needed for his anticlerical argument a populist basis because he had to appeal from the accepted opinions regarding the Church to the New Testament. The New Testament, while giving strong support to the demand for submission to absolute monarchs or to despots, does not give support to Marsilius' suggestion that the secular Christian rulers alone as distinguished from the priests ought to rule the Church in everything affecting men's fate in this world (punishment of heretics and apostates, excommunication, property, and so on); but the New Testament apparently gives some support to the view that decisions in such matters rest with the whole body of the faithful as distinguished from the priests alone. Marsilius' "whole body of the citizens" is merely the philosophic or rational counterpart of "the whole body of the faithful," and he needs such a counterpart in order to provide his anticlericalism with the broadest possible basis: both reason and revelation speak against the rule of priests. This explanation implies that the fundamental self-contradiction which is characteristic of the *Defender* is the conscious outcome of a conscious strategy. Both the explanation and its implication are defensible, yet they do not account for certain features of Marsilius' populist teaching or for the essential character of strategies like the one justly ascribed to Marsilius. They fail to account for the latter because it is not sufficient to conceive of Marsilius as a perhaps skillful but rather unscrupulous politician or advocate.

To find a way out of the difficulty, let us consider a Marsilian doctrine which is not affected by either political theology or antitheological preoccupations, his doctrine of monarchy or kingship. He says that kingship is "perhaps" the best form of government, but he makes it his business to discuss the question as to whether hereditary or elective monarchy is preferable. He devotes to this subject only one chapter, but that chapter is longer than the two chapters taken together which are apparently meant to establish popular sovereignty. He decides in favor of elective monarchy strictly understood, *i.e.,* of a monarchy in which each monarch, and not a monarch and his descendants, is elected. This decision might have recommended him to the pope but with greater likelihood to the German emperor, who was at that time engaged in a bitter fight with the pope and who soon became Marsilius' protector; it would not have recommended him to the French king, for instance.[18] Yet it was necessary for the success of his venture—the venture aiming at the eradication of papal plenitude of power and everything reminding of it —to obtain the good will of all secular princes. It can therefore be assumed that his preference for elective monarchy over hereditary monarchy belongs to his final or serious political teaching. He certainly never contradicts this preference as he contradicts the doctrine of popular sovereignty. His argument in favor of elective kingship can be reduced to a single consideration. The most important quality of the ruler is prudence, for the infinite variety of human affairs does not permit an adequate regulation by laws, and prudence does not come by inheritance. Prudence, *i.e.,* practical wisdom in contradistinction to mere cleverness, is not separable from moral virtue and vice versa. Prudence is also and especially required for the making of good and just laws. While prudence is then of the utmost importance, it is rare; nature generated only a part of the human race apt for prudence, and still fewer men actualize that potentiality. The foregoing consideration does not imply that hereditary kingship is illegitimate; it merely means that hereditary kingship is as such inferior to elective kingship. Hereditary kingship may even be preferable to elective kingship in most countries at all times and in all countries at the beginning of their political life, when all men are still uncivilized. For in most countries at all times and in all countries at the beginning or in their decay, prudence is as it were at best the preserve of a single family and there are therefore no prudent electors. Elective kingship is superior to hereditary kingship because the former is suitable to a perfect and civilized commonwealth, whereas the latter is suitable to a still imperfect or irremediably uncivilized society.[19]

Now, this very consideration leads to the conclusion that to a perfect or civilized commonwealth the rule of a number of prudent men, *i.e.*, aristocracy, is still more suitable than even elective monarchy, for there is no reason why, if there exists in a commonwealth a number of prudent men, as will be the case in a perfect commonwealth, all except one should always be deprived of the highest honor; those unjustly deprived of their fair share in government would justly engage in sedition. Marsilius devotes a whole chapter to the proof that the indispensable unity of government is in no way impaired if the government consists of a number of men instead of one man. Not only hereditary kingship but kingship as such is proper only at times and in places where there is an extreme paucity of men who are fit to rule a commonwealth as, *e.g.*, perhaps in Rome at the end of the republic. Monarchy is the proper kind of government in the household rather than in the perfect civil society. That aristocracy as distinguished from kingship is possible only under the most favorable conditions, and hence very rarely, in no way contradicts the fact that it is the most natural regime. If the priests were as they ought to be, Marsilius argues, the general council of the Church could consist only of priests, for the most important requirement for participation in such an assembly is thorough knowledge of the divine law, *i.e.*, the highest form of wisdom; but the priests are not as they ought to be. This amounts to saying that in principle aristocracy or the rule of the wise is preferable; only because the Church is no longer an aristocracy but, as Marsilius never tires of repeating, is now an oligarchy, is it in need of correction by the best part of the laity; and the laity is, in the Church, the popular element. Within his populist argument Marsilius indicates that the devising and examining of the laws is the proper business of the prudent men; the other members of society are of little use in this matter and would only be disturbed in the performance of their necessary work if they were called upon to do more than to act as "formal" ratifiers. Such popular ratification of the laws would indeed seem to be desirable, since it is likely to make the populace more willing to obey the laws.[20]

Marsilius' very vacillation between populism and absolute monarchy may be said to point to aristocracy as the right mean between these two faulty extremes. What speaks in favor of the legislative power of absolute kings redounds also to the benefit of a sovereign-government which consists of the prudent men of a city each of whom owes his position to cooptation by his peers rather than to popular election; and what speaks in favor of the legislative power of "the stronger or superior part of the whole citizen body" redounds to the benefit of what is in truth the stronger or superior part in every city which is not either too young or small or else too old or large for political excellence, namely, the most prudent and virtuous citizens. Marsilius abstains from arguing in favor of kingship while he argues emphatically in favor of popular sovereignty: the regime which he favors is somewhat closer, not indeed to democracy but to the "polity" than to kingship. At the same time his populist argument points, through its glaring defects for instance, from the "polity" to an aristocracy which is acceptable to the populace not only because of the inherent qualities of a genuine aristocracy as the rule of the most prudent and virtuous citizens, but also because it respects the susceptibilities of the populace. Marsilius presented the argument for aristocracy in the most subdued form because that argument did not provide a sufficiently broad basis for the anticlerical policy which he regarded as by far the most urgent task for his age. In addition, the argument in favor of aristocracy would have redounded in the opinion of the majority of his contemporaries to the benefit of the clergy, for if political power is shown to belong by right to the wisest, it would seem to follow that it belongs less to those wise in human wisdom than to those wise in divine wisdom.

The strategy which Marsilius employed can then be explained by the political impossibility which amounted to a physical impossibility of airing the fundamental political issue. He could have an easy conscience in proceeding as he did because he was satisfied that a government of priests was impossible or undesirable. For according to him the New Testament not only does not authorize government by priests, especially in secular matters, but positively forbids it. In the Christian law, and only in the Christian law, the action of the priest as priest is the most perfect of all. But this action requires a spirit and a way of life which are incompatible with rulership, for it requires contempt for the world and the utmost humility. Christ excluded himself and the apostles from worldly rule in every form. Paul forbade every priest to become entangled in any secular matter whatever, since no one can serve two masters. The New Testament recognizes in the strongest terms the duty of obedience to the human government "which beareth not the sword in vain," not so much for the defense of the fatherland as for executing wrath upon the evildoers, and the New Testament traces to sinful pride the view that bad rulers or masters may be disobeyed. Christian slaves are not permitted to demand that they be set free after six years' servitude as the Hebrew slaves are, for the Old Testament law in question acquires in Christianity a purely mystical meaning. Humility and contempt for the world can then go together perfectly with sincere obedience to worldly masters. Still, within the confines of political philosophy, Marsilius must put the accents somewhat differently than the highest Christian authorities had done. He almost goes so far as to defend the pagan rulers against the saying of Christ that they "lord it over" their subjects. According to Paul, only those that are "contemptible" in the Church, *i.e.*, those who possess wisdom in things which are not spiritual, ought to be judges in worldly matters. The demands of the Sermon on the Mount cannot be reconciled with the status and the duties of governors and their lay subjects.[21] The perfect Christian community was the community of Christ and the apostles in which there was community of goods; but that community was imperfect in other respects since it was meant to become universal and yet no provision was made for its unity in the future when it would have become a large society; it could become perfect only through the acts of Christian princes. One is tempted to express Marsilius' thought by saying that it was nature which perfected grace rather than grace which perfected nature. He even goes so far as to indicate that there is an opposition between human government and divine providence, the former rewarding in this world the just and the doers of good deeds and the latter inflicting suffering on them in this world.[22] Marsilius indicates the peculiarity of the Christian law by saying that belief in God's future judgment—*i.e.*, a belief which Christianity shares with all other religions—would induce the Christian priests not to defraud the poor, while belief in the Christian religion would induce the Christian priests to live in poverty. Evangelical poverty is indeed according to him the inevitable concomitant of radical contempt for this world or of radical humility. Within the confines of human reason, however, wealth, just as honor, comes to sight as something good since it is required for the exercise of moral virtue. But according to the Christian teaching, voluntary poverty is so far required for perfection that those who do not live in voluntary poverty are bad Christians. In spite of this, Marsilius can complain that the popes did not show proper gratitude for having been raised by the Roman emperors from extreme poverty to abundance of temporal goods. He appears to assume that Christian morality and the worldly morality of the gentleman contradict one another or that revelation is not simply above reason but against reason. This may be one reason why he regarded the New Testament law as especially difficult to fulfill.[23]

Marsilius has sometimes been celebrated as a defender of religious freedom. Yet he does not go beyond raising the question as to whether it is permitted to coerce heretics or infidels, while stating in the same context that he does not wish to say that such coercion is inappropriate. He does deny that such coercion can be exercised in this world on the basis of divine law. For according to Marsilius, no divine law has as such any coercive power in this world unless by virtue of a human law which makes it a crime to transgress the divine law in question. In addition, according to the Christian divine law which of course condemns heresy and infidelity and buttresses that condemnation by the threat of punishment in the other life, a man who is coerced into belief is not truly a believer; besides, Christian priests have not been given by Christ any coercive power. In spite of this, the Christian human legislator, not as Christian but as human legislator, may use coercion against heretics and infidels in this world. This right can be illustrated by the following parallel. The Christian divine law forbids drunkenness but does not as such require that coercion be used in this world against drunkards, yet it does not forbid the human legislator to prohibit drunkenness under penalties in this world. Similarly, the human legislator may enforce religious sobriety, *i.e.,* orthodoxy. Whether or not he does so will depend on his judgment on heresy, for instance. He may be guided by the biblical comparison of heresy to fornication and hence permit heresy as he permits fornication, although fornication, too, is forbidden by the Christian divine law. Or he may be guided by the biblical comparison of heresy to leprosy and hence take coercive action against heretics in compliance with the advice of experts (the priests), just as he takes coercive action against lepers in compliance with the advice of experts (the physicians). He may also be guided by the facts that the New Testament surely permits excommunication and that excommunication is bound to affect the excommunicated in this life.[24]

But apart from any theological consideration, *i.e.,* from any consideration peculiar to the Christian divine law, it is clear that if belief in divine judgment in the other world is conducive to virtuous conduct in this world, as even pagan philosophers admitted, it is not inappropriate for the human legislator to protect that belief and its corollaries by forbidding speech which may subvert that belief. This conclusion is not contradicted by Marsilius' teaching that human government is concerned only with "transeunt" as distinguished from "immanent" acts. According to that distinction (which may have been suggested to Marsilius by a passage in Isaac Israeli's *Book of Definitions*), those acts of our cognitive and appetitive powers are immanent which, like thoughts and desires, remain within the agent and are not performed by means of any of the locally moved members of the body, while the other acts of those powers are transeunt. In other words, human government is concerned only with acts the commission of which can be proved even if he who committed the act in question denies having committed it. From this it follows that speeches are transeunt acts. Since subversive speeches of the kind indicated may do harm to others and to the community as a whole, their prohibition clearly falls, according to Marsilius, within the jurisdiction of the human legislator.[25] Marsilius surely did not preach freedom from religion.

Any divine law would lose much of its value if everyone subject to it were free to understand its promises and threats as he pleases. The Christian divine law in particular, with its emphasis on faith as the necessary condition for eternal salvation, would have been given in vain, it would have been given for men's eternal perdition, if Christ had not provided that the one true meaning of his divine law is accessible to all Christians. The indispensable unity of faith is provided in a legally binding manner by the universal or catholic Church, *i.e.,* by the whole body of the faithful, in so far as it is the faithful human legislator who authorizes the general councils and gives their decisions coercive power. This provision causes no difficulty when there is a single human legislator of Christian faith whose jurisdiction extends over the whole world. Such a legislator was, according to an opinion adopted by Marsilius, the Roman people or derivatively the Roman emperor. Marsilius tries to preserve this dignity for the Roman emperors of his age. But he cannot conceal from himself or from his readers the fact that there existed in his time a number of faithful human legislators who did not recognize a superior or who were independent of one another. There was then no longer a guarantee of the unity of faith except within the borders of individual independent realms or commonwealths. Hence Marsilius regards it as advisable that the various Christian sovereigns should agree in recognizing the bishop of Rome as "the universal pastor," but in his opinion they are not obliged to do so.[26]

Yet, as he points out, a universal pastor or universal bishop is less necessary than a universal prince, for a universal prince is obviously more capable of keeping the faithful in the unity of faith than a universal bishop could be. As a Christian Marsilius seems then to be compelled, given his premises, to demand that political society be universal strictly speaking—and not only in pretense, or by courtesy, as the Roman empire was even at the peak of its power—so that it can discharge its duties to the Christian faith. He seems to be compelled, that is, to abandon the very last trace of his doctrine of popular sovereignty or of the Aristotelian preference for aristocracy which that doctrine partly represents; for neither democracy nor aristocracy as understood by Marsilius and Aristotle is feasible in any but fairly small societies. Yet in spite or because of all this, Marsilius denies that a universal prince is necessary. For Scripture does not demand a universal secular empire. Still less does reason demand it: peace among men is sufficiently guaranteed—we may understand this to mean that peace is guaranteed in the only possible way—if there exists unity of government within the particular commonwealths or kingdoms. In his only thematic discussion of the question concerning the desirability of a "world state," Marsilius refuses to decide it. He alludes to the difficulties obstructing world government which are caused by distance and by the lack of communication between the various parts of the world, as well as by the differences of languages and the extreme differences of customs. He refers to the view according to which all these things which separate men might be due to a heavenly cause, i.e., to nature which incites men, by means of these divisive things, to wars in order to prevent overpopulation. Marsilius makes it clear that, were it not for wars and epidemics, overpopulation would be inevitable if the human kind had no beginning and will have no end, i.e., if there is "eternal generation" or if the visible universe is eternal.[27] The Aristotelian doctrine of the eternity of the visible universe is irreconcilable with the biblical doctrine of the creation of the world. The Aristotelian doctrine of eternal generation is irreconcilable with the biblical doctrine that there was "a first man," with a doctrine which is the premise of the biblical doctrines that our first parents fell and that therefore man is in need of redemption. Marsilius does not declare that the Aristotelian doctrine is true. Nor does he declare that it is untrue because it contradicts the most fundamental and the most manifest doctrines of the Bible. The reader can therefore only guess whether Marsilius was a believer or an unbeliever until he considers Marsilius' discussion, presented in the thirty-eighth chapter of the *Defender* (II 19), of the question concerning the ground of the belief in the truth of the Bible.

Within the confines of political philosophy, Marsilius' tacit opposition to Thomas Aquinas shows itself most obviously in his teaching regarding natural law or natural right. Marsilius denies that there is a natural law properly so called. He presupposes that reason knows no other legislator than man and hence that all laws properly so called are human laws: reason is indeed capable of discerning what is honorable, what is just, and what is of advantage to society. But such insights are not as such laws. Besides, they are not accessible to all men and hence not admitted by all nations; for this reason they cannot be called natural. There are indeed certain rules regarding what is honorable or just which are admitted in all regions and are in addition enforced almost everywhere; these rules can therefore metaphorically be called natural rights. In spite of their being universally or generally admitted, they are not strictly speaking natural, for they are not dictated by right reason. What is universally admitted is not rational, and what is rational is not universally admitted. Among the rules which can metaphorically be called "natural rights" Marsilius mentions the rule that human offspring must be reared by the parents up to a certain time; he may have regarded this rule as not unqualifiedly rational since Aristotle had held that no deformed child should be reared. More generally, if wars are by nature necessary in order to prevent overpopulation, the distinction between just and unjust wars loses much of its force, and this grave qualification of the rules of justice cannot but impair the rationality of those rules of justice which are universally or generally admitted to obtain within the commonwealth. In other words, the universally admitted rules of right are not rational since there exists a natural necessity to transgress them or since man does not possess freedom of will to the extent to which both common opinion and the teaching of revelation assert it.[28]

One can understand Marsilius' denial of natural law best if one starts from the fact that he implicitly denies the existence of first principles of practical reason. The cognitive status of the first principles of action in Aristotle's *Ethics* is obscure. One way of removing this obscurity—the way preferred by Averroes and Dante—is to conceive of the first principles of action and therefore also of politics as supplied by theoretical reason or natural science: it is natural science which makes clear what the end of man is. Let the end of man be the perfection of his mind, *i.e.,* the actual thought of the metaphysician as metaphysician. The individual human being who is capable of pursuing this end will then deliberate as to how, given his circumstances, he can reach this end. This deliberation—an act of practical reason—will in many points differ from individual to individual, but there are certain universal rules of conduct with which all men must comply who wish to become perfect as men of speculation. Those rules are, however, not universal strictly speaking since only a minority of men is by nature capable of the contemplative life. But there is also an end which all men are able to pursue; this is the perfection of their bodies. This lower or first perfection requires among other things security in and through political society. Here a profound ambiguity enters: political society is required, although in different ways, for the sake of both man's first and his ultimate (theoretical) perfection. However this may be, political society in its turn requires a variety of "parts" (farmers, artisans, moneyed men, soldiers, priests, governors, or judges) and a certain order of these parts. It requires for its well-being that the legislators and the governors or judges possess prudence and if not all at any rate some of the moral virtues, especially justice. In agreement with Aristotle's procedure in the *Politics,* Marsilius deduces the necessity of those virtues from the purpose of civil society, and the necessity of that purpose from the end or ends of man. That is to say, deviating from the procedure which Aristotle had followed in his *Ethics* for educative or practical reasons, Marsilius does not take those virtues as ultimates, as choiceworthy for their own sake. It is because Marsilius treats prudence and the moral virtues less as choiceworthy for their own sake than as subservient to the two natural ends indicated that his political science is more obviously and more emphatically "demonstrative" than Aristotle's political science.[29]

Marsilius says much less than Aristotle even in his *Politics* about the highest end which is natural to man. For the reasons indicated above he lowered his sights. His doctrine of the commonwealth is reminiscent of the suggestion in Plato's *Republic* according to which the city of pigs is the true city. His doctrine of the human law is reminiscent of Maimonides' suggestion according to which the human law serves no higher goal than the perfection of man's body, whereas the divine law brings about the perfection of both the body and the mind.[30] But Maimonides held that the divine law is essentially rational and not, as it is according to Thomas, suprarational. One may say that Marsilius combines Maimonides' view of the human law with Thomas' view of the divine law and thus arrives, within the confines of political philosophy, at the conclusion that the only law properly so called is the human law which is directed toward the well-being of the body. Marsilius was driven to take this view to some extent by his anticlericalism. When antitheological passion induced a thinker to take the extreme step of questioning the supremacy of contemplation, political philosophy broke with the classical tradition, and especially with Aristotle, and took on an entirely new character. The thinker in question was Machiavelli.

## NOTES

1. Marsilius of Padua, *The Defender of the Peace,* trans. with an introduction by Alan Gewirth (New York: Columbia University Press, 1956), II. 13.24 (= 169th paragraph of Dictio II).

2. *Ibid.,* I. 9.2.

3. *Ibid.,* I. 11.2 beginning and 16.15 end.

4. *Ibid.,* I. 4.1; 1.7; II. 30.4 end (cf. I. 6.9 first paragraph).

5. *Ibid.,* I. 1.3–5, 7; 19.3 and 8–13.

6. *Ibid.,* I. 5.1; 15.10; 19.12 end. II. 1.4; 8.9 toward the end; 30.5 (paragraph 2).

7. *Ibid.,* I. 4.3–4; 5.11; 10.3.

8. *Ibid.,* I. 5.2, 3, 13; 10.3. II. 8.4 end. (But cf. the derogatory meaning of "sect" in II. 16.17.) See above, p. 178.

9. *Ibid.,* I. 5.12; 19.4 (102, 22, ed. Previté-Orton) and 5 beginning. II. 6.10 end; 10.6; 20.13. Note that Marsilius does not quote Deut. 33:10.

10. *Ibid.,* I. 5.1, 13. II. 13–14; 24.1 end; 30.4 (paragraph 1 end).

11. *Ibid.,* I. 1.1; 8.4; 10.4–5; 15.1; 17. II. 4.5; 8.9; 28 end. *Politics* 1255[b] 13–15; 1276[a] 1–3; 1282[b] 7–13; 1324[b] 7–9; 1333[b] 5ff. *EN* 1180[a] 24–35.

12. *Defender,* I. 5.1, 13; 8.3; 11 (esp. 11.6); 12.3, 4; 13.1, 3, 4. II. 17.10–12; 21.3 and 9 end. *Politics* 1281[a] 40ff. (esp. 1281[b] 23–25).

13. *Defender,* II. 2.3; 15.8; 16.1 and 9 beginning; 17.5, 7–8, 10; 28.3, 17.

14. *Ibid.,* I. 12–13. II. 23.9, 13 beginning; 24.11; 26.19; 28.29.

15. *Ibid.,* I. 5.1, 7; 8.1; 12.4. II. 2.8; 4.8; 8.7.

16. *Ibid.,* I. 4.4 (13, 20); 8.5; 10.2; 12.3; 13 end; 14 heading and end; 15.5–6; 16.21; 17.9. II. 5.4 (149 bottom); 8.6; 21.2; 30.4 (485, 19–21—one of the two central paragraphs of the chapter). III. 2.13. *Defensor Minor,* chap. 3 beginning. *Politics* 1296[b] 14–16.

17. *Defender,* I. 14.3; 15.4; 26.13. Cf. II. 3.15 and 30.6.

18. *Ibid.,* I. 9.5–7; 15.3 end; 16. II. 24.2.

19. *Ibid.,* I. 7.1; 9.4–7, 10; 11.3 (42, 14–15); 14.2–7, 10; 15.1; 16. 11–24 (esp. 16.17).

20. *Ibid.,* I. 2.2; 3.4; 9.10; 11.5 end; 12.2; 13.8; 14.9; 16.19, 21, 23; 17. II. 20.2 end and 13–14; cf. II. 3.15 with 30.6. Gewirth, *loc. cit.,* I, 254. The use of *regnum* suggested in I. 2 makes one expect a more monarchistic tendency than Marsilius actually has.

21. *Ibid.,* I. 10.3; 12.2. II. 4.13; 5.1–2, 4–5, 8 (paragraph 1); 9.10, 12; 11.2, 7; 28.24 (462, 9); 30.4 paragraph 1 end.

22. *Ibid.,* II. 4.6; 13.28; 17.7–8; 22.1 beginning, 15–16; 24.4; 27.2 (426 paragraph 2). Gewirth, *loc. cit.,* I, 81.

23. *Ibid.,* I. 6.3, 6; 15.21; 16. II. 11.4; 13.16, 23 end–24; 26.12 beginning.

24. *Ibid.,* I. 10.3–7. II. 5.6, 7 (154,

23–26 and 157, 28); 6.11–13; 8.8; 9.2–5; 10.3, 7, 9; 13.2 end.

25. *Ibid.*, I. 5.4, 7. II. 2.4 (3); 8.5; 9.11; 10.4, 9; 17.8 toward the end. Gewirth, *loc. cit.*, I, 284. See also above, pp. 174ff.

26. I. 19.10. II. 13.28; 17.2; 18.8 (paragraphs 1–2 and end); 19.1–3; 20.1–2; 21.11, 13; 22.6, 8, 10; 24.9, 12; 25.4–

6, 9, 15–18; 28.27; 30.8. *Defensor Minor*, chaps 7 and 12.

27. *Defender*, I. 17.10. II. 28.15.

28. *Ibid.*, I. 10.3–7; 12.2–3; 14.4; 15.6 end; 19.13. II. 8.3; 12.7–8.

29. *Ibid.*, I. 6–9; 11.3; 14.2, 6–7. Dante, *De Monarchia*, I. 14.

30. *Republic* 372ᵉ 6–7; *Guide of the Perplexed*, II. 40 and III. 27.

## READINGS

A. Marsilius of Padua. *The Defender of the Peace.* Trans. with an introduction by Alan Gewirth. New York: Columbia University Press, 1956. Discourse I, chaps i–xiii; Discourse II, chap. xii, secs 3–12.

B. Marsilius of Padua. *The Defender of the Peace.* Discourse I, chaps xiv–xix; Discourse II, chaps viii, xii, secs 1, 2, 13–33, and xix.

# NICCOLO MACHIAVELLI

## 1469–1527

"We are much beholden," said Francis Bacon, "to Machiavelli and others that wrote what men do, and not what they ought to do." It has long been known that Bacon spoke on behalf of modern man. Man is indebted to Machiavelli for modernity, for Machiavelli was the founder of the modern political orientation. His founding act, and the origin of our debt, was his effecting a break with the political philosophy of classical antiquity as well as with the ecclesiastical polity which based itself upon that tradition. Machiavelli overturned the tradition of classical political thought; he effected a revolution from the dominion of Plato and Aristotle, who had taught men what they ought to do. Machiavelli teaches what men do—herein lies his revolution, our debt, and his triumph.

For a long time, most men thought that Bacon spoke truly. Modern man was indeed in Machiavelli's debt. Machiavelli's teaching appeared as a great liberation from otherworldly patterns, a liberation from "points of duty higher than nature would well bear" (Bacon). Machiavelli's teaching, in guarding men from a vain thrust in the direction of unattainable goals, offered what appeared to be a great progress beyond the teaching of the classics. It made men sanguine about the goals of this life. Modern man, schooled by Machiavelli, learned his lesson well; he became liberated from unfulfillable duties. He thus looked about with a more tolerant eye at his nearer-to-hand aspirations. His liberation was a great moment of progress which looked forward to endless progress. Modern man was, as Bacon said of himself, much beholden to Machiavelli.

It has now been obvious for some time that modern man stands at the threshold of a most awesome reckoning. Modern political thought and the actions that flow from its premises have perhaps generated a contradiction of mortal proportions. The crisis of modern thought and modern life appears today only most incontrovertibly, and thus only most obviously, in the confrontation of armaments whose destructive might halts the imagination, rends the mind, and thus tends to paralyze the action of reasonable men. Modern thought is no longer certain that it has consummated a progress. This uncertainty puts it out of heart with itself. It looks with great distrust upon its liberation—the liberation that Machiavelli effected. If it is true that the specific character of the modern political horizon is due ultimately to the teaching of Machiavelli, then the crises of modernity can be seen only through an understanding of that teaching. "We are much beholden to Machiavelli . . . ." Modern man may no longer wish to regard himself as in debt to Machiavelli. But no one can say that his debt is not coming due.


Machiavelli's writings, only some of which were intended for publication, comprise an exceptional variety of forms. Since he fulfilled diplomatic duties for the Florentine republic, he wrote diplomatic dispatches to his superiors; and he composed various reports and memoranda relating to his legations. He responded to particular requests for advice and counsel with general as well as detailed proposals. He wrote fictional works in both prose and poetry: a novelette, comedies, poems, and fables. He wrote a history of Florence. A treatise on the principles of warfare was the only major work he saw published. He wrote short historical and political "portraits." His major works are *The Florentine Histories, The Art of War, The Discourses on The First Decade of Titus Livius* (referred to hereinafter as the *Discourses*), and the *Prince*. Of these major works, the *Prince* and the *Discourses* contain the most comprehensive and fullest exposition of Machiavelli's teaching regarding "political matters," human affairs, or *cose del mondo*—"things of the world." Machiavelli himself indicated the central importance of the *Prince* and the *Discourses* among his writings. In the dedicatory letter to the *Prince,* he says that, by reading it, the prince to whom it is addressed may understand *all* that Machiavelli knows and has understood. In the dedicatory letter to the *Discourses,* he indicates that the book contains *everything* he knows and has learned. In no other of his works are there assertions that the contents are equally comprehensive.

The titles of the major works themselves suggest this. *The Florentine Histories* is clearly a work dealing with a temporal, and therefore nonuniversal, phenomenon: this particular Italian city. *The Art of War,* in so far as it is descriptive of the constant rules and principles of human conflict, would seem to be a book of universal significance and therefore central for the understanding of Machiavelli's thought. But the art of war, no matter how far its rules may be universal and constant, is still a subordinate art. Universal and constant principles for a subordinate thing still make for a subordinate subject matter. The art of war is only one art, however necessary, that is practiced by political communities. The art of war is subordinate to the art of the political community as a whole—to the art of the statesman or the art of politics. The political art is the art of ruling, and the most emphatic kind of ruling is the rule of a prince. Thus the title of the *Prince* is immediately suggestive of the universal significance of the work. There is a problem regarding the importance of the *Discourses.* The title suggests a commentary or gloss on Livy's history of Rome; yet the book is primarily about republics. In the *Prince,* Machiavelli says he will not discuss republics, as he has done so elsewhere at length. Among Machiavelli's writings, this reference fits only the *Discourses.* In the first chapter of the *Prince,* Machiavelli divides all states into republics and principalities. If the fundamental political forms are republics and principalities, then the most comprehensive political teaching may be imparted by an analysis of republics and principalities. Machiavelli's political teaching is accordingly presented in the *Prince* and the *Discourses.*

Some writers on Machiavelli have alleged that there is evidence of internal "developments of his thought" and changes of opinion from one work to another. There is no satisfactory proof for these allegations. There is no convincing evidence that Machiavelli's thought is not unified, and that it was not mature when his first writings made their appearance. Excluded and distinguished, of course, are those deliberately partial, incomplete, and occasional statements which are found in legations, dispatches, letters, and minor, pamphlet-like works. Many of Machiavelli's writings were immediate political proposals, and most of them were political acts. Thus when one considers and weighs the importance of the difference of addressee and purpose in each case, the reasons for different statements in different cases are manifest.

A more serious problem arises from alleged inconsistencies, contradictions, or errors in Machiavelli's major works. As has been indicated above, and as will be shown, Machiavelli intended his great works to be of decisive political importance. They were meant to reformulate and redefine the horizon within which political thought and action would henceforth take place. They were intended as instruments of education and vehicles of new truth discovered or old truths recovered. In the introduction to the first book of the *Discourses,* Machiavelli indicates that he has discovered new orders and modes. In the sixth chapter of the *Prince,* he says, "there is nothing more difficult to carry out, nor more doubtful of success, nor more dangerous to handle, than to [make oneself a leader] and to introduce new orders. For the [leader] has enemies in all those who profit by the old order[s], and only lukewarm defenders in all those who would profit by the new order[s]."[1] Machiavelli's writing about "new orders" is presented as following from a concern with the common good. It is presented as a benefaction. But the common good is ambiguous. As indicated in the quotation above, some profit and some lose by the introduction of new orders. Machiavelli's fundamental teaching is presented in two works, the *Prince* and the *Discourses.* The one is addressed to the possessor of a principality; the other is directed to those who deserve to possess principalities. Do both profit equally from his teaching? However this may be answered, the introduction of new orders requires the displacement of the old orders. The alleged inconsistencies, contradictions, and errors must be looked at in this light. Whoever makes himself a leader, and introduces new orders, must guard himself from the strength of his enemies and the weakness of his defenders. His writing must do contrary things: encourage his friends and discourage his enemies. While he inspires the one, he must be careful not to arouse, or at least be careful to pacify the other. Thus he must write perhaps obscurely, from time to time inaccurately, sometimes inconsistently, but always cautiously.

A similar response may be made to the contention that Machiavelli wrote essentially for his times. That Machiavelli wrote many of his works to satisfy definite and momentary political needs cannot be denied. It is something else to assert that the principles underlying his solutions to the momentary problems were also only "for the times." Machiavelli's teaching was meant for his time, but it was also meant for mankind at any time. It is because the principles of his teaching were meant for mankind at all times that Machiavelli was able, perhaps compelled, to write for his time. Thus Machiavelli cannot be praised or blamed or excused on the grounds that he was a son of his time. He has presented too full (however cautious) an exposition of the grounds or principles of praise and blame for such an argument to be taken seriously. Furthermore, the entire cast of the *Discourses* appears to be a reflection on the problem of his time as such. To articulate the problem, he makes distinctions everywhere between his time and ancient times and all times, between "Florentines," "Romans," and "men." There is every reason to believe that Machiavelli could see well beyond his time.

The decisive principle of Machiavelli's political teaching is indicated by Bacon: Machiavelli wrote what men do, and not what they ought to do. This principle was in conflict with classical political philosophy whose intention was, according to Bacon, to teach man his duties, or what he ought to do. Machiavelli states his opposition to and liberation from the principles or intention of previous political philosophy in a famous passage in Chapter xv of the *Prince:* "And because I know that many have written of these things, I hope that writing of them also, I will not be held presumptuous since . . . I part in the greatest degree from the orders of others." [2] In the *Discourses,* Machiavelli indicates he has discovered new orders and modes; he says that he has entered upon a "way" hitherto traveled by no one. Machiavelli breaks from the principles of classical political thought because he has found new principles. The new principles are justifiable and even necessary because of the decisive inadequacy of the old ones. Classical political thought deserves to be supplanted because it is radically defective.

But only if Machiavelli and the allegedly defective tradition of political philosophy occupy the same arena can one speak intelligibly of one's supplanting or correcting the other. One alternative can be more adequate or better than another only if both are directed to the same end. What then is the purpose and effect of classical political philosophy? Most generally stated, classical political philosophy understood itself as providing the illumination to the crucial problems that arise from the fact that men naturally or characteristically live together in communities, and that life in communities generates antagonistic claims to exercise the final and authoritative role in the acts of the community as a whole. Classical political philosophy clarifies or elaborates the conflicting claims to rule that are raised whenever men associate together; it articulates the degree and sense of justice which each of such claims means to assert. By understanding and clarifying the unity and diversity in the claims which set men apart, it attempts to provide the answer to how men ought to live together, and is thus a guide to justice and the common good. Detached from the interests that animate these claims, classical political philosophy is the "deliverer" of the community, a nondivine benediction to mankind. [3]

Now Machiavelli is still within the arena of this view of political philosophy. Human association is in need of "detached" human guidance and illumination. It is those who "reason about political matters"—things of the world—who can supply that need. The illumination and guidance provided is a great benefaction. "I believe that the greatest benefit that can be rendered, and the one most gratifying to God, is that which is rendered to the fatherland." Machiavelli says in the *Dis-*

*courses* that he undertakes his "new way"—his new teaching—because of a natural desire to do those things which will be for the "common benefit of everyone." [4] Thus, in respect to a concern for the common good, Machiavelli and the tradition are united in a common arena; concern for the common good is not the defect of classical political philosophy.

The essential defect of classical political philosophy is that, in its concern for the common good, it sets goals impossible of fulfillment. It is "utopian" in its intentions and exacting in its prescriptions: classical political philosophy expects too much. Taking its bearings by the greatest excellences, it necessarily speaks primarily about what is most rare and hardly ever seen by living men. Plato, in the greatest example of utopian political thought, the *Republic,* even suggests that political life ought to be guided by what is never seen by living men. The best regime, the paragon for all political communities, is, according to Plato, invisible: a pattern laid up in heaven, it exists only in speech.[5] In agreement with the classical insight, but adrift from what it concluded therefrom, Machiavelli called these "utopian" standards and patterns children of the imagination. "And many are the imagined republics and principalities which have never been seen or known to exist in [truth]." Bacon, explicit advocate of Machiavelli, repeats, "As for the philosophers, they make imaginary laws for imaginary commonwealths; and their discourses are as the stars, which give little light because they are so high." [6]

The imaginary standards of classical political philosophy are bad standards (for political life) because they cannot be lived up to. They do not exist in the world of "truth." But political action emphatically takes place in the world of "truth." However sublime moral perfection appears as seen from the arena of political activity, political activity proper is not the realm of the sublime. Man cannot be expected to conform to impossible, *i.e.,* "unreal," prescriptions: an earthly being, man needs earthly standards—standards which reflect, indeed are shackled to, his very "unimagined" mortality, necessitousness, and "malignity." Thus only prescriptions which have a "realistic" basis have a chance of being fulfilled where men's lives, interests, and enemies are concerned. Machiavelli cites in this connection Cosimo De' Medici, who knew that one cannot rule a state with Pater Nosters. Any man, but especially a prince, who takes his bearings by considerations of moral perfection and plays the part of a good man in all things, might gain the love of his subjects and fellow men. But in this he will be deceived and through this error ruined. "[For] men have less scruple in offending one who makes himself loved than one who makes himself feared," and from this will to offend comes ruin.[7]

Classical political philosophy, therefore, which claimed to benefit mankind by its guidance, but which derived the source of its guidance from "unreal" or imaginary perfection, is inherently defective. It is at best useless and at worst cruel. It is cruel because pursuit of its prescription leads to ruin, not to benefit; it is useless because it is vain to expect superhuman virtue from less than superhuman beings. "For how we live is so far removed from how we ought to live, that he who abandons what is done for what ought to be done, will rather learn to bring about his ruin than his preservation. A man who wishes to make a profession of goodness in everything must necessarily come to grief among so many who are not good." [8]

Machiavelli thus turns from the "images" of traditional political philosophy to find a new foundation: ". . . since it is my intention to write useful things for those who understand, it appears to me more fitting to go back to the effectual truth of the thing than to imagination about it." [9] The effectual truth—the new "realistic" guide for political philosophy and political life—is to be found in what men do rather than in what they ought to do. It appears, however, that this (and Bacon's) statement of the new principle, though it is "presumptuous," is also very cautious. It does not indicate precisely Machiavelli's intention. Machiavelli does not merely teach what men "do." Indeed, as much as the traditional political writers before him, he speaks of the things men do only to provide an opportunity to reason about them— to show that what they did was or was not what they ought to have done. At the same time, however, it is certainly true that the range of things "done" that Machiavelli sees fit to report and analyze is more extensive than the range of the political writers before him. Machiavelli speaks openly where there was silence before, and it is from this fact that the precise significance of his intention emerges. The fabric of human doings is great and various. Machiavelli speaks everywhere of the mistakes and errors men have made; he is forever telling princes and republics what they "ought to do." The *Discourses* especially, but also the *Prince,* are set in motion by Machiavelli's reflection that there is something wrong with what his contemporaries do: these works thus appear as attempts to teach them what they "ought to do." [10]

In order to resolve this difficulty, we make the following suggestion. In claiming to base his political teaching on what men do rather than what they ought to do, Machiavelli was partially obscuring the true basis of that teaching. His explicit statement is a bold confrontation of the previous tradition. Still, it is only an abbreviated and "respectable" version of that which, fully stated, implies a radical reorientation of the entire human horizon.

Machiavelli presented his principles cautiously and obscurely because only such a presentation could secure the support of those who were as concerned as he was with correcting the bad political practice of his day. This bad political practice was due to bad principles of practice or to a bad interpretation of principles. The principles of his time were characterized by the highest standards, by a single and universal "truth" as to how men ought to live, and by a certain contempt for worldly considerations. The political practice founded on those principles was characterized by "great disorder," by "vice," and especially by an absence of the "love of liberty," which absence made "the world weak and gave it over as prey to the wicked."

Machiavelli's purpose is to overcome the contempt for worldly considerations; he desires to restore man to the earth, and the earth to man. He puts forward "what men do" in order to provide an antidote to these excessively uncompromising, rigid, and exalted standards of what men ought to do. His object is also to present to the "young" for imitation the "virtues" of the past in contrast to the "vices" of the present. His purpose thus appears to be to restore to practice its proper flexibility and horizon. Hence his political teaching would appear to seek to restore something of the past which had been lost sight of in his own time. What men did in ancient times is better than what they do in modern times; Machiavelli looks back to ancient times to correct the defects of modern times. Ancient practice, as distinguished from ancient political philosophy, is worthy of imitation. The imitation of ancient practice promises a rekindling of that "love of liberty" which will make the world strong again and take it out of the hands of the wicked. Thus Machiavelli attempts to correct the defective practice of his time by assaulting the principles of his time which made that practice possible or necessary. His assault on those principles takes the form of an affirmation that "human conditions" require greater latitude and flexibility than exalted standards permit. He appealed to the things men actually "do," and in particular to the things worthy of imitation "done" by ancient men. By thus appearing to correct defective modern principles by restoring consideration of ancient practice, he obscured his own innovation. His own innovation consisted in the fact that by setting up ancient practice for imitation, he was making ancient practice not only something from which to learn what men "do," but the new basis for what men ought to do.[11]

Now we may see the sense in which Machiavelli's "new foundation" is a transformation as well as a break with the political philosophy of Plato and Aristotle. According to this view, the only true standard for what men ought to do is the praiseworthy and the good. According to Machiavelli, "I know that everyone will [confess] that it would be

[most] praiseworthy . . . to possess all the . . . qualities that are [held] to be good, but . . . they cannot all be possessed or entirely observed, for human conditions [do] not [permit] it. . . ." [12] Men cannot be held accountable for always doing the praiseworthy and good things.

Now the tradition certainly was aware, as Machiavelli knew, that men and states sometimes must pursue courses which, while not praiseworthy, are still necessary and even "just." The tradition was aware of the problematic character of the "praiseworthy." But it had not directed its primary attention to this problem. The difficulty in the maxim that one must always choose the praiseworthy course may be seen as follows. First of all, there are various and even conflicting opinions about what the praiseworthy is. The praiseworthy appears first as a function or reflection of what men actually praise, but different men and different states praise different, even contradictory things. The requirement to follow the line of praise might lead to the requirement to follow contradictory courses.

Secondly, the same men, or the same states, praise on some occasions and at some times what they blame on other occasions and at other times. Some things which are praised in time of peace are blamed in time of war, and contrariwise. Neither classical political philosophy nor Machiavelli can leave it at the fact that what is praiseworthy appears first as that which is actually praised. However, although both the tradition and Machiavelli admit that there is a crucial difference between what is praised and what is praiseworthy, they draw different conclusions from the admission.

Praise is appropriate to the things thought to be good; and in different circumstances, different things appear to be good. Therefore, most generally stated, the relativity of praise may be said to be due to the fact that men have different and even conflicting opinions about what the good is. They praise those things which support, secure, or otherwise agree with what they regard as good. In particular, they praise those moral and political actions and those political arrangements and institutions which make possible, support, or secure the way of life which they regard as good. The variety of political institutions or arrangements is due then fundamentally to the variety of opinions about the good life. Each kind of political arrangement or each institution embodies a different opinion or image of the good life. The question naturally arises, which of these many opinions is the best one. Which way of life is the good life—and consequently, which regime or constitution is the best? This question, the essential one for classical political philosophy, was answered with the "utopian" and "imaginary" principalities and republics which Machiavelli rejected. The thought may be unfolded as follows. Aristotle, for example, in the *Politics,* said that in order "rightly" to investigate the best form of constitution, it is necessary first to say what is the best or most desirable way of life. According to classical political philosophy, the life which most fully and most perfectly consummated the highest human possibilities—the best life—was the philosophic or contemplative life: the way of life devoted to the "disinterested" quest for truth. Consequently, this view of the best life determined in the last resort the view as to what was the best constitution. The best constitutions were those patterned after the philosophic life; they were the "images" or reflections of philosophy.

By means of such an analysis, classical political philosophy was enabled to account for and to clarify the antagonistic claims to authority and rule which were raised within political communities. The conflict of rival claims was understood to result from the variety of partial, incomplete, or qualified versions of the best life. Each of these partial views had some hold of the truth, but each of them was related to the truth as opinion is to knowledge. The only unqualified claim was the one which took the measure of the highest in man's nature.

Since, however, cities or states, no matter what their constitution, do not philosophize, the analysis of classical political philosophy resulted in the conclusion that political institutions and arrangements were good to the extent that they were patterned after trans- or superpolitical ends. The solution to the political problem of the best regime was not to be solved on the political level. This palpable disproportion resulted in the articulation, by classical political philosophy, of a variety of "good," "legitimate," and "just" regimes, each with its own characteristic and determinative opinion of the best way of life, but each different from the truly best. Thus the rule of gentlemen was a legitimate substitute for the rule of philosophers, and thus the rule of the "old" was a legitimate substitute for the rule of the "wise." The nerve of the classical teaching, however, remained intact. Every constitution or political institution which was merely "good" or "legitimate" was so because of a certain approximation to what was simply best. The second-best arrangements were directed to, supported, or made possible the best. Thus classical political philosophy could recognize a hierarchy of various regimes, political institutions, or opinions of the good life. The ordering principle of this hierarchy was affinity to what was best. The lower members of the hierarchy were understood to be defective but tolerable approximations to the best. In this manner, the transpolitical, "utopian" standard of excellence, while not universally applicable in "actuality," provided the means of judging "actuality," the

goal of endeavor, and the image of human perfection which was universal and final. Because the various approximate opinions of the best
life and the best regime looked forward to the truly best, the truly best
cast its image backward: the highest in man was to provide the rule
and the measure. The philosophic life was the all-permeating principle
in whose terms "the political things" were to be understood.[13]

Thus, to return, when Machiavelli asserts that he has broken "in
the greatest degree" with the orders of those who preceded him, he is
asserting his break with that tradition which wanted to understand and
to direct the orientation of political things in light of the highest human
possibility. In turning the attention of men from what they "ought to
do" to what they "do," he perforce turned their attention from the
"ought" of classical political philosophy to the "ought" of his "effectual
truth." In this sense, Machiavelli's break with the tradition consists of
preparing a new image of man, a new articulation of the best way of
life, and consequently the "new orders and modes" in which to reformulate "things of the world."

This epoch-making revolution of thought appears at first as an
attempt to liberate the political and moral practices of his time from the
dominating political theology which claimed to be *the* single truth
which was universally applicable and which was to be universally applied. This liberation proceeded by attempting to restore the moral
basis of the legitimacy of a variety of political regimes, institutions, and
actions. Machiavelli wished to restore the order of the conventional to
its own. We have seen that classical political philosophy had provided
for this conventional realm, but it had also redeemed it by taking its
ultimate bearings by what was naturally best. What was by nature best
redeemed what was by convention legitimate. Classical political philosophy wanted to provide political life with an orientation by the naturally highest human possibility because it wanted to draw political life
upward. By setting so high a standard, it wished to provide for the
greatest possible upward reach. But it recognized that the highest or
the best could come to be only by the extremely improbable, if not
impossible, coming together of an untold number of favorable circumstances. This is an additional reason why it articulated a variety of "less
than best" regimes which were all variously "good" or "legitimate."
It was willing to show what is best, but only to hope for its materiali-
zation. By seeing what was highest, men might live as "high" as nature
and chance enabled them to do. Without seeing the highest, their reach
would inevitably be shortened.

Against the view that a higher aim, even if not attained, will raise the level of the result, Machiavelli had two objections. One he drew from the specific problem of his time; the other, the cause of his first objection, was based on his view of human nature.

As to the objection which arose out of considerations of the specific problem of his time, Machiavelli's argument may be outlined as follows. Classical political philosophy had been part of the patrimony inherited and appropriated from Greece and Rome by the Christian Church Fathers.[14] The fathers and those who followed them attempted a fusion of the political and moral teachings of pagan antiquity and biblical revelation. With respect to the decisive principle of classical political philosophy, they were not faced with an insurmountable obstacle. For the classical tradition had taught that the life of human beings in community—political life—must ultimately be oriented toward and guided by a transpolitical standard. The classics had found this standard in the philosophic or contemplative life—a "life more than human and almost divine." The Church Fathers, on the basis of biblical revelation, raised this standard and end of human terrestrial existence to the otherworldly goal of salvation and beatitude. The life of man in this world is redeemed by the life in the next world.

The transpolitical standard of the classics was determined by unassisted human reason. But whereas this standard, though universal in validity, admitted a certain legitimate and reasonable relativity in application, the transpolitical guide derived from biblical revelation presupposed and required the absolutization of all moral principles. The classics had derived the transcendent standard from considerations of the nature of man. The standard due to revelation required consideration of the "transnatural" or created man. Thus, for the classics, human action can be judged "legitimate" as approaching perfection—as having degrees of acceptability. But according to the absolutized standard of revelation, human action cannot ultimately be judged as having relative goodness since the consequence—salvation or its opposite—does not ultimately admit of relative degrees of attainment. Another way of stating this is that while the original classical tradition taught natural right, i.e., a "rightness" or standard that existed by nature, it did not teach natural law. Thus, while piety and impiety were topics for classical political thinkers, heresy was not. Biblical revelation claims to be the one universal truth applicable to men of all nations and men of all natures. All other religions are false: they have no "legitimacy," for there is no degree of salvation through them. The rational variety of legitimate regimes of classical political philosophy became ultimately assimilated into the one city of God.

According to Machiavelli, this combination of universal, absolutized moral demands with their final sanction in the next world, instead of making man as good as possible by having the goal at the highest, have resulted in the utmost disorder and ruin. As to the disorders resulting from the absolute and universalist quality of these standards, we may indicate Machiavelli's view as follows. Since there is only one true city or rather religion, then all who live outside of it live lives of deprivation. There can be no merely natural boundary to the Church's realm. All men may—indeed, since salvation cannot be due to any other religion, considerations of benevolence would seem to require that all men *must*—become citizens of the one true regime. Whether Machiavelli was correct in his view or not, the catholic claim of the Church, as opposed to the particularist political or civil religions of classical antiquity, seems to imply at very least a universal brotherhood of man independent of any political, natural, or racial boundary. Such a brotherhood promises "on earth peace, good will toward men." [15] Now according to Machiavelli, the actualization of such a brotherhood required, in its beginning, great destruction: "obliteration of all orders and all rites of the gentiles and destruction of all records of the ancient theology." Actualization of this realm requires the "persecution" of men as well as things, for since its purpose is to make in these respects "everything new," it must destroy the cause of the "happiness," "greatness," and "goodness" in ancient cities, and thus reduce their citizens to "despair." [16]

Such comprehensive transformations are alluded to by Machiavelli when he speaks of the new King David, "who heaped riches upon the needy and dismissed the wealthy empty-handed." Discussed in the same context is Philip of Macedon who "transferred inhabitants from one province to the other, as shepherds move their flocks from place to place" and "left nothing unchanged . . . so that there should be neither rank, nor orders, nor estate, nor wealth that should not be recognized as coming from him." Such ways are "most cruel." They are "enemies to a Christian and even to a human way of life." [17] What Machiavelli means to say is that such ways are unchristian because they contradict the Christian premises—benevolence, love, and peace—which set them in motion. However this may be, the universalist requirements of the Christian faith generated, not only in the beginning but in Machiavelli's times as well, great abuses. One example must suffice. Machiavelli speaks in the *Prince* of a "certain prince of the present time . . . who never does anything but preach peace and . . . faith but [who] is . . . a great enemy to both, and either of them, had he observed them, would have lost him state or reputation on many occasions." He speaks later of such a prince as one who "has become for fame and glory the first

king [of the Christians]. . . . With the money of the church . . . and
always under the pretext of religion, [Ferdinand of Aragon] had recourse to pious cruelty, driving out the Moors from his kingdom and
despoiling them. No more miserable or [rare] example can be [given].
He also attacked Africa under the same pretext. . . ." [18]

Machiavelli's analysis of the effect of Christian otherworldly sanctions takes as its point of departure what he regards as the center of that
teaching. According to Machiavelli, the support for the otherworldly
moral and political demands, with their sanction in the heavenly fatherland, is to be found in the principle that "it is evil to speak evil of the
evil." Machiavelli thus paraphrases that consummate statement of
otherworldly righteousness, from the Sermon on the Mount: ". . . resist not evil; but whosoever shall smite thee on thy right cheek, turn to
him the other also." Machiavelli's conclusion is that if the punishment
of the wicked is left to God, as the principle of not speaking evil of the
evil requires, then "the evil will do as much evil as they can, for they
do not fear a punishment which they do not see and in which they
do not believe." [19]

Furthermore, reliance upon and dedication to the heavenly fatherland renders one less concerned about one's life in the political communities of this world. It makes one care less about the good life possible
here and now. In particular, to live in obedience to rules of eternity
makes one uninterested in the political liberty of one's community for
the span of one's life on earth. Thus, according to Machiavelli, "as our
religion teaches us the truth, and the true way of life, it causes us to
attach less value to the honors and possessions of [the] world; whilst
the Pagans, esteeming those things as the highest good, were more energetic and ferocious in their actions. . . . Besides this, the Pagan religion
[beatified] only men who had achieved great glory, such as commanders of armies and chiefs of republics, whilst ours glorifies more the
humble and contemplative men than the men of action. Our religion,
moreover, places the supreme happiness in humility, [lowness] and a
contempt for [human things], while the other, on the contrary, places
the supreme good in [greatness] of [spirit], strength of body, and all
such other qualities as render men formidable; and if our religion
claims of us fortitude . . . , it is more to enable us to suffer than to
achieve great deeds. [This way of life, then,] seems to have made men
feeble and caused them to become . . . prey to [the wicked], who can
control them more securely, seeing that the [generality] of men, for
the sake of gaining Paradise, are more disposed to endure injuries than
to avenge them." [20] Thus again, life is not improved when men set for
themselves the highest standards. The consequence was that the "world

had become effeminate," incapable of political liberty and fit for servitude to tyrants. Accordingly, Machiavelli suggests that this was the reason there were fewer republics in his time as compared with ancient times. Those like Savonarola who said that the ease with which France overran Italy was due to the "sins" of the Italians "spoke the truth— but they were not the sins they believed," but rather those which Machiavelli related, *i.e.,* the "sins" of military weakness.[21]

In those communities which had somehow, miraculously, escaped servitude, there were divisions of a most disordering and enfeebling kind. Italy itself was "divided, overrun and insulted." Since the beginning of the sway of the Church in Italy, foreigners and barbarians had not only invaded the land, but had actually been invited by princes and republics no longer capable of waging their own battles. The vicars of the Church did not understand the art of war, for religion is the "art of peace." They had recourse, therefore, to foreign mercenary troops as buttresses to their temporal policies. Those rulers who resisted the temporal encroachments of the Church added to the disorders by similar practices. For, wishing to have troops upon whom they could rely when contending with the temporal forces of the Church, princes and republics would hire the Turks or other infidels, and thus could rely upon soldiers who had no fear of the Church's spiritual arm, *i.e.,* of excommunication. Foreign mercenary troops, as Machiavelli points out in the *Prince,* have no fear of God. Hence the ultimate cause of the division and disorder of the Italian cities and of Italy itself was the division produced in the minds of men by the conflicting demands of the otherworldly and worldly fatherlands. Allegiance to the heavenly fatherland made men weak, *i.e.,* not reliable as defenders of the terrestrial fatherland. For it made them subject to those foreign temporal powers which also controlled or pretended to control the way to the heavenly fatherland. Yearning for a home in the afterlife made men homeless on earth.

Machiavelli indicates that the Church, in temporal matters and as a matter of temporal policy, wished to keep Italy and Italian cities divided: "For having acquired and holding temporal dominion, yet she has never had sufficient power or [virtue] to enable her to seize the [tyranny of Italy and to make herself prince]. And, on the other hand, she has not been so feeble that the fear of losing her [dominion in temporal things] prevented her from calling in the aid of a foreign power to defend her against such others who had become too powerful in Italy."[22] But these temporal divisions and this weakness in Italian states only reflected the divisions fostered by the Church in men's minds. Thus the temporal policy of the Church, which kept

Italy weak, reflected its spiritual policy, which made its citizens weak. For if men had not become more disposed to suffer great things than to do great things, they would have shown how "little they are respected who live and rule as the prelates do . . ." and would not have allowed themselves to become "indebted to the Church and the priests for becoming irreligious and wicked." [23]

As it is, however, the subjects of the Church do not complain, and the princes of the Church "are kept in power, no matter which way they act and live." For entrance to the heavenly fatherland may be obtained only through the "ancient orders of the religion," [24] and the Church is the guardian of these ancient orders. Thus hope for the gain and fear for the loss of the heavenly fatherland give the ministers of the Church that spiritual dominion which they have "misused" in attempting to acquire the temporal ascendancy.

Machiavelli regarded this problem of the Christian cities of his time as a specific historical example of the general tendency of states to "change from a condition of order to one of disorder, and from disorder to order again . . . for virtue brings peace, and peace brings idleness, and idleness disorder, and from disorder comes ruin; and in like manner from ruin springs order, and from order virtue, and from that glory and good fortune." Machiavelli asserts that such causes made Italy by turns happy and wretched, "first under the ancient Tuscans, and afterwards under the Romans. . . ." [25] But since the ruin of Rome, nothing has arisen to redeem Rome's former greatness. One is compelled to wonder why this is so. Machiavelli indicated that the course of these changes from order to disorder is due to the natural impossibility that anything terrestrial remain in a state of changeless perfection or imperfection. The best can only decline; but when the worst state is reached, ascent must begin again. [26] But ancient Rome is destroyed, yet nothing has replaced her. Machiavelli indicates that the recovery from a ruined condition takes place unless it is prevented by some extraordinary force. One is compelled to wonder what extraordinary force prevented the attainment of former pagan greatness.

Machiavelli's answer has already been indicated. He presents it again in the *Florentine Histories*. "Literature follows arms, and in cities and provinces leaders of armies precede philosophers . . . nor can idleness enter any well-regulated community under a greater or more dangerous guise." Ancient Rome's martial virtue declined and idleness took its place. The authoritative element of Roman life turned its attention from the rigors of war to the blandishments of peace. Thus, in Roman youth, the love of war was replaced by the love of wisdom. It was in this way that Machiavelli understood Cato to have understood the danger to Rome. Cato, that consummate spokesman for pagan practice as opposed to pagan philosophy, seeing the Roman youth following the Greek philosophers Diogenes and Carneades with admiration, and "knowing the evil that would result to the country from this excusable idleness, ordered that henceforth no philosopher should be received in Rome." In Rome, the "idleness" that enabled philosophy to flourish was also the source of Roman decay. The Christian provinces and cities of Italy could not recover Rome's former greatness because the "ambitious idleness" of religion had substituted for the otherworldliness of philosophy in pagan times a new kind of "philosophy"—that of the heavenly fatherland. Thus "ambitious idleness" and "disarmed heaven" produced the "extraordinary force" which prevented the return from the disorder of Machiavelli's time to the virtue of the past.[27] For men thought more of the paradise which could only be obtained by the arts of peace than of the liberty which could only be obtained by the arts of war; and they never thought of imitating those ancient examples of virtue "which they judge to be not only difficult but impossible of imitation: as if the heaven, the sun, the elements and men had changed motion, their order and their power from what they were anciently." [28]

Machiavelli might be said to have provided much evidence for the view that he was opposed only to the corrupted Church, or to the corrupted interpretation of the Christian religion. That Machiavelli was opposed to the "corruption" and "wicked examples" of the "Court of Rome" requires no elaborate affirmation. One of the most shocking statements in this regard is in the chapter of the *Discourses* entitled, "Men are very rarely entirely good or entirely bad." Here Machiavelli shows how the evil "[Giovampagolo] Baglioni, who did not mind open incest and parricide . . . knew not how, or [better did not dare,] to rid himself of his enemy, [Pope Julius II] . . . an act for which everyone would have admired his courage, and which would have secured for him eternal fame as being the first to show these prelates how little esteem those merit who live and govern as they do; and as having done an act the greatness of which would have overshadowed [every] infamy and [every peril that might have resulted] from it." [29] Machiavelli contends that "if the princes of the Christian republic had maintained that religion in accordance with the orders of its founder, the Christian states and republics would have been much more united and happy than they are." As it is, through "the evil examples of the Court of Rome [Italy] has lost all devotion and all religion." [30]

Machiavelli certainly was opposed to the Church as it had become. But the full nature of his opposition does not become clear until one raises the question of whether Machiavelli regarded the "corruption" of the Church, and the corruption which the Church caused, as inevitable results of its doctrine. If this were his view, then any opposition to the "evils" resulting from the "corrupt" Church would also be opposition to the cause of these "corruptions"—the very foundation of the doctrine of the Church.

The authority of the Church rests upon the Bible, and the authority of the Bible rests upon its claim to be divinely revealed. The ultimate basis, therefore, of the Church's authority is beyond or above reason. Unaided human reason would thus seem to be incapable of examining the credentials and the institutions of ecclesiastical dominion. Machiavelli points to the problem in the *Prince,* when discussing the founders of new principalities. Moses is mentioned together with Cyrus, Romulus, and Theseus as being among the most excellent of those princes who have acquired principalities through their own virtues. "And although of Moses one ought not reason, he being a mere executor of things ordered by God, yet he ought to be marvelled at [if] only for that grace which made him worthy to speak with God." Moses (and thus the Bible) is set apart; one may not reason about him. But Machiavelli immediately qualifies his restraint. For, he says, if the other founders are considered, they will all be found "marvelous," and their actions and orders will not appear different from those of Moses who had so great a teacher. Unaided reason is not able to distinguish the life, actions, and orders of the biblical founder from those of the nonbiblical founders.[31]

Thus, "he who reads the Bible with discernment will see that Moses was compelled, in order to ensure that his laws and his orders were observed, to kill innumerable men who were moved solely by jealousy to oppose his designs." [32] If the Bible is read with discernment, Moses has not more "grace" and is not more "marvelous" than any other great ruler. Machiavelli says he "will never judge it to be a defect to defend any opinion with reasons without use of force or authority." [33] By reason alone, he cannot discern a reason for assigning Moses a higher place—a place beyond or above reason. The life and actions of the biblical Moses may be understood by anyone who understands political things in purely political terms, *i.e.,* in the same way as one would be compelled to understand nonbiblical figures. The Bible, which claims to be divinely revealed, reveals itself, in certain fundamental aspects, to a purely political analysis. It is in this way that Machiavelli suggests that the authority of the Church, which founds itself on the authority of the Bible, is also to be understood. The Church is a political phenomenon which must be understood in political terms. Its claim to be derived from super-rational sources, in so far as that claim rests upon the revealed character of Scripture, is not supported by a "discerning" examination of the Bible. One needs nothing more to understand the Bible than one needs to understand Livy's history of Rome.

Machiavelli has suggested in various places that other biblical characters also can and must be understood in purely political terms— by unaided human reason. He speaks of or alludes to David, Joshua, Solomon, Rehoboam, and others. Like that of Dante, however, his account of these matters is somewhat obscured by the fact that he intermixes mythical and biblical personages and events. In any case, he again asserts the super-rational character of Christian institutions in Chapter xi of the *Prince*. "But since [these principalities] are set up by superior causes, to which the human mind cannot reach, I will omit speaking of them; because, being exalted and maintained by God, it would be the part of a presumptuous and temerarious man to discourse upon them. Nonetheless. . . ." [34] This "nonetheless"—which substantially appeared in the discussion of Moses, who may not be reasoned about, but who "nonetheless" may be reasoned about—appears again. When speaking of ecclesiastical principalities, however, Machiavelli does not go forward from the "nonetheless" with the same kind of reflection that he had employed in speaking of Moses. Ecclesiastical principalities are not coordinate with other, secular principalities; they are unique. Here, the "nonetheless" is followed by a discussion of the growth of the temporal power of the Church. This subject does not reveal Machiavelli's attitude toward the fundamental problem of Christianity; however, it suggests that attitude. For the temporal powers of the Church were acquired, according to this discussion, not by poverty and humility but by money and force, *i.e.,* by unchristian means. The more revealing consideration and the one which requires, according to Machiavelli, a strict political analysis, would not be how the Church acquired its temporal powers by means of money and force, but how it acquired its money and force.

The authority of the Church is "sustained by higher causes," namely, the claim of access to a divine revelation of truths which unaided human reason is unable to discover. But according to Machiavelli, unaided human reason cannot discern the difference between the life and actions of a prince whose authority derives from divine revelation and a prince whose authority derives from no such source. In particular, unaided human reason is not able to distinguish between biblical and pagan claims to divine revelation. Thus, in the eyes of reason, biblical and pagan revelation are equally entitled or not entitled to authority. "For whoever considers Roman histories well, will see how greatly religion served to command the armies, animate the plebs, keep men good, and shame the wicked . . . and though Romulus could organize the Senate and establish other civil and military orders without the authority of God; yet it was very necessary for Numa, who pretended he held converse with a nymph who counseled him about the counsel he should give to the people. All this came about because he wished to introduce new and unaccustomed orders in that city, and he doubted that his own authority was sufficient. In truth, there never was one who ordered extra-ordinary laws for a people who did not have recourse to God, as otherwise they would not have been accepted. For there are many good things which are well known to the prudent, but have not in themselves reasons evident enough to enable the prudent to persuade others; and therefore wise men, wishing to remove this difficulty, resort to God. Thus did Lycurgus and Solon and many others who have had the same end as they did." [35]

It was for such reasons that Machiavelli rejected the principles of ecclesiastical polities of his time. We have already said that these principles were based in part on a fusion or assimilation of the political philosophy of classical antiquity and the Bible. Machiavelli's rejection of these principles is related to his rejection of classical political philosophy, and is based upon a view of political life which precludes its being guided by any transcendent standards.


According to Machiavelli, in order to understand the ultimate basis of political life (and thus to understand the disproportion between transcendent standards and political life), one must examine the beginnings of political life. Machiavelli's political teaching, particularly in the *Prince,* centers on an articulation of the beginnings. The *Prince* attempts to lay bare and to analyze the beginnings of states by analyzing their beginners or founders.[36] For the new prince, Machiavelli thus puts forward those points of view, or those elements or parts of political life, which are most revealing for an understanding of all of political life. For, according to Machiavelli, the most revealing and relevant political actions are those by which authority is established and states are founded. Accordingly, the *Prince* treats of political life as a whole by treating of its most decisive and determinative part. It tries to understand political life from the point of view of its rulers and founders, from the point of view of a prince and princely acts. But the ways and means by which principalities are gained and preserved differ. There is a hierarchy of ways and means, and to this hierarchy corresponds a hierarchy of princes. Thus, although the *Prince* as a whole is about a kind of man and activity, it has a fundamental and architectonic part which treats of the most fundamental and architectonic kind of prince. Machiavelli therefore returns to the beginnings in more than a single way. His concern with the beginnings leads him to analyze not only the founders and princes but also, so to speak, what is before the beginnings—the fundamental and decisive elements which especially characterize and determine the acts of princes. He is concerned to understand authority, hereditary and new; the use of force and arms; the relationship between fortune and virtue.

According to Machiavelli, situations other than the founding ones and men other than princes are only "imitations" of founding situations and of princes: they reflect the origins and the originators. "Let no one marvel, if in speaking of completely new princes and principalities, I bring forth the greatest examples. Because men walk almost always in paths beaten by others and follow by imitation their deeds . . . ." [37] Since, then, Machiavelli is concerned with the most architectonic, or most comprehensive and revealing, political acts, the main emphasis of the book is upon the foundation of a completely new principality by a completely new prince. It is this kind of prince who introduces or imposes "new orders and modes," or, as we may say, a completely new way of political life, in order to make a new state. All other political forms are derivative from the one in which there is an imposition of "new orders and modes." All mixed states are combined from unmixed elements which presuppose the same kind of original founding; all old states were once new and once required the imposition of new orders and modes; all hereditary authority presupposes the establishment of that authority; all old political orders and modes presuppose a beginning and a founding. The study and understanding of this kind of prince or founder and this kind of political situation, then, engenders an understanding of all political situations.

These features again indicate the divergence of Machiavelli's teaching from that of the classical tradition. Whereas the tradition taught that the crucial political considerations must ultimately be seen in light of the "end," for man and for society, Machiavelli wishes to understand all political things in light of the "beginning." For the classics it was the end that made everything intelligible; for Machiavelli it is the beginning. Machiavelli's "highest" type of prince is the beginning of the beginning—that which everything somehow imitates. For the classics, everything somehow reflects the end. Another point might be mentioned which is related to the above. For classical political philosophy, the primary task was an elaboration of the character of the various regimes. Machiavelli's teaching, however, centers on the character of the imposition of new modes and orders by which regimes come to be, or

rather about the very fact of the imposition. "The [principal] foundations of all states, whether new, old or mixed, are good laws and good
arms. And as there cannot be good laws where there are not good
arms, and where there are good arms there must be good laws, I will
not discuss the laws, but will speak of the arms."[38] Thus law appears
here as a secondary consideration with respect to arms. Lawfulness, we
might say, is secondary to force. Machiavelli revises this unrestrained
provisional statement, but the crucial emphasis is never replaced. We
must explain later, in another context, the meaning of this emphasis as
it applies to Machiavelli's understanding of the composite character of
man's nature. We may say here that this de-emphasis of the lawful,
and what it might be said to imply, is in part responsible for the fact
that Machiavelli nowhere in the *Prince* draws a distinction between a
prince and a tyrant. The word tyrant itself does not appear in that
work. Justice, as the root idea which allows and compels a distinction
between laws "imposed" by a tyrant and laws "imposed" by a prince,
does not appear among the "qualities" in Chapter xv of the *Prince* for
which a prince is praised or blamed. The statement prefatory to the
enumeration of these qualities is: "Leaving aside, then, those things
which concern only an imaginary prince, and speaking of those that
are real. . . ." To conclude this point, the central importance of "imposition" in the founding of new orders and modes, as contrasted with
the character of the new orders and modes, is indicated by Machiavelli
when he speaks of "examples" of most excellent princes: "It will not
be seen that they received anything from fortune but the occasion,
which gave them matter upon which to introduce whatever form they
thought fit."[39]

Examples of such princes and founders in the *Prince* are Moses,
Cyrus, Romulus, and Theseus. Each of these princes exercised the greatest human virtues in order to introduce new orders and modes and to
found new states. Their founding acts, being great benefactions to their
people and fatherlands, have gained them praise and glory that is
second only to that exaltation given to "those who have been gods."[40]
But it is precisely here, with the greatest possible examples and where
greatest praise and glory have been bestowed, that the character of
political life reveals itself most clearly. For Romulus "killed his own
brother, and consented to the death of Titus Tatius, whom he had
chosen as colleague in the kingdom, . . . in order to concentrate all
authority in himself."[41] The wedge of Machiavelli's analysis of political matters enters here.

Political society lives by its praise of the good, the virtuous, and the
just; yet at certain crucial moments these considerations are put aside.

"Everyone will confess that it is most praiseworthy" for a prince to do
every good and avoid every evil, but "human conditions" do not permit it. The foundation of a political society is one of these "human conditions"; for in founding a new state, "a new prince has enemies in all
those who profit by the old order." Thus, by this "natural and ordinary
necessity," "the new prince is compelled to offend with soldiers and innumerable other injuries those over whom he gains dominion; [for] it
is easy to persuade [people to do something], but [hard] to keep them
in that persuasion. And so it is necessary to order things so that when
they no longer believe, they can be made to believe by force. . . . Thus
it comes about that all armed prophets have conquered and unarmed
ones have failed." The founding of Rome's "civil and free life" required that Romulus have the sole authority. But he could gain that
sole authority only by extraordinary measures, *i.e.,* fratricide and
treachery. The good he did, the benefits he bestowed, "excuse" the evils
he did—"for no wise man will ever censure anyone for having used
any extraordinary [action in] establishing a kingdom or constituting a
republic." Romulus acted for the "common good" and for the "fatherland" and not for himself or for his heirs; but his great contributions
to the common good were inseparable from great evils: on great occasions and for great goods, the greatest men must do great evils. Machiavelli thus seems to contend that the "beginning" or the founding
of society justifies actions which can never be justified after it has been
established if that society is to "live well." The "beginner" or founder
of society must be excused for acts which can never be excused in
princes who rule in ordinary times and after the state has been established. Machiavelli recommends to new princes in new states that they
not try to imitate the actions of Marcus Aurelius, the emperor-philoso-
pher who became the ruler by hereditary right, and who was less
obliged to do injury and take other strong measures to secure his dominion. Hereditary princes of this kind are better loved and more
secure, since the dominion is old and has become customary and the
people have forgotten the injuries which were necessary in the beginning. But the new prince, on the contrary, ought to imitate the actions
of Septimius Severus, the emperor who was so far from being a philosopher that he was "a very fierce lion and a very crafty fox." The
moral order of political society owes everything to its foundation. But the
foundation of society is necessarily connected with evil; the morality
based upon the common good necessarily rests upon an immoral foundation which has been "forgotten" by those who admire the result, but
condemn its principal cause.[42]

Thus Machiavelli's analysis of the founders and the foundation of

political society reveals that neither the "absolute" principles of the
Bible nor the "transcendent standards" of classical political philosophy
are adequate guides to political life. For principles of morality cannot
be "absolute" if there must be right, just, or good abrogations of these
"absolutes" upon certain definite, if rare, occasions. Nor can the "highest standards" be the guides if the true character of political society
more often requires the virtues of Severus than those of Marcus, the philosopher. For the virtues of Severus, so far from reminding of the
life "more than human and almost divine," cause us to remember the
ways of the fox and the lion, *i.e.,* the life less than human and almost
bestial. It is by such thoughts that Machiavelli draws our attention to
his view that "there are two [ways] of fighting, the one by law, the
other by force: the first [way] is [proper to] men, the second [to] beasts;
but as the first [way] is often insufficient, one must have recourse to the
second. It is therefore necessary for a prince to know well how to use
. . . the beast and the man." [43]

At first sight, it would appear that "transcendent" and "absolute"
standards are inadequate to provide for the common good at the
foundation of political society, and they are therefore abandoned. The
common good, at least at the beginning of society, is the substitute for
all transpolitical standards, and all human virtue and excellence would
have to be seen in terms of the requirements of the common good. The
common good could not be more ultimately judged against the pattern
of some transcendent excellence.

The common good makes cruel and terrible demands, which can
be met in the beginning only by cruel and terrible men. The immorality
required for the foundation of society, however, is shown by Machiavelli's analysis of well-established societies to be unexpectedly wide in
scope. For extraordinary measures may be required not only at the
absolute beginning of the state, but from time to time, for example,
whenever dangers from wars or civil upheavals threaten. In such times,
there also are circumstances that hark back to the beginnings—to the
possibility that greater and more terrible evils will result if lesser evils are
not committed. Thus Manlius Torquatus, who commanded a Roman
army in "the most important" battle fought by Rome with any other
nation, ". . . killed his own son to secure the obedience of his troops."
Thus Brutus, who regained for Rome her liberty, not only condemned
his sons to death, but was present at their execution. Had he not given
this "rare" example of severity, his act of benefaction to Rome would
not have lasted long, and Rome would again have succumbed to tyranny.
For the ambition of his sons was such that their desire to lord it over
others could only be fulfilled by the slavery of the people, "for the freedom of the people appeared to have become but servitude to them."

Brutus was able to resecure Rome's liberty by deception. He "played the fool" to avoid destruction at the hands of the tyrant and awaited an opportunity favorable to his designs. In times of unusual danger, wise and public-spirited men resort to deceptions such as Brutus used. But also, in times which do not seem dangerous to most men, and which therefore seem less in need of extraordinary means, it might be the part of wisdom and public-spirited service to the common good to resort to extraordinary means and to invent the justification for doing so. "For there are many good things . . . seen by the wise," but not seen by others. Machiavelli gives an example of abstinence from strong measures which resulted in ruinous disorders: Piero Soderini, whose office in the Florentine republic gave him the opportunity to assume extraordinary authority, in order to be beforehand with those who would rule that city as tyrants, refused to take those extraordinary measures. For, though the ambitions of "those who were opposed to him gave him opportunity to destroy them . . . yet he believed that he could extinguish their malevolence by patience and goodness and put an end to their hostility by distributing some gifts. . . . What he did not know was that goodness alone does not suffice . . . and that malice cannot be placated by gifts." Thus, because Soderini had not imitated Brutus, he lost his position and Florence lost her freedom. "For one should never allow an evil to run on out of respect for good, when that good might easily be destroyed by that evil." [44]

Thus, by slow steps, Machiavelli's analysis proceeds to show that even less extreme and rare situations may sometimes warrant extraordinary measures for the common good. We move from "founding" to "preserving in rare cases," "preserving in more common cases," "preserving by anticipation of dangers." The analysis shows that the ordinary acts of states are similar to the extraordinary, and evoke similar practices. It is here that Machiavelli shows again why he regards the founding situation as most revealing for all political life. Political society as a whole is dominated and characterized by considerations, actions, and requirements which appear only most openly and severely at its beginnings. All of political life is of a piece so far as it is pervaded with the elements of the founding situation—life in political society tends only to obscure and to make less visible the true "human conditions."

Thus the common good must become the standard for political action (and the substitute for transcendent standards), not only because transcendent standards are inadequate at the beginning of political society. The common good must be the only standard throughout all of political life as a whole, for political life as a whole is set in motion by those same "natural necessities" which prohibited consideration of transcendent standards at the foundation. For "men afflict themselves in evil, and become weary of the good, and both these passions produce the same effects. For when men are no longer obliged to fight from necessity, they fight from ambition, which passion is so powerful in the [breasts] of men that it never leaves them, no matter to what height[s] they may rise. The reason [for] this is that nature has created men so that they desire everything, but are unable to attain [everything]; desire being thus always greater than the faculty of acquiring, discontent with what they have and dissatisfaction with themselves result from it. This causes the changes in their fortunes; for as some men desire to have more, whilst others fear to lose what they have, enmities and war are the consequences; and this brings about the ruin of one province and the elevation of another." [45]

Thus it is *nature* itself, according to Machiavelli, which makes it impossible for men to take their bearings by any form of transcendent standards. At the same time, it is nature itself which prevents the common good, as the replacement for transcendent standards, to be rooted in or referable to any natural right which might provide a moral orientation for society. Man is provided by nature "with a desire for everything" but is not provided by nature with a concern, or even a desire, for justice. Man is provided with "a natural or ordinary desire to acquire." He is not provided with a sense of restraint out of regard for the interests of others. "Men will always be wicked"—concerned with the gratification of their own ends—"if they are not *made* good by some necessity."

Part of this necessity is provided by the context of civil society itself. It is provided at its foundation by the new prince, who is compelled by a "natural and ordinary necessity" to hurt those over whom he gains dominion. It is later provided by the severity of laws and other institutions imposed by those founders who, "assuming men to be evil," made their foundations accordingly. And still later, it is provided by a salutary "return to the beginnings," *i.e.,* by a restoration of that atmosphere of terror which made men good at the foundations but has in the course of time lost its effect.

To sum up, then, nature cannot provide a standard of right for recognizing the common good because nature compels the collective self-interest embodied in the common good to conflict with other embodiments of collective self-interest, each with a legitimate claim to be recognized as the common good. Thus a "natural right" guide for the common good might appear in the distinction between a just war and an unjust war. A just war is defensive. Then if it is just to defend oneself, the attacker would be unjust. But the attacker might be a whole people who are faced with starvation and certain death in their own lands. Thus the natural right of preservation would conflict with the natural right of defense; the "natural necessity" to offend is contrary to an act of alleged natural justice: natural necessity denies natural right.

We said in our opening remarks that man was indebted to Machiavelli for modernity. But Machiavelli provided specifically only for the political orientation of modernity; equally massive in its effect and power is modern natural science and technology. We seem to have assumed that everything in modernity, including modern natural science, is due to the epoch-making achievement of Machiavelli. However the political and technological premises of modern life might finally be related, the assumption that they have a common ground is supported by the fact that the self-understanding and therewith the self-esteem of modernity has a well-marked focus. To use the formula of one of the latest of the moderns, modernity regards with pride its unparalleled, unswerving loyalty to the earth and to man. It is "man the measure" and "man the maker" and the earthly as opposed to the heavenly fatherland which command undivided devotion. "Realism" in science and freedom from otherworldly standards in action are the substance and aspiration of the modern soul as it sees itself at its best.

But the introduction of this substance and aspiration was the intention of Machiavelli's political teaching: classical political philosophy had reached too high. By putting man's guides in the heavens, classical political philosophy and the ecclesiastical polity which based itself on that tradition had made men homeless on earth and fully loyal only to the perfection existing in the other world. Machiavelli lowered the mark. He thus enabled man more easily to reach it. By liberating man from considerations of otherworldly perfection, he gave him expanded estimations of his own power as well as enlarged expectations for his own estate. No longer having to look up so high, man acquired a new dignity in his own eyes: he became not only lord of himself and his own destiny in the moral and political sphere, but was now free to become lord of nature itself. Hence Bacon, a father of modern natural science, rightly begins by acknowledging his debt to Machiavelli. By bringing down the "stars of the heavens" and enmeshing them in humanity, the merely human horizon and aspiration became themselves the heights. As transcendent goals for human life are abandoned (on the ground that they make men indifferent to the earth), human life as such is divinized, made into something transcendent; and it is thus that the sciences and the technological arts receive an imperious ordination to gratify a proliferation of human "needs." When human excellence, understood as an approximation or assimilation to nonhuman, nonwilled standards, loses its authority, and even its intelligibility, then what becomes authoritative and even sacred is the human-all-too-human as you find him, as he does, and as he needs: the "ought" is found not in what is looked up to, but on the contrary, everywhere one looks. By turning his back on the "ideal," modern man found comfort in the "real"; he thereafter made that his ideal.

Thus when human dignity is not understood as stemming from and restricted to that in man which is above or more than man, it becomes possible and even necessary to speak of the dignity of almost every human being and every human activity. Thus also we may examine the fate of the term "virtue" or "excellence." According to the classical view, legitimate claims to political power and authority must be based upon some superiority or excellence. In its view, even democracy —the rule of the common people or the poor—must base its claim not on individual poverty and limited wisdom—which are defects[46]—but on a collective wealth and wisdom superior to that claimed by the few rich and wise. But when excellence ceases to be anchored in something transcending mere man, or in the highest in man, then many things may be substituted to serve the function of providing a legitimate basis for political claims, *i.e.,* each of them becomes a kind of surrogate or surreptitious "excellence." So the defect of fear (fear of violent death) becomes in Hobbes the basis for establishing natural and political right and almost the cause of humanity itself. So the defect of pain (the pain of labor) is for Locke the source of natural and political entitlement. In Machiavelli, something of the classical orientation with respect to excellence remains. Machiavelli's rejection of the relevance of the "highest human possibility" to political life did not compel him to understand political life in terms of "the greatest evil" or even in terms of what is "low but solid." It suffices here merely to indicate his view that "glory" is the ultimate motive for the highest type of political man.

However this may be, Machiavelli can certainly be said to have prepared for the steps that were taken by political philosophers who followed him. He even indicated the unfinished character of his work and alludes to those who, coming later, would carry it forward. It was his rejection of the decisive premise of classical political philosophy that prepared the way for an ever more complete dedication of man to the earth.

Full devotion to the earth begins with Machiavelli's proposal to exhibit the guide in things as they are, not as they ought to be. Machiavelli also suggested that man begin to overpower and conquer chance.[47]

The *conquest* of the "actual" thus also would appear to be a substitution for dedication to the "ideal." These two strains of his thought, and ours, are inseparable. For modern science and technology as well as modern political aspirations are not simply dedicated to the earth and to man; they are dedicated to the earth and to man as they might *become* through transformation and conquest. Modern man is loyal to the earth and to man, not for what they are, but for what they ought to be.

## NOTES

Italian texts in Niccolo Machiavelli, *Opere,* ed. Antonio Panella (2 vols.; Milano-Roma, Rizzoli, 1939). English translations may be found in the Modern Library edition of *The Prince and the Discourses* (New York, 1940). For the *Florentine Histories: The Historical, Political and Diplomatic Writings of Niccolo Machiavelli* (Boston: James Osgood, 1882), Vol. I. For the *Discourse on Reforming the Government of Florence:* Machiavelli, *The Prince and Other Works* (New York: Hendricks House–Farrar, Straus, 1941).

1. Machiavelli, *Prince,* vi (Modern Library, p. 21). Reproduced by permission of Oxford University Press.

2. Trans. W. W.

3. Aristotle *Politics* 1282$^b$ 14–1283$^b$ 9; 1280$^a$ 10 f. Cf. 1253$^a$ 31, 1328$^b$ 12; *Nicomachean Ethics* 1179$^b$ 20, Plato *Republic* 368 ff., 427$^b$; *Theaetetus* 172$^c$–177$^c$, esp. 175$^c$ f.; *Sophist* 216.

4. *Discourse on Reforming Florence,* near the end; Discourses, I. Intro., (trans. W. W.).

5. Plato *Republic* 592$^b$, 472$^c$ ff. Cf. *Discourse on Reforming Florence,* near the end.

6. *Prince,* xv (trans. W. W.); Bacon, *Advancement of Learning,* near the end.

7. *Prince,* xvii (Modern Library, p. 61). Cf. *Discourses,* I. iii; II. xiv.

8. *Prince,* xv (Modern Library, p. 56).

9. *Ibid.* (trans. W. W.).

10. *Discourses,* I. Intro.; II. Intro. xvi, toward the middle. Cf. *Prince,* iii, near the end, xii–xiv, xxv, beginning, xxvi, *passim,* and poem at end.

11. *Prince,* xv, xviii, near the end, xxvi; *Discourses,* I. Intro., xii, II. Intro., ii, xvi ff. Cf. *Prince,* viii, near the end, with xiv, xvi, and the discussion of Hannibal near the end of xvii. For the variety of good practices, see also *Discourses,* III. xix–xxiii. Note Machiavelli's reference to the silence of the "ancients" and his own publication at the beginning of *Prince,* xviii. For a similar discrepancy, cf. *Discourses,* II. x. For the crucial importance of patterns of "imitation" to the "life and actions" of men, compare Machiavelli's discussions in *Prince,* vi, vii, near the end, xiv, near the end, xviii, xix, *passim* and esp. at the end; *Florentine Histories,* V. i, near the end, VI. xxix, VII. xxxiii; *Discourses,* II. Intro., near the end.

12. *Prince,* xv (Modern Library, p. 57).

13. Aristotle *Politics* 1279$^a$ 22 ff. Cf. the discussion in the *Rhetoric* 1365$^b$ 21–1366$^a$ 22 with *Nicomachean Ethics* 1095$^b$ 14 ff. Consider esp. *Politics* 1324$^a$ 25 ff.; *Politics* 1280$^a$ 10, 1323$^a$ 14 ff.; *Nicomachean Ethics* 1177$^a$ 3 f., 1177$^b$ 29 f. But for the relation between the community and philosophy: *Nicomachean Ethics* 1179$^b$ 30 ff.; cf. *Politics*

1288ª 16 f.; Plato *Republic* 493ᵉ f. For the legitimacy of the variety of regimes, see the discussion at *Politics* 1295ª 25 ff. Cf. *Nicomachean Ethics* 1134ᵇ 18 ff.

14. *Discourses*, II. v.

15. Luke 2:14. Cf. *ibid.*, 12:51; John 16:33. Compare also Eph. 6:15; Heb. 7:2; Phil. 4:7.

16. *Discourses*, II. v; I. xi, xii (trans. W. W.). Cf. *Florentine Histories*, I. i–v.

17. *Discourses*, I. xxvi (trans. W. W.).

18. The first reference is in *Prince*, xviii (Modern Library, p. 66); the second, *ibid.*, xxi (p. 82).

19. *Discourses*, III. i, toward the middle (trans. W. W.).

20. *Discourses*, II. ii (Modern Library, p. 285). Cf. II, Intro.; *Prince*, xi, beginning, xii, toward the end.

21. *Prince*, xii, toward the middle (trans. W. W.).

22. *Discourses*, I. xii; II. ii (Modern Library, p. 152). Cf. *Prince*, xi, xii, esp. near the end.

23. *Discourses*, I. xii (trans. W. W.); cf. III. xxix.

24. *Prince*, xi (trans. W. W.). Cf. *Florentine Histories*, I. ix–xix.

25. *Florentine Histories*, V. i–ii.

26. *Florentine Histories*, V. i. Cf. *Discourses*, I. vi, xxxvii; II. ii, iii, v, viii; III. i; *Prince*, vi.

27. *Florentine Histories*, V. i. Cf. *Discourses*, II. Intro.

28. *Discourses*, I. Intro. (trans. W. W.). Cf. *Prince*, xxvi.

29. *Discourses*, I. xxvii (Modern Library, p. 186). Cf. *Prince*, iii, near the end, and xi.

30. *Discourses*, I. xii (trans. W. W.). But cf. III. i.

31. *Prince*, vi (trans. W. W.).

32. *Discourses*, III. xxx (trans. W. W.). Cf. I. i, ix and II. viii.

33. *Discourses*, I. lviii (trans. W. W.).

34. Trans. W. W.

35. *Discourses*, I. xi (trans. W. W.).

36. *Prince*, i, iii, beginning, vi, xix, end. Cf. *Discourses*, I. i, beginning, x.

37. *Prince*, vi (trans. W. W.).

38. *Ibid.*, xii (Modern Library, p. 44). But cf. xviii, xxiv, xxv.

39. *Ibid.*, vi (trans. W. W.). Cf. *Discourses*, I. xvi–xviii, lv; III. viii.

40. *Discourse on Reforming Florence*, near the end.

41. *Discourses*, I. ix (trans. W. W.).

42. *Prince*, ii, iii, near the beginning, vi (Modern Library, p. 22); *Discourses*, I. ix (Modern Library, p. 139). Cf. *Prince* xvii, xviii, xix, esp. end; *Discourses*, I. xviii, xxvi; III. i.

43. *Prince*, xviii (Modern Library, p. 64).

44. *Discourses*, I. xlvi; II. xiv, xvi (trans. W. W.); cf. III. i, iii, ix, n. 30. Cf. *Discourses*, I. xi with *Prince*, iii, vi.

45. *Discourses*, I. xxxvii (Modern Library, p. 208); II. Intro. Cf. III. xxi; *Prince*, ix.

46. Aristotle *Politics* 1278ᵇ 6–1284ᵇ 34, esp. 1281ᵇ f. Cf. 1288ª 20, 1290ª 7 f.

47. *Prince*, xxv. Cf. *Discourses*, III. ix, xii. Consider also the implications of *Prince*, x, toward the end. Compare also the very beginning of *Prince*, xxv, with *Discourses*, III. xxxiii.

# READINGS

A. Machiavelli, Niccolo. *The Prince.* New York: Modern Library, 1940.
B. Machiavelli, Niccolo. *Discourses on the First Ten Books of Titus Livius.* New York: Modern Library, 1940.

# MARTIN LUTHER

## 1483–1546

# JOHN CALVIN

## 1509–1564

The great Reformers Martin Luther and John Calvin thought of themselves not as philosophers or politicians, but first and last as theologians and students of the Word of God. Accordingly, we should not expect to find them presenting a comprehensive political philosophy or a general theory of politics, for they did not see this as the task to which they were called. But the Reformation of the Church demanded the formulation of a general *theological* position, and this inevitably included some central affirmations about politics and political philosophy. And, willy-nilly, both Reformers were called upon to give much concrete political advice in practical situations and even to involve themselves in political activity in which their political opinions were elaborated and put to the test. They see their political affirmations as flowing directly from their theological premises and as derived from the same source, Holy Scripture. Their political teaching can only be understood properly in the light of their theology, for it was never meant to be viewed in isolation.

Their prime concern with politics is to define its proper sphere and place this in relation to its context. But it is impossible to mark out the frontier between theology and political philosophy without saying a great deal about both; and although Luther and Calvin take biblical theology as their standpoint, inevitably they are involved in saying much about the nature and function of politics. They discuss such subjects as the place of secular government in relation to God's scheme of salvation; the connection between sin and temporal authority; the relationships of divine law, natural law, and positive law; the multitudinous implications of the Christian doctrine of man; Church and State; the limits of political power; the mutual duties of ruler and subjects; and so on. In short, most of the great questions of political philosophy are at least touched upon, if only sometimes to show which tools—reason, tradition, experience, conscience, or Holy Scripture—are appropriate to the treatment of a particular problem.

Luther and Calvin are at opposite poles as far as mood and expression are concerned. Luther is flamboyant, vivid, impulsive, immensely readable, frequently exaggerating his true position or contradicting what he said elsewhere in order to put over a point forcefully. He wrote no one comprehensive exposition of his theology, and his political teaching must be culled from "tracts for the times," theological treatises, commentaries, sermons, and even hymns. In spite of some glaring surface contradictions and exaggerations, there is a profound underlying unity and coherence in his thought; his theology of politics is very carefully worked out and is, on the whole, consistent even if sometimes misleadingly articulated. Calvin is more restrained, dry, lucid, and systematic in his writing. His *Institutes of the Christian Religion,* first written when he was only twenty-five, but revised and expanded in successive editions up to 1559, is one of the greatest and most influential works of systematic theology of all time. In its final form it is the definitive statement of his theology, although much detail may be added from his voluminous sermons, lectures, commentaries, and correspondence.

In spite of certain significant theological and political differences, Luther and Calvin have broad general agreement. They accept the same authorities, adopt much the same method, and the structure and most of the conclusions of their thought are sufficiently similar to entitle us to treat them together, pointing out differences as they occur.

## A. The Basis of a Theology of Politics
### 1. Justification by Faith

The root and core of all reformed theology is the doctrine of justification by faith alone. All that is distinctive in the teaching of Luther and the Reformation may be traced back to a conviction of the radical perversity of man and his total alienation from God because of the immensity of his sin, together with a rejection of the currently accepted solutions to the problem of forgiveness and reconciliation. The Reformers went far beyond mere denunciation of the more obvious abuses of the indulgence system, and denied the very terms in which the problem of sin and redemption was being posed in the Roman Church.

Both Luther and Calvin believe in the total depravity of man. By this they do not mean that nothing that man can do can possibly be "good" in the generally accepted sense of the term, but rather that even what are, in the eyes of men, "good works" are pathetically and totally inadequate when measured against the standard of the righteousness which God requires of His servants. The evil that we do is the normal expression of our corrupted human nature and our own responsibility; but any good that we may do is God working through us, a gift of God's free grace for which we cannot claim merit. It is ridiculous to think of pleading our good works before Almighty God because they are hopelessly trivial in view of the condemnation of our sin which divine justice demands; they themselves are, without exception, stained with our corruption and wickedness; and besides, in so far as they are good, the goodness is God's and not our own. All men stand equally under the condemnation of God. "Even saints," wrote Calvin, "cannot perform one work which, if judged on its merits, is not deserving of condemnation." [1] Forgiveness and peace with God cannot be won or earned by anything man can do for himself.

The Reformers break with the medieval tradition not only in their more radical statement of the problem of sin and man's fallen condition, but also in the solution they present. We are justified before God, they claimed, not by works, or by the merits of the saints dispensed through indulgences, but *sola fide,* by faith alone. And faith is a gift of God, not something that man can create for himself. This does not mean simply that man must accept certain doctrinal statements, but rather that his only resource when faced by the judgment of God is to admit his total helplessness and the complete justice of the condemnation passed on him, and then, laying all his sin on Christ and relying on His work, to approach the throne of Grace clothed in the "alien holiness" [2] of Christ Himself. Our justification is an unmerited, gratuitous gift, to which any achievements of our own are simply irrelevant. The only righteousness of men which does not dissolve in the presence of God is the "passive righteousness" which is freely given with faith by God.

## 2. *The Authority of Scripture*

In arguing thus, Luther and Calvin find themselves returning to the teaching of St. Paul and St. Augustine and rejecting virtually the whole of medieval theology as Pelagian, that is, believing that man can in some sense earn his salvation by his own efforts. This break with scholasticism on the issue of justification is the starting point of Reformed theological thought. Luther is diverging from the whole medieval theological tradition when, as early as 1517, he can write: "It is false to state that the will can by nature conform to correct precept. . . . One must concede that the will is not free to strive towards whatever is declared good. . . . Man is by nature unable to want God to be God. Indeed, he himself wants to be God, and does not want God to be God." [3]

This leads him directly to the more academic issue: "Virtually the whole *Ethics* of Aristotle is the worst enemy of Grace. . . . No syllogistic form is valid when applied to divine terms. . . . The whole Aristotle is to theology as darkness to light." [4]

The failure to take the fallenness of man's condition with adequate seriousness, argued Luther, had led theologians to place undue reliance on reason. The true distinction and contrast between revelation and reason, theology and philosophy, had been lost in, for example, the Thomist synthesis. Reason had been regarded, at least in some of its operations, as exempt from the full effects of the Fall, and nature and Grace had been made complementary, thus evading the problem that the only nature we can know is fallen nature, nature in constant rebellion against Grace. The redemption of nature requires the restoration of its uncorrupted condition, not its fulfillment by the addition of a "supernature." Luther shows substantial agreement on the relation of reason and revelation with Ockham and the Nominalists, but finally rejects them, too, as Pelagians who "have not only darkened the Gospel, but have taken it clean away, and buried Christ utterly," [5] as the result of an unscriptural view of man's potentialities.

If reason can provide no proper tool for the treatment of issues of divinity, what is left of theology? Is the Queen of the Sciences to disappear, leaving behind her nothing but a formless pietism? The answer of the Reformers was unequivocal: the sole criterion of theological truth must be the revealed Word of God as expressed through the Holy Scriptures of the Old and New Testaments. Only thus can theology escape undue reliance on fallen nature or corrupted reason. Neither the tradition of the Church nor human philosophizing is to stand against Scripture. Reformed theology is to be *biblical* theology, basically nothing other than the exposition of the clear teaching of Scripture. Calvin, for instance, said of his *Institutes* that they were intended to be simply "the sum of what we find God wishes to teach us in His Word." [6] The authority of Scripture is self-authenticating, for it "exhibits as clear evidence of its truth as white and black things do of their colour, or sweet and bitter things do of their taste," [7] and this authority is further guaranteed to the individual believer by the working of the Holy Spirit in his heart. It is the clear sense of Scripture which is apparent to any fair-minded man, not any allegorical or spiritualized interpretation, which is the supreme rule of life and doctrine. The Reformers accuse their opponents not only of introducing alien authorities into theology in addition to Scripture and of subordinating the Word of God to the judgment of the Church, but also of refusing to be bound to its plain sense, and instead treating the Bible "as if it were a nose of wax, to be pulled around at will." [8] Rightly understood, the Reformers claim, the whole of the Bible shows itself to be a unity of witness to the revelation of God in Christ, free of obscurities and ambiguities. [9]

There is a distinction between Luther and Calvin in their doctrine of Scripture, but it is one which is nowhere formulated explicitly, and it can only be gathered in general terms from their differing approaches to exegesis. When Luther seeks to find a rule of life in Scripture he tends to understand this negatively: Scripture sets the limits within which positive guidance must be sought from reason, tradition, or history. The main concern of Scripture is to call men to salvation in Christ, but as far as life in this world is concerned it operates largely negatively, and requires to be supplemented in order to obtain an adequate ethic. Calvin, on the other hand, looks to Scripture for an unequivocally positive pattern of life and action. Where Luther sees Scripture as pointing to a relationship to Christ which may be expressed in many ways of life, Calvin tends to look for the one, immutable rule of Christian obedience. This distinction in the doctrine of Scripture is, however, far from absolute and must not be overemphasized. Much the same difference is to be found more clearly expressed in the different approaches of the two Reformers to the question of the "uses of the Law" (q.v.). Nevertheless, this disagreement is probably one of the sources of the greater radicalism of Calvin's concern with the form and workings of Church and State, and of the greater deference which Luther pays in these matters to reason and tradition.

If for no other reason than that the Bible contains a multitude of passages which are concerned with politics, it is obvious that Luther and Calvin, as biblical theologians, must have political doctrine in which they expound the teaching of Scripture on government, obedience, and so on, and relate this to the problems of the day. Neither

Luther nor Calvin makes any claim to being an original thinker. They think of themselves simply as *witnesses* to the truth which is available to all men in Holy Scripture. As they see it, their business is simply to take the passages relevant to any issue and explicate, correlate, and expound such passages in relation to the needs of the moment. In matters of politics and Church government the most pressing need is the recovery of the old, true, and apostolic orderings, and in this the Bible is the only guide.

### 3. Justification and Ethics

It has often been argued that the doctrine of justification by faith alone with its denial of the validity before God of human judgments of worth makes impossible any serious consideration of ethics and politics. If in the last analysis (that is, in the presence of God) good works can have no merit, why be good? Has not the whole basis of morality been in fact destroyed?

Not so, but far otherwise, is the answer of the Reformers. When a man knows himself to be justified by faith alone, his faith necessarily "becomes active in love" to his neighbor. "We do not become righteous by doing righteous deeds, but having been made righteous, we do righteous deeds." [10] The Reformers never understand faith as mere passive assent to a series of propositions.

Therefore, when some say that good works are forbidden when we preach faith alone it is as if I said to a sick man: "If you had health, you would have the use of all your limbs, but without health the works of all your limbs are nothing"; and he wanted to infer that I had forbidden the work of all his limbs; whereas on the contrary I meant that he must first have health, which will work all the works of all the members. So faith also must be in all works the master workman or captain, or they are nothing at all. [11]

The works of the faithful man are of special value because they are disinterested; he serves God and his neighbor for their own sakes, not because he hopes to win salvation for himself thereby.

And ethical standards are not abrogated. Although they are irrelevant to the question of salvation, they are nevertheless given and laid down by God for a purpose, and there is another sphere—the world—in which their proper validity remains totally unimpaired. The righteousness of those who are justified is, in Luther's phrase, a "passive righteousness," something with which we are endowed, but cannot earn. But there is also an active righteousness, no less necessary, and commanded by God, but confined, as it were, to the sphere of this world.

The justified man is accepted by God in Christ *as* righteous, but it is important to remember that this does not make him sinless or morally perfect in the eyes of men, although justification, to be sure, always struggles to express itself in acts of love. The Christian—and the Christian statesman—lives in two kingdoms, in both of which he must serve God, albeit in different ways. To a fuller consideration of the Reformers' teaching on these "two kingdoms" we must now turn, as it is central to their political thought.

## B. THE TWO KINGDOMS
### 1. The Dual Citizenship of Man

Man is a subject in two kingdoms, according to Calvin and Luther.

Let us observe that in man government is two-fold: the one spiritual, by which the conscience is trained to piety and divine worship; the other civil, by which the individual is instructed in those duties which as men and citizens we are bound to perform. To these two forms are commonly given the not inappropriate names of spiritual and temporal jurisdiction, intimating that the former species has reference to the life of the soul, while the latter relates to matters of the present life, not only to food and clothing, but to the enacting of laws which require a man to live among his fellows purely, honourably, and moderately. The former has its seat within the soul, the latter only regulates the external conduct. We call the one the spiritual, the other the temporal kingdom.[12]

Man, in short, belongs both to earth and to heaven, to the temporal and the eternal, subject to the secular law and recipient of the eternal Gospel, a being capable both of reason and of faith. In the spiritual kingdom he is wholly free, in the temporal kingdom he is totally in bondage. He is both a member of the Church, the eternal Body of Christ, and subject to the temporal authority of secular magistrates and laws. He is instructed in the temporal realm largely by reason, tradition, and the authority of the great minds of the past, and in the spiritual realm by the Word of God as recorded in Holy Scripture.

The clear distinction of these two realms is one of the primary and continuing tasks of theology, but it is far from being an easy one. The two kingdoms are not simply the Church and the State, as many medieval thinkers had suggested. Failure to distinguish, or the placing of a wrong division, leads to confusion and disaster in both realms, as we shall see in more detail. "Whoso then can judge rightly between the law and the Gospel, let him thank God, and know that he is a right divine." [13]

## 2. The Relation of the Two Kingdoms

While the two kingdoms must be clearly distinguished, we are not to think that they bear no relation to each other, or are wholly independent and self-sufficient. Just as Scotland and England were, between 1603 and 1707 (except for the Cromwellian period), united in the person of the crown while retaining their separate governments, so the spiritual and temporal kingdoms, although distinct from each other, have the same sovereign. Both are God's kingdoms, both expressions of His care and concern for men. In a sense we might say that they are complementary, although we must be careful to show what we mean by this in order to avoid confusion with medieval ideas which the Reformers disowned. God gives His good gifts both through the prince and the preacher, and each in his own way points toward heaven. Spiritual government leads us to love God; temporal government leads us to serve our neighbors. But love to God and service to one's fellows are ultimately so conjoined that it is impossible to do the one without at the same time also doing the other. Both law and Gospel, reason and faith, State and Church, philosophy and Scripture are necessary for life in this world. In spite of what often seems to be conflict and disharmony, we know that the two kingdoms belong together and are complementary.[14] But this union will only be fully realized at the consummation of all things, when the two will become one, and meanwhile the distinction must be maintained with care if dangerous confusion is to be avoided. "Now these two, as we have divided them, are always to be viewed apart from each other. When the one is considered, we should call off our minds and not allow them to think of the other." [15] The frontier between the two kingdoms is a division within every man. Properly considered, the two governments operate for the main part in different territories, by different means, and for different ends, and accordingly the question of the superiority of one to the other cannot sensibly be raised. They must and do cooperate, it is true, but only in such a way as not to confuse their separation and equality under God.

But it is far from easy to maintain the proper distinction, for "the Devil never stops cooking and brewing these two kingdoms into each other" [16] in order to bring chaos and disaster to earth. He acts either through human presumption or human idealism. On the one hand the secular power may seek to control the Church and dictate what is to be believed and taught; or the pope may seek to assert that all earthly authority flows through him. "Such people," says Luther, "want to be God themselves, and not to serve Him or remain subordinate to Him." [17] Law and Gospel may be confused together either by the "murdering and thieving bands of peasants" who undermine lawful authority as such, or by the pope who "hath not only mixed the law with the Gospel, but who of the Gospel hath made mere laws, yea and such as are ceremonial only. He hath also confounded and mixed political and ecclesiastical matters together; which is a devilish and hellish confusion." [18] On the other hand there are naively idealistic Christians who attempt to introduce the Gospel into spheres in which only law is appropriate—the religious enthusiasts and fanatics, notably the Anabaptists, who cannot see the bountiful hand of God in the temporal world, and so attempt to absorb the secular into the spiritual for the most laudable of reasons. They, too, are mistaken and are, albeit unwittingly, agents of the devil's confusion:

A man who would venture to govern an entire community, or the world, with the Gospel would be like a shepherd who should place in one fold wolves, lions, eagles, and sheep together and say, "Help yourselves, and be good and peaceful among yourselves; the fold is open, there is plenty of food; have no fear of dogs or clubs." The sheep, forsooth, would keep the peace and would allow themselves to be fed and governed in peace, but they would not live long.[19]

Working through the presumptuous and the naive, the devil has his way:

The people, the bishops, and the entire papacy ought to look after the Gospel and after souls. But they must rule in worldly affairs instead, wage war, and seek after temporal wealth, which in their shrewdness they are happy to do. Again, secular monarchs ought to look after their administration; but instead of that they must stand in Church, listening to Mass, and be altogether spiritual. Thus even now they are dabbling in matters of the Gospel and, following the pope's example, are forbidding what God has commanded, as, for instance, both kinds in the Sacrament, Christian freedom, and marriage. The results of this virtue are usually in evidence at the imperial diets too; thus the essential matters are postponed, or often simply omitted.[20]

One must, however, add that Luther himself from time to time transgresses his own conviction, as when he argues that " if every man had faith we would need no more laws," thereby "transferring the doctrine of the Gospel concerning spiritual liberty to civil order" illegitimately, by pretending that the man of faith can be wholly independent of secular government in this world.[21]

### 3. Church and State[22]

The two kingdoms are not identical with Church and State, but political government belongs wholly to the temporal realm, and it is created "for the purposes of this transitory life" only.[23] While it may show man his need of forgiveness, it cannot mediate justification, as can the Church. Nevertheless, it is in a fallen world a necessary institution, created by God as an instrument of His will and drawing its authority directly from Him, not by way of pope, Church, or people. In this the Reformers agree with medieval antipapalist theorists such as Wyclif, and with Marsilius and Ockham, except in so far as these thinkers spoke of popular sovereignty. Temporal government, for the Reformers as for the medieval antipapalists, has a very real dignity. Luther feels that in this emphasis he is restoring something long lost by the medieval confusion of the two kingdoms, so that he can write: "I might boast that, since the Apostles' time, the temporal sword and temporal government have never been so clearly described or so highly praised as by me." [24]

The term "Church" is somewhat ambiguous. It may be used to refer to the "Church Visible," that is, the empirically discernible body of baptized persons organized together for worship, instruction, and fellowship and subordinated to religious authorities; a group which contains many who are not, in fact, of God's Elect, and which may even exclude some of the Elect from its membership; a body which is manifestly imperfect and changeable. Or it may refer to the "Church Invisible," the eternal Body of Christ to which only the Elect, those who are justified by faith, belong, the true composition of which is known only to God. The Church Invisible is incorruptible, everlasting, and identical with the communion of saints. Both Reformers followed Wyclif and Marsilius in denying that the Church should be thought of as the hierarchy or priesthood. All Christians belong to the spiritual estate, and the ministry or priesthood is simply a particular function within the corporate priesthood of the whole body of believers.[25]

While both Luther and Calvin insist strenuously on the mutual independence of Church and State, it is important to realize that they mean rather different things by this. Luther, like Wyclif and Hus before him, lays greater stress on the invisibility of the Church, and is not overly concerned with its worldly independence except in relation to doctrine, preaching, and the sacraments. The secular government may organize the external polity of the Church as seems most convenient to it; it may do as it wills with the property of the Church; and the temporal authorities, if Christian, may even be recognized as "bishops" with authority over the external affairs of the visible Church, apart from the three matters mentioned above.[26]

Calvin, on the other hand, lays far greater stress on the "visibility" of the Church.[27] For him the true form of Church organization as well as true doctrine is to be found in Scripture, which also gives positive guidance for the outward behavior of Christian men. Control over outward morality cannot be surrendered entirely to the State; the Church must also exercise her discipline, with her own peculiar sanctions (notably excommunication), over her members, and even if they be governors or rulers in the secular realm, as Christians they are subject to the discipline of the Church. Discipline and polity are for Calvin the essential "sinews" of the Church, and belong to the essence of the Faith. Both Church and State are concerned with the maintenance of external morality, but they proceed in different ways appropriate to their different natures.[28] For Luther discipline and polity are matters of indifference as far as the realm of salvation is concerned.

We see, then, that Luther and Calvin both insist on the independence of Church and State, but they draw the division between these two "hierarchies" at very different points. The disputed territory covers most of the worldly functioning of the Church, and notably the form of external Church organization. For Luther, little binding guidance as to the government of the Church is to be found in Scripture, and he is willing to accept much that is traditional or seems expedient in the circumstances. For Calvin, Church polity must be conformable to Scripture, and neither tradition nor the temporal government is to be allowed to have authority in this matter. Now, if this disputed area is surrendered to the State, as by Luther, it becomes increasingly difficult for the Church to maintain its own autonomy (or rather, theonomy) at all, even within what Luther recognized as the proper sphere of the Church. And if it be granted to the latter, as by Calvin, the Church is constantly tempted to extend the sphere of "discipline" in such a way as to assert its superiority to, and authority over, the State.

In theory, if not always in practice, both these temptations are rejected by the Reformers. Although they differ in the delimitation of the two spheres, they agree that they are separate and not to be confused. But this does not mean that Church and State should not cooperate. Each is aided in its own proper work by the existence and support of the other. "The civil order is necessary for the well-being of the Church," wrote Calvin as the heading for the chapter on civil government in the first edition of the *Institutes,* and, on the other hand, the existence of a pure Church is advantageous to the State, for "all have confessed that no State can be successfully established unless piety be its first care."[29] Church and State are like the twins of Hippocrates: when one is sick the other sickens, too, and only together can they be in health.[30]

We may fill in some of the details of the cooperation of Church and State by looking at the functions which Luther and Calvin each attribute to the spiritual and temporal powers respectively. For both Reformers the temporal government is concerned not simply with the maintenance of social life and external morality, but also is charged with responsibility for the maintenance of the true worship and service of God. The State is entitled, and indeed obliged, if necessary to purge and reform the Church in accordance with the Word of God, restoring to it the form of the true Church, an essential part of which, it must be remembered, is the Church's independence of, and distinctness from, the secular power. This may appear to be a denial of the separation of Church and State, but two points should be noted: in the first place, the interference by the secular power in the proper realm of the Church (however this realm may be defined) is an emergency action and not a regular feature, and, in the second place, the temporal authority is only entitled to intervene in order to restore to the Church New Testament Christianity. The "godly prince" is bound to restore to the Church the form and function which it has in Holy Scripture. Otherwise his intervention is totally illegitimate. The proper and normal relation of Church and State is one of mutual support and encouragement between two equals.

The State then, has a dual function. It has duties both toward the civil community and toward the Church. Both Luther and Calvin see government as primarily a "dyke against sin" or "a remedy to vices." Luther is somewhat reluctant, as a theologian, to say much about how the State should restrain evil except in the most general terms, but Calvin does not hesitate to go into considerable detail: temporal government exists "to adapt our conduct to human society, to form our manners to civil justice, to conciliate us to each other, to cherish common peace and tranquility."[31] It must care for the poor, it must erect schools and pay the teachers, it must take care of the universities, and so on.[32]

With regard to the visible Church, the State should provide material support for pastors and the worship of the Christian community; it should "foster and maintain the external worship of God, defend sound doctrine and the condition of the Church." It must take care that "no idolatry, no blasphemy against the name of God, no calumnies against

His truth, nor other offences to religion break out and be disseminated among the people . . . in short, that a public form of religion may exist among men." [33] But the State has no arbitrary power or right to decide what is "sound doctrine" or the true Church. In such matters it must be bound by the clear teaching of the Word of God. But even if the teaching of Holy Scripture were as unambiguous as Calvin believed, it is difficult to argue that at the practical level he succeeds in maintaining the distinction of Church and State as clearly as, on his own premises, he ought.

It has always been difficult to separate with clarity the spheres of Church and State, and Luther and Calvin, as we have seen, do not entirely agree on this issue. Both, however, restrict the Church far more closely than had been the medieval pattern, and this they do on the ground that only so can the Church *be* the Church, and the State have the dignity and authority which are rightly its. They will have nothing to do either with a doctrine of the "two swords" or with any kind of caeseropapism. There can be only one sword, and that belongs to the secular government alone. Spiritual government denies its own nature if it usurps the proper function of the secular government, and the reverse is also true. In a profound sense Church and State together compose one unity, in as much as both are expressions of the sovereignty of God, but it is a disastrous mistake to attempt to realize this unity prematurely. Church and State should collaborate, it is true, but only as "separate but equal" servants of God.

## 4. Theology and Politics

Theology and secular learning, like Church and State, are to be limited to their proper spheres. Neither theology nor philosophy is now the Queen of the Sciences, but each is a "queen" within the confines of its own field. The theologian can make no pretension to being an authority on everything; he must recognize his competence as limited. "Why should I teach a tailor how to make a suit?" asks Luther. "He knows it himself. I shall only tell him how to do his work well in a Christian manner. The same is true of the prince. I shall only tell him he should act like a Christian." [34]

Theology is concerned with matters of faith, and its authority is Holy Scripture which in no sense sets out to be a politicians' (any more than a tailors') textbook. "In the apostolical writings we are not to look for a distinct exposition of those matters, their object being not to form a civil polity, but to establish the spiritual kingdom of Christ." [35]

Nevertheless, the theologian must tell the politician "he should act like a Christian," and Holy Scripture has a great deal to say about the behavior of rulers. Neither Luther nor Calvin had much hesitation in advising and rebuking rulers, often in the most forthright of terms. The limitation they place upon theology seems to be this: theology can offer no foolproof guidance through all the dilemmas of political life, no universally valid blueprint of the ideal society, and the theologian as such has no special qualification for the exercise of political power. Such matters can never be more than peripheral to theology. Theology cannot displace either the art or the science of politics. Political philosophy cannot be absorbed into theology any more than the State can be absorbed into the Church. There should, however, be something of a dialogue, if only to insure that neither oversteps its bounds. Let political philosophy never suggest that it can "penetrate to the heavenly kingdom of God," nor theology that it can rule the kingdom of this world.

If the political guidance to be received from theology and Holy Scripture is necessarily limited and inadequate, where are we to turn for guidance? Political activity, we are told, is based upon reason rather than revelation. As Luther puts it:

God made the secular government subject to reason because it is to have no jurisdiction over the welfare of souls or things of eternal value, but only over bodily and temporal goods, which God places under man's dominion. For this reason, nothing is taught in the Gospel about how it is to be maintained and regulated, except that the Gospel bids people honour it and not oppose it. Therefore the heathen can speak and teach about this very well, as they have done. And, to tell the truth, they are far more skilful in such matters than the Christians. . . . Whoever wants to learn and become wise in secular government, let him read the heathen books and writings.[36]

If we desire guidance in politics we must turn not so much to Scripture as to experience, reason generalizing on it, history sacred and profane, tradition, and philosophy. The very Aristotle whom Luther had labelled "this damned, conceited, rascally heathen" when considering his influence on theology,[37] becomes a most reputable authority when the question at issue is one of politics.

I am convinced that God gave and preserved such heathen books as those of the poets and the histories, like Homer, Demosthenes, Cicero, Livy, and afterwards the fine old jurists . . . that the heathen and godless, too, might have their prophets, apostles, and theologians or preachers for their secular government. . . . Thus they had Homer, Aristotle, Cicero, Ulpian, and others, even as the people of God had their Moses, Elijah, Isaiah, and others; and their emperors, kings, and princes, like Alexander, Augustus, etc., were their Davids and Solomons.[38]

But the ability to rule well is not simply the result of study of the right books and examples. Reason and political judgment are not dispersed equally among men. Ruling is a specialized craft for which pre-eminent gifts are required, for it is not simply a matter of following rules and principles. Very few are the truly original political innovators, the *viri heroici;* the average politician is compelled simply to "patch and darn and help himself with the laws, sayings, and examples of the heroes as they are recorded in books." [39]

## C. WHAT IS MAN?

### 1. Corruption . . .

Man, as we have already seen, is a fallen being. Created originally in the image of God, he rebelled against his Maker, and by the Fall this image has been radically distorted and changed out of all recognition. Man, the creature of God who was destined to enjoy perpetual fellowship with his Creator, has become estranged and alienated. Where order should be, disorder is now found, where harmony, strife. Since the Fall man has belonged to two kingdoms, not one, and in both the baneful consequences of corruption and sin can be traced.

Holding such views the Reformers are justly suspicious of "the great darkness of philosophers who have looked for a building in a ruin, and fit arrangement in disorder." [40] A theory of human nature derived from empirical observation cannot but project a radically false picture, based as it is upon the fallen man who "by [corrupted] nature has neither correct precept nor good will." [41] And a rational a priori doctrine of human nature would be in no better case, for it is involved in the corruption and limitation of human reason. Reason and observation can tell us many interesting and useful facts, but they are totally incapable of constructing a valid teleology. They can by themselves tell us nothing of value about the origin and destiny of man. They can describe the "ruin" and even instruct us in how to keep it in repair (and this is an important and useful function), but only revelation can describe the finished edifice and superintend the restoration.

But what do we mean when we say that reason is corrupted? Calvin joins issue with the philosophers who, he says,

generally maintain that reason dwells in the mind like a lamp, throwing light on all its counsels and, like a queen, governing the will—that it is so pervaded with divine light as to be able to consult for the best, and so endued with vigour as to be able perfectly to command; and, on the contrary, sense is dull and short-sighted grovelling among inferior objects, and never rising to true vision; that the appetite, when it obeys reason, and does not allow itself to be subjected by sense is borne to the study of virtue, holds a straight course, becomes transformed into will; but that when enslaved by sense, is corrupted and depraved so as to degenerate into lust.[42]

This position is to be rejected for two reasons, both largely based on the detailed picture of human depravity discerned by Christian experience. On the one hand, although reason is very often correct in general statements, it is normally subtly perverted by pride and selfishness in the particular advice it gives and, on the other hand, there is in fallen man a constant battle between reason and will: "The good that I would, that I do not; but the evil that I would not, that I do." The will is enslaved and at enmity with right reason; the reason aims high, but is quickly diverted into futility. Rejecting thus "the common dogma that man was corrupted only in the sensual part of his nature, that reason remained entire and will was scarcely impaired," [43] Calvin returns to Scriptural doctrine and the teaching of St. Augustine.

Nevertheless, "to charge the intellect with perpetual blindness so as to leave it no intelligence of any description whatever is repugnant not only to the Word of God, but to common experience." [44] While human reason is not to be relied upon in theology and is an inadequate guide in the sphere of salvation and in such matters "fails before it reaches its goal, forthwith falling away into vanity," [45] yet it has its proper place, and yields important results when concerned with "inferior objects," that is, the affairs of the secular realm. As examples of these, Calvin noticed "matter of politics and economics, all mechanical arts and liberal studies." [46]

Calvin then makes the somewhat surprising claim that "since man is by nature a social animal, he is disposed from natural instinct to cherish and preserve society, and accordingly we see that the minds of all men have impressions of civil order and honesty." [47] By this Calvin seems to argue that sociable instincts are one of the vestiges of the image of God, man's true nature, which are left to him. Man's total depravity before the throne of God does not mean that God has taken from him all resources for living in the temporal kingdom. Nevertheless, fallen man cannot be relied upon to use aright even the measure of reason and sociable instincts which has been left to him.

### 2 . . . . Coercion

Since man is alienated from, and hostile to, God he requires restraint if life in this world is to be possible. The pride and self-centeredness which cut man off from God are at the same time the roots of strife and hostility and alienation among men. Were man's reason, conscience, and will in harmony, education and enlightenment would be enough, and there would be no need of coercion. But since fallen man knows little about God or justice or goodness, and since he refuses even to follow the light that remains for him, restraint must be made the necessary basis of social life. All men, even justified men, are sinners who must in the earthly kingdom be forced to obey. Obedience to authority is, as we shall see in some detail, in itself a good, and the only foundation on which stable social and political life may be built. Man, in his pristine innocence, required no government; but fallen man must be harnessed and forced into outward conformity with the necessary rules of social living, for "if he is not governed, he excels in ferocity by far all savage beasts." [48] Coercion is at one and the same time a curb on sin, a constant reminder of the divine nature of the moral law, and the means whereby God in His mercy provides for man the great blessing of peaceful social life.

### D. AUTHORITY AND ITS LIMITS
#### 1. The State as the Servant of God

Luther and Calvin fight on three fronts when attempting to delimit and describe the secular government. In the first place they must oppose the fanatics such as the Anabaptists who deny that there is any place for civil government at all and who emancipate Christians from any obligations whatsoever toward the secular power. In the second place, they must refute the claims of the papacy to absorb secular power into the Church. Finally, they must curb the pretensions of those rulers whom "God Almighty has made mad. They actually think they have the power to do and command their subjects to do whatever they please . . . they presumptuously set themselves in God's place, lord it over men's conscience and faith, and put the Holy Spirit to school according to their mad brains." [49]

Against the Anabaptist view, Calvin and Luther prove theologically the *necessity* of civil government, as we have seen. Against the pope, they must prove the autonomy under God of the State. And against the presumptuous princes they must show the autonomy under God of the Church.

We have already seen something of the two Reformers' arguments for the necessity, the limits, and the independence of temporal government. God's sovereignty in the world is total. The necessity for temporal government is correlative to the necessity that God's Will should be observed among sinful men; its limits are defined by the fact that political authority is *delegated* authority, subordinate to, and dependent on, the sovereignty of God; its worldly autonomy arises from its direct dependence on the Will of God. In short, all political power flows from God and is to serve Him: "There is no power but of God: the powers that be are ordained of God .... He [the Ruler] is the minister of God." (Romans 13:1, 4) "We must firmly establish secular law and the sword, that no one may doubt that it is in the world by God's will and ordinance." [50] The origin of secular government lies in God's merciful will in shielding man from the full consequences of his disobedience, and not in human need. Its authority is a delegated authority from God and not from the people. In the thought of Luther and Calvin there is absolutely no room for any kind of social contract or notion of popular sovereignty. Secular government is an ordinance of God for the welfare of men in a fallen world. It must never under any circumstances be thought of as a human "device of government," or as in any way based on consent. It must answer for the use of its power always to God, and never simply to the people.[51]

The State, then, is "God's servant and workman" on earth. It is put there to express God's care for men, to punish the evil and protect the good, and for the well-being of the Church.[52] Coercion and restraint are not in themselves the be-all and end-all of temporal government. It exists to make possible for man the nearest approximation to the "good life" which is possible in a fallen world. We may say that it serves man, but it would be highly misleading to say it is man's servant. From man's point of view it is entitled to all respect, for "next to the preaching office [it] is the highest service of God and the most useful office on earth." [53] It may even be called *divine,* for rulers, both Luther and Calvin suggest, are sometimes even called in Scripture "gods" (*e.g.,* in Psalm 82).

## 2. Forms of Government

The question of the form and structure which secular government should assume as the servant of God lies on the delicate frontier between theology and political philosophy, and both Calvin and Luther show signs of uneasiness when they feel obliged to speak on the subject. Obviously certain theological and biblical insights are relevant, and indeed necessary, for the treatment of this question, but it is also obvious that other criteria apart from the Scriptures are also properly operative. The clarity of the division between theology and philosophy becomes

blurred by the tension between the Reformers' denial of their competence as theologians in this field, and their clear conviction that, again
as theologians, they have an indispensable contribution to make to the
discussion.

The legitimacy even of asking what is the best form of government
worried Calvin in particular. The authorities under which we live are
God's servants, ordained by Him, and this makes it presumptuous to
raise the question of their right. The fact that they are there proves
that they are installed in office by God and therefore entitled to respect
and obedience. The raising of abstract questions of right is quite improper for the private citizen. And the canny empiricism of both Reformers comes out clearly when they question the value of rational
speculation on this issue. The answer depends on circumstances. And,
although government as such is an indispensable good, the various forms
of government have within themselves so many possibilities for good
and evil that it is virtually impossible to say which is the best.

This subject is really a peripheral one for the Reformers. Government of some kind is essential for social living, and good government
can bring many temporal blessings to men. But even the cruellest of
pagan tyrannies is powerless to extinguish the flame of faith.[54] Nevertheless, both Reformers go beyond giving advice to rulers as to how
they should behave as Christians, and bring theological insights to bear
on the problem of what is the best form of State. They stop short of
constructing an ideal state, partly because they do not see this as a
theologian's—or a private citizen's—function, partly because they are
suspicious that such a project is presumptuous and tends to a glorification
of the State in itself and a disregard of its transitory and limited function. The doctrine of the perversity of man is the principal contribution
of theology in this field, and it acts as a curb on any kind of utopianism.
But the detailed consequences which Luther and Calvin draw from
this principle are radically different.

Luther sees the corruption of human nature as inevitably magni-
fied in a collectivity, and accordingly as a powerful argument in favor
of monarchic rule:

If wrong is to be suffered, it is better to suffer it from the rulers than that
the rulers suffer it from their subjects. For the mob has no moderation, and
knows none, and in every individual there stick more than five tyrants. Now,
it is better to suffer wrong from one tyrant, that is, from the ruler, than from
unnumbered tyrants, that is, from the mob.[55]

Luther does not really distinguish between democracy and mob rule,
which he sees as the negation of all orderly government. The mob can

never be either Christian or truly reasonable. Faith, justice, and reason may belong to individuals, but never to the mob, which carries everything to excess. Monarchy allows the possibility of rule by a Christian, just, and reasonable prince, but even the tyranny and unreasoning savagery of a bad prince cannot be as bad as the rule of the mob. Respect for, and obedience to, the secular authority is a prerequisite of stable social life, but cannot survive in the atmosphere of democracy. Monarchy is the best form of government, but not necessarily absolute monarchy, for Luther does not hesitate to place moral and religious limits on the exercise of political power, and is quite prepared to acknowledge the value of constitutional checks on the monarch on the pattern of the Imperial Diet vis-à-vis the Emperor.[56]

From the principle of the depravity of man, Calvin draws as his first conclusion that rulers must be ruled, or in other words, that there should be some system of "checks and balances." Accordingly, while he admits that all forms of government have weaknesses and are liable to perversion, he strongly prefers some kind of aristocratic rule, either based on popular franchise or not, because "owing to the vices or defects of men it is safer and more tolerable when several bear rule, that they may thus mutually resist, instruct, and admonish each other, and should any one be disposed to go too far, the others are censors and masters to curb his excess." [57] Checks and balances in the exercise of political power, operating *within* the government, are not seen by Calvin as in any way derogating from the sovereignty of God; indeed they are a constant curb on the rulers' inherent tendency toward presumption against God and tyranny over men.

Liberty and a republican constitution are great goods. But they are gifts of God and we may not demand them or set about obtaining them for ourselves. The Christian is to be no utopian revolutionary. Calvin values popular election—with safeguards against excess. Election is a feature of the properly ordered Church and also a great privilege and responsibility when it is extended into the realm of secular government. But in neither case does Calvin idolize democracy, and he has no use for notions of popular sovereignty. In the Church a properly conducted election can do no more than recognize God's prior calling of an individual to a particular ministry, and in the State the elective process is likewise the simple recognition that God has raised up a suitable person for a post. The power and authority flow from God and not the electors, and an elected magistrate is entitled to no less obedience and respect than a hereditary sovereign.[58] Liberty and the right to elect one's rulers are good, but not of ultimate importance for, as Calvin insistently reminds us, "It matters not what your condition among men, nor under what laws you live, since in them the Kingdom of Christ does not at all exist." [59]

### 3. "Let Every Soul be Subject unto the Higher Powers"

Since the political authority is God's servant and representative, by being obedient to it we are being obedient to God Himself: "Men ought to obey rulers as His officers and be subject to them with all fear and reverence, as to God Himself." [60] Even a bad magistrate, even a tyrant, must be obeyed. The prince's right to obedience is not conditional on his fulfillment of his duties toward his subjects as in Ockham and Marsilius, nor yet is it dependent on his standing before God, whose steward he is, as in Wyclif. We owe our rulers not only our obedience, but also our prayers and, let it be noted, our frank criticism if this is necessary.[61] This duty of obedience is clearly laid down in Holy Scripture, as in Romans 13: "Let every soul be subject unto the higher powers. . . . Whosoever therefore resisteth the power, resisteth the ordinance of God: and they that resist shall receive to themselves damnation. . . . Ye must needs be subject, not only for wrath, but also for conscience' sake."

This clear and unequivocal command of God expressed in Holy Writ is seen as in itself a completely adequate ground for the obligation of obedience. But many subordinate reasons are cited by Luther and Calvin to show that here God's Will coincides with the good of man. No government can be totally bad, and any government, however corrupt, is better than no government at all: "The form of civil government, whatever deformity and corruption it may have, is always better than the absence of princely authority." [62] Just as the misbehavior of one of the parties in a particular case does not justify the upsetting of the institution of marriage, so the misbehavior of the prince does not justify rebellion, which is interpreted as an attack on government as such. Secondly, each people receives the government it deserves: a good ruler expresses God's graciousness, a tyrant His wrath. We ought to be grateful for good government, but no tyranny can express a greater judgment than our sins deserve. Thirdly,

to suffer wrong destroys no man's soul, nay, it improves the soul, though it inflicts loss upon the body and property; but to do wrong [e.g. to resist] that destroys the soul, although it should gain all the world's wealth. . . . For the temporal power can do no harm, since it has nothing to do with preaching and faith and the first three Commandments." [63]

Obedience to an unjust ruler may be a cross we must bear in this world.

To repay evil with evil would, *for a private citizen,* be to disobey God, and harm his own soul. Resistance involves the unauthorized usurpation of God's power of judgment and condemnation, and is accordingly illegitimate (cf. sec. F2–3 below). Finally, in obedience lies the necessary basis of all stable social life. Luther is not abashed to point even to the Tartars and the Persians as examples of how much a deeply engrained habit of obedience contributes to the making of strong and healthy societies.

But in spite of all, the Christian can laugh in the face of the tyrant even as he obeys him, for "we know that if our earthly house of this tabernacle were dissolved, we have a building of God, an house not made with hands, eternal in the heavens" (II Corinthians 5:1), or as Luther expressed it in one of his great hymns:

> God's Word, for all their craft and force,
> One moment will not linger,
> But spite of Hell, shall have its course;
> 'Tis written by His finger.
> And though they take my life,
> Goods, honour, children, wife,
> Yet is their profit small,
> These things shall vanish all:
> The City of God remaineth.[64]

### 4. "We Ought to Obey God Rather than Men"

The Reformers' doctrine of obedience must not be understood simply as the exposition of Romans 13; to balance things and avoid distorting the witness of Scripture we must pay heed also to passages such as Peter's words before the council: "We ought to obey God rather than men" (Acts 5:29). The question of when we may, or must, disobey the "higher powers" is an important one, since disobedience to constituted authority is no light matter, as we have seen. The decision cannot be left to the whimsy or selfish judgment of the individual. Injustice, tyranny, and oppression are in themselves no excuse for disobedience. Nor are we entitled to disobey because obedience will cause suffering for us. Nevertheless, "we are subject to the men who rule over us, *but only in the Lord.* If they command anything against *Him* let us not pay the least regard to it." [65] We are not justified in breaking the clear command of God in order to be obedient to men.

In working out the implications of this position it is important not to forget the distinction between the two kingdoms. A magistrate who refused to convict a criminal on the ground that Christ said, "Judge not that ye be not judged," would not be obeying God rather than men; he would simply be confusing the Gospel with the law. He would, in fact, be being disobedient to God's law of love expressed in the form proper to his situation. But Luther gives two specific examples of circumstances in which disobedience would be permitted. The first is when we are called upon to commit an act of clear injustice against others:

Thus, if a prince desired to go to war, and his cause was manifestly unrighteous, we should not follow nor help him at all; since God has commanded that we should not kill our neighbour nor do him injustice. Likewise, if he bade us bear false witness, steal, lie or deceive, and the like. Here we ought to give up goods, honour, body, and life, that God's commandments may stand.[66]

We are to suffer injustice without complaint, but on no account to become partners in it; and the standard to be applied to determine what is just is the divine and natural law which is best expounded in Scripture, and applied by the reason and conscience to individual cases. The second case of justifiable disobedience is when the secular powers step out of their proper realm and presume to prescribe matters of belief and worship contrary to God's Word, thus claiming to "lord it over man's conscience and faith, and put the Holy Spirit to school according to their mad brains." [67] In such a case we should "pay not the least regard to it." And once again it should be noted that the criterion for justifiable disobedience is not simply the individual's personal conscience and pious feelings. These must not be trusted unless rooted in the Word of God.

But while disobedience is allowable, and indeed obligatory, in such situations, violent *resistance* never is. To resist with the sword would be to confuse the two kingdoms, presuming that the spiritual realm can justifiably assume the sword which belongs properly only to the temporal kingdom. In the absence of any doctrine of social contract, popular sovereignty, or government by consent, there is no basis for subjects to attempt to change governments by violence. Commands of the temporal ruler which clearly contravene the Word of God are in themselves illegitimate, but not even a concatenation of such acts destroys the authority of the government as such and justifies rebellion, or even the threat of force, as Calvin consistently and categorically pointed out in his letters to the persecuted French Protestants. Disobedience refers to particular commands; resistance is aimed at the overthrow of authority.

What, then is a Christian to do when faced by a government which constantly attempts to compel him to disobey the Word of God, and persecutes him for his scruples? Three possibilities are open to him. In

the first place, if disobedience involves great suffering, it may be possible
to fly to another, less tyrannical state, following the injunction of Matthew 10:23: "If they persecute you in this city, fly ye into another." Secondly, if flight is, for one reason or another, inadvisable or impossible,
one must simply suffer, refusing both to obey the illegitimate commands
and to disobey God by violently resisting the secular authority. In the
third place, Luther and Calvin each leave open a small loophole which
seems to provide a conditional justification of resistance in certain
clearly defined circumstances. Luther, at least in late life, was prepared
to admit that positive imperial law made it possible to envisage legitimate resistance to the emperor on the part of the electoral princes in a
number of cases. And Calvin makes much the same point:

> Now, if there are any who today are elected magistrates appointed to
> moderate the licentiousness of princes (like the Ephors who were at one
> time set over against the Spartan Kings, or the Tribunes of the People against
> the Roman Consuls, or the Demarchs against the Senate of the Athenians—
> and possibly it is the same power which the Three Estates employ today in
> every realm whenever they meet as an assembly of notables), then I am so
> far from forbidding them to withstand in their official capacity the fierce li-
> centiousness of Princes, that if they connive helplessly in the Princes' oppres-
> sion and baiting of the more lowly citizens, I would declare them guilty of
> criminal breach of faith because they deceitfully betray the liberty of the peo-
> ple, of which they know themselves the divinely appointed guardians.[68]

This short passage, destined to have fateful consequences in the
later development of Calvinist political thought, must be clearly understood. The subordinate magistrates are a part of the civil government,
but even if elected, are not in any sense the representatives of popular
sovereignty. Their authority, like that of the prince, comes from God,
and to fail to use it for its intended purpose of securing the common
good, even when this involves resisting the monarch, is to be disobedient
to God and invite His judgment. The question of whether the people
at large are entitled to support by force the subordinate magistrates, or
the estates, against the monarch is simply unasked. Calvin would find
this a very tricky question to answer.

Those who suffer patiently under an unjust tyrant should remember
that God is his judge, and he cannot escape God's condemnation. How
this judgment is expressed will be shown in section F.

### 5. Toleration

It is impossible to discover in the writings of Luther a consistent approach to the question of toleration and religious liberty. Even if we

may justifiably say that his thought develops, in general, from a reasonable toleration of dissent in his earlier period to a vehement espousal of persecution in the latter part of his life, he still bristles with contradictions and it is impossible to interpret the majority of his statements on this issue as more than impulsive and often thoughtless responses to particular situations.[69]

Luther denies the right of the papists to persecute him, and at the same time rejoices in being persecuted, as this is a necessary mark of the true Church: "I am not terrified because many of the great persecute and hate me. Rather, I am consoled and strengthened, since in all the Scriptures the persecutors and haters have commonly been wrong, and the persecuted right. The majority always supports the lie, and the minority the truth." [70] And yet later, when the majority was behind him, this principle was discarded and Luther had no hesitation in advocating in the most violent terms the persecution of dissident individuals like Carlstadt and Münzer, or groups like the rebellious peasants, the Anabaptists, and the Jews. In the early period he spoke much of the need to leave the Word free to accomplish its own work, and of the impossibility of enforced faith, and on this ground advocated general toleration in the conviction that the truth would win out. The toleration of heresy, he thought, could sharpen rather than weaken faith: "The Spirit wrote that the Jebusites and Canaanites should be left in the land of promise to give the Israelites exercise in war. . . . This refers to the heretic." [71] And toleration should be extended even to Jews.[72]

His attitude toward Jews, Romanists, and the dissident sects hardened rapidly, and his justifications of persecution are multifarious and often contradictory. In *A Treatise of Good Works* (1520) he lays it down that a prince is an example to the people, for the simple folk will believe as he does. It is therefore his duty to believe and maintain the true religion, and he has no power to decide what the true religion is.[73] In the *Commentary on Psalm 86* (1530) he discusses which heretics should be persecuted and concludes that the secular power should punish those who, on religious grounds, deny the dignity and authority of civil government and also those who deny doctrines which are found clearly in Scripture and are accepted throughout Christendom, for this is blasphemy. As to conflict between Lutherans and Romanists, Luther invites the secular ruler to judge between them on the basis of Scripture and bid the unscriptural party simply to keep silence.[74] But often Luther is far more all-inclusive and bloodthirsty in his demands for the punishment of his opponents. Sometimes he speaks of the death penalty for papists and Anabaptists, sometimes he thinks banishment sufficient. But in any case the Word should be supported by the sword of the civil magistrate. Some of Luther's utterances may be dismissed as obvious rhetorical exaggerations, but it would be more than difficult to argue that in this matter he does not create an "infernal confusion" between the two kingdoms he so clearly differentiated elsewhere.

Calvin's position is much more stable than that of Luther. It is the duty of the Christian magistrate to proceed against heresy even if it is not overtly seditious or blasphemous. The magistrate is God's lieutenant or deputy and accordingly must maintain the honor of God by all means in his power. For heresy is in itself an offense against Christian society, and as a direct assault on the honor of God it is more heinous than the worst offense committed by one man against another. The stamping out of heresy is demanded not only by natural law (as an attempt to undermine society) and Roman law (specifically in the measures against Donatists and Manichees included in the Code of Justinian) but is a specific requirement of Holy Scripture, for "God makes plain that the false prophet is to be stoned without mercy. We are to crush beneath our heel all affections of nature when His honor is involved." [75]

From the persecution of the saints at the hands of ungodly rulers neither Calvin nor Luther drew the conclusion that a godly prince should tolerate all manner of opinions. In their thought there is no trace of the relativism or indifference which is often the basis of toleration. Nor is their doctrine of the two kingdoms another way of stating the modern concept of the separation of Church and State. The truth is known, and its preservation against the assaults of skepticism is a matter of life and death with which both Church and State, each in its proper manner, must concern themselves. No compromise is possible when the truth itself is at stake.

### E. Law

Luther and Calvin recognize three modes of law: the divine law given directly by God in revelation; the natural law, which is available to, and binding upon, all men; and positive law, duly enacted and enforced by the proper secular authority. We will discuss each in turn.

### 1. The Law of God

The divine law is eternal, unchangeable, and absolute. It is the supreme and objective standard against which all human actions should be judged, expressed concisely in the Decalogue and elaborated elsewhere in Holy Scripture. It is given by God, according to Luther, for two purposes (known technically as the "uses" of the law), and to these Calvin adds a third. In the first place, since it reveals the righteousness of God and His demands on man, it convicts of sin and points to the need of forgiveness. The law, in this its "theological use," acts as a kind of mirror showing each man himself as he really is in his depravity and sinfulness, and eliminating the false self-understandings based on pride. In the second place, the law serves to restrain sinners from open evil and procure the "forced and extorted righteousness necessary for the good of society." In the third place (and here Calvin and Luther part company), for believers "it is the best instrument for enabling them daily to learn with greater truth and certainty what the will of the Lord is which they aspire to follow, and to confirm them in this knowledge." [76]

Are all the legal prescriptions found in Scripture to be reckoned divine law binding upon man? Luther and Calvin, like most other Christian thinkers, but in opposition to certain extreme sectarians, distinguish between time-bound and eternal divine law. Luther and Calvin have no hesitation in pronouncing the ceremonial law and most of the detailed economic and social legislation to be found in the Old Testament to belong to the former category and therefore to be obsolete. The ceremonial and ritual law has been abrogated by the Work of Christ (as the Epistle to the Hebrews argues), and there is no obligation on us to attempt to reproduce the polity or legal code of old Israel in modern times. These are certainly useful and instructive as examples of social and political arrangements agreeable to God, but they are conditioned by time and environment and are now simply not applicable. We have here a special instance of a social and economic system from which much may be learned, but which was never meant to be slavishly copied. It should be regarded, with much of the rest of the Bible, as a kind of commentary on the Decalogue. General guidance on such matters as the relation of Church and State may be found in both Old and New Testaments, and in this sense the Bible is the source of the "old orders" which must be recovered. And as to the external form of the Church, where Luther finds the structure of the New Testament Church as, at least in large part, time-bound, Calvin looks to the Apostolic Church as described in the Bible as a detailed pattern of the true form of the Church. Obviously in these matters, external criteria are being applied to Scripture in order to decide what is time-bound and what is absolute.

Both Reformers reject emphatically any "two-standard" conception of the law, such as had become accepted in the medieval Church: "There are not various rules of life, but one perpetual and inflexible rule." [77] All men are called to perfection, and all men stand under the judgment of the law. The old distinction between laws which are binding on all men, or all Christians, and counsels of perfection which guide the "religious," the athletes of the Spirit, is cast aside. The call to perfection lies at the heart of the law, but down the ages it had been clouded over, primarily by a misunderstanding of justification which assumed that salvation was possible simply by obedience to a series of outward regulations. Accordingly Christ is seen as the best expounder of the divine law since He "restored it to its integrity by maintaining and purifying it when obscured by the falsehood and defiled by the leaven of the Pharisees." [78] But to assert the unity and universality of the law is not to deny that particular obligations vary in relation to function: confusion has often arisen from the attempt to universalize standards which are in fact only appropriate in the exercise of a particular function in society. The same specific obligations are not binding upon a man in all his various official and private capacities. As a statesman or an executioner a man may be called upon to perform actions which would be wrong and improper for him acting as a father or a private citizen. The moral teaching of Jesus, by and large, deals with private morality and was not meant to be applied otherwise. But the varying functional standards through which God's law is expressed only apparently conflict, for love is the "queen and mistress" of all laws, and in specific situations all law must be tested by the rule of charity, for this is at the heart of all true law.

The divine law is a call to perfection and godliness; but perfection is quite unattainable by fallen man, and accordingly the law must point beyond itself to the forgiveness and atonement offered in the Gospel.

## 2. The Law of Nature

The natural law is, for both Luther and Calvin, ultimately identical with the divine law. Unlike Aquinas and most of the Scholastics, the Reformers never speak of natural law as perfected or complemented by a "supernatural" law. There is only one law, even if it may be looked at from various points of view. The law has a "spiritual use" (to convict of sin and point toward the Gospel) and a "civil use" (to curb public immorality), and for Calvin also a third use among the redeemed, but the law itself is always one and unchanged.

But the relation of the divine law and the law of nature *as we know it,* is not one of simple identity. It is important to notice that by the term "nature" in this context is meant the uncorrupted, ordered nature of man and the world before the Fall. Objectively considered, the law of nature is the law of God, absolute, unconditional, and binding on all men. Unlike the revealed law of God which was given to a particular people, the law of nature is in principle knowable by all men. It is

the true and eternal rule of righteousness presented to the men of all nations and all times, who would frame their lives conformably with the Will of God.[79] For although the Gentiles did not receive the written law of Moses, yet they received the spiritual law which is impressed upon all, both Jews and Gentiles, to which also all are under obligation.[80]

But since corruption extends not only to man's will but also to his reason and conscience, his understanding of the natural law is impaired. Accordingly there is a difference, even sometimes a conflict, between the divine law and the natural law as understood and interpreted by fallen man. Sin and corruption show themselves in man's constant attempts to revise and alter the law of nature in order to make it less contrary to his fallen will and desires. Sin obscures and darkens his comprehension of the law of nature, so that the divine law is revealed to remove the evasions introduced by man's fallen nature.

This is true of both "tables" of the law. With regard to the first table, the measure of the natural law available to fallen man teaches him simply that he ought to worship and serve God, but what this involves, *how* he is to serve God and who the true God is, he can now find only in the revealed divine law. With regard to the second table, a good example of the way in which the divine law expands, clarifies, and purifies the adulterated or stunted natural law is provided by the question of obedience:

Every man of understanding deems it most absurd to submit to unjust and tyrannical domination, provided it can by any means be thrown off, and there is but one opinion prevailing among men, that it is the part of an abject and servile mind to bear it patiently, the part of an honourable and high-spirited mind to rise up against it. Indeed, the revenge of injuries is not regarded by philosophers as a vice. But the Lord, condemning this too lofty spirit, prescribes to His people that patience which mankind deem infamous.[81]

Pride has perverted the subjective natural law so that authoritatively promulgated divine law has become the necessary means to the restoration of the objective and absolute law of nature.

How is the law of nature to be discovered and applied in specific situations? The law is not innate in man as such, but is an external objective standard set up by God, discoverable, at least in part, by the use of reason or, in Calvin, reason and conscience cooperating. Some men may be more reasonable than others, but it is never a simple business to find the natural law. Its discovery requires careful thought and consideration of all the issues, for "the noble gem called natural law and reason is a rare thing among the children of men." [82]

### 3. The Law of the State

The law of the state has as its purpose simply the maintenance of outward conformity with morality, and the discipline necessary for social life. It is related, it is true, to the divine-natural law, but is not directly deducible from it. The divine-natural law sets, as it were, the limits within which free play is given to the statesman to ordain such laws as may seem fit in the light of the circumstances and political necessities. Reason—fallen reason—must produce such legislation as the conditions seem to require without conflicting with the law of God. "But if it is true that each nation has been left at liberty to enact the laws which it judges to be beneficial, still these are always to be tested by the law of love, so that while they vary in form, they must proceed on the same principle." [83]

Positive law must be obeyed, even when it is patently far from perfect, save in extreme situations such as those discussed in section D 4. Luther, while maintaining this obligation of obedience, has a manly contempt for mere positive law—it is "sick law" as against the "healthy law" of nature. Its inescapable rigidity makes civil law inadequate:

> Whatever is done with nature's power succeeds very smoothly without any [positive] law; in fact it overrides all the laws. But if nature is missing and things must be done according to laws, that amounts to mere beggary and patch-work; and no more is achieved than is inherent in diseased nature. It is as if I set up a general rule that for a meal one should eat two rolls and drink a small glass of wine. If a healthy man comes to the table, he may well consume four or six rolls and drink a decanter or two of wine; thus he requires more than the law stipulates. But if a sick person comes to the table, he will eat half a roll and drink three spoonfuls of wine. Thus he will observe no more of such a law than his sick condition permits, or he will die if he has to observe this law.[84]

Lawmaking is a tricky and unsatisfactory business, and very few are the men who are adequately equipped to legislate, so: "Here one must patch and darn, and help oneself with the laws, sayings, and examples of the heroes as they are recorded in books. Thus we must continue to be disciples of those speechless masters we call books. Yet we never do as well as it is written there; we crawl after it and cling to it as to a bench or to a cane." [85]

It follows that legislation is a specialized and skilled craft in the details of which the theologian as such has no special competence. This principle, together with the Reformers' rejection of the Canon Law, leads to some radical consequences in Luther:

> What is the proper procedure for us nowadays in matters of marriage and divorce? I have said that this should be left to the lawyers and be made subject to secular government. For marriage is a rather secular and outward thing, having to do with wife and children, house and home, and with other matters which belong to the realm of government, all of which have been completely subjected to reason (Genesis 1.28). Therefore we should not tamper with what the government and wise men decide and prescribe on the basis of the laws and of reason. Christ is not functioning here (Matthew 5.31–32) as a lawyer or governor, to set down or prescribe any regulation for outward conduct.[86]

## F. Politics as a Vocation

### 1. Man and his Calling

All men have two types of callings from God. On the one hand, all men, though sinners, are called to salvation, into God's eternal kingdom. As regards salvation, all men are equal, all equally requiring God's free forgiveness. But as regards life in this world, equality disappears and is replaced by order and rank, and men find themselves in various "stations" or "vocations" in which they are required to serve God by serving their neighbor. Luther and Calvin both reject any possibility of a "religious" vocation in which service to God may be isolated from service to one's fellows. Each man has a variety of different functions in society which are to be seen as divine vocations. One man, for example, may have the vocations of husband, father, farmer, and citizen, each with its specific duties and obligations. In each, vocation acts as a curb on man's selfishness, forcing him to look outward and care for his fellows as well as himself. God's care for mankind is largely expressed through His placing of men in vocations, in each of which they are enticed into caring for their fellows and become, whether knowingly or not, "masks" or "veils" of God Himself, the instruments of His love.

Now, while vocations are in themselves good, men may and often do abuse their vocations by failing to do the appropriate duties or doing them improperly. Again, great confusion and disorder are caused if vocations are not kept distinct and separate. It would be quite wrong, for instance, for a magistrate to be as sharp and strict in his private relations as he is required to be when acting in his judicial capacity. Nor should we, spurred by ambition or love of novelty, abandon a vocation in which we find ourselves for another. This is presumption, and it is only at our peril that we neglect the duties which God has placed at our hand in order to seek something different. This teaching safeguards the stability of society and curbs sinful ambition, but it must not be allowed to conflict with the fact that God Himself often calls men to new functions, and *His* call must never be disregarded: "In everything the call of the Lord is the foundation and beginning of right action." [87]

The vocation of the statesman is a divine calling which is to have especial honor among men. Like any other man in *his* vocation, the statesman is God's "mask" or "veil," but he is entitled to peculiar honor because he is in a special sense the deputy of God. As far as men are concerned, in political life he stands in God's place.

Now, it is true that individual men are bound to obey the injunctions of the law. But God, whose nature is love, is not bound by this law, and often His love is expressed in ways which appear contrary to the law which is binding upon private individuals. Through vocation God frequently obliges men to do actions which appear to be contrary to the law, but are in fact, at a different level, expressions of the law of love. This is very apparent in the vocation of politics, where the statesman is obliged, in seeming contradiction both to law and Gospel, to resort on occasions to force, coercion, and violence. But: "The hand that wields this sword and slays with it is then no more man's hand but God's, who hangs, tortures, beheads, slays, and fights. All these are His works and His judgments." [88] And:

The Law of the Lord forbids to kill; but that murder may not go unpunished, the Lawgiver Himself puts the sword into the hands of His ministers. . . . Therefore it is easy to conclude that in this respect they are not subject to the common law, by which, although the Lord ties the hands of all men, still He ties not His justice which He exercises by the hands of magistrates—just as when a prince forbids all his subjects to beat or hurt any one, he nevertheless prohibits not his officers from executing the justice which he has specially committed to them.[89]

It is important to notice that this distinction between private and "vocational" moralities does not imply that they are not intimately related and connected. The statesman is not emancipated from the full rigor of the call to perfection as far as his private life is concerned, nor is he given *carte blanche* for his official actions. In both, albeit sometimes in different and seemingly discordant ways, he must express the love and justice of God.

## 2. *The Judgment of God*

The statesman, although he may be a "god" in the realm of politics as far as other men are concerned, entitled to obedience, respect, and honor, is in the eyes of God simply another sinful man. His authority and his dignity are borrowed and do not really belong to him at all, but to God. He is in a position of special temptation to assume that the gifts with which he has been entrusted are his own to be used as he may please, and he finds it difficult not to deny his dependence on, and subjection to, God. But should he become presumptuous, "he is not worthy to be compared to a louse or a maggot or any other vermin—for lice are still creatures of God, while he is a villain who was appointed by God His lieutenant but constantly mocks and forgets his sovereign Lord." [90]

How is God's judgment on the presumptuous—and that means, as far as men are concerned, unjust and tyrannical—ruler expressed? While it is certain that he will be judged in eternity, it is also true that God's judgment is expressed within history. Luther characteristically oversimplifies his true position when he argues that "it always happens, and always has happened that those who begin war unnecessarily are beaten" [91] for he admits elsewhere that God's judgment is not expressed in such simple terms. But nevertheless, retribution does come within history and, for example "tyrants run the risk that, by God's decree, their subjects may rise up . . . and slay them or drive them out." [92] This *fact* is not to be understood as in any sense a *justification* of resistance. Those who rebel are thereby guilty before God. But "the instrumentality of the wicked" can be "employed by God while He continues free from every taint." [93] If all his subjects were faithful Christians, the ruler need fear no insurrection; but since it is impossible for this to be so, he is wise to beware of the wrath of God expressed through the violence of the godless. The workings of God's Providence do not depend on the faithfulness of men. Or God may perhaps raise up foreign rulers and nations to subject the unrighteous prince:

Thus He tamed the power of Tyre by the Egyptians; the insolence of the Egyptians by the Assyrians; the ferocity of the Assyrians by the Chaldeans; the confidence of Babylon by the Medes and Persians, Cyrus having previously subdued the Medes, while the ingratitude of the Kings of Judah and Israel, and their impious contumacy after all his kindness, he subdued and punished —at one time by the Assyrians, at another by the Babylonians.[94]

Or God may curb the tyrant by the subordinate magistrates, as we have seen, or by a "Hero."

### 3. The Hero

Politics, according to Luther, is normally a matter of "patching and darning." Understandably, sooner or later the garment will wear out and require renewal. The last stage of decay is usually insufferable tyranny and oppression and the agent of renewal, the destroyer of the old garment and the tailor of the new is called a *Wündermann* or *vir heroicus*. Although it is presumptuous for private individuals to attempt to overthrow established authority or refashion the state, God entrusts to certain individuals at certain times this special vocation. Examples of such men cited are Samson, David, Jehoida, Cyrus, Themistocles, Alexander the Great, Augustus, and Naaman—all, perhaps significantly, non-Christians.

The hero receives his commission directly from God, who constantly instructs and guides him:

When David wanted to beat Goliath, they wanted to teach him; they put armour on him and equipped him. Yes, Sir. But David could not wear this armour. He had another master in mind, and he slew Goliath before he could know how he was to do it. For he was no apprentice either, trained in this craft; he was a master, trained for it by God Himself.[95]

The hero is not subject to the laws and rules which are binding on ordinary men, or even on ordinary rulers. He may lead a rebellion, and the people may justly follow him. He is endowed with rare gifts of reason and is privy to the counsels of God, so that he may even override the law, or at least improve it, for he is himself "the living law." Under his regime tyranny is destroyed, everything improves, and a new era is inaugurated. But he is no pattern for ordinary folk, and woe betide the man who, without a special calling from God, attempts to ape the hero.

The hero of Luther cannot justifiably be compared with the superman of Nietzsche, nor yet with the hero of Carlyle. His freedom from law and his powers of innovation and restoration flow, not from himself, but from God's choice of him, and his direct dependence on God. The glory, the worship, the power, and the sovereignty belong to God and not to him. His pre-eminent gifts are indeed *gifts,* and should not be held to imply any freedom from the taint of original sin. As proof of this, Luther points out that most of the heroes, their work finished, come to bad ends, having finally yielded to the sin of presumption.

Calvin, refusing to take as gloomy a view as Luther of the potentialities of secular government, sees the hero simply as a "Providential Deliverer" from oppression. Renewal is not his primary function, for this is a perfectly normal aspect of political activity. Since politics is not simply a matter of "patching and darning," no special God-sent tailor is required for the making of a new garment.

# NOTES

*Abbreviations:*
*WA—Weimarer Ausgabe* of the Works of Martin Luther.
*PE—Philadelphia Edition* of *The Works of Martin Luther.* 6 vols. in English. Philadelphia: A. J. Holman Company, 1915–32.
*AE—American Edition of Luther's Works.* Ed. Jaroslav Pelikan and Helmut T. Lehman. 55 volumes in process of publication by Concordia Publishing House, St. Louis, and Muhlenberg Press, Philadelphia.
*CR—Corpus Reformatorum,* in which Calvin's works edited by Baum, Cunitz, and Reuss comprise 59 volumes. Brunswick, 1863–1900.
*Ins.—*Calvin, *Institutes of the Christian Religion.* Citations, unless otherwise stated, are from the translation of Henry Beveridge. London: James Clarke & Co., 1949.

1. John Calvin, *Ins.,* III. xiv. 9.
2. Martin Luther, *Commentary on Galatians,* ed. P. S. Watson (London: James Clarke & Co., 1953), pp. 39, etc.
3. Luther, *Disputation against Scholastic Theology,* Clauses 6, 10, 17, *AE,* XXXI, 4 ff.
4. *Ibid.,* Clauses 41, 47, 50.
5. Luther, *Galatians,* p. 130.
6. Calvin, Preface to the French edition of the *Institutes.*
7. Calvin, *Ins.,* I. vii. 2.
8. Luther, *PE,* I, 367.
9. Luther, *The Bondage of the Will,* trans. J. I. Packer and D. R. Johnston (London: James Clarke & Co., 1957), pp. 70–74.
10. Luther, *Disputation against Scholastic Theology,* Clause 40, *AE,* XXXI, 4 ff.
11. Luther, *A Treatise of Good Works, PE,* I, 199.
12. Calvin, *Ins.,* III. xix. 15.
13. Luther, *Galatians,* p. 122.
14. Calvin, *Ins.,* IV. xx. 2.
15. *Ibid.,* III. xix. 15.
16. Luther, *Commentary on Psalm 101, AE,* XIII, 194.
17. *Ibid.,* p. 195.
18. Luther, *Galatians,* p. 123.
19. Luther, *Secular Authority: to what extent it should be obeyed, PE,* III, 237.
20. Luther, *Psalm 101, AE,* XIII, 174.
21. Luther, *Of Good Works, PE,* I, 199; Calvin, *Ins.,* III. xix. 15.
22. The term "the State" is used here, and throughout this chapter, simply as a synonym of "the civil government."
23. Calvin, *Sermon 1 Tim. 6:13–16, CR,* LIII, 618.

24. Luther, *Whether Soldiers, too, can be Saved*, PE, V, 35.

25. Wyclif, *Select English Works*, ed. Arnold, III, 447; *Tractatus de Ecclesia*, ed. Loserth, *passim;* Calvin, *Prefatory Address of the Institutes to the King of France*, sec. 6, etc.; Luther, *To the Christian Nobility of the German Nation*, PE, II, 61 ff.

26. Luther, *To the Christian Nobility of the German Nation*, p. 68.

27. Calvin, *Ins.*, IV, i. 7.

28. *Ibid.*, xi. 1, 3; xii.

29. *Ibid.*, xx. 9.

30. Calvin, *Homilies on I Samuel 38*, CR, XXIX, 659.

31. Calvin, *Ins.*, IV. xx. 2.

32. Calvin, *Letter to the King of England*, CR, XIV, 40.

33. Calvin, *Commentary on Isaiah*, CR, XXXVII, 211; *Ins.*, IV. xx. 2, 3.

34. Luther, *WA*, 10.iii. 380.10.

35. Calvin, *Ins.*, IV. xx. 12.

36. Luther, *Psalm 101, AE*, XIII, 198.

37. Luther, *To the Christian Nobility of the German Nation*, PE, II, 146.

38. Luther, *Psalm 101, AE*, XIII, 199.

39. *Ibid.*, p. 164.

40. Calvin, *Ins.*, I. xv. 8.

41. Luther, *Disputation against Scholastic Theology*, Clause 34, *AE*, XXXI, 4 ff.

42. Calvin, *Ins.*, II. ii. 2.

43. *Ibid.*, 4.

44. *Ibid.*, 12.

45. *Ibid.*

46. *Ibid.*, 13.

47. *Ibid.* Cf. Luther, *Galatians*, p. 490.

48. Calvin, CR, XXX, 487.

49. Luther, *On Secular Authority*, PE, III, 230.

50. *Ibid.*, p. 231.

51. Calvin, *Commentary on Romans* (Edinburgh: Calvin Translation Society, 1844, 1849), on 13:4.

52. Luther, *On Secular Authority*, PE, III, 245. Calvin, *Ins.*, IV. xx. 2, 3.

53. Luther, *Commentary on Psalm 82, AE*, XIII, 51. Cf. *Ins.*, IV. xx. 25.

54. Calvin, *Ins.*, IV. xx. 8; *Romans* 13:1–3; *Commentary on I Peter* (Edinburgh: Calvin Translation Society, 1855), on 2:13–14. Luther, *A Treatise of Good Works*, PE, I, 263–64.

55. Luther, *Whether Soldiers, too, can be Saved*, PE, V, 45.

56. *Ibid.*, pp. 45, 48, 50; *On Secular Authority*, PE, III, 237; *Psalm 101*, AE, XIII, 160–61.

57. Calvin, *Ins.*, IV. xx. 8. Cf. *Sermons on Deuteronomy*, CR, XXVII, 453–60.

58. Calvin, *Ins.*, IV. iii. 13–15.

59. *Ibid.*, xx. 1.

60. Luther, *Psalm 82, AE*, XIII, 44.

61. Luther, *WA*, LII, 189; Calvin, *Commentary on Psalm 82*, on vs. 2.

62. Calvin, *Commentary on I Peter*, on 2:14.

63. Luther, *A Treatise of Good Works*, PE, I, 263.

64. Luther, *"Ein'feste Burg,"* trans. Thomas Carlyle.

65. Calvin, *Ins.*, IV. xx. 32. (Italics supplied.)

66. Luther, *Of Good Works*, PE, I, 271.

67. Luther, *On Secular Authority*, PE, III, 230.

68. Calvin, *Ins.*, IV. xx. 31 (trans. D. F.)

69. The Reformers' attitudes to toleration are expounded and discussed with great penetration and balance in the works of R. H. Bainton, in particular in his article on "The Development and Consistency of Luther's Attitude to Religious Liberty," *The Harvard Theological Review*, vol. XXII, no. 2; in the Introduction to his edition of Castellio's *Concerning Heretics* (New York: Columbia University Press, 1935); and in his books *The Travail of Religious Liberty* (London: Lutterworth Press, 1953) and *Hunted Heretic: The Life and Death of Michael Servetus, 1511–1553* (Boston:

Beacon Press, 1953). The paragraphs which follow rely much on these works, from which several citations have been borrowed.

70. *WA*, 7.317 (1521).
71. *WA*, 1.624 f. (1518).
72. *WA*, 2.336 (1523).
73. *PE*, I, 265 (1520).
74. *AE*, XIII, 61 ff.
75. Calvin, *Commentary on Deuteronomy*, chap. xiii.
76. Luther, *Galatians*, pp. 297 ff; Calvin, *Ins.*, II. vii. 8–12.
77. Calvin, *Ins.*, II. vii. 13.
78. *Ibid.*, viii. 7.
79. *Ibid.*, IV. xx. 15.
80. Luther, *Romerbrief*, 37.15 f.
81. Calvin, *Ins.*, II. ii. 24.
82. Luther, *Psalm 101, AE*, XIII, 161.
83. Calvin, *Ins.*, IV. xx. 16.
84. Luther, *Psalm 101, AE*, XIII, 163.
85. *Ibid.*, p. 164.

86. Luther, *Commentary on the Sermon on the Mount, AE*, XXI, 93.
87. Calvin, *Ins.*, III. x. 6. Cf. *Commentary on the Harmony of the Gospels* (Edinburgh: Calvin Translation Society, 1845–46) under Matt. 22:21 and Luther, *Whether Soldiers, too, can be Saved, PE*, V, 34; *Commentary on the Sermon on the Mount, AE*, XXI, 23.
88. Luther, *Whether Soldiers, too, can be Saved, PE*, V, 36.
89. Calvin, *Ins.*, IV. xx. 10. From the word "Therefore" this citation is found only in the French from the edition of 1541.
90. *CR*, XLI, 395.
91. Luther, *Whether Soldiers, too, can be Saved, PE*, V, 37.
92. *Ibid.*, p. 48.
93. Calvin, Heading of *Ins.*, I. xviii.
94. *Ibid.*, IV. xx. 30.
95. Luther, *Psalm 101, AE*, XIII, 156.

# READINGS

A.  Luther, Martin. *Commentary on Psalm 101*, vol. XIII, pp. 146 ff., of the American Edition of *Luther's Works*. Ed. Jaroslav Pelikan and Helmut T. Lehmann. St. Louis: Concordia Publishing House, and Philadelphia: Muhlenburg Press, 1956—.

Calvin, John. *Institutes of the Christian Religion*. Ed. J. T. McNeill. Trans. F. L. Battles. *"Library of Christian Classics."* Philadelphia: Westminster Press, 1959. II. ii. 1–4, 12–16, 22–24; III. xix. 15; IV. xx.

B.  Luther, Martin. *The Open Letter to the Christian Nobility of the German Nation. The Works of Martin Luther.* 6 vols. Philadelphia: A. J. Holman Company, 1915–32. Vol. II, pp. 61 ff.

Luther, Martin. *Secular Authority: To what Extent it Should be Obeyed*, in *ibid.*, vol. III, pp. 223 ff.

Luther, Martin. *Whether Soldiers, too, can be Saved*, in *ibid.*, vol. V, pp. 32 ff.

Calvin, John. *Institutes.* I. xv. 4, 6–8; IV. x. 1–12; xi.

Calvin, John. *Commentary on Romans.* Edinburgh: Calvin Translation Society, 1844, 1849. On Romans 13.1–5.

Calvin, John. *Commentary on the Harmony of the Gospels.* Edinburgh: Calvin Translation Society, 1845–46. On Matt. 5:31; Matt. 22:21; Matt. 26: 52–56.

# RICHARD HOOKER

## 1553–1600

Hooker's great work, *The Laws of Ecclesiastical Polity,* was conceived as an extended attack on the position of the Calvinistic Puritans of his day. But we should notice that this Puritan position was in many somewhat inconsistent ways different from that of Calvin himself. The Puritans in England, the Huguenots in France, and Knox and his followers in Scotland all claimed to be disciples of Calvin and attributed high authority to his writings. But in fact they altered much of their master's system of doctrine, especially his political teaching, and by emphasizing certain aspects, neglecting others, and introducing alien concepts, they produced a distinct and far less consistent political theology.

The heart of their innovation lay in a thoroughgoing disparagement of the validity of human reason even in the spheres which Calvin had recognized as proper to it, together with the assertion of the exclusive authority and total adequacy of Holy Scripture as the guide in *all* things. John Knox, for instance, showed in his *The First Blast of the Trumpet against the Monstrous Regiment of Women* (1558) no embarrassment at defending almost entirely with Scriptural arguments the strictly political and legal proposition that no woman may hold political power.[1] And the English Puritans suggested as a principle for the guidance of Parliament "that nothing be done in this or any other thing, but that which you have the express warrant of God's Word for."[2] Such statements remove all limits to the scope of scriptural authority and leave the autonomous reason without place or function. As a result of this innovation, the understanding of what Scripture is undergoes a change. It is no longer simply the record of God's mighty acts to which faith clings, the raw material of dogma, the guide to the imitation of

Christ, the herald of salvation, the "earthen vessel" in which God's treasure is to be found. Now it is looked upon as a totally infallible and adequate compend of moral and political guidance, a textbook in which the statesman discovers how to rule and the philosopher how to escape the delusions of corrupted reason. The considerable degree of critical acumen with which Luther and Calvin had approached Scripture almost disappears and is replaced with a new kind of bibliolatry.

This change made theocratic claims almost inevitable. The Church is the guardian of God's Word, and it is the duty of the ministers to preach it. And since this Word is the only sure guide in politics, as in everything else, kings and magistrates should submit themselves to the guidance of the Church and its ministers in all things. Thomas Cartwright, the Puritan divine against whose works so much of *The Laws of Ecclesiastical Polity* is directed, was further then he knew from the teaching of his master, Calvin, when he wrote that kings should "throw down their crowns before" the Church "and lick the dust from off her feet." [3]

But it was the question of resistance which brought the conflict between Calvin and his successors into the open. Calvin's far from unequivocal suggestion that the "subordinate magistrates" might curb the power of kings,[4] although based more on constitutional law than scriptural authority, became the banner which the radical Calvinists nailed to their mast. The *Vindiciae contra Tyrannos,* written by an unknown French Huguenot in the last quarter of the sixteenth century, asserted that even if only *one* magistrate were prepared to resist one of those kings who "toss the poor people like tennis-balls," it was the duty of all Christian subjects to take to arms to overthrow the tyrant. In defence of the right, and indeed obligation, of resistance, the author of the *Vindiciae* argues that the Old Testament shows political society to be based on two covenants or contracts, the one between God, the king, and the people, constituting a "People of God," the other between the king and the people by the terms of which the people promise to obey and the king to rule justly. The Bible, the *Vindiciae* claims, shows sovereignty to be vested by God in the people and only delegated by them to the monarch and magistrates. On similar premises Knox, writing to his followers in Scotland, had asserted emphatically the duty of revolt against an ungodly prince and appealed even to the commons to disown the tyrant. Old philosophical ideas such as popular sovereignty and contract which had been commonplaces in the Middle Ages, but rejected by the Reformers, were now reappearing in a new, ostensibly biblical, guise. Holy Scripture and Calvin were still the avowed authorities, but now the tone and terminology were often far different.

The godly were now called not so much to suffering and passive obedience as to the creation everywhere of Christian commonwealths on
earth despite all difficulties and opposition.

It was against such biblical radicalism that Hooker launched his
powerful counterattack. He might have appealed to Calvin against the
Calvinists, and indeed he does so on occasion,[5] but he was not a Calvinist of any sort and was not interested simply in scoring debating points.
For him the authority of Calvin was not final. Nor could he enter controversy on the basis of a shared understanding of the authority of
Scripture, for he could not admit that "in Scripture all things needful
to be done must needs be contained." [6] Much of what he wished to say
concerned matters in which Scripture alone was not, he claimed, the
sole authority. In matters of ecclesiastical and civil government, for
instance, there must be an appeal to reason for "there is as yet no way
known how to determine of things disputed without the use of natural
reason," [7] and even Christ used to exercise His reason in argument. In
the natural sphere at least, reason and the great "reasoners" of the past
must have a proper authority. Accordingly, Hooker finds himself able
to invoke freely against his opponents the authorities of antiquity, notably the Fathers and the Scholastics, particularly Aquinas. Since the
Puritans had chosen to argue, they could not escape from reason by
pleading the absolute authority of Scripture or faith.[8]

*The Laws of Ecclesiastical Polity* is a long work in eight books
covering an immense field. The first five books were published during
Hooker's lifetime, but the remaining three had to wait for publication
until the middle of the next century. The authenticity of these three
books is now beyond doubt, although Book VI as we have it is just a
fragment.[9] Stylistically the *Ecclesiastical Polity* is a masterpiece of prose,
and it is probably the first great work of philosophy and theology to be
written in English. If its original intention is polemical, it yet ranks as an
important work of political philosophy since it rises above immediate
conflicts to abiding matters of principle.

In Book I Hooker, relying heavily on the authority of Thomas
Aquinas, expounds the metaphysical basis of his thought. It is not
misleading to suggest that he gives to metaphysics the place which the
Reformers had given to dogmatics in their political thought. The world,
he holds, is an ordered cosmos in which everything works toward an
end proper to it. Every end is itself a means toward some further end,
except the final end, the *summum bonum,* God, who is good in Himself,
and cannot be a means to any further good. This cosmos is governed by
law, which is defined as "a directive rule unto goodness of operation," [10]
given by a superior. But "the being of God is a kind of law in His work-

ing; for that perfection which God is giveth perfection to that He doth." [11] The law laid down by God for Himself and all other things is the eternal law, and from it all other laws flow.[12] This eternal law is not an expression of an *arbitrary* will of God but is reasonable, for reason is inherent in the Godhead.[13] Thus Hooker rejects at the very start the voluntarism of the Nominalists and Reformers. Reason lies at the heart of things and is always directed toward goodness, since goodness is of the essence of God.[14] The acts and edicts of God are always both good and reasonable, and this "reasonable goodness" of God expresses itself through the various laws which bind all created things and are derived from the eternal law. These laws take different forms in relation to the beings and operations over which they have force. Natural law binds all created things. Celestial law has reference to angels. The law of reason obliges all rational creatures, who are bound also by the divine law which is known through revelation. Human law is law enacted by men and derived from rational or divine law. All these derived laws together comprise a "Second Law Eternal." Some may be broken, and thence springs evil which, however, cannot change the cosmos into a chaos, for evil and sin are at least permitted by God, and may be said to fall under the first law eternal, God's unchanging purpose.[15]

Man, like all other created things, necessarily seeks his perfection. All men pursue goodness since evil cannot be desired as such.[16] The perfection which man seeks takes a threefold form: "sensual" (or physical), intellectual, and spiritual.[17] Each mode of perfection is desired naturally by man, but spiritual perfection, the beatific vision which is the crown of man's striving, is attainable only by supernatural means provided by God to remedy the damage caused by the Fall.[18] Nature and supernature are two complementary orders to which man belongs. Accordingly his perfection must be both natural and supernatural.

How does man know what his perfection is? The good is known by means of reason,[19] or general acceptance, that is, the reason of many.[20] By following reason we are in fact following the commands of God. It is the will rather than the reason of man which is corrupted by sin, for reason points clearly to a perfection which fallen man finds himself unable to achieve by himself. Nature can take him so far, but supernatural assistance is necessary if true bliss is to be attained.

Man, then, is bound by a number of different laws. As a sensual or physical organism he operates in accordance with the same kind of law that binds all created things; as an intelligent being, he is bound by the law of reason; as an eternal soul he is bound by supernatural law. And within this basic scheme, Hooker sees many subdivisions and mixed modes of law. Man's many functions have each their proper law, and there are many different authorities which may impose laws in various spheres. There is supernatural law, moral law, political law, ecclesiastical law, and the law of nations, each produced by a different legislator.[21] All these laws are fundamentally God's laws and arise from the eternal law, but the authority to enact some of them is delegated by God to men or societies, while in others God Himself remains both legislator and enforcer.

Within this system of laws we must distinguish the mutable from the immutable. The eternal law is unchanging, and it is the direct expression of the reason and will of God. Again the "laws" which are the formulations of the great dogmatic truths of the Christian faith are eternal. If we wish to know whether a law may be altered, we must consider in each case the end to which it is directed.

The Jewish ceremonial law is abrogated, for instance, because the purpose of the sacrificial system was fulfilled by the coming of Christ. Thus even some laws laid down by God are mutable.[22] Some matters are indifferent, and are subjected entirely to human legislators; others are the subjects of immutable divine or natural laws. As regards laws made by men, change is always possible, either to increase their effectiveness in achieving a desired end, or to lay them aside when a specific end is achieved or no longer desired. But the changing of law is always dangerous and unsettling, only to be approached with great caution even if it is sometimes necessary.[23] In both the making and the changing of laws, the eternal law must be the guide.[24]

The immediate controversial edge of this analysis of law was the criticism it offered to the extreme Puritan position that there is only one true law, that of God, which is to be found clearly stated in Scripture, and which governs the whole life of man. On this thesis depended all the radical Puritan claims which offended the conservatism of Hooker. The fundamental purpose of Scripture, he claimed, is to teach supernatural duties, and for this end it is entirely sufficient.[25] But the natural and supernatural order complement each other. The achievement of bliss depends on the fulfillment both of natural and of supernatural duties. The former are discovered primarily by reason, but the latter, as a result of the Fall, are beyond reason's scope. Accordingly natural reason and Scripture "both jointly and not severally either of them be so complete that unto everlasting felicity we need not the knowledge of anything more." [26] This is not to deny that there is much in Scripture that is in fact concerned with natural rather than supernatural duties, nor yet that Scripture may often correct faulty reasoning, but simply to state emphatically that the possession of Scripture does not free us from the arduous process of reasoning to discover our duties in moral and political matters.[27] The perfection of Scripture is relative to its super-natural purpose, and it is misleading to seek in it alone an absolute, political, ecclesiastical, or moral ideal, or to treat it as the final authority in every trivial decision. Such a procedure in fact degrades Scripture and blinds a man to its proper sense.[28] Scripture presupposes rather than replaces natural and rational laws.

Men are by nature free and equal, but a life that is not social is a brutish existence in which man cannot advance toward perfection.[29] Accordingly men have a natural inclination to society. Social life is founded on this inclination and on a social contract, "an order expressly or secretly agreed upon touching the manner of their union in living together." The maintenance of society demands government, the function of which is to curb strife, restrain evil, and harmonize the conflicting interests of men.[30] But government has as its purpose not simply the maintenance of social life by means of coercion; it also concerns itself with the search for the *"summum bonum."* Thus Hooker looks on political organization not only as the remedy for human sinfulness, a consequence of the Fall, but also as a condition of human perfection (in the Christian rather than Aristotelian sense).[31] On this issue he stands both in the classical and Christian traditions. Both reason's knowledge of man's nature and the knowledge of his depravity stemming from revelation show the necessity of the state. Government, like society, is based on a contract,[32] and most legitimate political power arises from consent, although this may take several forms. A man may consent personally and explicitly; he may give his assent through properly appointed representatives; or consent may be assumed from traditional usage.[33] But although consent is the best basis for political power, all political power need not be rooted in consent. A conqueror, for instance, has power over those he has subjected, limited solely by the law of God and the law of nations. And there are men who are specially called by God and exercise power by pure divine right.[34] But power which in the beginning was based on conquest or divine right may, in the course of time, become freely accepted so that in reality if not in origin it becomes government by consent.[35] Whatever the origin of political power, those who govern are God's lieutenants, and their authority, even if delegated from the people, is His.[36]

Normally, then, political power belongs to the people and is entrusted to the government by contract and consent. This is by far the best form of power.[37] Such power is limited either by the terms of the original "pact of submission," or, if these are not known or have fallen into desuetude, simply by what has become traditionally acceptable in the society.[38] The legitimate acts of the civil authorities are the acts of the whole community, and express what we might be inclined to call a general will. It ill befits citizens or factions to seek exemption from what are in fact their own actions.[39]

Human nature being what it is, seeking perfection and yet corrupted and blinded by sin, some kind of government is necessary. But there are many kinds of government, and nature "leaveth the choice as a thing arbitrary." [40] Hooker's deep respect for whatever is established and traditional restrains him from talking much of the best form of government. The best is hardly to be attained, and rash attempts to achieve it often do more harm than good. It is no trivial thing to tamper with the established order.[41] Hooker has his preferences, to be sure: by and large he is satisfied with the Elizabethan Settlement both of politics and religion. He thought a properly limited monarchy, allied to a church ruled by bishops, both governing by consent, to be the best possible arrangement, but he hesitated to suggest that this arrangement should be imposed elsewhere or in different circumstances.[42]

Much of the *Ecclesiastical Polity* is devoted to an important discussion of the relations of Church and State. The principles of ecclesiastical government, like those of civil, are to be found out by reason. Against Cartwright's claim that "the discipline of Christ's Church that is necessary for all times is delivered by Christ and set down in the Holy Scriptures. . . . [It] is to be fetched from thence and thence alone. And that which resteth upon other foundations ought to be esteemed unlawful and counterfeit," [43] Hooker affirms categorically that matters of church polity, unlike matters of dogma, must be decided simply by reason guided, it is true, by the law of nature and without infringing scriptural prohibitions. The Scriptures allow a large field of variation, and are quite inadequate if looked upon as a guide in specific issues of polity.[44]

Church and State cannot rigidly be separated, thought Hooker. Religion assists and encourages both subjects and rulers in the exercise of their respective functions. It is the spring of justice and harmony.[45] Religion—almost any religion—is politically useful, but it is not adequate to think of religion simply as a political device, or to suggest, with Machiavelli, that that religion is best which is most useful for the achievement of certain political ends.[46] Nevertheless, the Christian religion is both the true religion and also ultimately the most politically useful, as it curbs the selfish ambitions of statesmen and the rebellious restlessness of subjects. Since the State is a condition of man's reaching his perfection, and this perfection culminates in the supernatural, "in all Commonwealths things spiritual above temporal ought to be provided for." [47] In nations where Christians are in a minority, the Church is inevitably separate from the State, for citizenship does not imply churchmanship. But in "Christian Commonwealths" Church and State have the same "substance," the whole body of the people, but they are to be looked on as different "accidents" or functions.[48] Church and State stand to each other in much the same relation as faith and reason. The Church complements the State, and together they guide man toward his supernatural destiny. The State is concerned with the good life of man, but this necessarily involves that the State should have a concern for the Church and for true religion.

At this point agreement with Aquinas ceases. In Church as in State, Hooker argues, sovereignty in all matters which are not the subjects of direct divine revelation belongs to the whole body of members. He is as emphatic as Wyclif or Luther in denying that authority in the Church belongs simply, by divine right, to the pope or the hierarchy. Power over external religious matters is vested in the whole body of the faithful, although it may well be delegated by them to one or a few men. In Church as in State, government is by consent.[49] In a Christian commonwealth the social contract whereby power is entrusted to the political authorities is also understood religiously so that it is common and quite natural for supreme power in ecclesiastical as in civil matters to be granted to the same person or persons. Holy Scripture does not, as the Puritans and Calvin himself thought, condemn such an arrangement. The idea of a Christian commonwealth is unknown to the New Testament, while in the Old we find ecclesiastical and civil power united in Israel.[50]

Hooker's teaching on the relationship of Church and State raises the question of toleration in a peculiarly awkward form. His conception of the visible Church is a "comprehensive" one and he is unwilling to assert that heretics and papists are, even if misled, outside the Church in an ultimate sense.[51] Matters absolutely essential to salvation are, for the main part, virtually self-evident, and most disputes among Christians concern doctrines which are, to a greater or a lesser extent, indifferent to salvation.[52] But the State, as we have seen, cannot be aloof from matters of religion, although its concern is inevitably primarily with outward observance and profession. It cannot make true by edict a doctrine which was false before, although it can create a duty where none existed before. Human laws cannot force a man to believe, although they can and do force men to act *as if* they believed. Human laws oblige only outwardly, yet in many circumstances it is inconvenient for public unity that certain opinions should be expressed or acted upon. The civil authorities should have a care for the maintenance of true religion, but they have no right to decide what pure religion is, and in any case religious opinions are unenforceable. Within the Church, therefore, a considerable degree of doctrinal diversity is inevitable and should be tolerated. But, on the other hand, the civil authorities are charged with the maintenance of a stable social order, harmony and unity in Church and State. They cannot tolerate actions which are subversive of these things, disputes which split society into warring factions, or the expression of opinions which are likely to incite people to illegal or antisocial actions. Private opinions and feelings cannot be controlled and therefore must be tolerated. But in so far as opinions and feelings are publicly expressed or give rise to action, they fall within the proper scope of human law, and toleration must be limited by consideration of the common good.[53] The "judicious" Hooker disliked all religious persecution, but unconditional toleration seemed to him a political and theological impossibility.

## NOTES

1. In Laing's edition of the *Works*, Edinburgh, 1846, vol. IV.
2. *The First Admonition to Parliament*, in *Puritan Manifestoes*, ed. Frere and Douglas (London, 1907). Quoted in A. P. D'Entreves, *The Medieval Contribution to Political Thought* (Oxford: Oxford University Press, 1939), p. 104.
3. In his *Replye to an Answere* (1573).
4. Calvin, *Institutes*, IV. xx. 31.
5. *E.g.*, Richard Hooker, *The Laws of Ecclesiastical Polity*, Preface, iii. 4.
6. *Laws*, II. viii. 5. Cf. III. vii. 2.
7. *Ibid.*, III. viii. 17.
8. *Ibid.*, II. iv. 7; vii. 4.
9. On the authenticity of bks VI–VIII see R. A. Houk, *Hooker's Ecclesiastical Polity, Book VIII* (New York: Columbia University Press, 1931), and C. J. Sisson, *The Judicious Marriage of Mr. Hooker and the Birth of the Laws of Ecclesiastical Polity* (Cambridge: Cambridge University Press, 1940).
10. *Laws*, I. viii. 4.
11. *Ibid.*, ii. 2.
12. *Ibid.*, 4, 6; iii. 4.
13. *Ibid.*, ii. 4, 5; iii. 4.
14. *Ibid.*, ii. 4; xi. 2.
15. *Ibid.*, iii. 1.
16. *Ibid.*, viii. 1; vii. 6.
17. *Ibid.*, xi. 4.
18. *Ibid.*, xii. 1, 3; xv. 2.
19. *Ibid.*, viii. 1.
20. *Ibid.*, vii. 3.
21. *Ibid.*, xvi. 5.
22. *Ibid.*, II. x. 4; I. xv. 1.
23. *Ibid.*, IV. xiv. 1.
24. *Ibid.*, I. xvi. 2; IV, xiv. 1, 2; V. vii. 1.
25. *Ibid.*, I. xiv. 1; II. viii. 5.
26. *Ibid.*, I. xiv. 5.
27. *Ibid.*, xiii. 2; II. viii. 5.
28. *Ibid.*, I. xv. 4; II. viii. 6.
29. *Ibid.*, I. x. 1.
30. *Ibid.* and VIII. ii. 18.
31. *Ibid.*, VIII. ii. 18.
32. *Ibid.*, I. x. 3.
33. *Ibid.*, 8; VIII. ii. 9; vi. 8.
34. *Ibid.*, VIII. ii. 5.
35. *Ibid.*, 11.
36. *Ibid.*, 6.
37. *Ibid.*, 5, 9; I. x. 3.
38. *Ibid.*, VIII. ii. 11.
39. *Ibid.*, Preface. v. 2.

40. *Ibid.*, I. x. 5; cf. III. ii. 1.
41. *Ibid.*, V. ix. 1–2; IV. xiv. 1–2;
V. vii. 1, 3.
42. *Ibid.*, III. xi. 16.
43. Thomas Cartwright and others, *A Directory of Church Government*, opening sentences.
44. *Laws*, III. ix. 1–2.
45. *Ibid.*, V. i. 2.
46. *Ibid.*, ii. 3–4.

47. *Ibid.*, VIII. i. 4; iii. 2; V. lxxvi. 4.
48. *Ibid.*, VIII. i. 5.
49. *Ibid.*, i. 8.
50. *Ibid.*, 1, 5, 14, 18; iii. 2, 6; iv. 9.
51. *Ibid.*, III. i. 10–11; *Sermon on Justification*.
52. *Laws*, Preface. iii. 2.
53. *Ibid.*, VIII. vi. 5; V. lxii. 15; lxviii. 7.

# READINGS

A.   Hooker, Richard. *The Laws of Ecclesiastical Polity,* in *Hooker's Works.* Ed. John Keble. Rev. R. W. Church and Francis Paget. 7th ed. 3 vols. Oxford: Oxford University Press, 1888. Bk I, chaps ii–v, viii, x–xii, xv–xvi; bk V, chaps i–ii; bk. VIII, chaps i–iii.
B.   Hooker, Richard. *The Laws of Ecclesiastical Polity.* Preface, bks I, II, chaps vii–viii, bk VIII.

# FRANCIS BACON

## 1561–1626

To Francis Bacon, Baron Verulam, Viscount St. Albans, no worldly thing was more important, or more worth penetrating, than the problem of political philosophy, the nature of the best "state or mould of a commonwealth." [1] More precisely, the most precious thing on earth was a result of the meeting of the mind of man with the nature of things. That meeting would truly take place when the mind of man could subdue nature so as to force out of nature the most nearly perfect human thing, the commonwealth which Bacon outlined in the *New Atlantis*. Although the *New Atlantis* is Bacon's most important political work, we can see its importance only if we realize that political things meant to him much more than is usually granted. To be convinced of that, one must understand Bacon's express practice of using old words and phrases to describe new things. [2]

Bacon denies, for example, that there is such a thing as "fifth essence." The "fifth essence" is a term that had been applied to an element in the stars and the celestial regions, different from the four known elements: water, earth, air, and fire. This view of heaven, which can be traced to Aristotle, is treated with great scorn by Bacon, who calls Aristotle's heaven a "fantastic heaven." Yet, in a dialogue called *Advertisement touching an Holy War,* one of Bacon's characters suggests that the Socrates of the dialogue, a man named Eupolis, may be the "fifth essence." "Eupolis" means the "good city," or, perhaps more clearly, the "well-governed country." What Bacon denies to the heavens, a fifth element or essence, he seems to grant to the well-governed country. His real quarrel with Aristotle, then, is not that Aristotle suggested something fantastic, but that he looked for the fantastic in the wrong place.

The truly fantastic is to be found in man's political world, the world of man's creation.[3]

There is another old expression, "final cause," that Bacon uses to describe something new. The final cause is the end for which things exist, and Bacon said that the search for final causes had corrupted natural philosophy. He treats that search as scornfully as he treats the search for the "fifth essence." Yet Bacon does not scorn when he grants that the search for final causes may be legitimate when relating to the "human things." Full understanding of that search leads to the notion that man is that in which the world centers, "with respect to final causes." Certainly to discuss final causes as comprehensible only in the human things, presumably the man-made things, is to change radically the meaning of final causes. The final cause, that for which all things exist, is the things which man makes, and the best thing that man can make is the best commonwealth, the commonwealth of the New Atlantis, the happy land, the land of all earthly things worthiest of knowledge. That thing, however, does not exist, except in Bacon's mind, and is his construction in principle. It remains for mankind to construct it in practice.[4]

The dependence of the highest things upon human construction is a sign of the elevation of the man-made, the artificial, over the natural. Bacon's natural philosophy was materialist and was akin to that ancient materialism, especially the materialism of Democritus, which he acknowledged as his intellectual heritage.[5] Few of those who have followed him, however, have acknowledged his own acknowledgment, except Shaftesbury.[6] Although the materialist and atheist teaching of Democritus naturally led to a denial of the fruitfulness of any search for final causes, it could not of itself lead to the creation of human or political final causes. As a materialism Bacon's is altogether novel in that it defines a possible supreme human end, albeit an end affected with what we now call utopianism. The Baconian formulation, although novel, was influenced by the work of two political philosophers who preceded him, Machiavelli and Giordano Bruno.

Bacon appeared to accept Machiavelli's formulation that political philosophy ought to concentrate on what men do and not on what they ought to do. Like Machiavelli, he took as his starting point the extreme situation. Bacon believed that nature was at its truest and most intelligible when "vexed" and "tortured" by experiments, just as Machiavelli saw the origins of the good political order in extremes, in violence and crime. Men are made up of desires, and out of those desires states and commonwealths have their origins. Man has a mind, and with that mind he may subdue nature, but only by submitting to it and by understand-

ing it at its most irregular, in marvels or miracles. Submission to nature
enables man to conquer nature. Man himself has no natural goal or
end: the cosmos is alien and incomprehensible. The guide to all things
is in the appetite that is in all things to take in and to expel. Like
Machiavelli, Bacon was a hedonist, but a hedonist who rejected the
apolitical conclusions of classical hedonism.[7]

When Machiavelli speaks of concentration on what men do rather
than what they ought to do, however, he contrasts his own procedure
with that of the creators of imaginary commonwealths. Bacon, while
commending this statement of Machiavelli, was himself the creator of
an imaginary commonwealth. The significance of this fact emerges
when we realize that, much as Bacon was indebted to Machiavelli for
his starting point, the course his political thought took was quite a different one. The fact that Bacon's most important political works
are neither works about the nature of the prince nor discourses
on an ancient historian, but that one (*Wisdom of the Ancients*) is an
analysis of ancient myths and the other (*New Atlantis*) a refutation of
a Platonic myth, tells us something of Bacon's difference from Machiavelli. Before we see the importance of these myths, however, we must
recognize that, at the very point of inception, in the very scheme of
Bacon's plan, there is a difference from Machiavelli. The importance of
fame or glory, the end for which the selfish perform unselfish acts, is,
for Machiavelli, overwhelming. Bacon, however, apparently wavers
between the love of fame or of wisdom as the highest passion and fame
or wisdom as the highest good. That wavering is only apparent, however, for those who wish true fame achieve it only as lovers of wisdom.

It is as if Bacon had said to Machiavelli that the things for which
men are most grateful are not the feats of heroes or even the actions of
the founders of commonwealths. The things that have made men grateful are those which have most "relieved man's estate" (a Baconian
phrase), *i.e.,* inventions. It is true that in the popular essays Bacon refers
to the founders of states and commonwealths as the first "marshalls of
sovereign honour," but in more recondite places he points out that the
ancients made inventors gods, while they made heroes only demigods.
Moreover, if such honor has not always been forthcoming, it is because
there have been very few inventors, and their work was largely accidental. In this respect, the beasts had done better than men. Small wonder that he borrowed much of the symbolism of the *New Atlantis* from
the ancient religion of Egypt, hinting, at least, at what a more forthright
Bruno had said quite openly, though perhaps less effectively. Egypt,
which to Christians stood for the darkness of the material world, was
an object of great admiration, where beasts who made inventions were

accorded their due. In Bacon's own utopia, moreover, the statues are for the inventors, not for heroes.[8]

A practical aim of Bacon's teaching is to promote inventions. The ancient suspicion of technological progress is replaced by something like faith in technological progress. Faith in technological progress would issue in inventions, the creation of which requires a new method, the method of Bacon's *Novum Organum,* in principle the method of modern natural science.[9] Politically what was required was a veritable "New Model Army" of Baconian followers who were prepared to experiment and had faith, not only in their scientific results, but also in the political beneficence of their scientific results. Bacon's teaching demanded a following, just as Machiavelli's did, but it was a different kind of following. It was not an army of statesmen but an army of inventors. There was no conclusive reason to believe that Bacon's followers would understand his teaching. That they do so was not even necessary. The old distinction between philosophers and nonphilosophers was to be replaced by a new, threefold distinction between philosophers, experts, and the public. A teaching which issues in inventions demands a large group of experts or technicians, people who, because of shared experience and what is now called collective research, can help to make man's lot easier. Such people would not have to know the truth about the cosmos or about man. They would not really have to understand Bacon's political philosophy, but only the methods by which inventions could be made. They would, of course, have to be subordinate to those who understood which inventions truly would contribute to the relief of man's estate, since inventions can also be destructive. Bacon had his own techniques for preventing destructive inventions from triumphing over constructive ones. That such protective techniques do not exist today need not obfuscate Bacon's superior judgment in adopting them. The inventors themselves had to be men skilled in method. Therefore Bacon's emphasis on method marks a departure from the political philosophy of Machiavelli. Without denying the loftiness of statesmanship, Bacon suggests that the methods which he presents can become methods for all human invention, including political invention. Although Bacon does not say that statesmanship will be easier when aided by modern invention, the conclusion follows from the assurance that the method of the *Novum Organum* can be applied to all human knowledge.[10]

In order for inventions to multiply, Bacon had to convince the powerful that inventions were politically innocent. He made a distinction between the pure knowledge of nature and the "proud knowledge of good and evil," and tried to protect his own knowledge not only from the consequences of the doctrine of the Fall, but also from persecution.[11] Yet it is clear that, if there is a passage from Bacon's scientific method to all human knowledge, in all its branches, there must be inventions that are not politically innocent. Ultimately the pure knowledge of nature affects and must affect the proud knowledge of good and evil. Yet, when applications are made to kings and patrons, applicants must speak with great care lest kings and patrons understand the revolutionary character of their proposals. The very fact that Bacon regarded his teaching as issuing in inventions meant that that teaching must have a large following, and that that following must have a large public approval. Not so much to protect himself as to protect his teaching, Bacon hesitated to spell out his political philosophy. To some extent he could not spell it out, for, while there were some things that he considered settled, such as the rightness of his method, there were other things that could not be known until the inventions that were to be made actually succeeded in relieving man's estate. For example, Bacon set great store by the future of medicine, not only for health but also for longevity. If human life could be free of natural death, and he certainly hinted at that possibility, the scarcely predictable consequences of that freedom would force some reservations regarding any final political teaching.[12]

There were certain things about the final political teaching that Bacon did claim to know. One was that the scientific method, issuing in inventions, compelled a view of history quite different from that of Machiavelli. For this view, Bacon seems to have been indebted to Giordano Bruno, a philosopher whom he rarely mentions. The act which brings fame to the hero is time-bound, whatever may be said of the fame itself. The hero helps his country, and the country may rise and fall. Inventions, on the contrary, belong to mankind and remain with mankind. They transcend what was called the eternal recurrence, and Bacon, following Bruno, considered it his duty to refute the assertion of eternal recurrence. The doctrine of eternal recurrence referred to the cycle of birth, growth, decay, and death, and referred to that cycle in plants and seasons, as in human life and in states and commonwealths. All human things were seen as transient, and that view, which sees the green of spring come and go, was held by Bacon to be "natural." Though it was natural, it was incorrect. It was the principal source of man's despair of the future. Among the reasons for hope for the future Bacon lists, with particular emphasis, the abandonment of man's natural acceptance of recurrence. The cycles do not follow their course, and the great age of modernity, Bacon's own age, is greater than the great age of antiquity.[13]

The idea that the greatness of modernity must defy the cycles that have dominated historical thought is an idea of which Giordano Bruno was aware, and from which he took comfort, apparently, during his days of persecution. Bruno spoke of the fruits of modern science, and he believed that his discovery of the infinite universe would aid substantially in gathering those fruits. In a famous fable, men blinded by the human ineptitude to grasp the divine are cured of that blindness and have a greater clairvoyance regarding human change than they had had before. Good and evil may still alternate, but, because of Bruno's new science, each good will be a little better than the last good, and each evil a little less than the last evil. Thus Bruno contrasts his own teaching, which brings tolerance in matters of opinion, precisely because it brings unity in matters of science, with the exploits of Columbus and his followers, who insist on imposing their own beliefs on others. Bruno hoped to find a way out of the ineluctable force of human change.[14] In seeking that way, Bacon was his disciple.

While Bruno believed, however, that in order to transcend recurrent changes in the human things it would be necessary to shock men and to destroy the power of the Christian Aristotelians who dominated the schools, Bacon believed that civil peace alone could bring scientific progress and, therefore, political progress. Thus he compared himself to a certain miller who prayed for "peace among the willows, for when the windmill wrought, the water-mill was less customed." [15] The operation of the windmill, in Bacon's figure of speech, religious controversy, was cheaper and easier than the operation of the water mill, which stood for the advancement of science. Bacon saw that progress required conjoint experience and collective research, which in turn required well-stocked institutions of learning, which themselves required civil peace. To promote it he taught what may be called a provisional political philosophy. He does not use the term "provisional morality" later used by Descartes, but he advocates a moral and political way that is certainly calculated to serve men until they reach the island utopia of the *New Atlantis*.

That political way is provisional both practically and theoretically. In the former respect, of course, there is nothing new about it. Political philosophers have always realized that men had to live in their own societies, and those might not be the best possible societies. Bacon's view was novel in that he denied the possibility of imagining the best political order before great progress had been made in conquering nature. That progress would enable men to know what they might wish for, *i.e.,* it would reveal to them how far they might reach out in envisioning the good for man. Bacon, standing at the fountainhead of the scientific revolution, thus had to profess ignorance of the final good for man.[16] He claimed to know enough, however, from the alien character of the cosmos and the possibility of conquering nature by means of his improved method, to be sure that men could learn what to wish, and that it would be generally good. While he had some vision of his own utopia, much of his work is concerned with the state or commonwealth that would lead man to that utopia. Knowing how much civil and religious conflict would disturb science, Bacon sought to join freedom with custom or tradition. His provisional teaching may therefore be characterized as conservative, and issuing in the maintenance and extension of three institutions: crown, church, and empire.

Concerning the first two, little need be said. Bacon was a monarchist because monarchy existed, because it gave private men time from politics for philosophy and science, and because it was convenient to write under a monarch to whom Bacon's writing "resembled the peace of God; it passeth understanding." What passes understanding also passes censorship, and, if a monarch is no brighter than James I, monarchy may well consort with freedom. Whether Bacon was a true monarchist, who thought as highly of the prerogative as he pretended, is by no means certain. As to his Anglicanism, Bacon saw that the Anglican Church was that of the *politiques* in Britain, the people who wished to put down religious controversy and unite the nations. He saw its leadership as less intolerant than that of either the Puritans or the Catholics, and thus he held it to have settled religious controversies "for all time." There is, of course, a deeper reason for his adherence. Obviously a man who sees "final causes" and "fifth essences" as related only to the things that man creates must see his own teaching as divorced from theology. Bacon's very plea that the knowledge of nature might bypass the Fall, for it was not the knowledge of nature that was condemned by the Fall, but the proud knowledge of good and evil, would naturally lead him away from religious controversy. That church which permitted the separation of philosophy from theology would be regarded by Bacon as the Christian church which was closest to the true church. He saw that separation in the Anglican rather than the Roman Church, for the power of the Scholastics to dominate learning was, he thought, very great. He also tried, however, to make the Church of England more tolerant. He was spared the necessity of joining in Bruno's complaint that learning was dominated by the "vulgar" because he believed that in Britain the problem had been solved.[17]

Bacon's imperialism is somewhat more complex. While both his monarchism and his Anglicanism may be regarded as cautious, his imperialism was bold. It is perhaps the sole evidence in his provisional teaching for his own Machiavellian statement that the middle way, useful in all other pursuits, is baneful in politics. To Bacon, to amplify the bounds of empire was a duty, a duty that had been neglected in political philosophy prior to his own. What such a concept of duty does to traditional political principles is not hard to imagine. A duty of imperialism implies that the best societies are not small cities but great empires. It places values upon "greatness," not only in terms of power but also in terms of size. Nations with growing populations, like Britain, had a better opportunity for greatness than nations with small populations, populations that could not maintain their empires, like Spain. The fulfillment of such a duty would demand conduct rather aggressive than just, and valor itself would become the virtue of warfare, regardless of the justice of the war. Indeed, the search for the just war, a problem so meaningful to the Schoolmen and to Bacon's contemporary, Grotius, takes on quite a different meaning in Bacon, when he characterizes an apprehensive war (or what is popularly called a "preventive war") as a defensive and just war. Any war against any nation that is bent on conquest (like Turkey or Spain) would then be a just war because it would be a quarrel on apprehension of war. In other words, if nation A is to do its duty by amplifying its empire, nation B, observing that amplification, will be doing its duty by going to war against nation A. Perhaps this is the Baconian form of the "state of nature" doctrine among sovereigns, and, in a state of nature, action is selfish and the solution imperialist. The very concept of the just war seems to fall before the imperialist solution to the problem.[18]

When Bacon says that the problem of the extension of empire is neglected in political philosophy, we may justly ask why he seems to overlook its treatment in Machiavelli. Machiavelli approved of warlike actions and imperial goals, and the historical precedent that he most emphatically holds up for emulation by founders of modes and orders is warlike and imperial Rome. Yet Bacon did consider the study and discussion of the duty of amplifying empire a neglected study. It is not altogether easy to see why. The one clear difference between the imperialism of Bacon and that of Machiavelli relates to the importance of naval power. Bacon's imperialism is emphatically a naval imperialism, as that of Machiavelli is not. That seems rather a small difference, hardly justifying Bacon's claim to be the first to regard imperialism as a civic duty. We must remember, however, that the kind of people who could bring about a successful naval imperialism were, around 1600, "new men." They were the kind of people who could follow the advice which Bacon scattered so freely in his *Advancement of Learning* to learn how to get along in the world, to practice the arts of rhetoric and business management, and the courtier's art. They were the people who could bring the comforts and luxuries from the far corners of the world to the London shops. They were the men who were not ashamed to exact usury, which Bacon defended. They were those who could think of imperialism rather in terms of economic gain than in terms of despotic power. They were the true representatives of the spirit of capitalism, to which Bacon, at least as much as Calvin and perhaps more, contributed.

Bacon's imperialism was, in a sense, a link between his provisional teaching and his definitive teaching because, alone among the props of his provisional teaching, it offered the way for the new man. It was directed less to kings, lords, and clerics than to merchants. Bacon's aggressive society was a society peopled by those who would be guided by his architecture of fortune, by recommendations on how to get along in the world, a study which he considered neglected in earlier political writings. Such people were to be the bulwark of the new naval imperialism. They were to man the ship to take mankind to the New Atlantis. That ship was primarily a British ship, and Bacon saw the achievement of his utopia chiefly as a British achievement. Britain was ripe for the just war. She had the most warlike breed of men. The kingdom of heaven was like a mustard seed, a small seed, from which a great tree would grow. Bacon's idea of imperialism was one that he compared with that mustard seed. From the little seed that was Britain would grow a great empire.[19]

We should do less than justice to Bacon, however, in imagining that his imperialism was a narrow design for one nation. Its aggressive quality was designed for something much more important than British imperialism, namely, for the rule of mankind over nature. This quality may well have been the link between provisional and definitive teaching. That definitive teaching was only partly complete in Bacon's own writing, but it was expected to transcend both place and time. The transcendence takes us back to the problem of the old myths. The *Wisdom of the Ancients* (*De Sapientia Veterum*) is a collection of ancient fables, with Bacon's own interpretations. That Bacon considered it a very important writing is indicated by his statement in the Preface that even in his own time anyone who had a new truth to bring forth would have to bring it forth in just such a manner. While pretending to interpret old myths or fables, Bacon is really presenting his own teaching as far as the structure of the myth permitted invention. Old fables are held to be a commerce between earliest antiquity, which is buried in oblivion, except for what the Bible tells us, and the historical things. This link between the historical things and the first things is, however, something more, for, as the biblical comparison indicates, it is a link between the divine things and the human things. As the only divinity which can be understood is the man-made divinity, however, the old fables are presented as the way to divinity through the study and the conquest of nature.

Whether the pre-Homeric authors of the fables thought of them as Bacon did, saw, for example, the wooing of Juno as the search for political understanding, the quest for Eurydice as philosophic quest, or the riddles of the Sphinx as the source of the Baconian distinction between the kingdom over nature and the kingdom over man, does not really matter. In distinction to biblical tales, these tales represent a more natural way of looking at man and the world, and suggest that, if it had not been for Aristotle and Christianity, it might not have been necessary to wait for Bacon until man could create the society which conquered nature. Bacon follows Bruno in saying that the present age is "antiquity," the old age of the world, where men know more than those who were called the ancients.[20]

The myth of greatest importance to Bacon, however, is one partly of his own creation, partly a refutation of a Platonic myth, and is found in the *New Atlantis*. This work is a description of an island utopia in the Pacific, and it is formally incomplete. It ends, rather abruptly, at the end of a description of the institution called Solomon's House, which is the most important and most powerful institution in the land, an academy of scientists. Some writers have concluded that Bacon got tired of the work and did not bother to finish it. He did bother, however, to translate it into Latin, "for the benefit of other lands," and while that would not have been so great a chore for Bacon as for some, he would have done it only if he thought the work had some merit. Bacon left a number of incomplete works unpublished. The *New Atlantis* was not one of them. The work is, moreover, intended as a refutation of a Platonic dialogue, the *Critias,* which is also formally incomplete. When we understand just why the *New Atlantis* is formally unfinished, we shall have taken a stride toward understanding it.

The *New Atlantis* differs radically from some of the island utopias which preceded it, like More's *Utopia*. Discovery of the latter was said to depend on chance, and people could not be told where to find it. The travellers to the New Atlantis also depended on chance, but once they spotted the island it was easy of access, and the land was seen from evening to morning, just as the children of Israel knew in the evening that the Lord had brought them out from Egypt, and in the morning they should see the glory of the Lord. That Bacon intended the New Atlantis to mean the Promised Land is quite clear. He calls it a "happy

land," a "blessed land," a "land of angels." He says that, in the language
of the natives, it is called "Bensalem," which means the Perfect Son.
Bacon's imagery of the sea, moreover, signifies the triumph of navigation and therefore of science. Unlike Shakespeare's *Tempest,* or *Pericles,*
in which the most important sea images are characterized by storms, in
the *New Atlantis* the travellers find their way to the island in a calm
sea. The imagery is comparable to that suggested by the phrase "peace
among the willows." So much the modern utopia demanded.

The story of Atlantis, an island somewhere in the west, as it comes
to us in Plato, is the story of a technological paradise. The people of
Atlantis, corrupted by luxury, fought against an old Athens (nine
thousand years old when Solon was supposed to have told the story),
were defeated, and the armies did not return. Later the island was punished by Zeus with extermination and remained a shoal rendering navigation impossible. Unlike Atlantis, which was destroyed by an earth-
quake, never to revive, the old Athens perished in a flood, the people of
the mountain surviving and later constructing another Athens. Bacon
deliberately turns Plato's myth upside down. He admits that the old
Atlantis was destroyed, but by a flood, suggesting that there, too, mountain folk survived and later built the Inca and Aztec civilizations. The
New Atlantis, like the old Athens, defeated an Atlantic army, but
treated it more humanely than the Athenians and allowed it to return
home. The New Atlantis, moreover, survived a flood. It had something
which the old Athens did not have, a means of surviving floods. It had
Baconian science, and with the aid of Baconian science, it was able to
transcend the vicissitudes of time. By vicissitudes, Bacon referred to both
natural catastrophe and political decay. The New Atlantis is a trans-
historical regime, and Bacon uses it to deny the view, shared even by
Machiavelli, that societies come and go. Bensalem does not come and
go. Its very age contests the Christian view of the age of the world which
prevailed in Bacon's own time, *i.e.,* less than six thousand years.

Upon their arrival at the island, the travellers are first warned,
though they approach Bensalem in sickness and want, that they must
not land. After a very mild inquisition into their customs, however,
they are permitted to land and remain on shore. They are introduced
to the strange island by a Christian priest, who is the Governor of
Strangers' House. He discusses the miracle which brought the Bible to
Bensalem and the ways by which Bensalem, unknown to Europe,
knows about Europe. By means of secret expeditions, Bensalem learns
the things about Europe that seem to them worth knowing: the inventions and progress in the sciences. The governor also tells the travellers
of the past when the famous monarch of Bensalem, King Solomona,

founded the establishment called Solomon's House. The travellers meet
a Jewish merchant named Joabin, who is clearly higher in the hierarchy
of Bensalem than the Christian priest. Joabin explains to them the most
important festival of Bensalem, called the feast of the Tirsan, or father
of the family, and favorably contrasts the marriage customs of Bensalem with those of Europe. He ushers in a still more important functionary, one of the Fathers of Solomon's House. This functionary is
dressed in robes worthy of the high priest in the Old Testament, rides
in a splendid chariot, and blesses the people in a manner reminiscent of
Christ, or of the pope. He also consents to talk with one of the travellers,
and the narrator of the tale himself is chosen for this honor. The official tells of the organization and the functions of Solomon's House,
clearly the ruling body of the island, and gives the narrator permission
to publish for the benefit of others.

The story of Bensalem is not without dramatic quality. The island
is hardly affected by what the travellers do, but the travellers, in the
course of the narrative, undergo great change. They come upon an
island, blessed but inhospitable, which saves them but does not welcome
them. They wonder whether they will see Europe again, but when they
are given permission to stay, and when they learn of the conversion of
Bensalem to Christianity, they want to remain. Yet they are not ready
to stay, and the discussion of the festivals and of the role and rule of
Solomon's House represents a kind of initiation. They are toughened
up for a life in utopia. In the course of the acclimation of the travellers,
or what may more properly be called their conversion, the leadership
passes from the captain of their ship or "principal man" of the company
to the narrator, who is clearly the most learned man on board. Their
notion of rule must approach that which prevails in Bensalem itself
before the travellers are ready to become citizens of Bensalem. The
change appears to be the process whereby Western and Christian society
is transformed into universal society. The names, the images of Bensalem are drawn from a variety of sources. While the journey itself is a
journey to the west, the images are predominantly Eastern and are
drawn from Palestine, Egypt, Persia.

By suggesting that one may go eastward by journeying westward,
Bacon suggests that vicissitudes of space as well as of time may be transcended by the well-governed regime. The authenticity of the miracle
which brought the Bible to the city of Renfusa ("of the nature of
sheep") in Bensalem before it was brought to the West is attested by a
member of Solomon's House. His claim to judge rests on his knowledge
of natural philosophy, and the biblical teaching is accepted only so far
as it accords with the universal teaching of natural philosophy. What

follows politically is the virtually absolute power of the scientific fraternity, the academy of Solomon's House.

The exercise of the collegiate power required, however, the support
of an ally. Solomon's House could decide which inventions might be
given to the state and which might not. We today well know, as Bacon
foresaw, that a science which seeks to "imitate the thunderbolt" must
have some protection as to its use and abuse.[21] Society itself would have
to have certain safeguards. These are of two kinds: the safeguard of the
collegiate power, which, by deciding which inventions might be revealed, limits public knowledge; and the safeguard of paternal power,
which enforces virtue. We might call these the safeguard of public ignorance and the safeguard of public spirit. As for the latter, Bacon's *New
Atlantis* seems to suggest a certain civil religion, a festival of which is
the feast of the Tirsan. The Tirsan is the father of a family, having
thirty living descendants over the age of three. His feast is a mixture of
pagan feasts, but it differs from the ordinary celebration of abundance
because it is a reward for longevity as well as fertility. Its symbols are
suggestive of Osiris and Isis, Egyptian divinities. It brings about the
union of piety, or reverence for age, and nature, or reverence for fertility and abundance. The Tirsan himself is awarded not only honors
but also powers. Bacon places great stress on the monogamous character
of Bensalem, calling it "Virgin of the World," once a designation of
Isis, but otherwise incomprehensible in an utopia famous for fertility.
Its significance lies in the severe character of the Tirsan's feast, as well
as the other festivals of Bensalem. Bacon elsewhere distinguishes between the "affections," which are natural to all men, and the "per-
turbed affections," which are what he calls passions. Since the feast of
the Tirsan glorifies the unperturbed affections, it is a celebration not
only of age and fertility but also of virtue. Its rewards are rewards given
by the real rulers of Bensalem, the Fellows of Solomon's House, to those
whose pleasures are faithful and simple.

The political importance of the feast of the Tirsan lies in the union
of old, patriarchal power with new, vigorous science. The civil religion,
adding piety to science, renders secure the rule of science; at the same
time, the rulers had to secure the civil religion by the works of science.
Progress would convince men of the value of virtue. If all men are
guided by affections, but those affections which contribute to the good
life are the ones which leave the mind free of perturbation, then the
best life is the philosophical life, the life most free of perturbation, and
especially of the most powerful source of perturbation, namely, superstition. In that view Bacon followed Lucretius, but he went further in
trying to construct a society in which the citizens generally might be

relatively free from perturbation. Their freedom would rest, however, not on knowledge but on illusion.

While Bacon claimed that his science would go far to "level men's minds," he also made it clear that he could be understood by all only in terms of "works." All men would never really understand Baconian science.[22]

While paternal power is definitely subordinate to collegiate power, it appears to replace royal power. It is the "state," not the "king," which gives the travellers leave to remain in Bensalem, and Elizabeth I objected to the use of the word "state." Kings are mentioned in the *New Atlantis,* but the rule of those kings withers. Those who rule achieve or approach the forms of immortality recognized as possible by Bacon— the Tirsan achieves the immortality that belongs with regeneration and approaches corporeal immortality that transcends death. The Fellows of Solomon's House may achieve the immortality that comes from fame. The latter are a very restricted body, representing a small fraction of the populace. When the travellers are told that one of the Fathers of Solomon's House is to visit the city where they are staying, they are also told that the populace of the city have not seen one of those fathers for twelve years. While recruitment is not according to birth, and membership in the ruling group is, in that sense, democratic, the gap between ruler and citizen is enormous. There are, apparently, thirty-six fathers and fellows. Bacon was so sure of agreement on the part of the fellows as to scientific truth and its proper utility that he did not propose an odd number of members of the house or try to make a majority always possible.

What would prevent one member of the ruling group from trying to seize power, from giving the dangerous inventions to the state? What would prevent the people from demanding them in a national crisis? Bacon tells us little of that. There is an element of faith in the construction of his utopia, as there is generally in modern utopian thought, a faith that a threefold distinction between philosophers, experts, and the wider public may be preserved. Preservation of that distinction presupposes that experts will look up to philosophers and will be guided by them, or that knowledge will remain subordinate to wisdom. Under such conditions men would not indurate the brain to propagate communism or split the atom to destroy worlds, for knowledge would be kept in the service of the good of man. To know the good of man might require more knowledge of the affections than Bacon possessed; but he claimed to know at least the ways of life that the society of Bensalem would protect and secure.

We should now understand more clearly the attempted refutation of Plato. The *Critias* ends abruptly as Zeus calls the gods together to speak to them in a place where they could see all the world of becoming. He had called them to punish Atlantis, and his unwritten speech presumably would deal with that punishment and with the destruction of Atlantis. Bacon's work also ends with a speech, but the speech is given. It is not about the destruction of something that becomes and passes away, but about how to avoid destruction. It is not given by Zeus, but the man who gives it is almost divine. He blesses the people in a Christlike or papal manner, his fellowship has the power of "natural divination," and he looks upon mankind with pity. He and his predecessors have established a commonwealth, where they also see but transcend the world of becoming. He knows the secrets of Zeus, and he may tell them. Some things, however, he does not tell because he cannot, for natural philosophy can issue fully into political philosophy only when man has discovered how to imitate the thunderbolt.

The means by which the Fellows of Solomon's House see the world of becoming are presented in the form of freedom to travel. Bensalem is actually a closed society. Travel restrictions are adopted which correspond rather closely with those found in Plato's *Laws*. Capricious travel, so necessary in order to reach the New Atlantis, is banned from that society once one arrives. As in the *Laws*, contact with imperfection could corrupt even Bensalem. Travel then is restricted to the highest and the wisest, in this case called "Merchants of Light." While Platonic travellers seek the "divinely guided men" who may grow up in corrupt countries as well as uncorrupted ones, the Baconian travellers seek light. That suggests, of course, that European science, a science which to Bacon depended on chance, may have something to teach a science which depends on a systematic mastery over nature. Only the wisest, however, may see and choose the benefits of accidental science. As Bensalem tends to become a universal society, deliberate science will have taken all it could from accidental science, and the dangers of external corruption will be eliminated.

What then would happen to the mercantile and imperialist spirit of Bacon's provisional teaching? While Bensalem is opulent, it is a hospitable society which keeps rather a leisurely pace. Through the mingling of youthful science and old society, it is able to temper its luxury with simplicity and obedience. Such a society is not one which we usually associate with the supremacy of commerce and bears little resemblance to hungry, commercial Britain. It seems that the spirit of commerce, and, indeed, the spirit of imperialism, are no longer needed with the fruition of Baconian science. Science would furnish the luxury associated with commerce, and the universality of Bensalem would render the aggressive spirit of imperialism unnecessary.

Bensalem is a peaceful society. While Bacon certainly had no superstitions, he pretends to copy not warlike Rome, as Machiavelli did, but a
more peaceful civil religion, that of the Egyptian Osiris. Bensalem,
moreover, apparently has not been at war for many years, since it seems
to have known the rest of the world simply through its Merchants of
Light. The king whose forces once defeated the old Atlantis was named
Altabin, which suggests in its Latin source that he was twice lofty. He
permitted his enemies to return home with a promise never to fight
against the New Atlantis again, a promise which Machiavelli would
have thought mad, and which Bacon seems at least to have considered
foolish. He was lofty for his statesmanship and for his humanity. After
Altabin, and with the establishment of Solomon's House, rulers arose
who were thrice lofty, suggested by the mythical figure of Hermes
Trismegistus (thrice lofty). They were lofty also because of wisdom.
Under their rule the armament of Bensalem prospered, including even
unquenchable fires, more violent cannons, imitations of the flight of
birds, and ships that go under the water. Whatever has since been done
with these dire instruments, there is no indication that the rulers of
Bensalem used them. They had them because Bensalem, with its alien
civil religion and its hedonistic utopia, would have needed mighty defenses in a hostile world. But Bensalem seems to have fought no wars
since Altabin.

What happens to the warlike spirit can best be seen by referring to
two other treatments of the problem. One is found in Bacon's discussion of the myth of Perseus in the *Wisdom of the Ancients*. The fable is
said to deal with war, but Bacon's treatment is entirely devoted to a
crusade and says nothing of merely defensive war. In fact, the interpretation of the fable appears to be the description of a Christian crusade
and of a countercrusade or defensive war by the opponents of Christianity. The war is less a real war than a campaign of proselytism, ending with a victory over the minds of men. Probably more important
than the treatment of this fable is the dialogue on the *Holy War,* which
is, like the *New Atlantis,* formally incomplete. The dialogue begins
with a discussion of war against infidels and whether such a war is a
just war, and ends with recommendations for war against the "unnatural." The skeptic in the dialogue, a courtier named Pollio, suggests that
if the interlocutors really want to have a holy war, they must organize
it as a crusade and find a pope named Urban to conduct it, as an Urban
conducted the First Crusade. The name "Urban" refers to the Latin
word for city but came to mean not merely any city, but the best city,
Rome. The name of the Socrates of the dialogue, "Eupolis," also refers
to the best city (but Greek, not Roman). The crusade which Bacon advocated, the only holy war which he could really support, was the cru-

sade conducted by the best city, or the well-governed country, whether
it be called Eupolis or Bensalem. The possibility that such a holy war
might actually be armed conflict is not precluded, but the holy war is
primarily a crusade for emancipating the world from the obscurantist
traditions.

The holy war, moreover, solves the problem raised several times in
the *Wisdom of the Ancients:* the problem of the relation between natural and political philosophy. Orpheus journeyed to hell to regain his
wife, Eurydice. He rescued her but looked upon her prematurely as he
was leading her to the light. He then turned to the beasts and stones,
eschewing the company of women, and subdued the forest with his
lyre. At this he was successful, until the Thracian women drowned out
his music with their rebellious din and killed him. Orpheus, Bacon says,
was a man "wonderful and wholly divine." He was a "complete philosopher." Complete philosophy meant, to Bacon, natural and political
philosophy. The powers of darkness represented nature, and, but for
his impatience, Orpheus would have mastered nature and rescued
Eurydice, who represents the things for which philosophy cares. His
failure to do so brought melancholy, an affection not suitable to philosophy. Even in his melancholy, however, Orpheus subdued other alien
forces, beasts and stones, as men found states and commonwealths. The
subjugation, however, was temporary, as states founded without the
completion of natural philosophy must be temporary. The din of the
Thracian women was too strong for Orpheus. The Thracian women
were followers of Dionysus, and they represented not only frenzy, but
primarily religious frenzy. This was the most violent of the passions,
and the one most likely to destroy the commonwealth.

What would have happened if Orpheus had not been impatient?
He would have kept Eurydice, but would he still have subdued the
beasts and stones? And would he have needed to compete with the
Thracian women? In the fable there are three alien forces, and they
stand for nature (the infernal powers), man (beasts and stones), and
the religious rites that men have created (the Thracian women). The
first two might be subdued; the third would have to be destroyed.
Eurydice, whom the philosopher loves, must also stand for mankind,
however. The road Orpheus takes leads, through contemplation, to the
darkest and most recondite of nature's secrets. Then it leads back to the
light, taking humanity with it. There is a certain ambiguity in the suggestion that there are two imitations of mankind in the fable, but Bacon
did not invent the fable and had to take it as he found it. Clearly, if
Eurydice stands for the things for which philosophy cares, as he says,
then she stands for final causes, and these can be related only to humanity in Bacon's teaching.

The science of politics, Bacon says elsewhere, is a secret science, not only because it is hard to know, but because it is not fit to utter. That means that while the knowledge is only difficult the teaching is also, in a sense, shameful. The reason that political knowledge is shameful is that it may be destructive of much that men hold dear if it is not communicated with care and circumspection. Thus in another fable Bacon speaks of nakedness as meaning political secrets, and in the *New Atlantis* the nakedness of the prospective bride and groom may be understood as relating shame to politics. Here Bacon refers to Orpheus' care for his own wife. With her return he would win (or rule) mankind. It would not then be possible for the flutes of the Thracian women to drown out his lyre. In other words, once the mastery of nature, a universal goal, had been achieved, the universal society might be created, and man could have his utopia.

Yet the melancholy of Orpheus is not necessarily merely the result of his despair. We are told that the Father of Solomon's House had eyes as if he pitied man. And in another work, the *Refutation of Philosophies,* the philosopher, lecturing before an international congress, also had eyes of pity for man.[23] Why should that be necessary inside utopia? Bacon seems to have seen something that not all of his successors have seen. Mankind could, he believed, be free of old religious superstitions. But new civil institutions would have to be put in their place, and only a very few men would be really free, because very few men could be really wise. The universality of human affections, by which philosophy must steer its course, does not lead, in Bacon's thought, to the inference of natural equality. There may be much value in the relief of man's estate, in the lessening of illness and poverty. Yet one must still pity man, whose lot is miserable, for there is something more important that man cannot have, perhaps happiness, perhaps wisdom, perhaps God.

## NOTES

1. Cf. opening of Francis Bacon, *Instauratio Magna* with *New Atlantis,* ed. A. B. Gough (Oxford: Blackwell, 1915), p. 13.

2. *Advancement of Learning,* II.vii.2 (paragraphing according to 5th Oxford edition, ed. W. A. Wright [Oxford: Oxford University Press, 1900]).

3. *Descriptio Globi Intellectualis,* in *Works,* ed. J. Spedding, R. L. Ellis,

and D. D. Heath (Boston: Little, Brown, 1861—), VII, 313; *Holy War, Works,* XIII, 191 ff.

4. *Novum Organum,* I.48 and II.2; *Redargutio, Works,* VII, 52; esp. "Prometheus," in *De Sapientia Veterum (The Wisdom of the Ancients), Works,* XIII, 44 ff.

5. See especially *Cogitationes de Natura Rerum* and *Principiis atque*

*Originibus, Works,* V, 203 ff. and 289 ff. See also the fables of "Cupid" and "Coelum," in *De Sap. Vet.*

6. Cf. Shaftesbury, *Characteristics,* Miscellany II. 2 (1732 ed., III, 69).

7. *Works,* II, 254; III, 31, 45, 77; VI, 327; IX, 211; XII, 119, 213, 275, 318; XIII, 124, 222. See also the fable of "Sphinx," in *De Sap. Vet.*

8. *Essays,* 55, "Honour and Reputation." (All essays are numbered according to the last edition edited by Bacon personally. He changed the numbering from earlier editions.) See also *Works,* VI, 145; "Prometheus," in *De Sap. Vet.; New Atlantis, passim; Novum Organum,* I.129.

9. Alfred N. Whitehead, *Science in the Modern World* (New York: Macmillan, 1925), pp. 60 ff.

10. *Novum Organum,* I. 79, 80, 120 ff.; *New Atlantis, passim.*

11. See *Advancement of Learning,* I.

12. See especially *Historia Vitae et Mortis, Works,* III, 331–502.

13. See Bruno, *On the Infinite Universe and Worlds* (a translation is printed in Dorothea W. Singer, *Giordano Bruno, His Life and Thought* [New York: Henry Schuman, 1950], pp. 243–45, 283, 285 ff.); *Opere Italiane,* ed. G. Gentile [Bari: Laterza, 1925–27], I, 24 ff.; II, 23, 86; *Eroici Furori* (in Michel's edition, with French translation, *Des Fureurs Héroïques* [Paris, 1954], 114, 205–7, 311). Bacon, *Novum Organum,* I. 84, 92.

14. For the nine blind men see *Eroici Furori,* pp. 415 ff.; for passage on Columbus see *Cena de la Ceneri* in *Opere Italiane,* I, 24.

15. "Peace among the willows" comes from a personal letter to Toby Matthew in February, 1610, in J. Spedding, *Life and Letters of Lord Bacon* (1861). As this letter accompanied Bacon's present of the *De Sap. Vet.,* it furnishes a clue to that work.

16. Probably the strongest statements of our ignorance of what to wish are in the *Redargutio, Works,* VII. See also *Novum Organum,* I. 70, 117, 120–22.

17. See especially Essays 3, 17, 18; *Advancement of Learning,* II (Oxford ed.); J. Spedding, *Life and Letters of Lord Bacon,* prints the *Advertisement touching the Establishment of the Church of England,* which Bacon did not publish, I, 74 ff. See also letters at I, 48; III, 48–50; V, 373.

18. See Essay 29 and *True Greatness of the Kingdom of Britain, Works,* XIII, 231 ff. For imperialism as a duty, see the Latin translation of Essay 29 in *De Augmentis Scientiarum, Works,* III, 120; also see the piece about the Spanish war in *Life and Letters,* VIII, 483. *Holy War* is in *Works,* XIII, 191 ff. The statement about the middle way is from *De Sap. Vet.,* "Icarus."

19. See, in general, the discussion of the architecture of fortune, in *Advancement of Learning,* II. xxiii. See also Essays 34, 36, 41 and the citations in n. 18.

20. *De Sap. Vet., Works,* XII, 427 ff. and XIII, 1 ff.

21. The phrase comes from the *Redargutio, Works,* VII, 93.

22. Cf. *Novum Organum,* I. 122 with I. 128.

23. *Works,* VII, 59.

## READINGS

A.  Bacon, Francis. *New Atlantis.*
    Bacon, Francis. *Wisdom of the Ancients.* Preface, Fables 11 "Orpheus," 16 "Juno's Suitor," 26 "Prometheus."
    Bacon, Francis. Essay 29 "Of the True Greatness of Kingdoms and Estates."
B.  Bacon, Francis. *Wisdom of the Ancients.* Fables 1 "Cassandra," 5 "Styx," 7 "Perseus," 10 "Acteon and Pentheus," 6 "Pan," 12 "Coelum," 22 "Nemesis," 24 "Dionysus," 28 "Sphinx."

Bacon, Francis. *History of the Reign of Henry VII.*
Bacon, Francis. *Advertisement touching an Holy War.*
Bacon, Francis. *Of the True Greatness of Britain.*
Bacon, Francis. Essays 6 "Simulation and Dissimulation," 10 "Love," 11 "Of
    Great Place," 13 "Goodness and Goodness of Nature," 14 "Nobility,"
    16 "Atheism," 17 "Superstition," 19 "Empire," 41 "Usury," 51 "Fac-
    tions," 55 "Honour and Reputation," 58 "Vicissitude of Things."
Bacon, Francis. *Advancement of Learning,* in *Selected Writings.* New York:
    Modern Library, 1955. Bk II, pp. 345–78, section on "Civil Knowledge."

# HUGO GROTIUS

## 1583–1645

Hugo Grotius was a citizen of Holland. A veritable prodigy of learning as well as a man of action, Grotius was diplomat, lawyer, magistrate, scholar, and teacher; but essentially he was a jurist. He regarded his greatest work, the *De Jure Belli ac Pacis* (1625) or *The Law of War and Peace,* as a legal treatise rather than as a treatise in political theory; and he explicitly distinguished his intention as that of a jurist from Aristotle's intention in the *Politics* as that of a political scientist.[1]

Grotius' work is not, however, simply a treatise on positive law. Nor is it—in spite of its title—limited to the treatment of the law of war and peace, which is to say to international law as we know it today. On the contrary, it is, as its subtitle indicates, a general treatise on "the law of nature and of nations" (*jus naturae et gentium*), and on the main points of "public law" (*jus publicum*). And although it is true that Grotius focuses upon the law of war and peace, he constantly places that particular branch of jurisprudence within the framework of a general juristic analysis of law and government.

So far as the history of political theory is concerned then, Grotius' work is of importance because, in the first place, it is an excellent example of a juristic as opposed to a specifically philosophic or theological teaching on politics; and in the second place it is a superb specimen of the numerous treatises on natural public law which were written by jurists and theologians in western Europe from the sixteenth through the eighteenth century. (Other important examples of such works are *On Laws and God as Legislator* (1612), by the Spanish Jesuit Francisco Suárez; *On the Law of Nature and Nations* (1672), by the German jurist Samuel Pufendorf; and *The Law of Nations* (1758), by the Swiss diplomat Emmerich de Vattel.) The practical importance of such works may be gauged by the fact that Grotius, Pufendorf, Vattel, and others were authorities for statesmen and lawyers, including the founding fathers of the United States.

The idea that man is by nature a rational and social animal is the central principle of Grotius' treatise. The work begins with a restatement of the centuries-old struggle between classical conventionalism and classical natural right. Grotius assigns the task of pleading the case for conventionalism to Carneades, who was head of the later Academy at Athens. Carneades is made by Grotius to argue that men have imposed laws on themselves only for reasons of expediency and self-protection; that such laws necessarily vary from place to place; that there is no law of nature, strictly speaking, because all men are impelled by their natural desires toward ends which are advantageous ultimately only to themselves; and that, consequently, there is no justice which is natural to man. To this doctrine, which was also accepted by the Epicureans, Grotius opposes what is basically a Stoic doctrine. That is, he begins by accepting the proposition that men are, in the beginning of their lives, impelled by natural desire merely to preserve their own being, as distinguished from being impelled by pleasure or pain. But he denies that this desire constitutes the definitive quality of man. Indeed, for Grotius the original desire to preserve one's natural constitution is in effect an instinctive or unconscious attempt to realize one's full nature: to grow and to develop as a rational being. The rational faculty, which defines man because it decisively distinguishes him from all the other animals, is more excellent and more natural than are any of the original natural desires. And it is the rational faculty, in turn, which perceives that justice is a virtue, a good in and for itself, apart from any considerations of self-interest or expediency. Thus men are naturally impelled to seek society with others; they naturally come to possess speech and reason; and they naturally are inclined to behave justly, even though it is true that many men in fact do not always follow their true nature.[2]

It is in relation to this central conception of man as a rational and social animal that right and political society are understood by Grotius. Right (*jus*), in its primary meaning, is that which is just. Right thus understood has, according to Grotius, a negative rather than a positive meaning: it is that which is not unjust. What is unjust is anything that is in conflict with the nature of society between beings endowed with reason. Thus for Grotius, who quotes Cicero and Seneca to support his statement, men act justly only when they act in conformity with their natural attraction to and desire for society. For example, since to steal what belongs to others is destructive of all trust, and therefore of society, to steal is against the natural order to which man belongs.

A second meaning of right is a quality of or belonging to persons, and usually refers to the rightful power to have or to do something. Kinds of rights are liberty or power over oneself, the power of a master over a slave, the power of a father over his son, and power over property. The rights, in each case, are in fact objective laws which define how the power in question may be exercised; and in some cases, the law of nature itself specifies the right. For example, the law of nature permits a person to kill a robber escaping with stolen property, if the property cannot be otherwise recovered. But it is important to notice that by making this second sense of right pertain specifically to the abstract "person" (*persona*), Grotius was believed by several of his contemporary jurists to have departed significantly from the traditional or Roman sense of the term "right" (*jus*). And it has been argued, in recent years, that Grotius' second definition of right is a precursor of the strictly modern idea of subjective "rights," which holds that the person possesses intrinsic "rights" simply as a human being and not as embodying certain objective qualities such as those of the ruler, the father, or the landowner. Even so, however, it must also be said that Grotius goes only a short distance toward the full idea of subjective rights; the specifically philosophic statement of that idea, and therefore of individualism as we know it in the modern age, begins with Thomas Hobbes, whose first major work, the *De Cive,* was published less than two decades after Grotius' work.

The third meaning of right is law, that is, a rule of action which obliges to what is correct and which carries with it some sanction.

Having defined three senses of *jus* or right, Grotius next divides right in the sense of law into two kinds: natural and volitional. The first kind, the law of nature (*jus naturale*), is defined in relation to the essential nature of man as "a dictate of right reason which points out that an act, according as it is or is not in conformity with rational nature, has in it a quality of moral baseness or moral necessity; and that in consequence, such an act is either forbidden or enjoined by the author of nature, God."[3] But lest we think, because of the last clause, that the law of nature itself depends simply on God's will, Grotius states in the Prolegomena that the law of nature would be valid even if there is no God or if the affairs of men are of no concern to Him. This statement—which Grotius, it should be noted, instantly acknowledges as blasphemous—constitutes an indication that a desacralization of natural law is conceivable to Grotius without thereby necessarily destroying its essential validity as a rule of reason to reasonable creatures. But even this cautious statement, because it suggests the possibility of the independence of natural law from both revealed and natural theology, was interpreted by a number of Grotius' contemporaries as marking a decided break with medieval and classical doctrines. The point we are mainly concerned with here is that Grotius' suggestion of the possibility of a secularized natural law which would still be fully binding on man was, at the beginning of the seventeenth century, very controversial although not unique. The doctrine of the dependence of man and the political order on the divine order was still, for most jurists as well as theologians, the essence of natural law.

Grotius offers two proofs of the existence of the law of nature. The first is a priori, that is, the demonstration of the necessary agreement of an act or a thing with the rational and social nature of man. This proof, although very difficult, is the basis of certain knowledge of what men are bound to by their intrinsic nature, for such a proof proceeds strictly by reasoning about that nature. The second proof is a posteriori, that is, it proceeds by supplying evidence of that which is believed by all nations, or at least by learned men from all civilized nations, to be binding on all men. In developing this general line of proof Grotius quotes Cicero to the effect that "the agreement of all nations upon a matter ought to be considered a law of nature" and Aristotle to the effect that "in order to find what is natural we must look among those things which according to nature are in a sound condition, not among those that are corrupt." [4] Furthermore, in developing the a posteriori line of proof for particular principles of the law of nature, Grotius cites scores of examples and arguments taken from the writings of ancient philosophers, historians, poets, rhetoricians, and theologians, as well as from the Bible. In so doing, Grotius bases his own argument on the idea of the *consensus gentium,* or agreement of peoples; for, as he argues, when so many learned and wise men, who also happen to represent different nations, such as the Jews, the Greeks, the Romans, and so on, affirm the same principles as being true or certain, it must be due to the operation of a "universal cause." That cause must be either a correct conclusion drawn from the principles of nature themselves by these learned men, or else the common consent of civilized mankind. In either case, such evidence serves to confirm that which is in principle discoverable, via the a priori proof, concerning the nature of man, law, and political society.

The second kind of law is volitional. It is divided into human and divine law. Human volitional law is of three kinds. First is the law which is not directly dependent on the civil power; it is less comprehensive than the municipal or civil law and comprises the commands of a father, a master, and all similar commands. Second is the municipal or civil law (*jus civile*), which emanates from the civil power and which therefore regulates the relations of men and things within a particular political society. Third is the law of nations (*jus gentium*), which receives its obligatory force from the will of all or of many nations. The law of nations is distinguished from the law of nature not by subject matter but by reason of its being changeable, whereas the law of nature is unchangeable, and by reason of its being based on will and not simply on what is discerned by reason as being in accordance with the rational and social nature of man. These distinctions and their importance may be understood by taking an example: the question of the responsibility for actions. Grotius states that according to the strict law of nature no person is responsible for another's acts, except in the limited case where one person inherits the property of another. Nevertheless, the law of nations—that is, the law developed by the will of all or many nations—has modified this strict principle to the effect that all the subjects of a political society are responsible for the debts of the ruler, and their possessions are considered to have a charge against them to fulfill his obligations. The reason Grotius gives is that unless this concession is made, rulers, because they alone would then be responsible for their acts, would be encouraged to licentious actions since they are practically immune from having their own property seized as repayment. And on the other side, those to whom debts are owed by the ruler would thus unjustly be deprived of redress—unless, that is, a charge may be levied against the property of his subjects.

In contrast to his exceedingly elaborate and detailed analysis and definition of the nature and the kinds of law, Grotius' treatment of more specifically political phenomena, such as the nature and origins of political society or the nature and exercise of political power, is very sketchy, and it relies heavily on the authority of philosophers, historians, jurists, and so on. For example, when Grotius defines municipal law (*jus civile*), he indicates that it emanates from the civil power (*potestas civilis*), that the civil power is that power which rules over the civil order or state (*civitas*), and that the civil order is "a complete association [*civitas coetus perfectus*], joined together for the enjoyment of rights and for the common interest." [5] Later, when he provides a slightly more extended treatment of the civil power, Grotius is content, so far as the meaning or purpose of the civil order or state is concerned, to refer the reader to his proposition that the civil order is a "perfect association [*perfectus coetus*]." [6] But he provides practically no independent argument as to what precisely is meant by this and why this should be so. The reason seems to be first, that Grotius, as a jurist, is less concerned with such questions than with questions concerning the char-

acter of law, above all in its *relation* to the operations of the civil power;
and second, that he simply accepts two general classical ideas: (1) that
only within the civil order can man fully realize the potentiality of his
rational and social nature; and (2) that ruling, as such, is as necessary
and natural to the civil body as is the rule of reason necessary and natural
over the human body.

The latter point is shown strikingly well by the way in which
Grotius treats the civil power and its parts: he relies essentially on the
concepts and the distinctions of Aristotle, as provided in the *Politics* and
the *Ethics*. Thus Grotius says that the civil power has three aspects or
branches. The first branch is concerned with the general framing of
laws, both secular and religious, and is called "architectonic," for it
embodies the overarching and directive aspect of the civil power.[7] The
second branch concerns the particular interests of the society which are
public in nature. Such interests are the making of war, peace, and
treaties; the levying of taxes; and the exercising of the right of eminent
domain over the property of private citizens. Of this branch Grotius
says that Aristotle calls it the "political" branch, properly speaking, or
the branch which "deliberates" about specific policies and the framing
of specific decrees. The third branch of the civil power concerns the
private interests of the citizens and the possible controversies which may
arise among them. Its function, as contrasted to framing general laws
or deliberating concerning particular public policies, is to adjudicate
conflicts of private interests by the public authority. It therefore is called
the "judicial" branch.

Grotius concept of the nature and locus of the supreme power
(*summa potestas*) in the civil order also links him to the classical tradition and separates him from the modern idea of "sovereignty," as the
latter emerges in the writings of men such as Hobbes. Although supreme
power is defined initially as that power whose actions are not subject to
the legal control of another and cannot therefore be rendered void by
the operation of another human will, it is also true that every political
society, and therefore its supreme power, is subject to the limitations set
by the law of nature and the law of nations. As Grotius puts it, the
mother of municipal law is that obligation which arises from consent;
but since the obligation arising from consent derives its force from the
law of nature, above all that part of the law of nature which dictates
that men live in civil society and be guided by the rules of justice, nature
itself may be considered the "great-grandmother" of municipal law.
He also says that they are in error who argue that the standard of justice
which is applicable in the case of individuals is inapplicable to a nation
or a ruler. Such a view is only a particular application of a false doctrine

of law, which fails to see that law is not founded simply on expediency but on natural justice as well.[8]

Although it is true that in the case of most states it is the benefit or good of those who are governed which is the primary consideration in judging whether the supreme power is properly constituted, this does not mean that the supreme power ultimately resides in the governed or that there is a relation of mutual dependence between rulers and ruled. On the contrary, in a monarchy, for example, the possession of the supreme power means in essence the possession of rights and powers which are intrinsic to the ruling function. It is of course quite possible that the king may misconstrue those rights and misuse those powers. But Grotius vigorously opposes the conclusion that the people thereby automatically has a right to assume the supreme power or to dethrone the ruler. Thus the general right to revolution does not exist, strictly speaking: the end of civil society being public tranquility, this end necessarily takes precedence even over the right to protect oneself against the abuse of power by the ruler. Consequently, the waywardness of the supreme power is usually to be borne, even though one ought not, if at all possible, to do acts which are against the law of nature even if they are commanded by the supreme power. And here Grotius, typically, reverts to the authority of antiquity when he quotes Cicero, who says, "To me, peace on any terms between citizens seems more advantageous than civil war." [9]

Grotius constantly seeks to make a distinction between the nature of the supreme power in itself and the absolute possession of it. Thus in some cases, and above all in the case of absolute hereditary monarchy, the supreme power is held with full proprietary right. This means that when a people so ruled is transferred from one monarch to another there is not, strictly speaking, a transfer of the individuals but of the perpetual right of governing them in their totality as a people. But in other cases—in fact, perhaps the majority of cases—the supreme power is not held absolutely. Such is the case of a king who has the supreme power because it was conferred on him by the will of the people. Even in such a case, however, the actual *exercise* of the supreme power, once granted, is plenary.

The supreme power is in principle a unity, or is indivisible, and consists of the parts enumerated above as constituting the three branches of civil power. In fact, however, there are numerous historical examples in which the supreme power is divided. A notable example would be Rome under the emperors, where it happened that one emperor administered the East, another the West, and even that three emperors governed the whole empire in three divisions. A different type of division may occur when a people, in choosing a king, reserves to itself certain powers and confers others on the king absolutely. Thus in the time of Probus at Rome, the senate confirmed the laws made by the emperors, took cognizance of appeals, appointed proconsuls, and assigned military officers to the consuls. Still a third type of division is cited from the account given in Plato's *Laws* where, because the Heraclids had founded Argos, Messene, and Sparta, the kings of these states were bound to govern within the provisions of the laws which had been previously laid down.

Finally, Grotius generally follows Aristotle's idea that the civil order or state changes when the supreme power changes from one kind to another, as when there is a change from aristocracy to democracy, or democracy to monarchy; but he distinguishes this "political" issue from the juristic one of how the laws and the government are related to one another with respect to the definition of supreme power.

We have now to glance briefly at Grotius' application of the general principles set forth above to the question of just war, which is the main theme in his doctrine of international law.

The crucial question is whether war can ever truly be just. To this Grotius replies in the affirmative, arguing from the general principles of the nature of man and society, and buttressing these principles by exhaustive and exhausting citations from history, both sacred and secular, from the *jus gentium,* and from divine volitional law (that is, the Bible). The gist of his argument is that not all use of force is prohibited by natural and volitional law, but only that use of force which is in conflict with the principles of society, that is, which attempts to take away the rights or possessions of another. Thus war may be waged justly, but only to achieve or to re-establish the natural end of man, which is peace or the condition of tranquil social life, and not for personal or collective self-aggrandizement. But this kind of definition of the scope of just as opposed to unjust war is too general to serve effectively as a guide. Grotius must, therefore, set forth with his usual detail the various categories of just and unjust war.

As for just wars, they fall into two general categories: those waged in defense of self and property, and those waged to prosecute injuries and to inflict deserved punishment. The treatment of the first category requires Grotius to enter into a very elaborate discussion of the origin and types of property, for it is only by knowing what belongs to whom that one can decide when a war is just. The treatment of the second category requires him to set forth the nature of pacts, contracts, and promises, for it is only by knowing what is owed to whom that one can decide when a war is just with respect to such matters.

As an illustration of Grotius' doctrine on just war it is instructive to consider his argument concerning the application of the law of nature to cases where a particular ruler has not been directly injured by the depredations of another ruler. The governing principle, says Grotius, is that rulers are free to serve the interests of human society by punishing those who "excessively violate the law of nature," even though no direct injury has been done to those who mete out the punishment. This principle he derives from the fact that those who hold the civil power are subject to no other legal power, yet are bound to observe *and to enforce* the law of nature wherever possible. He then quotes Seneca to the effect that "if a man does not attack my own country, but yet is a heavy burden to his own, and although separated from my people he afflicts his own, such debasement of mind nevertheless cuts him off from us." And he cites Aristotle's authority for the proposition that against men who are truly barbarians war is sanctioned by nature, that is, that a "war of civilization" is, in extreme circumstances, just. In adopting this position Grotius explicitly takes issue with writers of the fifteenth and sixteenth centuries, such as Francisco Victoria, who had taught that whoever metes out punishment must either have suffered injury in his own person or state, or have jurisdiction over him who is attacked.[10] The basic difference—and it is one which links Grotius more to the writers of classical antiquity than either to moderns such as Hobbes or theologians such as Victoria—is that for Grotius the power of punishing is derived not merely from civil jurisdiction but from the law of nature itself.

Grotius' work appeared, as we have noted, less than two decades prior to the *De Cive* (1642) of Thomas Hobbes. But in spite of this proximity in time, and in spite of a superficial agreement, such as the common use of the concept of the "law of nature," the fact is that Grotius still looks mainly to the classics of antiquity whereas Hobbes explicitly sets out to build anew. The basic disagreement concerns the question whether man is indeed by nature a rational and social animal; in turning to Hobbes we turn to the iconoclast who states the essence of the modern view of man and natural law.

## NOTES

1. Hugo Grotius, *The Law of War and Peace,* Prolegomena, 57; II.ix.8.
2. *Ibid.,* Prolegomena, 3–10, 16–30; I.ii.50.
3. *Ibid.,* i.10.
4. *Ibid.,* 12.
5. *Ibid.,* 14.
6. *Ibid.,* iii.7.
7. Cf. Aristotle *Ethics* VI. viii, which Grotius cites.

8. *The Law of War and Peace,*        9. *Ibid.,* I. iv.19.
Prolegomena, 15–23.                         10. *Ibid.,* II.xx.40.


# READINGS

The best text of *The Law of War and Peace* is the translation of Grotius' work prepared as part of the series titled, "Classics of International Law," sponsored by the Carnegie Endowment for International Peace. The translation, by Francis W. Kelsey, is complete and was published in 1925 by the Clarendon Press, Oxford.

A. Grotius, Hugo. *The Law of War and Peace.* Prolegomena, secs 1, 2, 5–22, 28, 30, 39–42, 45–50, 57–58; bk I, chap. i, secs 1–13; chap. ii, sec. 1; chap. iii, sec. 5, par. 7–sec. 7, sec. 8, pars 1–6, 13–14, sec. 9, secs 13–14, sec. 16, par. 1, sec. 17, sec. 24; chap. iv, sec. 1, par. 3, sec. 2, par. 1, sec. 7, pars 1–2.

B. Grotius Hugo. *The Law of War and Peace.* Prolegomena; bk 1, chap. i; chap. ii, secs 1–4, 6; chap. iii, secs 1–9, 13–17, 24; chap. iv; bk II, chap. i, sec. 1, pars 1–2, secs 2–3, sec. 11, sec. 17; chap. ii, secs 1–2; chap. iii, secs 1–4; chap. v, secs 1–5, 7–9, 27–29; chap. viii, sec. 1; chap. x, sec. 1; chap. xi, secs 1–3; chap. xii, secs 7–12; chap. xiv, secs 1–6, 9; chap. xv, secs 1–3; chap. xx, secs 1–4, 18, 40, 48; chap. xxii, secs 1–3, 11; bk III, chap. i, secs 1–3; chap. ii, secs 1–2; chap. iii, secs 1, 4, 6.

# THOMAS HOBBES

## 1588–1679

Hobbes presented his political philosophy thematically in three books, *The Elements of Law* (1640), *De Cive* (*The Citizen,* 1642), and *Leviathan* (1651). The most manifest differences among the books concern the development and elaboration of theological doctrine in the later books.

Hobbes's intention can be seen as twofold: (1) to put moral and political philosophy, for the first time, on a scientific basis; (2) to contribute to the establishment of civic peace and amity and to the disposing of mankind toward fulfilling their civic duties. These two intentions, theoretical and practical, were in Hobbes's mind closely connected. This latter intention, the civic or civilizing intention, identified Hobbes with the tradition of political philosophy that he associated with the names of Socrates, Plato, Aristotle, Plutarch, and Cicero. The entire tradition, according to Hobbes, had failed, however, both in its quest for truth and in its inability to lead men toward peace. Hobbes's emphatic break with the tradition was decisively prepared by Machiavelli and, following Machiavelli, Bacon. The classics failed, according to Machiavelli, because they aimed too high. Because they based their political doctrines on considerations of man's highest aspirations, the life of virtue and the society dedicated to the promotion of virtue, they rendered themselves ineffective; as Bacon said, they made "imaginary laws for imaginary commonwealths." Machiavelli's "realism" consists in a conscious lowering of the standards of political life, taking as goals of political life not the perfection of man but those lower goals actually pursued by most men and most societies most of the time. Political schemes framed in accordance with men's lower but more powerful motives are much more likely to be realized than the utopias of the classics. However, unlike Machiavelli, Hobbes elaborated a code of moral or natural law, natural law as a morally binding law, determining the purposes of civil society. But, following Machiavelli's "realism," he separated his doctrine of the natural law from the idea of the perfection of man.[1] He attempted to deduce the natural law from what is most powerful in most men most of the time: not reason, but passion. Because of what he regarded as his discovery of the true roots of human behavior, his knowledge of human nature, and his scientific way of proceeding, Hobbes believed that he had succeeded where all others had failed, that he was the first true political philosopher. In accordance with these convictions he recommended that his books be established in the universities as authoritative and continually attacked the doctrines of Aristotle, "whose opinions are at this day and in these parts of greater authority than any other human writings," as both subversive and false.[2]

For Hobbes, scientific knowledge meant mathematical knowledge, or geometrical knowledge. Hitherto, he wrote, geometry has been the only science that has attained indisputable conclusions. The term geometry was sometimes used by Hobbes to refer to all the mathematical sciences, the study of motion and force, mathematical physics, as well as the study of geometrical figures. Philosophy, or science, proceeds in either of two ways: (1) with the compositive method, or "synthetically," by reasoning from the first and generating causes of all things to their apparent effects, or (2) with the resolutive method, or "analytically," by reasoning from apparent effects, or facts, to possible causes of their generation. The first principles of all things are defined by Hobbes as body, or matter, and motion, or change of place: "every part of the Universe, is Body; and that which is not Body, is no part of the Universe: and because the Universe is All, that which is no part of it is Nothing. . . ." In accordance with the synthetic or geometrical mode of proceeding one would begin with the laws of physics in general, from them deduce the passions, the causes of the behavior of individual men, and from the passions deduce the laws of social and political life. However, it is by means of the analytic method, the analysis of sense experience, that one arrives at adequate definitions of the first principles themselves.

The analytic method is especially important for political philosophy. For Hobbes expected the moral and civil science which he elaborated to be able to be convincing not only to natural philosophers, but also to any man "that pretends but reason enough to govern his private family." This expectation is reasonable because the facts upon which his analysis is based are known to all normal men by experience. Hobbes invites his reader to test the truth of what he wrote by looking into himself and considering whether what Hobbes says about the passions, thoughts, and natural inclinations of mankind apply to him; then by learning to "read" and know himself, through the similitude of passions and situations he will be able to read the passions and thoughts of all other men. Although his conception of scientific method influenced Hobbes's formulations, presentation, and analysis of human experience, he indicates that it is not to his conception of science but to his understanding of common prescientific experience that we are to look in order to determine the truth and importance of his political philosophy. He suggests that the adequacy and correctness of his judgments of, or insights into, what are the fundamental human experiences can be considered and understood independently of his physics.[3]

Human behavior, according to Hobbes, is to be understood primarily in terms of a mechanistic psychology of the passions,[4] those forces in man, which, so to speak, push him from behind; it is not to be understood in terms of those things which could be thought of as attracting man from in front, the ends of man, or what for Hobbes would be the objects of the passions. The objects of the passions, Hobbes says, vary with each man's constitution and education and are too easy to disguise. Furthermore, good and evil, the words with which men characterize the objects of their desires and aversions, are strictly relative to the man using the words, "there being nothing simply and absolutely so; nor any common Rule of Good and Evil, to be taken from the nature of the objects themselves. . . ." What men really mean when they say something is good is that it pleases them. Yet it is true that as the passions issue in actions, men are guided by their imaginations and their opinions of what is good and evil; but the thoughts do not control the passions; on the contrary, "for the Thoughts are to the Desires, as Scouts, and Spies, to range abroad, and find the way to the Things Desired." [5]

Hobbes was in agreement with the tradition, stemming from Socrates and including Thomas Aquinas, that the goals and character of moral and political life should be determined by reference to nature, especially human nature. However, he determined the way in which nature sets the standards for politics very differently than did the tradition, namely, through the construction of a theory of "the state of nature." The theory of the state of nature, deduced, Hobbes says, from the passions of man, is one way of dealing with the old psychological problem, a problem of decisive importance for political philosophy: Is man by nature social and political? Hobbes denies that man is nat-

urally social and political.⁶ The grounds of this denial are made evident
by the theory of the state of nature, that prepolitical condition in which
men live without civil government, or without a common power over
them to keep them in fear.

If man is not by nature social and political, then all civil societies
must have grown out of presocial and prepolitical states of nature, *i.e.,*
the state of nature must have existed among the progenitors of all
men now living in civil society. Hobbes did not believe that there ever
was such a state all over the world, but, he said, in many places of
America "at this day," during civil wars, and between independent
sovereigns such a state actually exists. The historical question, however,
is not very important for Hobbes. The state of nature is deduced from
the passions of man; it is meant to reveal and clarify what it is about
man's natural inclinations that we must know in order to form the right
kind of political order. It serves primarily to determine the reasons, the
purposes, or the ends for the sake of which men form political societies.
These ends being known, the political problem becomes one of how to
organize man and society in order to realize the ends most effectively.

What would the condition of mankind be if there were no civil
society? How would men be related to each other? First of all, Hobbes
argues, men are much more equal both in faculties of body and mind
than has hitherto been recognized. The most important equality is the
equal ability all men have to kill each other. This is most important because the most important concern of men is their own self-preservation.
Self-preservation, in turn, is most important because fear, the fear of violent death, is the most powerful passion. Equality of ability leads to
equality of hopes and to competition among men, among all who desire
the same things. This natural enmity is intensified by the diffidence, or
distrust, men without government have for each other as they anticipate
how each would like to deprive all others of whatever goods (including
life) they have, so that each is led to think of subjugating all the rest until
there is no power left capable of threatening his security. Contrary to
what is said "in the Books of the old Moral Philosophers," Hobbes says,
happiness, or felicity, consists in a continual progress of the desire from
one object to another. Since this is so, what men seek constantly is some
means of securing the way to their future desires. Men seek not only to
procure, but also to be insured of a contented life for themselves "So
that," Hobbes says, "in the first place, I put for a general inclination of
all mankind, a perpetual and restless desire of power after power, that
ceaseth only in death." ⁷

The problem of civil life is further complicated by the presence
in our nature of the love of glory, or pride, or vanity. All pleasures which

are not bodily, or sensual, pleasures Hobbes calls pleasures of the mind. All pleasures of the mind are directly or indirectly derived from "glory-ing." Glorying is based upon the good opinions a man receives or has of himself or of his power. The opinions are always based upon compari-sons with others. Every man desires to have others value him as he values himself, and consequently, upon signs of contempt and undervaluing, he becomes quite ready to destroy those who slight him. Even when men gather for pleasure and recreation they seek it mostly through those things which stir laughter. And laughter, Hobbes says, is caused by sudden glory, being pleased by some sudden act of one's own, "or by the apprehension of some deformed thing in another, by comparison whereof they suddenly applaud themselves." This bleak picture is not relieved by any reference to a sense of honor or nobility. Honor and dishonor, properly understood, according to Hobbes, have nothing to do with justice or injustice. Honor is nothing else than an acknowledg-ment or opinion of someone's power, *i.e.,* superiority, especially one's power to help or harm ourselves. Even reverence is defined by Hobbes as the conception we have of another being who, having the power to do good or hurt to ourselves, does not have the will to do us hurt. The emphasis is not upon admiration or love, but fear.

These three great natural causes of quarrels among men, competi-tion, distrust, and glory, make the state of nature really a state of war, "and such a war, as is of every man, against every man." In such a state,

men live without other security, than what their own strength, and their own invention shall furnish them withal. In such condition there is no place for industry; because the fruit thereof is uncertain: and consequently no culture of the earth, no navigation, nor use of the commodities that may be imported by sea; no commodious building; no instruments of moving and removing such things as require much force; no knowledge of the face of the earth; no account of time; no arts; no letters; no society; and which is worst of all, continual fear, and danger of violent death; and the life of man solitary, poor, nasty, brutish, and short.[8]

Furthermore, there is no appeal to justice in the state of nature; nothing there can be unjust, for justice and injustice are such only in terms of some preceding law and there is no law outside of civil society. In short, man is not by nature social; on the contrary, nature dissociates man. The state of civil society, then, is radically conventional. This does not mean that there are not present in men certain natural impulses or forces that drive them toward civil life. It does mean that the antisocial forces are as natural as, and, when unmitigated by convention even more powerful than, the forces promoting civil life. Instead of serving as a direct guide to human goodness, nature indicates what man has to run away from. The only redeeming thing about the state of nature is the possibility of getting out of it. With Hobbes we are already in an atmosphere congenial to the idea of the conquest of nature.

Fear of death, desire for comfort, and hope of obtaining it through their industry incline men to peace. Reason, working along with these passions of fear, desire, and hope, suggests rules for peaceful living together. By comparing these passions with the three great natural causes of human enmity, we see that fear of death and desire for comfort are present both among the inclinations toward peace and among the causes of enmity; vanity, or the desire for glory is absent from the former group.[9] The task of reason then is to devise means of redirecting and intensifying the fear of death and the desire for comfort, so as to overpower and cancel out the destructive effects of the desire for glory, or pride. By understanding human nature mechanistically, we become capable of manipulating and finally, Hobbes seems to hope, conquering it. Hobbes calls these rules of reason Laws of Nature, the Moral Law, and sometimes the dictates of reason. In using these names he admits he is bowing to traditional usage, for him the rules are merely conclusions or theorems concerning what conduces to self-preservation. Properly speaking, only commands of the civil sovereign are laws. These rules, however, in so far as they are commanded by God in the Scriptures, may be called laws.

All the laws of nature and all social and political duties or obligations are derived from and subordinate to the right of nature, the individual's right to self-preservation. To the extent that modern liberalism teaches that all social and political obligations are derived from and are in the service of the individual rights of man, Hobbes may be regarded as the founder of modern liberalism. Social, moral, and political rules and institutions in the service of individual rights can be expected to be much more effective than the utopian schemes of Plato and Aristotle. For the individual rights themselves are derived from the most powerful selfish passions and desires of men, the desire for comfortable living and, most powerful of all, because it is the fear of what is worst of all, the fear of violent death, the passion underlying the right to self-preservation. Because the rights are backed up by the passions, they can be, in a sense, self-enforcing. As the foundations of the traditional doctrines of moral restraint and contempt for selfishness become discredited, the way is opened for a new legitimation or sanctification of human selfishness.

The right of nature is the blameless liberty to do or refrain from doing whatever one can to preserve one's life.[10] The right to an end also implies a right to the means to that end. Because men differ in intelligence and prudence, some understand the requirements of preservation better than others. Yet these intellectual differences are not decisive for Hobbes. Regardless of his intelligence, no man, Hobbes argues, is sufficiently interested in the preservation of others; hence in the state of nature, each man must be the sole judge of the means necessary to his own preservation. Therefore, each man has a natural right to whatever means he judges conduce to his preservation. In the universal enmity of the state of nature, anything not under a man's own power can be regarded as a danger to his preservation, and therefore there is nothing which cannot be regarded as a means to his preservation. Hence, in this state "every man has a right to everything." No man is secure in such a state. The laws of nature, as distinguished from the rights of nature, are precepts of reason which instruct men as to what they ought to do to avoid the perils to their own self-preservation that follow equally from their natural rights and from their irrational desires.

For the securing of their own self-preservation, the first and fundamental law of nature enjoins men to seek peace and to defend themselves against those from whom peace cannot be obtained. All the rest of the moral law, the laws of nature, is directed toward establishing the conditions of peace. The first law of nature derived from the fundamental law is that each man ought to be willing to divest himself of his right to all things when others are also willing, and ought to be satisfied with just as much liberty against other men as he allows other men against himself. This mutual laying down of rights is accomplished by what has come to be known as the social contract. Civil society is constituted by the social contract, wherein each one of a multitude of men obliges himself, by contract with each of the rest, not to resist the commands of that man or council that they have recognized as their sovereign. Each man contracts only with a view to what is good for himself, and above all with a view to the security and preservation of his life. Therefore it cannot be presumed that any man has contracted away those rights whose loss would defeat the purpose of all contracts. No one, for instance, can be regarded as having laid down his right to resist anyone who attempts to deprive him of his life.

When a man has by contract or covenant given away or renounced any right, he is obliged or bound not to hinder those to whom he granted or abandoned that right from enjoying the benefit of it. In other words, according to the next law of nature, men should perform their covenants. If this principle did not hold, society itself would dissolve. This principle, fidelity to contracts, according to Hobbes, is the basis of all justice and injustice; for where no covenant has preceded, no rights have been relinquished or transferred, and each man has a right to everything. Thus injustice, or injury, is nothing other than the non-performance of covenants, exercising a right that one has already legally relinquished. All genuine legislation then becomes a form of self-legis-lation, and injury is like a self-contradiction, willing to do that which one has already willed not to do.[11] All duties and obligations to others derive from covenants. But covenants, contracts where one or both of the parties promise to perform in the future, depend upon trust. There is no trust and no valid covenant where there is a reasonable fear of non-performance on either side. There is then no trust in the state of nature. Therefore, before it is correct to use the terms just or unjust, there must be some coercive power, the sovereign, which can compel all contractors equally to perform their covenants. The sovereign must see to it that terror of punishment is a greater force than the lure of any benefit which could be expected from a breach of covenant. No moral force is appealed to in order to establish conditions of trust; once again fear is the passion to be relied upon. According to Hobbes, intelligent calculation of self-interest is all that is required to make a man just. The fact that he acts under compulsion does not make him less just, for self-interest is the only basis of morality. One consequence of this kind of reasoning is a broad-ening of the traditional notion of a just war. For Hobbes, as for Bacon, the intention to rectify a previous injury is not necessary to justify war; the subjective criterion, fear of a neighboring nation's strength, is suffi-cient.

Hobbes addressed himself directly to Aristotle's idea of distributive justice. The doctrine that some men by nature are more worthy to com-mand and others more worthy to serve is the foundation of Aristotle's political science, Hobbes wrote. The doctrine is false because in the state of nature all men are equal, the inequality found now among men has been introduced by the civil laws. Furthermore, the doctrine is danger-ous because it contributes to pride. Distributive justice properly conceived is the justice of an arbitrator and consists not in distributing to each in proportion to his virtues and vices, but in treating all as equal. For, Hobbes said, if nature made men equal, that equality ought to be acknowledged. Even if nature made them unequal, men will always consider themselves equal and thus will enter into conditions of peace only on equal terms. Therefore, for the sake of peace, such equality ought to be admitted, even if it does not exist. Hence it is a law of nature that all men should acknowledge each other as equal by nature. The natural differences between men are then either nonexist-ent or politically irrelevant. One purpose dominates Hobbes's discussion of the laws of nature: to make men sociable and peaceable, and accord-

ingly to end or reduce to a mimimum the friction, resentment, and hostility generated among men by pride, partiality, and excessive self-love in
general. Among the laws of nature are rules for the arbitration of controversies and for the impartial distribution of disputed property. Ingratitude is forbidden. Expressions of hatred, contempt, or disesteem,
even by judges for convicted criminals, are not to be allowed. Lest one
think that not all men are able to comprehend all these laws of nature,
Hobbes asserts that they can all be comprehended, even by those who are
too neglectful or too busy to learn them, through the rule: Do not do
unto others what you would not have them do unto you.[12] The moral
law is not directed toward the perfection of our natures. Aristotle was
wrong about virtue and vice. Because his opinions were merely the
opinions received during his own times and still received by most unlearned men, Hobbes said, they were not likely to be very accurate.[13]
Virtue, if it means anything more than a man's power, is the habit of
doing what tends to our own self-preservation, and to its fundamental
condition, peace; vice is the contrary.

The essential defect of the laws of nature, the dictates of reason, is
that they bind men in their consciences only, and the actions and wills
of men are determined not by conscience or reason but by fear of punishment and hope of reward. There is fear of invisible powers, God or gods,
in the state of nature, but this fear is not powerful enough.[14] What is
needed, according to Hobbes, is the establishment of conditions that
really make it safe to obey the laws of nature, otherwise one who obeys
such rules only puts himself at the mercy of those who do not obey.
In short, civil or political government, visible powers, are required.
Security requires first of all the cooperation of many men, a multitude
large and powerful enough both to make the breaking of covenants
and invasion of each other's rights very dangerous, and to provide defense against foreign enemies. There is no set limit to the size of a civil
society. The size should be great enough to deter any enemy from risking war, and therefore depends upon the size of the enemy. These requirements and the antisocial elements in man's nature indicate that
the unity achieved through consent, many wills agreeing in one object,
one common good, is not sufficient to bind men together. Political society, or the commonwealth, requires a real unity, or union.

This union, like justice and injustice, is defined by Hobbes in legal
terms. The commonwealth must be constituted as one legal person by
a great multitude of men, each of whom convenants with all the others
to regard the will of this legal, civil, or artificial person as his own will.
This legal person, the sovereign, "is" the commonwealth. In practical
terms this means that every subject should regard all actions of the

sovereign power as actions of his own, all legislation by the sovereign as his own self-legislation. In fact, the sovereign power, the power of representing and commanding the wills of all, can be vested in one man or in a council. Hobbes was the first to define the commonwealth as a "person." He found this necessary for the following reasons. Since the only legitimate obligation is ultimately self-obligation, the freedom of man in the state of nature must survive, in some form, in his subjection to the government.[15] This is accomplished through the legal fictions that the sovereign is a "person" with a will that can represent the wills of all his subjects, and that the sovereign's legislation is self-legislation of the subject. Through such a union the powers and faculties of every subject can be brought to contribute fully to the maintenance of peace and the common defense.

The social contract has two parts: (1) a covenant of each member of the future civil body with each of the others to acknowledge as sovereign whatever man or assembly of men a majority of their number agrees upon; (2) the vote determining who or what is to be the sovereign. All those who are not parties to the contract remain in the state of war and are, therefore, enemies of the rest.

The validity of the covenant is in no way affected by whether it was entered into under duress, fear of death and violence, or not. The body politic, Hobbes says, can be founded "naturally" as well as through institution. All paternal and despotic government arises in the first way, through fear of the sovereign himself, e.g., when he is a conqueror in war; all government by institution arises through mutual fear of the individuals. Fear is the motive in both cases. Both foundations are equally legitimate: there is no difference, as far as right is concerned, between foundation by conquest and foundation by institution. In the acquisition of sovereignty by conquest, it makes no difference whether the war was a just war or not. Since no one can really transfer his strength and faculties to another, the social contract in fact obliges all not to resist the will of the sovereign power. That all citizens have not explicitly entered into such a covenant is obvious; but anyone who lives in a commonwealth accepting the protection of the government, the sovereign, is to be regarded as having tacitly entered into the covenant. Apparently, for Hobbes, that exactness in political life which corresponds to mathematical exactness in theoretical matters is legal exactness. And just as controversies are put to rest in mathematics, so evidently he hoped that the political controversies that had always disturbed the peace of the political world could be put to rest by an exact deduction, from the social contract, of the rights and duties of sovereign and subject.

The social contract is binding only when the end for the sake of which it is entered into, security, is realized. Obedience is exchanged for protection. Not that men can ever be made completely safe from injury by others. It is sufficient for each citizen to know that anyone who intends to injure him has more to fear from punishment by the sovereign than he has to gain from his crime.

The first right of the sovereign is the right to punish or the right to wield the police power. This follows from the fundamental renunciation of the right of resistance agreed to by all the citizens. No subject can be freed from his subjection by claiming that the sovereign has committed a breach of covenant, for the sovereign has made no covenant with any subject, the subjects have covenanted only among themselves. Since the sovereign has not covenanted with anyone, he alone retains the right to all things that all men had in the state of nature. Consequently he can neither injure anyone nor commit injustice, since injustice, or injury, in the strict or legal sense is nothing but nonfulfillment of covenant, assuming a right which one has already convenanted away. Furthermore, since the sovereign represents the will of each of the subjects, anyone accusing the sovereign of injury is accusing himself, and to do injustice to oneself is impossible. Hence the sovereign cannot justly be punished in any way by his subjects. The right to make war and peace, which includes the right to levy taxes and to compel citizens to take up arms for their country's defense, is also annexed to the sovereign, for these rights must be in the hands of the same power that can punish those who will not obey.

The legislative power must also be in the sovereign's hands for the same reason: men will not obey the commands of those they have no reason to fear. The power of the sword, the punitive power, and the legislative power must be in the same hands. The civil laws of each commonwealth are nothing else than the commands of the civil sovereign. They prescribe what goods a man may enjoy, *i.e.,* they define what is and what is not private property. They determine what actions a man may do without being molested by his fellows, *i.e.,* they prescribe what is good, evil, just, unjust, honest, and dishonest. They contribute to peace by attempting to determine all controversial questions before controversy arises.

The judicial power, for the same reason as the legislative power, is also committed to the sovereign. Because the sovereign must be able to determine the means of discharging his functions, the executive power, and the power of appointing all counselors, ministers, magistrates and officers, also is invested in him. Furthermore, because all voluntary actions of men depend upon their wills and their wills upon their opinions of the good and evil, or reward and punishment, they will receive from acting or omitting to act, the sovereign is to be judge of all doctrines and opinions which may be delivered to the citizens. The criterion of censorship is what doctrines are conducive to and what repugnant to peace. This power of absolute censorship applies to religious opinions as well. As a matter of fact religion is defined with a view to this power by Hobbes. Both religion and superstition are defined as "fear of power invisible." The difference between them is that the former is allowed by the public authority, the latter not allowed. The opinions which, according to Hobbes, have most disturbed the peace of the Christian world, are the opinions that lead citizens to believe that they owe obedience to others besides those to whom the supreme civil authority is committed. We shall take up this subject again in our discussion of Hobbes's teaching regarding Christianity.

It is clear from this list of powers that the power of the sovereign is absolute, *i.e.,* no greater power can be conveyed by men to any man. The sovereign is not bound to obey the civil laws, for they are only his commands and he can release himself from them at his pleasure. No one can claim any property rights against him because all property is derived from the laws, *i.e.,* his will. Opposing the sovereign's will in any particular case would be opposing the ground of all property and, hence, self-defeating. When citizens are allowed to sue the supreme authority, the question cannot be whether the sovereign or his ministers had a right to do what was done, but rather what it was that the sovereign in fact willed in this matter. That absolute power is really implicit in all governments can be seen through the cases of generals who are granted absolute powers temporarily in wartimes. Only the possessor of absolute power can grant absolute power, even temporarily. And when, for example, a constitutional assembly prescribes limits to the powers of a government, the exercise of the power of limitation is itself an exercise of absolute power. The objection that such an absolute power has never been acknowledged by citizens anywhere is, as arguments from practice generally are, invalid, for practice may be faulty practice. The art of making and maintaining commonwealths consists in following certain definite rules like the rules of arithmetic and geometry. Hobbes believed himself to be the first discoverer of those rules.

There are certain rights of the subject that are unalienable, *i.e.,* that cannot be transferred or resigned by covenant. For there is no obligation of man which does not proceed from some act of his own, and every act of his own is presumed to aim at some good to himself; therefore no contract, including the social contract, should be so construed as to deprive a man of the condition of all good for himself, his life, and the means of securing it. Every man may justly disobey any command to kill or wound himself or to abstain from anything that he requires to live. The right to self-preservation remains inviolable. But are not soldiers required to sacrifice their lives in war? And is not the fear of violent death in a sense the basis of all legitimacy, and therefore a sufficient motive to justify civil disobedience? Hobbes faced this problem and concluded that to run away from battle out of fear is dishonorable and cowardly but not unjust. It is the sovereign's task to see that the fear of desertion outweighs the fear of battle. To refuse the sovereign's command to fight against an enemy is not unjust if a man finds a suitable substitute. For a condemned man to resist an executioner lawfully doing his duty is just. No man in a criminal trial is bound to testify against himself, for no covenant, including the fundamental covenant, can oblige a man to harm himself. No man is obliged, e.g., to execute his own parent, or a benefactor, or to do any act that is so shameful that it would result in his being so miserable and despised that he would grow weary of his own life.[16]

It is clear that these inviolable liberties of the citizens could be extended and construed as providing standards for distinguishing good from bad sovereigns, i.e., as providing citizens with standards by which they could legitimately criticize, judge, and thereby weaken the sovereign authority. If given institutional form they could lead to limited sovereignty. Hobbes tried his best to guard against the revolutionary principal inherent in all attempts to set forth the principles of government: he who sets forth principles justifying authority by that very act provides standards for justifying the alteration or abolishment of that authority when it departs from those principles. Despite these exceptions to the obligation of obedience to the sovereign, the sovereign's absolute right remains: he may rightfully punish with death any refusal or resistance, however just. If the sovereign exercises his right contrary to right reason, however, he, like every man in the state of nature, sins against the laws of nature and therefore is answerable to their author, God, for his iniquity. Furthermore, Hobbes admits, there is a certain natural punishment for negligent government, i.e., rebellion.

In all matters where the laws are silent, the subject retains the right to do or forbear as he wishes. And sometimes a sovereign may prudently forbear to exercise his right, though that in no way diminishes the right. There is no valid reason for sovereigns to desire to oppress their subjects, for the strength of sovereigns is directly dependent upon the strength and well-being of their subjects. Certainly, Hobbes admitted, such absolute power can be abused, but there is no condition of human life without inconveniences. "The obligation of subjects to the sovereign, is understood to last as long, and no longer, than the power lasteth, by which he is able to protect them." [17] And there is no avoiding the fact that he that has the power to protect all also has the power to oppress all. Following the book of Job, Hobbes compared the sovereign to Leviathan, whom God called "King of the Proud." Only the greatest of earthly powers can govern the pride of man. Hobbes's *Leviathan* is also such a Leviathan in so far as it rules the minds of men and crushes and roots out the seeds of human pride.

There are three kinds of commonwealths, differing as the respective sovereign powers differ. When that power is committed to one man, the government is a monarchy; when committed to an assembly of men where every citizen has a right to vote, it is a democracy; when committed to an assembly where only a part of the citizens have a right to vote, it is an aristocracy. The ancient Greek and Roman writers also distinguished between good and bad governments. They called bad rule by one man tyranny, bad rule by the people, or many, anarchy, and bad rule of the few oligarchy. Good and bad governments were distinguished according to whether the rulers ruled primarily for the sake of the common good or common advantage, or for their own selfish advantages. These moral distinctions, according to Hobbes, are unsound. They indicate only the subjective like or dislike of those who use them. Those who dislike monarchy call it tyranny, likewise anarchy is a name for democracy disliked, oligarchy a name for aristocracy disliked. This rejection of what Hobbes calls Aristotle's distinction between governments which rule for the benefit of the subjects and those which rule for the benefit of the rulers makes the distinction between a tyrant and a legitimate monarch politically meaningless. Both subjects and rulers, Hobbes argues, share equally in the first and greatest benefits of all government, peace and defense. All suffer equally from the greatest misery, civil war and anarchy. Since the ruler's strength and power always depend upon the strength and power of his subjects, both suffer the same disadvantages if the ruler weakens the subjects by depriving them of money and goods.

A deeper ground, perhaps, for the rejection of the distinction was Hobbes's conviction that no ruler or bearer of the sovereignty could be expected not to pursue his private advantage, the advantages of family and friends, as much and even more than the public advantage. On the basis of Hobbes's reduction of good and evil to pleasure and pain and his doctrine of sovereignty, the age-old political controversies about what form of government is best become much less important. These controversies were necessarily connected with the question about what over-all purposes civil society should serve, *e.g.*, liberty, empire, or wealth. Contrary to the misleading doctrines of Aristotle and Cicero and other Greek and Roman writers, who were, according to Hobbes, prejudiced in favor of popular government, the power of the government and the liberty of the citizen in each form of government is the same. The sovereignty is absolute in every commonwealth. The goal, or purpose, of each form of government is the same, peace and security. The decisive political, or practical, questions tend to become technical or administrative questions, such as under what kind of administration of the sovereign powers peace and security are most conveniently produced.[18]

Since those who bear the sovereign authority, being men, will always be most concerned with their private interests, the public interest will be most advanced where it is more closely united with private interests. This occurs under monarchy, which is therefore the best form of government. In democracy, where each man bears some part of the sovereignty, the number of those capable of enriching and serving themselves at the expense of the public interest is at a maximum. In a monarchy there can be only one Nero, in a democracy there can be as many Neros as there are orators flattering the populace. A monarch may promote unworthy persons but often will not. In a democracy the promotion of unworthy persons cannot be avoided. For within democracy there is always keen competition between popular orators, or demagogues, and the power of each demagogue is dependent upon his power to control and dispense patronage. Those who did not endeavor to benefit and attach as many people as possible, worthy and unworthy, to their side, or faction, would soon be overwhelmed by those who did. From this it is easy to understand the chief defect of democracy, the tendency to breed factions and civil wars. An aristocracy in this regard stands somewhere between the other two forms. It becomes better the more it approaches monarchy, worse the more it approaches democracy. As far as the actual exercise of the sovereign powers is concerned, one can doubt whether democracy is really ever anything different from an aristocracy of orators or a temporary monarchy of one orator. Those who complain of lack of liberty under monarchy do not understand what they really want. For the liberties of a subject, as defined by the doctrine of sovereignty, are the same under all governments, but under a democracy the accusers of monarchy would be rulers as well as subjects. It is not liberty but dominion or power and its attendant honor that they want. The true cause of their disaffection is that monarchy deprives them of the opportunity to show off their wisdom, knowledge, and eloquence in deliberating, or seeming to deliberate, about matters of the greatest importance. The love of liberty, according to Hobbes, turns out to be only a mask for the desire for praise, for vanity.[19] Despite these criticisms and others, like irresolution from divided counsels, the difficulty of proceeding secretly, and so on, democracy has a certain privileged position within the framework based upon the idea of the state of nature and the doctrine of sovereignty. This may be seen as follows.

The institution of monarchy or aristocracy requires a previous official nomination or designation of certain particular persons as sovereign. Democracy, however, can be instituted directly by the separated individuals themselves. Hence the original or first form of all instituted government is democracy. Since all men in the state of nature are equal in rights, and all legitimate obligation is ultimately self-obligation, the first part of the social contract, in order to be binding, must be an agreement of each man with every other man to accept as sovereign that person or persons designated by a majority of all of them. This first agreement of every man with every other man constitutes the multitude as a democratic people; the act nominating the sovereign, each man having one equal vote, is a democratic act. One could say that only a democratic procedure is consistent with the equality of men in the state of nature. In accordance with a principle often enunciated by Hobbes, that whoever has the power to dispose of the sovereignty is the true sovereign, one could say that the people, as a democratic people, are the ultimate sovereign of every instituted commonwealth. Hobbes guarded against this conclusion by addressing himself to a more fundamental argument, namely, as all contracts depend upon the consent of the contractors, they may be dissolved by the same consent. Hence the people by withdrawing their consent may dissolve the government. First of all, Hobbes answers, the original contract obliges each man to all of the others, not to a majority, even an overwhelming majority. So long as one man dissents to the dissolution of the contract, no others have a right to dissolve. It cannot be imagined, Hobbes said, that all the people with no exception would combine against the supreme power. But there is a distinct obligation to the sovereign himself, for every man by agreeing to acknowledge the sovereign's acts as his own has transferred his natural right to use his powers as he sees fit to the sovereign. He cannot take away what now belongs to the supreme power without committing injustice against the sovereign.[20]

The traditional arguments for the mixed regime, or limited government, are rejected by Hobbes as being based upon an insufficient understanding of what a true union is. Where, for example, the sovereignty is supposedly divided between a monarchical executive, an aristocratic judiciary, and a popular body with power of the purse, the liberty of the subject is as much restricted as it can be under any government, so long as the three branches are in agreement. The advantage of such a division of powers would then be seen to exist in the disagreement or mutual checking of the three powers; but that disagreement, according to Hobbes, constitutes civil war and the dissolution of the government. He acknowledged that many governments have lasted a long time thinking wrongly that they were governments of this kind. But in the limited monarchies and temporary dictatorships known to history, the true sovereigns were not the monarchs but the assemblies that limited the monarchs. A genuine body politic, he argues, is constituted not by agreement, or concord, but by union, the uniting of the wills (and thereby the strength and power) of all in the will of one legal person, the sovereign.

A true monarchy, according to Hobbes, is a hereditary monarchy, for the true sovereign of an elective monarchy is the electing body. The chief difficulty for monarchies is the problem of succession, especially the problem of who is to appoint the royal successor. The present possessor of the sovereignty is to determine his successor. Hobbes works out detailed rules about what is to be understood as the will of the monarch in any case where he has not expressly indicated who shall inherit his power. He proceeds, speaking generally, from the presumption that the nearest in kinship is the nearest in affection and thereby should be understood as successor.

Hobbes defines law in terms of will, not reason. Counsel, on the other hand, bases itself on reasons, reasons deduced from the benefit to be gained by the one counseled. Counsel aims, or pretends to aim, at the good of another. But law is command, not counsel, and a command is expected to be obeyed only because it expresses the will of the one commanding. Since the object of every man's will is some good to himself, every command aims at the good of the one commanding. Law is a command addressed to one who has been obliged formerly to obey, a command from one who has already acquired a right to be obeyed. Civil law is such a command issued by the commonwealth, the sovereign. More fully, civil laws are those rules, commanded by the commonwealth to every subject through some sufficient sign of its will, which are to be used by the subjects for distinguishing right from wrong. Hobbes's political teachings, the laws of nature themselves, are merely counsel until commanded by some civil sovereign.

Custom in itself has no power to create law. Customary law derives its authority from the tacit consent of the present sovereign. The common law and the law of equity were said to be guided by the standard of right reason, a standard which, because it is considered to be independent and above all political authority, could be and was used to check and question the unreasonable actions of all civil authorities.

Hobbes reinterprets the traditional understanding of the common law in such a way as to make appeals to any authority higher than the civil sovereign impossible. He agrees with the lawyers that the law can never be against reason. But whose reason, he asks? Not the reason of scholars, or wise men, or subordinate judges, but the reason of that artificial person, the commonwealth, he answers. In his discussion of the common law, Hobbes does not distinguish the reason of the commonwealth from its will. In every just decision, the judge refers to the reason which moves the reigning sovereign to make or consent to the law governing the case under consideration; the judge does not recur to the reasons that influenced the sovereign under whom the law in question was first promulgated. Hobbes's approach would seem to lead to the idea of the absolute supremacy of current statute law. The canon of the church, or ecclesiastical law, also is law only in so far as it is constituted by the civil sovereign. All laws, of course, require interpreters, *i.e.,* judges, to apply the laws to particular cases. The sovereign is the supreme interpreter of the law and constitutes all subordinate interpreters, or judges, as such.[21]

Nothing which mortals make, says Hobbes, can be immortal. Yet with the help of a very able architect, commonwealths can be so constructed as to prevent their perishing from internal disorders. Hobbes describes those forces in the nature of man which have always tended toward the dissolution of peace and civil order. Yet those forces are not to be counteracted by way of moral reform, by appeals to what had been regarded as the nobler part of man's nature. Hobbes appeals instead to enlightened self-interest and, on the basis of knowledge and manipulation of the mechanism of the passions, relies on the devising of the right kinds of institutions. There was no need for him, as there was for Aristotle, to distinguish the kinds and levels of peoples in order to determine what kind of government is suitable for each. He aimed at devising a scheme of government which was to be right for all times, peoples, and places. By building his edifice upon the lowest common denominator of human motivation, he could expect it to stand firm anywhere and everywhere. For when commonwealths "come to be dissolved, not by external violence, but intestine disorders, the fault is not in men, as they are the Matter; but as they are the Makers, and orderers of them." [22]

One great mistake is often made at the very beginning of a commonwealth when men, in order to gain a kingdom, are content with less power than is necessary for maintaining peace and defense. Then, when the public safety requires the exercise of those renounced powers, their resumption appears as an act of injustice. This, in turn, disposes large numbers of men to rebellion and connivance with foreign powers, which always welcome an opportunity to weaken their neighbors. Thus William the Conqueror's pledge not to infringe the liberty of the Church led to Thomas Beckett's defection and his enlisting the support of the pope against Henry II. And because neither the senate nor the people of Rome claimed the whole power, the seditions of the Gracchi developed, then the wars between senate and people under Marius and Sulla and Caesar and Pompey, and finally popular government itself in Rome was destroyed and the monarchy was instituted. Thus it is a breach of his duty for the sovereign to lay aside any of his rights.

Furthermore, it is a breach of his duty to allow the people to be misinformed or ignorant of the grounds of his rights. The first task in this regard is to purge the commonwealth of "the poisons of seditious doctrines." The first group of seditious doctrines proceed mainly from the words of unlearned divines, who, misconstruing Scripture, induce men to think that sanctity and natural reason cannot stand together. They teach that every private man is the judge of good and evil actions. This is true in the state of nature, but in civil society the civil law and the sovereign are the measure and the judge of good and evil.

A second doctrine repugnant to civil society states that whatever a man does against his conscience, including those things he is commanded to do by his sovereign, is sin. If the commanded act is sinful, it is the sovereign's sin and he is answerable to God for it. It is not the subject's sin. On the contrary, disobedience to the sovereign is sin. For by disobeying, the subject arrogates to himself the knowledge and judgment of good and evil, conscience and judgment being really one and the same thing. Third in order is the doctrine that faith and sanctity are not to be attained by study and reason but by supernatural inspiration or "infusion." If this doctrine is granted, Hobbes said, he cannot see why every Christian is not a prophet, obliged to take his own inspiration rather than the law of his country for the rule of his action. This doctrine, too, leads men to set themselves up as judges of good and evil. Then there is that group of "eloquent sophistries" penned by Aristotle, Plato, Cicero, Seneca, Plutarch, and the rest of those maintainers of the Greek and Roman anarchies, the "sophistries" taken over by the lawyers to serve their own interests, such as the doctrine that sovereigns are subject to their own laws; that the supreme authority may be divided; that private men have absolute rights over property which exclude interference from the sovereign; and, finally, the doctrine, also held by many divines, that tyrannicide is lawful and even laudable. This last amounts to saying, according to Hobbes, that it is lawful for men to rebel against and to murder their kings so long as they call them tyrants first. Finally, there is that doctrine rooted in the fear of darkness and ghosts, and drawn out of the "darkness of school distinctions," the doctrine of the division of civil, or temporal, power from spiritual, or ghostly, power. That the distinction has no significance and that no man can serve two masters Hobbes attempts to prove by Holy Scripture in his theological discussion.[23]

Rooting out seditious and false opinions is not enough. It is the duty of the sovereign to have the true grounds of his rights taught to the people. This meant, first of all, adopting Hobbes's books as the authoritative texts on morals and politics in the universities. Apparently Hobbes regarded his as a long-range educational project, for, he said, he was not very interested in whether his books would be adopted "at this day." Nevertheless he looked forward to his books being officially recommended by some sovereign for teaching in the universities, "the fountains of civil and moral doctrine." One should begin, he said, with young minds uncorrupted by the doctrines of Athens and Rome. Those who are properly educated, after they leave the universities as preachers, gentry, men of affairs, and lawyers, in the conduct of their everyday affairs will transmit the true grounds of civil right to the people. The difficulties in the way of teaching the people are usually overestimated, Hobbes thought. For, first of all, it is not too hard to learn what appeals to one's own selfish interests and secondly, in a judgment reminiscent of Machiavelli's estimation of the people, Hobbes remarks that the people lack the pride and ambition that obstructs the minds of the rich, the powerful, and those with a reputation for learning. In spite of his exaltation of sovereignty and monarchy, Hobbes evidently expected that some day his doctrines would be popular.[24]

There is not much said in a positive way about the good society which Hobbes looked forward to, once the conditions of peace are established. The emphasis in Hobbes is upon the extreme situations like civil war, where all law and order break down, upon the dangers to peace resulting from attempts to question and restrict the sovereign authority, upon negative standards rather than positive standards. Yet evidently he looked forward to a much milder regime than his total arming of the sovereign power would suggest. In the first place he looked forward to a nonimperialist society. This, however, is inconsistent with his doctrine that independent sovereigns and nations are necessarily in a state of nature with respect to each other and, hence, naturally obliged to do all they can to subdue or weaken their neighbors. The policies are inconsistent so long as there is no world state. However this may be, he also looked forward to a state with laws encouraging husbandry and fishing, laws against idleness and inordinate expense and consumption, and laws to encourage and honor industry, navigation, mechanics, and the mathematical sciences. Public burdens are to be distributed equally. Men are to be taxed according to what they spend or consume: frugality is to be rewarded, luxurious waste discouraged, and each man is to pay the commonwealth in proportion to the benefit he derives from its protection. There is to be equality before the law, strict penalties against corrupt judges, and easy access to courts of appeal. The safety of the people is to be the supreme law, and safety is to be understood as including all the contentments and delights of life a man can earn lawfully without hurting the commonwealth.[25]

The peace of civil society depends upon the sovereign's having the power of life and death over his subjects. If men believe that there are other powers capable of granting greater rewards than life and inflicting greater punishments than death, they will obey such powers and the authority of the sovereign will be destroyed. Eternal life and eternal torment or "eternal death" are greater goods and evils than natural life and natural death. Because, or so long as, men believe in the power of other men, acting as ministers of powers invisible, to grant them eternal bliss or eternal torment, theology, according to Hobbes, cannot be separated from political philosophy.[26] We must confine ourselves to a rough sketch of Hobbes's Christian theology, omitting the numerous passages from Holy Scripture that he cites as authorities.

Although from the Creation God has ruled over all men through the power of nature, the kingdom of God, in most places of Scripture, contrary to the interpretation of most divines, signifies a political kingdom with definite subjects, the Jews. Adam and all those living up to the Flood and Noah and his family after the Flood were commanded by God directly through His voice. The first in the kingdom of God by covenant was Abraham with whom God made a contract, offering Abraham the land of Canaan as an everlasting possession in return for his obedience and the obedience of his posterity. Thus God was instituted as the civil sovereign of the Jews. God needed to speak only to Abraham, the father, lord, and civil sovereign of his family, for the wills of all his family and seed were involved in his will. As the family and seed of Abraham received the positive commands of God from their earthly sovereign, Abraham, so in every commonwealth those with no supernatural revelation to the contrary ought to obey the laws of their own sovereign in all the external acts and professions of religion. Every sovereign, as did Abraham, has the right to punish anyone who pretends to a private revelation in order to oppose the laws. As was Abraham in his family, so only the sovereign in a Christian commonwealth can be the authoritative interpreter of the Word of God. God's contract was renewed with Isaac and Jacob, but was suspended while the Jews were under the sovereignty of Egypt.

The contract was renewed again by Moses at Mount Sinai. Since Moses could not inherit Abraham's authority, his authority was grounded in the consent of the people and their promise to obey him. Again, only Moses, as civil sovereign under God, was called up to God, not Aaron, the chief priest, nor any other priest, nor the aristocracy of seventy elders, nor the people. By Moses throwing over the calf made by Aaron, and by Moses' control of those who prophesied in the camp, it was shown that all priests and prophets in a Christian commonwealth derive their authority from the approval and authority of the sovereign. The kingdom was a sacerdotal kingdom: Moses ruled as God's high priest and viceregent on earth. The kingdom was inherited by Aaron and then by his son Eleazar. After the death of Joshua and Eleazar it was said that there was no king in Israel. This was true only as far as the exercise of the sovereign power was concerned. The right to govern, the sovereign power, was still lodged in the high priest. The powers of the judges were extraordinary or temporary emergency powers. By deposing Samuel, the high priest, the people deposed the peculiar kingdom of God and instituted a monarchy of the usual type. Solomon's treatment of Abiathar, his dedication of the temple, and the whole of biblical history show that from the first institution of the kingdom of God until the captivity, the supreme religious authority was in the same hands as the civil sovereignty. And after the election of Saul, the priest's office was ministerial with respect to the sovereign, not magisterial. During their captivity the Jews had no commonwealth, and after their return everything was so confused and corrupted that nothing of value for state or religion can be learned from those times.

The "office of our Blessed Savior," the Messiah, wrote Hobbes, is threefold: Redeemer, Teacher, and King. Christ on earth was Redeemer and Teacher, not King. He never did anything to call into question the civil laws of the Jews or Caesar, nor gave anyone else warrant to do the same. He is to be King only after the general resurrection; the kingdom he claimed is to be in another world. He never actually commanded anyone. As Redeemer he was sacrificed to ransom men's sins, and as Teacher he counseled men about the path to salvation, *i.e.,* eternal life. The meaning of the Trinity is that the one person of God was represented at three different times and on three different occasions. Moses represented God the Father, Christ God the Son, and the apostles and their successors, by receiving and transmitting the Holy Spirit, represented God the Holy Ghost. So long as there was no Christian com-

monwealth, no civil sovereign converted to Christianity, the ecclesiastical power was in the hands of the apostles and those they ordained as
ministers. They had no power of command, their office was only to instruct and advise men to believe and have faith in Christ. That Jesus is
the Christ is the sole article of faith necessary for a Christian. If commanded by an infidel sovereign to profess the contrary with one's
tongue, martyrdom is not necessary; confession is but an external thing,
a sign of obedience to the law. If commanded by the sovereign to do
actions such as worshipping false gods, which, in effect, deny the Lord,
the sin is not that of the obedient subject but of the sovereign. It is never
just for Christians, or anyone else, to attempt to depose even an infidel
or heretical king once he has been established; for that would be a violation of faith and thereby against the law of nature which is the eternal
law of God.

The first Christian emperor was Constantine, who was also the
supreme bishop of Rome, just as all Christian sovereigns are supreme
bishops in their own territories. This office adheres essentially to the
sovereignty. Hobbes educes long arguments, especially against the writings of Cardinal Bellarmine, to oppose the claims of the popes of Rome.
All priests in a Christian commonwealth are only the sovereign's ministers, deriving their authority from him, the chief priest. Where a
foreigner has authority to appoint teachers or priests, he does it only by
the authority of the sovereign in whose domains the teaching or ministry takes place. In fact, "church" as the word is used in the Bible
means nothing else than a Christian commonwealth. From all this it is
clear that the distinction between spiritual and temporal government
is false. All government in this life, both of the state and of religion, is
temporal and under the command of one civil sovereign.[27]

Hobbes says that the doctrine concerning the Kingdom of God has
so much influence on the kingdom of man that it should not be decided
by any but those that have the sovereign power. However, since his own
country is in a state of civil war, he writes, and the authority is undecided, he will set forth his own novel doctrine tentatively. The Kingdom
of God, wherein men shall enjoy eternal life, shall be a kingdom under
Christ here on earth and at the time of the general resurrection. Hell
is also on earth, and Satan is any earthly enemy of the church. The
torments of Hell signify metaphorically that grief of mind, envy,
caused by the sight of others enjoying that eternal felicity which the
tormented, because of their disbelief and disobedience, have lost. The
sinners will also have bodily pains and will die a second death. For
everlasting fire and everlasting death do not mean that the tormented
will be granted everlasting life, which everlasting torments would re-

quire. What is meant is rather that the tormenting fire will burn eternally and the supply of sinners to be tormented and killed will not fail, because the sinners will eat, drink, generate, and die perpetually after the resurrection as before. In fact, under Hobbes's interpretation it becomes difficult to see how the life of sinners is in any way changed by the resurrection. Eternal death then turns out to be not so much, if at all, worse than natural death. The over-all conclusion that Hobbes evidently wanted the readers of his theology to draw was that there was really no essential difference between the Word of God as revealed in the Scriptures and the word of Hobbes set down in his political philosophy.[28]

However, one is forced to raise the question of whether Hobbes believed in the truth of his theology. He does say about God that "it is manifest we ought to attribute to him, existence: For no man can have the will to honor that which he thinks not to have any being." But the relation between truth and worship or honor is by no means unambiguous. For, he writes, "all words and actions that betoken fear to offend, or desire to please, is worship, whether these words or actions be sincere or feigned: and because they appear as signs of honoring, are ordinarily also called Honor." Because of these and many other statements, Hobbes became notorious as an atheist during his own lifetime.[29]

Perhaps the most charitable conclusion that one can draw from his theology is that in his dauntless zeal to destroy all opinions which he believed to be inimical to a proper understanding of the rights and duties of man, Hobbes showed that, for him, nothing was more sacred than the pursuit and promulgation of the philosophic truth.

# NOTES

1. Thomas Hobbes, *Leviathan,* ("Everyman's Library" [New York: Dutton, 1950]), chap. xi, p. 79. Spelling has been modernized in quotations in this chapter.

2. See, *e.g., Leviathan,* chap. xxxi, end, and *The Elements of Law,* ed. Ferdinand Toennies (Cambridge: Cambridge University Press, 1928), 1.17.1.

3. *The Metaphysical System of Hobbes,* selected by Mary W. Calkins (Chicago: Open Court, 1948), *Concerning Body,* chaps i and ii, esp. ii.7;

*Leviathan,* chap. xxxiv, pp. 339–41, chap. lvi, The Introduction, pp. 4–5; A Review, and Conclusion, p. 627. It is difficult to determine whether Hobbes conceived of his materialism as simply true, *i.e.,* as "metaphysical," or as "methodological," *i.e.,* an assumption required for proceeding scientifically.

4. *Leviathan,* chap. vi. Cf. *Elements,* 1.7.1–1.10.11.

5. *Leviathan,* chap. vi, p. 41; chap. vii, p. 59.

6. *De Cive (The Citizen), The Eng-*

*lish Works of Thomas Hobbes,* ed. Molesworth (1839–45), vol. II, chap. i.2; see especially the note.

7. *Leviathan,* chap. xi, pp. 79–80.

8. *Ibid.,* chap. xiii, pp. 103–4.

9. *Ibid.,* chap. xiii.

10. *Elements,* 1.14.6.

11. *Ibid.,* 1.16.2; *De Cive,* chap. iii.3.

12. *Leviathan,* Chap. xiv, pp. 107–8; chap. xv, pp. 128, 130–31; chap. xxvii, p. 251; chap. xlii, pp. 435–36; chap. xxvi, pp. 231–32.

13. *Elements,* 1.17.14 and 1.13.3.

14. *Leviathan,* chap. xiv, p. 117.

15. *Ibid.,* chap. xxi, p. 183.

16. *Ibid.,* chap. xv, pp. 128–30; chap. xxi; chap. xxviii, pp. 258–59; *De Cive,* chap. vi.13.

17. *Leviathan,* chap. xxii, p. 187.

18. *De Cive,* chaps x.2 and x.16.

19. *Ibid.,* chap. x, esp. x.7, x.8, and x.15.

20. *Ibid.,* chap. vi.20.

21. For a confrontation of Hobbesian with premodern traditional jurisprudence, compare chap. xxvi, "Of Civil Laws," of the *Leviathan* with Thomas Aquinas' *Summa Theologica,* I-II, Qq. 90–97 (published by the Henry Regnery Co. as *Treatise on Law*), which Hobbes's chapter may have been written in opposition to. See also his *A Dialogue between a Philosopher and a Student of the Common Laws of England, The English Works of Thomas Hobbes,* Molesworth ed., VI.

22. *Leviathan,* chap. xxix, pp. 275–76.

23. *Ibid.,* chap. xxix.

24. *Ibid.,* chap. xxx, pp. 288–96; *De Cive,* chap. xiii.9.

25. *Leviathan,* chap. xxx, pp. 296 ff. and *De Cive,* chap. xiii, esp. xiii.14.

26. *Leviathan,* dedicatory epistle; chap. xv, end; chap. xxxviii, beginning; *De Cive,* chap. xvii.27.

27. *Leviathan,* chaps xl–xliii.

28. *Ibid.,* chaps xxxviii and xliv.

29. *Ibid.,* chap. xxxi, p. 312; chap. xlv, p. 570; chap. xii; chap. xlv: cf. chap. xxvii, pp. 249–50 and chap. xliv, pp. 558–59; chap. xxxix, p. 406; chap. xlii, p. 435; chap. xl, p. 417; chap. xlvi, pp. 591–92.

# READINGS

A. Hobbes, Thomas. *Leviathan.* Chaps xiii–xv, xvii–xviii, xxi, xxiv, xxvi–xxx, xlvi.

B. Hobbes, Thomas. *Leviathan.* Chaps vi, x–xii, xvi, xix, xx, xxii–xxiii, xxv, xxxi–xxxii, xxxv, xliii.

# RENE DESCARTES

## 1596–1650

Descartes has long been celebrated as "the founder of modern philosophy," but never of modern political philosophy. His epochal beginning
appears to stand in splendid isolation from the older modern political
tradition founded by Machiavelli: he never even composed a thematic
discussion of political things. This suggests that modern philosophy
and modern political philosophy are separate in origin and perhaps
divergent in intention. A link between Descartes and the modern political tradition is visible, however, in his relation to Francis Bacon, the
first great and avowed advocate of Machiavellian politics directed to the
mastery of fortune or nature in human affairs. Copying even the language of Bacon, Descartes asserted that philosophy founded in a new
method and directed to "the mastery and possession of nature" would
attain the greatest glory for philosophy and the greatest benefit to society. His political teaching, therefore, is mainly concerned with the
paramount political necessity, the establishment of harmonious relations between philosophy or science and society, or with the "Enlightenment" version of that relationship, the ruling relationship of modern
times. Accordingly, d'Alembert, a prime mover of the French Enlightenment, could declare in the *Encyclopédie* (1751) that Descartes "laid
the foundations of a government more just and more happy than has
ever been seen established." [1]

Descartes' political teaching is partially obscured because of the
notorious caution of his manner of writing: "I have composed my
philosophy in such a way as not to shock anyone, and so that it can be
received everywhere, even among the Turks." [2] His caution is evident in
the fact that he never published praise or blame of any political philoso-

379

phy in his own name, but only an anonymous praise of Bacon's *Great Instauration* and *New Atlantis;* whereas in private letters he accepted "the principal precept" of Machiavelli, "noticed nothing bad" in his *Discourses on Livy,* and thought Hobbes's politics in his *On the Citizen* superior to his metaphysics.[3]

Descartes' political teaching is part of "the highest and most perfect moral science" which is the end of philosophy altogether. "The whole of philosophy is like a tree, the roots of which are metaphysics," namely, knowledge of God and the human soul; "the trunk is physics, and the branches which come from the trunk are all the other sciences," but principally medicine, mechanics, and morality. "Just as it is not from the roots nor from the trunk of trees that one gathers the fruits, but only from the extremities of their branches, so the principal utility of philosophy depends on those of its parts that one can only learn last." [4] The ultimate branch is "the perfect moral science . . . which, presupposing an entire knowledge of the other sciences, is the last degree of wisdom." Yet it is almost universally held that nowhere in his published or unpublished writings can one find Descartes' "perfect moral science." This difficulty is inseparable from another that arises from inspection of the tree of knowledge. Man is treated twice, once as the second metaphysical root and once as the highest branch. But in each of the published versions of his metaphysics Descartes treats first the human soul and then God. Moreover, the simile omits any reference in the "roots" to the metaphysical principle coeval with the soul, namely, corporeal substance, from which the "trunk" presumably must grow. Hence, the poetic simile of the tree of knowledge is deceptive as regards its least visible part.

We are forced then to seek for a nonpoetic argument according to which man is the beginning and end of the tree of knowledge and "the perfect moral science" its "principal utility." Only in the *Discourse on Method* (1637) does Descartes offer an account of the beginning and end of his philosophy, of all the parts and their true order. Nevertheless, this writing is customarily depreciated today because of its popular character. Yet precisely its popular rhetoric is the first sign that the *Discourse* alone treats the peculiar difficulty of Descartes' supreme goal: the "perfect moral science" will come into full existence only by an unprecedented political cooperation between philosophy and the public.

Descartes writes that he began with the opinion of his Jesuit teachers that study would yield "a clear and certain knowledge of all that is useful to life." By the criterion of utility, he examined and rejected the learning of the schools and the whole of ancient philosophy. One science alone, mathematics, he excepted; what "astonished" him was that "no loftier edifice had been built on the firm and solid foundations" of mathematics.[5] In place of that wonder at the fundamental perplexities that confront the mind that was the beginning of philosophy for the ancients, Descartes substitutes astonishment at a hitherto undreamed-of possibility of human "creativity" that will banish wonder: "I shall reveal to you secrets so simple that you will henceforward wonder at nothing in the works of our hands." [6] As contrasted with mathematics, "philosophy," which ought to supply the "foundations" of the sciences, is wholly disputable, useless, and uncertain. "Theology"—a term that Descartes uses here and everywhere to signify revealed theology exclusively—"shows the way to gain heaven," to which he "aspired as much as any other." But "revealed truths" are "above our intelligence": hence they are not clear and assured knowledge useful for life. The only moral writings he so much as mentions in his critique of the tradition are "the writings of the pagans"—they too lack foundations.[7]

Descartes opposes the goal of the classic tradition since he abandons the "speculations," or the quest for knowledge for its own sake, in favor of "useful knowledge." The justification of the rejection of the classic view appears from the treatment of the one discipline in the critique that treats of man's end. The "writings of the pagans" comprise the moral teachings of the Stoics especially, but also those of Platonic and Aristotelian political philosophy. While the pagan writings contain many "exhortations to virtue which are most useful," the "superb and magnificent palaces" of virtue are "built on sand and mud." What the pagans "called by such a beautiful name," *i.e.,* "virtue," is "often only insensibility, or pride, or despair, or parricide." [8] Pagan virtue which claimed to be a mean, and the excellence of man, is therefore often an extreme, and an inhumane, presumptuous, poor-spirited, and even criminal extreme. As extremes the pagan virtues cannot be distinguished from the passions. "There is nothing in which the defective nature of the sciences that we have received from the ancients appears more clearly than in what they have written on the passions." [9]

Descartes replaced the distinction made by the ancients between the passions and the virtues with the distinction between good and bad passions. The basis of the ancient distinction was the view that the soul has parts, that certain parts are capable of listening to and obeying reason, and that by their means reason can establish and rule a natural hierarchy within the soul. Reason is autonomous because reason has its own proper object, or because "all men by nature desire knowledge," regardless of the utility of knowledge. Descartes rejects this view of a natural order of the soul: the ancients had not seen the acute "de-

pendence of the mind" or reason on the passions or "on the temperament and the disposition of the organs of the body." [10]

Descartes' twofold reflection on the power of the passions and the
promise of mathematics leads directly to his argument for a new method
which is at the same time his primary political reflection. Since the
virtues are replaced by certain passions, the "useful for life" must be
understood as that which serves the ends of the passions. Among the
passions, however, distinctions must be drawn between good and bad,
useful and useless, noble and ignoble passions. More precisely, what is
required is a comprehensive passion, or a passion that can supply a principle of order to the other passions, hence necessarily the passion capable
of mastering the other passions. This most useful passion will thus be
the noblest and most perfect master passion. Descartes begins his argument for method with the principle "there is less perfection in works
composed of several portions, and carried out by the hands of various
masters, than in those on which one [master] has worked." [11] What is
made wholly by one master is wholly in the power of that master: thus
he begins as the Stoics had done, with what is wholly in one's own
power, without restricting this to "one's own thoughts." His principle is
articulated by a series of examples of masters that culminates in reason
as a form of mastery. But since it is "the will of some men using reason"
that leads to perfect mastery, reason is in the service of the will, or as
Descartes will later say, of the supreme passion he called "generosity."

The examples are seven: (1) the single architect of a building; (2)
the single engineer of the buildings of a city; (3) the general case of the
single "prudent" legislator who gives laws to a people; (4) the special
case of the single divine legislator, God, who made "the ordinances" of
"the state of the true religion," or of Christendom, which "must be in-
comparably better regulated than all the others"; (5) the special case
of the single human legislator of pagan Sparta—the only human legislator ever praised by Descartes—even though many of the Spartan laws
were "very strange and even contrary to good morals"; (6) the simple
reasonings made naturally by a single man of "good sense"; and (7)
the final, hypothetical case of a single man who had perfect use of his
unaided reason from infancy, unaffected by "appetites or preceptors." [12]

The series of examples is an ascent: it ascends from lower practical
arts concerning inanimate things to the highest (including the divine)
practical art of legislation, and thence to the highest theoretical "mastery," the use of unaided human reason. Since all the masters are authors
of "works," "work" must include the highest use of reason: mastery is
neutral to the distinction between thinking and making, philosophy
and technē. Philosophy is henceforth described, as previously by Bacon,

as "architecture": the organic simile of "the tree of knowledge" is deceptive. The first meaning of "perfection" in the series is the unity of the "work" deriving from the singleness of the master. To this he adds a second, the magnitude of the subject matter on which the master works. Therefore, Descartes' mastery will be as comprehensive as the series, or such a theoretical mastery of the whole or nature, the object of greatest magnitude, as will also comprehend the highest practical mastery, "legislation" of the greatest magnitude. Political science, the architectonic or master art according to Aristotle, is replaced by philosophy understood as theoretical mastery, or "architecture." To unity and magnitude Descartes adds, by the final example, a third ground of perfection, namely, that source within the master from which perfect mastery proceeds: the unaided use of human reason. All three grounds take their place in the definition of that master passion that Descartes calls the highest virtue, "generosity": the sensation in oneself of "a firm and constant resolution . . . never to fail of one's own will to undertake and execute all the things [one] judges to be the best . . . which is to follow perfectly after virtue." [13] Evidently "generosity" has not the sense of "liberality" of its English counterpart.

Yet the final example is hypothetical—the master who had perfect use of his unaided reason from infancy, unaffected by "appetites or preceptors." Of himself Descartes observes that he was sufficiently free from the passions to be able to reflect, at the outset of his chief reflections in the *Discourse* and *Meditations,* because of chance rather than virtue. As for his preceptors, he speaks of "the religion" in which he had been "instructed from his infancy." He must therefore find a procedure or a method that will purge the mind of all opinions and beliefs that depend on "appetites and preceptors." Only the construction of a method, and not the natural use of natural reason, can overcome the natural disproportion between the rate of growth of the appetites or passions and that of reason. For the prejudices received from our appetites or passions beginning in childhood govern our sense perceptions and cannot be corrected by reason which naturally serves those passions. Hence all previous philosophy that began with sense perception and lacked a method for purging the mind of prejudices necessarily went astray. Method can master the natural defects or disproportions of man's nature by taking as its model mathematics, which is certain because it owes nothing to the senses or to the body. But to be the comprehensive mastery as well as to master the body, method must become comprehensive mastery of all body, *i.e.,* mathematical physics.

That Descartes' highest example of mastery, or "generosity," necessarily includes politics or "legislation" becomes fully evident from his immediately following reflection on "reformations." [14] The first rule of method demands the rejection of all opinions that are not "clear and distinct," or the "reformation" of those uncertain opinions that are the "foundations" of one's own life. As contrasted with this private "reformation," Descartes asks whether it is desirable that states and nations be reformed by a private individual, and if desirable whether it is legitimate and possible. But the opinions a private individual must necessarily doubt are also the ruling or constitutive opinions and therefore "foundations" of states.

The connection of private and public reform is peculiarly evident in that private reform of defects in "the body of the sciences" can lead, and perhaps ought to lead, to reform in "the order established in the schools" to teach the sciences, and the schools are the authoritative repository of the opinions that are the "foundations" of the "great bodies," *i.e.,* states and nations. Descartes thus agrees with the classic view that opinion is the element of society, the binding ligament that gives it unity and motion. Publication of his private reform would necessarily raise the question, therefore, of whether he intended a public reformation: again he agrees with the classics that philosophic questioning when made publicly tends to erode the element of opinion in which society lives. Moreover, the jeopardy to the foundational opinion of society is unprecedented in the case of Descartes' philosophy, because his method demands the blanket attainder of all opinion that lacks the certitude of mathematics. Yet Descartes did publish his method, even writing in a popular mode and in the vulgar tongue, and thereby indicated that he intended a public reformation.

Descartes' political intention in the *Discourse* remains obscure without at least brief clarification of the three chief features of its rhetoric. Descartes is often believed to be a political conformist because his provisional morality begins: "the first [rule] was to obey the laws and customs of my country, retaining constantly the religion in which God has given me the grace to be instructed from my infancy." [15] Apart from the provisionality of the rule, it is less often observed that in the center of the same paragraph he says that "in the corruption of our morals there are few people who wish to say all that they believe." He was "forced to add these rules" of provisional morality because otherwise "pedagogues and the like would say of him that he is without religion and faith and seeks to overthrow all that with his method." [16] This prudential character of its rhetoric blurs the meaning of the principal literary feature of the *Discourse.* Just as the argument on supreme mastery leads to "my way," the way of the individual Descartes which is unprecedented, unrepeatable, and needless of repetition, so likewise his act of publication is entirely unique. The form of the *Discourse* is therefore that of an autobiography of the first and final founder of philosophy. Its third rhetorical feature, its popularization of philosophy, becomes intelligible when one learns in what sense the founder is in need of nonphilosophers.

Descartes' act of publication is premised, firstly, on the desirability of the reform of existing states, which is evident "from their diversity alone," but ultimately on the desirability of a permanent reform of the relations of philosophy and the public. Since "diversity alone" evidences imperfection, there will be but one good regime characterized by the perfect relation of philosophy and the public. His particular criticisms of contemporary society imply the general character of the permanent reform. The prime authority for existing "foundations" breeds civil war: "the controversies of the schools, by insensibly making those who practice themselves in them more captious and obstinate, are possibly the chief causes of the heresies and dissensions that now exercise the world."[17] The entire reflection on mastery, Descartes' famous day in the "stove," begins with a reference to the "wars" in Germany and ends with a reference to the war in Holland: it is framed by the post-Reformation wars between the Catholic and Protestant powers of Europe. The "state of the true religion," or Christendom, exhibits not the unity of its founder but self-diremption.

The question of the legitimacy of public reformation by private individuals is subordinate for Descartes to that of its possibility, for the reason that "fortune" is a title to legitimate political power. He "absolutely disapproves of those turbulent temperaments who never fail to plan some new reformation, although they are not called by fortune nor by birth to the management of public affairs."[18] This unusual constriction of the bases of legitimacy to fortune and birth is still more surprising if one considers fortune as a claim to legitimacy: if fortune legitimates, then every attempt to seize power has the prospect of legitimacy, since an individual cannot know he has been "called by fortune to the management of public affairs" prior to success. Since chance or fortune set Descartes himself on the right path to the discovery of the true "foundations," his project is blessed with legitimacy from its inception. To show the legitimacy of supreme mastery Descartes must show the possibility of the total mastery of fortune. But "one must entirely reject the vulgar opinion that there is outside of us a Fortune that makes things happen or not happen." As with Machiavelli, whose stamp on Descartes' treatment of the goddess Fortuna is unmistakeable, it is nature that must be mastered. Still the immediate issue is but the difficulty of public reformation by a private man: it will be solved for Descartes by the attractive power for all men of the "fruits" of his philosophy and the strategy used to advertise them.

Once the general principles of physics are known, the "project" of Descartes becomes a "practical philosophy" "very useful for life" that can supplant the "speculative philosophy taught in the schools." By the "mastery and possession of nature" man can invent "an infinity of artifices that would enable us to enjoy, without any pain, the fruits of the earth, and all the comforts that are to be found there." [19] The fruits of the tree of knowledge will undo the consequences of the Fall in the garden, or, more precisely, will effectively deny its truth. The *Discourse* culminates then in a promise of a heaven on earth, or it imitates Bacon's writing on method, the *New Organon,* whose subtitle refers to "the kingdom of man." The science that leads to human happiness is not the traditional study of the excellence of the soul, moral and political science, and still less the "theology" that "shows the way to gain heaven," but medicine, the science of the body. "Health is without doubt the first good and the foundation of all the other goods of this life." Medicine is also the means to the prolongation of life, but above all it is the science that produces "wisdom," the ultimate fruit: "the mind depends so much on the temperament and on the disposition of the organs of the body that if it is possible to find some means which generally renders men wiser and more skillful than they have been hitherto, I believe that it is in medicine that one must search." [20]

To govern the relations between society and the philosophy that promises such fruits, Descartes asserts that there is a "law that obliges us to procure so far as it is in us, the general good of all men." [21] This law, the only categorical obligation ever asserted by Descartes, is stated but once in his writings, and no argument is ever offered for it. He declares that the law obliged him to publish his philosophy lest he "sin," but he never claimed to derive the law from "revealed truths." To account for this amazing mixture of bold assertion and resounding silence, we observe first that Descartes invoked the law only when he had discovered "general notions regarding physics": he did not regard his metaphysics, which contained what he claimed were the first demonstrative proofs of the existence of God and of his perfections, as of sufficient benevolence to the public to require publication. Indeed, immediately after expounding his metaphysics in the *Discourse* (Part IV), he turns to his physics in which he "discovered many truths more useful and more important than all [he] had learned before, or even hoped to learn." [22] In the context of the discussion of publication in the *Discourse* (Part VI), Descartes tacitly reformulates the law as a hypothetical obligation only, which binds those who desire the end or the fruits of the new philosophy to seek the means to that end. The means are the required experiments, or the exchange of experiments between qualified people, or the political conditions that will sanction and promote such an exchange. The hypothetical character of the obligation appears in Descartes' "promise" that he would "show so clearly the utility that the public could receive" from his philosophy that he "would oblige all those who desire in general the good of men, that is to say, all those who are in fact virtuous and not merely seem so, not only to communicate to me [the experiments] they have already made, but also to aid me in the search for those that remain to be made." [23]

The "good of men"—the term lacks the sense of community of "the common good"—now comprises chiefly what all men have always sought as individuals or through society, namely, the satisfaction of needs, comfort, health, and long life, and this drastically lowered view of the common good is the standard of virtue. Thus Descartes, in common with the founders of modern political philosophy, reversed the relation of virtue and the common good as understood by the classics, revising both in the process. The "law" of benevolence is doubly hypothetical in that it obliges one to seek the means only if one accepts the desirability of the end of utility, but also only if the true means, the true physics or the science of "fruits," is available. It has its locus therefore not primarily in the relations of citizens to each other or with the sovereign, but in the mutual relations of philosophy or science and society. For this reason, but even more for the additional one that philosophy or science must be the principal donor and society the beneficiary of utility, Descartes did not offer any teaching on justice or natural right. "Generosity," the highest virtue of philosophers or scientists, excludes or replaces justice because it is based on a view of the soul different from that of either the ancient or modern teachers of natural right.

Descartes' first beginning in a new method is completed by a mathematical physics that forced him to re-examine the status of the soul and its knowledge in the metaphysical argument most fully presented in the *Meditations* (1641). In his second famous beginning, he resolves to doubt absolutely, or rather to reject absolutely, every opinion or source of opinion in the slightest degree dubious, in order to find a "foundation" for the "sciences." To attain the maximum of doubt, he supposes that God, who at least sometimes permits him to be deceived, always deceives him; or rather that an omnipotent and evil genius causes him always to be deceived. This supposition is customarily regarded as the apogee of Cartesian doubt. Yet for those who would make bold to proceed to doubt the existence of a God so powerful, Descartes proceeds with equal boldness to substitute the supposition that man and

his thinking are caused by fate or chance or by a continuous chain of
antecedent causes. The true extremity of doubt therefore derives from
the view that man is caused by a nature devoid of a ruling intelligence,
or by a mechanistic physics, since Descartes makes clear in the same
passage that man is more likely to be deceived the less intelligent is the
cause of man's being and thinking. He thus supposes the absolute enmity of God or nature to man's need for knowledge. But man cannot
be absolutely deceived by either cause: for even in the case of maximum
deception, man knows that he must exist in order to be deceived.
Therefore, no external superhuman or subhuman power can deprive
man of the power to think with necessity the truth of his own existence.
Hence the thought or intuition "I think, therefore I am," the "first
principle of philosophy," implies that there is no external omnipotent
being.

This principle is the "Archimedean point" that establishes the existence of the knowing ego within the whole, whose enmity is overcome
by the mathematical physics of the mastery of nature. Only following
the determination of the principle does Descartes ask what mind or
thinking is: the "cogito" is therefore prior to, and independent of, any
determination of the materiality or immateriality of the human mind.
Descartes compromised the absolute autonomy of the thinking ego,
according to most contemporary scholars, by proceeding to prove the
existence of an omnipotent God who is possessed of an infinity of infinite perfections: God is therefore the first principle or cause of all
things, and so of man and man's knowledge. Descartes made the difficulty of interpreting his metaphysics almost insuperable by also asserting that the finite human mind cannot know anything infinite, and by
concluding therefore that "God is incomprehensible." [24]  Resolution
of these difficulties will vary as one agrees with most contemporary
scholars that Descartes published his essential thought with complete
candor, or with earlier men such as Leibniz who said, "Descartes took
care not to speak so plainly [as Hobbes], but he could not help revealing
his opinions in passing, with such address that he would not be understood save by those who examine profoundly these kinds of subjects." [25]
However this may be, Descartes never claimed to derive from the knowledge of God any knowledge of man's duties or rights; whereas from
"the infinite perfections of God" he did claim to derive "the laws of
nature."

Descartes' metaphysical argument furnished him with one source
of the understanding of the soul that underlies his theory of "generosity." The second source of his view of the soul is physics, or the "medicine" that treats "the machine of our body," most fully presented in his

final publication, the *Passions of the Soul* (1649). According to his metaphysical argument, the free will is a function of mind or soul, an immaterial substance, separate from corporeal substance, yet able to act on corporeal substance, specifically on the human body, in a manner that Descartes admittedly did not adequately explain. This metaphysical view is reflected in the first part of the definition of generosity, which is the "knowledge" that "nothing truly pertains to [man] but this free disposition of his volitions, nor any reason why he should be praised or blamed except that he uses it well or badly." However, according to the physical argument, the heat of the heart "is the corporeal principle of all the movements" of "the machine of our body," while "the first cause" of the error of "the ancients" is the belief that "the soul gives movement to the body." Hence the metaphysical argument would repeat the ancient error. On the physical argument, thinking or consciousness is awareness of the motions of the (wholly corporeal) animal spirits, which awareness Descartes did not adequately explain; and the will is not free but acted on by the passions: "the principal effect of all the passions in men is that they incite and dispose their soul to will the things to which they prepare the body." This second or physical view is reflected in the second part of the definition of generosity, "that [man] is sensible in himself of a firm and constant resolution ... never to fail of his own will to undertake and execute all the things that he judges to be the best, which is to follow perfectly after virtue." "Resolution" Descartes understands as a species of courage which is a "certain heat or agitation" of the animal spirits that "disposes the soul powerfully to bear itself to the execution of the things that it seeks to do." This physiological view of the soul best explains why Descartes can say he speaks in the *Passions of the Soul,* whose first part treats "the whole nature of man," "as a physicist." [26] (The seventeenth-century English philosopher Henry More openly avowed the physiological interpretation of the Cartesian soul, which doctrine he called "Nullibism." [27])

However we view these alternatives, we may say that "generosity" is awareness of one's identity in the quality of one's will or resolution. The freedom of the will "in a certain measure renders us like God in making us masters of ourselves, provided that we do not through cowardice lose the rights which He gives us." [28] Since cowardice deprives man of rights, they belong to the brave or resolute, hence peculiarly to the "generous." Yet "cowardice has some use when it exempts us from taking the pains that we might be incited to take by probable reasons, if other more certain reasons, which have caused them to be judged useless, had not excited this passion." [29] Hence very certain reasons may perhaps deprive the generous of their God-given rights. However this

may be, no argument nor any scriptural basis is ever offered by Descartes
for the existence of these rights, nor does he ever mention them again.

The political meaning of generosity emerges by contrast with Aristotle's virtue of "magnanimity," of which generosity is a revised version,
according to Descartes. Magnanimity is a cultivated habit or disposition
of the soul, whereas Descartes chooses the new name "generosity" precisely because it is not cultivated but an ingenerate, or congenital, temperament at least partly physiological. Generous minds, or "strong and
noble minds," have their strength from birth, or by nature, hence are
"masters" by nature, a natural nobility or aristocracy. Whereas magnanimity was for Aristotle a comprehensive moral virtue and therefore
distinct from and lower than theoretical virtue, generosity is Descartes'
highest virtue simply: since its supreme object is "mastery of nature"
through mathematical physics, the very distinction between theory and
practice becomes doubtful. Magnanimity comprehends and presupposes
the other virtues, hence in particular the virtue of justice, and is therefore
"a kind of ornament to the [other]virtues." [30] Generosity, on the other
hand, does not presuppose the other virtues, and Descartes does not
mention justice as a virtue or passion; generosity is rather "the key to all
the virtues." [31] Therefore, Descartes does not offer any kind of natural-
right teaching. As contrasted with the ancients, the absence of any
natural order of the soul precluded a natural-right teaching of the traditional type. He shared with Hobbes, the chief founder of modern
natural-right doctrine, the view that reason serves the passions. In the
decisive context of the comparison of man and the brutes, reason is a
"universal instrument" [32]: what distinguishes man from the brutes is
a unique means, not a specifically different end. But as contrasted with
Hobbes, he viewed political society from the perspective of the strong
or generous minds whose sense of the strength of their resolution, their
strongest passion, is unique to them. Hence he rejected the egalitarian
perspective of Hobbes's *On the Citizen* according to which the passion
for self-preservation is the strongest passion of all men, and therefore
the basis of natural rights.

Generosity is a political passion or virtue not merely because its
object is that mastery of nature which is productive of goods for all
men. Knowledge of generosity is the primary part of that "wisdom," or
perfect moral science, that teaches man to be master of and hence to
enjoy the passions, by which man "tastes the highest sweetness in this
life." [33] "Epicurus was not wrong, when considering in what beatitude
consists . . . to say that it is pleasure in general." However, the "satisfaction and contentment" of the consciousness of one's own strength in the
mastery of nature are not incompatible with the pleasure of glory ac-

corded by others for the benevolent results of mastery: the highest philosophic and political rewards may coincide in the same soul. Descartes does not "profess to scorn glory as did the Cynics" [34] and the Epicurean tradition. The quest for glory may indeed disturb "contentment" or "repose" of mind, but glory as respect of "the people" or the vulgar for "the exterior of our actions" is also pursued for the sake of safety and hence "repose." The true glory is the recognition of other "strong and noble minds" for the benevolence of what is not visible externally, the perfect moral science or "wisdom." "It is a reason to esteem oneself to see that one is esteemed by others." [35] The primary self-esteem or generosity is accordingly enhanced by the esteem or glory that is granted for benevolence, and benevolence thus understood becomes the substitute for justice.

Descartes' "reformation" begins with the transformation of philosophy into the project of mastery of nature, of virtue into the science of the passions, and of perfect theoretical and practical virtue into the single virtuous passion of generosity. Since mastery of nature is a means to a practical end for all men, philosophy must bear a novel relation to society. The relation is a compound of a threat to the traditional foundations of society and a promise of benevolence by the fruits of mastery of nature. Yet this jeopardy is redeemed by the fact that the "universal doubt" that method demands is so far from doubting the view that the good is the useful that it is in fact based on this view, and the useful is needed by all societies always. Therefore, Descartes' project can be welcomed by all societies except those based on traditional virtue or piety, or it is relatively neutral to the differences among types of regimes. The support of the project of science by the most liberal as well as the most tyrannical regimes in modern times offers some evidence for this neutrality. For this reason primarily Descartes never articulated a view of the best regime. The convergence of the goals of philosophy and society is not destroyed by the fact that the useful sought by the generous minds is not identical with the useful sought by society. For the final wisdom of the passions, and the prize of glory, sought by the generous, demands the same means, i.e., the advancement of science, that is required to achieve the useful fruits sought by society. The fundamental premise of the harmony of philosophy and society is that all men are ruled by the passions.

The common means, the advancement of science, cannot be achieved without a certain transformation, or new "legislation," of social institutions. Science will advance only if the free exchange of "experiments" or free communication is sanctioned within the borders of society, but also between societies; it will achieve its promise only if society also promotes science by the endowment of scientists with safety, income and deference. This free exchange cannot be limited to exchange of knowledge: societies, or more precisely, the political authorities, are not competent judges of knowledge. Hence society must not only sanction the competent or the scientists as judges but must sanction all communication of doctrines. Society therefore necessarily surrenders control of its opinions, *i.e.,* its "foundations," since the ruling opinions of society are necessarily affected by the free communication of doctrines. Moreover, society will be profoundly affected by "the infinity of artifices" or technology of science. Society cannot have knowledge of science but only belief in the benevolence of science. But since society had originally no acquaintance with the benevolence of science, nor its social requirements, it was necessary for Descartes, following Bacon, to "enlighten" society regarding both.

"Enlightenment" may be said to have three meanings. It is an unprecedented type of political action undertaken by the founders of modern philosophy and continued by most of their followers that forges the bond between philosophy or science and society in the common enterprise of "the mastery of nature." It may also be said to be the rhetoric employed in forging the bond, and the relationship established by it. Since the optimum condition of the progress of science demands the cooperation of the scientists of various countries, and hence freedom of communication among them, and requires as well the spread of knowledge of the conditions of the advancement of science, Enlightenment implies "open societies" linked with each other in the common enterprise of "the mastery of nature." It is necessarily antithetical to any societies, or elements in a society, that seek the autonomous cultivation and preservation of their own morality and way of life. Thus Enlightenment is by intention a universal politics, potentially of global magnitude, and the first of philosophic origin.

Because it is a compound of a promise and a threat, the Enlightenment rhetoric is divisive of society, both at the time of its inception and after its victory. Descartes indicates its promise to three kinds of men. In the *Discourse* especially he appeals to the men of "good sense" or "the public," a broad middle range of mankind that thinks itself adequately provided with "good sense," which Descartes provisionally and deceptively equates with reason. The truth underlying this flattery is that the men of good sense reason well on "matters that especially concern [them]" and regarding which errors of judgment "punish them soon afterwards":[36] their rationality is rooted in their self-interest or self-preservation in the here and now, and not what will punish them in another life. Descartes' rhetoric advertises to them that they are the beneficiaries of the project that produces "the fruits of the earth without pain," and of the social conditions of the progress of the project. They are the natural allies of the second group, the generous minds, or the scientists who build on his foundations and the *philosophes* who propagate his reformation. One may distinguish as a third group the political rulers proper who necessarily welcome Descartes' advocacy of knowledge useful for society, as well as his opposition to the political ambitions of "reformers" who believe God has given them "sufficient grace and zeal to be prophets." [37]

He invites these groups to join in common opposition against those opponents who draw their beliefs from "the ancient books, their histories and their fables." Together with "reformers" and "prophets" he places those who, believing themselves "devout" and "great friends of God," though in fact "only bigots and superstitious," have "committed the greatest crimes that can be committed by men, as betraying cities, killing princes, and exterminating entire peoples, only because they did not follow their opinions." The popular support of these zealous leaders comes from "the weak minds," a term used repeatedly by Descartes to designate those who are prone to "superstition," and whose "consciences" are agitated by "repentances and remorse," [38] the human type most opposed to "the strong and noble minds." But these latter have a remedy available, the science of the passions: "even the weakest minds could acquire a most absolute empire over all their passions if one employed enough industry to train them, and to conduct them." [39] Behind the zealous stands the authority of "the school," or scholasticism: "the monks have supplied the opportunity for all sects and heresies through their theology, that is to say, their scholasticism, which before all must be exterminated." [40] Because of this alliance of friend against foe, d'Alembert could "regard [Descartes] as a chief of conspirators who first had the courage to raise himself up against a despotic and arbitrary power."

Yet Descartes' Enlightenment rhetoric must vanquish more fundamental enemies to ensure the lasting success of his project. Not only his "preceptors" or the books of Latin Christendom "corrupt the natural reason," but so also do the "Greek and Latin books." [41] He made plain that his only rivals on the plane of his endeavor, or those alone "whose writings we possess" who sought out "the first causes and the true principles," were "Plato and Aristotle." Hence those whose "prejudices" most oppose his project are those who have "most studied the ancient philosophy." His rhetoric has then the function of opposing the whole tradition of humanistic learning, which required him to oppose tradition simply. Since the view that the good is the old or the traditional

can never be fully eradicated, Enlightenment rhetoric has a permanently divisive social function. Descartes succeeded in turning the questioning of the identity of the good and the old by classic philosophy
against the classics by identifying them as the old or the tradition. The
classic tradition appeared to him, as it had to Stevin and Grotius, as a
corruption of the wisdom of the golden youth of the world in some
pre-Socratic *siècle sage.*[42] Since Descartes knew that some less than philosophically precise belief regarding the whole is required as a foundation for society, he sought to supply a substitute for tradition that
would foster the project of science. By a scientific "fable of the world,"
or by what purported to be a scientific account of the genesis of the
heavens and the earth, of the visible universe and all its phenomena, he
established the belief that science is master of the whole; and by the
promise of the progress of science toward infinite benefits he and Bacon
established the "idea of progress," or the belief that the good is the
future whose benevolence owes nothing to tradition, to nature, or to God.

It was not Descartes but Bacon who first proposed a "project" that
promised maximum benevolence to society by a universal method, and
hence inaugurated the politics of Enlightenment. Descartes following
Bacon may be said to have accepted but revised Machiavelli's earlier
fusion of the highest glory or mastery with the highest benevolence
through a political teaching devoted to the mastery of chance or nature
in human affairs. It was initially Machiavelli's "realism" that taught
that reason does not by nature seek the pure truth but serves the passions,
or that "the natural force of man's judgment" does not suffice, as Bacon
put it, and hence reason must be "equipped" with the artifact of method,
or that reason must be "conducted" by the "work" or art of method, as
Descartes said. Precisely Machiavelli's incipient critique of the impurities
of natural reason demanded that nature be remedied, or rather mastered,
by art, or by the construction of a method. Whereas Machiavelli thought
that the understanding of man must descend to include that of the beast
in order to ascend to the mastery of human nature, Bacon thought that
a first mastery of the human understanding itself must be gained by
descending to learn from the mechanical arts so that the ascent to the
mastery of all nature "be done as if by machinery." Hence on the basis
of Machiavelli's "realism," Bacon attempted to surpass Machiavelli, as
is especially evident in the *New Organon* (Book I, section 129). For the
"endeavor to establish and extend the power and dominion of the
human race itself over the universe" through a universal method is more
benevolent than the teaching of political modes and orders. "The benefits of discoveries may extend to the whole race of man, civil benefits
only to particular places; the latter last not beyond a few ages, the former

through all time;" "civil reformations" usually begin in violence, but discoveries confer benefits without causing sorrow to any.

This argument in its entirety is a germinal part of the project of Descartes. The genealogy of Descartes' project is especially visible in the amazingly similar statements of the doctrine concerning "reformation" of political bodies by a private individual in the *Prince* (chapter vi), the *New Organon* (Book I, section 129), and the *Discourse* (Part II). According to Descartes, Bacon did not see with sufficient clarity that the new method must be mathematical to be certain or "systematic," or that it required a new mathematics and a mathematical physics and a corresponding determination of the soul. By these momentous amendments,[43] but on the foundation laid by Machiavelli, Descartes became "the founder of modern philosophy."

## NOTES

1. J. d'Alembert, *Discours préliminaire de l'Encyclopédie,* ed. L. Ducros (Paris, 1930), p. 104.

2. René Descartes, *Oeuvres,* ed. C. Adam and P. Tannery (Paris, 1910), V. 159. Quotations within this chapter have been translated by the author.

3. *Ibid.,* XI, 320; IV, 531; IV, 67.
4. *Ibid.,* IX B, 14–15.
5. *Ibid.,* VI, 6–7.
6. *Ibid.,* X, 505.
7. *Ibid.,* VI, 8.
8. *Ibid.,* VI, 8.
9. *Ibid.,* XI, 327.
10. *Ibid.,* VI, 62.
11. *Ibid.,* VI, 11.
12. *Ibid.,* VI, 13.
13. *Ibid.,* XI, 446.
14. *Ibid.,* VI, 13–15.
15. *Ibid.,* VI, 22–23.
16. *Ibid.,* V, 178.
17. *Ibid.,* IX B, 18.
18. *Ibid.,* VI, 14–15.
19. *Ibid.,* VI, 61–62.
20. *Ibid.,* VI, 62.
21. *Ibid.,* VI, 61.
22. *Ibid.,* VI, 41.
23. *Ibid.,* VI, 65.
24. *Ibid.,* VIII, 9; IX A, 37; IX B, 33.
25. G. W. Leibniz, *Philosophischer*

*Briefwechsel,* I, 506.
26. *Oeuvres,* XI, 446, 330, 332, 327, 326.
27. *Philosophical Writings of Henry More,* ed. F. I. MacKinnon (Oxford: Oxford University Press, 1925), pp. 183–96. Descartes, "the prince of the nullibists," "befooling" his readers with his "jocular subtilty," contended that "incorporeal spirits" exist, "but would be found to do it only by way of an oblique and close derision of their existence, saying indeed they exist, but then hiddenly and cunningly denying it, by affirming they are no where" or "null ibi."
28. *Oeuvres,* XI, 445.
29. *Ibid.,* XI, 462–63.
30. Aristotle *Nic. Eth.* 1124a.
31. *Oeuvres,* XI, 454.
32. *Ibid.,* VI, 57.
33. *Ibid.,* XI, 488.
34. *Ibid.,* VI, 9; XI, 483.
35. *Ibid.,* XI, 482.
36. *Ibid.,* VI, 9–10, 12–13.
37. *Ibid.,* VI, 61.
38. *Ibid.,* IV, 529; VI, 24–25.
39. *Ibid.,* XI, 370.
40. *Ibid.,* V, 176.

41. *Ibid.*, VI, 77; IX B, 7, 9, 11; X, 495, 503.

42. *Ibid.*, X, 373, 376.

43. For these steps, see especially J. Klein, "Die griechische Logistik und die Entstehung der Algebra," *Quellen und Studien zur Geschichte der Mathematik, Astronomie, und Physik,* B III (1936), 207–25.

## READINGS

A.  Descartes, René. *Discourse on Method.* Trans. L. J. Lafleur. New York: Liberal Arts Press, 1951.

B.  Descartes, René. *Meditations.* Trans. with introduction by L. J. Lafleur. New York: Liberal Arts Press, 1951.

# JOHN MILTON

## 1608–1674

While an undergraduate at Cambridge, John Milton delivered seven Latin orations that reflect, as they might be expected to reflect considering their style and language, not only the extent of his reading of the authors of classical antiquity, but also the considerable extent to which, even as a schoolboy, he consciously accepted their authority as teachers. Later, when he dared to break the law respecting the licensing of printing and, in the same act, to advise Parliament of the necessity of its repeal, he entitled his speech, which was to become his most famous prose work, the *Areopagitica,* thus reminding his addressees of the classical example of Isocrates and the Athenian Areopagus. He sought to reform English education by patterning it after the "ancient and famous schools of Pythagoras, Plato, Isocrates, Aristotle and such others." For almost twenty years he expounded and defended a political teaching knowingly derived from the doctrines and institutions of ancient Greece and Rome.

He also insisted, however, that this was not a case of introducing something wholly alien to English tradition, of revolting in order to make a new beginning by establishing government on wholly new principles. Indeed, he argued in his most comprehensive political work, *The Ready and Easy Way to Establish a Free Commonwealth,* that it did not require "the introducement of . . . exotic models" at all; there was model enough to be found in the English past. As he had written in an early anti-episcopal tract: "There is no civil government that has been known, no not the Spartan, not the Roman, though both for this respect so much praised by the wise Polybius, more divinely and harmoniously tuned, more equally balanced as it were by the hand and scale of justice, than is [or was] the commonwealth of England: where, under a free and untutored monarch, the noblest, worthiest, and most prudent men, with full approbation, and suffrage of the people have in their power the supreme, and final determination of highest affairs." [1]

The virtue of this free commonwealth consisted in part in the fact that it had a mixed constitution; it was not a monarchy, aristocracy, or democracy, but a mixture that recognized the claim of each of these, a balance, "divinely and harmoniously tuned." The best and least barbarous commonwealths "have aimed at a certain mixture and temperament, partaking the several virtues of each other state. . . ." [2] Although he was to become an avowed enemy of monarchy, early adopting views wholly republican and therefore, in this respect, more in the spirit of his classical models than of English tradition, his attachment to the idea of the mixed constitution remained fixed throughout his political career. A politics knowingly derived from ancient Greece and Rome is a constitutional politics, and the cause of constitutional government, the cause that England was chosen by God to promote in the world of the seventeenth century, had no greater friend than John Milton. Even at the last moment before the restoration of the monarchy and with it the prelacy, when it appeared that the "good old cause" was doomed, it was Milton who insisted that the way to a free commonwealth was clear and easy: ". . . and if the people, laying aside prejudice and impatience, will seriously and calmly now consider their own good both religious and civil, their own liberty and the only means thereof . . . and will elect . . . men not addicted to a single person [i.e., a king] or house of lords, the work is done; at least the foundation firmly laid of a free Commonwealth, and good part also erected of the main structure." [3] The task here is to understand the form and purpose of this free commonwealth.

Even though he did not originate it, no name has been more closely associated with the doctrine of the mixed constitution, or more precisely in this case, mixed state, than that of the Greek historian Polybius. In his famous description of the Roman constitution, a description preceded by a somewhat enigmatic commentary on it, Polybius seems to combine the idea of the mixed constitution of Plato and Aristotle with a new idea, that of the division of power. Whereas Aristotle's was a mixture of oligarchy and democracy achieved by giving political power to the middle, and most moderate, class in an effort to achieve moderation, Polybius' Roman mixture seemingly involves elements of monarchy, aristocracy, and democracy, each wielding a part of the power of the state and each associated with a particular institution, the monarchy with the consulate, the aristocracy with the senate, and the democracy, but vaguely, with the popular assemblies. Without going into the question of Polybius' intention, we must attempt to grasp what Milton himself meant by the term. Did he mean by it, like Aristotle in the fourth book of the *Politics,* a regime that blends democracy and oligarchy so as to avoid the disadvantages of each and to combine the advantages of each, and yet possesses an undivided citizen body ultimately sovereign in all respects; or did he mean by it a regime in which the sum total of political power is divided into a monarchic, aristocratic, and democratic element?

Milton was not a mere spectator of the tremendous political events of his time, he was an active supporter of both the Parliament's cause against Charles I and, later, of Cromwell. Much of his political writing was presented in pamphlets written in haste and for immediate practical purposes, whether to defend himself and the English people or to make a final effort to prevent the restoration of the monarchy. In these circumstances it is not surprising that his views on some questions changed under the buffeting of the events of the civil war and its aftermath. One of these was his opinion of monarchy; another was his opinion of the character of the common people.

Milton was at no time a democrat, but he seems to have had a higher opinion of the political capacity of the common people in the beginning than he had later on. In 1644 in the *Areopagitica* he attacked the licensing of printing because, among other reasons, it was a reproach to the common people, assuming them unreasonably to be in "such a sick and weak estate of faith and discretion, as to be able to take nothing down but through the pipe of a licenser." But in his *Second Defense of the People of England,* a vindication of the nation for deposing, then executing Charles I, and thereby delivering the "commonwealth from a grievous domination," he drew a distinction between those valorous, magnanimous, and steadfast persons who were capable of great deeds and fidelity to a great cause, and the vulgar multitude.[4] At one point early in his political career he reproached an opponent for his use of the term "mutinous rabble," but he later used the term "rabble" himself, and meant thereby the common people who, he said, were dull and ignorant of the art of government, and fickle and excitable. Only a few men desire liberty, he said in this first *Defense of the English People,* and only a few are capable of using it: "Far the greatest part of the world prefers just masters—masters, observe, but just ones."[5] Yet in his *Second Defense* of the same English people, he also asked Cromwell to ensure that "all the citizens alike should have an equal right to be free." [6] In the light of these conflicting statements, perhaps the surest guide to his appraisal of the character of the common people is to be found in the place he assigned them in the constitution. In 1641 he spoke of political power being exercised only "with full approbation and suffrage of the people," but it was not until 1660 in *The Ready and Easy Way* that he spoke in any detail of the manner in which this consent was to be given, and here, in the context of a description of the election of members of the General Council, or legislature, it becomes quite clear that the role of the people is minimal. They exercise some power in a well-balanced state, but no one could describe that state as a democracy. Nevertheless, one of the reasons for his latter-day refusal to permit a king in his mixed state is his attachment to the principle of popular sovereignty.

Milton was not always a republican. Whereas in *Of Reformation,* written in 1641, he found it necessary in order to promote religious reform to argue that episcopacy was not the only form of church government compatible with monarchy, eight years later he said that a king may be deposed when he acts unlawfully, and even when he does not act unlawfully, because he "holds his authority of the people." The people choose kings in the first place and they may reject them: freeborn men have the "right . . . to be governed as seems to them best." [7] (But may other nations, especially a nation of barbarians or a "rabble concourse" legitimately be ruled by a king or even a despot? This is suggested in both the *First Defense* and *The Ready and Easy Way*.) Kings do not hold their titles from God, but from the people: "So that we see the title and just right of reigning or deposing, in reference to God, is found in Scripture to be all one; visible only in the people, and depending merely upon justice and demerit." [8] It is popular sovereignty that is derived from God, as he says in *Paradise Lost,* Book XII:

> . . . but Man over men
> He made not Lord; such title to himself
> Reserving, human left from human free.

Milton may have begun by supporting the monarchy, but he quickly became a republican, and an avid republican.

Popular sovereignty is, however, perfectly compatible with the acceptance of monarchy, even of hereditary monarchy, since the people may delegate the governmental power to a royal family while retaining the sovereign power to withdraw it. But by 1651, the year he published the *First Defense,* Milton had found in contemporary events sufficient practical reasons for rejecting monarchy, even in its limited sense of constitutional monarchy. His experience as an Englishman during the preceding decade had confirmed the argument he knew from the writings of Plato and Aristotle that monarchy tends to degenerate into tyranny—indeed, according to Milton, of all the forms of government monarchy is most likely to do so. Nothing written by the friends of the king could dissuade him; in fact, he became increasingly republican in the course of replying to the various promonarchical pamphlets. Finally, he could see nothing around a king but a corrupting luxury, a dissoluteness, a style of life that made the people abject, debauched the "prime gentry," and bred a servile nobility that aspired not to public service but to service as "stewards, chamberlains, ushers, grooms, even of the close-stool. . . ." Monarchy, in short, debases men's character. It is, as a student of Aristotle could be expected to argue, a form of government not suited to free men. To be ruled by a king, to commit all to his paternal care, is to act "more like boys under age than men." "How unmanly must it needs be . . . to hang all our felicity on him, all our safety, our well-being, for which if we were ought else but sluggards or babies, we need depend on none but God and our own counsels, our own active virtue and industry. . . ." [9] It was for these reasons that Milton was a republican. This does not mean, of course, that Milton refused to provide for the exercise of executive power; the mixed state provided for a magistracy, and if in 1641 this was a king, in 1660 it was a Council of State, chosen by the legislature.

It is clear that neither the people as a whole nor the king and his retinue were to exercise the decisive political power in the mixed state; this role was reserved for the "noblest, worthiest, and most prudent men," as he said in Of Reformation. It is also clear that these words did not refer to a titled aristocracy ruling through a house of lords, for there is no house of lords in the free commonwealth, and Milton had contempt for the idea that a title conferred nobility on its possessor. By noblest, worthiest, and most prudent men, he meant those men truly distinguished in their character and by their public service. "To these accomplished men and chosen citizens," he advised Cromwell in the latter's capacity as Lawgiver or founding father, "you doubtless might properly commit the care of our liberty. . . ." [10] He meant men for whom public service was not a means of amassing power, position, or wealth, but a sacred duty. "And what government comes nearer to this precept of Christ, than a free Commonwealth; wherein they who are greatest, are perpetual servants and drudges to the public at their own cost and charges, neglect their own affairs; yet are not elevated above their brethren; live soberly in their families, walk the streets as other men, may be spoken to freely, familiarly, friendly, without adoration." [11] Such men are likely to be found among the "middle sort," for, and once again Milton agrees with Aristotle, the "rest are most commonly diverted, on the one hand by luxury and wealth, on the other by want and poverty, from achieving excellence, and from the study of laws and government." [12]

It is clear, then, to whom Milton entrusts the decisive political power in the free commonwealth: not to a "single person" or to the people, but to a true aristocracy to be found among men of the middle class; and it is necessary now to see how he would effect this. The ablest and noblest men are to rule with the consent or, as he said in 1641, with "full approbation and suffrage" of the people, and they are to exercise their rule initially through a General Council or legislature. "For the ground and basis of every just and free government (since men have smarted so oft for committing all to one person) is a general council of ablest men, chosen by the people to consult of public affairs from time to time for the common good." Unlike the Roman republic described by Polybius, this legislative body not only makes the laws, raises and manages the public revenue and, generally, performs as a legislative body, but it also controls the army and navy. Furthermore, it elects, from among its own members as well as from outside, a Council of State, an executive body or magistracy, that carries on "particular affairs with more secrecy and expedition. . . ." Finally, there is local government, organized in every county in the land and exercising the powers of a kind of subordinate commonwealth, and especially with the full power to elect judges and administer justice.[13] Here, then, are the elements of a Polybian mixed state: monarchy, or the magistracy, embodied in the Council of State; aristocracy represented in the General Council or legislature; and democracy represented in the electoral process, specifically in the election of local officials and, more significantly, members of the General Council. These are the institutions of the free commonwealth, a state constructed with a view to striking a balance of some sort.

But what sort of balance? Is it a balance of legislative against executive against judicial, that is, a dividing up of power in order to prevent anyone or any one group from becoming too powerful? Or is it a balance of monarchy and aristocracy and democracy, the power of each being exercised through one of the constitutional institutions? There is, of course, no monarch, but there is a magistracy; there is no distinct popular assembly, but the people (or at least some of them) do vote. In what sense is this a balanced state? The answer to this question requires, at a minimum, a closer analysis of the institutional factors involved.

The ablest men rule with the consent of the people, but this consent is expressed only in the election of the General Council and of local officials. Milton weighed the possibility of balancing the General Council with a popular assembly, or some other popular institution, such as the Spartan ephors or the Roman tribunes, but he rejected it on the ground that "these remedies either little availed the people, or brought them to such a licentious and unbridled democratie, as in fine ruined themselves with their own excessive power." [14] On the basis of the experience of the Roman republic, which, he said, degenerated into the tyranny of Sulla because the people, not content to have only their tribunes, gained control over the choice of first one, then both consuls, then the censors and praetors, Milton rejected popular assemblies in favor of the democratic suffrage, or quasi-democratic suffrage, alone. His mature judgment convinced him against the possibility of balancing class against class by balancing institution against institution: the attempt to do this led either to a wholly unpopular constitution or to an unbridled democracy, and not to a balanced state.

But it appears that the suffrage is not democratic, and even if it were, the electoral machinery seems to be designed to minimize the influence of the common people. Members of the General Council are selected by a series of electoral commissions working with a list of nominees provided initially by a kind of electoral college. "Another way [to effect a balance] will be, to well-qualify and refine elections: not committing all to the noise and shouting of a rude multitude, but permitting only those of them who are rightly qualified, to nominate as many as they will; and out of that number others of a better breeding, to choose a less number more judiciously, till after a third or fourth sifting and refining of exactest choice, they only be left chosen who are the due number, and seem by most voices the worthiest." [15] The democratic element in the constitution seems especially weak, moreover, and scarcely sufficient to balance off the power of the aristocracy in the General Council, when we give due consideration to the fact that this council, the principal governing body under the constitution, is elected in perpetuity. Except upon "the death or default" of a member, there are to be no elections after the original one. He prefers a perpetual parliament (and it is only with the greatest reluctance that he concedes the unpopularity and infeasibility of this arrangement and accepts as a substitute an assembly one-third of whose members are elected annually) because the necessity to choose successive parliaments breeds commotions, novelty, change—that is, instability—especially because the newly elected legislators will initiate change merely in order to have something to do, or to appear to have something to do. Because the General

Council is both "foundation and main pillar of the whole state," to make an unnecessary change in it is to endanger the entire structure.

He was aware that this constitution would be attacked for its alleged failure to erect safeguards around the interests of the people, and he pointed out that one safeguard was to elect trustworthy men to the council, men who would exercise a just rule, and this could be done by a well-educated electorate (without regard, apparently, to the number of people comprising it). At this point it is possible to see an important difference between Milton and those political writers who taught that by such devices as a mixed state, but meaning thereby a division or balancing of power, men could build an indestructible commonwealth whose viability depended in no way upon the presence of citizens of good character. Milton's free commonwealth pretended to immortality,[16] but its excellence and durability depended on the presence of men of good character, in fact, it depended absolutely on the rule of truly virtuous men. The educating of these men could not be left to chance but must be assumed as a major public duty: "To make the people fittest to choose, and the chosen fittest to govern, will be to mend our corrupt and faulty education, to teach the people faith not without virtue, temperance, modesty, sobriety, parsimony, justice; not to admire wealth [the principle of the commercial society] or honour [the principle of monarchy] . . . to place every one his private welfare and happiness in the public peace, liberty and safety."[17] Who or what institution was to teach the people "faith not without virtue," becomes something of a problem because of his notion of the proper relation of Church and State, although, as we shall see, the apparent problem is readily resolved by his understanding of moral training and Christian liberty. Certainly it is clear from *Of Education,* with its outline of educational reform, and from the *Second Defense,* where he called upon Cromwell as Lawgiver to make "a better provision for the education and morals of youth,"[18] that the provision of moral training is a public duty. The excellence and durability of the free commonwealth, then, depended not on institutional devices, however soundly contrived, but on the character of the men comprising it. Thus, the true safeguard of the people's interest consisted not in a balance of institutions, but on their character and the character of the men governing.

Milton made one concession. "But to prevent all mistrust, the people . . . will have their several ordinary assemblies . . . in the chief towns of every county [and these will be as effective] toward the securing of their liberty, as a numerous assembly of them all formed and convened on purpose with the wariest rotation [*i.e.,* with the most frequent elections]." These local assemblies will have the power to "declare and publish their assent or dissent by deputies within a time limited sent to the Grand Council. . . ." [19] This does not mean that each county has a veto over decisions taken by the General Council, but that a majority of counties must assent to the decisions.

These are the institutions of the mixed state or free commonwealth, a form of government held by the wisest men in all ages to be the noblest and most just, "the most agreeable to all due liberty and proportioned equality," and also a form of government "plainly commended, or rather enjoined by our Saviour himself. . . ." [20] It is a form of government not only derived from the teachings of the wise men of classical antiquity and patterned on a model found in the English past, it is a form of government enjoined by Christ. But the question persists: what sort of balance does it strike? If this arrangement were meant to strike a balance between the various powers of government, executive, legislative and judicial, it is ill conceived. A moment's reflection on the method of selection of the executive is sufficient to reveal the lack of true balance and the extent to which the legislative is the decisive power. This is altogether proper, he says, because although it is important to have the executive power exercised by men not in the legislature, the legislative power is supreme. [21] Certainly if this strikes a balance between aristocracy and democracy, it does so not by establishing each class in an institutional stronghold, but rather by regulating the electoral franchise. In this respect it resembles less what is usually said to be the mixed state of Polybius than it does the polity of Aristotle, the rule of the middle class effected mainly through a moderate property qualification for voting. [22] This is intended to produce a suffrage wide enough to achieve popularity, and thereby, it is hoped, stability, but restricted in such a way as to minimize the full power of numbers, for, as Milton said, nothing is more natural than that "the less should yield to the greater; not number to number, but virtue to virtue, and counsel to counsel." [23] Monarchy finds no place in the mixture, and the only dividing up of power is to be found in the quasi-federalism, because Milton, as Plato and Aristotle before him, knew that power cannot be divided among classes. ". . . the balance therefore [would have to] be exactly so set, as to preserve and keep up due authority on either side, as well in the Senate as in the people," [24] and this is impossible. Give the people the tribunes and they end up with the consuls, censors, and praetors as well; either all this or nothing. Constitutional government is not a balance of class against class, but a mixture of aristocracy (or oligarchy) and democracy, made possible through the rule of the "middle sort." Among the "middle sort" are to be found the "most prudent men," the men most skillful and virtuous.

While it is clear that Milton was indebted to the writers of classical antiquity for his model of constitutional government, it is not altogether clear that he shared fully their understanding of the purpose of this constitution. True, Polybius had praised Lycurgus for introducing stability into Sparta, thus interrupting the "regular cycle of constitutional revolutions," and Milton had asked first Cromwell, and after Cromwell's death, General Monk, to imitate Lycurgus. It is also true that he believed that, properly established, the free commonwealth would endure forever, that is, until Christ came to establish His commonwealth. But for both the ancients and Milton stability was merely a necessary condition of the goals of political life, it was not the purpose of political life, and therefore they would agree that institutions are laid down with a view not only to stability but to this purpose. For, assuming a solution to the problem of succession, the most stable constitution might very well be the absolute rule of one man over a completely degraded population. It is when we look to the purpose of political life that Milton seems to part company with his classical authorities, and the obvious reason for this seems to be his Christianity.

Not only religious questions in general but questions of doctrine in particular were of decisive importance to Milton, so that his efforts to reform the constitution of England were at least matched by his efforts to reform the religious life of the English, and it would be difficult to say to which he assigned priority. The bishops were as great a threat to the well-ordered constitution as was the king, and a much more immediate threat than that posed by the common people. Just as the bishop of Rome did not hesitate to seize that city and make himself temporal ruler over it, so, Milton feared, the English bishops would assert a tyrannical temporal rule over England. The bishops and the entire establishment should be abolished. Not only can a Christian understand the truth of the Scriptures without the assistance of a bishop, but bishops with political power are destructive of Christian liberty. ". . . what numbers of faithful and freeborn Englishmen, and good Christians, have been constrained to forsake their dearest home, their friends and kindred, whom nothing but the wide ocean, and the savage deserts of America, could hide and shelter from the fury of the bishops." Episcopacy is a "wen" on the body of the constitution, its ceremonies and ecclesiastical courts are "leeches" that suck the revenue and riches of the country.[25] Milton wrote as many pages devoted to the reformation of these things as he did on the reformation of political things.

Yet it is difficult to separate the two in his thought, that is, to speak of political reform without reference to religious reform, and this despite the fact that according to Milton himself the two powers, ecclesiastical and civil, are "totally distinct." It would not be altogether accurate to say that he saw only one problem, that of the relation between the ecclesiastical and the civil. Yet what was in need of reform was not the Church alone or the State alone, but the relation between them. Thus he advised Cromwell to "leave the church to itself, and have the prudence to relieve yourself and the magistrates from that burden, *which is one half, and at the same time, most remote* from your own province. . . ." [26] What he meant by this paradoxical statement can perhaps be understood from the epistle dedicatory (addressed to Parliament) to *A Treatise of Civil Power in Ecclesiastical Causes.* Here he wrote: ". . . both commonwealth and religion will at length, if ever, flourish in Christendom, when either they who govern discern between civil and religious, or they who so discern shall be admitted to govern." [27] Religious matters are not properly the concern of civil authority as is shown by the outrages committed by Archbishop Laud and his coadjutors, backed by the power of the State; on the other hand, religious matters are properly the concern of civil authority in a negative sense: it is the duty of the civil authority to maintain the separation. But Milton also means more than this. He also means that Cromwell, as a Christian lawgiver, can best promote the Christian religion—and it is his duty to promote it—by establishing and maintaining a separation of civil and ecclesiastical powers. His assistance is required to establish a free commonwealth, and the free commonwealth, more than any other form of government, will promote the liberty of conscience, "which above all other things ought to be to all men dearest and most precious. . . ." [28] It is difficult to distinguish Milton's religious teaching from his political teaching because his political reforms are guided by his religious doctrine, and, to a lesser extent, his religious reforms are guided by political considerations. (His political reforms are undoubtedly laid down with a view to Christian liberty, but there is also a civil liberty, which is independent of Christian liberty, and which is jeopardized by, among other things, an established church. With respect to civil liberty, an established church is similar to a titled nobility, because both offer preferments on a basis other than merit, and both limit the access to position by those whose only claim is merit.) It is his doctrine of Christianity, and specifically his doctrine of Christian liberty, that provides the final cause or purpose, and therefore the form, of the mixed constitution. Liberty is the goal of political life, without regard to whether it is the acknowledged goal of the majority of a particular people. Indeed, Milton knew that in 1660 the "inconsiderate multitude" seemed to be "mad" for the restoration of the monarchy, with its trappings and its religion so inimical to liberty, and that many who had once supported the cause of liberty had become "zealous backsliders." But it was neither just nor reasonable that their voices "against the main end of government should enslave the less number that would be free." Better and more just if the "able and worthy" minority were to compel the multitude, if necessary by force of arms, "to retain . . . their liberty. . . ." [29]

Milton's idea of liberty is complex, and not only because, while customarily dividing it into two parts, spiritual (or Christian) and civil liberty, in one place in the *Second Defense,* he adds a third, domestic or private liberty, and refers to the *Areopagitica* as the place where he treats not civil but this domestic liberty. It is complex because this befits the difficulties of the subject. Nowhere in his work is it reduced to a simple statement, and nothing he wrote can qualify as a treatise on the subject. The closest to it is the *Areopagitica,* but this deals, admittedly, with only one aspect of liberty. As he says in the *Second Defense,* there is, first, liberty in the sense of a means to the end, virtue: "to form and increase virtue, the most excellent thing is liberty." But in the next sentence he calls upon Cromwell to "make a better provision for the education and morals of youth," [30] a statement sufficient in itself to remind us of something we learn from the *Areopagitica* as well, that the free commonwealth is not a pluralistic society. We know, for example, that it does not tolerate "popery and open superstition," but only "neighboring differences, or rather indifferences." The citizen of the free commonwealth is assured the liberty to become virtuous, but he is not assured the liberty to define virtue in any way that happens to please him.

There is, secondly, liberty in the negative sense of liberty from government. The free commonwealth exercises no authority in ecclesiastical matters, nor, as we know, does it require the licensing of printing, thus providing a liberty of the press. The limited nature of that liberty, however, may best be seen from Milton's summary of the argument of the *Areopagitica* in his *Second Defense.* "Lastly, I wrote, after the model of a regular speech, *Areopagitica,* on the liberty of printing, that the determination of true and false, of what ought to be published and what suppressed, might not be in the hands of the few who may be charged with the inspection of books, men commonly without learning and of vulgar judgment, and by whose license and pleasure, no one is suffered to publish any thing which may be above vulgar apprehension." [31] Those "who are inclined to freedom of inquiry" have the liberty to communicate "without the private inquisition of any magisterial censor," but only at their own peril. Milton's distinction is the one made later by the common law, where the liberty of the press consisted in being able to publish without previous restraint, "and not in freedom from censure for criminal matter when published." [32] Finally, the General Council, in part because of the extent of the powers exercised at the local level, promises to restrict its governing mostly to the area of foreign affairs. This negative liberty is at least compatible with, and is probably required by, Christian liberty, which Milton defines in part as the release, through the agency of Christ, "from the rule of law and of men." What this means can perhaps best be understood from the following passage in *A Treatise of Civil Power in Ecclesiastical Causes,* written in 1659:

. . . the state of religion under the gospel is far differing from what it was under the law: then was the state of rigor, childhood, bondage and works, to all which force was not unbefitting; now is the state of grace, manhood, freedom and faith; to all which belongs willingness and reason, not force: the law was then written on tables of stone, and to be performed according to the letter, willingly or unwillingly; the gospel, our new covenant, upon the heart of every believer, to be interpreted only by the sense of charity and inward persuasion: the law had no distinct government or governors of church and commonwealth, but the Priests and Levites judged in all causes not ecclesiastical only but civil . . . which under the gospel is forbidden to all church-ministers. . . .[33]

This passage serves to introduce liberty in its exalted sense.

Men may think they are free, they may boast they are free, and they may indeed be free in the negative sense, but they may still be slaves. They may be slaves in the decisive respect of being unable to use properly the negative freedom they are given, and they are slaves if they are ignorant of right and wrong, or if they think power consists in violence, or dignity in "pride and haughtiness." They are slaves if "unnerved through luxury," if controlled by their lusts and not by their reason, if, in short, as he makes abundantly clear in the *Second Defense,* they are not masters of themselves. Liberty from law is not enough. "Unless your liberty be of that kind, which can neither be gotten, nor taken away by arms; and that alone is such, which, springing from piety, justice, temperance, in fine, from real virtue, shall take deep and intimate root in your minds; you may be assured, there will not be wanting one, who, even without arms, will speedily deprive you of what it is your boast to have gained by force of arms." [34] The liberty that can neither be won nor lost by force of arms, and the liberty on which all other liberties depend, is Christian liberty in the full meaning of the term. This is the liberty known only to the truly free man, and this is the liberty that constitutes the end or goal of political life.

Such a liberty became possible only through Christ, because it was

Christ who changed man's condition from "legal to evangelical," from one of "servility toward God" and toward God's law to one in which man is permitted to exercise a faculty he shares only with God. True, this is a liberty to "serve God," but it is a liberty to serve God "according to the best light which God has planted in [one] to that purpose," [35] and what this signifies in fact is the liberty to seek the truth. Truth came into the world with Christ, "and was a perfect shape most glorious to look on," but was later scattered about in a thousand pieces. The liberty of man consists in the search for these pieces, which means the search for what is unknown by what is known. Not only is it the liberty of man that consists in this life of seeking after truth, but it is also the dignity or the virtue of man. For in all things, God directs his offers "not to an indolent credulity, but to constant diligence, and to an unwearied search after truth. . . ." [36] To actualize Christian liberty is to seek the truth within the limits of Scripture, the seeker being guided by the Holy Spirit, and to seek the truth within the limits of Scripture guided by the Holy Spirit, "which no man can know at all times to be in himself," [37] is to seek the truth within very broad limits. It is almost to seek the truth within no limits at all.

That this is so appears from the following consideration: how a Christian judges of the power of unassisted reason will depend to some extent on what he regards as the consequences of the Fall, of man's first disobedience to God. According to Milton, man indeed lost paradise by his Fall, but the acquisition of the knowledge of good and evil elevated man above the level of his previous existence to a point where he was more like God. Milton's poetic description of the expulsion from Eden is not reminiscent of the scene of anguish depicted in, for example, Masaccio's fresco.

> Some natural tears they dropped, but wiped them soon;
> The World was all before them, where to choose
> Their place of rest, and Providence their guide:
> They hand in hand with wand'ring steps and slow,
> Through Eden took their solitary way.[38]

With the coming of Christ and the release from the Mosaic law, paradise is regained, but not the paradise of Eden, for that original state of innocence is lost irrevocably. Man now knows good and evil. The world, moreover, has known Socrates, "wisest of men," and even Christ, who rejects Satan's offer of the earthly kingdom of Athens at the height of its intellectual power, knows the intellectual beauty of classical antiquity. He rejects it because it is not "true wisdom," but, "being built on nothing firm," is mere conjecture or fancy. It is possible to distinguish the life of the truly free man, seeking truth within the limits of Scripture guided by the Holy Spirit, from the life of the philosopher of pagan antiquity, but it is not easy; not many questions open to the latter are closed to Milton. Without the liberty to winnow and sift "every doctrine," he said, and to think and write about it, "according to . . . individual faith and persuasion," men are "still enslaved, not indeed, as formerly, under the divine law, but, what is worst of all, under the law of man, or to speak more truly, under a barbarous tyranny." [39] Not many pagan thinkers held the life of the intellect in higher esteem: for what is "more delightful, what more happy than those conferences of learned and most eminent men, such as divine Plato is said to have held very frequently under that famous plane tree. . . ." [40] Happiness, for this Christian, consists in friendship, and friendship consists in seeking the truth together. It is the duty of the free commonwealth to promote this, for the free commonwealth is a "place of philosophic freedom," as England was once thought to be. The purpose of political life, which determines the form of political life, exists outside or beyond political life.

The free commonwealth honors the pursuit of knowledge and educates its citizens in such a way that they are equipped to pursue knowledge and, thereby, to exercise the freedom that Christ gave them. The free commonwealth is built not only on certain institutions but on self-governing men, men who have learned to rule themselves. How many men will learn to rule themselves and to be truly free, Milton does not say, although he wants all men to have the right to try.

## NOTES

1. *Of Reformation in England, The Complete Works of John Milton*, ed. F. A. Patterson (New York: Columbia University Press, 1931–38), III, i, 63. Cited hereafter as *Works*. Spelling has been modernized throughout.

2. *Ibid.*

3. *The Ready and Easy Way to Establish a Free Commonwealth, Works*, VI, 125.

4. *Works*, VIII, 3–5, 151.

5. *Defense of the English People, Works*, VII, 393, 75.

6. *Works*, VIII, 239.

7. *The Tenure of Kings and Magistrates, Works*, V, 14.

8. *Ibid.*, p. 18.

9. *Ready and Easy Way, Works*, VI, 120, 122.

10. *Second Defense, Works*, VIII, 235.

11. *Ready and Easy Way, Works*, VI, 120.

12. *Defense of the English People, Works*, VII, 393.

13. *Ready and Easy Way, Works*, VI, 125–26, 144.

14. *Ibid.*, p. 130.

15. *Ibid.*, p. 131. Milton is not specific concerning the method of election of local officials, but it appears that here, too, it is the "nobility and chief gentry"

who are to exercise effective power. *Ibid.*, p. 144.

16. "Now is the opportunity, now the very season wherein we may obtain a free commonwealth and establish it forever in the land." *Ibid.*, p. 125.

17. *Ibid.*, p. 131.

18. *Second Defense, Works,* VIII, 237.

19. *Ready and Easy Way, Works,* VI, 132, 144.

20. *Ibid.*, p. 119.

21. *Eikonoklastes, Works,* V, 132.

22. Aristotle *Politics* 1294$^b$ 3–8.

23. *Second Defense, Works,* VIII, 153–55.

24. *Ready and Easy Way, Works,* VI, 130.

25. *Of Reformation in England, Works,* III, i, 48–49, 54.

26. *Second Defense, Works,* VIII, 235. Italics supplied.

27. *Works,* VI, 2.

28. *Ready and Easy Way, Works,* VI, 142.

29. *Ibid.*, pp. 140–41.

30. *Works,* VIII, 237.

31. *Ibid.*, pp. 133–35.

32. Blackstone, *Commentaries,* IV. xi. 13.

33. *Works,* VI, 25.

34. *Second Defense, Works,* VIII, 237–41.

35. *Ready and Easy Way, Works,* VI, 141.

36. *Christian Doctrine, Works,* XIV, 9.

37. *Treatise of Civil Power, Works,* VI, 6.

38. *Paradise Lost,* XII.

39. *Christian Doctrine, Works,* XIV, pp. 11–13.

40. *Seventh Prolusion, Works,* XII, 263–65.

## READINGS

A.  Milton, John. *The Ready and Easy Way to Establish a Free Commonwealth.*
    Milton, John. *A Second Defense of the People of England.*
    Milton, John. *Areopagitica.*
B.  Milton, John. *Of Reformation in England.*
    Milton, John. *Of Education.*
    Milton, John. *The Tenure of Kings and Magistrates.*
    Milton, John. *A Treatise of Civil Power in Ecclesiastical Causes.*

# BENEDICT SPINOZA

## 1632–1677

Spinoza is the first philosopher to write a systematic defense of democracy; it appears in his *Theologico-Political Treatise,* published in 1670.
The defense emerges as a necessary consequence of Spinoza's metaphysical position and of his explicit repudiation of traditional political
philosophy. The most detailed statement of the metaphysical foundations
of political thought is contained in the *Ethics,* Spinoza's major work,
a study of the fundamental structure of reality or Substance, and so of
the relationship between human existence and eternal order. Spinoza's
rejection of traditional political philosophy is most clearly stated in the
opening pages of the *Political Treatise* and leads him to replace what he
regards as the imaginary and useless conceptions of traditional philosophers by the realistic, scientific analyses of political life characteristic
of such men as, above all, Machiavelli.

Spinoza's scientific metaphysics preserves to some extent that aspect
of the classical political tradition according to which an eternal order
underlies and regulates the merely human order. According to the
classical understanding, the eternal order first becomes accessible
through an analysis of this human order. But Spinoza's analysis, in
keeping with his acceptance of modern scientific procedures, entails an
initial disregard of the human order, so that the eternal order may become visible. Observation of political phenomena, as distinguished from
order, attempts to eliminate the distortion of the merely human perspective: political phenomena are recorded and analyzed exactly as the
phenomena of any other science. The human order is then "deduced"
from the scientifically revealed eternal order.

The "classical" element in Spinoza's thought, we may suggest, is a revision from the Stoic viewpoint of one strand in the Socratic teaching: Spinoza continues to recognize the need for, and the possibility of, an improvement in the human order in the light of our vision of the eternal order, but he combines this recognition with a Stoic conception of the relationship between the philosopher and eternity. This results in a curious combination of Socratic "activism" and Stoic "passivity." Philosophic fulfillment comes from contemplation of the eternal order, of which man is but a part, and in terms of which his social and political concerns are illusory temptations from serenity. But serenity depends upon the successful reconstitution of the social and political, or human order.

The influence of the Stoics upon Spinoza is visible in his "metaphysical" definition of freedom, which, in accord with his determinism, seems to identify the highest form of activity as a passive resignation in the consequences of the eternal order. In the political sphere, although it is true that Spinoza preserves the aforementioned Socratic activism, he transforms it from the activity of gentlemen to the activity of scientists, or of politicians who have been decisively influenced by a scientific understanding of political affairs. The gentleman hearkening to the philosopher is replaced in the practical sphere by the scientific politician, with a corresponding change in the practical political teaching. Freedom is conceived in the practical sphere as the intelligent expression of human power. But human power is explained in terms of a general conception of power, a conception common to every existent thing. The common conception of power makes possible a method of study which is common to all things. The combination of the conception of power and the method of study in turn produces the scientific metaphysics which purports to explain the fundamental principles of reality, the principles which are common to every aspect of reality, whether human or eternal.

The new or scientific metaphysics changes the practical political teaching because it begins from a new conception of human nature. In ignoring the "merely" human perspective, scientific metaphysics explains man in terms which are common to the human and to the nonhuman. The new scientific realism takes its bearings by the common, by what the traditional philosophers would have called the base. It does so because these common elements may be mastered by its universal method: the new conception holds forth a promise of success in political dilemmas which was not available to the excessively exalted vision of the traditional philosophers. The mastery of power, itself the greatest power, proceeds in an identical manner in both the human and the nonhuman realm. Spinoza is a student of Machiavelli, who taught that Fortuna could be mastered by strong men, and even that, through the development of an effective method, man's nature (perhaps nature itself) might be changed.

Both Spinoza and Machiavelli emphasize their intention to set out on a new way which is useful because powerful, and powerful because initiated in an understanding of men as they are, not as one would wish them to be. By stripping man of his fantasies, by beginning with man as he is in the nakedness of his natural existence, the new way is lower than the old (classical and Judaeo-Christian) way, which "lost its way" by aiming too high. The heights, or freedom and virtue based upon the control of nature by human power, can be won only through the suitably low beginning. Such a beginning in turn prefigures the replacement of the old height by a new height. The new or lower height recognizes man's debased nature, which is due to the dominance of passion over reason. To reach the heights, reason must regulate passion. Passion is best regulated by the invocation of other passions: man can be regulated, in brief, only by means of those elements which are common to all men. The regulation of men is based fundamentally on the approval of those who are to be regulated. The scientific conception of power and the universal method of analysis lead us, by way of the new conception of man, to a rejection of classical aristocracy in favor of democracy.

Reason liberated from passion is science. This liberation involves a change in the classical conception of reason. Stoic passivity is transformed into an active mastery based upon the understanding of Substance. Thus man comes into conflict with traditional religion as well, for religion also counsels a resignation to the eternal order through the mediation of obedience to God's revealed word. The initial attempt by Machiavelli to free reason from traditional religion in the sphere of politics is continued by both Hobbes and Spinoza in a similar way: both try to modify the claims of religion by a radical reinterpretation of Holy Writ.

Spinoza also retains Hobbes's (and Descartes') admiration for mathematics as the model for the new reason whereby false utopias will be replaced by a scientifically regulated will to power. In the application of "mathematical" analysis to the human order, Spinoza dissolves this order into its individual atoms in such a way that natural man is strictly presocial. For both Hobbes and Spinoza, the state of nature is consequently characterized by a primacy of the individual, that is, the multiplicity of individuals, each striving to exist in so far as its power permits, constitutes the initial *datum*. Society arises when man, the intelligent individual, recognizes the advantages of union in compromise; he recognizes that society, or the man-made instrument for the satisfaction of desires, is in general an efficient augmentation of his individual power.

There is, however, an essential difference between the thought of Hobbes and Spinoza, which is at least partially explained by the difference in their metaphysical orientation. Hobbes continues in the materialist tradition. The intelligible order, although not invented by man, is a human interpretation of the sequence or pattern of motions. The scientific expression of this interpretation begins with, and is deduced from, definitions of primary movements and of the laws of thought whereby these definitions may be combined. But man is in effect a kind of motion which differs in its internal structure from other kinds of motion. Man, as the interpreter of motions, is not explained entirely in terms of nonhuman motions. The importance of man is indicated in the political sphere by the fact that, by "natural right," Hobbes means fundamentally *human* right. Since order is relative to the decision of the individual to accept common definitions, the decisive autonomy of the individual can never be totally transformed into the security of community.

For Hobbes, the individual's need for self-preservation is more primitive than, and indeed the condition of, society, philosophy, and religion. Therefore self-preservation remains even within society in a form which is common to all individuals in the state of nature. But for Spinoza, in accord with the Stoic tradition, the eternal order is prior to, and independent of, the individual, or the decisions of the individual. For Spinoza, the transition from the state of nature to the political society is in no sense, as it is in part at least for Hobbes, the creation of order or of the conditions of power. Society is rather the condition for philosophy, or for the discovery of order. Thus philosophy, rather than the autonomous passion common to all individuals, is for Spinoza the most powerful safeguard of the individual's self-preservation.

Because Hobbes preserves in society the radical autonomy of the individual, whose passionate striving to exist interferes with his success in doing so, it is necessary to counterbalance this natural and inexpugnable pluralism by a strongly centralized government. Hobbes is a monarchist for the sake of the individual; the monarch is better able than the individuals to provide a remedy for what underlies their common fear. Furthermore, a natural autonomy means that individuals are radically equal. This equality is best preserved in a community which is as homogeneous as possible, one in which factionalism is restricted if not altogether eliminated. The monarch is a symbol of the equality of the social units in the very fact of being the unification of their social will. His will, one and indissoluble, is the reflection of the will of each individual subject as equal to every other subject. Thus monarchy is the most secure, and therefore the best of regimes.

Spinoza, on the other hand, conceives of individuals as representing, from the human viewpoint, the articulation of the eternal order into a hierarchy of parts and wholes. He is therefore able to accept natural (as distinct from conventional) differences in men as politically fundamental. The inexpugnable character of these natural differences will always necessitate a variety of kinds and functions among men in society, and therefore of opinions, which cannot be destroyed in the unity of the governing power, except at the price of destroying the social order itself. Spinoza is therefore an advocate of democracy, in which, for the sake of philosophy (which guards the interests of all), freedom of speech must be permitted in order to reflect and to satisfy the natural differences in men. In so far as democracy is the embodiment of the correct philosophical teaching, it will regulate the opinions of men by means of religious, social, and political institutions, but will not insist on uniformity of opinion.

Thus, the philosopher is by nature the "highest" man, because he is most powerful and the best safeguard of the power of nonphilosophic individuals. But, in order for philosophy to be preserved, the philosopher must support the democracy (which is in fact the manifestation of his political teaching). Otherwise, when opinion is tyrannized, philosophy is destroyed by dogma and superstition. Conversely, in order for the democracy to be preserved, it must support the freedom of philosophy. The interests of philosophy and democracy coincide, when both are properly defined.

We have already observed that Spinoza's political teaching is intended to be a deduction from his analysis of Substance. As Spinoza tells us in the *Improvement of the Understanding*,[1] he wished to direct all sciences to one end. The end of the political science is therefore identical with the end of the natural or metaphysical sciences. The fundamental principles of all sciences are the properties of Substance, and therefore all sciences proceed according to the method whereby these properties are discovered. Since men are parts of, and thus determined by, Substance (Spinoza calls such parts "modes"), the laws governing their behavior may be deduced from the general laws of substantial parts or modes.

By equating "right" with "power," and "power" with the struggle of every mode to persist, Spinoza, unlike Hobbes, denies the peculiarly human character of political phenomena;[2] as we have seen, the "human" viewpoint leads to illusions. It is in the perspective of these equations that we shall have to understand the *Theologico-Political Treatise*, in which the principles of political science are formulated on the basis of an accommodation (explicitly alluded to by Spinoza) to the (illusory) assumption that man has a special status in the universe. This also explains Spinoza's detailed concern with theology in a political book, since the traditional ground for believing in man's special status, and so for the propagation and preservation of unscientific illusions, is (in his view) religion. In the same perspective, we also understand Spinoza's remark that the entire doctrine of the *Political Treatise* follows from the premise that the desire for self-preservation is necessarily universal.[3] This premise is the proximate cause of human activity, and so it functions in the scientific presentation of political philosophy as the middle term between Substance and the structure of the best forms of government.

All sciences are to be pursued by the use of the method that is applied in mathematics; in this respect, Spinoza follows the new movement in philosophy as exemplified by Descartes. Only those conclusions are acceptable which have been deduced from adequate (clear and distinct) ideas. Ideas are adequate when they express the nature of a mode, or aspect of Substance, as it is in itself, rather than as it appears to man. By analogy from mathematics, the internal structure of the mode, though deducible from the properties of the more general structure of Substance, can be understood merely as it is, as it stands forth before the light of our understanding, and not as tending, or seeming to tend, toward some end or good beyond its intrinsic "what-ness" or determinate structure.

Thus Spinoza banishes teleology from philosophy. The attempt by the philosopher to understand how things are, as they have been determined by the laws of Substance, must not be obstructed by the fact that the philosopher has himself been determined toward the "end" of understanding. In order to acquire a true understanding of reality, the philosopher must see things as they are, and not as they appear to him because of the influence of his passions on his reason. Without such an accurate understanding he cannot achieve that mastery of reality which his passions desire.

The understanding of political phenomena is consequently different from political action based upon correct understanding. There is no reason or purpose for the properties of a sphere, for example, beyond the necessity intrinsic in the idea of a sphere that, if it is to exist at all, it must exist in a specific way. The same holds true for mankind. The study of man, as a branch of philosophy, proceeds in the same way as the study of spheres, stones, or horses. As Spinoza says in the *Ethics,* "I shall consider human actions and appetites just as if it were a question of lines, planes and solids."[4] Mathematical deduction is as appropriate to the study of man as it is to the study of stones. But stones do not engage in political activity. Man's rational nature has both a scientific and a nonscientific manner of expression. The nonscientific manner reaches its fullest development in political society, or the organization of individual power in terms of subjective feelings and desires. This subjective element is itself conditioned by man's tendency to draw a false analogy between his own purposive activity and the activities of natural things. Man reads purposes into the activities of natural things, and thereby develops religion, together with its degenerate form, superstition.

The scientific study of political phenomena requires a careful study of religion as the most decisive way in which political behavior in pre-scientific societies is conditioned. Similarly, a scientifically constructed appeal for radical political change must make accommodations to the existent forms of subjective, religious belief. The philosopher must study human passions and their modifications exactly as if they were properties of the atmosphere, but he must also consider the practical side of politics from the human or contingent viewpoint. This viewpoint, although present in both political treatises, predominates in the *Theologico-Political Treatise,* as is immediately obvious from the fact that it contains Spinoza's exhaustive treatment of religion, a subject which is touched on only lightly in the *Political Treatise.*[5] It is essential to notice that this difference between the two treatises is compatible with the fact that Spinoza's most complete statement of his political teaching is to be found in the *Theologico-Political Treatise,* precisely because it is a combination of theoretical and practical considerations.

For this teaching, two questions are paramount: (1) On the basis of the scientific understanding of human nature, what is the form of the best state (*optima respublica*)? (2) How may men be persuaded to change their present laws and customs in order to bring society into closer correspondence with the model of the best state? The *Theologico-Political Treatise,* and not the *Political Treatise,* is designed to persuade as well as to instruct. The main concern of the *Political Treatise* is in fact not the best state simply, but rather the more practical question of the best version of the three principal kinds of government: monarchy, aristocracy, and democracy.[6] Its consequently greater emphasis upon positive laws and institutions, together with an initial frankness about the scientific character of the aims and methods of political philosophy, makes it resemble much more closely than the *Theologico-Political Treatise* the present-day model of a theoretical work in political science. But Spinoza is not a present-day political scientist; he considers it part of his scientific enterprise to move men toward conduct that is theoretically justified. Political philosophy is not scientific unless it is useful. Thus the most theoretical work is the one which leads men toward the theoretically correct activity.

The *Theologico-Political Treatise* is from Spinoza's viewpoint his most complete theoretical treatment of political philosophy because it is least concerned with positive laws and institutions and most concerned with the universal motivations of human behavior. In a somewhat similar sense, one may say that Plato's *Republic* is a more complete account of his political theory than the *Laws,* precisely because the *Laws* is more concerned with the details of legislation than with the nature of the human soul. But the *Theologico-Political Treatise* is much less obviously universal in its intention than is the *Republic.* For our present purposes, the "local" character of Spinoza's treatise may be explained as due to his accommodation to the pervasive influence in his time of Holy Scripture. Since men act from passion rather than from reason,[7] they can be moved to reconstruct religious beliefs, upon which political society rests, only by a modification of the prevailing passions through a judicious replacement of the objects which gratify them.

We can thus understand the religious exterior of the *Theologico-Political Treatise.* Spinoza cannot simply reject Scripture without cutting himself off from those whom he hopes to influence. The starting point of any public appeal must of necessity be the contemporary historical situation. But the ground from which the contemporary historical situation is considered itself transcends that situation. It is the ground of the philosophical comprehension of nature; in Spinoza's famous phrase, the philosopher who stands on this ground sees the historical world *sub specie aeternitatis.* The same point may be stated as follows. According to Spinoza, human nature functions in accord with intelligible and unvarying principles. When one understands thoroughly the contemporary situation, one sees that it is rooted in the human situation as such. The roots of the contemporary situation are the principles of human nature, which are not themselves altered by the variety of historical situations. The correct theoretical analysis of contemporary society and religion requires a correct theoretical analysis of society and religion as such. The fundamental political book is a *theologico-political* treatise because it is based upon the recognition that the relationship between religion and politics is not just an accident of history, but stems from man's nature.

We turn now to a more specific consideration of the two political treatises. The link between the two works is a negative one: the absence from the *Political Treatise* of an extensive discussion of religion. But Spinoza's politicization of religion, when it is not explicitly stated, can be deduced from his theory of human nature. The two treatises are compatible with each other, just as both are compatible with the *Ethics.*

The precise form of Spinoza's religious views cannot be established here; but it is quite clear that he never challenges man's need for religion. One may agree with the statement that the *Ethics* as a whole constitutes Spinoza's exposition of a free man's worship. In his political writings, he makes it clear that there is a distinction between the religion of philosophers and the public religion. In the *Political Treatise,* he tells us that, although freedom of religious diversity is to be allowed among the people, this freedom is restricted to private belief and worship. But when discussing the rights of supreme authorities in general, and the form of an aristocracy in particular, Spinoza advocates a national religion, determined by the state, and therefore with uniform public rites. Throughout the treatise, he emphasizes the danger to public stability from a diversity of religious sects and modes of worship. This emphasis is characteristic of Spinoza's approach to each aspect of political legislation, and is a direct consequence of his view of human nature.

Since men are moved to act by passion rather than by reason, it would be folly to construct a state in which freedom rests merely upon a presumption of reason or good faith. The primary passions are fear of pain and hope of pleasure. Since each man desires nothing more deeply than his own self-preservation, the struggle to maximize pleasure and minimize pain makes men enemies by their very nature; to *fear* and *hope* may be added the basic passion of *hatred*. When men come together to form societies in an effort to safeguard individual existence through collective power, they do not for that reason change their natures, but continue to be creatures of passion. They continue to be motivated by fear and hope, and so the danger of hatred persists within society. For this reason, Spinoza continuously advises the need for the preservation of unity within the state. Political association is natural, but one of its principal functions is to curb man's passionate nature. This will best be done by playing upon the primacy of fear and hope. The principle of the state is the desire for self-preservation, and it is by this desire that men are to be led to obedience.

But the emphasis upon passion, both in the case of the individual and of the state, is compatible with Spinoza's claim to legislate according to reason and his belief that men are free only when they obey through reason rather than through fear. Man's right is identical with his power, and his power is limited by passion. Since passion can be controlled only by other passions, it is both rational and in the interest of freedom to construct the state on this basis. Society must rectify the condition of the prepolitical state of nature, wherein men are so divided by passion as to have almost no right at all. Freedom is life in accord with reason. In accord with the classical element in his thought, Spinoza conceives of the state as such as a direct expression of the rational order of the universe. Thus, in at least a qualified sense, it is reasonable to obey the law in society.

Society itself exists as the result of a common agreement by individuals to surrender their power to a sovereign authority for the sake of enhancing each man's power of self-preservation. Within society, the will of the sovereign authority is in effect the will of the reasonable individual. In the best society, the will of the individual is externalized in the best, or most reasonable, laws. To disobey the sovereign authority is to contradict oneself, to be unreasonable, to go contrary to one's best interests. Because of man's selfishness and passionate nature, if each citizen has the right of interpreting the laws, the state will be dissolved by self-interest. So each of us is bound in all things to the one mind of the commonwealth, even when we regard its decisions as iniquitous. Reason teaches us to acquire individual independence by surrendering it to the will of the state. Consequently, the most powerful and independent state may truly be said to be constituted according to the principles of right reason, which reveal the end that is in the interest of all men.

The need for unity, however, does not make men slaves to a monolithic tyranny. Since obedience is predicated upon self-interest, it is in the best interest of the sovereign authority to be reasonable: the state should avoid causing indignation among the people. It does not have the right to do so, for it does not have the power to do so, since an indignant populace is a threat to the sovereign authority's might. Just as the reasonable citizen will understand that his freedom is dependent upon a strong and united commonwealth, and that this strength and unity is not in itself an obstacle to his private freedom of thought and belief, so, too, will the sovereign authority in a reasonable state understand that it does wrong when it acts against the dictates of reason.

Spinoza is not here contradicting his regular assertions that passion is governed by passion rather than by reason. It is reasonable to appeal to self-interest rather than to religious or philosophical argument. The wrong act of the sovereign is one which causes its own ruin. Therefore, the sovereign authority is bound to act in such a way as to preserve fear and reverence among the populace. Although the social compact is no longer binding when it violates the general interest, Spinoza expressly says that the right to decide when it does so rests solely with the sovereign authority.[8] Only the sovereign authority has the power to know what is in the general interest. Nevertheless, this power is itself subject to the limitations of public passion. The sovereign authority acts in the general interest by transforming public passion into virtue and obedience, and this is done by means of good laws. Good laws are in the best interest of every citizen; therefore, they are reasonable, and, as reasonable, not to be feared. So the best commonwealth gains obedience, not by fear, but by reason. "That state is best where men pass their lives in concord, and the laws are preserved inviolate." [9] It should be understood that by reason, Spinoza has so far meant calculation in the interest of the individual.

The Spinozist state, then, transforms passion into the servant of reason by the rational understanding of man's passionate nature. Philosophy is the highest power for all men, even though its teaching must be presented in a form suited for the public mind. Philosophy is in the general interest: it is no exaggeration to say that the ultimate end of the state is philosophy. The title page of the *Theologico-Political Treatise* tells us that "freedom of philosophizing" is necessary for the preservation of piety and the public peace. The freedom of the citizen within the best state is the political manifestation of philosophical freedom. Within the state, there is a unity of citizen and sovereign. That unity depends upon rational institutions, which make the magistrates the political surrogates of the philosophers, just as the institutions are the public face of philosophy. As Spinoza says, "men are to be so led that they think themselves not to be led but to live by their own mind and by their own free opinion." [10]

On this basis, Spinoza rejects monarchy in favor of democracy. Democracy imitates the state of nature by limiting the right of the chief magistrates to the amount of their power. In the state of nature, there is a natural heterogeneity of human types which underlies the heterogeneity in amounts of power, and is itself the visible expression of the articulations in the structure of Substance. One man has not sufficient power to rule the state: monarchies are concealed aristocracies. The heterogeneity of the state of nature is in political terms the condition of the natural inequality of men. But this does not mean that one man (or a few men) has the right to rule his fellows. Since "right" is equivalent to "power," and the power of any single man is insufficient to rule (to preserve itself in accord with its best interests), the politically significant characteristic of the state of nature is not the superiority of one individual to another, but rather the variety of kinds.

This variety of human types can no more be suppressed than can the character of Substance itself. The desire of the individual must be reflected in the legal and institutional structure of the regime itself; otherwise individuals will not accept the identity of their will with that of the state. The democratic regime, or the synthesis of human types which remains faithful in its structure to the difference of those types, imitates the state of nature. But an imitation is not an identity. We may say that the democratic regime rationalizes the state of nature, or fulfills what is implicit in the state of nature. The variety of types in the state of nature contains an implicit rational inequality which is different from brute or physical inequality.

To take a simple example: The man who is able to dominate his neighbors by physical force in the state of nature may be unable to cope with threats to his power that transcend the realm of brute force. The man of superior physical strength is in fact less powerful than the man of greater intelligence. Nevertheless, he is powerful enough to destroy, under certain circumstances, the conditions, not just for his own survival, but for the survival of those who excel him in other ways. The rational democratic regime must balance the powers of strength and intelligence in order to preserve both. Spinoza conceives of this balance in such a way as to make his version of democracy differ considerably from that of most present-day writers. As his treatment of the scope of sovereign power indicates, Spinoza tends to emphasize the freedom of institutions rather than of individuals. He tends to conceive of institutions as the rational embodiment of checks upon the irrational power of the multitude. As a consequence, the freedom of individuals tends to be reserved for the private, rather than the public, sphere of the regime.

When Spinoza assesses the political intelligence of the multitude, he points out that, if they could moderate themselves, and suspend judgment when they are ignorant, they would be more fit to govern than to be governed. In his discussion of democracy in the *Political Treatise,* he says that the name "democracy" does not designate the number of voters, from whom the officeholders are chosen, but rather that there are laws which specifically determine who will be eligible to vote. In the very conception of democracy, the emphasis is upon institutions rather than upon individuals. According to Spinoza, the chief difference between an aristocracy and a democracy consists in this: in an aristocracy, the patrician governing council perpetuates itself by electing new members. In a democracy, all citizens are eligible to vote and hold office. But restrictions of age and property may reduce the number of citizens in the democracy's supreme council to less than are contained in the council of an aristocracy. This modification, in itself an expression of Spinoza's conservative understanding of democracy, is the only essential difference between the two councils. When Spinoza attributes the political ignorance of the multitude to inexperience, he is not advocating individualistic liberalism, but rather the educative function of free institutions to which individuals are subordinate (and which make them truly individuals).

Spinoza's deviation from Hobbes may be summarized in the observation that he moves from the commonly understood to a subtly understood definition of self-preservation. We have followed this transition in our analysis of the way in which a subtly understood implication of the state of nature replaces a commonly understood generalization from the most explicit form of the state of nature. The transition becomes politically manifest in the rejection of an absolute monarchy in favor of a conservative (virtually aristocratic) democracy. The principle of the conservative democracy which embodies the philosophical significance of this transition is freedom of philosophy: philosophy is the subtly understood power of self-preservation.

In order to keep philosophy free, that is, powerful, we must correctly mirror in our political regime the differing kinds of human types. Since philosophy is the understanding of the structure of Substance, it cannot flourish unless it has access to this structure. This access is obtained by observation of the differing kinds of human institutions and activities; consequently, the political regime must allow for a variety of opinions, as has already been indicated. It is important to remember that the political regime has as its highest good the preservation of philosophy. For this is not at all the same as to say that the highest good is the "freedom" of the individual. The latter statement implies a lack of natural order on the basis of which individuals may be classified. Spinoza is neither a Christian, a modern liberal, nor an existentialist: freedom is for him possible only on the condition of philosophy, and so, in the fullest sense, only the philosopher is free. The free society is absolutely dependent, not on freedom of speech in the sense of anyone's speech, but on freedom of philosophical speech. This is the heart of Spinoza's "conservatism," and it is explicitly visible in the *Theologico-Political Treatise*.

Because of the various subordinate ends of this treatise (the most important being to free philosophy from religious or popular control), however, the aforementioned explicit visibility is frequently obscured and needs to be explicitly indicated. The *Theologico-Political Treatise* is a revolutionary work. On the other hand, Spinoza wishes to initiate practical changes without disrupting the order of society. His revolution is intended as a bloodless substitute for the bloody extravagances which have been caused by the triumph of superstition over religion. In order to bring a nation to change its ways one must present instructions which are intelligible to it. Spinoza accepted the traditional distinction between the minority of philosophers and the overwhelming majority of the unphilosophical multitude. The problem of speaking in the presence of the vulgar, to say nothing of the potential philosophers who are still under vulgar influences, led Spinoza to practice great caution in the midst of his daring. In the short view, his caution was largely ineffective, but, in the long run, it seems to have been surprisingly efficient, as may be estimated by considering the change in interpretations of Spinoza during the past hundred and fifty years.

Spinoza instructs his readers in the treatise *On the Improvement of the Understanding* to speak in a manner intelligible to the multitude and to accommodate themselves to the capacity of the many as much as possible. In the *Theologico-Political Treatise* he indicates that the vulgar include all those who are not at least potential philosophers; together with the vulgar are linked all those who suffer from the same passions as the vulgar.[11] Spinoza asks men of this sort not to read his book, but it is obvious that his request cannot be enforced. The book is surely addressed to the leaders of the multitude, for it is through these leaders that the multitude may itself be changed. Spinoza, commenting on the literary form of Scripture, says that, to instruct a nation (or mankind), one must "accommodate to the maximum the reasons and definitions of his teaching to the plebeian capacity, who form the greatest part of the human genus." But this is exactly the purpose of the *Theologico-Political Treatise*: to change mankind's views about religion and to teach a new political doctrine. In the most general sense, the treatise as a whole is an accommodation to the ordinary understanding, certainly in those cases about which the many are most concerned.

Of course, philosophers are free, in their private capacity, to make the needed corrections in order to see more clearly the theoretical teaching; but precisely if they have done so will they submit their public speech and actions to the laws of the republic which the theoretical teaching advocates. Thus we must distinguish between those aspects of the *Theologico-Political Treatise* which are designed to persuade the vulgar, those which express the principles of the best republic, and those which describe the republic itself. In the third case, we ought never to forget Spinoza's words in the crucial passage concerning freedom of speech and thought: "No one can act contrary to the decrees of the sovereign power and keep it safe; but in all things one may think and judge, and consequently even speak, provided that one speaks or thinks only and solely from reason, not from guile, anger or hatred, and that he does not try to introduce anything into the state solely on the authority of his decree." [12]

To obtain the best republic, one must first purify religion, for reasons which have already been discussed. Fifteen of the twenty chapters of the *Theologico-Political Treatise* are dedicated to this task. The argument of these chapters is much too complex to be more than summarized here. So long as we understand clearly the reasons for the complexity of the subject, we are justified, in an introduction to Spinoza's political thought, in restricting ourselves to his simple but crucial conception of religion and its relation to sound political principles.

For reasons of persuasion, Spinoza accepts initially the divine origins of Scripture. He moves, however, on a path from a conventional beginning to an unconventional end. Scripture must be studied in a way analogous to the study of nature. In contrast to the position of Maimonides, the principles for the interpretation of Scripture must be drawn from Scripture itself, and not from a prior philosophical position. When we approach the Bible without bias, we find that the speculative views uttered by the prophets are like the contradictory and inadequate opinions of other nonphilosophers. A scientific analysis of Scripture, based upon historical, linguistic, and biographical data and detailed study of internal contradictions and errors in the Scriptural compilations themselves, free us from the notion that the book has authority in speculative matters. But the moral teaching of Scripture is everywhere the same and easily understood. The prophets disagree on speculative matters, but they are in complete harmony as regards the Divine Law of morality. In this respect they prefigure the citizens of the best republic. The Divine Law, as the evident universal teaching of Scripture, must be the foundation of our understanding of Holy Writ.

True religion has authority solely over action; any religion which claims to exercise theoretical authority is superstition: "The end of philosophy is nothing but truth; of faith, however, as we have abundantly shown, the end is nothing other than obedience and piety." [13] Since "obedience" means obedience to God's law, the content of obedience is determined by the definition of piety. What is piety? The answer, as derived from Scripture, is clear, distinct, and simple. First, piety requires assent in a minimal number of theoretical propositions, as for example that an omnipotent God exists, upon whom our salvation depends. Second, true virtue consists entirely in love of God and neighbor. Love of God is expressed by love of one's neighbor (and by conforming to the public modes of worship). To love one's neighbor is to respect his rights. Since his rights are determined by positive law, piety not only demands that we obey the laws of the state, but consists in such obedience.

The true teaching of Scripture has been interpreted to make piety virtually identical with law-abidingness and patriotism. By restricting the authority of religion to morality (the precise rules of which are defined by the political order), Spinoza has freed reason from the dangers of superstition without destroying the beneficial results of faith. Reason and revelation are shown to agree, both with respect to the content of morality or religion, and also concerning the sense in which they are independent of each other and the sense in which they are related. The universal covenant, which replaced the special covenant between God and the Jews (and by means of which we have innate knowledge of God as the source of morality), is the religious manifestation of these innate ideas from which reason deduces the principles of morality. Finally, revelation alone provides man with the proof that salvation rests upon his obedience to these principles. Since the principles of morality are most adequately expressed, according to Spinoza's political argument, in the laws of the best regime, religion in effect furnishes proof that piety consists strictly in obedience to the right political order, and more generally to one's legally constituted government.

In the closing chapters of the *Theologico-Political Treatise* Spinoza demonstrates that the political teaching of natural reason is in harmony with revealed morality, as has just been noted. Natural reason teaches us the *jus naturale,* which pertains to every finite being. Activity originates in the struggle for self-preservation. For example, fish use the water and eat smaller fish by a natural right which is simply an expression of their determinate being. As Spinoza says, "nature, taken absolutely, has absolute right to all things it can get or do. In other words, natural right is coextensive with power." [14] Thus, in the state of nature, wrongdoing is impossible: nothing which one can do is prohibited, for all occurrences are natural. Wrongdoing becomes possible only within a society, as the violation of the law. Wrongdoing is a violation of the fundamental desire for self-preservation. That is, man is by nature a political animal, because political society is necessary for human survival and perfection. Society is created by reason and is the instrument whereby reason perfects itself. The perfection of reason is the perfection of man as such: the perfection of his power. In order to perfect his power, man is led, not merely into society, but to an effort to understand, and to actualize, the best society.

It is rational to moderate one's behavior according to circumstances. Men have a variety of natures, and this, together with the fact that so few are philosophers, requires that the best society be acccommodated to the nature of the majority. A fundamental accommodation of this sort is the recognition that all men are moved by their calculation of goods (pleasures) and evils (pains), but that few are capable of making such calculations accurately. The social compact on which the best regime is based can be preserved only by an appeal to self-interest: "everyone has by nature the right to act with guile, nor is he required to observe his pacts, unless in the hope of a greater good or in fear of a greater evil." [15] Spinoza must demonstrate, both to the few and (in a sense) to the many, that his best regime is so great a guarantor of goods as to make disobedience to it a contradiction of self-interest.

In accord with the primacy of self-interest, Spinoza formulates his preference for a democracy. The state exists for the sake of the individual, but it is for the individual's sake that he subordinates individuality to the common power. In his chapter on aristocracy in the *Political Treatise,* Spinoza says that it is right to treat all citizens as equals, because the power of each, with respect to the entire state, is negligible. The same conception of equality is applicable to democracy. Each individual cedes to the state all of his power, so that the democracy is "a collective assemblage of men which has collectively the highest right to all things within its power." Whether "from a free spirit or in fear of the highest punishment," [16] each citizen will thereafter be required to obey the sovereign authority. If all people agree to transfer all of their power to one government which expresses the will of all, then all are participating in self-government. This is nothing other than seeing to one's self-preservation. Since democracy gratifies this natural desire by being compatible with the variety of natures having a common general goal, democracy is preferable to other regimes.

One striking feature of Spinoza's democracy is that it gives to the sovereign power the right "to make whatever laws about religion that it decides." [17] Spinoza does not intend, of course, to abolish religion. He wishes, rather, to avoid subjecting the state to "the diverse judgments and passions of everyone. . . ." [18] Furthermore, when clergymen are granted political power, it tends to corrupt them, to the detriment of both Church and State. The form of the democracy must be such as to balance the need for public harmony and stability with the excellence of private freedom in speech, thought, and faith. The right of the sovereign authority to make religious legislation follows from the natural right of the state to supervise all matters concerning the self-preservation of its citizens. This right is expressed in the form of a contract according to which the sovereign power is alone responsible for the articulation of legal codes; but its actions must obviously be tempered by the danger of losing power. Spinoza discusses this question, together with the relationship between statesmen and priests, within an analysis of the first Jewish commonwealth as established by Moses.

Spinoza deduces specific political doctrines from that analysis. The first Jewish commonwealth ought by no means to be copied in its entirety, since the exclusive covenant with God upon which it was based is no longer valid. The new demands which follow from the universal covenant are symbolized by Spinoza's remark that the Jewish constitution is useless for states desiring foreign relations. The doctrines to be learned from study of the Jewish commonwealth may be summarized as follows: (1) there must be a separation of the religious and political functions; (2) speculative matters must not be referred to the Divine Law, for religion must consist in actions only; (3) the sovereign power must have entire right to decide what is lawful and what is not; (4) more harm than good ensues from a change in the form of government. The third conclusion is sufficiently important to merit an entire chapter. "Religion acquires its force as law solely from the decrees of the sovereign. God has no special kingdom among men except in so far as He reigns through temporal rulers." [19] Inner piety cannot be legislated; outer piety is manifested in justice and charity. God cannot be conceived as a lawgiver; His precepts become law only through the mediation of the duly constituted authority.

Despite the power of the sovereign to legislate as it wishes with respect to religion, Spinoza emphasizes that freedom of religious belief is necessary for the well-being of the sovereign power itself. This emphasis is in effect identical with Spinoza's defense of free speech. Suppression of thought is impossible; far better to allow discussion in most affairs than to force men into secret factionalism. Since the true end of government is liberty, men should be free to discuss even the laws, short of inciting to sedition. Freedom to discuss the laws is inseparable from freedom of religious discussion, and freedom of discussion in general is necessary for the progress of the arts and sciences. The health of philosophy depends upon such freedom. There are disadvantages to free speech, but the advantages are far more weighty. It should not be overlooked, however, that such freedom is not unrestricted. Those citizens who are most capable of speculative thought and speech will be restrained by considerations of private and public good from advocating doctrines which contradict the public laws and customs. Interest and reason thus combine to provide a balance between liberty and restraint. The test of the legitimacy of speech is thus the law. Since the law must be preserved, action must submit to the law's censorship. Censorship is both direct and indirect, depending upon the degree of understanding of the individual citizen, that is, upon his power to speak and think. Since power is equivalent to right, freedom and discretion are rendered compatible.

Jewish political virtue forms one element in Spinoza's best regime, but it is not sufficient. Its defect may be summarized in Spinoza's remark that the Jews despised philosophy, and that life for them was one long school of obedience to the elaborate law which differentiated them from all other men. Christianity, on the other hand, may be used to show that the apolitical character of religion leaves room for philosophical speculation. Philosophers and apostles alike argue rationally; the *logos* of Christianity can be compared with the *logos* of philosophy; but the law or *nomos* of Judaism cannot be. The virtue of obedience therefore suffers from an intrinsic defect which must be remedied by the possibility of philosophy. Despite his synthesis of elements of Judaism and Christianity, Spinoza is able to show that each separately, when correctly interpreted, is equivalent to his definition of the true universal religion.

We noted initially that the difference between the *Political Treatise* and the *Theologico-Political Treatise* lay in the relative silence of the former with respect to religion. It should now be clear that there is a second fundamental difference between the two treatises. The *Theologico-Political Treatise* is concerned with the political status of philosophy, as the *Political Treatise* is not. This concern is inseparable for Spinoza from a concern with religion and ultimately with superstition. The fully adequate treatment of political science is then the one which deals with the way in which philosophy must be preserved from superstitious corruptions of religion. The defense of democracy is essentially a defense of those conditions which make possible the development of philosophy. The details of Spinoza's conception of democracy, which are perhaps most fundamentally characterized by the aforementioned balance of liberty and restraint, express his understanding of the impossibility of sundering freedom from danger.

The political philosophy of Spinoza is of special interest today because it combines the acceptance of modern science with the traditional conception of the normative function of philosophy. Like Machiavelli and Hobbes, Spinoza believed that he had understood correctly man's nature, and therefore that his analysis of the political situation was the one true political teaching. Like Descartes and Hobbes, Spinoza saw no contradiction between mathematics and the mathematical mode of reasoning on the one hand, and the possibility of constructing a detailed philosophy on the other, a philosophy which would express the truth about the principles of every aspect of man's experience. In a more immediate political sense, Spinoza's version of democracy, apart from its historical importance, reminds us in a detailed and luminous manner of the difficulties which must be faced by all those who love freedom, and especially of the impossibility of preserving freedom when a love of speculation is absent.

## NOTES

1. Benedict Spinoza, *Improvement of the Understanding,* in *Works,* ed. van Vloten and Land (3rd ed.; 4 vols. bound as 2; The Hague: Nijhoff, 1914.), I, 7. Quotations in this chapter have been translated by the author.
2. *Ethics* I. iii. 6–9.
3. *Political Treatise,* II. iii. 18.
4. *Ethics* I. iii. Preface.
5. *Political Treatise,* II. viii. 46.
6. *Ibid.,* p. 31.
7. *Ibid.,* ii. 4–6.
8. *Ibid.,* iv. 6.

9. *Ibid.,* v. 2.
10. *Ibid.,* x. 7.
11. *Theologico-Political Treatise,* II, v, p. 92.
12. *Ibid.,* xx, p. 306.
13. *Ibid.,* xv, p. 249.
14. *Ibid.,* xvi, p. 258.
15. *Ibid.,* p. 261.
16. *Ibid.,* p. 262.
17. *Ibid.,* p. 268.
18. *Ibid.*
19. *Ibid.,* xix, p. 295.

## READINGS

A. Spinoza, Benedict. *Theologico-Political Treatise,* in *The Chief Works of Benedict Spinoza.* Trans. with an introduction by R.H.M. Elwes. New York: Dover, 1951. Preface, chaps iv, vi–vii, xii–xx.
   Spinoza, Benedict. *Political Treatise,* in *ibid.* Chaps i–v, viii.
B. Spinoza, Benedict. *Theologico-Political Treatise,* in *ibid.* Chaps i–iii, v, viii–xi.
   Spinoza, Benedict. *Political Treatise,* in *ibid.* Chaps vi–vii, ix–xi.
   Spinoza, Benedict. *Ethics,* in *ibid.* Bk I, appendix; bk III, preface; bk IV, propositions 7, 37 (scholium 2).
   Spinoza, Benedict. *Epistle 50,* in *ibid.* (to Jarig Jellis; numeration according to van Vloten's ed.).

# JOHN LOCKE

## 1632–1704

Near the beginning of his *Two Treatises of Government*,[1] John Locke used the following words to describe the political doctrine of Sir Robert Filmer, an author with whom he strongly disagreed: "[Filmer's] system ... is no more but this: *That all government is absolute monarchy.* And the ground he builds on is this: *That no man is born free.*"[2]

Locke's own political teaching may be stated in opposite terms but with similar brevity, in this way: *All government is limited in its powers and exists only by the consent of the governed.* And the ground Locke builds on is this: *All men are born free.*

The theme of human freedom characterizes those of Locke's works which are most important for an understanding of his political thought: in *A Letter Concerning Toleration* (1689), he wrote of religious freedom; in the *Two Treatises of Government* (1690), of political freedom; and in *Some Considerations of the Consequences of the Lowering of Interest and Raising the Value of Money* (1691), of economic freedom. Each of these works is an instructive examination of the principle of human freedom, but since this principle receives its fullest and most political statement in the *Two Treatises,* this chapter will be confined almost entirely to a description and analysis of that work.

Book I of the *Two Treatises* (usually referred to as the *First Treatise* or *Of Government,* and now infrequently published and seldom read) is devoted primarily to a discussion and refutation of the argument advanced by Filmer that kings rule by a divine right inherited from Adam. Book II of the *Two Treatises* (usually called the *Second Treatise* or *Of Civil Government,* and often published and read as if a separate work) begins with a brief summary of the argument of the

*First Treatise;* having refuted the principle of divine right, which many then considered to be the foundation of princely power, Locke acknowledged his responsibility to explain what he considered to be the true foundation of government.

Locke's inquiry begins with the great question: What is political power? To answer that question—"to understand political power right" (§4)* and to explain the "true original, extent, and end of civil government" [3]—is the major concern of the *Second Treatise.* We are first presented with a definition:

*Political power,* then, I take to be *a right* of making laws, with penalties of death and, consequently, all less penalties for the regulating and preserving of property, and of employing the force of the community in the execution of such laws and in the defense of the commonwealth from foreign injury, and all this only for the public good [§3].

But we are told at once that to understand this definition we must first consider "what state all men are naturally in," and that is "a state of perfect freedom" and "a state also of equality." Natural freedom derives from natural equality,

there being nothing more evident than that creatures of the same species and rank, promiscuously born to all the same advantages of nature and the use of the same faculties, should also be equal one amongst another, without subordination or subjection [§4].

But though this state of nature is a state of liberty, "yet it is not a state of license. . . . The state of nature has a law of nature to govern it which obliges everyone" (§6). The natural liberty of man is not to be understood as meaning that men are not restrained by any law, for "in all the states of created beings capable of laws, where there is no law, there is no freedom" (§57). "The natural liberty of man is . . . to have only the law of nature for his rule," "to be under no other restraint but the law of nature" (§22).

And reason, which is that law, teaches all mankind who will but consult it that, being all equal and independent, no one ought to harm another in his life, health, liberty, or possessions. . . . And being furnished with like faculties, sharing all in one community of nature, there cannot be supposed any such subordination among us that may authorize us to destroy one another, as if

* All references in the text of this chapter are to sections of the *Second Treatise.*

we were made for one another's uses, as the inferior ranks of creatures are for ours [§6].

Thus the dictates of the law of nature in the state of nature seem very different from what we were previously taught by Hobbes. According to Hobbes, the state of nature is a state of war "of every man against every man." But Locke does not equate the states of nature and war; he instead speaks of

the plain difference between the state of nature and the state of war which, however some men have confounded, are as far distant as a state of peace, good will, mutual assistance, and preservation, and a state of enmity, malice, violence, and mutual destruction are one from another [§19].

Our first impression of Locke's state of nature, then, is of men living together amicably, in the first ages of mankind, before the advent of civil society, enjoying natural freedom and equality in an atmosphere of peace and good will, under the beneficent rule of the law of nature.

But let us now examine in greater detail the main elements of this first impression. What is the state of nature? How peaceful is it? And what is the law of nature which governs it?

Our first observation on closer inspection is that the state of nature is not limited to the original, prepolitical condition of man. In fact, when Locke first answers the question whether the state of nature ever existed, the example he offers is not at all one of prepolitical men, but rather of men who are essentially, and to an unusual degree, political:

It is often asked as a mighty objection, where are or ever were there any men in such a state of nature? To which it may suffice as an answer at present that, since all princes and rulers of independent governments all through the world are in a state of nature, it is plain the world never was, nor ever will be, without numbers of men in that state [§14].

All princes and rulers—civilized men living in a civil relation with many other men—are in the state of nature. A subsequent example is of a Swiss and an Indian, at least one of them a man with political experience, meeting in the woods of America; of them Locke says, "they are *perfectly* in a state of nature in reference to one another" (§14, italics supplied). If, as we see, the phrase "state of nature" is sometimes not related to the condition of prepolitical man, what, then, in precise terms, is the state of nature? Locke provides this brief definition:

Men living together according to reason, without a common superior on earth with authority to judge between them, is *properly the state of nature* [§19].

The state of nature is more comprehensive than a description of the condition of man prior to the advent of civil society. It is a certain form of human relationship; its existence, when it exists, is without reference to the degree of political experience of the men in it; and it may exist at any time in the history of mankind, including the present: "wherever there are any number of men, *however associated,* that have no ... decisive power to appeal to, there they are still in the state of nature" (§89, italics supplied).

Using the terms of the definition of the state of nature, we can derive a definition of its opposite. That would be a state of men living together *with* a common superior on earth with authority to judge between them. In other words, the opposite of the state of nature is civil society:

Those who are united into one body and have a common established law and judicature to appeal to, with authority to decide controversies between them and punish offenders, are in civil society one with another; but those who have no such common appeal, I mean on earth, are still in the state of nature. . . [§87].

This makes clearer the sense in which the state of nature and the state of war are not to be confounded. They are not identical and yet they are not opposites. Their difference lies in the fact that they are not things of the same kind. It would be as wrong to confuse the state of nature and the state of war as to confuse civil society and the state of war; such a confusion would reveal a misunderstanding of their definitions, for the definition of the state of war does not include the essential term ("a common superior") of the definitions of both the state of nature and civil society.

The words that define the state of war introduce a wholly different element, that is, the *use of force* without right, without justice, without authority. "The use of force without authority always puts him that uses it into a state of war" (§155); "it is the unjust use of force then that puts a man into the state of war with another" (§181); "whosoever uses force without right ... puts himself into a state of war with those against whom he so uses it. . ." (§232). And, finally, "it is such force *alone*" (§207, italics supplied) which establishes the state of war; that is, the existence of the state of war does not depend on the presence or the absence of a common judge:

Want of a common judge with authority puts all men in a state of nature; force without right upon a man's person makes a state of war, *both where there is, and is not a common judge* [§19, italics supplied].

Since the use of force without right defines the state of war, its opposite, the state of peace, would be defined as the condition of men living together where there is *no* use of force without right (or, the same thing, where force is used only with right). Now we may state fully the sense in which the state of nature and the state of war differ:

1. The state of nature is characterized by the absence of a common judge and by the absence of any law but the law of nature.

2. Civil society, its opposite, is characterized by the presence of a common judge with authority to enforce civil law.

Then, in addition, either within the state of nature or within civil society:

3. The state of war exists if force is used without right.

4. Or the state of peace, its opposite, exists if there is no use of force without right.

This means that in the state of nature, and also in civil society, at some times a state of peace may prevail and at other times a state of war, and that however clearly we may have distinguished the state of nature and the state of war one from another, we have not at all disposed of the essential question: Will there be war in the state of nature?

But before we turn to that question we must first understand how it is that the state of war can exist within civil society, where there is a common judge with authority to prevent the use of force without right. As a matter of fact, just before Locke says that a state of war can exist "both where there is, and is not, a common judge," he gives a definition which seems to say the opposite, which seems to exclude the state of war from civil society:

But force, or a declared design of force, upon the person of another, *where there is no common superior on earth* to appeal to for relief, is the state of war. . . [§19, italics supplied].

The resolution of this difficulty lies in the fact that even in civil society the power of the civil authority cannot always be operative:

Thus a thief, whom I cannot harm but by appeal to the law for having stolen all that I am worth, I may kill when he sets on me to rob me but of my horse or coat, because the law, which was made for my preservation, where it cannot interpose to secure my life from present force, which if lost, is capable of no reparation, permits me my own defense and the right of war, a liberty to kill the aggressor, because the aggressor allows not time to appeal to our common judge. . . [§19].

The state of war can exist within civil society only when the force of the common judge is rendered ineffectual. It is as if the parties—even though they be fellow citizens met on the king's highway—were for the moment in the state of nature, without a common judge to settle their differences. Thus we see that the state of war can occur in civil society only to the extent that the state of nature can occur within civil society. Speaking precisely, the state of war cannot exist where civil authority is presently and effectively enforcing the law of society. The state of war can occur only in the absence of such civil authority; the state of war can exist only in the state of nature or something temporarily approximating it. What seems to be the state of war in civil society is rather this: the state of war in the state of nature within civil society. The state of nature is "the state all men are naturally in"; civil society is a human contrivance which obscures, for the most part, the inescapable fact that the state of nature persists, at least partially, and is ineradicable. As we shall see later, Locke makes use of this concept of the recurrence of the state of nature and the state of war within civil society; it is in those terms that he asserts the right to resist the exercise of arbitrary, tyrannical power. Thus Locke is able to speak of the state of war occurring in civil society and also, without contradicting himself, to speak of "civil society being a state of peace amongst those who are of it, from whom the state of war is excluded. . ." (§212).

In the manner just described, war can indeed occur in civil society as well as in the state of nature—with, however, these decisive differences: war is more likely to begin in the state of nature than in civil society and, once begun, is also more difficult to terminate there, because force cannot give way to "the fair determination of the law" (§20), as it does in civil society.

Let us now return to consideration of the state of nature in the more limited and more revealing sense of the original, prepolitical condition of man, and let us ask once again: Will there be war in that state? Of numerous passages we might cite, perhaps these will suffice to indicate the answer to the question:

I easily grant that civil government is the proper remedy for the inconveniences of the state of nature, which must certainly be great where men may be judges in their own case, since it is easy to be imagined that he who was so unjust as to do his brother an injury will scarce be so just as to condemn himself for it [§13].

The state of nature is "not to be endured," because of "those evils which necessarily follow from men's being judges in their own cases." In the state of nature, "everyone has the executive power of the law of nature" (§13), and although the law of nature is "intelligible and plain to a rational creature and a studier of that law" (§12), "yet men, being biased by their interest as well as ignorant for want of study of it, are not apt to allow of it as a law binding to them in the application of it to their particular cases" (§124).

If the executive power of the law in any state should be in the hands of ignorant and biased men who misapply it against others and refuse its application to themselves, will the enforcement of the law in that state differ in any significant way from the use of force without right? Locke provides many similar passages to support the conclusion that the state of nature will frequently be indistinguishable from a state of war.

But this conclusion seems incompatible with the earlier description of the state of nature ("men living together according to reason"), unless we entertain the possibility that Locke was urging on his readers the very strange doctrine that reason sometimes counsels men to kill other men. The conclusion seems also to contradict the teaching of the law of nature that "no one ought to harm another in his life, health, liberty, or possessions" (§6). What then is the law of nature and what are the obligations it imposes?

The obligations of the law of nature are stated in two ways. Every man is obliged to preserve himself, and every man is obliged to preserve all mankind:

Every one, as he is bound to preserve himself and not to quit his station will-fully, so by the like reason, when his own preservation comes not in competi-tion, ought he, as much as he can, to preserve the rest of mankind, and may not, unless it be to do justice on an offender, take away or impair the life, or what tends to the preservation of the life, the liberty, health, limb, or goods of another [§6].

We have in this passage direct, explicit statements of unselfish obliga-tions of restraint in relations with our fellow men, but, as we see, they are not without qualification. Under the conditions of the original state, will a man's "own preservation" come often "in competition"? When it does, what then is his obligation? To what extent will he be able to act "to preserve the rest of mankind"? What considerations will guide him when he undertakes "to do justice on an offender"? By the law of nature "he is bound to preserve himself"; he also has the duty, "as much as he can, to preserve the rest of mankind." Will his two duties conflict?

Many passages indicate that there is a surprisingly close connection between self-preservation and the obligation to preserve all mankind. In example after example the execution of the duty to preserve others is coupled with the right to kill another man who threatens or might threaten one's own preservation. The aggressor against me is to be treated as one unfit to associate with human beings, as a savage beast, as, therefore, a threat to *all* mankind. It is

reasonable and just I should have a right to destroy that which threatens me with destruction; for, by the fundamental law of nature, man being to be preserved as much as possible, when all cannot be preserved, the safety of the innocent is to be preferred; and one may destroy a man who makes war upon him, or has discovered an enmity to his being, for the same reason that he may kill a wolf or a lion. . . [§16].

In this formulation there seems to be no conflict between the duty to preserve oneself and the duty to preserve all mankind as much as can be. But the possibility of misjudgment is obvious, if a man is forced to judge not only "who makes war upon him," but also who has "an enmity to his being," and, on the basis of that judgment, to destroy him. Thus a zealous effort to fulfill the obligation to preserve the rest of mankind may in practice be indistinguishable from an excessive concern for self-preservation and may itself, in the absence of other restraint, become an unprovoked threat to peace and the preservation of others.

Aggression against others is indeed a violation of the law of nature: it exposes all to increased danger; it jeopardizes preservation. If the law of nature is misunderstood, as it will be by those who do not study it, that is, by those who, driven by their strong desire for self-preservation, do not consider sufficiently the importance of the conditions of general peace for their own preservation, destruction of life will be the general result.

The connection between the law of nature and the desire for self-preservation is profound. "The first and strongest desire God planted in men, and wrought into the very principles of their nature, being that of self-preservation," [4] men are assured that in pursuing that desire they are also fulfilling their obligation to God and nature:

For the desire, strong desire of preserving his life and being, having been planted in [man] as a principle of action by God himself, reason, which was the voice of God in him, could not but teach him and assure him that, pursuing that natural inclination he had to preserve his being, he followed the will of his Maker. . . .[5]

A course of conduct which tends toward self-preservation, then, is not only in accord with reason, which is the law of nature, but it is, one may say, the very definition of reasonable behavior. In this sense, the law of nature is known to all men, and, in this sense, men cannot but follow its dictates. But in another sense, that of understanding the means by which that desire might be fulfilled, men are ignorant of the law of nature "for want of study of it," and therefore they unwittingly behave contrary to its dictates, contrary to reason, that is, contrary to their interest in their own preservation. However the law of nature may be "writ in the hearts of all mankind" (§11), in one sense, in the other there is little likelihood that men in the state of nature can know how to obey it. The law of nature is both known and not known. Men must discover and contrive the conditions that will enable them to fulfill their natural desire for self-preservation.

The source of the law of nature is thus to be found in the strongest desire of men. The law of nature has peace and preservation as its end. It will be obeyed because of the universal desire for preservation; it does not rely for enforcement on obligations to others. Although some relation to earlier teachings may be seen in this, compared to classical and medieval concepts of the law of nature it is indeed "a very strange doctrine" (§9), for this law of nature concerns itself neither with the excellence of man nor with the love of God and of man for his fellow man. Locke, it must be said, does not explicitly deny the importance of excellence or love; he simply disregards them. For that matter, he barely uses or does not use at all, in the *Second Treatise,* such words as *charity, soul, ethics, morality, virtue, noble,* or *love.* They are not essential to his explanation of the foundation of civil society. For that task he names other, more powerful and universal forces in human nature—and, above all, the strongest. It is as if he had said: I do not deny that men are often moderate and just, and that some strive for excellence; nor do I deny that some are moved by fear or love of God, and love and charity for their fellow man. I assert only that when we consider the true foundations of political society, the real origins of government, none of these is of sufficient consequence to merit mention. What counts is what is universal and powerful, what exists with controlling force within every man, what can be relied upon to govern the behavior of man.

The basis of the law of nature is that strongest desire implanted within every man. The desire for self-preservation determines how men will behave; since men are not able to behave otherwise, such behavior can never be wrong ("God and nature never allowing a man so to abandon himself as to neglect his own preservation" [§168]); men must be acknowledged to have a *right* to do what they are unable not to do. No government is securely grounded in nature which does not permit and even encourage men to act as they cannot help acting. This unvarying principle of action governs the behavior of men in varying circumstances and conditions; an understanding of it as the basis of the law of nature, therefore, is the necessary foundation of an inquiry into the nature of political power. And so when we read Locke's statement that the civil laws of political society "are only so far right as they are founded on the law of nature, by which they are to be regulated and interpreted"

(§12), we must keep in mind the content of that law of nature, if we are to appreciate its political significance:

The obligations of the law of nature cease not in society but only in many cases are drawn closer and have by human laws known penalties annexed to them to enforce their observation. Thus the law of nature stands as an eternal rule to all men, legislators as well as others. The rules that they make for other men's actions must, as well as their own and other men's actions, be conformable to the law of nature, i.e., to the will of God, of which that is a declaration, and the fundamental law of nature being the preservation of mankind, no human sanction can be good or valid against it [§135].

The first impression of Locke's state of nature seems very unlike Hobbes's state of nature, as was said. But, in fact, we have discovered three significant similarities. However Locke may have distinguished the state of nature and the state of war, the state of nature is the home— and the only home—of the state of war: the state of nature is "an ill condition" "not to be endured." Secondly, the source, content, and end of the law of nature can be stated, briefly and not inaccurately, in the word *self-preservation*. And finally, Locke's teaching is not unlike Hobbes's in the assertion that "civil government is the proper remedy for the inconveniences of the state of nature."

Yet we must not lose sight of the validity of that first impression. There is, notwithstanding their similarities, a deep and significant difference in the two teachings: Locke's state of nature is *not* as violent as Hobbes's. If, as it seems, force will commonly be used without right in Locke's state of nature, it is not because most men are vicious or savage and bloodthirsty; Locke does not, as Hobbes does, speak of every man as the potential murderer of every other man. The main threat to the preservation of life in the state of nature lies not in the murderous tendencies of men but rather, as we shall see, in the poverty and hardship of their natural condition.

Since the defects of the state of nature differ in the two accounts, the remedies proposed by Locke and Hobbes differ accordingly. The main consequence of the crucial difference in the two accounts is the fact that the civil government Locke propounds has a character far less violent and absolute than Hobbes's. And the most obvious sign of the difference is the very much greater attention Locke gives to the subject of property.

The beginning of Locke's discussion of property has three elements: (1) an assertion or supposition about the original divine donation of

the world to man; (2) a question, stemming from the assertion or supposition, concerning the origin of private property; and (3) the promise
of an answer to the question:

. . . 'tis very clear that God . . . has given the earth to the children of men,
given it to mankind in common. But this being supposed, it seems to some a
very great difficulty how anyone should ever come to have a property in anything. . . . I shall endeavor to show how men might come to have a property
in several parts of that which God gave to mankind in common, and that
without any express compact of all the commoners [§25].

In the original universal common of which Locke speaks, "nobody has originally a private dominion exclusive of the rest of mankind" (§26). Every man has an equal right to every part of what is
common. This cannot mean, however, that everyone has a share in the
ownership of everything; it can only mean that originally there was no
ownership, there was no property. If in the universal common any man
has a right to help himself to any part of the common without the consent of the others, then the others have no property, for it is the nature
of property "that without a man's own consent, it cannot be taken from
him" (§193). The assertion that the world was given to mankind in
common means, simply, that in the beginning no one owned anything.
The original universal common was a state of universal propertylessness.
That is why Locke proceeds at once to the question: How did anyone
"ever come to have a property in anything"?

The answer lies in this, that there was one exception to the otherwise
universal common; that sole exception was the person of each man
himself:

Though the earth and all inferior creatures be common to all men, yet every
man has a property in his own person. This nobody has any right to but
himself [§27].

Furthermore, every man owns not only his own person but also his
own labor, which is the immediate extension of his person: "the labor
of his body and the work of his hands, we may say, are properly
his" (§27). The property which every man has in his own person and in
his own labor is the original and natural property; it is the foundation of
all other property in the state of nature. All other property, then, was
derivative from that original, natural, and underived property.

In the earliest times there were vast uncultivated territories and very
few men; there were therefore ample supplies of natural provisions
fit for food—fruits and wild beasts. In this setting of abundance (and
even superabundance) of provisions, the apples you gathered were yours,

for you had combined what belonged only to you (your labor in gathering them) with something that belonged to no one (the apples hanging on the trees or lying on the ground). Another might contest your property in them, claiming that, by removing those apples from the common state, you had deprived him of the opportunity to take them for himself. Although this objection would otherwise be valid, it is fully overcome by a reminder of the condition of abundance, in the form of a decisive and always present qualification: whatever you remove from the natural common and mix your labor with is yours *"where there is enough and as good left in common for others"* (§27, italics supplied). In the state of nature, you come to own unowned apples simply by picking them, if there are so many more unowned apples left on and under the trees that anyone else may have as many simply by picking them himself. Another who contests your property in the picked apples is really not claiming the apples that were common. If apples alone are all he wants, there are enough and as good still left for his taking. By claiming the apples already in your possession, he is really seeking only the labor you have mixed with them—and to that labor he never had any right:

For this labor being the unquestionable property of the laborer, no man but he can have a right to what that is once joined to, at least where there is enough and as good left in common for others [§27].

Property in land is, in the state of nature, acquired in the same way. "As much land as a man tills, plants, improves, cultivates, and can use the product of, so much is his property" (§32). And if the objection is raised, that by thus enclosing the land he deprived another, the same rebuttal, based on the same qualification, applies:

Nor was this appropriation of any parcel of land by improving it any prejudice to any other man, since there was still enough and as good left, and more than the yet unprovided could use. So that, in effect, there was never the less left for others because of his enclosure for himself. For he that leaves as much as another can make use of does as good as take nothing at all [§33].

This property is a combination of what is private—labor—and what is common—the land. Why then does the combination of the private and the common produce a result that is wholly private?

Nor is it so strange, as perhaps before consideration it may appear, that the property of labor should be able to overbalance the community of land. For it is labor indeed that puts the difference of value on everything. . . [§40].

When there is so much land for so few people, however much one may enclose, more than enough remains for the others: it is as if nothing had been taken. What is taken is of little or no account; land without labor "would scarcely be worth anything" (§43). This is another way Locke has of stating why the combination of the private and the common results in private property: the private component, labor, constitutes almost entirely the value of the thing; the materials, the common element, are "scarce to be reckoned in." Labor gives title to property in the state of nature primarily because "labor makes the far greatest part of the value of things we enjoy in this world" (§42). If the addition of my labor made something valuable which was, without it, "almost worthless" (§43), then surely, my labor being the only thing of value in it, it must be acknowledged that the labor made it mine.

There are two reasons why the natural provisions are, in themselves, almost worthless. The first is that an apple can provide no benefit to a man until it is picked or in some way appropriated, nor a deer until it is hunted and caught. The fruits and beasts, as they exist in nature, before any addition of human effort, are useless to man. As an apple on another continent is of no use, so it is with an apple ten feet away, until the addition of labor.

The second reason why the natural provisions are almost worthless is precisely their very great abundance, which would constitute a surplus supply when the number of human beings is relatively very small. In speaking of the provisions as worthless, Locke does not mean that they are unimportant for survival. The air we breathe and the water we drink are vital, but where air and water are superabundant, we would not pay for a breath or a drink. The natural materials, like anything that is present in practically unlimited abundance, could not command a price or a barter equivalent. This seems to indicate that Locke had in mind some early form of the law of supply and demand; it should not surprise us, therefore, to find in his economic writings the statement that value or price is determined by "quantity and vent" (very roughly equivalent to supply and demand) and "no other way in the world":

He that will justly estimate the value of any thing, must consider its quantity in proportion to its vent, for this alone regulates the price. The value of any thing . . . is greater, as its quantity is less in proportion to its vent. . . . For if you alter the quantity, or vent, on either side, you presently alter the price, but no other way in the world.

For it is not the being, adding, increasing, or diminishing of any good quality in any commodity, that makes its price greater or less; but only as it makes its quantity, or vent, greater or less, in proportion one to another.[6]

The original condition was an abundance of almost worthless provisions; it was not an actual plenty but only a potential plenty, to be
made actual by human labor and invention. What seems at first to be
a kind of paradise, a vast expanse of fertile land well stocked with "the
fruits it naturally produces and beasts it feeds," all "produced by the
spontaneous hand of nature" (§26), "the common mother of all" (§28),
and with very "few spenders" (§31) to consume this abundance, is in
fact a compound of too much of what is almost worthless and not
enough of what is necessary to make it valuable—human labor. The
general "penury" (§32) of the primitive state of nature is comparable to
the condition of the Indians, America's "needy and wretched inhabitants" (§37),

who are rich in land and poor in all the comforts of life; whom nature having
furnished as liberally as any other people with *the materials of plenty,* i.e., a
fruitful soil, apt to produce in abundance what might serve for food, raiment,
and delight, yet *for want of improving it by labor* have not one-hundredth
part of the conveniences we enjoy [§41, italics supplied].

A second major cause of the penury of the state of nature is that
"the greatest part of things really useful to the life of man . . . are
generally things of short duration, such as, if they are not consumed
by use, will decay and perish of themselves. . . " (§46). This natural fact
of spoiling was perhaps the major limitation of property in the state of
nature.

Nature does severely limit property in the state of nature: "As much
as any one can make use of to any advantage of life before it spoils, so
much he may by his labor fix a property in. Whatever is beyond this is
more than his share and belongs to others" (§31). The possession of land
was similarly limited:

whatsoever he tilled and reaped, laid up and made use of before it spoiled,
that was his peculiar right; whatsoever he enclosed and could feed and make
use of, the cattle and product was also his. But if either the grass of his enclosure rotted on the ground, or the fruit of his planting perished without
gathering and laying up, this part of the earth, notwithstanding his enclosure, was still to be looked on as waste, and might be the possession of
any other [§38].

Locke seems to have derived from the natural fact of spoiling a kind of
rule to assure the fair distribution of goods in the state of nature.
The reasoning is plausible, but consideration of two questions reveals
the inadequacy of that interpretation of Locke's discussion of spoiling.
First, why is such a rule necessary? Second, would it be effective?

The foundation of property in the state of nature, as has been explained, must be a superabundance of natural provisions. Your labor in picking an apple makes it your property if enough apples and as good are left for others. But when there is such an abundance, what need is there for a rule to limit accumulation? The quantity you take can make no difference to me, so long as you leave me enough and as good; nor would I care whether what you have taken spoils or not in your possession. If you are so foolish as to waste your labor acquiring more than you can use, you cheat yourself but you do not cheat me.

Some means of limiting accumulation is required only if there is less than a superabundance, only if what is taken leaves less than enough for others. But whether a rule based on spoiling would serve to limit accumulation even in that case depends on whether it is applied to perishable or durable goods. Suppose that a man achieves an effective local monopoly of nuts, leaving not one for others; since they might "last good for his eating a whole year" (§46), he could take that long to eat his way through his supply without any spoiling. The spoiling rule would be ineffective in limiting possession of these scarce, durable goods. It would not achieve a fair distribution of them.

Any rule limiting accumulation is unnecessary when there is a very great plenty of provisions. If, under other conditions, such a rule is necessary, one based on spoiling is ineffective in the case of durable goods. The spoiling rule can be necessary *and* effective as a means toward fair sharing only in the case of a scarcity of perishable goods. But, as we have seen, the establishment of property in the state of nature, by mixing labor with the natural provisions, depends entirely on a very great abundance, one which automatically achieves the leaving of enough for others. If there is not enough for everyone, not even labor can establish a right to a part of the whole, to the exclusion of all other men. And if labor cannot establish a title to property when there is a scarcity, then nothing can. There is no other way in the state of nature. Title may be transferred by barter or purchase, but only labor can begin property. In short, if there is a scarcity of perishable provisions in the state of nature, there cannot be natural property. There can be only possession of what is common. The conclusion is that even when the scarce perishable thing is in your possession, any other man still has as good a claim to it as you have. In the struggle for possession which would ensue, right would be established by the might of the stronger, and it would be difficult, if not impossible, to keep more for yourself than could be quickly consumed.

The fact of spoiling does indeed limit possessions in the state of nature and keep every man in a state of penury. "Nothing was made by

God for man to spoil or destroy" (§31), we are told, but if all the denizens of the state of nature had become so demented as to devote their entire labor to spoiling as much as they could, the results of their combined efforts would be as nothing compared to the extensive spoiling and waste occurring throughout the vast territory "left to nature" (§37). When we consider "the plenty of natural provisions there was a long time in the world, and the few spenders" (§31), the spoiling that could not be blamed on man is appalling. The spoiling of things by the hand of man is dwarfed by the spoiling that occurs beyond his reach. Natural spoiling can be lessened only by an alteration of the prevailing conditions.

However much Locke deplored wastefulness and destruction, his discussion of spoiling does not point toward a moral rule of fair dealing with other men in the state of nature. It indicates, rather, the massive scale of waste under the rule of nature; it points toward the necessity of discovering some means of liberation from that harsh rule.

The third factor contributing to the penury of the earliest stage of the state of nature is the lack of cultivation of the land: "land that is left wholly to nature . . . is called, as indeed it is, *waste*" (§42); the extent of this natural waste can be lessened, therefore, by the spread of agriculture. One is mistaken to think that a man deprives others by enclosing land to cultivate it for his own use. Because cultivated land is much more productive than uncultivated land, all his neighbors will benefit:

. . . I have heard it affirmed that in Spain itself a man may be permitted to plough, sow, and reap, without being disturbed, upon land he has no other title to but only his making use of it. . . . The inhabitants think themselves beholden to him who by his industry on neglected and, consequently, waste land has increased the stock of corn which they wanted [§36].

Agriculture then is a major step toward alleviating the penury of man's condition in the state of nature, but it is limited in its effectiveness by the fact of spoiling. Unless there is some way for a man to dispose of his surplus crops before they spoil, he will surely grow no more than his own family can consume; if he grows more, the surplus will only rot or be taken from him by others. Thus there will be no surplus, which is the necessary basis for the improvement of man's condition, and no "increase of mankind," which is the main intention of nature.

In brief, what was needed was some invention that would make it reasonable for a man to produce more than was necessary for his own family's immediate wants, more than they could consume before it spoiled. And that invention was money, which, according to Locke, came into existence through a natural sort of progression in the state of nature. Men first bartered perishable foods for more durable foods, like nuts; later they traded goods for "a piece of metal, pleased with its color" (§46). Finally they arrived at an agreement that scarce but durable things, like gold and silver, would be taken in exchange for the perishable goods.

And thus came in the use of money, some lasting thing that men might keep without spoiling, and that by mutual consent men would take in exchange for the truly useful but perishable supports of life [§47].

By this invention of money, men solved the basic economic problems of the state of nature—with what far-reaching political consequences we shall presently see.

It is important to understand that Locke did indeed mean that money came into use in the state of nature, before civil society. The use of money came in "by mutual consent" (§47) that men would exchange it for perishable goods. This "tacit and voluntary consent" does not presuppose the existence of civil society; it was made "out of the bounds of society and without compact, only by putting a value on gold and silver, and tacitly agreeing in the use of money. . ." (§50). This tacit agreement could not in itself establish civil society,

for it is not every compact that puts an end to the state of nature between men, but only this one of agreeing together mutually to enter into one community and make one body politic; other promises and compacts men may make one with another and yet still be in the state of nature [§14].

Money was introduced in the state of nature, but its use hastened the end of the state of nature. Money so altered the conditions of the state of nature that it was no longer possible for men to live together without greater protection for their possessions. Money enabled men to enlarge their possessions; money made it profitable for a man to "possess more land than he himself can use the product of" (§50). Without money, a man can have no incentive to enlarge his holdings and produce a surplus, however favorable all other circumstances may be:

Where there is not something both lasting and scarce, and so valuable to be hoarded up, there men will not be apt to enlarge their possessions of land, were it never so rich, never so free for them to take [§48].

But, "find out something that hath the use and value of money amongst his neighbors, you shall see the same man will begin presently to enlarge his possessions" (§49).

Introduction of the use of money completes the reversal of all of the original economic conditions of the state of nature. Unowned land becomes scarce because enclosed holdings are enlarged. The increased production can support an increased population, that is, a more plentiful labor supply. The early condition, in which possession was limited to "a very moderate proportion" (§36), gives way to larger possessions. The prevailing equality of penury is replaced by an economic inequality: "as different degrees of industry were apt to give men possessions in different proportions, so this invention of money gave them the opportunity to continue and enlarge them" (§48). Locke, we see, has done more than he promised; he has not only shown the origin of private property, he has justified the inequality of possessions:

... it is plain that men have agreed to a disproportionate and unequal possession of the earth, they having, by a tacit and voluntary consent, found out a way how a man may fairly possess more land than he himself can use the product of, by receiving in exchange for the overplus, gold and silver, which may be hoarded up without injury to anyone, these metals not spoiling or decaying in the hands of the possessor. This partage of things in an inequality of private possessions, men have made practicable ... only by putting a value on gold and silver, and tacitly agreeing in the use of money [§50].

If we now consider the objection that might be most appropriately raised at this point—that an inequality of possessions is *not* fair—we are led directly to the central theme of Locke's whole political teaching: *increase*. The conditions of the first stages of the state of nature were hostile to any prospects for increase in the supplies of goods men need for their comfort, convenience, and preservation. The question then was how to share the very little that could be wrested from the tight fist of nature. This meant that whoever took a little more than did his neighbors, "took more than his share and robbed others" (§46). But when some men, by invention and industry, created the new conditions for the production of plenty, there came to be very much more to share; and although the new conditions required an inequality of possessions proportionate to the "different degrees of industry" among men, no one was cheated. Those who had a smaller share of the greatly increased whole were better off than those who had earlier shared, on an equal basis, in the pitiful little of the original condition. The poorest of men in a society having agriculture and money is richer than the most fortunate in the primitive, preagricultural state of nature. Consider the "needy and wretched" Indians in America, who do not cultivate the soil: "a *king* of a large and fruitful territory there feeds, lodges, and is clad worse than a *day-laborer* in England" (§41, italics supplied).

It is difficult to exaggerate the importance Locke ascribed to the combination of agriculture and money. As he described the problem in an early essay, nature is utterly powerless to provide the conditions in which nature's own main intention—the increase of mankind—might be fulfilled:

The inheritance of the whole of mankind is always one and the same, and it does not grow in proportion to the number of people born. Nature has provided a definite profusion of goods for the use and convenience of men, and the things brought forth have been bestowed in a definite manner and quantity deliberately; they have not been fortuitously produced nor are they increasing in proportion with men's need or avarice. . . . Whenever either the desire or the need of possession increases among men, there is no extension, then and there, of the world's limits. Victuals, clothes, adornments, riches, and all other good things of this life have been given in common; and when any man snatches for himself as much as he can, he takes away from another man's heap the amount he adds to his own, and it is impossible for anyone to grow rich except at the expense of someone else.[7]

This passage may be said to state the problem which Locke solved in the *Two Treatises*. The world remains constant; it is not within nature's power to extend its limits by even one square yard. But without such extension, how can there ever be sufficient support for the increase of mankind? And how can there be any improvement in the condition of men generally if "no gain falls to you which does not involve somebody else's loss"?[8] The answer Locke provides is shocking in its audacity. What is completely beyond the power of nature is well within the power of *any* farmer:

. . . he who appropriates land to himself by his labor does not lessen but increase the common stock of mankind. For the provisions serving to the support of human life produced by one acre of enclosed and cultivated land are (to speak much within compass) ten times more than those which are yielded by an acre of land of an equal richness lying waste in common. And therefore he that encloses land, and has a greater plenty of the conveniences of life from ten acres than he could have from a hundred left to nature, *may truly be said to give ninety acres to mankind* [§37, italics supplied].

Men, by their labor, invention, and arts, make *increase* possible, and thereby solve the economic problems that beset them in the state of nature. But at the same time they also make the continuance of the state of nature impossible. The state of nature, however dangerous and inconvenient, is tolerable when its conditions are a plenty of raw provisions, few men, lots of room, and a general equality of weakness. But the consequences of *increase* are to make unowned provisions scarcer, men more numerous, and open space harder to come by; and in this new situation there is generated a new inequality of power among men, based on the new inequality of possessions. Under these new conditions, labor can no longer give title to property or be the measure of value, and spoiling ceases to limit acquisition. Now, for the first time, there is the possibility of possessions too extensive to protect by the means available in the state of nature. The sovereignty of nature dissolves and men must institute a new form of rule of their own making to take its place. Men are "quickly driven into society" (§127) for the protection of their property.

The possessions of the "industrious and rational"—those men upon whose powers of increase the well-being of all depends—must be protected from the "fancy or covetousness of the quarrelsome and contentious" (§34). The final step in the long process of the liberation of man's powers of increase from the restraints of nature is government. "The increase of lands and the right employing of them is the great art of government," and the prince is called "godlike" who "by established laws of liberty [secures] protection and encouragement to the honest industry of mankind. . . ." [9]

And so we have seen that Locke's discussion of property is an account of the development of the state of nature through several economic stages to the point where men can no longer live together without the authority and power of a common judge to protect the enlarged possessions made possible, to the benefit of all, after the introduction of money. Locke's theory of property explains the necessity for the transition from the state of nature to civil society. We have moved very far now toward an understanding of Locke's answer to the great question: What is political power?

Although Locke addresses himself to the question of the nature of political power throughout the *Two Treatises,* it must be acknowledged that his approach is quite indirect. The *First Treatise* is, in large measure, a demonstration that Filmer's patriarchal power cannot be transformed into political power; and the first half of the *Second Treatise* is mostly devoted to a description of the natural powers and the natural state of man, as opposed to his political powers and political state. It is only thereafter that Locke takes up directly and in detail the discussion of political power and political society. It remains for us, therefore, to see how Locke moves from the nonpolitical base he has established to the political consequences.

The relevance of the prepolitical to the political is made immediately obvious in Locke's statement that "the great and chief end . . . of men's uniting into commonwealths and putting themselves under government is the preservation of their property" (§124). (Here, and in many places other than the chapter called "Of Property," Locke uses the word *property* in the comprehensive sense, which includes "life, liberty, and estate" [§87]). In the state of nature, property is "very unsafe, very unsecure" (§123), because there are lacking three things necessary to its preservation: "an established, settled, known law" (§124); a "judge with authority to determine all differences according to the established law" (§125); and the "power to back and support the sentence when right, and to give it due execution" (§126). Political society, the opposite of the state of nature, is designed to remedy these three defects. The character of political society derives from the fundamental intention to assure the preservation of property by providing a power to make law and judge controversies and a power to execute the judgments and punish offenders.

Any number of men can make a compact to leave the state of nature and "enter into society to make one people, one body politic under one supreme government" (§89). Only those who make such an express compact with one another are in political society together; those who do not join are, in relation to the society and its members, still in the state of nature.

The substance of the compact that all the members make with one another in order to form a political society is an agreement to transfer the powers that each had in the state of nature "into the hands of the community" (§87). In the state of nature, every man has two natural powers: "to do whatsoever he thinks fit for the preservation of himself and others within the permission of the law of nature" and "the power to punish the crimes committed against that law" (§128). These two natural powers of every man are "the original of the legislative and executive power of civil society" (§88). The second power, the power of punishing, every man, upon entering political society, "wholly gives up, and engages his natural force . . . to assist the executive power of the society, as the law thereof shall require" (§130). But Locke does not say that the first power, which includes judging what is necessary for preservation, is wholly transferred; he says it is given up "so far forth as the preservation of himself and the rest of that society shall require" (§129). We must be alert, therefore, for the answers to these questions: To what extent is the transfer of this power to society required? Why is this power not wholly transferred? and, What are the rights and obligations of a member of society if, as may happen, the preservation of "himself" conflicts with the preservation of "the rest of that society"?

The natural powers of men in the state of nature are transformed by compact into the political powers of civil society. These political powers are limited, however, by the purpose for which they were made. Since the purpose was to remedy the uncertainty and danger of the state of nature by providing settled laws for the protection of the property of all the members, the exercise of unlimited power is not and cannot be considered political power:

Absolute arbitrary power, or governing without settled standing laws, can neither of them consist with the ends of society and government, which men would not quit the freedom of the state of nature for, and tie themselves up under, were it not to preserve their lives, liberties, and fortunes, and by stated rules of right and property to secure their peace and quiet. It cannot be supposed that they should intend, had they a power so to do, to give to any one, or more, an absolute arbitrary power over their persons and estates. . . . This were to put themselves into a worse condition than the state of nature, wherein they had a liberty to defend their right against the injuries of others and were upon equal terms of force to maintain it. . . [§137].

Locke's insistence on the limited nature of political power reveals both his agreement and very great disagreement with Hobbes. Locke, starting from the principle of self-preservation as the rock-bottom foundation of civil society, shows again and again that absolute arbitrary power is no remedy at all for the evils of the state of nature. To be subject to the arbitrary power of an uncontrolled ruler without the right or strength to defend oneself against him is a condition far worse than the state of nature; it cannot be supposed to be that to which men consented freely, for "no rational creature can be supposed to change his condition with an intention to be worse" (§131). Therefore, Locke says, absolute monarchy is "no form of civil government at all" (§90). The great error of Hobbes is not his premise but his political conclusion that the only remedy for the state of nature is for men to make themselves subject to the unlimited power of the mighty leviathan, a conclusion which contradicts the premise that the fear of violent death or the desire for self-preservation is the first principle of human action. Locke's conclusion—limited government based on the consent of the governed—is more true to that premise than Hobbes's own conclusion.

Political society is a human invention and contrivance, but this artificial thing, once made, has a nature of its own and hence has an applicable natural law. It is "acting according to its own nature" when it is "acting for the preservation of the community" (§149), for, not surprisingly, "the first and fundamental natural law . . . is the preserva-

tion of the society" (§134). The first obvious consequence of this natural
law of society is that all of the rights of its members must be consistent
with the preservation of the society. No society can concede to any of its
members any right that would lead to its destruction. To do so would
threaten the preservation of its members, whose safety depends so much
on the protection the society affords them. For this reason also, the
commitment made by the members must be permanent. Once a man
has become a member of a commonwealth, he "is perpetually and in-
dispensably obliged to be and remain unalterably a subject to it, and can
never be again in the liberty of the state of nature" (§121), so long as
the government survives. And the power of the society must be all-
inclusive, reaching to every member and all controversies under the
law:

... there and there only is political society where *every one* of the members
hath quitted this natural power, resigned it up into the hands of the community in *all* cases that exclude him not from appealing for protection to the
law established by it. And thus *all* private judgment of *every* particular
member being excluded, the community comes to be umpire by settled standing rules, indifferent and the same to *all* parties, and by men having authority
from the community for the execution of those rules, decides *all* the differences that may happen between *any* members of that society concerning *any*
matter of right, and punishes those offenses which *any* member hath committed against the society with such penalties as the law has established [§87,
italics supplied].

The power of the community over its members seems sweeping—one
might even say, unlimited. It is here that we see clearly the fundamental
difficulty inherent in the attempt to develop a theory that political power
is limited because it has its source in prepolitical natural powers and
rights. If the members of a community retain some of their natural
power, relying on it rather than on the power of the community for
their protection, can political society function as intended? On the
other hand, if all power is put into the hands of the community, what
then will remain to protect the members from possible abuses of that
concentrated power?

Another natural law applicable to the body politic—and, in fact, to
all bodies composed of discrete elements—might be called *the law of
the greater force*. This law is the basis of Locke's doctrine of majority
rule. As was said, political society is formed by the unanimous agreement of its members to make one community; but although every political society is founded on the basis of unanimity, no such unanimity

can be expected in other matters. The immediate consequence of this first unanimous agreement and the impossibility of continuing unanimity is that a part of the society, the majority, will rule:

For when any number of men have, by the consent of *every* individual, made a community, they have thereby made that community one body, with a power to act as one body, which is only by the will and determination of the majority. For that which acts any community being only the consent of the individuals of it, and it being necessary to that which is one body to move one way, it is necessary the body should move that way whither the greater force carries it, which is the consent of the majority; or else it is impossible it should act or continue one body, one community, which the consent of *every* individual that united into it agreed that it should; and so *everyone* is bound by that consent to be concluded by the majority [§96, italics supplied].

The first proposition of this argument is that the greater force within any society will rule it. Locke seems to assume that the majority will be the greater force and that therefore the majority will rule. The same form of argument is advanced in Locke's discussion of conjugal society. When man and wife differ, the male, "as the abler and the stronger" (§82), will naturally rule. But on the basis of the law of the greater force, we would have to say that in the unusual but possible case of a husband who is not stronger and abler than his wife, he will not rule by nature. In the same way, in any body politic in which the majority is not the greater force, the rule will not naturally fall to it. But we know and Locke certainly knew that the majority of the people are not always the greater force in civil society, because inequalities of an economic, political, and social nature grow up under government; sometimes, therefore, one man is the greater force, as evidenced by the fact that the entire society is subject to his rule. Why then did Locke seem to assume that the majority would be the greater force?

In any body made of discrete elements, the majority will necessarily be the greater part of the whole only when all the parts are equal, and necessarily the greater force only when all are equal in force. Locke means that the majority will rule society at those times when the members are all equal or practically equal in force. We know that in the state of nature men are on "equal terms of force," while, after some time in political society, one man may become "100,000 times stronger" (§137) than other men. Locke's doctrine of majority rule, then, is that at those times when men in society are closest to the state of nature and therefore are most nearly equal in force—as, for example, when they first agree to leave the state of nature and make a community—the majority, being the greater force, will rule. "The majority [have], *upon men's first uniting into society,* the whole power of the community *naturally* in them" (§132, italics supplied); we shall see that there is another decisive time when the majority must rule, another time when men in society are very close to if not in the state of nature, that is, a time when society is briefly without government.

Thus far we have been following Locke's own procedure in speaking of political society without reference to any forms of government. Locke distinguishes political society and government, but he does not mean that political society can exist without government (except for very brief periods on extraordinary occasions). Men join political society in order to be ruled by a settled law, and that purpose can be accomplished only by establishing legislative and executive powers, which is precisely how Locke expresses the act of making government. Political society will continue only if government is formed practically at once. Political society and government may be separable in the mind, but they do not exist independently: political society requires government.

Political society without government can do nothing but make government. The performance of that task requires a profound decision, a choice of the form of government. Forms of government differ primarily according to how and into whose hands the legislative power is placed. "The first and fundamental positive law of all commonwealths is the establishing of the legislative power" (§134); the making of this fundamental law or constitution—an act of political society necessarily without government—is the great act that is naturally and necessarily determined by the majority of society. The majority may retain the legislative power, and then the government is a democracy; or may entrust it to some few men, and then the government is an oligarchy; or may put the power into the hands of one man, under one set of terms or another, and then it is one form of monarchy or another. But in every case, only majority consent can found the government; all forms of government (remembering that absolute monarchy is not a form of government), from "perfect democracy" to "hereditary monarchy" (§132), are equally founded on majority consent. Locke's doctrine of majority rule does not necessarily eventuate in a preference for one form of government over others.

The people are the parties to the social compact, each man agreeing with all the others to make one society. Nothing is said of a compact between the people and the government. The powers of government are only entrusted, without being relinquished, to those who become its officials; they have only a fiduciary power. The supreme power to preserve themselves and the society remains always with the people themselves. This power they cannot give away, "no man or society of men having a power to deliver up their preservation, or consequently the means of it." The people "will always have a right to preserve what they have not a power to part with" (§149). And yet, though the people remain the supreme power, Locke also says that when the legislative power is established, *it* is and remains the supreme power so long as the government continues to exist and function. Further, "this legislative is not only the supreme power of the commonwealth, but sacred and unalterable in the hands where the community have once placed it" (§134). To explain the apparent massive contradiction of having two supreme powers requires recalling the distinction between society without government and society under government. The supreme power remains always in the hands of the people, "but not as considered under any form of government" (§149). The people exercise the supreme power *actively* only in society without government; but when government exists, the supreme power is in the hands of the legislative, where the people have placed it. The people and the legislative are both supreme, but not both at the same time. Under government, the supreme power of the people is completely latent and never to be exercised until by some calamity or folly the government ceases to exist: "this power of the people can never take place till the government be dissolved" (§149). As long as government exists, the legislative is the actively supreme power. But the latent power of the people persists, and if the government should come to be dissolved, then once again there is society without government; at such a time, the supreme power will be wielded directly and actively by the people (meaning, of course, by the majority) and to accomplish one purpose only: to form a new government as quickly as possible by deciding on a constitution and placing the legislative power in new hands.

The fundamental principle of the separation of powers is clearly expressed by Locke. In "well ordered commonwealths" the chief powers are separated "because it may be too great a temptation to human frailty, apt to grasp at power, for the same persons who have the power of making laws to have also in their hands the power to execute them" (§143). But Locke applies this principle only to the separation of the legislative and executive functions; he speaks of the judicial as a part of the legislative and does not urge their separation. Locke does distinguish one other political power, "the power of war and peace, leagues and alliances" (§146). But though this power, which Locke names the "federative" power, is distinguishable from the executive power, they must nevertheless be placed in the same hands, "both of them requiring the force of the society for their exercise," which force cannot safely be placed "under different commands" (§148).

The legislative power is superior to the executive power, "for what can give laws to another must needs be superior to him" (§150). But,

where the legislative is not always in being, and the executive is vested in a single person who has also a share in the legislative, there that single person in a very tolerable sense may also be called supreme. . . . Having also no legislative superior to him, there being no law to be made without his consent, which cannot be expected should ever subject him to the other part of the legislative, he is properly enough, in this sense, supreme [§151].

This is not a denial that the legislative *power* is supreme, but it is a reminder that the legislative *body* need not be the supreme branch of government. This is the first indication of the surprising scope Locke concedes to the power of the person who is the executive—surprising because his doctrine of legislative supremacy seems so emphatic and unqualified.

However much the executive exists to perform the subordinate role of enforcing the law as set down by the legislators, it is necessary to add that at some times he must act without the direction of the law:

. . . the good of the society requires that several things should be left to the discretion of him that has the executive power. For the legislators not being able to foresee and provide by laws for all that may be useful to the community, the executor of the laws, having the power in his hands, has by the common law of nature a right to make use of it for the good of the society. . . [§159].

The executive may act not only without the sanction of the law, he may also make the laws "give way" (§159) to his power where blind adherence to them would be harmful, and he may even go so far as to act contrary to the law for the public good. "This power to act according to discretion for the public good, without the prescription of the law and sometimes even against it, is that which is called *prerogative*" (§160). The danger inherent in the executive's prerogative is no less obvious than the necessity for it. The prerogative has always grown most extensively in the reigns of the best princes. The people trust a good and wise prince even while he acts beyond the limits of the law, not fearing for their safety because they see that his purpose is to further their good.

Such godlike princes, indeed, had some title to arbitrary power by that argument that would prove absolute monarchy the best government, as that which God himself governs the universe by, because such kings partake of his wisdom and goodness [§166].

But even godlike princes have successors, and there is no assurance that one of them, claiming the precedent, will not make use of the enlarged prerogative to further his own private interests at the peril of the people's property and safety. "Upon this is founded that saying that the reigns of good princes have been always most dangerous to the liberties of their people" (§166).

According to this argument, what characterizes the wisest and best princes is not their obedience to and enforcement of settled law, but their service to the people. The scope of executive discretion is limited only by the proviso that it be used for the public good; "a good prince who is mindful of the trust put into his hands and careful of the good of his people cannot have too much prerogative" (§164). But since exceeding the bounds of constitutional or legal powers on the pretext of serving the people has been the constant practice of tyrants from time immemorial, "the public good" seems a dangerously vague and inadequate test of whether the prerogative is being properly used. The good prince and the tyrant are alike in that they both act outside the law and even contrary to it. The difference between them lies entirely in whether their lawlessness is beneficent or the opposite. The good prince breaks the law the better to serve the people; the tyrant uses his power "not for the good of those who are under it, but for his own private separate advantage" (§199). But is there a practical way to ascertain a ruler's intention? It is not always easy to determine whether the law has been broken, but it is certainly easier than to determine whether it has been broken for a good purpose. Has not Locke made it uncommonly difficult to distinguish the good prince from the tyrant? Locke does not seem to think so. The important thing is not how the question would be answered in theory, but how it is judged in practice; and in practice, he tells us, the determination is made "easily" (§161). But before he tells us how it is made, he tells us by whom it is made. To the question, who shall decide whether the powers of government are being used to endanger the people, Locke answers, "The people shall be judge" (§240).

The meaning of *the people shall be judge* is inextricably intertwined in Locke's argument with the people's *right to resist* tyranny; these two themes will, therefore, be considered together. The right of resistance, as asserted by Locke, must not too readily be equated with what has come to be known as a right of revolution. If we recall the fundamental natural law of society, it is clear that there can be no right to endanger the preservation of society. Revolution is a threat to the preservation of society. Whatever the right of resistance is, it must be consistent with the preservation of society.

The people shall be judge, says Locke. Of what shall they be judge?

They shall be judge of whether they must actively resume the supreme power because the government has been dissolved. How did they get the right to make that judgment? They have always had it and are absolutely incapable of surrendering it. At this point Locke begins again to draw on his earlier discussion of the state of nature and the state of war and the rights that exist in them, in the following fashion. When a prince or anyone in a position of political power uses that power, contrary to the trust reposed in him by the people, to further his interests at their expense, he makes his good separate from theirs; he separates himself from their community; he puts himself outside their society, into a state of nature with them. Further, by using force against them without authority or right, he places himself in the state of war with them.

The tyrant wars on the people. By using the force they entrusted to him against them, he effectively destroys their government. He can no longer be considered their political ruler in any meaningful sense of the word *political*. The people thus have a natural right to defend themselves against his aggression, and their resistance is perfectly consistent with the preservation of society. They are defending society; it is the tyrant who has rebelled:

rebellion being an opposition, not to persons, but authority, which is founded only in the constitutions and laws of the government, those, whoever they be, who by force break through, and by force justify their violation of them, are truly and properly *rebels*. For when men, by entering into society and civil government, have excluded force and introduced laws for the preservation of property, peace, and unity amongst themselves, those who set up force again in opposition to the laws do *rebellare*—that is, bring back again the state of war—and are properly rebels. . . [§226].

Locke rarely uses the word *revolution* throughout this discussion, preferring the word *rebellion,* thus maintaining a strictly literal usage: according to his argument, there is no right to *overturn,* there is only a right to resist upon the *return of war.*

Locke's teaching on this subject is addressed to those who have political power, and above all to princes, for they are the most likely rebels; "the properest way to prevent the evil is to show them the danger and injustice of it who are under the greatest temptation to run into it" (§226). He thus reverses the usual discussion, which considers the people to be the likeliest source of revolution. Why does not Locke direct his teaching also to the people, warning them against the use of force to depose their rulers? Has not Locke simply played a trick on his readers by a clever reversal of terminology? The prince is called a rebel, and the people who try to depose him are called the defenders of society; and the whole argument rests on Locke's insistence that the people shall judge whether the government has been dissolved—an extremely intricate and technical question. And does their resort to force really mean anything more than that the people oppose the policies of their present government and wish to replace it, either with a new form or by putting it in new hands? Does not Locke's teaching foment popular revolution, inciting and justifying the people, whenever they shall be displeased, to rise up with the cry of tyranny on their lips to depose their properly appointed rulers?

Locke denies that he has provided any new ground for revolution. He has argued that there is no legal or constitutional right to do anything that endangers the preservation of society and government while the government exists. He has denied any right to resist authority where it is possible to appeal to the law: "force is to be opposed to nothing but to unjust and unlawful force" (§204). This right to resist is not a political right, but a prepolitical natural right which may not be exercised so long as a duly constituted government functions.

Further, the people are not disposed to stir up trouble; they generally prefer to avoid the danger of disorder: "revolutions happen not upon every little mismanagement in public affairs. Great mistakes in the ruling part, many wrong and inconvenient laws, and all the slips of human frailty will be borne by the people without mutiny or murmur" (§225). And Locke is vehement in his condemnation of those individuals who do foment revolution against a just government; they are, he says, "guilty of the greatest crime I think a man is capable of" (§230).

But Locke's most instructive defense against the charge that he promotes the tendency to revolution is more profound than, but not unrelated to, these previously mentioned. In the state of nature, all men have the power to judge what is necessary to their preservation; this power of judging they cannot wholly give up into the hands of society. It may be called inalienable because, try as he might, it is impossible for a man to surrender his power to judge whether his life is in danger. No oaths, no threats, no doctrines can accomplish it. In the state of nature or in civil society, there is no sort of surgery that can remove from a living man the desire for self-preservation and the consequences of it. But though this right to judge is reserved by all men "by a law *antecedent and paramount* to all positive laws of men," recognition of this right does not make "a perpetual foundation for disorder; for this operates not till the inconvenience is so great that the majority *feel* it and are weary of it and find a necessity to have it amended" (§168, italics supplied).

The three questions, of when the prerogative is improperly used, of how to distinguish the tyrant from the good prince, and of when the government is dissolved, all turn out to be the same question—Is the government threatening the people's safety? And *that* is the question of which only the people shall be judge. Locke sees no difficulty in assigning it to them, nor any possibility of assigning it elsewhere, because however difficult it may be to answer theoretically, the people answer it easily—not by reasoning but by *feeling*. Locke denies that his words influence this situation. His arguments or doctrines have no effect on the matter. "Talk . . . hinders not men from feeling" (§94). His hypothesis—in fact, anyone's hypotheses—can have no influence in such a matter; the natural forces are unaffected by doctrines,

for when the people are made miserable, . . . cry up their governors as much as you will for sons of Jupiter, let them be sacred and divine, descended or authorized from heaven, give them out for whom or what you please, the same will happen. . . . If a long train of abuses, prevarications, and artifices, all tending the same way, make the design visible to the people, and they cannot but feel what they lie under and see whither they are going, it is not to be wondered that they should then rouse themselves and endeavor to put the rule into such hands which may secure to them the ends for which government was at first erected. . . [§§224, 225].

Whether there will be resistance to the rulers depends entirely on what the people see and feel. When the great majority of the people have been made to feel that their lives are in grave danger, "how they will be hindered from resisting illegal force used against them, I cannot tell."

This is an inconvenience, I confess, that attends all governments whatsoever, when the governors have brought it to this pass to be generally suspected of their people; the most dangerous state which they can possibly put themselves in, wherein they are the less to be pitied, because it is so easy to be avoided [§209].

The resistance of the people when they feel themselves in danger is the only effective limit on the use of the prerogative. A wise prince understands this limit and always avoids actions that make the people suspect his intentions. When he must act without the sanction of the law and even contrary to it, he is attentive to the necessity to make his good intention so manifest that the people see and feel it. If he fails in this, and the people come to suspect him and rouse themselves to replace him, then, though he may for a time be able to maintain his place by force, his political power is gone.

When a king has dethroned himself, and put himself in a state of war with his people, what shall hinder them from prosecuting him who is no king, as they would any other man, who has put himself into a state of war with them [§239]?

The king is no king, the government is in fact dissolved, and the in-equalities associated with government are nullified. The return to the use of force, the state of war, "levels the parties" (§235). At such a moment there are no political superiors and inferiors. The outcome will be determined by the greater force.

And so the argument has come full circle. Man's desire to preserve himself leads him out of the war of the state of nature and into political society. But men in political society face a new and more terrible dan-ger, tyranny or absolute arbitrary power, the augmented power of one man or a few men who bring back a far worse war than the war in the ordinary state of nature. Under tyrannical rule, the odds against the individual are vastly multiplied and defense is almost impossible. Men have, at bottom, only the protection of their natural force and natural desire for preservation. This strongest desire, which gave rise to political society originally, is also its chief defense; when the people feel that soci-ety, their greatest safety, is threatened, they will resist those who would destroy it. Mankind's political enterprise is an unending struggle to climb out of and avoid falling back into the state of nature, with all of its fearful evils.

There are two places in the *Second Treatise* where Locke speaks of "godlike" princes. In one he speaks of the princes who are allowed the largest prerogative, who have the greatest freedom from the control of the laws. They are like God, who governs the universe as an absolute monarch, because they "partake of his wisdom and goodness" (§166). But in the earlier passage, the prince is said to be wise and godlike who rules "by established laws of liberty." Such a prince is like God as Creator, for established laws of liberty are the means of bringing about "the increase of lands," which is a kind of creation, as we have seen, although not a creation out of nothing. This increase is not only the cause of domestic prosperity but also the source of the power to preserve the society against the hostile attacks of other societies. The godlike prince whose law-abidingness brings increase "will quickly be too hard for his neighbors" (§42).

This mention of power and hostile neighbors reminds us that every society is in the state of nature with all other societies, and that power is the basis of safety. But the necessities of life in the international state of nature, especially the demands of war, require at times extraordinary actions in response to unanticipated situations that cannot be regulated by law. So that a powerful people, made powerful by the material increase resulting from the encouragement of the desire for comfortable preservation under the protection of established laws of liberty, must face always the possibility of battle, a situation in which citizens must be dutiful, public-spirited, and ready to sacrifice treasure and perhaps even their lives, under the discretionary command of the executive-federative power, for the defense of the society as a whole.

The fact that those princes who rule most by law and those who rule least by law are both called *godlike* expresses the dilemma that cannot be fully resolved so long as society is understood to be founded on the principle of self-preservation. It remains a question, unresolved by Locke, whether the preservation of society as a whole and the preservation of the individual members can ever be made sufficiently compatible. For instance, can the preservation of society be made consistent with self-preservation in those moments of severest trial which often determine the fate of political societies? Can the principle of self-preservation provide the basis for the development of patriotism, public spirit, and especially the sense of the duty to give up wealth and even life in defense of one's country? Locke is profound and comprehensive on the reasons for founding political society, but those reasons turn out to be such that he is prevented by their very character from considering in what direction society should develop after the founding is secure. He does not supplement his fundamental principle; he does not discuss other reasons for continuing a society, after its founding, reasons which might grow up within a society that perhaps could not have existed at the time of its founding. There is no discussion, for example, of the bonds that grow up among fellow countrymen. He speaks often of societies, rarely of countries; often of the law of nature, rarely—if ever—of traditions, customs, institutions; often of rights, rarely of duties; often of "the people," rarely of peoples. When he speaks of Englishmen, he does not speak of their love of England, but of their "love of their just and natural rights." [10] What little Locke says of education in the *Two Treatises* has nothing to do with developing a sense of public duty; education is spoken of as having no purpose loftier than preparing children to take care of themselves.

There is a revealing passage in this regard, in which Locke speaks of the absolute character of martial discipline:

The preservation of the army, and in it of the whole commonwealth, requires an absolute obedience to the command of every superior officer, and it is justly death to disobey or dispute the most dangerous or unreasonable of them. . . [§139].

"The sergeant" can "command a soldier to march up to the mouth of a cannon or stand in a breach where he is almost sure to perish." "The general . . . can condemn him to death for deserting his post, or for not obeying the most desperate orders." He can hang him "for the least disobedience." And this extraordinary power of the military commander is justified "because such a blind obedience is necessary to that end for which the commander has his power, viz., the preservation of the rest. . ." (§139). The preservation of the rest of the society may explain very well the right of the general to command; but why must the soldier obey *desperate* orders? From Locke's words only one reason emerges: if he disobeys, the general may hang him. But does not the effectiveness of an army demand a better reason than that? What sort of army will that be in which the fear of punishment is the only support of discipline in combat? The question is whether Locke's soldier (unfamiliar with un-Lockean words such as *honor, gallantry, duty,* and *valor*) will fight for the sake of others when his fear of the enemy exceeds his fear of his own commanding officers. Neither in this passage nor in any other in the *Two Treatises* does Locke explain the basis for a soldier's duty to give his life for his country.

Locke's great theme was freedom and his great argument was that there is no freedom where there is no law. In man's natural condition there is no law, or at least there is no known and settled law. To be free, therefore, men must be lawmakers. But through ignorance of human nature and the society best suited to it, the results of their lawmaking efforts have too often been not to improve but to worsen their condition. The task of making mankind free requires an understanding of the nature of man.

The one most powerful force in human nature, and therefore the one most significant for political understanding, is the desire for self-preservation. It is at once the greatest obstacle to, and the greatest force for, peace among men. Properly guided, it provides assurance of safety in the midst of plenty. Ignored or defied, it causes violence, anarchy, and a fearful destruction of life and property. The task of reason, therefore, is to understand, pacify, and direct this passion constructively, always in awareness of the imminent peril should a feeling of uneasiness set it in the course of violence.

The desire for preservation can be diverted, directed, or cajoled, but there is no way to diminish or eradicate its overwhelming power. For this reason, men are not wholly governable, and the task of making mankind free under law can never be completed. The "remedy" for the evils of the state of nature never fully accomplishes its cure. Men live, partially at least, always and inescapably in the natural nonpolitical condition and always in danger of relapsing into a far worse condition, for men cannot be taught to have feelings contrary to their strongest desire. Government is powerless to change human nature; it must accommodate itself to what cannot be changed. The government that will not accommodate itself to this passion in every man must be prepared to struggle against it endlessly with force and terror. But the wise ruler will do more than accommodate himself; he will channel and guide, encourage and protect, the desire for preservation, and make of it the very foundation of law, freedom, safety, and plenty for his people.

Locke sought to free mankind from every form of absolute arbitrary power. He sought to present the true and complete account of man's making of civilization out of the almost worthless materials furnished to him. In this account, the chief force that spurs man on to his own liberation is a passion, the desire for preservation. As the reader of this volume well knows, the ancient political philosophers considered the passions arbitrary and tyrannical; they thought that the tendency of the passions is, above all, to enslave men. They taught, therefore, that a man is free only to the extent that the reason in him is able, one way or another, to subdue and rule his passions. But Locke recognized passion as the supreme power in human nature and argued that reason can do no more than serve the most powerful and universal desire and guide it to its fulfillment. Only when this ordering of things is understood and accepted as the true and natural ordering is there any prospect of success in mankind's struggle for freedom, peace, and plenty. That, above all else, is Locke's political teaching.

John Locke has been called America's philosopher, our king in the only way a philosopher has ever been king of a great nation. We, therefore, more than any other people in the world, have the right and the duty and the experience to judge the rightness of his teaching.

## NOTES

1. In his last will and testament, Locke referred to the several editions of the *Two Treatises of Government* printed in his lifetime as "all very incorrect." Before he died, he had prepared at least one corrected copy, of the third printing, to be used by the publisher in the printing of any future editions. (One such copy, with marginal corrections and additions in Locke's own hand and that of his assistant, is now in the possession of Christ's College, Cambridge University.) From the edition of 1713 on, this corrected text was the basis of most printings; but, for some unknown reason, late in the nineteenth century editors returned to the text of the first edition. Most

editions now in print in the United States and England follow this "very incorrect" text. The most notable exceptions are John Locke, *Two Treatises of Government* and Robert Filmer, *Patriarcha*, ed. Thomas I. Cook (New York: Hafner, 1947); John Locke, *The Second Treatise of Government*, ed. Thomas P. Peardon (New York: Liberal Arts, 1952); and John Locke, *Two Treatises of Government*, ed. Peter Laslett (Cambridge: Cambridge University Press, 1960).

All quotations from the *Two Treatises* in this chapter are from a photocopy of the Christ's College text; I have taken the liberty, however, of Americanizing the spelling and modernizing the punctuation. For those few passages in which the Christ's copy text is obscure, I have consulted Laslett's edition and its very helpful critical apparatus. Readers will find that the passages presented here differ only in small ways from the texts of the three editions named above (but see n. 9, below).

2. *First Treatise*, sec. 2.
3. Title page of the *Two Treatises*.
4. *First Treatise*, sec. 88.
5. *Ibid.*, sec. 86.
6. *Some Considerations of the Lowering of Interest and Raising the Value of Money*, in *The Works of John Locke in Nine Volumes* (12th ed.; London, 1824), IV, 40–41.

7. The Latin text and English translation of this passage appear in John Locke, *Essays on the Law of Nature*, ed. W. von Leyden (Oxford: Clarendon, 1954), pp. 210 and 211; some minor revisions of the translation were provided by the senior editor of the present volume. Reprinted by permission of Oxford University Press.

8. *Ibid.*, p. 213.
9. *Second Treatise*, sec. 42. This passage is one of the most important of those added by Locke in the Christ's College copy. It does not appear in most editions now available (for reasons explained in n. 1, above) and is misprinted in several editions in which it does appear. It is erroneously printed as "the increase of lands and the right of employing of them," rather than the correct text, "the increase of lands and the right employing of them." Examination of the handwritten text leaves no doubt that the superfluous "of" is a printer's error, with what distortion of the meaning of the passage the attentive reader will readily see.

10. Preface to the *Two Treatises*.

# READINGS

A. John Locke. *Second Treatise*.
B. John Locke. *First Treatise*.
    John Locke. *Some Considerations of the Consequences of the Lowering of Interest and Raising the Value of Money*.
    John Locke. *A Letter Concerning Toleration*.

# MONTESQUIEU

## 1689–1755

Charles Secondat, Baron de Montesquieu, was born and died in France. His most famous writings are *The Persian Letters* (1721), *Considerations on the Greatness and Decline of the Romans* (1734), and *The Spirit of the Laws* (1748).

## 1. INTRODUCTION

Montesquieu's mature teaching must be gathered primarily from *The Spirit of the Laws,* as he himself indicates in its preface. His other writings ought therefore to be related to this one. Yet its thirty-one books seem lacking in over-all plan or coherence, from which the inference has been drawn that Montesquieu was not a systematic philosopher and had no mature teaching in the strict sense. The preface, however, contains a manifest claim that the work as a whole has a design and is based on long-meditated principle. Thus the design, and hence a systematic teaching, either does not exist, or it exists in an unapparent manner. If we are compelled to choose, we prefer assuming that the writer's clear reference to the existence of a design is more authoritative than any reader's denial that the design exists. Montesquieu strongly suggests that the design is not immediately apparent when he speaks of the need to look for it. *The Spirit of the Laws* is therefore an obscure work. One important reason for disguising unorthodox views was the possibility of reprisals by Church and State. But d'Alembert's *Eulogy of Montesquieu,* written shortly after the latter's death, explains the obscurity more broadly. According to d'Alembert, Montesquieu sought to instruct both the wise and the unwise in such a way as to keep from the unwise important truths the direct statement of which could do needless harm. Apparent disorder and obscurity were instruments of this purpose. Montesquieu himself tells us that his principles can be discovered by reflecting upon the details; our task, then, is to approach the whole and its principles through the parts and details.

The philosophy introduced in the preface and Book I has a double aim: to comprehend the diversity of human laws and mores (unwritten laws), and to assist wise government everywhere. The first is theoretical, the second practical, and their connection arises from within the problem of "law" itself. In his famous opening formulation, Montesquieu defines laws, in the most extensive sense, as the necessary relations deriving from the nature of things. Laws are relations; they exist objectively and by necessity. They "govern" the action of all things—of God on the world, of bodies on each other, and so on. This universal lawfulness is the background against which human law must be viewed. But the term "law" is equivocal: in human enactments it implies a law *maker,* a *promulgation* of the law to those who are to obey it, and law *enforcement,* with attendant sanctions. Then do laws "govern" all things in the universe exactly as they may govern human beings? The classic exposition for the affirmative had been St. Thomas Aquinas' treatment of law in the *Summa Theologica.* Human enactment or positive law was understood in terms of its connection with eternal law, natural law, and revealed law. Law, as such, was an ordinance of reason, made, promulgated, and enforced for the common good by the community's ruler. Its ultimate source was the mind of God.

Montesquieu's opening definition of law takes issue with the Thomistic tradition, first, by appearing to leave no room for the miraculous, and, second, by depicting the universality of sheer, blind necessity rather than governance rationally aimed at good. Human law, as human reason applied to man's governance,[1] seems curiously out of place in such a world. But it is precisely the extent to which human affairs are swayed by mechanical causes that Montesquieu undertakes to demonstrate. By abandoning both divine and natural teleology and indicating the limits of purposive human action as well, he hopes to establish a science of human affairs consistent with Cartesian and Newtonian physics. It is difficult to say with assurance what view of God he considered compatible with this view of law and nature.

Before there were human laws there was man. To comprehend the diversity of human laws we must visualize them emerging from man's nature as he acts within particular natural and social settings. The variety of actual settings will account for the variety of human affairs, and indeed for the histories of all nations, provided we know the general principles involved, and provided due allowance is made for exceptional individuals, for political skill, and for chance. Human science requires historical studies, and these studies form the link between theory and practice. Political practice, or statesmanship, demands that each society be understood and treated in its particularity, *i.e.,* in the light of its history. But historical particulars are intelligible only in the light of general causes, proximate and ultimate, and therefore sound historical knowledge requires theory or philosophy.[2] This is how law as "legislation" and law as "necessary relations among things" are connected.

What were men like before there were human laws, and why did such laws arise? At first men were hardly distinguishable from brutes. Lacking in language and reason, they were led by instinctive physical fears and wants to preserve themselves individually and then to associate with each other; only later could they consciously desire to remain in society. But society breeds discontents. Groups seek to become privileged in the possession of its advantages, and, encouraged now by a sense of their own strength, proceed to war upon each other. From war comes law, right, or the just (*droit*). Law arises as a means of suppressing war, whether within or among societies. Within societies, the relations between rulers and ruled (political law) and of citizen to citizen (civil law) are established in such a manner as to unite the war-torn community. The idea of the right, the just, the obligatory originates with the idea of law and does not precede it. Man does not by nature or originally have a conscience or sense of duty.

This account, derived from the second chapter of Book I, omits reference to the "anterior relations of equity" ascribed to men in the first chapter. These relations or duties preceding all positive law are peculiar in character. They enjoin a bare minimum—to obey positive laws, to be grateful for benefits received, to remain dependent on the being that has created man, and to repay evil with the same evil. Their slightness practically guarantees that they be felt by men everywhere. Yet they are not included in the account of man's nature and earliest behavior in Chapter ii. This suggests that they are brought into existence by primitive social requirements similar to those engendering law. In any case, such obligations fall far short of prescribing the fullness of justice or human good by which societies must be guided.

If man does not begin by knowing justice, neither does he have any natural end or perfection. Montesquieu explicitly denies that any particular form of government or set of laws is required by, or most in accord with, nature: "Law, in general, is human reason in so far as it governs all the peoples of the earth; and the political and civil laws of each nation ought only to be the particular cases in which this human reason is applied." [3]

The laws of each nation must be related to its form of government, its physical circumstances (*e.g.,* climate, geography) and social conditions (*e.g.,* liberty, mores, commerce, religion). And all the relations laws have or ought to have, taken together, constitute their spirit (*esprit*).

By this passage the classical quest for the best state, Thomistic natural law, and Lockean natural right are all rejected as guides to the ordering of political society. Stark relativism emerges as the conclusion of Montesquieu's introductory book. But it is not subjectivism. Montesquieu grants that a certain set of laws may *be,* not merely be thought to be, objectively better or worse for a given people. He maintains, however, that there is an ultimately irreducible variety of norms as well as of actual political configurations. These norms, in short, are not themselves capable of being judged in terms of what is absolutely best or worst politically. It would follow that the study of history is more important to the discovery of specific norms than the study of philosophy. Yet history, as the study of facts and causes, cannot by itself yield any norms whatsoever. How, then, are valid specific norms derived?

*The Spirit of the Laws* is an analysis of the different things to which laws can be related. These things, taken up one after the other without apparent order, occupy Books II through XXV of the work, while Books XXVI and XXIX return to a level of generality akin to that of Book I. Books XXVII, XXVIII, XXX, and XXXI, however, seem to be adjuncts to the main body of the work rather than intrinsic parts, the latter three serving to illuminate the constitution of modern France by laying bare its historical origins.

## 2. Forms of Government

Montesquieu turns first to an examination of political structures, *i.e.,* of the means for repressing social strife. Every government has both a nature and a principle to which its laws must be related. We know its nature when we know who rules and how; the passions that give it motion are its principle. The main species of government are the republic (either democratic or aristocratic), monarchy, and despotism. Their domestic and then their external affairs comprise the subject matter of Books II through X.

Before taking up the details, several general observations are in order. We note first that Montesquieu does much more than merely supply information about the various forms of government as they have actually existed. He tells us that his chief objective is to construct the laws, institutions, and practices whereby each form is perfected. This by itself may be consistent with the relativism he purports to espouse. But he also compares the various forms with each other in such a manner as to point toward their ultimate comparative merit. Is this possible without some absolute standard of political good and evil?

Let us begin with the democratic republic. In a properly constituted democracy, the sovereign people will delegate authority to do what they themselves cannot do. They need to be guided in foreign affairs and the preparation of legislation by a council or senate, and can have confidence in it only if they choose it. They need magistrates but are admirable at discerning the worth of individuals for this purpose. Legislation itself, however, will be by the people directly.

Democracy does not require that all citizens be eligible for public office but that all participate in the selection of the officers. Senators and lower civil magistrates are to be chosen by lot, not vote, and from among volunteers drawn from those who are not needy: the poor are not eligible. Military and high civil magistrates are to be elected by all, again from among those who are better off. Members of the popular courts, finally, are chosen by lot from among all volunteers, rich or poor. Thus democracy is not the simple rule of the majority, nor simple rule by lot. It is a mixture. Indeed, the poor are obviously less privileged, and the well-to-do more so, than sheer numbers would admit—a fact strengthened by the implication that public offices would be left unsalaried and attendance at popular assemblies uncompelled. Democracy needs the conservatism as well as the self-support and leisure of the well-to-do. But it also needs merit, the procuring of which is aided by the use of the techniques of election and examination of candidates.

The principle of democracy is virtue. Where all participate in making laws which they must themselves obey and in choosing their own rulers from amongst themselves, a very high degree of public spiritedness or devotion to the common good is needed. Virtue, in short, is patriotism, love of the republic and the laws, and from it stem the particular citizen virtues of probity, temperance, courage, and patriotic ambition. To preserve virtue, the extremes of wealth and poverty must be avoided by setting legal minima as well as maxima to the possession of property. Virtue needs near-equality, and more than that, a relatively low general level of wealth, assuring frugality and precluding luxury. This condition must both exist and be loved. Other methods of sustaining virtue are a censorial senate of elders, elected for life to preserve the purity of mores; strong paternal powers; sumptuary laws; the public accusation of unfaithful wives; and, in general, the mutual surveillance of all in points of conduct.

Democracy can subsist only in a small city-state, the familylike cohesion of which engenders a continual preference for public over private good. Its public assemblies are not representative. But it is inconsistent with an independent clergy—*i.e.,* a state within the state—and probably only consistent with pagan religion and morality. Solon's Athens, Sparta, Carthage, the later Roman republic are all adduced in illustration of democracy. No Christian, nor for that matter nonpagan or nonancient commonwealth, is so named.

Democracy's most attractive feature is the moral greatness of its citizens. Democracy also assures its citizens a high degree of freedom and security under law. On the other hand, it must, perforce, set limits to both their greatness and freedom. Its poverty, its smallness, its restriction of privacy, its reliance on unquestioning public devotion, and the mutual surveillance of its citizens prevent the more complete development of human talents—especially in the area of philosophy and the fine arts. Democracy means intellectual and artistic mediocrity.[4] Montesquieu acknowledges a distinction between productive, commercial republics, like Athens, and military republics, like Sparta. The first choice for democracy seems to be something between the two: the citizen body should consist of farmers who both work and fight. Nevertheless, a democracy based on the commercial spirit as its principle is possible, provided its laws keep this economical temper from being destroyed by excessive wealth. Montesquieu gives the impression, however, that the health of a commercial democracy is very difficult to sustain. The brilliance of Periclean as distinguished from Solonian democracy in Athens was predicated upon extremes of wealth, moral corruption, and freedom, *i.e.,* on political decadence rather than health.

The aristocratic republic is a regime wherein only a part of the people is sovereign, as best exemplified in the early Roman republic and modern Venice. Aristocracy depends upon political and economic inequality between the sovereign nobles and the nonparticipating people. That the nobles should identify their own interest with the interest of the people, in this way most closely approximating the virtue of democracy, is rare but not impossible. The more probable principle of aristocracy, however, is a spirit of moderation in the nobles restraining them from seeking inordinate superiority over each other or the people. The laws and institutions conducive to such restraint are difficult to secure. In general, the larger the number of nobles, and the smaller and poorer the body of those without political rights, the healthier the aristocracy. Democracy can therefore be considered the perfection of aristocracy. It is characterized by a broader concern and provision for the common good than aristocracy. Its members are, on the average, more virtuous, freer, and more secure, or, from the other side, less humiliated and exploited.

We should note that Montesquieu radically alters the standards and names used in the traditional Aristotelian classification of regimes. Aristotle classified in terms of the holders of sovereign authority and the purpose of their rule. Good regimes are ruled for the common good, bad ones for the advantage of the rulers themselves. Thus a clear distinction is made between oligarchy and aristocracy, both being rule by the few. Montesquieu has only two (not four) types of republic, depending on whether the whole or part of the people rules. Each type is perfected in a certain way, and actual instances of either would bear greater or less resemblance to this perfection. But, as in Machiavelli, the clear-cut distinction between virtuously and viciously motivated regimes is no longer primary. Thus Montesquieu uses the term "aristocracy" for regimes that Aristotle would have called "oligarchies." He also calls "democracy" the regime that Aristotle would probably have called "polity," and even instances as "democracies" regimes that Aristotle considered mixed aristocracies (*e.g.,* Carthage). One might conclude that Montesquieu's revised classification has two effects: first, it casts doubt on the adequacy of classifying regimes according to the goodness of their rulers' motives; second, it elevates the worth of popular regimes, or of the popular element in mixed regimes, thereby teaching that the common good is best achieved through widespread popular participation in government. We might be led to question this by Montesquieu's high praise of the "singular institutions" of Plato's *Republic* in Book IV, but the consequence of this concession is not an adherence to the classical preference for aristocracy.

Republican government has its natural place in a small society, and the expansion in the size, power, and wealth of a republic leads necessarily to the breakdown of its spirit and institutions. This is the lesson Montesquieu drew above all from his study of Rome, in opposition to Machiavelli's favoring of Roman imperialism in the *Discourses.* But the smallness required by republics poses a crucial problem of defense. The solution to this problem on a republican basis is the confederation, whereby several republics gather together to form a larger defensive whole. The modern Dutch republic and the ancient Lycian confederation are illustrations of this device. Montesquieu seems to have regarded confederation as an association of societies, not directly of individuals, and refers to the possibility of the confederation's dissolving while its component societies remained. But he also explicitly favors—as in the

Lycian case—a highly centralized rather than loose association of the member states.

In monarchy, one person governs according to fixed and established laws. This requires that there be powers intermediate between the monarch and the people, hence the nobility, church, and cities. There must also be an independent depository or guardian of the laws, such as the French *parlements*. Together, these forces—by their privileges and independence—are able to restrain the actions of both the monarch and the people. Nevertheless, when the monarch combines the legislative and executive powers in his own person (as in France), the government inclines toward despotism. Cautiously, though clearly, Montesquieu gives evidence of regarding a balanced monarchy as one in which something like the old French Estates-General shared legislative power with the monarch.[5]

Unless monarchy has such a structure as this, it is not a stable regime. Montesquieu claims that the ancient world had no proper conception of monarchy. This conception arose out of the Germanic conquest of Rome, its two main components being an independent, hereditary, privileged nobility and representative government. The closest the ancients came to it was the monarchy of the heroic age described by Aristotle, but there the people had direct legislative power and were able, ultimately, to strip the king of his powers. Regarding the classification of monarchies, Montesquieu explicitly takes issue with Aristotle. He rejects the classical principle of classifying regimes on the basis of the intentions or virtues and vices of the rulers. To have a good monarchy it is not enough to have a good monarch. Government has a nature or constitution only if its structure does not depend on so unreliable a circumstance as an important individual's natural or nurtured moral endowment. Nevertheless, Montesquieu himself admits later that the moral character of a monarch is as vital to the liberty of his country as are its laws.

The principle of monarchy is honor, not virtue. Montesquieu is very severe in his moral criticism of the courts and principal men of monarchies everywhere. He speaks of their miserable character and of their trumpery spreading to all levels of society. Yet the object most sought in monarchies—honor, or superiority of condition and person— serves as a substitute for the incentives of virtuous action. Ambition for distinction on the part of all classes and individuals elicits conduct that redounds to the public benefit while aiming only at private or selfish good. In addition, the code of honor sets unofficial limits to the arbitrariness of king and subjects alike.

The honor-seeking criticized by Montesquieu cannot simply be identified with the activity attributed by Aristotle to the magnanimous or proud man. Monarchy's system of mores and manners is vulgarized honor, or honor that seeks to be recognized by many, that depends so much more on recognition by others, that succumbs to, rather than resists, the vices (*e.g.,* gallantry) that are popularly taken for signs of boldness. On the other hand, Montesquieu seems less willing than Aristotle to accept the mental horizon of the magnanimous man himself, in so far as that horizon is bounded mainly by self-esteem, and encourages action less out of love of the public good than out of self-esteem and the desire for the highest honors.[6]

The laws supporting honor in monarchies must grant hereditary privileges to the persons and property of the nobility. Luxury should be permitted as a means of supporting the poor, and commerce on the part of nonnobles favored. Monarchy is more inherently set on ambitious war and conquest than is the republic and naturally requires a larger territory. But immoderate expansion weakens the power of honor and encourages despotic power. In general, monarchy is less moral, less just, less stable than democracy. It must guarantee vast, hereditary inequalities. Nevertheless, it is compatible with, and even requires, a structure of written and unwritten law that protects person and property in their very inequality. As for France itself, Montesquieu never advises its turning toward either republican virtue or English liberty. Yet *The Persian Letters* reveals his awareness of the decay of the monarchy caused by royal absoluteness, aristocratic corruption, and middle-class wealth.

Despotism exists where one man rules as he wishes without law. In describing this type of government, Montesquieu usually takes his illustrations from the empires of the Near East and southern Asia, just as in *The Persian Letters* it was expedient to speak of the despotisms of Europe, theological or secular, via explicit or implicit comparisons with those of the east. Despotism makes use of a chief political steward or vizier who rules while the despot riots. Its principle is fear, aroused by the exercise of brutal force especially on the great, who otherwise would oppress the masses. In this way despotism fulfills a certain public function, but it also depends on its subjects lacking virtue, honor, and learning, for these are dangerous to the regime. It is the most inhumane, vice-ridden, and stupid of governments, yet it prevails amongst mankind. Moderate government requires special conditions and special skills and is thus achieved only with difficulty. In Asia especially, climate and geography combine to make despotism inevitable. It naturally thrives among a numerous but timid population occupying an immense territory. Then only one man ruling through force can keep the country together and prevent that only greater evil, anarchy. And in such cases despotism is intrinsically incapable of essential amelioration: its very existence depends on the permanent use of cruel and sanguinary violence.

Of the four forms of government, two republican, Montesquieu clearly regards democracy as best and despotism worst. It is more difficult to decide precisely why. To illustrate: democracy is praised more for the virtue of its citizens than for the freedom and security it affords them. Yet this virtue is called a passion or sentiment, something every citizen feels by being brought up within such a community. This means that the virtue founded on reason or understanding rather than passion, which we may call rational virtue, has no status either in democracy or in the political forms inferior to it. In short, all virtue having political significance remains on the level of passion and prejudice. But if democratic virtue is not substantively on a higher level than the desire for freedom and security, ought the political philosopher to cherish democracy primarily because of its virtue?

There is another way to the same difficulty. Politically considered, the passion of virtue is valuable because it makes for a healthy democracy. Its function is therefore instrumental to something other than itself, which is the truly desired object. A democracy might be likened to a family, in which something like collective selfishness animates its members, who identify their own with the common good. This thought is consistent with the view of human needs presented in Book I. There virtue is never presented as a natural need of the soul, desirable for its own sake in the same way that health of the body is desirable. Society originates and remains in the service of bodily needs, such as self-preservation, economic security, and sexual satisfaction. If so, the virtue as well as the liberty and equality of democracy would have to be valued as the political means by which such needs are best satisfied. We shall return later to the relation between political life and the goods of the soul.

### 3. POLITICAL LIBERTY

Up to this point in the analysis, no form of government with liberty as its principle has been introduced. The situation is remedied in Books XI through XIII and the last chapter of Book XIX. Modern England is the one country whose laws have liberty as their direct object. Liberty, politically speaking, is the right to do what the laws permit. It has two aspects: a balanced constitution and the citizen's sense of legal security, with the former contributing to the latter. Its first requirement is the separation of the three powers of government—legislative, executive, and judicial—so that they rest in different hands. If any two or all are combined in the same hands, power will be too much concentrated and insufficiently checked.

Montesquieu does not divide the powers of government in exactly the same way that Locke did. Locke had distinguished the function of carrying on foreign policy and called it "federative," and had subsumed both the execution of domestic laws and the trial of lawbreakers under the heading "executive." What Montesquieu does is to join into one power the execution of domestic laws and foreign policy, while also granting independence to the judicial power. His purpose, in short, is to guarantee the citizen even greater security than was possible within Locke's system.

One must carefully distinguish between Montesquieu's and the traditional or Aristotelian analysis of the powers of government. Aristotle speaks of the deliberative, magistrative, and judicial functions. The first has to do with deliberating about common affairs or the most important common affairs, such as making war and peace (and foreign policy in general), lawmaking, judging the greatest crimes, and appointing magistrates. The magistrative pertains to the authority to issue instructions and orders in more limited areas, such as strategy or finance. The judicial has to do with judging offenses and adjudicating disputes other than the greatest. It is clear from this that Aristotle included within the deliberative sphere functions that Montesquieu would have distributed among all three of his powers. Moreover, Aristotle thinks of the magistrative function in terms of several independent magistracies, whereas Montesquieu conceives of the executive power essentially as a unity. Above all, Aristotle does not make a principle of the distribution of the three powers among different men—rather the opposite, as his deliberative function shows. The utmost in liberty, whether in the form sought by Locke or Montesquieu, did not seem to him consistent with the needs of any healthy regime, much less with the needs of the regime dedicated to the good life.

Political liberty in its relation to the constitution requires not only that the three powers be separated but that they be constituted in a certain way. The judicial power should be given to *ad hoc* juries composed of the defendant's peers, with judgments being determined as precisely as possible by written law. The legislative power must be divided. Its main part should go to the duly elected representatives of the whole people, and only those in so base a condition that they are thought to have no will of their own should lack voting rights. Those distinguished by birth, riches, or honors ought to comprise a body of nobles who protect their hereditary privileges by serving as the second half of the legislature. The executive should be a monarch whose check on the legislature would consist of a veto power and whose ministers, in turn, could be examined and punished by the legislature, though he himself could not legally be removed.

Montesquieu regards the England so described as not only freer but more just and in some respects wiser than the ancient republics or his own democracy. Its first advantage is the clear-cut separation of powers and the checking mechanism built into the legislative and executive branches. The second is the representation of public opinion through one branch of the legislature, which can then proceed to discuss legislative matters and abstain from executive decisions in a manner impossible to the ancient city-state. In addition, the judicial power is less menacing and more just. Finally, the single executive—though not comparable in wisdom to a body like the Roman senate—will nevertheless possess a great amount of concentrated power and sufficient motives to wield that power vigorously. Constitutional government of this type could not be expected to work without a considerable amount of internal friction, so that some sacrifice of quality and smoothness in governmental operation is the necessary cost of liberty.

Montesquieu makes the ambiguous claim that such liberty is established in the laws of England, whether or not this liberty is actually enjoyed by the English people. Nevertheless, he clearly adheres to the logic of liberty as he understands it rather than to the actualities of mid-eighteenth-century England. If he did not draw attention to the very limited and irregular suffrage of the people and very irregular distribution of seats in the House of Commons, it was undoubtedly because he thought those actualities deficient from the viewpoint of liberty. Similarly, if he refused to describe those tendencies toward the merging of executive and legislative powers that later became known as cabinet government, it may well have been because he thought they were harmful to liberty.

The main advantage of England over that freest of ancient commonwealths, the Roman republic, is its having weakened the direct and massive power of the people and granted both nobles and commoners an almost impregnable, mutually limiting authority. But the main distinctions between what liberty meant to England and what it meant to any ancient republic are still to be seen. For it is not enough to have a proper constitution: proper laws are also necessary if the citizen is to enjoy the maximum in legal security. Here the criminal laws are crucial, having a function similar to that of the Bill of Rights in the Constitution of the United States. Montesquieu distinguishes four kinds of crimes: those against religion, against morals, against tranquility, and against security. The net result of his analysis is to make it impossible in a free state to prosecute sacrilege by legal means, or to punish moral turpitude except in sexual matters. Limitations are also set to the dangerous charge of treason, and writings should be considered criminal only when they prepare treasonable action. Finally, legal procedures and penalties must be so devised as to insure just treatment as far as possible.

Now the distance separating the republic founded on virtue and modern England begins to appear in its true dimensions. They have a basic resemblance: both are republics—a fact that England's monarchical past tends to obscure. They illustrate Montesquieu's judgment that the best of governments will have a massive popular foundation which will guarantee its concern for the common good. But England embodies individualism, each citizen being left alone to live as he pleases. Religion is a private concern of the individual; so also is the choice of his way of life. Philosophic inquiry has the privacy it needs, the arts and sciences have freedom of expression. England departs from the conformity, rigor, and inquisitiveness of democratic virtue. Far from being a requirement of modern England, virtue is even dangerous to it.

The analysis of England must be taken one step further. Its liberty is not only of actions and thoughts but of passions. To be free is mainly to follow one's appetites for money, prestige, and power.[7] England is capitalistic: the moral limits on endless competitive acquisition have been removed. The parallel in the field of ambition is party politics. England is the modern Athens—a commercial rather than a military or agricultural republic. Aided by its naval power, its imperialism is commercial rather than militaristic. But how does the spirit of commerce keep from destroying itself through excessive luxury and dissoluteness? High taxes keep men working, and frivolous expenditure is considered blameworthy, though whether on religious or business grounds is not clear. Furthermore, the extreme intensity of competition and the constant opening of new economic opportunities make dissoluteness the exception rather than the rule. Nor can the dissolute still have the influence they had within the narrower confines of the city-state. In sum, avarice and ambition constitute the moral foundations of the English system, not its deadly enemy. Each man's sense of self-interest supports his love of liberty and his patriotism.

In England the liberty of the impassioned many guarantees the liberty of the thoughtful few. Montesquieu does not deny that the vices of Englishmen deserve the bitter satire of a Juvenal, but he himself does not provide that satire. This is because the English system derives benefits for all from the vices it allows and encourages. The utmost in legal security, participation in government by all, and activity in commerce produce a citizen proud of his independence, hopeful of getting ahead, but completely blind to the fact that he is a slave to vulgar passions. England is a secularized society, interested in earthly goods. It does not need a common religion or democratic virtue to bind the community together, and thus can permit more privacy and freedom of expression than ancient Athens itself. With a novel constitutional system by which the striving for selfish interest is given permanent form, England has discovered how to postpone internal breakdown almost indefinitely.

## 4. Nature

The full significance of England and commerce for Montesquieu's thought can only be appreciated if one understands his conception of natural or primitive man and of the natural setting in which he first existed. The second chapter of Book I had led us to expect a historical treatment of human development out of the state of nature. This approach appears in the first passages of the third chapter, too, but then our attention is abruptly transferred from what is natural to man in the sense of "original" to what is natural in the sense of "best." In other words, we begin to think about advanced and later human things. This change of subject is carried forward in Books II through XIII, where the perfected forms of government are discussed. Books XIV through XVIII, however, are meant to satisfy the original expectation. Their subject is man's natural setting and beginning, the importance of which might explain the central location of these five books in the work as a whole. The topics treated are, first, the effects of climate on body and soul and its relation to diverse forms of slavery; second, the relation between geography and primitive human society. Material gathered from the references to primitive conditions in other books will help us complete the picture of what man was and is by nature.

Montesquieu displays the full strength of his ateleological naturalism in the first book on climate. Temperature, by influencing the human body, influences the mind and the passions. In hot climates, men are more sensible to pleasures and pains and hence more sensuous, more timid, more slothful. A cold climate has opposite effects, while the temperate zone is indeterminate. Thus are awakened dissimilar tendencies and needs, different moral possibilities, while the virtues themselves—e.g., courage, temperance, justice—vary radically with climate in their practicability and desirability. In general, the legislator's problem is to assure that at least the minimum conditions for society be met. But Montesquieu does not ask which climatic conditions produce the best human beings. As the relevant book titles indicate, he even stresses the connection between climate and human slavery, not human freedom. Climate sets natural limits to the extension of free, moderate, or non-despotic government, or, more generally, man is the subject, not the master, of climate. It is strange, therefore, that Montesquieu gives so little attention in Book XIV to temperate climates and their effects, for there is an obvious connection between these areas of indeterminacy and civilization—unless he means to indicate the rare and accidental character of that which supports the highest human things.

Given the variations caused by climate, what was the earliest human society like? Montesquieu does not speak openly about original family relations, but he suggests that they harbor some of mankind's deepest secrets. In all probability, the family as a stable unit did not exist originally but had to develop out of the condition of promiscuity. Incest prohibitions had themselves to be developed, thus providing a basis for peace and mutual care. The male ruled the family through his superior strength, and the female remained in a subordinate and even servile position. Under these conditions, polygamy was very widespread, whereas only in hot climates is it an enduring necessity, together with the institutions of the seraglio which preserve it.[8]

Primitive societies are either savage or barbarous, depending on whether, as hunters, the men remain in isolated tribes or, as herders, they are able to unite into a horde. Their loose organization permits each man considerable freedom, and the absence of money makes for near-equality of possessions and thus little exploitation. Political authority is in the hands of the strong, the sage, and the old. Wars are severe, and slave-taking a normal practice. The punishment of crime, too, is crude and cruel. Finally, religion and frequently priests already wield strong influence.

This picture of primitive man can help to clarify the true meaning of natural law. Natural law consists of those rights and duties of individuals or nations that ought to be respected everywhere because of the good they produce. In this sense natural law is natural to mankind. But it is not natural in the sense of being originally known to men or originally intended on moral grounds. It has two poles: on the one hand, the right to self-preservation and freedom of individuals and nations; on the other, the mutual obligations binding the members of the family. Only these ought to be universal among mankind. In point of fact, the various articles of natural law differ in the degree to which they are actually respected, and also in the time of their origin in human history.

On two heads Montesquieu's version of natural law went far beyond

the practice of even civilized nations. Private slavery, he claims, is
legitimate in only one case: that of a mild, contractual slavery within a
political despotism. As for the necessity of harsh slavery, he inclines to
the view that free labor can be obtained to do even the worst of jobs
in even the most torrid climates. He argues against Aristotle that slavery
is bad for both master and slave, and that no men are by nature born to
be slaves. He also refuses to grant the claim of the Roman jurists that
capture in war and indebtedness are sufficient grounds for enslavement.
At the same time, however, he admits that all men have a deep-seated
desire to enjoy the servile services of other men.

Montesquieu seems to have thought that the work of Christianity
in ending slavery within Europe could be spread abroad with the help
of cosmopolitan enlightenment and an appeal to humane sympathies.
He is less sanguine about the possibility of ending warfare, even within
Europe. In spite of the modern mitigation of warfare itself, and the
greater lenience of peace settlements, Europe is hardly more peaceably
inclined than ever and remains armed to the teeth. Montesquieu maintains that the only just war is one of self-defense, and the only just
treatment of a conquered territory that which aims to preserve the conquest rather than to destroy or oppress the vanquished. Yet he is forced
to admit that international relations have always been and will always
be conducted on the basis of self-interest and force rather than agree-
ments or consideration for the rights of others.[9] Decent nations neglect
this fact at their own peril. The conclusion seems necessary that it will
be more difficult to persuade mankind to give up war than slavery.

These examples also show that natural law, as dictates of reason
for human good, to some extent calls for the restriction of self-regarding
tendencies that are natural to man. Those natural laws observed everywhere (*e.g.,* regarding the family) probably did not originate out of
rational and just intent but out of some of the self-regarding passions
themselves. Those natural laws which are much less observed probably
constitute dictates of reason that fail to spread precisely because they
lack sufficient basis in the human passions. It would appear, therefore,
that man's natural or original endowment did not itself immediately
provide for his becoming a moral and reflective being.

Machiavelli and Bacon had raised the question in modern times
as to whether natural and social necessities, and chance, set any limits
to what human knowledge, will, and power could achieve. Locke had
implied that men could establish free societies on the English model
everywhere: what they had a right to do—*i.e.,* to replace old regimes of
every kind with the new individualism—was capable of accomplishment. Montesquieu shares this admiration for modern freedom, and

even goes beyond Locke in devising safeguards for it. But the English model is absolutely impossible in Asia and highly improbable even in most of Europe.

Asia is the natural home of every kind of slavery—private, marital, and political. Because Asia lacks a temperate zone and because the character of its natural barriers does not dispose it to form moderate-sized states, it has favored despotisms in the south, despotic conquests of the south by the north, and virtual immobility in its way of life and mores over many centuries. Opportunities for moderate government are much greater in Europe—hitherto the most interesting area of the world by far. But Montesquieu does not recommend revolutions against the old European monarchies in an attempt to imitate English liberty. This liberty is peculiar: on the one hand, it seems to depend on things easily subject to imitation, *e.g.,* the emancipation of the selfish passions and the establishment of a constitutional mechanism; yet England's insular position, its particular history, its climate all have a special kinship to its laws. Even in this case, then, Montesquieu attempts to restore to the modern position a prudent recognition of the necessity for a variety of political orders. He sets limits to what conscious human effort can achieve, but it must also be said that these limits go considerably beyond what the classics thought necessary or wise.

## 5. COMMERCE

We now have some conception of man's deficient natural beginnings and of the highest point he can attain, the regime of modern liberty. The two are connected by the development of commerce. Montesquieu was the first great political philosopher to consider commerce worthy of expansive empirical treatment within his major work. Of the various elements which enter the spirit of laws, it is the only one with a separate book devoted to its history or "revolutions."

In his analysis of primitive societies, Montesquieu regards the introduction of agriculture as the cause of the introduction of money. There is a constant interplay between man's needs and his knowledge: new needs encourage the searching for new knowledge, new knowledge encourages the growth of new needs. The art of agriculture implies the prior existence of numerous specialized skills and increases the need for some material to serve as a means of exchange and standard of value: money. Once the metallic form of money is invented, the opportunity for increasing inequalities among men is vastly enlarged. But internal exchange is still not international trade, and apart from conquest, the main source of a people's multiplying wealth, measured in terms of the variety and abundance of commodities, is international trade. Trade leads to riches, riches to luxury, luxury to the perfection of the arts. In his history of commerce Montesquieu mentions the poetry of Homer and draws attention to the perfection of taste and the fine arts in the ancient Greek cities. In the book on primitive societies there is no mention of poetry.

Montesquieu calls commerce the communication of peoples. In two ways this communication is connected with the civilizing of man, *i.e.,* with the reduction of barbarism. The first is through wealth and the arts, the second through philosophy. The tribe or nation that fails to participate in commerce is characterized by inbred superstition, prejudice, and ignorance, as well as by barbaric mores. Thus the original or "natural" condition of human societies is gravely defective. Commerce lays the basis for breaking out of this parochialism. It encourages the comparison of different ways of life. It makes possible the questioning of ancestral beliefs. It enables men to discover more of nature. In short, it makes possible philosophy, the coherent or conscious quest for knowledge of nature and man. It is curious that Montesquieu does not point to the philosophy of ancient Greece. Even more startling is his failure to draw attention to the great revolution in natural philosophy that he considered the most important feature of modernity. But the motto from Vergil prefixed to the first book on commerce is sufficiently indicative: "the things that mighty Atlas taught" (*Aeneid* I. 740) refers to a variety of topics within the study of nature. It was the revival of commerce that encouraged the revival of philosophy as well as the softening of European barbarism in early modern times. Commerce and knowledge together put an end to the Middle Ages.

Commerce develops by a combination of needs, inventions, and accidents. Montesquieu describes its principal varieties, its frequently awkward origins, its dependence on technology, its discovery of ways to outwit tyrants, its modern global extension, and finally its complex financial arrangements. The effects of commerce are to soften and polish barbaric mores (at the same time that it corrupts pure mores), to encourage the arts and sciences, to conduce toward peace by linking nations via their needs, and to raise standards of living. Of these, Montesquieu seems least interested in the last regarded as an end in itself. Nor is he solicitous of the merchant's profit-making: the greatest benefits of commerce are the less obvious, unintended consequences of the merchant's selfishness.

The book linking Montesquieu's discussion of natural or primitive man and his extensive discussion of commerce deals with the "general spirit" of nations. It begins by warning against the attempt to force all nations into the same mold, then proceeds to point out that moral virtues and vices are different from political virtues and vices, and ends by revealing modern England's foundation in the selfish passions of avarice and ambition. The idea that the political "virtues" required of its citizens by a defective political order might in reality be moral vices was a cornerstone of classical political philosophy: only rarely, if ever, were the good man and good citizen identical. But Montesquieu has in mind something far more disconcerting: the highest human things are brought about through the action of moral vices, and the *best* political order depends upon such vices. This understanding of human life Montesquieu learned from Machiavelli and his followers, not from the classics. The latter condemned commerce as institutionalized avarice, they had harsh words for moneylending, the regimes they favored had an agricultural, not a commercial base. But this amounted to wanting the fruits of commerce—the sciences and arts—without commerce itself. If popular or vulgar activities generate and nourish the highest activities of man, endangering them jeopardizes the higher things, which cannot endure independently. Remove commerce and travel, as in the Middle Ages, and you ruin philosophy. Philosophy is sustained by cosmopolitanism, and cosmopolitanism by commerce. Philosophy is freest in highly commercial England.

Montesquieu's view does not imply that the things produced indirectly through the actions of the multitude are, or ever can be, in complete harmony with the character of the multitude itself. Philosophy is a case in point. Can the people or societies as a whole be made philosophical? Are they capable of enlightenment in the radical sense? Montesquieu's answer is given in the book on the "general spirit" of each people. The general spirit is formed by climate, religion, the laws, political maxims, past examples, mores, manners. The spirit or mind of no nation is formed by reason. Nations live by passion and prejudice, not understanding. Enlightenment to make human life less barbaric or inhumane is possible, but even such enlightenment must be supported by an appeal to the passions, whether of self-interest or pity, and to the prejudices peculiar to the society addressed. Or again, England offers the greatest opportunity and security for philosophy and the arts, but England itself is neither philosophical nor poetic. Societies believe, whereas philosophers question, and societies protect philosophy more out of a concern for their own than for its freedom. Philosophy and society are therefore never bound in true amity. On his side, the philosopher is morally obliged to consider both the good and harmful social effects of his writings: hence the style of writing attributed to Montesquieu by d'Alembert, and its peculiar concealment of philosophy itself.

At the outset of the work, Montesquieu distinguishes between the tasks of the philosophical moralist and of the legislator.[10] For Aristotle, political aims had to be understood in terms of the quest for complete good: ethics and politics formed parts of a single study, with the former preceding the latter. For Montesquieu, however, ethics and politics have a much less direct relation, and as a legislator, he himself never systematically reveals the true or philosophical morality. Strictly speaking, the political world never is nor can be guided by this morality. For political virtues, like political vices, are all passions. If so, no nonphilosopher can be morally virtuous in any degree. But this is a more radical doctrine than that of the classics, who regarded men of popular or merely habitual virtue as animated by a very incomplete but nevertheless real knowledge of virtue. He concludes, for this and various other reasons we have seen, that man by nature is not a rational any more than he is a sociable or philanthropic being: the elements of the human soul do not naturally tend toward moral and intellectual perfection. It follows that the utopias and near-utopias of classical political philosophy are based on false premises. They judge and try to guide human nature by standards foreign to it and are utopian for this very reason. The philosophical legislator gains immeasurably in effectiveness by concealing his philosophical ethics and making prudent use of the real passions and opinions by which intellectual elites and greater multitudes can be moved. Yet his function changes therewith: before he was only an educator of philosophers and statesmen, now he is himself a political manipulator of men. The standards to which he appeals are those that the average man is best equipped by nature to understand. Their double root is self-preservation and pity. Their highest reach is political liberty, not excellence.

### 6. Religion

In Book I Montesquieu had vaguely suggested that God assisted man by a special revelation, and that man's being drawn toward the Creator (after forming an idea of Him) is the first of natural laws in importance, though not in time. As it turns out, religion is the last element of the spirit of laws to be discussed in the work. The two topics immediately preceding it—commerce and propagation—are concerned with the needs of the body. And in the book succeeding it, religion is treated in such a way as to obscure the distinction between the truly divine law of Jews and Christians on the one hand and the religious laws of gentiles on the other. It is also true that the work has little dependence on sacred history as such, though it sometimes draws examples from that history. With respect to the Christian Middle Ages, it is far more interested in the feudal than the Christian component.

Montesquieu claims, in this work, to be a political writer, not a theologian. But he also claims that the two capacities are perfectly consistent: Christianity is not only true but the greatest worldly good mankind could possess. He argues, against Bayle, that Christians make the best citizens. Yet the qualifications he attaches to the assertion make it clear that he considers the Christian counsels of perfection incompatible with political life, so that the most perfect Christian would make a very poor citizen. It is this view that engenders Montesquieu's praise of the ancient Stoic sects and the great Roman emperors, the Antonines, who were of their number. The Stoics were above all citizens, *i.e.,* not saints. And the main function of religion and civil laws is to make men good citizens and thereby to assist each society in satisfying its needs. For the truest and holiest dogmas can have very bad consequences if not linked to the principles of society, and the most false dogmas admirable consequences when so linked.

Montesquieu is critical of the social and political effects of Christianity on several counts. Christianity opposed commerce and moneylending in the Middle Ages; by fostering conventual chastity, it discouraged marriage and propagation; it was hostile everywhere to polygamy and divorce; it promoted civil disobedience in the name of a higher law; it turned Christian against Christian and Christian against non-Christian through an intolerant zeal for universality.[11] But it also had salubrious effects in restraining the schemes of despots and monarchs and assisting both the abolition of slavery and the mitigation of warfare in Europe. Montesquieu tries to correct its excesses. Unlike Locke, however, he does not make freedom of conscience a natural and universal right of man. A universal invitation to the establishment of religious diversity is not wise. One need not admit a new religion into a society if one can exclude it; but where any religion is already established, it should be tolerated.

### 7. Conclusion

The main virtue of the legislator, according to Montesquieu, must be moderation. He stresses the deliberate skill required by statecraft—its need for determining the kind of law to be applied, for understanding the network of relations comprising the spirit of laws and their connection with the complex particulars of each society.[12] Although Europe remained his main interest, he extended the purview of scientific explanation and evaluation in human affairs to all times and places. The phrase he applied to the Stoic emperors suits him even more aptly: he watched over humankind.

Montesquieu's philosophy delineates and relates the parts played by blind necessity and reasoned choice (another kind of necessity) in the formation of laws. His emphasis on the variety of political orders and the priority of particulars in statecraft derives from the classics. But he joins with Machiavelli and Locke in rejecting classical virtue as the ultimate political guide. This rejection foredoomed his effort to stem the revolutionary, universalistic tendencies of Lockean liberalism. Indeed, since liberty's portrait, unlike virtue's, must necessarily have widespread appeal, his elaborate description of English liberty itself became an instrument of that liberalism. The same rejection had another effect: by making a labyrinth of the relation between ethics and politics, it encouraged a political science that would lose interest in morality and statesmanship.

The surface of *The Spirit of the Laws* is both simple and disorderly, the interior difficult and coherent. What we have said may suffice to establish the truth of the claim that it has a design. Its systematic teaching, even its mystifying title, will continue to elude us until that design is fully understood.

## NOTES

1. See quotation on pp. 471–72 below.
2. Montesquieu, *The Spirit of the Laws,* ed. Gonzague Truc (2 vols.; Paris: Collection des Classiques Garnier, n.d.), Preface.
3. *Ibid.,* I. iii. (trans. D. L.).
4. *Ibid.,* V. ii–iii.
5. *Ibid.,* XI. viii.
6. *Ibid.,* III. vi.

7. *Ibid.,* XIX. xxvii, beginning.
8. *Ibid.,* XVIII. xiii; XXVI. xiv; XVI, ii.
9. *Ibid.,* X. ii–iii; XXVI. xx.
10. *Ibid.,* I. i, end.
11. *Ibid.,* XXI. xx; XXIII. xxi; XXIV. xiii; XXV. x.
12. *Ibid.,* Preface; I. iii; XXVI, i; XXIX. i.

## READINGS

A. Montesquieu. *The Spirit of the Laws.* Preface, bks I–V, XI, XII, XIX (11, 27).
B. Montesquieu. *The Spirit of the Laws.* Bks XIV, XV, XVIII, XX, XXI, XXIV, XXVI.
Montesquieu. *The Persian Letters.*
Montesquieu. *Considerations on the Greatness and Decline of the Romans.*

# DAVID HUME

## 1711–1776

David Hume is best known as a skeptic, as an acute and thoroughgoing critic of human reason. Indeed, it is sometimes claimed that Hume's philosophy dealt the deathblow to natural right and eliminated the possibility of rational judgments of "value." Thus Hume's theory is presented as a challenge to the very existence of political philosophy, one which must be confronted. But we are faced with a paradox. Hume was himself the author of a comprehensive political doctrine, purporting to be the truth about such subjects as the laws of nature, justice, the obligation to civil obedience, and the best kind of government.

Our first subject, it appears, must be Hume's teaching concerning the foundation and authority of normative judgments. This must be prefaced by a brief consideration of his theory of the principles and operations of the understanding.

Turning his observation inward upon the human mind, Hume finds there a collection and succession of what he calls "perceptions": the taste of an apple, the idea of a triangle, a notion of justice, esteem for a prudent action, anger, and so on. A perception is whatever is present to the mind, and nothing is present to the mind but its perceptions. Indeed, the mind is nothing but a heap or bundle of perceptions.

Perceptions are of two kinds. There are *impressions,* what is in our mind "when we hear, or see, or feel, or love, or hate, or desire, or will." There are *ideas,* what is in our mind "when we reflect on a passion or an object which is not present." The difference between impressions and ideas is a difference in their degree of force and vivacity: impressions are more "strong" and "lively" than ideas.

All ideas, Hume says, are derived from impressions. Now it is true that the imagination is very free, and we can picture golden mountains and winged horses that we have never seen; but those ideas are compounded out of other ideas. And as to "simple ideas," those irreducible ideas that admit of no distinction or separation, we find that it is not in our power to imagine any which does not correspond to and represent some impression we have previously experienced. As a blind man can form no idea of purple nor a deaf man of a flute's sound, so in general, "we can never *think* of anything which we have not seen [or in some way sensed] without us or *felt* in our own minds." All our simple ideas are but images or copies of impressions.[1]

We cannot have *knowledge* in the fullest sense and absolute *certainty,* Hume says, concerning matters of fact and real existence, but only concerning "the relations of ideas." This may be explained as follows: It is laid down as an "established maxim" that whatever is conceivable is possible. Now the contrary of every assertion of matter of fact is always conceivable. I can imagine that the sun will not rise tomorrow; hence, I have no knowledge that it will. I cannot be certain that the objects before me continue to exist when I close my eyes, for it is imaginable that they do not. We cannot have knowledge of that which can be thought to be otherwise. Knowledge then can be only of that which cannot be thought to be otherwise—of that which càn be thought only as it is. For example, the contrary of the proposition, "The angles of a triangle are equal to two right angles," is not conceivable; the relation between "the angles of a triangle" and "two right angles" must be thought to be what it is. Since the realm of possibility is where the imagination is free, then necessity must be located where the imagination is bound.

The only objects of knowledge then are those relations of ideas that "depend entirely on the ideas which we compare together." We can know only what is necessarily implied in our ideas; in a sense, we can take from our ideas only what we have put into them. For example, the proposition, "Where there is no property, there is no injustice," is certain, when the idea of injustice is simply the violation of property. But this is nothing more than unpacking what we have previously packed. And Hume appears to think that even the demonstrations of mathematicians are merely more lengthy and complicated forms of this kind of extraction process. Let us also note that the objects of knowledge are the relations of ideas *considered as ideas.* By comparing ideas we can learn nothing about that which is not ideas. We can have no knowledge, strictly speaking, of the world of realities, but only of the world of ideas.[2]

The principle, "Whatever is conceivable is possible," deserves further examination. Now there are many statements, Hume says, whose contrary is conceivable but that we are nevertheless entitled to accept with complete assurance; for example, that all men shall die. Indeed, Hume regards all matters of fact as parts of a system of universal necessity.[3] What then is meant by saying that "whatever is conceivable is possible" or "not absolutely impossible" or "possible, at least in a metaphysical sense"? Moreover, why is this principle, which seems not to be self-evident, to be considered an "established maxim"?

In answer it can be said that at a certain point in the history of philosophy it began to be thought that the disorder, contradiction and ignorance that prevailed in philosophy was a disgrace, and that it should be ended and the edifice of human reason erected on a completely unshakeable foundation. But an unshakeable foundation could be assured only by allowing the utmost sway to skepticism to begin with. In order that philosophy should be indubitable it is necessary to begin by doubting all that can be doubted.

Now Hume's "established maxim" is to be understood as an instrument of this kind of preliminary skepticism. The starting point of philosophy is the determination to doubt. The area of doubt is most extensive when the area of the merely possible is most extensive. Thus arises the necessity of regulating our reasoning by this "established maxim," which widens the possible to that which it is possible to conceive, and as a consequence, restricts the necessary to what it is necessary to conceive. Indeed, the maxim might be considered to be preliminary skepticism in its most naked form: it compels us to doubt wherever we are not obliged to affirm. Whereas Descartes, in whose philosophy the necessity of universal doubt is most clearly urged, employed that "freedom of the mind" whereby "it supposes that no object is, of the existence of which it has even the slightest doubt," in Hume the mind supposes (one could say) that no object is, the existence of which it is not forced to acknowledge.

Hume's principal concern is not with that kind of reasoning that through intuition or demonstration discovers the relations of ideas, but rather with "probable reasoning," by which we discover matter of fact and real existence, and which guides us all our lives and indeed composes most of our philosophy. Now all our reasoning about matter of fact is based, he says, on the relation of cause and effect. Without causation we cannot go beyond our senses and memory; by causation we are enabled to infer the existence of objects and occurrences beyond our experience. So the discussion of probability resolves itself into an examination of causation.

Hume begins by raising "sceptical doubts" concerning cause and effect. Consider a particular instance of the inference from cause to effect. For example, we see a billiard ball moving across a table and striking another. We conclude that the second one will begin to move. What is the basis for this conclusion? It is not made known to us by reason, for it is possible to conceive of the movement not following the collision. It must then be founded on experience: we have seen balls collide and set in motion in the past. But it still remains conceivable that they might not do so in this case. The inference is then based on experience together with the assumption that the future will resemble the past. But what is the basis of this principle? Not reason; for it is conceivable that the future will not resemble the past. Experience then; but how can we learn from experience the very principle that alone makes it possible to learn from experience?

We seem to be at a dead end. But now Hume presents his "sceptical solution" of these skeptical doubts. When we have observed one event succeeding another in a number of instances, the mind gets in the habit of considering them together. So when I see one billiard ball striking another my imagination, falling into a familiar groove, is led to think of the second ball's moving. And I not only form this conception but I *believe* in it; which means simply that it feels different from ideas I do not believe in. What its feeling is like is hard to describe; the idea is conceived in a stronger, or more vivid, or firmer manner, so that it forms a part of what we call "reality," along with impressions and the ideas of the memory. In sum, "all reasonings [about causation] are nothing but the effects of custom; and custom has no influence, but by enlivening the imagination, and giving us a strong conception of any object."

Another question is considered: the idea of *cause* and its origin. We observe, for instance, one billiard ball striking another, causing it, as we say, to move. From what impression is the idea of cause derived? What we observe is that the collision of the balls and the motion of the second are contiguous events, that one occurs prior in time to the second, and finally that on repetition this conjunction of events is found to be constant. That is all. Yet there is more to the idea of causation than contiguity, priority and constant conjunction; we commonly suppose that there is a *necessary* connection between the two events. From what impression can this come? Hume answers, from nothing in the objects, but from something in the mind, namely, the feeling of being compelled or determined to pass in the imagination from cause to effect.

We mistakenly transfer this impression to the objects themselves; but in fact, necessity lies not in the objects but in ourselves.[4]

The argument that has been sketched above follows a pattern that recurs frequently in Hume's philosophy. What is accepted unquestioningly by common sense—here causation, elsewhere the existence of a world of objects not dependent on our perception of them, and elsewhere even the continued existence of a personal self—is found to have no rational basis. But it is dissolved only to be restored. Nature is too strong for reason. And an account is given of the way in which reason is overcome.[5] But the overcoming is of a dubious nature. The "sceptical doubts" are not refuted. Nor are they simply shaken off in the name of common sense, in the manner of Dr. Johnson refuting Berkeley by kicking a stone. They receive a "solution," but a "skeptical" solution. What is "restored" is not quite what has been dissolved. Thus, the inference from cause to effect is a habit; the belief in what is inferred is an inexplicable feeling; the idea of cause is a mistake.

By thus reducing causal reasoning to a matter of custom and sentiment Hume exposes himself to difficulties in attempting to distinguish and justify correct reasoning. For example, by observing a number of instances of the conjunction of objects a habit of mental transition is engendered, although they may have in reality no essential connection. We may, to use Hume's example, come to regard all Irishmen as dull, in the face of clear evidence to the contrary. This is prejudice, and the judgment must be called in to rectify the imagination. But how is this possible? Hume explains that the general rules called "prejudices" are corrected by other general rules called "rules of logic," based on observation of the nature and operations of the understanding and enabling us to distinguish the essential from the nonessential. Habit is overcome by habit. But it would seem that a habit could be overcome only by a *stronger* habit. Yet Hume says that these rules of reasoning are derived from the observation not of a greater number of instances but of the "more general and authentic operations of the understanding." [6]

Another problem: how it is that we can arrive at a judgment concerning cause and effect after only one careful experiment? The habit of making a mental transition from one object to another must, it would seem, vary in proportion to the number of instances of their conjunction we have observed, and after one instance would be slight at the most. How can habit exceed experience? Hume answers that we subsume our single experiment under the principle that similar objects in similar circumstances produce similar effects, and the habit of transition is produced artificially. The principle itself is of course habitual; the uniformity of nature is reduced to a habit of expecting in the future what we have been accustomed to in the past. It is a full and perfect habit, based on millions of experiments.[7] But, we must ask, is our experience of uniform succession perfect? And if not, then once again, how can habit exceed experience?

The problems put above may be summarized as follows: If the ground of inference is habit, then (it would appear) habit is reason enough for an inference, and inference cannot go beyond habit. Hume cannot allow these consequences. His theory is intended not only to explain the "reasoning" of animals but also to justify the methods of Newton.[8] The question is whether he does solve the problems without bringing in anything but habit and feeling.


We are now able to proceed to Hume's treatment of the foundation and authority of normative judgment. As in his discussion of causation, he begins with "sceptical doubts," which lead to the conclusion that "moral distinctions [are] not derived from reason."[9]

One line of argument is designed to show that virtue and vice are not objects of the understanding. The understanding has, Hume says, two operations: the comparison of ideas, by which it discovers the relations of objects, and the inference of matter of fact, by which it discovers their existence. So if virtue and vice can be discovered by the understanding they must consist in either *relations* or *matters of fact*.

First, Hume undertakes to show that virtue and vice cannot be relations. The ultimate object of moral approval and disapproval is a mental action in respect of external objects; for example, the passion of affection for one's children, or the volition to take somebody else's property. If moral good and evil are relations they must therefore be relations obtaining between internal actions and external objects, and capable of obtaining *only* between internal actions and external objects. For if, for example, moral good were a relation that could also apply between external objects, then irrational and inanimate objects could be morally good. Now there appears to be no relation that is so restricted. Consider, for instance, the relation of *fittingness*. A moral theory that Hume seems especially interested in refuting asserted that there are certain natural fitnesses and unfitnesses of things to one another, and that the virtue of an action lies in its fittingness to the situation. Hume's objection is that fittingness (supposing such a relation to exist) can obtain between external objects which, however, cannot be called virtuous.

Indeed, the relations that actually do exist between internal actions and external objects in instances of virtue and vice are found to exist between external objects, where they clearly do not constitute virtue and vice. Suppose, for example, a tree that grows up and chokes out the tree from whose seed it itself grew. The relations here are precisely the same as one finds in the case of a child strangling its parent. We do not regard the former case as an instance of vice; but if vice consisted in the relation it would be so.

Are virtue and vice then matters of fact? Hume bids the reader to take an example of a vicious action, murder, perhaps, and to "examine it in all lights, and see if you can find that matter of fact, or real existence, which you call *vice*. In whichever way you take it, you find only certain passions, motives, volitions and thoughts. There is no other matter of fact in the case. The vice entirely escapes you, as long as you consider the object."

Hume concludes that virtue and vice are neither relations nor matters of fact; that is, they are not objects of the understanding, and hence the sense of morality does not consist in their discovery.

Another and more prominent line of argument is summarized as follows: "Morals excite passions, and produce or prevent actions. Reason of itself is utterly impotent in this particular. The rules of morality, therefore, are not conclusions of our reason."

By the impotence of reason Hume means this: An action is the result of a propensity or an aversion to some object, and this propensity or aversion is excited (usually, at least) by the pleasure or pain given by or expected from the object. Now reason can inform us of the existence of objects and of the relations among them, but if the objects are indifferent to us, if they arouse no propensity or aversion, this information has no influence on the will. So reason *alone* cannot produce or, by the same token, prevent any action. As Hume puts it in a famous sentence, "Reason is, and ought only to be the slave of the passions, and can never pretend to any other office than to serve and obey them." Yet it is clear that reason *in conjunction with passion* may have a strong (if "oblique" and "mediate") influence on the will. It may *prompt* passion by informing it of the existence of its object. For example, I am of the opinion that behind a garden wall there is tasty fruit, and my desire for it is founded on that opinion. And reason may *direct* passion to its object, by tracing the connection of causes and effects. I may hit on the expedient of getting a ladder and climbing the wall. In such a case the part of reason may be great and even decisive. Thus, if I learn that my opinion about the existence of the fruit or the best way to get it is incorrect, my passion and volition cease. But reason's role remains a ministerial one, for it does not supply the impulse that moves us.[10]

The "calm and indolent judgments of the understanding" are then not sufficient to influence the will. And the crux of Hume's argument is that "those judgments by which we distinguish good and evil" are sufficient to influence the will. He denies that moral cognition is separable from a propensity or aversion to action. He denies, that is, that one can know what is morally good without feeling an inclination to it.

The following celebrated passage from Hume may at once be elucidated by and help to elucidate the preceding argument.

In every system of morality which I have hitherto met with, I have always remarked that the author proceeds for some time in the ordinary way of reasoning, and establishes the being of a God, or makes observations concerning human affairs; when of a sudden I am surprised to find, that instead of the usual copulations of propositions, *is,* and *is not,* I meet with no proposition that is not connected with an *ought,* or an *ought not.* This change is imperceptible; but is, however, of the last consequence. For as this *ought,* or *ought not,* expresses some new relation or affirmation, 'tis necessary that it should be observed and explained; and at the same time that a reason should be given, for what seems altogether inconceivable, how this new relation can be a deduction from others, which are entirely different from it. But as authors do not commonly use this precaution, I shall presume to recommend it to the readers: and am persuaded, that this small attention would subvert all the vulgar systems of morality, and let us see that the distinction of vice and virtue is not founded merely on the relations of objects, nor is perceived by reason.[11]

Morality, we see, is concerned with duty and obligation; the morally good is essentially what one *ought* to do. And this cannot be found out by reason. For example, consider once again the thesis that virtue consists in fittingness. In one place Hume concedes for the sake of argument that the relation of fittingness exists and is discoverable by reason. But this, he says, is not sufficient to show that it is virtue; it must be shown that there is a connection between fittingness and the will. For the morally good has the character of law; it is obligatory. That is to say, it is "forcible," it influences the will. Reason may (it is assumed) discover the fitting, but it cannot discover it as morally good. For the morally good is what we ought to do, and what we ought to do is what we are compelled or impelled to do. The only way to know compulsion is to suffer it; we can discover what influences the will only by feeling that influence.

Now this identification of the obligatory with the forcible is not self-evident. It seems to rest upon the need to make the obligatory *effectively* obligatory. Hume seems, in other words, to be following the lines laid down by Hobbes and Locke in trying to erect morals on a foundation that "the passions not mistrusting, shall not seek to displace." In the same way that Hume found the certainty of knowledge by identifying the necessary with what must necessarily be thought, so he finds the efficacy of morality by identifying the virtuous with what one is compelled to pursue. As the human imagination was made the ground of science so the human affections are made the ground of morality.

We turn now to the "sceptical solution of these sceptical doubts" concerning morality, which is that "moral distinctions are derived from a moral sense." Since virtue and vice are not discovered by reason, it follows that we distinguish them by some sentiment or impression that they excite. The vice of a vicious action "entirely escapes you, as long as you consider the object. You can never find it, till you turn your reflection into your own breast, and find a sentiment of disapprobation, which arises in you, towards this action. Here is a matter of fact, but 'tis the object of feeling, not of reason. It lies in yourself, not in the object." "Morality, therefore, is more properly felt than judged of. . . ."

More precisely, Hume asserts not merely that virtue and vice are *discovered* by sentiment, but that they are *constituted* by sentiment. It is not that virtue is approved because it is virtue, but that virtue is virtue because it is approved. When an action is said to be virtuous, nothing is meant but that it gives rise to a feeling of approbation, just as when an object is said to be the cause or effect of another, nothing is meant but that they are habitually united in the imagination.

The sight of virtue, Hume observes, is pleasing, and that of vice displeasing. He further declares that the very sentiment of moral approbation is pleasing and that of disapprobation displeasing. Indeed, he identifies the approbation and the pleasure. He denies that the approbation is an inference from the pleasure. He silently passes over the possibility that the pleasure is a consequence of the approbation. Rather, he reduces the approbation to the pleasure. "To have the sense of virtue, is nothing but to feel a satisfaction of a particular kind. . . ." We see then that the moral sense is not a distinct and peculiar faculty, and that moral sentiments are pleasures and pains.

Moral sentiments are, however, pleasures and pains of a particular kind, differing in their feeling from other pleasures and pains in the same way as, for instance, the pleasure given by a beefsteak differs from the pleasure given by a poem. These peculiar pleasures and pains (1) arise only from the consideration of the characters and actions of rational beings and (2) arise when these are considered "in general, without reference to our particular interest." Thus we may esteem an enemy for those very qualities that make him dangerous to us.

In sum, "virtue is distinguished by the pleasure, and vice by the pain, that any action, sentiment, or character gives us by the mere view or contemplation." [12]

Those qualities or characters that are esteemed as virtuous are found by Hume to be of four kinds. First, qualities that are useful to others: *e.g.,* justice, generosity, beneficence, honesty. Second, qualities that are useful to the one possessing them: *e.g.,* prudence, frugality, industry, temperance. Third, qualities that are immediately agreeable to others: *e.g.,* modesty, wit, decency. Finally, qualities that are immediately agreeable to the one possessing them: *e.g.,* a proper self-esteem, love of glory, magnanimity. It might be added that a quality may fall into more than one of these classes. For example, courage is not only *useful* to its possessor and to the public but also gives an immediate pleasure to its possessor.

In short, the objects of moral approbation are those qualities that are either immediately pleasant or productive of pleasure, either to their possessor or to others. The good is fundamentally identical with the pleasant. But it is *not* identical with one's own pleasure. In making moral judgments we do not value others for their value to ourselves. Approbation is not bestowed on qualities because they give pleasure to us but, on the contrary, because they give pleasure to others, including the one who has them. Yet, in another sense, we should note, it can be said that we approve of what pleases us, because our very approbation consists in being pleased.

Why do we approve of those "virtuous" qualities? Hume sometimes replies that we are moved by "humanity" or "benevolence." But this is not to be understood as an "original instinct" or desire for the good of others. It is the manifestation of a more general and extremely important principle of human nature: *sympathy,* or "that propensity we have to receive by communication from others their passions, sentiments, etc." It must be noted that sympathy is not the same as pity, and has no connotation of affection or good will. It is a mere conduit through which pains, pleasures, passions, and so on, are transmitted from one person to another.[13]

The object of moral approbation then is a source of pleasure; the sentiment of approbation is itself a pleasure; and the pleasantness of the sentiment is borrowed from that of the object. Thus Hume is enabled to reject what he calls the "selfish morality," and yet to avoid affirming the existence of general benevolence toward men apart from their relation to ourselves. He does this by postulating the operation of sympathy, which makes the pleasures and pains of others our own, but does so as it were mechanically, without the interposition of either good will to our fellows or calculations of self-interest.

At the bottom of Hume's denial that moral good and evil can be found out by reason is the demand that morality be in accordance with the passions, or, to use his own formulations, the identification of the obligatory with the forcible, and the insistence that moral judgments have a direct and immediate influence on the will. His own theory meets that demand. The principal motives to action are pleasure and pain; the judgments of moral approbation and disapprobation are nothing but pleasures and pains. Thus, virtue is essentially "amiable" and vice essentially "odious," and consequently desired or shunned. A moral judgment is therefore not only a sentiment of praise or blame, *i.e.,* a feeling of pleasure or pain, but also an "opinion of obligation" or a "sense of duty," *i.e.,* a propensity or aversion.

In requiring that morality be in accordance with and built upon the passions, Hume is following Hobbes and Locke. But he does not follow them in their conclusions. They represent what Hume calls the "selfish system of morals," which he criticizes severely. As Hume understood it, the basic premise of the "selfish system" is that the fundamental and ruling passion is self-interest. Hume denies this. (1) It exaggerates the power of reason. To show that such passions as friendship that appear to be disinterested are really only manifestations of self-love, philosophers must hypothesize very intricate and refined reasonings, reasonings much too intricate and refined to have in fact much influence on the passions. (2) Moreover, not all desires can be subsumed under the desire for one's own good. For example, there are affection for one's children and hatred of one's enemies and many others. These are original instincts or impulses quite as much as the desire of one's good is, and they pursue their objects independently of any consideration of advantage. (3) Indeed, far from all passions being reducible to self-interest, the action of self-interest itself presupposes the existence of other passions, at least sometimes and perhaps always or almost always. Self-interest moves us to desire a pleasing object, for instance, a beefsteak. But why does the object please? Because it gratifies some other desire, for instance, hunger. Without desires other than self-interest there would be nothing or little for self-interest to concern itself with. (4) Nor is self-interest necessarily the strongest or dominant passion. When placed in competition with some other particular passion, self-interest does not always command priority. And a man may prefer his lesser good to his greater, *knowing* it to be lesser. The desire for a lesser good may overcome the desire for one's acknowledged greater good.[14]

The "selfish morality" is based on an excessively simplified understanding of the passions. Hobbes, to take the clearest example, finds his starting point in a single passion, the fear of death or the desire for self-preservation; this is the strongest or most fundamental passion. Virtue consists in obedience to the laws of nature, which are dictates of reason for avoiding death and preserving life. Fear of death is the strongest passion because death is the greatest evil. It is presupposed that all men by natural necessity always seek what they think to be their own greatest good.

Hume, on the other hand, says that there is no such natural necessity. Passion supplies no single incontrovertible axiom to reason, and hence reason can furnish no authoritative guidance to conduct. " 'Tis not contrary to reason to prefer the destruction of the whole world to the scratching of my finger. 'Tis not contrary to reason for me to choose my total ruin, to prevent the least uneasiness of an Indian or person wholly unknown to me." [15] The standards of moral judgment are not "dictates of reason" derived from passion; they are themselves passions, *i.e.,* moral sentiments.

Moreover, since no passion is "axiomatic," a morality in accordance with the passions must be marked by breadth and complexity. Hume rejects the kind of narrowing of virtue characteristic of modern natural-law teaching; he declines to "fetter his moral sentiments by narrow systems." From the moderns Hume appeals to the ancient moralists, such as Cicero, who are "the best models." The modern natural-law teaching, in basing morality on the passions, as Hume does, failed, however, to do justice to the full range of human passions. A morality truly in accordance with the passions takes its standard from the "common and natural course" of the passions.[16]


According to Hume morality is distinguished and determined by sentiment. A character is virtuous or vicious in so far as it excites a certain pleasure or pain, and if it excites such pleasure or pain it is virtuous or vicious. It follows that, since we can never be mistaken as to our feelings of pleasure and pain, moral judgments are "perfectly infallible."

This appears to lead into a chaos of subjectivity. For the sentiments of different men differ, as do the sentiments of the same man at different times, depending on their particular situations. For example, we seldom have much affection for someone who works against our interest, even if he is acting in accordance with the general rules of morality. We receive a stronger and livelier pleasure from the common diligence of a servant than from the noblest qualities of Marcus Brutus.

Hume is, however, not a relativist. Morals are a matter of taste, but there is right and wrong taste. This is accounted for as follows: The variation in our sentiments arising from the variation in our situation makes us uncertain. Moreover we find that the sentiments of others based on their particular situations contradict our sentiments based on our particular situations. Now this contradiction and uncertainty makes it impossible for men "to converse together on any reasonable terms. . . ." In order, therefore, to communicate with one another we are obliged to seek a common and less variable point of view from which to judge the qualities of persons. The point of view we adopt is that of those who are immediately connected with those persons. For example, our affection and admiration for Brutus would, we know, be much greater than that for our servant were they equally near to us, and we dispense our esteem accordingly. In making moral judgments we overlook our present situation and even our own interest. We "correct our sentiments."

It needs to be asked how this is possible on Hume's ground. How can a sentiment arising from a real situation be overcome by a sentiment arising from a hypothetical situation? Hume in effect concedes that it is not: "The passions," he writes, "do not always follow our corrections." What is regulated by the transposition of situations is not so much our feelings as our "abstract notions" and "general pronouncements." [17] But, we must ask, does this not imply an abandonment of the principle that moral judgment is a matter of sentiment?

The problem with which we have been concerned—the status of normative judgments in Hume's philosophy—may now be approached by considering the question of the extent to which such judgments stand on a different footing from judgments about matter of fact. There are passages in which Hume indicates that they differ radically in kind. For example, he writes that reason, which gives knowledge concerning truth and falsehood, differs from taste, which is the source of moral sentiment, in that the former "discovers objects as they really stand in nature, without addition and diminution," whereas the latter "has a productive faculty, and gilding or staining all natural objects with the colors, borrowed from internal sentiment, raises in a manner a new creation." The standard of reason is "eternal and inflexible," whereas the standard of the other arises from the "frame and constitution of animals."

It is doubtful, however, that the contrast so vividly drawn will survive further examination. For if "morality is more properly felt than judged of," yet in the same way "all probable reasoning is nothing but a species of sensation. 'Tis not solely in poetry and music we must follow our taste and sentiment," but in the experimental sciences as well.[18] Virtue and vice are not matters of fact; or rather, they are *internal* matters of fact, *i.e.,* our sentiments of moral approval and disapproval. But the same is true of the connection between cause and effect. "Objects have no discoverable connection together. . . ." The causal relation is nothing in the object but something in the mind.

Hume of course attempts to supply a more secure foundation for causal reasoning than mere feeling, to distinguish prejudice and fantasy from solid reasoning and to give rules to guide the conduct of inquiry. But, as we have just seen, he undertakes a similar task for morality, to escape from the contradiction and variation of moral judgment and to determine the standard of correct taste in morality. And in both cases he encounters similar difficulties in doing so.


The "state of nature" is, in Hume's opinion, a fiction of the philosophers. But in tracing the origin of government it is permissible to begin by hypothesizing man in a "savage and solitary condition." We find that more than any other animal he is at once necessitous and weak. He needs food, clothing, and shelter. Yet he is ill-equipped by his natural abilities to obtain and secure them. Society alone can compensate for his weaknesses. By joining forces with others he is able to carry out projects for which he alone is not powerful enough; the division of labor induces greater skill in the arts; and mutual helpfulness is a shield against accident and bad fortune. Only in society can his wants be met—including the new wants that society itself engenders.

The origin of society cannot however be attributed to such calculations of advantage as these, which are far beyond the capacity of uncultivated men to make. It is due to another need with a more obvious remedy, namely, sexual desire. This draws together man and woman; parental affection continues to unite them; and a family society arises, ruled by the parents. It is in the family that men learn by experience the advantages of society and are at the same time fitted for it.

There are, however, certain factors that make society difficult to maintain. First, the passions of selfishness and confined generosity. A man commonly loves himself better than any other single person. And although the total of his affection for others is usually greater than his self-love, it is restricted mainly to his relatives and friends. Secondly, the scarcity and instability of external goods. External goods do not exist in enough quantity to satisfy everyone's needs and desires. And they may be taken from their possessor and become useful to someone else, unlike useful bodily attributes. These internal and external circumstances co-incide to produce the chief impediment to society, the "insatiable, per-petual, universal" desire of acquiring possessions for ourselves and those near to us. The other passions are more easily restrained or are not so dangerous. Vanity, for example, is a social passion, and "a bond of union among men."

We cannot expect this propensity to be controlled by our natural moral sentiments. These conform themselves to the natural course of the passions and tend to reinforce them. The remedy is an artifice found out by reason: "a convention entered into by all the members of the society to bestow stability on the possession of those external goods, and leave every one in the peaceable enjoyment of what he may acquire by his fortune and industry." This is the first law of nature: abstinence from the possessions of others.

This convention or agreement is not of the nature of a promise or contract. It is rather a common sense of common interest, arising grad-ually among men and gaining force by repeated experience of the inconvenience of transgressing it. Once it is established there arise the ideas of justice and injustice, and the ideas that follow from them, property, right, and obligation.

If the fundamental rule of justice is the stability of property, there are needed some other rules to determine what goods are the property of what persons. The most obvious rule was that of present possession, and afterwards others presented themselves: occupation, prescription, and so on. Now in operation these rules depend on chance and must often result in a disproportion between men's property and their wants and desires. Yet the fitness or suitability of property to persons can never, Hume insists, be accepted as a rule. The rules of justice are set up to end contention and discord, and nothing is more productive of conten-tion and discord than questions of fitness and suitability. To allow the adjustment of property to persons without stirring up trouble, the natural expedient is to permit the transfer of property by consent. This is the second law of nature, and grows up in much the same fashion as the first.

The third law of nature is the obligation of promises, and it arises as follows: The advantage of mutual helpfulness is obvious. If I help you harvest now and you in turn help me harvest later, both of us are bene-fited. But if men were left to follow the natural course of their passions selfishness and confined generosity would lose them the advantage. I might help you and you not help me. Or more likely, I would decline to help you lest you might not help me in return. A little experience shows the remedy: Men invent a "certain form of words" called a promise, by which a person expresses a resolution to do something and exposes himself to the penalty of mistrust if he fails to perform.

Such is the origin of the rules of justice. The "natural obligation" to their observance, Hume says, is self-interest. But since Hume rejects the "selfish system of morals" he must account for their "moral obligation" on a different basis. Why is justice a virtue and injustice a vice? The answer is that we recognize that justice is beneficial to society. We may not always act justly. But in viewing the injustice of others we regard it as pernicious and come to share the uneasiness of those who will feel its bad consequences. This applies to some extent even to our own actions. And this shared uneasiness or sympathetic pain is identical with the sentiment of moral blame. It is reinforced by other means: the "artifice of politicians" dispensing public praise and blame, education, which teaches us to regard justice as honorable, and by a care for our reputation. But all this without antecedent moral distinctions would be in vain. In sum then, the original motive for the establishment of justice is self-interest, but the source of its moral approbation is "a sympathy with public interest." [19]

The advantages of society and hence of the rules of justice are great and obvious. Yet a strict observance of them cannot be expected. For one thing, one's interest may sometimes be better served by an act of injustice. More frequently, however, our infractions are due to our tendency to regulate our desires and wills in accordance with the appearance of objects rather than their real value, and to prefer a lesser good near at hand to a greater good that is more remote. We are thus apt to seize an immediate advantage gained by an act of injustice at the expense of the real but remote advantage to be gained from justice. The principal safeguard devised by men to prevent themselves from giving way to this weakness is *government*. Men's natural propensity to prefer the contiguous to the remote is incurable, but it can be made harmless by changing their circumstances and situations. Some men are made rulers, *i.e.*, they are placed in a position where they have an immediate interest in the impartial administration of justice and no interest or only a remote one in the contrary. The rest of men are ruled, *i.e.*, they are so constrained and restrained by the rulers that their immediate interest is in adherence to justice. As with the laws of justice, the original motive and the natural obligation to obedience to government is self-interest, and the moral obligation comes from sympathy with the public interest.

The fundamental and principal object of government is the administration of justice, *i.e.,* the protection of property and the enforcement of contracts. But they go beyond this, to undertake useful large-scale projects that individuals would be unable or unwilling to attempt. So government not only protects men as they pursue their interest but also requires them to pursue it.[20]

The duties of obedience to government and the observance of the rules of justice are called by Hume "artificial virtues," as distinguished from "natural virtues." The basis of the distinction is this: The natural virtues are those to which men are impelled by some original instinct or natural impulse, and which are given moral approbation because they are signs of such an instinct or impulse. For example, quite apart from any considerations of duty or of utility there is a natural affection of parents for their children. The artificial virtues on the other hand are not practiced because of any such propensity. On the contrary, it appears that our natural instincts if left unrestrained would lead us into all kinds of inequity and insubordination. The artificial virtues appear as laudable only after thought and reflection, for they are virtues only as a consequence of human contrivance. To take a clear example, suppose that in accordance with the terms of a will a fortune is taken from a deserving person and handed over to an undeserving one. Neither private happiness nor, at first glance, public happiness is thereby advanced. But the virtue of the act appears when it is considered as a part of a vast scheme which must be adhered to inflexibly even in such hard cases because the operation of the scheme as a whole is beneficial.

In another sense, however, the "artificial virtues" are natural. They arise necessarily out of man's situation. And they are a product of reason, which is part of man's nature as much as passion. Thus, as we have seen, Hume does not hesitate to speak of the "laws of nature." [21]

The artificial virtues are not to be regarded as contrary to the passions. They are contrary only to their "heedless and impetuous movement." Thus, government does not eradicate the propensity to prefer an immediate advantage to a remote one; it only gives it a new turn so that it destroys its own bad effects. Indeed the passions are better satisfied by being controlled and directed. In particular, acquisitiveness is much more fully gratified by being subjected to the restraints of justice than by being left to itself.[22]

Since justice and government are contrivances aimed at human benefit, it is clear that in very rare and extreme cases it is permissible to suspend their obligation. The common rule is the inflexible observance of justice and blind submission to government. But, for example, in a besieged city the rights of property may have to give way to public necessity. And, as the universal sentiment of mankind declares, when only public ruin would be the result of continued submission to government the ties of allegiance are loosened and rebellion is proper. Men's interest in that security and protection that can be afforded only by political society is at once the "original motive" to the institution of government and the "immediate sanction" of obedience to it. When rulers have become so oppressive that government no longer affords that security and protection, the sanction cannot remain in force. The effect ceases with the cause.

This admission of the right of disobedience in extraordinary emergencies raises the following difficulty: Since men are so inclined to follow "general rules" and to adhere to maxims after the reasons for them have ceased to exist, might not the "moral obligation" to obedience, derived from sympathy, survive the "natural obligation" founded on interest? Might not men be bound to obey a government that is destructive of justice? Hume says not. Our knowledge of human nature, of past history, and of present times informs us that those human imperfections that political society is set up to guard against are inherent in all men, not excluding rulers, and that we may reasonably expect them sometimes to act cruelly and unjustly, even against their immediate interest. This observation, being based on many examples, has itself the character of a general rule, and hence can serve as the basis of an exception to the general rule of obedience. Thus, it is that the general opinion of mankind thinks it no crime to resist great oppression.[23]

In the wise framing of political institutions, Hume says, "every man must be supposed a knave," *i.e.,* to be always seeking his own interest. The alternative to this supposition is to rely on the good will of rulers for the security of property and liberty; in other words, to rely on chance and to have no security at all. Good constitutions will not depend on the existence of great private virtues; they will ensure that the private interests of men, even of bad men, will be so controlled and directed as to serve and produce the public good. Such is the aim of free government, which Hume calls the "happiest" society.

The power of a free government is as great as that of any other government, but it is divided among several parts, perhaps a monarch, an hereditary aristocracy and a popular assembly, who have such checks on one another as to prevent any one from overcoming the others and gaining absolute control. Since arbitrary power is always oppressive to some extent, a free government must act according to general, equal, and previously known laws. There should be both a popular assembly and a smaller "aristocratic" senate. The senate furnishes wisdom, and it is kept honest by the other body. It is expedient for the popular assembly to be chosen in frequent elections by an electorate with a fairly high property qualification. Aristocracy is favorable to peace and order, but it tends to become oppressive. It is well to modify it with an element of democracy, so regulated as to avoid democracy's peculiar faults, such as turbulence. It is of great importance to protect the state against ecclesiastical encroachment and religious disturbances. There must be a union of the civil and ecclesiastical power and a dependence of the clergy on the civil government. Toleration of dissenting sects is necessary in order to "allay their fervor and make the civil union acquire a superiority above religious distinctions."

Liberty in the sense of free government is, Hume says, "the perfection of civil society." Yet authority is essential to its very existence, and when the two conflict, as they often do, authority should perhaps be given the preference. On the other hand, it may reasonably be said that what is essential can and will take care of itself, and needs less protection than what tends to society's perfection and is apt to be neglected or overlooked.

Despite Hume's esteem for free government, he thought that in recent times even absolute monarchy had improved so much that it met the ends of civil society almost as well as any kind of government. Modern civilized monarchies had borrowed institutions and manners from free governments and closely approached them in gentleness, stability, and the security given to property. They might improve even more.

This reflection illustrates the need for care in laying down eternal, permanent truths in politics. We should be cautious in prophecy. Likewise, we should be forbearing in historical judgment, and not, for example, blame former ages for religious intolerance, since they had no experience to show that toleration, although "paradoxical" in principle, is "salutary" in practice. We should judge of other times by the maxims prevailing in those times. To put it more generally, "the world is still too young" for it to be fully known what human nature is capable of or the effect of changes in men's "education, customs, or principles." [24]

Hume's views on politics have often been characterized as "Tory." For example, Thomas Jefferson held Hume's *History of England* responsible for undermining the principles of the free English government and spreading "universal toryism over the land." Hume would reply, of course, that what was offensive was his refusal to sacrifice historical truth to "the plaguey prejudices of Whiggism." His theoretical teaching concerning the nature, objects, and proper form of government has seemed to be very close to that of the great "Whig" philosopher, Locke. Yet if Hume was philosophically a "Whig," he was, as he put it, "a very sceptical one." This appears most obviously perhaps in his attack on the "fashionable system of politics" and the "creed" of the Whig party, the social-contract theory, and in his warning against and distrust of innovation.

The social-contract theory as Hume understood it taught that the powers of government are derived from the consent of the governed, that the obligation to obedience is based on the exchange of promises in the contract setting up government, and that subjects are released from their obligation when government becomes oppressive and thus breaks the promises made on its side. One argument against this theory is the following: The original motive of the duty to keep promises is the same as the original motive of the duty to obey rulers; promises serve our interest one way and government another. The latter duty does not then depend on the former. If promises had never been invented, government would still be necessary. Indeed, so far is government from depending on fidelity to promises that government was established in large part to enforce that fidelity.

Hume's principal objection is that the contract theory is contrary to the practice and sentiment of all mankind. He will concede that government in its first beginning must have been founded on consent. Men are very nearly equal in physical strength, and, until educated, even in mind; none could subject a multitude to his rule by force. Subjection to government could have arisen only when men voluntarily gave up their natural liberty and submitted to be ruled for the sake of peace and order. And this may be called an "original contract." But no government of which we have any record has been formed by the voluntary consent of the people; their beginnings are rather conquest or usurpation. As a rule, it is precisely when a change of government occurs that the people are least consulted.

The natural sentiments of all men contradict the contract theory. So far are rulers from regarding their authority as based on the consent of the ruled that they are inclined to treat that view of things as seditious. And the ruled usually think of themselves as born to obedience to a particular government.

So Hume opposes Locke's version of the modern natural-law teaching. But he opposes it from a position of fundamental agreement with its intention. The aim is to order political society in such a way that its ends are served by the natural action of the passions, without excessive reliance on extraordinary goodness, *i.e.,* on chance. As Hume says, "All plans of government which suppose great reformation in the manners of mankind are plainly imaginary." Now Hume's objection to the contract theory is precisely that it supposes such a reformation of manners. It overestimates the power of reason, or more precisely, it too readily assumes that men will correctly perceive and steadily follow their real interests. If they did, no government would in fact exist except on the basis of consent. But since they do not, other foundations must be admitted and allowed to be just. The contract theory, which is intended to be consonant with the passions of men, leads to conclusions that are contrary to universal experience and sentiment. For example, it denies the legitimacy of absolute monarchy, which is as "common" and "natural" a form of government as any.

The contract theory teaches that when rulers become so oppressive as no longer to provide for the security and protection of the ruled, the latter are no longer bound to submit. Hume agrees, as we have seen. But the doctrine of an original contract is not needed to reach this conclusion in theory, nor to assure it in practice. In such extreme cases men can be counted on to resist, without reference to any theory; the doctrine of passive obedience is as remote from their common sentiments as that of the social contract. The latter is, however, not only unnecessary but even pernicious. In the normal course of events the duty of the ruled is "blind submission." Yet the contract theory draws our attention from the general rule and directs it to the exceptions, exceptions we may be "but too much inclined of ourselves to embrace and extend." A voluntary allegiance is a precarious allegiance.

The bonds of allegiance ought not to be dissolved but held tight. Human society is a continuing body, gaining and losing members every moment, and hence stability in government is essential. It is necessary for the sake of peace and order that there be government and rulers. It is desirable of course that the form of government be good and that the rulers be suitable. But to make the superiority of a form of government or the suitability of a particular ruler the overriding standard is to open the door to that very strife and disorder that government is meant to exclude. Hence the claims of the established order should be given the greatest weight.[25]

Every government, Hume says, is founded on opinion. The main support of the rule of the few over the many, *i.e.,* of the weak over the strong, is the opinion that those in authority have a right to that authority. This opinion is usually the fruit of time and habit. Custom is the great guide of human life; most men never think of inquiring into the reasons for the authority of the form of government to which they have become habituated. Or, if they should, they are satisfied to be told that it has prevailed for a long time and that they are treading in the path of their forebears. "Antiquity always begets the opinion of right." That foundation of government truly in accordance with men's natural inclinations is not contract but custom.

From the above consideration it appears that there are limits to what can be done in the way of innovation and, more important, since novelty, too, has its charms, to what ought to be done. Violent innovation is never justified. To shake the authority of custom and antiquity gives it not to reason, which is an uncertain guide with little sway over man, but to every man's private interest, disguised as reason.

The wise statesman therefore "will bear a reverence to what carries the marks of age." In attempting to improve a constitution he will adapt his innovations to the "ancient fabric," so as not to disturb society. His caution may be reinforced by reflection on the limits of human foresight. Political measures have many consequences that cannot be foretold; one must be guided by experience; one must learn of errors by feeling their inconvenience when it appears. Time not only strengthens political institutions; it also perfects them.[26]

Hume begins, we see, from the most fundamental principles of the modern natural-law teaching, and draws consequences that are to a large extent like those of Locke. At the same time, and working from the same principles, he rejects important elements of Locke's teaching and becomes a strong advocate of conservatism. His political doctrine thus presents something of a paradoxical appearance and perhaps contains a certain tension, reflected in his maxim that there is "nothing of greater importance in every state than the preservation of the ancient government, especially if it be a free one."[27]

## NOTES

1. David Hume, *Treatise of Human Nature*, ed. L. H. Selby-Bigge (Oxford: Clarendon, 1896), I. i. 1; *Enquiry Concerning Human Understanding,* ed. L. A. Selby-Bigge (Oxford: Clarendon, 1894), 2.

2. *Human Understanding,* 4. I. first two pars; an earlier and less satisfactory statement is in *Treatise,* I. iii. 1.

3. *Treatise,* I. iii. 11, beginning, and 12. 5.

4. *Ibid.,* 2, 3, 4, 6, 7, and 14; *Human Understanding,* 4, 5, and 7.

5. *Treatise,* I. iv. 2 and 6.

6. *Ibid.,* iii. 13.

7. *Ibid.,* 8. 13 and 14; 12. 3.

8. *Ibid.,* I. iii. 15 and 16.

9. *Ibid.,* III. i. 1; also *Enquiry Concerning the Principles of Morals,* appendix I.

10. *Treatise,* II. iii. 3.

11. *Ibid.,* III, i. 1, last par.

12. *Ibid.*, next to last par., and 2.
13. *Principles of Morals*, 10. 1. and 10. 5; *Treatise*, III. iii. 1.
14. *Principles of Morals*, appendix II; *Treatise*, II. iii. 3, last par., and 9. 8.
15. *Treatise*, II. iii. 3. 6.
16. *Ibid.*, III. ii. 1, next to last par.; cf. *Principles of Morals*, appendix IV.
17. *Treatise*, III. iii. 8 next to last par., and iii. 1. 14 ff.; *Principles of Morals*, 9. I.
18. *Principles of Morals*, appendix I, last par.; *Treatise*, III. i. 2. 1; I. iii. 8. 12.
19. *Treatise*, III. ii. 2–5; *Principles of Morals*, 3.
20. *Treatise*, III. ii. 7; *Essays*, "Of the Origin of Government"; *Principles of Morals*, 4.
21. *Treatise*, III. ii. 1.
22. *Ibid.*, 2. 13; 5. 9; 6. 1.
23. *Ibid.*, 9; *Essays*, "Of Passive Obedience."

24. *Essays*, "On the Independency of Parliament," "That Politics May Be Reduced to a Science," "Of the Origin of Government," "Idea of a Perfect Commonwealth," "Of Civil Liberty"; *History of England*, end of chap. xxiii, Appendix to the Reign of James I. On religion see *History*, beginning of chap. xxix, and chap. lxvi (1678).
25. *Essays*, "Of the Original Contract," "Of Passive Obedience," "Idea of a Perfect Commonwealth"; *Treatise*, III. ii. 8–10.
26. *Essays*, "Of the First Principles of Government," "Of the Original Contract," "Idea of a Perfect Commonwealth," first two pars, "Of the Coalition of Parties," par. 5, "Of the Rise and Progress of the Arts and Sciences," par. 25.
27. *Essays*, "Of the Liberty of the Press," par. 6.

## READINGS

A. Hume, David. *Enquiry Concerning Human Understanding*. Secs 2, 3, 4, 5, 6, 7.
   Hume, David. *Treatise of Human Nature*. Bk III, parts i and ii.
   Hume, David. *Essays*. "Of the Origin of Government," "Of the Original Contract," "Of the First Principles of Government," "Idea of a Perfect Commonwealth." (A good selection of Hume's essays on politics is found in *David Hume's Political Essays*. Ed. Charles W. Hendel. New York: Liberal Arts Press, 1953.)
B. Hume, David. *Treatise of Human Nature*. Bk I, parts i and iii.
   Hume, David. *Enquiry Concerning the Principles of Morals*. Secs 1, 3, 4, 5, 9; appendices I, II, and III.
   Hume, David. *Essays*. "Of the Liberty of the Press," "That Politics May Be Reduced to a Science," "On the Independency of Parliament," "Whether the British Government Inclines More to Absolute Monarchy, or to a Republic," "Of Parties in General," "Of the Parties of Great Britain," "Of Civil Liberty," "Of the Rise and Progress of the Arts and Sciences," "Of the Balance of Power," "Of Some Remarkable Customs," "Of Passive Obedience," "Of the Coalition of Parties," "Of the Protestant Succession."

# JEAN-JACQUES ROUSSEAU

## 1712–1778

Rousseau begins the *Social Contract* with the celebrated words: "Man was born free, and everywhere he is in chains. . . . How did this change come to pass? I do not know. What can make it legitimate? I believe I can resolve this question." With this statement he poses the political problem in its most radical form and at the same time suggests the revolutionary principle that almost all existing regimes are illegitimate. Civil society enchains man and makes him a slave to law or other men whereas he was, as man, born to freedom, to the right to behave as he pleases. What is more, civil society, as it is now constituted, has no claim on the moral adhesion of its subjects; it is unjust. Rousseau's political thought points away from the present in both directions: to man's happy freedom of the past and to the establishment of a regime in the future which can appeal to the will of those under its authority. It is the task of the philosopher to make clear what man's nature truly is and, on this basis, to define the conditions of a good political order. Rousseau's thought has an externally paradoxical character, seeming at the same time to desire contradictories—virtue and soft sentiment, political society and the state of nature, philosophy and ignorance—but it is remarkably consistent, the contradictions reflecting contradictions in the nature of things.[1] Rousseau undertook to clarify the meaning of modern theory and practice, and in so doing he brought to light radical consequences of modernity of which men were not previously aware.

Modern politics, according to Rousseau, are based on a partial understanding of man. The modern state, the Leviathan, is directed to its own preservation and, consequently, to that of its subjects. It is, hence, totally negative, taking into account only the condition of happiness, life, while forgetting happiness itself. Any political system which takes into account only one side of human existence cannot satisfy men's longing for fulfillment or call forth their full loyalty. And it is further Rousseau's argument that the modern state based on self-preservation constitutes a way of life precisely contrary to that which would make men happy. The life of the big nations is characterized by commerce and, consequently, by the distinction between rich and poor. Each man can pursue his gain within the framework laid down by the state. Money is the standard of human worth, and virtue is forgotten. Calculation of private advantage is the basis of human relations; this may not lead to perpetual war, but it destroys the foundations of trust and easy sociability and leads to selfishness and poor citizenship. But, most of all, because there is scarcity and the needs and desires of all men in society cannot be satisfied, the rich are protected and the poor oppressed. Civil society is a state of mutual interdependence among men, but the men are bad and the majority are forced to give up their own wills to work for the satisfaction of the few. And, since these few control the laws, the many do not even enjoy the protection for which they are supposed to have entered into society. The result of the oversimplified and one-sided concentration on preservation is the destruction of the good life which is the only purpose of preservation.[2]

This is the basis of Rousseau's attack on the Enlightenment. The progress of the arts and sciences was believed to be the condition, perhaps the sufficient condition, of a progress of civil society and of an increase in human happiness. Prejudice would be vanquished by learning, manners softened by the arts, nature conquered by science. Sound government could be assured by grounding it on the passions of those who take part in it. The hopes of the Enlightenment are those of modern man, according to Rousseau, and it is the picture of human society painted by the Enlightenment that is the starting point for his revolution in political thought. Rousseau not only denies that progress in the arts and sciences improves morality but asserts, on the contrary, that such progress always leads to moral corruption. The arts and sciences require an atmosphere of luxury and leisure in order to flourish. They themselves emerge, in general, from vices of the soul; at best idle curiosity is their source, and most often they come from the desire for unnecessary comforts which only weaken men and satisfy unnecessary wants. The society dominated by the arts and sciences is one full of inequality, both because the talents needed to pursue them become grounds of distinction among men, and because great sums of money are needed to support them, as well as workers to man the implements devised by those arts and sciences. Society is transformed to support the arts and the sciences and their products, and this very transformation creates a life full of vain self-regard and injustice.[3]

The first stage of Rousseau's reflection leads to admiration of the past. The situation of modern man is new, but in classical antiquity models of civil society can be found in which men were free and governed themselves. The old republic, the *polis,* above all Sparta, was the refuge of real men and provided long periods of peace, stability, and independence. Rousseau revives the quarrel between the ancients and the moderns in restating the case for the ancient city. That city was not founded on comfort, self-preservation, or science but on virtue—the science of simple souls. Virtue in the classic sense meant good citizenship and the qualities that necessarily accompany it. Only on the basis of courage, self-sacrifice, and moderation can a city in which the great majority govern themselves be founded. Rousseau is a republican; he is a republican because he believes men are naturally free and equal. Only a civil society which is a reflection of that nature can hope to make men happy. The requirements of a free society were best met by the Greek cities and Rome, although they were not perfect, and Rousseau's ultimate solution is an improvement upon them. They were small so that everyone could know everyone else and hence have both common interests and trust. They were governed by the people so that the rulers and ruled were one and the same; there were thus no fundamental differences of interest between governors and governed. The laws were of ancient date and men grew used to their heavy weight by force of long habit. The rule of law is necessary to civil society, and just laws require a stern moral code to support their burden equally; only strict mutual surveillance and habits of justice can ensure their operation. The primary consideration of the government is the virtue of the citizens. The civil society which is to function as a society must be a unity in which the individuals give up their private wishes for the sake of the whole. Society cannot be conceived of as the balance of conflicting interests if men are to be free and not the pawns of interest groups in power. Not enlightenment but severe moral education is the prerequisite of sound civil society. Rousseau's taste and his analysis of the injustice of modern society lead him back to Greece.[4]

But he is led even further. His teaching is not merely a revival of those of Plato and Aristotle. If he admires the practice of antiquity, he does not accept its theory. No political teaching can suffice which merely describes how to construct a stable order or how to make the citizens content. It must also legitimate the authority exercised by the government; it must state the grounds of the citizen's duties and rights. The central political question is always: What is justice? and this leads necessarily to the question: What is natural? For, outside the limits of the positive law, when the problem is to found or reform a regime, the only standard can be nature and, more specifically, the nature of man. And it is concerning this question that Rousseau differs from his predecessors, or, rather, he joins the moderns in their denial that man is by nature political. Following the current of modern science in general, as well as of political science, Rousseau rejects the notion that man is directed by nature toward an end, the end of political life. The city or the state is a purely human construction originating in the desire for self-preservation. As such, man is conceivable without political society, although in this later age it may have become necessary for him.

Justice, as it can be seen in nations, consists in maintaining the privileges of those in positions of power. All known states are full of inequalities of birth, wealth, and honor. These inequalities can perhaps be justified in terms of the preservation of the regime, but that does not make them more tolerable for those who do not enjoy them. The laws institute and protect these differences of rank. If there are natural inequalities, those existing in the nations do not reflect them; they are the results of human deeds and of chance. They cannot be morally binding on those oppressed by their weight.

If civil society is not natural, then one must go to a time prior to civil society to find man as he is naturally. This investigation is necessary in order to determine the origins of the state; if civil society is not natural, it is conventional; therefore, if there is to be any legitimacy in the laws of civil society, its conventions must be founded on that first nature. Rousseau makes an attempt to describe man in the *state of nature*. Other modern thinkers who agreed that civil society is conventional tried to do the same thing and to ground political right on a prepolitical natural right. But, according to Rousseau, they never succeeded in reaching the primitive state of nature. They were not radical enough in their own rejection of the naturalness of civil society. They denied that attachment to the common good and the political community are parts of human perfection, and they tried to derive the rules of politics from the individual unattached to any state. But they, in describing that individual, described in fact the man living in civil society. They were cryptoteleologists in the sense that they tried to understand man as he is naturally from the point of view of his complete development in civil society. But, if man is truly not a political and social being, then his nature must have been transformed in order for him ever to have come to the point where he could live in civil society. The earlier thinkers, in stripping man of his social nature, saw in him many characteristics which are results of communal living, for example, envy,

distrust, unlimited desire for acquisition, and reason. To know the
natural man requires an almost superhuman effort of the mind, for we
have no contact with him, we are civilized men worn by the corrosion
of civil society.

There is a road from natural man to civil man, and the passage of
that road is not like that from embryo to man where the first step is
directed to the last and illuminated by it. The movement is not a necessary one, so we are in need of a history of the human species. For the first
time, history becomes an integral part of political theory. Man is a different being at different epochs, although for Rousseau he still has a primeval nature which dominates all transformations brought about by time.
Rousseau's awareness of the disproportion between natural man and
civil man, which is implied in a rejection of the naturalness of civil
society, forces him to an investigation of primitive man. The other
teachings which do not discover the truly natural lead only to a deeper
enslavement to the vices engendered by civil society. The investigation
he undertakes proceeds in two ways: the first is by means of what we
would today call anthropology. The primitive, which was formerly
despised as inferior and imperfect, now seems to throw light on that
earlier period and hence becomes an object of serious scientific interest.
But, because the so-called savages or primitives already live in societies,
they are no more than signposts on the road back. More important is
the second way: introspection to uncover the first and simplest movements of the human soul.

Since man is not primarily political and social, he must be divested
of all qualities that are connected with life in a community if we are to
understand him as he is by nature. The first and most important of
these is reason. Reason depends upon speech, and speech implies social
life. Hence, the definition of man can no longer be that he is a rational
animal. At first one can say only that he is an animal like other animals.
He roams the forest in search of nourishment. He seeks to preserve his
being, but he is not a ravenous beast naturally hostile to every other
member of his species as Hobbes understood him to be. Hobbes could
only assert this by attributing to the first men the unlimited desires of
political man. Actually this first animal-man has only the simplest
needs of the sort that are usually easily satisfied. He cannot think far
into the future. He is not frightened of death because he cannot conceive it; he only avoids pain. He has no need to fight his fellow creatures
except when there is a scarcity of the bare necessities. He is idle by
nature and stirs himself only to satisfy his natural wants. Only a being
with foresight who has needs beyond the natural seeks wealth. Locke's
industrious natural man is also a construction drawn from already

developed society. It is in this idleness that the true pleasure of the animal is enjoyed; he senses the sweetness of his own existence. He has only two fundamental passions: the desire to preserve himself and a certain pity or sympathy for the sufferings of others of his kind. The latter prevents him from being brutal to other men when such "humaneness" does not conflict with his own preservation. He has no virtues because he needs none. One cannot say that he has morality; whatever he does, he does because it pleases him to do so. But he has a certain goodness; he does no harm.

Considered in this way, it may be said that all men are by nature equal. They have, practically speaking, only physical existences; if there are differences in strength, they have little meaning because the individuals have no contact with one another. From man's natural state can be derived no right of one man to rule another. The right of the stronger is no right, first, because the enslaved can always revolt in his turn; no moral obligation is established by a stronger man subjugating a weaker one. Second, one man could never enslave another in the state of nature because men had no need of one another, and it would be impossible to hold a slave. Nor does the family provide a source for political right because in the state of nature there is no family. The relations between man and woman are casual, and the mother instinctively takes care of the children until they are strong enough to fend for themselves; there is no authority or duty involved. The state of nature is a state of equality and independence.

There are two characteristics which distinguish man from the other animals and take the place of rationality as the defining quality of humanity. The first is freedom of the will. Man is not a being determined by his instincts; he can choose, accept, and reject. He can defy nature. And the consciousness of this liberty is the evidence of the spirituality of his soul. He is aware of his own power. The second, and least questionable characteristic of man, is his perfectibility. Man is the only being which can gradually improve its faculties and pass this improvement on to the whole species. All the superior faculties of the mind seen in civilized man are proofs of this. They are now a permanent part of the species, but they did not belong to it naturally. On the basis of these two fundamental characteristics of man, it can be said that natural man is distinguished by having almost no nature at all, by being pure potentiality. There are no ends, only possibilities. Man has no determination; he is the free animal. This constitution leads him away from his original contentment toward the misery of civil life, but it also renders him capable of mastering himself and nature.

Natural man, then, is a lazy beast, enjoying the sentiment of his

own existence, concerned with his preservation and pitying the sufferings of his fellow creatures, free and perfectible. His motion toward
the civilized state is a result of unforeseeable accidents which leave unalterable marks on him. He is forced into closer contact with other men
by natural catastrophes. He develops speech and begins to maintain a
permanent establishment with his woman and children. He is softer and
his needs are now greater, but his existence is intrinsically pleasant.
There are, as yet, no laws, no state, no inequality. The needs of men are
not such as to make them competitors. But men have at last become
dependent on one another, and the first experiences of cooperation or
common ends bring to consciousness what obligation or morality might
be. Man's freedom still comes first, and he can withdraw from any
engagement he might have made when it is to his advantage; but he
also sees the advantage in getting help from others and the necessity of
doing his share if he is to receive in kind. However, he is still so independent as to be unwilling to sacrifice any of his freedom in order to
guarantee the fulfillment of contracts.

In addition to the first consciousness of moral obligation, man in
this new communal situation begins to practice vengeance. Because men
are in daily contact with one another there is more occasion for friction;
and, because there is no law, each man is judge in his own case. The
natural pity which was the root of humanity in the state of nature is
weakened as a result of the conflict between self-love and pity; in any
such case the former always wins. But it is not these battles which cause
men to form civil society; it is the foundation of private property. The
founder of political society and the man who brought the greatest evils
to mankind was the first who said, "This land belongs to me." The
cultivation of the soil is the source of private property. Only what a man
has made or that to which he has added his work can in any sense be said
to belong to him. With the foundation of private property forethought
also arises. When the fields and streams of themselves provided nourishment, clothing, and housing, man did not think to the future. But the
farmer must do so, and the desire to increase and protect his crops both
multiplies his desires and causes him to seek power.

And, further, in the foundation of private property, we have also
discovered the origin of inequality. For different men have different
skills and talents which enable some of them to increase their possessions. Soon all available land is enclosed, and some have more than
they need, others less. Men recognize property as something real, but
their own need is also something real. There is no judge between these
different claims, and there is no natural law to resolve them because
the situation is man-made, not natural. A state of war necessarily ensues
between the haves and the have-nots.

At this stage man has developed all his powers, and he has made himself miserable. The greatest change in his nature is that formerly he lived entirely for himself within himself. Now he lives for others, not only because he is physically dependent on them but because he has learned to compare himself with them. His soul has become enslaved to other men, and this is more of a bond than his need of them to help him satisfy his desires. He seeks money and honor instead of reflecting on his real wishes. Man has become vain, and in the search to gratify that vanity there are endless sources of quarrel. Vanity (*amour-propre*) has taken the place of the original self-love (*amour de soi*); instead of physical desires which must be appeased, he is now possessed by infinite yearnings for possessions he can never use and a glory he despises as soon as it is gained.

It is now that someone among the rich, aware of the constant danger to his property and the wretched condition of the people, suggests a contract for the establishment of civil society. This clever man sees the possibility of guaranteeing his questionable right to property by the consent of other men and of maintaining peace by a mutual pact to protect each and all against aggression. The natural passion of pity has been extinguished, and the only substitute for it in the new conditions is a morality defining men's duties, backed up by a recognized authority. Nature no longer suffices. The frightful state of war makes this step necessary and ensures the acquiescence of the poor. But it is a swindle. The rich give an appearance of legitimacy to their control of their property and are able to enjoy it peacefully. The inequality which has gradually come into being is made lawful, and the oppression of the poor is maintained by public force. Hobbes is right when he says that the men who are constrained to found civil society are hostile to one another and afflicted by infinite desires. He is wrong only in asserting that this is the nature of man. There was an earlier state which defined the essential character of man's freedom and which makes it impossible for him legitimately to deliver himself over to the will of anyone else. Locke is right when he asserts that the purpose of civil society is to protect property. He also is wrong only in asserting that property is natural to man, and that the inequalities stabilized by civil society conform to real standards of justice. Every man has a natural right to preserve himself and to act in accordance with this right. Civil society has no natural ground to legitimate a command which contradicts the natural right. But all civil societies issue such commands; natural right cannot be their legitimation. Man is naturally free, and civil society takes his freedom away from him; he is dependent on the law, and the law is made in favor of the rich—at least in its origin it was meant to favor them.[5]

So the political problem is posed in the presentation of the history of its birth. Man, free by nature, needs government to organize and regulate the life in common to which he has become committed. But precisely because he has developed terrible passions which necessitate government, a just government is rendered factually difficult because the men who form the laws are under the influence of those passions, and the citizens continue to possess those passions and have every interest in altering the government for the sake of their satisfaction. Only the most severe moral education can obviate this difficulty, a moral education almost never to be found. And, from the point of view of right, civil society demands a devotion to the common good, a subordination of the individual to the whole, while man by nature is a selfish, independent animal. At any point where he senses a conflict between society and himself he is naturally and properly motivated by his selfish interest. How can civil society rightfully call upon a man to sacrifice himself for it? How can one selfish individual demand that another obey him? No contract can bind to the point of sacrificing that for which it was made, and no man willfully contracts away the freedom which is the core of his being.[6]

Civil society cannot be grounded on natural right; nature dictates only self-interest. Nature is too low to comprehend civil society; the study of nature leads to its rejection as the standard, at least for society. This was what Rousseau's predecessors had not understood, according to him. Civil society requires morality because man's natural character does not suffice to bind him, *in foro interno,* to the more stringent demands of political life, and his newly inflamed passions make him even less fit for society. A society which was based on each man's calculation of his interest would only cause those passions to develop further, for his interest is already determined by his passions, and would lead inevitably to tyranny or anarchy. Hence, since morality is not natural to man, he must create it. It is the basis for this project that Rousseau sets down in the *Social Contract;* in it he tries to resolve the problem posed by the conflict between the individual and the state, or self-interest and duty. Nothing can bind man's freedom, but civil society is bondage. The act of establishing civil society is identical with that of establishing morality or binding commitments to others. Since nature does not provide the basis for the agreement, it must be a convention. Traditionally, conventions were considered to be of a lower order than natural laws, precisely because they are man-made and changeable; conventions differ everywhere and seem to be the result of arbitrary will and chance. The man who obeys convention would seem to be the prisoner of other men. But, if man is free, his capacity to make conventions is the sign of that freedom; his will is not limited by nature. To this extent, man the maker of morality and the state is the fulfillment of the notion of man as the free, undetermined being. If the simply arbitrary character of conventions could be avoided, then one could say that a conventional civil society is at once the fulfillment of man's nature and worthy of his respect and obedience.

As Rousseau puts it in his own forceful formulations: "[The difficulty is] to find a form of association which defends and protects with all the common force the person and the goods of each associate; by which each, uniting himself to all, obeys nevertheless only himself and remains as free as before." [7] The solution is that every man give himself entirely to the community with all of his rights and property. The deposit is made with the whole, with no individual; in this way no one puts himself into the hands of another. The contract is equal, for each gives all. No one reserves any rights by which he can claim to judge of his own conduct; hence there is no source of conflict between individual and state, for the individual has contracted to accept the law as the absolute standard for his acts. The social contract forms an artificial person, the state, which has a will like the natural person; what appears necessary or desirable to that person is willed by it and what is willed by the whole is law. Law is the product of the *general will*. Each individual participates in legislation, but law is general, and the individual in his role as legislator must make laws which can conceivably be applied to all members of the community. He makes his will into law but now, as opposed to what he did in the state of nature, he must generalize his will. As legislator he can only will what all could will; as citizen he obeys what he himself willed as legislator. Although men of diverse tastes and understandings go to make up the sovereign legislative body, none can impose his will on the others unless the others could have willed it themselves. The law is produced by the will of each thinking in terms of all. The primary function of the social contract is to constitute a regime which can express the general will.

Civil society is simply the agreement among a group of men that each shall become a part of the general will and be obedient to it. As a result, each remains as free as he was before, because he obeys nothing but his transformed will. The conventional liberty of civil society satisfies the primary natural right of man—freedom. As long as the society is organized so that the laws can be made impersonally, no man can make a claim against it on the basis of natural right. Man in the state of nature had a right to all that he willed; neither the will nor the reason of other men could legitimately issue commands to him. There is no eternal reason which can and should control our actions. Each man has his own judgments based on his personal experience and affected by his particular will. This fact is reflected in the notion of the general will; man is a being who wills, and the capacity to do what he wills is the essence of freedom. Willing is, as such, independent of what is willed. The natural law, or any other rational command directed toward the common good, is a limitation on freedom drawn from a questionable source. Therefore, the general will contains no specific directives; it can determine itself to do whatsoever occurs to it; it is in itself empty; it is pure will. This is another aspect of the preservation of the natural freedom. The general will is formal, and the only thing which distinguishes it from the particular will is that it can only will what all could conceivably will. This sets some limitation on what society as a whole can do, as opposed to the complete license of nature, and Rousseau believes that these purely formal limitations are sufficient to guarantee decency, or that the generalized will is in itself moral. He considers that he has discovered the true principle of morality that others had only sensed and had tried to base on dubious and arbitrary interpretations of nature or on revealed religion. Man's freedom, which seems to be independent of, and opposed to, moral rule is the sole source of morality. With this discovery, Rousseau completes the break with the political teaching of classical antiquity begun by Machiavelli and Hobbes. His immediate predecessors had maintained the notion of natural law which limited the human freedom which they themselves taught.[8]

The movement from the natural state to the civil state produces a very great change in man. Formerly he was an amiable beast; now he has become a moral being. All of his capacities come into play, his ideas are developed and extended, and his sentiments are ennobled. In the state of nature man acted only from instinct; now he must consider his action in relation to principle so that the words *choice* and *freedom* take on a moral sense. If a man continues to act according to his private will, he can be said to degrade himself to the level of the animals. He gives up his freedom, both in the sense that he is a mere tool of his passions and in the sense that he destroys the possibility of a just society and hence puts himself in the power of others. Society is justified, therefore, in forcing him to be free, in constraining him to exercise his will in the proper way. Education and punishment are the instruments of this constraint. But the truly human dignity emerges in the conscious choice of the general will over the private.

The social contract constitutes the sovereign. Rousseau uses the term "sovereign" to indicate that the source of all legitimacy is in the people at large as opposed to the monarch or the aristocrats or any other

segment. There must be a government, and it may be monarchic, aristocratic, or democratic, but its right to rule is derived from the people
and exercised only so long as it pleases them. Since nature and revealed
religion have been set aside, only the voice of the people can establish
law; every enactment must return to them, to their will. The will of
the people is the only law. The government is obedient to the law alone,
and each citizen is constantly a member of the lawmaking body. Every
citizen finds himself in a double relation to the state, as a lawgiver, in
so far as he is a member of the sovereign, and as a subject of the law, an
individual who must obey.

Several consequences follow from the fact that the sovereign is the
only source of legitimacy. In the first place, sovereignty is inalienable.
No man or group of men can be given the right to make laws in the
place of the citizen body at large. They would be acting according to
their individual wills, and their enactments would not be binding. This
means that representative government is a bad form of government.
Others take the responsibility from the citizens, and they lose their citizen virtue as well as their freedom. If a nation is so large that the citizens
cannot hope to meet in a common body, then representation becomes
an unfortunate necessity, a necessity which weakens the expression of
the general will. If any legitimacy is to be preserved in such a case, the
representatives must be elected by local assemblies in which all citizens
meet, and the representatives must be given complete instructions. They
must have no independent judgment, and for every new question which
arises they must return to those who elected them. Otherwise there is
no general will. The general will requires constant consultation.[9] It can
be consulted only by vote, so that the system suggested by Rousseau
turns out to be majoritarian. But it is not a simple majoritarianism; the
laws can only be properly instituted if the citizens possess the virtue to
suppress their private wills. The individuals must be citizens in the
classical sense, and this requires a very severe, self-imposed morality.
Rousseau is not a libertarian in the modern sense of the word; every
man cannot live as he likes, for that would end the possibility of agreement and destroy the sources of the moral energy necessary to self-
control. Rousseau despised democracy as it is usually practiced because
it means a wild anarchy of self-interest. A formalistic insistence on the
vote of the people is meaningless without the establishment of its moral
preconditions. Sparta was right in its concentration on the habits of its
citizens as over against the modern laxity which leaves the private life
to the individuals. The tastes and manners of the citizens affect all their
judgments, and certain habits make free government altogether impossible. Rousseau re-establishes the Greek city but brings to light the true

principle which motivated its insistence on austere virtue: virtue is not itself the end; it is a means to freedom.

Moreover, in addition to virtue, the expression of the general will must be guaranteed by the suppression of faction. Each citizen alone cannot hope to have his private will prevail and recognizes that if everyone voted according to his passions there would be no order. It is only when he belongs to a group large enough to influence the vote decisively that his private will overcomes his sense of the general will in seeing what he personally can gain. Thus, parties must be forbidden, and extremes of wealth and poverty must be prevented. In so far as possible, informed citizens must vote as individuals, and the result of such a vote can be considered a general will.

Rousseau was aware of the tension that exists between the stability that law requires and the constant reconsideration implied in the assembly of the people. There is no law or institution which cannot be revoked if the state is going to be governed by the actual wills of its present citizens. Every assembly must begin with the question: Does the sovereign please to preserve the present form of government?[10] But the idea that the law is a product of one's will weakens the almost religious awe that is necessary to maintain the respect for law. Old institutions and the sacredness of the law are restraints on the expression of selfish interest; the man who never conceives of the possibility of altering the established way is more likely to behave according to the commands he never questioned than the one who is accustomed to easy change. This is a difficulty never entirely resolved by Rousseau, but which he attempts to do away with by making the process of change difficult, by making the individuals who suggest it responsible for its effects, and by an education in the respect for good institutions. But the possibility of change cannot be obviated if the citizens are to be conscious of their freedom and able to judge what preserves it and what destroys it.

The sovereign is by its nature also indivisible. The notion of the general will makes it impossible for there to be a separation of powers which is anything more than a delegation for the execution of functions previously defined by the sovereign and ultimately dependent upon it. The sovereign power is a unity which cannot be divided without destroying it. No authority is anything but derivative from it.

The social contract is an agreement to form a civil society and establishes the instrument of authority—the sovereign. But the institution of this body does not give the body motion; the new society must have activities and ends; it needs laws. The character of the laws is undetermined by the contract; the contract only sets up the legitimate organ of legislation. The particular enactments can vary according to the interests of the society. The laws must, like the general will, be only general. They cannot refer to particular persons or acts. If they did, the persons involved would not partake in the general will; they would be alien to it, since their wills did not take part in forming the law. The law can establish regulations distinguishing diverse duties, honors, and classes, but it cannot say to whom these regulations should apply. It considers the citizens as a body and acts as abstract.

The laws must have sanctions imposed by men, since there are no other sources of them on earth; these sanctions must include the power of life and death in so far as the vicious need repression. Otherwise society would be of advantage to the unjust rather than the just. And there is no limitation on the scope of the law. Whatever does not touch the needs of civil society itself should be left to the citizen's free determination, but there is no means of establishing in advance what will be necessary for society's preservation. There are no reserved rights on behalf of the citizens. If there were, the citizens could withdraw from the contract at critical moments. And, since civil society entails a whole way of life, the apparently most trivial matters of private enjoyment can have a political effect. The manners of the society are of as much or more concern than the institutions of government, because manners underlie institutions and give them their force.[11]

To find a code of laws which fits a people, which is complete, and which will be obeyed is not a task for primitive men; such a code cannot arise from the mere gathering together of a group of men who constitute themselves as a sovereign. The private wills are still too dominant; they are not repressed by the habit of civil life. Practically speaking, it is only after a people has lived with its laws and habits for a long time that it can be said to be a people, a group with common interests and a general will, something more than an agglomeration. It is only afterwards that the body of the people is prepared to judge if its laws are good. But the society needs laws from the beginning if the strongest are not to take over and impose their private wills on the mass of the people and make slaves of them. Hence, for the formation of a real civil society a legislator is needed. This extraordinary man must discover the rules appropriate to the society in question, and he must force or persuade the people to accept them. He himself cannot be a member of the state, and he has no authority; he presents the laws which must be approved ultimately by the general will. His is a labor of love from which he can win only honor. Rousseau has in view men like Moses and Lycurgus who established a people and along with it justice. He returns in this, too, to a classic view in that he does not believe in piecemeal reform or in the gradual automatic triumph of reason in politics. Conscious, statesmanlike action is necessary; the whole order must be founded at one time according to rational plan, and only greatness can compass the task. The greatest political task is the establishment of a regime, and nothing can do away with the need for extraordinary virtue to accomplish it. The very greatness of the legislator makes his success more difficult, because he cannot be understood by those whom he wishes to convince. He must learn the language of the vulgar, and that is chiefly the language of divine inspiration or religion. The people can be impressed and persuaded by the accents of piety and the semblance of miracle. This is one of the few ways to still the voice of private interest long enough for the many to learn to appreciate the advantages of law. Religion is used for political purposes and, in Rousseau's view, should not become independent of political control. The religion should not contain teachings which do not conduce to the ends of the regime. Rousseau was perfectly aware that impostors could play the role of legislator and that the "strong man" is always a danger. But in looking to the origins of regimes, he could see only means such as these to establish orderly and legitimate ones. Regimes are made by men, and good ones require great men and unusual means.[12]

Although the formal conditions of legitimacy are the same everywhere, Rousseau wanted to preserve a realm for the activity of statesmanship. He knew that politics could not be made an abstract science as some modern theory wanted it to be. He tried to combine the clarity and certainty of modern political science with the flexibility of the classical art of politics. The fact of difference of circumstance means that many nations cannot enjoy liberty and that many others can only have a diluted form of it. A regime that could be realized everywhere would be of such a low order that the few who can enjoy a good one would be deprived of it without the others gaining by it. Legislation must be made at the right moment, and a primitive people uncorrupted by decadent habits is most eligible for it. The climate and the territory, its extent and character, must be taken into consideration. The traditions of the people and their manners determine the range of possibilities. The fact that the general will is formal allows for these differences. There is no doctrine of natural law which limits the statesman's activities and forces him to mitigate his judgments about what most conduces to the common good. That there are different peoples implies that the determinations of the general will will differ. The diversity of life is preserved, but man is not left without moral guidance; in the diversity there is the unity which is everywhere the same, the general will. But there are no universal substantive commands implied in the general will; a great variety of opposed principles can legitimately be emitted by it; it can make laws which lead to widely varying styles of life and action. According to the *Social Contract* and the political philosophy underlying it, there is no one best regime or scheme of laws. Different arrangements can equally well allow for the existence of a general will in different circumstances.[13]

The general will is only the expression of a desire that something be done. The force to do it is also necessary. This necessity brings into being the distinction between the legislative and the executive, between the sovereign and the government. Since the sovereign can legitimately make laws only about general objects, the application of the laws to particular acts or persons is not of its domain and belongs rather to the government. The government receives its instructions from the general will and uses its authority to determine the acts of the citizens according to the sense of the sovereign. It is the intermediary between sovereign and individual citizen and is totally derivative. This distinction is new in Rousseau and works a fundamental break with his predecessors, especially those of classical antiquity.[14] It prefigures the distinction between state and society so important today. For the classical thinkers the arrangement of the offices—the government—was the primary consideration. The form of government determined the form of society, and with a change of government a new society would be constituted. Loyalty was not owed to the country, the people, or the society but to the government. In Rousseau's scheme the existence of the sovereign prior to the existence of government means that the latter is only a secondary phenomenon from the point of view of right and fact. The contract constitutes the society which antedates the government and maintains itself in spite of changes in the government. Hence, the most interesting object of study is the society, and loyalty is owed primarily to it rather than to the government. The primary fact of politics is not the government of men; government is a necessary evil because men need direction in the exercise of their freedom. The less government, the better, and there is a great pre-occupation with limiting the scope of the government and preventing it from contradicting the general will. Government is always viewed with suspicion, and the citizens must be careful that the exercise of its functions does not unjustly inhibit them in the exercise of their liberty. The government institutes inequalities of rank and authority which are necessary to it, but those differences do not establish real differences of worth among the citizens who are all equal. The government is always completely dependent on the will of the people and can be reduced to its original equality with them.

It is easy to see how later thinkers were able to develop on this basis such notions as "the withering away of the state" without believing that the fundamental advantages of society would be lost; and it is less shocking to think of changes in government on this basis. The older tradition taught that the establishment of government is the fundamental act in the formation of a community, and that the destruction of government is equivalent to the destruction of society. Hence, the inequality which government implies is coeval with society, and it follows that the authority of government is not derivative from the people as a whole or the general will. The superior men do not owe their superiority to the people. This difference leads in Rousseau's thought to a certain deterioration in the respectability of government and more concentration on the rights of the citizens than on the effectiveness of execution.

Government must be powerful enough to dominate the particular wills of the citizens but not powerful enough to dominate the general will or the laws. The more inhabitants a country has, the more the particular wills are powerful, and the harder it is for the individuals to identify themselves with the community. Hence the government must be more vigorous in populous lands, especially when the extent of the territory is great. The more persons sharing the authority of government, the less vigorous the government; monarchy is the most vigorous of governments and democracy the least. It follows that difference of size of nations means that different sorts of government are required. One cannot speak of the best government. The difference between democracy, aristocracy, and monarchy is one of number, and consequently of vigor. The classic notion, that the difference is one of virtue and that the choice between the three forms of regime is the decisive political act, is tacitly denied by Rousseau. As a rule, aristocracy has the fewest inconveniences. Democracy requires too much virtue, is almost no government at all, and the identification of the collective private wills with the general will is too easy. Monarchy is too concentrated and the problems of succession are too great. Aristocracy is a sort of mean between the inconveniences of the two, but it can become the worst of regimes. There are three possible sorts of aristocracy: hereditary, natural, and elective. The first is the worst sort in Rousseau's view, based as it is on wealth and conventional inequality; and its members are under the delusion that their rights are independent of the will of the people. They have a collective interest of class which divides the community. Contradicting the whole tradition of political philosophy, Rousseau denies that a true aristocracy is a politically identifiable class.[15] In primitive societies the best-equipped to rule are chosen almost naturally, and this is an excellent solution but inadequate for more developed societies. Election is the sole legitimate mode of selecting a limited number of governors, for it guarantees that they will be in constant submission to the general will.

In this way, aristocracy becomes little more than an expression of the fact that in most societies not everyone rules so that some limited number of men must be chosen. There are no criteria of birth or wealth for the selection of those few, and the aristocracy does not represent a way of life. Rousseau, of course, tries to make provision for the selection of the truly best and to avoid demagoguery, but his notion of aristocracy is not far from our present-day notion of popular or democratic government. Above all, no classes are allowed to establish special rights for themselves and, consequently, no special way of life may be connected with their class privileges. Rousseau tries to preserve differentiation and special privilege for political talent, but the fundamental principle of political right is equality, and privilege should never become identified with the conventions of traditional aristocracy which preserves mediocrity under the guise of superiority. His thought entails a wholesale condemnation of the encouragement of the class differences which were central to classical thought.

The death of a government occurs when the particular wills substitute themselves for the general will. This can lead either to anarchy or tyranny—anarchy when the individuals go off each in his own direction, tyranny when the private will of a single man directs the government. The entire political problem is, in sum, to establish the proper relation between the particular and the general will. The transformation of man in his passage from the state of nature to the civil state and his discovery of his free capacity to will is the crucial event for him, and the first and continuing preoccupation of the statesman is to guarantee the preservation of that transformation. For this purpose the ancient city serves best: because it is small enough to permit an aristocratic government and for the citizens to share a common heritage and a common way, because the particular wills can more easily be submerged in custom, and because the statesman can control the entirety. The question of the size of a nation is not a matter of mere technical limitations as has been most often supposed in modern thought, but has to do with the nature of human possibilities. Rousseau believed that revolutions could restore conservative antiquity on new, self-conscious grounds. His thought is an amazing union of the radical, revolutionary progressivism of modernity with the discretion and restraint of antiquity.

As has been said, Rousseau began his critique of modern thought from the point of view of human happiness. A political solution which does not fulfill humanity is only an abstraction, nor can the proper place of the political be distinguished except against the background of the whole man. And that raises the question whether the solution of the *Social Contract* is as completely satisfactory as that book itself would seem to indicate. The question is whether all men, especially the best men, can find complete satisfaction within a possible civil society. That the *Social Contract* provides a basis, from Rousseau's point of view, for establishing orders in which most men can live satisfactorily when laws have become necessary for them, there is no doubt. But whether these orders can realize a perfect justice that commands the attachment of the minds and hearts of the best is not entirely clear. There are two reasons drawn from Rousseau's writings which make this question unavoidable.

The first is purely political and has to do with property. Rousseau never envisioned as universally feasible a common use of the fruits of the earth. Private property is almost inextricably bound up with civil society and attaches men to it. But private property is not natural and is always a source of inequality. Private property is the root of power in civil society, and it cannot help influencing the establishment of laws. Even in a society where there are not the extremes of wealth and poverty, the distinction exists, and the tendency is always toward aggravating these differences. A man's life is very different if he is born to poverty or wealth, and money has a great deal to do with his capacity to remove external impediments to his freedom. Society protects the rich more than the poor, and the poor have much less to lose and perhaps much to gain in the destruction of the established order. Rousseau recognizes this in being willing to weight the procedures of voting somewhat in favor of the solidly entrenched rich who have the preservation of the regime at heart, if only selfishly. As soon as the equality of persons is the basis of political right, the legitimacy of the inequality of private property becomes highly questionable. Rousseau did not believe that real equality of wealth could be maintained without constant revolution and the destruction of the advantages of political life, but his view of private property is not wholly unlike Marx's. Private property is a perpetual question mark standing after the words "legitimate civil society." [16]

But more important is the doubt raised by the investigation of man's nature and Rousseau's own life as he saw fit to describe it for the public. Man is naturally an idle animal whose real pleasure is in sentiment, especially the sentiment of his own being. The movement of time and events does not entirely efface that nature. But civil society requires effort and work; one has little time to exercise the sentiments. The good citizen wants the esteem and affection of his fellow citizens; he looks to their opinions rather than living within himself as does the savage. Above all, civil society demands virtue, and virtue is hard. Virtue means living according to principle, conscious repression of the animal and sentimental in man. Virtue is necessary for civil society, but it is unclear whether it is good in itself—whether, as for the ancients, it is the specific human perfection, desirable for itself in addition to its effect of preserving society. The natural man had a goodness which caused him to care for his fellows; this was a pleasure for him just as was the satisfaction of his personal needs. He never did anything because he had to, but because it flowed naturally from him. Rousseau makes a distinction between the moral and the good man.[17] The moral man acts from the sense of duty and has the character of the trustworthy citizen. The good man follows his natural instincts, that first nature uncorrupted by vanity; he is the sentimental friend and lover. Rousseau put himself in the class of the good men, and his *Confessions* are the revelation of the life, actions, and feelings of such a man. He is not a reliable citizen; he is useless to society. He is idle. Finally, he is a solitary walker who dreams and recovers the sense of his existence under the layers of convention that have caused it to be utterly lost. He goes away and lives in the country, alone, untouched by civil society. This is another solution to the human problem, impossible for most men who do not have the strength of soul and intellect necessary to free themselves from their dependence and to think through the false opinions of society; but it is more satisfactory and more pleasant because it is closer to that first nature.

One can say that there are two roads from the state of nature and that they do not meet, the one leading to civil society, the other to the condition of men like Rousseau. One looks forward to the future and to a transformation of man, the other longs passionately for a return to nature. There is no harmonious solution to the human problem; there are unsatisfactory alternatives at tension with one another: the statesman versus the dreamer or the poet. They are mutually exclusive. One is left with a sense of incompleteness or imperfection in Rousseau's view of human life. Civil society does not satisfy much that is deepest in man. The dreamer cannot live well with his fellows. And, in the state of nature, where this split had not occurred, man was not really man. But Rousseau resisted the temptations to which his successors succumbed. Because he was aware that man's morality was purchased at the sacrifice of his sweetest natural sentiments and is partly only a means to the preservation of the state, he did not try to absolutize that morality to the exclusion of all else that is human. He did not teach that history, for all its power, would overcome the force of man's nature. He did not believe that man could become entirely social. And he did not neglect the importance of the political to give himself up to romantic longings for the lost past. All of these possibilities are to be found in his thought, but each was given no more than its due. For this reason one feels that he presented the human problem in its variety with greater depth and breadth than any of his successors.

## NOTES

1. Rousseau's awareness of the paradoxical character of his works is well illustrated in the *Letter to M. d'Alembert,* in *Politics and the Arts. Letter to M. d'Alembert on the Theatre by Jean-Jacques Rousseau,* trans. with notes and an introduction by Allan Bloom (Glencoe, Ill.: The Free Press, 1960), p. 131, n.; and in Rousseau's *Lettre à M. Beaumont,* sixth paragraph.

2. *Discourse on Political Economy,* in *The Social Contract and Discourses,* trans. with an introduction by G. D. H. Cole ("Everyman's Library" [New York: Dutton, 1950]), pp. 306–8, 323–24. This volume will be cited hereafter as Cole's Rousseau.

3. *Discourse on the Arts and Sciences,* in Cole's Rousseau, pp. 144–74.

4. *The Government of Poland,* in Rousseau, *Political Writings,* trans. and ed. by Frederick Watkins (New York: Nelson, 1953), chap. ii, pp. 162 ff.; cf. *Discourse on the Origin and Foundation of Inequality among Men,* in Cole's Rousseau, pp. 176–88.

5. The preceding pages summarize the argument of the *Discourse on the Origin of Inequality.*

6. *Social Contract,* I.ii–v, in Cole's Rousseau, pp. 4–12.

7. *Ibid.,* I.vi, p. 13.

8. *Ibid.,* I.vii, pp. 16–18.

9. *Ibid.,* III.xv, pp. 93–96. Cf. *Government of Poland,* chap. vii, pp. 187–205.

10. *Social Contract,* III.xviii, p. 101.

11. *Discourse on Political Economy,* p. 298.

12. *Social Contract,* III.vii, pp. 37–42; cf. *Government of Poland,* chap. ii, pp. 163–65.

13. *Social Contract,* III.viii, p. 77; *Letter to M. d'Alembert,* p. 66.

14. *Social Contract,* I.vii, pp. 16–18, III.i, pp. 54–60; *Discourse on Political Economy,* pp. 289–97.

15. *Discourse on the Origin of Inequality,* p. 265, n. 1.

16. *Ibid.,* pp. 234–35.

17. See Rousseau's *Les Rêveries du promeneur solitaire,* sixième promenade (Paris: Garnier, 1960), pp. 75–86.

## READINGS

A.  Rousseau, Jean-Jacques. *Discourse on the Arts and Sciences,* in *The Social Contract and Discourses.* "Everyman's Library." New York: Dutton, 1950.

Rousseau, Jean-Jacques. *Discourse on the Origin and Foundation of Inequality among Men,* in *ibid.*

Rousseau, Jean-Jacques. *Social Contract,* in *ibid.,* bks I and II.

B.  Rousseau, Jean-Jacques. *Discourse on Political Economy,* in *The Social Contract and Discourses.*

Rousseau, Jean-Jacques. *Social Contract,* in *ibid.,* bks III and IV.

Rousseau, Jean-Jacques. "The Confession of Faith of the Savoyard Vicar," in *Emile.* "Everyman's Library." New York: Dutton, 1933. Bk VI.

Rousseau, Jean-Jacques. *The Government of Poland,* in *Political Writings.* Trans. and ed. F. Watkins. New York: Nelson, 1953.

Rousseau, Jean-Jacques. *Letter to M. d'Alembert on the Theatre,* in *Politics and the Arts.* Trans. with notes and an introduction by Allan Bloom. Glencoe, Ill.: The Free Press, 1960.

# WILLIAM BLACKSTONE

## 1723–1780

Sir William Blackstone was not a political philosopher, but an English lawyer and judge. His major piece of writing is not a book on justice or even on law, but a set of *Commentaries on the Laws of England*. He was not original or inventive, but deliberately the opposite; and he often treats important and difficult questions in what seems to be an obscure or superficial way. Indeed, Blackstone is fairly widely regarded as having been contradictory or confused on important points of political philosophy. He is thought to exhibit a character that is amiable if a bit pompous; a style that is crisp and sometimes elegant; an intellect not strong in theory but capable of sound practical judgment and intrinsically bent to compromise—in short, to present himself a thorough Englishman. There is considerable ground for this view, but it is insufficient, and the reasons for its insufficiency are the reasons for giving note to Blackstone in a history of political philosophy.

When Blackstone first offered a course of lectures on the laws of England at Oxford University in 1753, he set a precedent that was intended to have a major effect on English legal and, more broadly, civic education.[1] Although the *Commentaries* are addressed to officers of every description and subjects of every order, they are aimed particularly at the lawyer and the gentleman. The lawyer was to be lifted from the confines of mere practice and directed to the elements and first principles upon which his practice was based. The gentleman was to be rescued from his dishonorable ignorance of the laws that it was his duty to safeguard, improve, and administer. In both cases what was required was academical instruction in the laws of the land which would enable the student not only to learn the outlines of the positive law but

536

also to comprehend, and even himself to form, arguments "drawn *a priori,* from the spirit of the laws and the natural foundations of justice." [2] Blackstone invites examination of the laws of the land, their natural foundations, and the intervening "spirit of the laws." It is true that he also discusses divine law, for example, in his introductory treatment of law in general, but divine law typically makes an early and brief appearance, soon collapsing into natural law; and Blackstone makes little or no use of it in explaining, as distinguished from supporting, the laws of England. Religion does indeed have an important place under the laws of England, and Blackstone is a warm friend of the established Church; but what is relevant is the influence of the Church in making men sober, industrious, and good citizens.[3]

Blackstone's highest theme, then, deals with the relation between natural law and conventional law, as this relation presents itself to one who is a lawyer in the best and highest sense. The plan or organization of the *Commentaries* is characterized by a symmetry which contains, as a whole and in each of the parts, a movement or progression from the natural to the conventional.[4] Following an Introduction, the four volumes of the *Commentaries* are divided into two parts, each comprising two volumes or books. First are "Rights," divided into the Rights of Persons (Book I) and the Rights of Things (Book II); there follow "Wrongs," divided into Private Wrongs (Book III) and Public Wrongs (Book IV). The argument as a whole moves from individual rights to public wrongs.

The first chapter of Book I begins with what Blackstone calls the absolute rights of individuals, which are those that appertain and belong to particular men as individuals and "would belong to their persons merely in a state of nature. . . ." The "first and primary end" of human laws is to maintain and regulate these absolute rights.[5] Blackstone spends little time, however, with the natural liberty of mankind, even in this first chapter, but moves quickly to the subject of civil rights and specifically the absolute rights of Englishmen, which are treated under the familiar Lockean headings of personal security, personal liberty, and private property. The remainder and by far the bulk of Book I deals with relative rights, that is, the secondary and more artificial rights of individuals as they stand in legally established relationships to other individuals, first the public relationships of governors and governed, then the private relationships of master and servant, husband and wife, parent and child, and the like, which are consequent on civil society. Although the right of property is discussed, as has been said, in the first chapter of Book I as one of the absolute rights of individuals, Blackstone treats property in a separate and subsequent book, subsequent, it may be noted, even to the relations of govcrnment. The reason for this is that the natural origin of rights of things is, compared to rights of persons, both less clear and less relevant to civil society. It is less clear because Blackstone finds the natural origin in occupancy or possession, and he seems to leave open the difficult question of what kind of right mere possession can be or grant; it is less relevant because, whereas natural personal rights, such as self-defense, are more or less regulated by positive law, the natural right to acquire property is substantially replaced or superseded by conventional rights to hold and transfer property.[6]

"Wrongs," the subject of the second part of the *Commentaries*, are said "for the most part [to] convey to us an idea merely negative, as being nothing else but a privation of right."[7] The second part contains no chapters comparable in philosophical intention to the first chapters of Books I and II, because wrongs are defined by and derivative from rights. The last pair of books is not, however, merely a mirror image of the first pair. Book III describes how the law provides for the redress of private wrongs relating to both persons and property (civil injuries), reflecting therefore the discussion in both Book I and Book II and bringing to a conclusion, as it were, the whole subject of individual rights. Public wrongs (crimes and misdemeanors), the subject of Book IV, constitute that part of the law that is most artificial. Rights are the basis of Blackstone's jurisprudence, and there are, strictly speaking, no rights of the public but only rights of individuals. In Book IV, however, political society, which is a means to the end of protecting individual rights, is treated—as it can and must be treated for many practical purposes—as if it were an end. That end is "the government and tranquillity of the whole," or more simply, peace; "for peace is the very end and foundation of civil society."[8] Without entering into detail, we may say that Blackstone's description of the several species of crimes and misdemeanors, for example crimes against God and religion and against the king and government, contains his negative or indirect discussion of the kind of artificial public or common good that must be constructed for the sake of the peaceful enjoyment of individual rights.

"The only true and natural foundations of society," Blackstone asserts, "are the wants and fears of individuals"[9]; but it is not Blackstone's procedure to enter into any detailed or exhaustive examination of these wants and fears or of the natural liberty of mankind from which he begins. Rather he hastens on (not, we may imagine, to the displeasure of his English gentlemen and lawyers) to a discussion of civil rights, as if to define the rights of man in terms of the rights of Englishmen. The rights of Englishmen, however, are all rights *under law*. Personal liberty, to give but one example, "consists in the power of loco-motion, of changing situation, or removing one's person to whatsoever place one's own inclination may direct; without imprisonment or restraint, *unless by due course of law*." [10] But if the law were amended to permit arrest and imprisonment for indefinite periods on suspicion of executive officials, would that not constitute an abridgment of the Englishman's right of personal liberty? Putting the point more generally, Blackstone says, following Montesquieu, that in England as perhaps nowhere else, "political or civil liberty is the very end and scope of the constitution"; but he goes on to say that "this liberty, rightly understood, consists in the power of doing whatever the laws permit. . . ." [11] Blackstone seems to present a circular argument: defining good law as that which best maintains individual liberty and defining individual liberty as that which is permitted by law. This circularity or ambiguity is present throughout the *Commentaries,* not because of a defect in Blackstone's powers of reasoning or some irrational commitment to the English legal system, but because the theoretically sound argument, the argument taken from nature, tends to be practically self-defeating.

Even self-defense, "justly called the primary law of nature," is strictly confined, although "it is not, neither can it be in fact, taken away by the law of society." [12] The principal of law is "that where a crime, in itself capital, is endeavoured to be committed by force, it is lawful to repel that force by the death of the party attempting." Blackstone immediately goes on to warn that "we must not carry this doctrine to the same visionary length that Mr. Locke does; who holds, 'that all manner of force without right upon a man's person, puts him in a state of war with the aggressor; and, of consequence, that . . . he may lawfully kill him that puts him under this unnatural restraint.'" This principle may be just "in a state of uncivilized nature," but "the law of England, like that of every other well-regulated community, is too tender of the public peace, too careful of the lives of the subjects, to adopt so contentious a system; nor will suffer with impunity any crime to be *prevented* by death, unless the same, if committed, would also be *punished* by death." [13] The law of England does, however, provide an exception to this rule of justifiable homicide, and that is, in the terminology of the law, excusable homicide. Where, for example, a man protects himself from assault and in the course of the quarrel kills his assailant, he is excused from legal penalty, provided that "certain and immediate suffering would [have been] the consequence of waiting for the assistance of the law" and that "the slayer had no other possible (or, at least, probable) means of escaping from his assailant." [14] A man attacked must turn his back and flee, if he can, and later bring his assailant to court. The presumption is always in favor of the law of civil society, not the law of nature.

The maintenance of government and therefore law itself is an even more delicate case. Blackstone is often pointed to as an exponent of parliamentary sovereignty, in contrast, for example, to American ideas of limited government. In Parliament, consisting of king, lords, and commons, lies "that absolute despotic power, which must in all governments reside somewhere. . . ." Parliament can deal with matters outside the ordinary scope of law, it can remodel the succession to the crown, it can alter the established religion, it can change the constitution of the kingdom and Parliament itself. "It can, in short, do every thing that is not naturally impossible. . . ." [15] It is true that Blackstone frequently seems to assume that Parliament cannot do what it ought not to do (for example, substitute an elective for a hereditary monarchy); and he emphasizes "the true excellence of the English government, that all the parts of it form a mutual check upon each other." [16] But however great the safeguard provided in practice by the English system of mutual social and political checks, in the end Blackstone must return to the first principle of civil society, which is that Parliament, or the legislature, can do what it likes.

Is there not, however, a still more fundamental principle? "It must be owned that Mr. Locke, and other theoretical writers, have held, that 'there remains still inherent in the people a supreme power to remove or alter the legislative, when they find the legislative act contrary to the trust reposed in them. . . .'" Blackstone insists that, "however just this conclusion may be in theory"—and it *is* just in Blackstone's theory for precisely the same reasons that it is just in Locke's—"we cannot practically adopt it, nor take any *legal* steps for carrying it into execution, under any dispensation of government at present actually existing." Such a devolution of power to the people at large presumes a dissolution of government, a reduction of the people to their "original state of equality," and the repeal of all positive laws. "No human laws will therefore suppose a case, which at once must destroy all law, and compel men to build afresh upon a new foundation; nor will they make provision for so desperate an event, as must render all legal provisions ineffectual." [17] The ultimate resort to first principle, to what Blackstone calls elsewhere the "law of nature" or "the God of battles," [18] is at the foundation of law because it enforces, as no law and no internal checks can do, the limits on political authority. Yet the law cannot provide for or even suppose this ultimate resort and is, in fact, in tension with it: the maintenance of law and therefore the effective maintenance of individual rights depends upon a putting aside, as if for once and all, of the original state of lawless equality out of which civil society arose and into which it may, in desperate event, relapse. Mr. Locke and his theoretical friends are not wrong, but they may endanger the polity precisely because of their clear expression of its true foundation. "For civil liberty rightly understood, consists in protecting the rights of individuals by the united force of society: society cannot be maintained, and of course can exert no protection, without obedience to some sovereign power: and obedience is an empty name, if every individual has a right to decide how far he himself shall obey." [19] Blackstone is not fearful that his constant emphasis on law and law-abidingness will incapacitate the people for the resumption of their original right should that be necessary. Where the sovereign power becomes tyrannical and threatens desolation to the state, "mankind will not be reasoned out of the feelings of humanity; nor will sacrifice their liberty by a scrupulous adherence to those political maxims, which were originally established to preserve it." [20]

The origin of civil society, Blackstone suggests, is anarchy; its tendency, tyranny. There have been times when the rights of Englishmen were "depressed by overbearing and tyrannical princes; at others so luxuriant as even to tend to anarchy, a worse state than tyranny itself," says Blackstone, as befits a lawyer, "as any government is better than none at all." [21] But the objective is to avoid both, as the British constitution has generally done. In support of this objective, Blackstone's jurisprudence acknowledges the extremes, while resisting their pull, for either is fatal to liberty. Stated positively, Blackstone seeks to maintain between the ground and the tendency of civil society the central position of law, particularly the law as it is understood by judges and administered in their courts. In a list of five "auxiliary subordinate rights," which serve principally as "barriers" to protect the three great primary rights, Blackstone gives central place to the right of every Englishman to apply to the courts for redress of injuries. The law (not Parliament or the people at large), Blackstone says here, is in England "the supreme arbiter of every man's life, liberty, and property. . . ." In this "distinct and separate existence" of the judiciary lies "one main preservative of the public liberty; which cannot subsist long in any state, unless the administration of common justice be in some degree separated both from the legislative and also from the executive power." In particular, "were it joined with the legislative, the life, liberty, and property, of the subject would be in the hands of arbitrary judges, whose decisions would be then regulated only by their own opinions, and not by any fundamental principles of law; which, though legislators may depart from, yet judges are bound to observe." [22]

Blackstone here expresses again the principle of mutual checks, but our present concern is with his comment that there are "fundamental principles of law; which, though legislators may depart from, yet judges are bound to observe." This seems curious when we consider what may be called Blackstone's basic (though not exhaustive) definition of law: "the will of one man, or of one or more assemblies of men, to whom the supreme authority is entrusted . . . is in different states, according to their different constitutions, understood to be *law*." [23] Law is the will of the sovereign; but good law, and therefore law properly speaking, requires something more. Not only consent, for "even laws themselves, whether made with or without our consent, if they regulate and constrain our conduct in matters of mere indifference, without any good end in view, are regulations destructive of liberty. . . ." The good end in view is genuine civil liberty, which is "no other than natural liberty so far restrained by human laws (and no farther) as is necessary and expedient for the general advantage of the publick." [24] How far and in what respects the general advantage requires restraint of natural liberty is not a question that can be answered, except in a way that reformulates the question, by some general principle or rule. It is a matter of judgment. And free government depends on the maintenance within it of a central place for the judiciary, that peculiar body of men who are capable, by tradition, political position, and training, of judging well. While providing disinterested protection of the lives, liberties, and properties of the subjects, the judiciary also serves as a brake on the unwise use of parliamentary and popular authority and as a source (or at least a mouthpiece) of instruction in the true principles of civil liberty.

The fundamental principles of law to which judges must adhere, and which mitigate the view of law as the will of the sovereign, consist of or are drawn in the first place from custom. In English law, "the goodness of a custom depends upon it's [sic] having been used time out of mind; or, in the solemnity of our legal phrase, time whereof the memory of man runneth not to the contrary. This it is that gives it it's [sic] weight and authority: and of this nature are the maxims and customs which compose the common law, or *lex non scripta*, of this kingdom." When in his Introduction Blackstone turns from a discussion of the nature of law to the laws of England, he does not begin with a contracting people or a sovereign legislature but with these common laws, of which judges are the "depositaries" and "living oracles." Written laws or statutes are merely declaratory or remedial of some defect in the common laws, which are "the first ground and chief corner stone of the laws of England. . . ." [25]

In innumerable ways throughout the *Commentaries* Blackstone recognizes, strengthens, and uses the authority of the old. He is often taken for a mere patriot or conservative, even though he gives ample indication that neither his praise of what is English nor his devotion to what is old is to be taken simply at face value.[26] Certainly Blackstone does emphasize the bindingness of precedent and the deference owed by the present generation to former times. He chooses, for example, to defend on the ground of authority rather than reason and justice the decision of the lords and commons to regard James II as having merely abdicated the throne, rather than as having subverted the government and broken the original contract. While making clear his own opinion that the decision was reasonable and just, in avoiding "the wild extremes into which the visionary theories of some zealous republicans would have led them," he fears that such speculation, if carried too far, "might imply a right of dissenting or revolting from [the decision], in case we should think it to have been unjust, oppressive, or inexpedient." [27] Blackstone was as perceptive as those commentators who have pointed out that there is a defect in this argument because on Blackstone's own principles the present generation does have a right at any time to be judge of whether the contract has been broken. Blackstone's implicit argument is that if desperate circumstances arise, as they did in 1688, it must be hoped that the original right will be exercised as wisely and moderately as it was then, when the fabric of government and law was maintained while a revolution was made. But the exercise of this basic right is to be discouraged. The stability of any polity, not least a polity whose fundamental principles contain an intrinsic tendency toward instability, depends upon a widespread opinion of the bindingness of the old.

It is the duty of the judge, and the concern of Blackstone as his teacher, to articulate and maintain the integrity of the system of positive law as it stands. The reader of the *Commentaries* is frequently told of the nicety with which the old rules of law were framed, "and how closely they are connected and interwoven together, supporting, illustrating, and demonstrating one another." [28] He is cautioned that the very number and complexity of English municipal laws which vex him, whether as student or litigant, testify to the extent of the country, its commercial prosperity, and above all the liberty and property of the subjects.[29] He is reminded that every science has its terms and rules of art, the reason of which may not be immediately visible. Many of these artificial rules reflect the lawyer's preoccupation with forms and procedures, arising out of his trained understanding that if laws are cast in a certain form, promulgated in a certain way, and enforced according to certain processes, the likelihood of doing substantive justice is increased. The legal art provides the framework within which judgment is exercised and justice done. Thus, lawyer-like, Blackstone says that municipal law is "something permanent, uniform, and universal" and describes the procedure of trial by jury as "the most transcendent privilege which any subject can enjoy, or wish for. . . ." [30] But his concern with the integrity, or rationale, of the English legal system goes deeper than forms and procedures, important as they are and large a place as they inevitably occupy in an analysis of English law.

The *Commentaries* are full of intricate and seemingly endless "explanations" of the old rules of law, many of them apparently irrelevant or even in opposition to present needs and modern principles. Dizzy with the effort to comprehend the reason of a system where, for example, a brother of the half blood may never succeed as heir to the estate of his elder brother even if they have the same father,[31] the reader is likely to conclude that the old maxim of the common lawyer that "what is not reason is not law" [32] is maintained only by an unshakable determination to assert, however artificially and at whatever cost in Latin maxims and patchwork fictions, that what is English law is reason. If there is any consistent underlying principle it seems to lie in Blackstone's emphatic intention to draw his students away from "the rage of modern improvement." Yet "modern improvement" is the very foundation of the *Commentaries;* but it is essential to the modern enterprise itself that reform should wear a conservative cloak.[33] The weight and influence of the old is to be preserved and used to support the new.

We inherit an old Gothic castle, erected in the days of chivalry, but fitted up for a modern inhabitant. The moated ramparts, the embattled towers, and the trophied halls, are magnificent and venerable, but useless. The inferior apartments, now converted into rooms of convenience, are chearful and commodious, though their approaches are winding and difficult.[34]

Blackstone helps to remodel the old castle, by means of which its comfort is improved, for example by relaxing some of the old legal restrictions on commerce; but he is careful to warn against reform that might loosen some apparently useless stone or weaken some inconvenient timber and cause the whole edifice, the pleasant apartments as well as the noble shell, vital damage.

Blackstone is therefore an extremely cautious reformer, but his metaphor also has a deeper significance. Civil society consists of a set of conventional, and in a sense arbitrary, rules and regulations whose purpose is the regularization and thereby the protection of natural rights. But the effectiveness of that conventional system depends upon its becoming confounded, for many practical purposes, with nature. Too persistent inquiry into the grounds of the conventional system may reveal too clearly and widely that it *is* a conventional system and not a set of natural rules, thereby encouraging self-destructive appeals from the artificial system to its natural foundation. "It is well if the mass of mankind will obey the laws when made, without scrutinizing too nicely into the reasons of making them." [35] And of course the older and better established the laws, the less likely that their reasons will be questioned. The general tendency to "mistake for nature what we find established by long and inveterate custom" [36] can be a trap for the academic student of law, but it is absolutely indispensable to the maintenance of law.

The classic case, because the most modified or artificial of individual rights, is the right of property, and Blackstone provides two versions of its origin. In his introductory discussion of property in general, he finds the origin in sheer possession or occupancy. He then shows how men's desire to hold their property in greater security drives them by stages from a "savage state of vagrant liberty" to civil society, and to civilization, with its increasingly complex and artificial system of law establishing property rights.[37] The second version of the origin of property begins at the peak of the hierarchy rather than its base and describes a conquering general seizing lands, partitioning them among his followers, and eventually establishing a hierarchical military system.[38] English law, and English history as well, is presented here as a combination of these two developments. Thus the basic pattern of land law is feudal tenure, of which "the grand and fundamental maxim" is "that all lands were originally granted out by the sovereign, and are therefore holden, either mediately or immediately, of the crown." [39] But this fundamental maxim is a fiction; a fiction to which our ancestors consented under William only in order to establish a then generally useful military system; a fiction that later Norman lawyers made the engine of ecclesiastical tyranny; a fiction, now much modified and adapted to a commercial society, that signals the recognition that a man can most effectively preserve what is his own by consenting to regard it as the king's.

Indeed, the hereditary monarch is himself a kind of fiction, or he is an altogether artificial entity, the prime sign and example of the replacement of men's natural equality by that "due subordination of rank" that government requires.[40] While Blackstone praises the modern freedom to discuss the limits of the king's prerogative, "a topic, that in some former ages was thought too delicate and sacred to be profaned by the pen of a subject," he discusses it nevertheless with "decency and respect." "For, though a philosophical mind will consider the royal person merely as one man appointed by mutual consent to preside over many others, and will pay him that reverence and duty which the principles of society demand, yet the mass of mankind will be apt to grow insolent and refractory, if taught to consider their prince as a man of no greater perfection than themselves. The law therefore ascribes to the king . . . certain attributes of a great and transcendant [sic] nature; by which the people are led to consider him in the light of a superior being, and to pay him that awful respect, which may enable him with greater ease to carry on the business of government." [41]

Thus the merely conventional superiority of the king is widely regarded, thanks partly to certain laws and writings about law, as a natural superiority; his conventional title to the throne a natural title; his contractual right to the loyalty of his subjects a natural right. As subjects we stand in awe of the king, without considering that he is our servant; we accept our subordinate rank in society, without considering our original equality; we accept the property that the laws assign us, without considering our original right to seize what we can. In sum, we obey, without considering our right to rid ourselves of the sovereign who commands and the law he administers; for to exercise this right would be the destruction of the security of our persons, our liberty, and our property. "The moated ramparts, the embattled towers, and the trophied halls," Blackstone says, "are magnificent and venerable, but useless." It is true that the noble and chivalrous purposes that they once supported and displayed are now displaced; newer and better ends are expressed in the comfortable apartments. But these apartments cannot provide for themselves that magnificence and venerability with which their own outer walls must be reinforced if the modern edifice is to stand. The Gothic labyrinth of hierarchy and duty, to which Blackstone provides the key, is the indispensable means to the regulation and thus the preservation of human equality and individual rights.

## NOTES

1. The four volumes of the *Commentaries on the Laws of England* first appeared in 1765, 1766, 1768, and 1769. The edition used here is the eighth, published in 1778 and the last published during Blackstone's lifetime; except where otherwise indicated, citations are to volume and page. The authenticity

of the changes made by the editor of the ninth edition, on which many modern editions are based, is somewhat doubtful; but the differences are minor, and numerous standard editions reproduce the entire text with original pagination. The useful edition of William G. Hammond (San Francisco: Bancroft-Whitney, 1890) contains a collation of all changes in the first eight editions.

2. *Ibid.*, I, 32.

3. See *ibid.*, III, 100–103; IV, chaps iv, viii, xxviii.

4. In an early sketch of the ground covered later in the *Commentaries,* Blackstone remarks that he follows in many respects the plan of Sir Matthew Hale (*The Analysis of the Law . . . of England,* 3rd ed., 1739); but he emphasizes that he has chosen "to extract a new Method of his own, [rather] than implicitly to copy after any." *An Analysis of the Laws of England* (3rd ed., 1758), p. vii.

5. *Commentaries,* I, 123–24.

6. *Ibid.,* II, 3, 8–9, and *passim.* In Blackstone's significantly loose formulation, "The original of private property is probably founded in nature . . . : but certainly the modifications under which we at present find it, the method of conserving it in the present owner, and of translating it from man to man, are entirely derived from society. . . ." I, 138.

7. *Ibid.,* III, 2.

8. *Ibid.,* IV, 7; I, 349.

9. *Ibid.,* I, 47.

10. *Ibid.,* 134; italics supplied. For the definitions of the rights of personal security and property, see I, 129, 138.

11. *Ibid.,* 6.

12. *Ibid.,* III, 4.

13. *Ibid.,* IV, 181–82; cf. III, 168–69. Italics original. The passage here from Locke is not a direct quotation but a paraphrase. See *Second Treatise,* secs 18–19.

14. *Ibid.,* IV, 184.

15. *Ibid.,* I, 160–61.

16. *Ibid.,* I, 154–55. See I, 50–51:

". . . as the legislature of the kingdom is entrusted to three distinct powers, entirely independent of each other; first, the king; secondly, the lords spiritual and temporal, which is an aristocratical assembly of persons selected for their piety, their birth, their wisdom, their valour, or their property; and, thirdly, the house of commons, freely chosen by the people from among themselves, which makes it a kind of democracy; as this aggregate body, actuated by different springs, and attentive to different interests, composes the British parliament, and has the supreme disposal of every thing; there can no inconvenience be attempted by either of the three branches, but will be withstood by one of the other two; each branch being armed with a negative power, sufficient to repel any innovation which it shall think inexpedient or dangerous."

17. *Ibid.,* 161–62. Italics original.

18. *Ibid.,* 193.

19. *Ibid.,* 251.

20. *Ibid.,* 245.

21. *Ibid.,* 127.

22. *Ibid.,* 141, 269.

23. *Ibid.,* 52. Italics original. An obvious misprint in the text of this passage has been corrected.

24. *Ibid.,* 125–26.

25. *Ibid.,* 67, 69, 73.

26. See *ibid.,* 172, 190–91; IV, 3–5.

27. *Ibid.,* I, 212–13.

28. *Ibid.,* II, 128; cf. II, 376.

29. *Ibid.,* III, 325–27.

30. *Ibid.,* I, 44; III, 379; cf. Blackstone's discussion of equity at I, 62, 91–92; III, 429–41.

31. *Ibid.,* II, 227–33.

32. *Ibid.,* I, 70.

33. *Ibid.,* 10. For some of Blackstone's suggestions for reform, see III, 381–85 (trial by jury); IV, 235–39 (capital punishment); IV, 388–89 (corruption of blood).

34. *Ibid.,* III, 268.

35. *Ibid.,* II, 2.

36. *Ibid.,* 11.

37. *Ibid.,* 6–8.
38. *Ibid.,* 45 ff.
39. *Ibid.,* 53.
40. *Ibid.,* I, 271; cf. I, 208–9; IV, 105;

and Blackstone's discussion of allegiance, I, 366–70.
41. *Ibid.,* I, 237, 241.

## READINGS

A.  Blackstone, William. *Commentaries on the Laws of England.* Introduction, I. i; II. i.
B.  Blackstone, William. *Commentaries on the Laws of England.* I. ii, iii, vii, xii, xiv; II. iv, xiii, xiv; III. i, iii, viii, xxiii, xxvii; IV. i, iv, vi, xiv, xxviii, xxxiii.

# ADAM SMITH

## 1723–1790

The major writing of Adam Smith is contained in two books, *Theory of Moral Sentiments* (1759) and *An Inquiry into the Nature and Causes of the Wealth of Nations* (1776). His major professional employment was to serve, for thirteen years, as Professor of Moral Philosophy in the University of Glasgow. His fame now rests upon the foundation he laid for the science of economics. In all of this there is not much of political philosophy to be seen, even allowing for the inclusion of jurisprudence in the Morals course. Smith's contribution to economics, however, has the character of a description and advocacy of the system now called liberal capitalism; and the ligaments between the economic order and the political system, close under any circumstances, are exceptionally broad and strong in the world as seen and molded by Adam Smith. The close conjunction of economics and political philosophy, even or perhaps especially if tending toward the eclipse of the latter, is a powerful fact of political philosophy; the men, like Smith, who were responsible for it would have a place in the chronicle of political philosophy on that ground alone.

Smith is of interest for his share in the deflection of political philosophy toward economics and for his famous elaboration of the principles of free enterprise or liberal capitalism. By virtue of the latter, he has earned the right to be known as an architect of our present system of society. For that title, however, he has a rival in Locke, whose writing antedated his own by roughly a century. Our thesis will be that, although Smith follows in the tradition of which Locke is a great figure, yet a distinct and important change fell upon that tradition, a change that Smith helped bring about; that to understand modern capitalism adequately, it is necessary to grasp the "Smithian" change in the Lockean tradition; and that to understand the ground of engagement between capitalism and postcapitalistic doctrines—primarily the Marxian—one must grasp the issues of capitalism in the altered form they received from Adam Smith. To state the point in barest simplicity: Smith's teaching contains that formulation of capitalist doctrine in which many of the fundamental issues are recognizably those on which postcapitalism contests the field.

It would be vastly misleading to suggest that the initiative in modifying the classic modern doctrine was Smith's. To avoid that intimation, we must cover all of what follows with a single remark on the obligation of Smith to his senior friend and compatriot, David Hume. Smith's moral philosophy, as he in effect admits, is a refinement upon Hume's which differs from it in respects that, although very significant, are not decisive.[1] A thorough study of the relation between the doctrines of Smith and Hume would disclose in full the connection between liberal capitalism and the "skeptical" or "scientific" principles upon which Hume wished to found all philosophy. The broadest conclusions that would emerge from such a study can be deduced from an examination of Smith's doctrines alone, precisely because they do reflect so deeply the influence of Hume.

Many of Smith's fundamental reflections are contained in the *Theory of Moral Sentiments,* wherein he sets forth his important understanding of nature and human nature. He does this in the course of answering the following question: What is virtue, and what makes it eligible? The premise of his answer is that, whatever virtue may turn out to be, it must have very much in common with, perhaps it must simply coincide with, that by reason of which men or their actions deserve approbation. The question, What is virtue? is never distinct from the question, What deserves approbation? Approbation and disapprobation are bestowed upon actions. The spring of any action is the sentiment (or emotion, or affection, or passion—they are synonymous) which is the motive for committing the act. Approbation of any action must ascend to the passion which truly explains the action.

The sentiment or affection of the heart from which any action proceeds, and upon which its whole virtue or vice must ultimately depend, may be considered under two different aspects, or in two different relations; first, in relation to the cause which excites it, or the motive which gives occasion to it; and secondly, in relation to the end which it proposes, or the effect which it tends to produce.

In the suitableness or unsuitableness, in the proportion or disproportion which the affection seems to bear to the cause or object which excites it, con-

sists the propriety or impropriety, the decency or ungracefulness of the consequent action.

In the beneficial or hurtful nature of the effects which the affection aims
at, or tends to produce, consists the merit or demerit of the action, the qualities
by which it is entitled to reward, or is deserving of punishment.[2]

Propriety and merit are thus the attributes of the passion behind
each action that determine the virtuousness of the action. These bear a
certain similarity to the "agreeable and useful" of Hume, but Smith
believed his own doctrine to be original in that it avoids the final reduction of all approbation to utility, which Smith rejected on the
Humean ground that "utility" is not as such recognizable by immediate
sense and feeling, but only by a sort of calculation of reason. Smith believed he had been able to ground morality on a phenomenon of the
passions alone, a belief to which the name of his book testifies. If sense
and feeling are indeed immediate—unmediated in the sense that nothing is between them and the root of the fundamental self—then there
is considerable value in bringing down the analysis of the virtues to
its true bottom in the passions. In Smith's doctrine, the clue to that reduction is in the phenomenon of Sympathy, the criterion of propriety
and merit.

Sympathy is a word used by Smith in its literal meaning, an
etymological parallel of compassion: "feeling with," or a fellow feeling.
It is a fact of which, perhaps, no further mechanical account can be
given, that the passions of one human being are transferred to another
by the force of imagination at work in the recipient. The man who
sees or merely conceives the terror, hatred, benevolence, or gratitude of
another must to some extent enter into that passion and experience it
himself, for he must imagine himself in the other's circumstances, and
therefrom everything follows. Of chief importance in the foregoing is
the qualification "to some extent." If the impartial spectator, cognizant
of what stimulated the terror, hatred, or other passion of the agent,
feels in his own breast the same measure of that passion as moved the
agent to his action, then the spectator literally sympathizes with the
agent and approves his act as consistent with "propriety." The spectator
experiences sympathetically the passion of the agent; and if he experiences it in the same degree, he further experiences the "sentiment of
approbation"—for that, too, is a passion.

Propriety, however, is not the only ground of moral virtue. Not
only the suitableness of the agent's passion to its cause, but the aim or
tendency of that passion, its effect, has a bearing on the moral quality
of the act in question. Smith refers to "the nature of the effects which
the affection aims at, or tends to produce." The "or" is disjunctive, and

we must later discuss the important difference between the effects that the sentiment aims at and those that the act it inspires actually tends to produce. For the present it is enough to note that when an action falls upon some human being, it will cause him to feel gratitude or resentment because it will be either beneficial or harmful, pleasurable or painful. If an impartial spectator, informed of all the circumstances, would sympathize with the gratitude felt by the object human being, then the spectator would judge the agent's act to be meritorious, and the second condition of moral virtue would have been met. In brief: if the actual or supposed impartial spectator should sympathize with the passion both of the agent (propriety) and of the patient (merit), then the agent's act may be pronounced virtuous on the basis of the spectator's feeling of approbation.

If Smith's elaboration of the sympathy mechanism did nothing more than show how a rather strict morality could be educed from the passions and the imagination alone, it would have a certain interest. In fact, it points toward a much wider circle of consequences. Sympathy cannot be separated, in Smith's formulation, from imagination. Together they define an undoubted natural sociality of man. By the exercise of two subrational capacities, sympathy and imagination, each man is by his nature led or compelled to transcend his very self and, without indeed being able to feel the other man's feeling, is able and is driven to imagine himself in the place of that other and to participate, how vicariously is a matter of indifference, in the feelings which are the fundamental phenomena of the other's existence. Smith, it will be recalled, wished to know not only what virtue is but what makes it eligible. Why—in principle—do men choose to be virtuous, when to be virtuous means to be deserving of approbation? Smith's answer is that it is of the nature of a human being to desire the approbation and love of his human congeners.[3] The first sentence of the *Theory of Moral Sentiments* intimates the withdrawal that is in progress from the doctrine of the war of all against all: "How selfish soever man may be supposed, there are evidently some principles in his nature, which interest him in the fortune of others, and render their happiness necessary to him, though he derives nothing from it except the pleasure of seeing it." The combination of imagination, sympathy, and the need for the love and approbation of other men is the ground for Smith's asseverations that nature formed man for society.[4]

Not only does Smith thus teach a natural sociality of man, but also the natural character of the moral law. He can with ease refer to "the natural principles of right and wrong,"[5] understanding by "right" not merely what benefits or avoids bringing harm to the agent. He can do so because the ground of moral action and perception is the inner constitution of human nature; not in the antique sense of man's highest possibilities, it is true, but in the sense of human psychology—the instincts, sentiments, mechanisms of sympathy that are the efficient causes of human behavior. These are perfectly natural, and the sentiments of approbation are equally so; hence the principles of right and wrong are incontestably natural.

Smith's version of natural right depends very heavily upon the construct of the "impartial spectator," the imaginary being who is supposed to represent all mankind in viewing and judging each individual's actions. Judgment rendered from such a point of view implies that no man may rightly prefer himself to the extent of making exceptions from the general rule in his own behalf. "As to love our neighbour as we love ourselves is the great law of Christianity, so it is the great precept of nature to love ourselves only as we love our neighbour, or what comes to the same thing, as our neighbour is found capable of loving us." [6] Recourse to the imagined judgment of general humanity at the same time directs conscience toward the imagined surveillance maintained over each man at all times by a supposed all-seeing humanity. The constructive standard of "universal mankind" is fundamental to the version of natural right and natural sociality taught by Smith. It is also a premonition of the postcapitalistic construct of "all mankind" as the focus of right and history.

It is true that Smith taught the natural sociality of man and the natural basis of the moral law, but this modification of the modern natural law doctrine did not mean a return to antiquity. It must be repeated that natural right for Smith rests upon the primacy of the subrational part of the soul, and that natural sociality as he understood it is not an irreducible principle of man but the product of a mechanism at work. Later on, Kant was to speak of the same phenomenon as man's asocial sociality. Natural sociality in this sense does not, as it did for Aristotle, point toward political society. It rather resembles gregariousness. It is a compassion with one's fellow species-members that has everything in common with the alleged unwillingness of horses to tread upon a living body (of any species) and the distress of all animals in passing by the cadavers of their like. [7] To claim on the basis of it that man is by nature a social animal is by no means to claim equally that he is a political animal. Man is tied to humanity by the bonds of immediate sense and feeling, but he is tied to his fellow citizens as such by the weaker, superinduced, bonds of calculation or reason, derivative from considerations of utility. As we have seen, the viewpoint of moral judgment for Smith is that of "man" or universal mankind, the homogeneous class of species-fellows. The moral law is natural in such a sense as to overleap the intermediate, artificial frontiers of political society and regard primarily the natural individual and the natural species. Under that law, the perfection of human nature is "to feel much for others and little for ourselves, . . . to restrain our selfish, and to indulge our benevolent affections. . . ." [8]

Political society, however, is not directed toward this humane perfection of human nature but toward the safeguard of justice very narrowly conceived. "Mere justice is, upon most occasions, but a negative virtue, and only hinders us from hurting our neighbour. The man who barely abstains from violating either the person, or the estate, or the reputation of his neighbours, has surely very little positive merit." Justice means to do "every thing which [one's] equals can with propriety force him to do, or which they can punish him for not doing." [9] Justice, in brief, closely resembles compliance with the law of nature as seen by Hobbes and Locke. Smith understood it so himself. He concluded the *Theory of Moral Sentiments* with a passage on natural jurisprudence, justice, and the rules of natural equity, meaning by all of them "a system of those principles which ought to run through, and be the foundation of the laws of all nations." (He closes by promising to take up this theme in a later work. His only other book is the *Wealth of Nations*.)

We shall not sufficiently understand Smith's version of man's natural sociality if we do not grasp thoroughly the difference between man conceived as a social animal and as a political animal. [10] It is helpful for this purpose to consider further the problem of justice, the singularly political virtue which might even be synonymous with obeying the positive law. Justice, in the context of Smith's moral theory, is a defective virtue. He prepares for the exceptional treatment of justice by dividing moral philosophy into two parts, ethics and jurisprudence, the subject of the latter being justice. The defense of justice means the punishment of injustice; and the punishment of injustice is based upon the unsocial passion of resentment, the desire to return evil for evil, the command of "the sacred and necessary law of retaliation" which "seems to be the great law which is dictated to us by Nature." [11] Political society is based upon a moralistic paradox, one of many we will encounter: sociality rests upon latent animosity, without which the state could not exist.

In the second place, justice, equal to rendering another no less (or more) than what is his due, does not command gratitude and therefore in Smith's system is not attended with merit—or with "very little." Considering both the nature of justice and the safeguard of it, it is a defective virtue in that it cannot, or almost cannot, deserve fullest approbation, on the grounds of merit as well as propriety.

In the third place, although there is a sense in which political society is natural, it is a weak sense. The national society is indeed the protector and the matrix of ourselves, our homes, our kin, our friends, and Smith does not for an instant dream of the withering away of the state. "It is by nature endeared to us." But "the love of our own nation often disposes us to view, with the most malignant jealousy and envy, the prosperity and aggrandisement of any other neighbouring nation."

The love of our own country seems not to be derived from the love of mankind. The former sentiment is altogether independent of the latter, and seems sometimes even to dispose us to act inconsistently with it. France may contain, perhaps, near three times the number of inhabitants which Great Britain contains. In the great society of mankind, therefore, the prosperity of France should appear to be an object of much greater importance than that of Great Britain. The British subject, however, who, upon that account, should prefer upon all occasions the prosperity of the former to that of the latter country, would not be thought a good citizen of Great Britain. We do not love our country merely as a part of the great society of mankind: we love it for its own sake, and independently of any such consideration.[12]

These reservations and qualifications upon political sociality deserve notice. They will appear in a swollen incarnation conjured by Marx a century later, when the replacement of political man by the species-animal reaches a climax.

It would be misleading to suggest that Smith's doctrine of man's sociality was a relapse into the Middle Ages or into antiquity. It would be more misleading to suggest that, in Smith's view, human nature is simply dominated by a natural sociality of any description. We have given attention to the mechanical or psychological bond of sympathy, at the basis of Smith's moral theory, in order to show the change in emphasis between the preparation of capitalism in Locke's doctrine and the elaboration of it in Smith's. But the theme of man's natural directedness toward preservation is not by any means made to languish by Smith. On the contrary: "self-preservation, and the propagation of the species, are the great ends which Nature seems to have proposed in the formation of all animals."[13] There is no reason to doubt that Smith meant this in all its force. We are able to gather, therefore, that if we use "altruism" and "egoism" in their literal sense, man can be described, according to Smith, as being by nature altruistic and egoistic—a species-member moved by love of self and fellow feeling with others.

It is one of the outstanding characteristics of Smith's system that sociality, withal of a certain description, and self-centered concentration upon preservation are shown as profoundly combined in a natural articulation of great strength; and this is achieved simultaneously with a rehabilitation of morality upon natural grounds: "Nature, indeed, seems to have so happily adjusted our sentiments of approbation and disapprobation, to the conveniency both of the individual and of the society, that after the strictest examination it will be found, I believe, that this is universally the case." [14] When it is borne in mind that Smith's teaching aims at the articulation of morality and preservation, and that the practical fruits of his doctrine are intended to be gathered by emancipating men, under mild government, to seek their happiness freely according to their individual desires, the accomplishment as a whole commands great respect. The reconciliation of the private good and the common good by the medium not of coercion but of freedom, on a basis of moral duty, had perhaps never been seen before.

In this wide and symmetrical edifice Smith perceived what appeared to him to be an irregularity or a class of irregularities. He observed that at certain points a disjunction develops between what man would by nature be led to approve as virtuous and what he is led by nature to approve as conducive to the preservation of society and the human species; and this notwithstanding the over-all truth of the passage quoted immediately above. It will be recalled that the elements of a virtuous act are propriety and merit, and that both rest upon a ground of sympathy. If men did not desire the sympathy of others, as well as respond to the impulse to sympathize with them, there would be no morality and no society. But the natural tendency of men is to sympathize especially with joy and good fortune; and it goes without saying that men not only desire to be sympathized with but to be sympathized with by reason of their prosperity, not their adversity. But the wish to be sympathized with on the grandest scale becomes, as a consequence, the foundation of ambition, which is the aspiration to be conspicuous, grand, and admired. To this aspiration the multitude of mankind lends itself, for it naturally sympathizes with eminence, that is, wealth and rank. But wealth and rank are not, as Smith occasionally said, necessarily conjoined with wisdom and virtue. He remarks, "This disposition to admire, and almost to worship, the rich and the powerful, and to despise or, at least, to neglect persons of poor and mean condition, though necessary both to establish and to maintain the distinction of ranks and the order of society, is, at the same time, the great and most universal cause of the corruption of our moral sentiments." [15]

Merit, we remember, is the quality of an act that the impartial spectator would pronounce worthy of gratitude. The decisive quality of such an act is the propriety of the agent's passion in committing it, his benevolent intent toward the patient, and the patient's pleasure in the benefit conferred, in consequence of which he desires to reciprocate a benefit to the agent. The conjunction is perhaps complicated, but through it all one condition stands out clearly: benefit must be conferred on the patient. Now Smith observes that there is a gap of sorts between the intention and the consummation. That gap is Chance. Because of mere chance good will miscarries, and the benevolent agent produces nothing or worse than nothing for his intended beneficiary. On other occasions the agent, intending nothing or possibly worse than nothing, happens to be the source of a benefit to the patient. Contrary to sound morality, the first agent's act goes without the approval of sympathy and the stamp of virtue while the second agent's act wins applause and gratitude. The universal tendency of men to regard the issue rather than the intention is said by Smith to be a "salutary and useful irregularity in human sentiments," for two reasons. In the first place, "to punish . . . for the affections of the heart only, where no crime has been committed, is the most insolent and barbarous tyranny." To try to live a common life while holding men culpable or laudable for their secret intentions would mean that "every court of judicature would become a real inquisition." In the second place, "Man was made for action, and to promote by the exertion of his faculties such changes in the external circumstances both of himself and others, as may seem most favorable to the happiness of all. He must not be satisfied with indolent benevolence, nor fancy himself the friend of mankind, because in his heart he wishes well to the prosperity of the world." [16] Smith goes on to speak of the utility to the world of the cognate inclination men have, to be troubled in spirit even when the ill they have wrought is wholly unintended, a subject that he illuminates with some healthy remarks upon the fallacious sense of guilt, illustrated by the "distress" of Oedipus. In sum, nature has wisely provided that our sentiments direct us toward the preservation of our kind where a conflict between preservation and either moral virtue or sound reason is brought on by the divergence of intent and issue.

Further in the same vein, Smith notes that when a man conquers fear and pain by the noble exertion of self-command, he is entitled to be compensated with a sense of his own virtue, in exchange for the relief and safety he might have had by giving way to his passions. But it is the wise provision of nature that he be only imperfectly compensated, lest he have no reason to listen to the call of fear and pain and to respond to their promptings. Fear and pain are instruments of preservation; a man or a species indifferent to them would die. The self-command that dominates them does not, as it ought not, bring with it a sense of self-esteem sufficient to outweigh the anguish of suppressing those violent passions.[17] Evidently moral virtue neither is nor ought to be simply its own reward; nor therefore can it be unqualifiedly eligible or eligible for its own sake. It must yield, according to the dictate of nature, a certain precedency to preservation.

In an important passage,[18] Smith unfolds further the paradoxy of natural morality as he conceives it. He is led to contrast "the natural course of things" with "the natural sentiments of mankind." It is in the natural course of things that industrious knaves should prosper while indolent men of honor starve, that great combinations of men should overweigh small ones, and finally that "violence and artifice prevail over sincerity and justice." The natural sentiments of man, however, are in rebellion against the natural course of things: sorrow, grief, rage, compassion for the oppressed, and at last despair of seeing the condign retribution of vice and injustice in this world—these are man's natural sentiments. The natural course of events, though, for all its offensiveness, has something weighty to recommend it. In allotting to each virtue, without favor or accommodation, the reward proper to it, nature has adopted the rule "useful and proper for rousing the industry and attention of mankind." Toil and moil happen to be indispensable to human survival, and the only way to draw them forth is by appropriate reward and punishment. The natural course of events supports the preservation of the race at the expense of precise morality; the natural sentiments of mankind are stirred by "the love of virtue, and by the abhorrence of vice and injustice." Nature is divided, but not equally divided against itself. The cause of unmitigated virtue can be heard only upon a change of venue to a jurisdiction in a world beyond nature.

Smith pursues his theme of the price in goodness and reason that must be paid to get the world's fundamental business done. He takes up the question, of much importance to his doctrine, whether the utility of actions is the basis of their being approved. If the answer were a simple affirmative, then it would follow that the principle of virtue (approbation) is rational: the calculation of usefulness. But we know that in his view the principle of virtue and approbation is not reason but sentiment and feeling, via sympathy. Yet it is evident that mankind exhibits a steady tendency toward those measures of labor and government which are the supports for the preservation of the race. Smith explains this by recurring to a delusion imposed upon men by nature, a delusion that does the work of reason better than reason could have done it. When we look upon the power or wealth in a man's possession, our minds are led in imagination to conceive the fitness of those objects to perform their respective functions. At the same time we sympathize with the imagined satisfaction of the possessors of those prizes. It is only a step from that to desiring ourselves to be happy in greatness, and thence to putting forth the immense exertions that eventuate in wealth and government. Upon consideration, it appears that we are led to pursue prosperity and power by a psychological motive, and thus to generate wealth and order among men as by-products of subjective "drives," as we would say. Moreover, and conjunctively, we act under the influence of the appetite for the means to gratification, not even for the gratification itself, when we seek after wealth and power. Both are desirable for the happiness they supposedly give their possessors. In fact, happiness is not at all or very little promoted by the possession of power and riches, those "enormous and operose machines contrived to produce a few trifling conveniencies to the body, consisting of springs the most nice and delicate, which must be kept in order with the most anxious attention, and which in spite of all our care are ready every moment to burst into pieces, and to crush in their ruins their unfortunate possessor." [19]

Smith's reason for depreciating distinction of wealth and place is of interest: "In what constitutes the real happiness of human life, [the poor and obscure] are in no respect inferior to those who would seem so much above them. In ease of the body and peace of the mind, all the different ranks of life are nearly upon a level, and the beggar, who suns himself by the side of the highway, possesses that security which kings are fighting for." [20] It is in this context that Smith announces, in the *Theory of Moral Sentiments,* the notion and the expression of the "invisible hand," very famous from its elaboration through the central argument of the *Wealth of Nations.* The passage deserves extensive quotation:

And it is well that nature imposes upon us in this manner. It is this deception which rouses and keeps in continual motion the industry of mankind. It is this which first prompted them to cultivate the ground, to build houses, to found cities and commonwealths, and to invent and improve all the sciences and arts, which ennoble and embellish human life; which have entirely changed the whole face of the globe, have turned the rude forests of nature into agreeable and fertile plains, and made the trackless and barren ocean a new fund of subsistence, and the great high road of communication to the different nations of the earth. The earth by these labours of mankind has been obliged to redouble her natural fertility, and to maintain a greater multitude of inhabitants. It is to no purpose, that the proud and unfeeling landlord views his extensive fields, and without a thought for the wants of his brethren, in imagination consumes himself the whole harvest that grows upon them. The homely and vulgar proverb, that the eye is larger than the belly, was never more fully verified than with regard to him. The capacity of his

stomach bears no proportion to the immensity of his desires, and will receive
no more than that of the meanest peasant. The rest he is obliged to distribute
among those, who prepare, in the nicest manner, that little which he himself
makes use of, among those who fit up the palace in which this little is to be
consumed, among those who provide and keep in order all the different
baubles and trinkets which are employed in the œconomy of greatness; all of
whom thus derive from his luxury and caprice, that share of the necessaries
of life, which they would in vain have expected from his humanity or his
justice. The produce of the soil maintains at all times nearly that number of
inhabitants which it is capable of maintaining. The rich only select from the
heap what is most precious and agreeable. They consume little more than the
poor, and in spite of their natural selfishness and rapacity, though they mean
only their own conveniency, though the sole end which they propose from
the labours of all the thousands whom they employ, be the gratification of
their own vain and insatiable desires, they divide with the poor the produce
of all their improvements. They are led by an invisible hand to make nearly
the same distribution of the necessaries of life which would have been made,
had the earth been divided into equal portions among all its inhabitants, and
thus without intending it, without knowing it, advance the interest of society,
and afford means to the multiplication of the species.[21]

Beyond this there is no advantage in multiplying the evidence of
Smith's belief that the dominant end of nature with respect to man,
namely, the prosperity of the species as a whole, is achieved by mitiga-
tions of morality and reason. Since this is a point which postcapitalistic
thought was to take up polemically and against which it was to bring
its ultimate, most ambitious dialectic, it deserves to be examined with
some attention.

That nature's end for man is advanced by the guidance of his sentiments rather than his reason follows from the premise that the passions
are more governing than the mind, and every animal persistently desires its own uninterrupted being. A man's nature is more immediately
reflected in what he feels than what he thinks; moreover, the difference
between the two is not the profound one anciently conceived but is
rather such as can be composed by their being both subsumed under
"perceptions." Smith does not employ the language of "impressions and
ideas" used by Hume in the enterprise by which the operation of the
mind was given a unified appearance as the distinctions among sensation, emotion, and reason were blurred. If Smith had done so, he would
more explicitly have concurred in Hume's definition of the self as "that
succession of related ideas and impressions, of which we have an intimate memory" and of "ideas [as] the faint images of [impressions] in
thinking and reason." [22] The reduction of the self, the ego or the real
man, to his actuality or to the traces of what he has actually perceived

rather than to his soul and its powers or "faculties" is part of the doctrine that rejected innate ideas and therewith all but the nominal essences. This doctrine, with its echoes of Hobbes and Locke, is interlaced with the view that the lines of force along which nature produces and communicates its motions penetrate him and govern him more through his passions than through his reason.[23]

In any event, Smith's formulation is that nature did not leave it to man's feeble reason to discover that and how he ought to preserve himself, but gave him sharp appetites for the means to his survival as well as for survival itself, thus insuring him in his preservation. But it is this same primacy of sentiment over reason, or at least the equal subsumption of them both under something like perception, that is the basis for the concessions which must be made against morality on behalf of preservation.

It will be recalled that Smith's moral doctrine begins with approbation: the virtuous is so because it is in fact or in principle approved by the sentiment of mankind. We now understand that a difficulty exists because nature teaches man to approve both what conduces to morality and what conduces to preservation. The instruction of nature is occasionally equivocal. Evidently the attempt to derive the Ought from the Is is vexed by the fact that, although what is virtuous is actually approved, it does not follow either that everything which is approved is virtuous or that everything which is virtuous is approved. It is from this circumstance that the "irregularities" or concessions previously mentioned have their origin. What, then, is to be gained by the psychological or "behavioral" derivation of a natural morality? It is that by this method, moral virtue may be deduced from the character of "man as man," *i.e.,* in abstraction from his character as a political being and attentive only to his character as a "natural" one. Smith's moral philosophy aims at comprehending the basis of virtue as that basis may be said to exist in a fully actual state at every moment in "the bulk of mankind" [24] as such. That is to say, Smith's starting point is the natural equality of men in the sense elaborated by Hobbes. The contrast with classical antiquity throws light on the modern position. The famous scheme of Plato's *Republic* makes a high principle of the division of labor or distribution of functions in the political society because virtue in one social class could not well be measured by the same rule against which it must be measured in another class. Aristotle's *Politics* distinguishes the virtue of slaves, freemen, and men of excellence; the *Nicomachean Ethics* cannot be regarded as a manual of the excellence of the bulk of mankind. The ancient moralists coldly concentrated upon the distinction between the politically weighty people and the entire populace that dwelt within the frontiers. Only democracy has the merit of making possible the effacement of that distinction, and we are entitled to deem the "humanization" of moral virtue—its universalization or reference to what is actually present in "all men as men"—as the democratization of morality.

Democracy is the regime that minimizes the distinction between rulers and ruled, the fundamental political phenomenon; and in that sense it can be said that democracy or liberal democracy tends to replace political life by sociality (private lives lived in contiguity) at the same time that it diffuses political authority most widely. The abstraction of morality from the demands of political life proper is in a way impossible: political life has to be lived, and support for it must be provided in the form of economic organization, the use of force for suppressing crime and rebellion, the legitimation of conventional inequalities in the interest of order, and so on. Where morality is radically "human" or "natural" in the sense of those words that is opposed to political, the indispensable provision for political life will have the character of an inroad on morality, or an irregularity. It is not our contention that the moral basis of Smith's social doctrine is contrived to produce an abstraction from the conditions of political existence. It is rather, on the contrary, that in order to mitigate or forestall that abstraction, which his premises threaten to enforce, he must have recourse to "irregularities" of nature or exceptions to his premises.

There is hardly a better way of illustrating the elusive relation between rectitude and politics than by the following passage from Churchill's *Marlborough*:

The second debate in the Lords . . . drew from Marlborough his most memorable Parliamentary performance. It is the more remarkable because, although he had made up his mind what ought to be done and what he meant to do, his handling of the debate was at once spontaneous, dissimulating, and entirely successful. As on the battlefield, he changed his course very quickly indeed and spread a web of manœuvre before his opponents. He made candour serve the purpose of falsehood, and in the guise of reluctantly blurting out the whole truth threw his assailants into complete and baffling error. Under the impulse of an emotion which could not have been wholly assumed, he made a revelation of war policy which effectively misled not only the Opposition but the whole House, and which also played its part in misleading the foreign enemy, who were of course soon apprised of the public debate. He acted thus in the interests of right strategy and of the common cause as he conceived them. He was accustomed by the conditions under which he fought to be continually deceiving friends for their good and foes for their bane; but the speed and ease with which this particular manœuvre was conceived and accomplished in the unfamiliar atmosphere of Parliamentary debate opens to us some of the secret depths of his artful yet benevolent mind.[25]

It is apparent that dissimulation cannot be made the principle of morals; it is also apparent that morality which makes no serviceable distinction between dissimulation in a noble cause and common mendacity will end either in the precisianism that condemns it all as vice or in the latitudinarianism that peers unsuccessfully for the line between vice and virtue. Ancient moral philosophy could in this respect be described as very politic. It recognized in prudence a subtle virtue that animated the others from its seat in the mind. In palliation of the Odysseanism of the ancients' moralizing, it should be said that departure from the straitest morality was countenanced by them in the ultimate interest of something higher, for they did not conceive moral excellence to be the greatest of all excellences. The Smithian subtractions from morality cannot be in the interest of anything higher, for there is nothing higher: "The most sublime speculation of the contemplative philosopher can scarce compensate the neglect of the smallest active duty." "The man who acts solely from a regard to what is right and fit to be done, from a regard to what is the proper object of esteem and approbation, though these sentiments should never be bestowed upon him, acts from the most sublime and godlike motive which human nature is even capable of conceiving." [26] To state the case somewhat simplistically, the ancients and the moderns alike conceded something in mitigation of strict moral virtue, the ancients without repining because they had in view a higher excellence, Smith with mixed feelings because his aim could not exceed moral virtue in worth.

Smith's aim, a free, reasonable, comfortable, and tolerant life for the whole species, found its hope, its basis, and its expression in the science of economics as he to a considerable extent launched it. Anything like a detailed account of Smith's economics would be far out of place here, and we shall confine ourselves to selected themes. His teaching in the *Wealth of Nations* is above all famous for its defense of free enterprise on a broad and simple line: The welfare of the nation cannot be separated from its wealth, which he conceives in the modern mode as the annual national product. But the annual product of the nation is the sum of the annual products of the individual inhabitants. Each inhabitant has an undying interest in maximizing his own product and will do everything possible to accomplish this if left in freedom. Thus all should be accorded this freedom, and they will simultaneously maximize the aggregate product and keep each other in check by the power of competition. His renowned attack on mercantilistic capitalism—the system of invidious preference for the merchant interest—is part of his argument that the common interest is served not by differential legislative stimulation of enterprises but by allowing nature automatically to convert the individual self-interest into the good of all:

As every individual, therefore, endeavours as much as he can both to employ his capital in the support of domestic industry, and so to direct that industry that its produce may be of the greatest value; every individual necessarily labours to render the annual revenue of the society as great as he can. He generally, indeed, neither intends to promote the public interest, nor knows how much he is promoting it. By preferring the support of domestic to that of foreign industry, he intends only his own security; and by directing that industry in such a manner as its produce may be of the greatest value, he intends only his own gain, and he is in this, as in many other cases, led by an invisible hand to promote an end which was no part of his intention. Nor is it always the worse for the society that it was no part of it. By pursuing his own interest he frequently promotes that of the society more effectually than when he really intends to promote it. I have never known much good done by those who affected to trade for the public good. It is an affectation, indeed, not very common among merchants, and very few words need be employed in dissuading them from it.[27]

We have no difficulty recognizing the natural reconciliation of the individual and common interest for which the *Theory of Moral Sentiments* has prepared us. Nor are we unprepared for the moral "irregularities" that Smith conceived to be incidental to that reconciliation. They fall under two or three main heads in the argument of the *Wealth of Nations*. In the first place, the prosperity of each and all cannot be disconnected from their productivity, and their productivity rests upon the division of labor. But the division of labor inevitably stultifies the working classes, much if not the bulk of mankind. The laborer's "dexterity at his own particular trade seems . . . to be acquired at the expense of his intellectual, social, and martial virtues. But in every improved and civilized society this is the state into which the labouring poor, that is, the great body of the people, must necessarily fall, unless government takes some pains to prevent it."[28] In his discussions he tries not to exaggerate the likelihood that the government will succeed.

In the second place, a large part if not the preponderant part of the economic life of the nation must come under the regulation of the class of merchants and manufacturers. His animadversions upon them as a body of men are sometimes shockingly severe. The burden of his objection against them is that their preoccupation with gain puts them in illiberal conflict with the other orders of society and with the nation as a whole—except by inadvertence.[29] The wisdom of government is necessary to prevent their mischief, *i.e.,* their interested interference, and to give free rein only to their useful activities, *i.e.,* their productiveness. Smith was not the dogmatist that some advocates of *laissez faire* were later to become.

In the third place, the annual addition to product is believed by Smith to be generated by labor. The "exchangeable value" or price of each commodity, once land has been made private property and capital has been accumulated, "resolves itself" into wages, rent, and profit. In this way, landowners and the employers of labor "share" in the produce of labor. Smith is at pains to argue that the profits of capital are not a wage for the "supposed labour of inspection and direction," which he said is often "committed to some principal clerk." [30] He was far from attempting to conceal the contribution to output that results from the accumulation of capital. On the contrary, he dwelt upon it; but he described it as taking effect by an "improvement in the productive powers of labour." [31] In the course of his investigations into what we now call national income accounting, he certainly gave later generations some reason to regard him as holding a labor theory of value, with concomitant beliefs about distribution. As for rent, that is "a monopoly price" [32] for the use of land, by the exaction of which the owner is enabled to share in the annual product of labor. We cannot fail to notice how little trouble Smith gave himself to justify this "sharing" and this "resolving." On the contrary, by a certain invidiousness of expression ("As soon as the land of any country has all become private property, the landlords, like all other men, love to reap where they never sowed, and demand a rent even for its natural produce." [33]) he indicates a reserve as to its perfect propriety. He seems to think, it is true, that when the facts of distribution are recited, the intimation of possible inequities may be fully balanced by a statement of the broad, compensatory benefits: he speculates whether it might not be true "that the accommodation of an European prince does not always so much exceed that of an industrious and frugal peasant, as the accommodation of the latter exceeds that of many an African king, the absolute master of the lives and liberties of ten thousand naked savages." [34] But Smith manifestly did not imagine himself to be addressing the multitude of laboring poor in detailed defense of capitalism, as Marx was to address them in detailed denunciation. Smith freely hinted at his notion that something like one of his moral "irregularities" lay around the root of the distributive order, but it was much outweighed by the correlative advantages for all—and he loathed the men of "system" who would be incapable of grasping such a simple computation.

Smith did not refer to the complex of free enterprise as "capitalism" but as "the system of natural liberty," or the condition in which "things were left to follow their natural course, where there was perfect liberty." [35] Nature meant for Smith the humanly unhindered or unobstructed, and this more amply means what is not confounded by the misplaced interventions of human reason: letting nature take its course, letting men do as they are instinctively prompted to do, as far as that is compatible with "the security of the whole society." [36] It is easy to conceive and to grant that natural is in distinction to artificial, human, or constrained to obey a forecontrived design. Thus freedom is all on the side of nature, as opposed to constraint on the side of human reason. At the same time, however, nothing in the world is so unyielding and hence constraining as the necessary dictate of deaf and dumb nature, while the source of man's freedom resides in his power of reason, the origin of his various contrivances.[37] Smith's manner of confronting this difficulty is in effect to declare for the freedom of reason harnessed in the service of the more binding freedom of nature: calculation at the command of passion. Smith's doctrine is pervaded by the consequences of the fact that the superordinate element, nature conceived as the free motive of passion, is the symbol of man's unfreedom, as Kant was to emphasize so elaborately.

It is a distinguishing characteristic of Smith's doctrine and of liberal capitalism at large that they do not conceive freedom to be important primarily because it is the condition for every man's existence as an individual moral being, the ground of his self-legislating will in action or of his humanity. Liberty continued to mean for Smith what it had meant to Locke, to Aristotle, and to the long tradition of political philosophy: the condition of men under lawful governors who respect the persons and property of the governed, the latter having to consent to the arrangement in one way or another. This view of liberty is primarily political and belongs to the libertarianism of Locke, not of Rousseau. The capitalistic project is not animated by a search for methods of institutionally liberating the inner drives of every man in the interest of the moral will. It is animated by a search for methods of institutionally liberating every man's natural instinct of self-preservation in the interest of external, politically intelligible freedom and peaceful prosperous life for mankind as a whole. Therefore Smith had no difficulty in conceiving man as free while both in thrall to nature and subject to forms of law which guarantee his external freedom but can scarcely aim to be the basis of his internal emancipation from that same nature.

Smith is thus at liberty to repose his trust in a wisdom of nature that shows itself even or especially in the folly and injustice of man: the moral hygiene that produces a multitude, in fact a race of self-legislators was not indispensable to his plan, nor was political life a species of psychotherapy for bringing on man's subpolitical emancipation. Smith was thus resigned to receive the benefits of civil society even if they must be mediated by certain undoubted ills, and he was prepared to do so indefinitely if the benefits are vast and the ills unavoidable. In this respect he anticipated the mechanisms of philosophy of history as it would emerge, but not its ends: good through ill and reason through folly, but no Elysium at a rainbow's end.

It is important for us to see more exactly what Smith's doctrine has in common with philosophy of history as that was later to develop. There is, to begin with, his belief in a "natural progress of things toward improvement"—animated by "the uniform, constant and uninterrupted effort of every man to better his condition," bettering his condition being understood in "the most vulgar" sense.[38] Smith illustrates this in an account of the progress of Europe from medieval disorder to the comparative regularity of modern times. The anarchy of old persisted because the great landed proprietors had troops of retainers who comprised, in fact, private armies. Nothing could produce order which did not dissolve those armies. The basis for their existence was the fact that the grandees had abundant income in kind which, under the primitive conditions of commerce then prevailing, they could not dispose of by exchange or sale. They accordingly were compelled to feed it to crowds of men who became their dependents and inevitably their soldiers. What brought down the entire system was the enlargement of trade, which enabled the magnates to convert their produce into money and thence into luxuries for their personal delectation instead of into the military basis of their political power.

A revolution of the greatest importance to the public happiness, was in this manner brought about by two different orders of people, who had not the least intention to serve the public. To gratify the most childish vanity was the sole motive of the great proprietors. The merchants and artificers, much less ridiculous, acted merely from a view to their own interest, and in pursuit of their own pedlar principle of turning a penny wherever a penny was to be got. Neither of them had either knowledge or foresight of that great revolution which the folly of the one, and the industry of the other, was gradually bringing about.[39]

Smith speaks of the ascendancy of the Roman Church from the tenth through the thirteenth century. He regards it as signalized by the temporal power of the clergy, and that in turn as resting upon the influence of the clergy with the multitudes of men. The inferior ranks of people were bound to the clergy by ties of interest, the multitudes depending upon a charity which was bestowed freely because, once again, the clergy had no other means of disposing of an enormous produce from their lands. When such means presented themselves, the constitution of the Catholic Church underwent a profound alteration:

Had this constitution been attacked by no other enemies but the feeble efforts of human reason, it must have endured for ever. But that immense and well-built fabric, which all the wisdom and virtue of man could never have shaken, much less overturned, was by the natural course of things, first weakened, and afterwards in part destroyed. . . .

The gradual improvements of arts, manufactures, and commerce, the same causes which destroyed the power of the great barons, destroyed in the same manner, through the greater part of Europe, the whole temporal power of the clergy.[40]

By these same instrumentalities, the species of mankind at large is drawn together, probably upward as well as onward. Smith regards the geographical discoveries as of unparalleled significance for the species: "The discovery of America, and that of a passage to the East Indies by the Cape of Good Hope, are the two greatest and most important events recorded in the history of mankind." The communication and commerce of the species as a whole was thereby in principle achieved for the first time in the memory of man, and with that epochal event came the supreme occasion for enabling all mankind reciprocally "to relieve one another's wants, to increase one another's enjoyments, and to encourage one another's industry."[41]

Smith believed that, to a large extent, nature speaks to history in the language of economics, and that the broad course of history so instructed is probably toward an easier, more cultivated, more rational and secure life for the generality of mankind. At the same time, he imagined that the advance of civilization was synchronous with the generation of a tremendous industrial mob, deprived of nearly every admirable human quality. Civilization is not an unqualified good, or more accurately, it comes at a price. This famous theme, of which Rousseau was the virtuoso, was developed by Smith with concern but without agitation. He proposed to palliate the ill with a wide system of almost gratis elementary schooling for the masses and with the encouragement of an unheard-of number of religious sects (as many as three thousand), each necessarily to be so small that every member of it would be conspicuous to the surveillance of his fellow communicants. All would maintain a vigil upon each other's morals that, far from being in any danger of flagging through lack of interest, would itself require to be moderated by febrifuges: courses of education in science and philosophy and artistic spectacles such as theater.[42] Smith repeatedly recommends the intellectual and moral state of much of industrial mankind to the most serious attention of government, not only out of philanthropy but for obvious reasons of state.

Our thesis, with a summary of which we shall now conclude, has been this: Within a short time of the completion of Locke's work, intelligent men began to reflect on and to draw out what would today be called the "moral implications" of his doctrine.[43] How far he had mitigated Hobbes's teaching of the natural ferocity of man and thereby turned political philosophy in the direction of economics has been shown above in the chapter on Locke. But the chief teaching of the modern school of natural law was not thereby impaired: nature continued univocally to mean preservation, with the supporting rights to whatever pertains thereto. Now this came to be regarded as insufficient, and the reduction of man to his affections was thought to imply that man is affected not only toward himself but toward his species. Perhaps Locke was not given enough credit for the important mitigation mentioned above, which is in this direction, but in any event the theme was made emphatic by Smith (at about the time of Rousseau's *Second Discourse*). The reduction of human life to its emotional foundations was enlarged to become the ground of duties as well as rights. It cannot be denied that those duties were consciously made to revolve about the preservation of the species; but it cannot either be denied that duties are different from rights, and the two require somehow to be reconciled with one another. In the course of reconciling the duties of moral virtue with the rights of nature, which is to say preservation, Smith had recourse to the tension between nature and the moral order derived from it, leaving the reconciliation inevitably imperfect. From this germ grew the teaching as to the moral imperfection of the natural or best order of society—the free, prosperous, and tolerant civil society. In its self-understanding, capitalism thus anticipated the chief postcapitalistic criticism of capitalism: civil society is a defective solution of the human problem.

Our second point, inseparable from the first, is that the self-understanding of capitalism also anticipated an astonishing proportion of what was to be proposed by the nineteenth century as the alternative to capitalism. We have tried to show how the direction of capitalism was toward the construction of a universal mankind, both as the ground of duty (the universal spectator) and as the ultimate beneficiary of economic progress—thus as the ultimate society. The engine of that progress was the ignoble desires and strivings of man, channeled through the economic institutions of production and distribution that opened up to him from time to time. An expectation of good through evil, reason through unreason, progress, a belief in the tendency of the interest of mankind to supersede that of particular political society, in the preponderance of economic influence on human affairs, in the primacy of labor in the process of production, in the preoccupation of civil society with the defense of property, this and more which Marxism would trumpet was present to the doctrines of capitalism in one measure and form or another, as it has been our purpose to show. A strange light is cast on Marx's theory that capitalism contains the seed of its own negation. It might perhaps be said that according to its own self-understanding, the ground of capitalism coincides to a remarkable degree with the seed bed of its own negation; but the seed itself is an alien thing, namely, philosophy of history, something that was generated not by the working of any economic institutions but by an act of human speculation.

Perhaps Smith is to be blamed for not having extracted a metaphysic from that "wisdom of nature" which he believed to guide the human process and to which he so often recurs, a metaphysic that would historicize the consummation of the whole human career. Perhaps he ought to have perceived the potency in such a metaphor as the "wisdom" of nature and gone on to postulate still higher wisdoms by which the laws of nature itself might be brought under orders. He never reached that point, however, for he did not question the belief that there is an unchanging horizon within which all change takes place, that horizon or framework being Nature.

Philosophy of history will be a subject of later chapters. For the present we may observe that when Rousseau's teaching of the malleability of human nature received its due cultivation and enlargement, it proved to be the little leaven that leavened the whole lump. The paradoxes and irregularities that liberal capitalism was willing to abide because of their origin in man's nature could not be tolerated by the nineteenth century since it no longer saw a need to tolerate them. The nature that gives rise to inconveniences must away, and itself submit to be superseded by the law of the change of nature, namely, History. It is this fissure, narrow but bottomless, that divides capitalism from communism.

## NOTES

1. *Theory of Moral Sentiments,* in *The Essays of Adam Smith* (London: Alexander Murray, 1869), part VII. sec. II. chap. iii *ad fin.,* p. 271. Comparison of such a representative passage from Hume as part V of *An*

*Enquiry Concerning the Principles of Morals* with, for example, part I of *Theory of Moral Sentiments* will suggest the broad agreement between the two doctrines.

2. *Theory of Moral Sentiments,* I. I. iii. p. 18.

3. "The chief part of human happiness arises from the consciousness of being beloved." *Ibid.,* I. II. v. p. 40.

4. For example, *ibid.,* III. II. p. 105. Cf. above, pp. 356–59, concerning Hobbes's denial of the natural sociality of man.

5. *Theory of Moral Sentiments,* V. II. p. 177.

6. *Ibid.,* I. I. v. p. 24.

7. From Rousseau, *Discourse on the Origin of Inequality,* First Part. Readers of Rousseau's two *Discourses* will be struck by the similiarity of themes and views between them and the *Theory of Moral Sentiments.* The division of human nature between self-love and compassion, and the qualified goodness of civil society are but instances.

8. *Theory of Moral Sentiments,* I. I. v. p. 24.

9. *Ibid.,* II. II. i. p. 75.

10. The reader is urged to refer to the treatment of this subject in the chapter on Aristotle.

11. *Theory of Moral Sentiments,* II. I. ii. p. 65; II. II. i. p. 75.

12. *Ibid.,* VI. II. ii. pp. 202, 203–4.

13. *Ibid.,* II. I. v. p. 71n.

14. *Ibid.,* IV. ii. p. 166.

15. *Ibid.,* I. III. iii. pp. 56–57.

16. *Ibid.,* II. III. iii. pp. 96–98.

17. *Ibid.,* III. iii. p. 129.

18. *Ibid.,* III. v. pp. 147–49.

19. *Ibid.,* IV. i. p. 161, and throughout the book.

20. *Ibid.,* p. 163.

21. *Ibid.,* pp. 162–63.

22. Hume, *A Treatise of Human Nature,* I. I. i and II. I. ii.

23. Hume's remark is characteristically uncompromising: "[the reason] can

never oppose passion in the direction of the will." *Ibid.,* II. III. Smith makes two remarks, in the form of allusions, which deny man's unique rationality: "mankind, as well as . . . all other rational creatures" (*Theory of Moral Sentiments,* III. v. p. 146) and "that great society of all sensible and intelligent beings" (*ibid.,* VI. II. iii. p. 209.)

24. *Theory of Moral Sentiments,* III. v. p. 142.

25. Winston S. Churchill, *Marlborough: His Life and Times* (4 vols in 2 bks; London: Harrap, 1947), vol. III. bk II. p. 303. Reproduced by permission of Charles Scribner's Sons and George Harrap & Co., Ltd.

26. *Theory of Moral Sentiments,* VI. II. iii. p. 210; VII. II. iv. p. 275.

27. *An Inquiry into the Nature and Causes of the Wealth of Nations* (New York: Modern Library, 1937), IV. II. p. 423.

28. *Ibid.,* V. I. iii. 2. p. 735.

29. *Ibid., e.g.,* I. conc. pp. 249–50; IV. III. ii. p. 460.

30. *Ibid.,* I. VI. pp. 48–49.

31. *Ibid.,* II. intro. p. 260. Also II. II. p. 271, etc.

32. *Ibid.,* I. XI. p. 145.

33. *Ibid.,* I. VI. p. 49.

34. *Ibid.,* I. I. p. 12. Also, Introduction and Plan of the Work, p. lviii.

35. *Ibid.,* IV. IX. p. 651; I. X. p. 99.

36. *Ibid.,* II. II. p. 308.

37. Smith commonly juxtaposes "naturally" and "necessarily," the latter often used apparently as an intensified form of the former. Cf., *e.g., ibid.,* pp. 8, 86, 357, 414, 421, 422, 591, 674, 723 and footnote, 754, 756.

38. *Ibid.,* II. III. pp. 326, 325.

39. *Ibid.,* III. IV. pp. 391–92.

40. *Ibid.,* V. I. iii. 3. p. 755.

41. *Ibid.,* III. VII. iii. p. 590; also IV. I. p. 416.

42. *Ibid.,* V. I. iii. 2. pp. 736–38; V. I. iii. 3. pp. 747–48.

43. The reader's attention should be

drawn to the work of Bernard Mandeville (*c.* 1670–1733) whose *The Fable
of the Bees* (1714) had the subtitle
"Private Vices, Public Benefits." Controversy raged around him, and Smith
added his rebuke by dealing with him
in a chapter "Of Licentious Systems"
(*Theory of Moral Sentiments,* VII. II.
iv), at the same time admitting that
Mandeville was not mistaken in all
respects.

## READINGS

A.   Smith, Adam. *An Inquiry into the Nature and Causes of the Wealth of
Nations.* Book I, chaps i–x; chap. xi, intro. and conc.; book V, chap. i.
B.   Smith, Adam. *An Inquiry into the Nature and Causes of the Wealth of
Nations.* Book III; book IV, chaps i, ii, vii.

*Note:* Although it would be desirable to draw the student's attention to passages
of the *Theory of Moral Sentiments,* "assignments" from that book would be
unrealistic because of its unavailability in print.

# THE FEDERALIST*

## 1787–1788

Immediately after the 1787 federal convention Alexander Hamilton turned to the difficult task of securing New York's ratification of the proposed Constitution. As part of his strategy, he planned a series of short essays to expound the virtues of the Constitution. Hamilton secured the collaboration of John Jay and, ironically only after several others declined his invitation, of James Madison as well. *The Federalist* was published serially in groups of two and four essays in the New York City press. The essays were intended to influence the election of delegates to the state ratifying convention and, since for this election universal manhood suffrage was adopted, the essays were therefore addressed "to the People of the State of New York." But *The Federalist* was further intended to instruct and inspirit favorable delegates and to persuade or mollify unfavorable delegates to the convention. To this end, even before completion of serial publication in the press, the essays were published as a book and circulated to leading supporters of the Constitution throughout the country. Thus *The Federalist* was at once addressed to the widest electorate but also to those able and educated men who actually would determine the fate of the Constitution. It seems clear that its authors also looked beyond the immediate struggle and wrote with a view to influencing later generations by making their work the authoritative commentary on the meaning of the Constitution. While *The Federalist* was the most immediate kind of political work, a piece of campaign propaganda, it spoke also to thoughtful men then and now, with a view to the permanence of its argument.

* Alexander Hamilton (1757[5?]–1804); James Madison (1751–1836); John Jay (1745–1829).

The reading of *The Federalist* is further complicated by the fact that it was written by two men (Jay's small contribution may be disregarded here) whose individual opinions and subsequent careers radically diverged.[1] This fact has encouraged many readers to see fundamental inconsistencies in the work where they do not exist, on the presumption that a work written jointly by Hamilton and Madison must contradict itself. Like the belief that *The Federalist* was merely a propaganda piece, the belief that it was the inconsistent work of incompatible authors has depreciated *The Federalist* as a theoretical writing. But *The Federalist* presents itself as the work of one Publius who claims to supply a consistent, comprehensive, and true account of the Constitution and of the regime it was calculated to engender. As will be seen, Publius makes good his claim.

Apart from the fact that Hamilton and Madison had motive and capacity to achieve a remarkably consistent Publius, *The Federalist* has a literary character which made it possible for them to agree quite easily on much of what had to be said. *The Federalist* deals largely with factual matters. Whatever their differences, Hamilton and Madison could agree as to what the convention had done and what kind of country would be the result. Similarly they could readily agree on how to make the Constitution seem most attractive or least noxious to those they were seeking to persuade. The Federalist was a commentary on and a plea for a constitution. Its authors were therefore not *primarily* obliged to deal with the most controversial subject, namely, the standard by which they themselves deemed the Constitution good. This is, of course, not to say that Publius stays only at the surface or says only what his readers want to hear. In fact, Hamilton and Madison go very far, as Publius, in suggesting the theoretical grounds upon which a wise acceptance of the Constitution should rest. That is what makes *The Federalist* an illuminating work. But the literary character of *The Federalist* did not oblige them to push so far in the discussion as to lay bare their ultimate differences. Unfortunately, what helps explain Publius' consistency explains also why *The Federalist* falls short of those great works in which theoretical matters are pressed to their proper, that is, farthest limits.

One last observation on Publius leads directly to the teaching of *The Federalist*. We know that Hamilton took his pseudonyms seriously; they were meant to convey the character of his argument.[2] Shortly before Publius appeared, a series of essays in support of the Constitution had been initiated under the pseudonym "Caesar." It has often been thought that Hamilton was also Caesar, but scholarship has now made this seem unlikely. In any event, Caesar's first two essays were very poorly received and the series was abandoned by its author. The choice of "Publius" is especially revealing when compared with the ill-fated Caesar essays, whether the latter were written by Hamilton or not. Publius, the educated reader knew, was the Publius Valerius Publicola described in Plutarch. Publius like Caesar was a "strong man," but between them there was one enormous difference: Caesar destroyed a republic, Publius saved one. Unlike Caesar, Publius makes his contribution to the republic in a way compatible with its continued existence. He brings to its salvation qualities it cannot itself supply, but leaves it essentially intact after his efforts. Whoever wrote them, the Caesar papers had to founder. The Constitution was in fact not Caesarist, and the public to be persuaded was then profoundly hostile to a Caesarist appeal. The character of Publius on the contrary was exactly appropriate to the situation and perfectly characterized the argument of *The Federalist*. Publius, with a capacity and knowledge that the people cannot themselves supply, brings to the people the constitution that will preserve, indeed will safely found the republic.

In the first essay Publius supplies the outline of the work.

[1] *The utility of the UNION to your political prosperity*—[2] *The insufficiency of the present Confederation to preserve that Union*—[3] *The necessity of a government at least equally energetic with the one proposed, to the attainment of this object*—[4] *The conformity of the proposed Constitution to the true principles of republican government*—[5] *Its analogy to your own State constitution*—and lastly, [6] *The additional security which its adoption will afford to the preservation of that species of government, to liberty, and to property.*[3]

Publius then finds it necessary to explain the order of his work. "It may perhaps be thought superfluous to offer arguments to prove the utility of the UNION," he says, since it is thought that it "has no adversaries." Publius justifies his opening theme on the ground that there are in fact secret adversaries. But apart from this peculiar justification, it is possible to see Publius' other grounds for the organization of his work. In particular it is clear why he begins with the utility of the union. For one thing, he gets off on the right foot by beginning with a subject on which he is in accord with nearly all his readers. Further, a proper and full statement of the agreed end of union turns out, as a full statement of the end always does, to contain the clearest implications for what must be done to achieve the end. Therefore, by the time Publius has fully stated the value of union, he has introduced all his major arguments on disputed matters in the amiable context of the undisputed end. Rightly stated, the end of union is palpably inconsistent with the "imbecility" (*i.e.,* weakness) of the Confederation and requires an "energetic" government. Publius wants to extort from the "general assent to the abstract proposition" [4] that union is good and the Confederation inadequate, acquiescence in what is necessary to sustain the union. Publius is able to convert "general assent" into intelligent and detailed assent by instructing his readers on what is logically implied in their vague commitment to union. The first three branches of Publius' work therefore make this argument: to desire union is necessarily to despise the present Confederation and to welcome the energetic government union needs. All that remains is to show that the union under this energetic government, the proposed Constitution, is satisfactorily republican. Hence Publius must teach a republican way more fully to enjoy the "utility of Union" than hitherto thought possible.

This, as will be seen, is both Publius' most difficult political task and his most important theoretical teaching. A closer look at the organization of the work reveals its importance. The work is actually divided among the six "branches of the inquiry" in the following way: (1) "the utility of Union"—14 papers; (2) "the insufficiency of the present Confederation"—8 papers; (3) the necessity of energetic government—14 papers; (4) the republicanism of the Constitution—48 papers; (5) and (6)—1 paper. By the time he has reached the last paper, Publius claims to have "so fully anticipated and exhausted" the last two branches that he only brings together the appropriate arguments and concludes the work. The book is therefore written in fact under four "heads." But the organization may be stated still more simply. As has been seen, the first three heads deal with one theme, the immediate political question of what is to be done about the union—showing why it is good, what is inadequate in the Articles of Confederation, and what kind of government will be adequate to the end of union. The proposed Constitution being adequate to that end, all that remains is to show that this Constitution conforms to the *true* principles of republican government. And this is the work of the fourth, and by far the largest branch of the inquiry. The organization of the essays stated in its simplest form therefore is: union and republicanism. The organization of the essays perfectly conveys *The Federalist's* teaching. *The Federalist* teaches a new and true republicanism which involves crucially a new view of the problem of union. [5]

Americans were already living under republican governments, and under a confederal union of these republics; but, in the view of *The*

*Federalist,* the principle of these republics and their confederal union was old and false. The Confederation was therefore necessarily foundering, and the individual republics were tending to "the mortal diseases under which popular governments have everywhere perished." [6] The Constitution contains the new and true principle of republican union which will rescue republican government in America. The proud conclusion of the famous tenth essay summarizes the teaching: "*In the extent and proper structure of the Union,* therefore, we behold a *republican* remedy for the diseases most incident to republican government." (Italics supplied.)

*The Federalist* is remarkable for the conjunction it achieves between discussion of the most urgent political matters and of theoretical matters. This is nowhere more evident than in the treatment of republican union. The right arrangement of union was the first political problem of the day; but what *The Federalist* has to say on this practical question is based on its most novel and important theoretical teaching. The opposition to the Constitution also rested upon a theoretical view. Indeed, one of the remarkable features of the debate over the Constitution was the extraordinary intrusion of theoretical considerations into the settlement of the practical question. The great attack on the Constitution was the charge that the new union was antirepublican. Certain features of the Constitution were regarded as specifically antirepublican, but the main thrust of the opposition resulted from the more general argument that only the state governments, not some huge central government, could be made effectively free and republican. This rested on a widely held belief, popularized in the way men understood Montesquieu, that only small countries could enjoy republican government. The reasoning that *The Federalist* had to oppose ran as follows.

Large countries necessarily turn to despotism. For one thing, large countries need despotic rule simply in consequence of largeness; political authority in the parts breaks down without more forceful government than the republican form admits. Further, large countries, usually wealthy and populous, are warlike or are made warlike by envious neighbors; the conduct of wars inevitably nurtures despotic rule. And even if large countries try to be republican, they cannot succeed. To preserve their rule, the people must be patriotic, vigilant, and informed. This requires that the people give loving attention to public things, and that the affairs of the country be on a scale commensurate with popular understanding. But in large countries the people are baffled and rendered apathetic by the complexity of public affairs, and at last become absorbed in their own pursuits. Finally, even the alert citizenry of a large republic must allow a few men actually to conduct the public business; far removed from the localities and possessed of the instruments of coercion, the trusted representatives would inevitably subvert the republican rule to their own passions and interests. Such was the traditional and strongly held view of the necessity that republics be small. It followed that such small republics could only combine for limited purposes into confederacies which respect the primacy of the member states. But its opponents regarded the Constitution not as a proper confederacy, but as "calculated ultimately to make the states one consolidated government," which is to say, one large republic; hence the Constitution was *necessarily* antirepublican. That is, the Constitution was denounced as resting on a novel and false view of republican union.

*The Federalist,* understandably then, asks its readers to "hearken not to the voice which petulantly tells you that the form of government recommended for your adoption is a novelty in the political world; that it has never yet had a place in the theories of the wildest projectors; that it rashly attempts what it is impossible to accomplish." [7]

While the readers are urged to hearken not, *The Federalist* does not deny the charge of novelty; on the contrary, it extols novelty as "the glory of the people of America."

Happily for America, happily, we trust for the whole human race, [the leaders of the revolution did not fear to depart from old ways but rather] pursued a new and more noble course. They accomplished a revolution which has no parallel in the annals of human society. They reared the fabrics of government which have no model on the face of the globe. They formed the design of a great Confederacy, which it is incumbent on their successors to improve and perpetuate. [8]

But one must expect, we are immediately told, some flaws in these achievements. It turns out that "they erred most in the structure of the Union." But this was to be expected because *"this was the work most difficult to be executed."* (Italics supplied.) The right republican union, then, is a more difficult work to accomplish than a revolution without parallel and the creation of state governments without previous model. But the Constitution will accomplish this most difficult work. It will fulfill and therefore save "the new and more noble" way of life America has brought to the world. This "more perfect Union" rests upon the new and true republicanism which it is Publius' task to expound.

Publius states his most important claim in the conclusion of the famous tenth essay: he presents "a republican remedy for the diseases most incident to republican government." Again, Publius praises Thomas Jefferson for displaying equally "a fervent attachment to republican government and an enlightened view of the dangerous propensities against which it ought to be guarded." [9] Publius thus claims to be the wholehearted but cool-headed partisan of republicanism. But the word republican does not tell us enough about the kind of regime which Publius advocates. That is, the question immediately arises: what *kind* of republic? How may Publius' republic be fitted into the traditional distinction of three kinds of rule, by the one, few, or many? The answer is obvious: Publius espouses a *democratic* republic. Indeed, what is remarkable is the extent to which Publius gives the word republic, in the key passages, an exclusively democratic content. For example, "the republican principle . . . enables the majority to defeat [a minority faction's] sinister views by regular vote." And this must be a majority "derived from the great body of the society, not from an inconsiderable proportion, or a favored class of it." [10] While it is true that the word republic always meant the absence of monarchy and implied the importance of the whole body of citizens, it did not imply universal or nearly universal manhood suffrage: earlier usage always distinguished between aristocratic or oligarchic republics and democratic republics. But Publius' exclusively democratic idea of republicanism obliges him explicitly to deny the appellation republic to all those aristocratic and oligarchic regimes formerly so styled.[11] In short, in so far as it accepts the old threefold distinction of regimes, *The Federalist* treats its republican regime as belonging overwhelmingly to the democratic kind of rule. However much its regime departs from the character of a "pure democracy," *The Federalist* emphatically and rightly denies that the departure removes the Constitution from the class of democratic governments into the monarchical or aristocratic class.

Publius' new and true republicanism is therefore a new and true democratic teaching. For many reasons, which cannot be discussed here, the democratic character of *The Federalist,* and of the Constitution it expounded, has been obscured. This has been to miss the most important thing about *The Federalist.* It is necessary and appropriate, however, to examine one argument frequently made in support of the view that Publius' Constitution did not establish a democratic regime. In a famous passage in the tenth essay, Publius is thought himself to have radically distinguished republics from democracies, and hence himself to have withdrawn the Constitution from the democratic class. This is not quite accurate. Publius distinguishes a republic from "a *pure* democracy," [12] and that is a very different thing. By a pure democracy, Publius says he means "a society consisting of a small number of citizens, who assemble and administer the government in person." As Publius compares the two, a republic "varies from a pure democracy" only in that it is "a government in which the scheme of representation takes place." This and this alone is the distinction Publius makes. The perfect synonym for Publius' use of republic is therefore representative democracy. The principle of representation, however, introduces an impurity into the republican form from the point of view of pure democracy. But this does not mean that republics are opposed in kind to democracies; rather, republics are, so to speak, "impure" democracies.

On the crucial question of where sovereignty is lodged, namely, with the many, republics and pure democracies alike belong to a more inclusive class. The apparent difficulty raised by *The Federalist*'s distinction between republics and pure democracies is resolved when we see that this larger class or genus is what Publius calls *popular* government. And by popular government Publius means what is meant today by the term democracy. That is, Publius sees popular government as including all the forms of rule by the many, as distinguished from the various forms of rule by the few or the one. We may seek aid in understanding Publius from Madison and Hamilton individually. On the crucial question of the locus of political authority, Publius, Madison, and Hamilton all speak of a republic, democracy, and popular government interchangeably. Publius in the tenth essay speaks identically of a *republican* remedy for the disease of faction, and a remedy that will "preserve the spirit and form of *popular* government." On June 6 at the federal convention, Madison discussed the identical remedy as "the only defense against the inconveniences of *democracy* consistent with the *democratic* form of government." Hamilton styled the republic created by the Constitution a *"representative democracy."* [13] Publius must be understood, then, as having undertaken, in the fine phrase G. L. Pierson applied to Tocqueville, to "make democracy safe for the world." This is how Publius' greatest claim is to be understood. To save popular government from its "mortal diseases" while preserving both "the spirit and the form of popular government is . . . the great object . . . [of] our inquiries." Publius claims to rescue "this form of government . . . from the opprobrium under which it has so long labored," and therefore to recommend it "to the esteem and adoption of mankind." [14]

The foregoing is not intended, however, to depreciate the importance of Publius' distinction between republic and pure democracy. On the contrary, the peculiar property of a republic, that it is a *representative* democracy, is the foundation of *The Federalist*'s teaching; it "promises the cure for which we are seeking." [15] But the democratic character of *The Federalist*'s republicanism must be emphasized in order to grasp its central contention. Publius claims to cure the hitherto incurable ills of popular government, while remaining perfectly consistent with the principle of popular government, that is, lodging sovereignty with the many.

Publius helps us to see what is new in his teaching. In the fourteenth essay, which continues the assault on "the error which limits republican government to a narrow district," [16] Publius explains why men so long committed that error. What Publius now knows about republicanism was hitherto veiled from men by both the ancient and modern examples of it. The possibilities latent in the popular republican form were veiled because "most of the popular governments of antiquity were of the democratic species." While

in modern Europe, to which we owe the great principle of representation, no example is seen of a government *wholly popular,* and founded, at the same time, wholly on that principle. If Europe has the merit of discovering this great mechanical power in government, by the simple agency of which the will of the largest political body may be concentred, and its force directed to any object which the public good requires, *America* can claim the merit of making the discovery the basis of *unmixed* and *extensive* republics. It is only to be lamented that any of her citizens should wish to deprive her of the additional merit of displaying its full efficacy in the establishment of the comprehensive system now under her consideration.[17]

The ancients had many wholly popular governments but mostly of the *pure* democratic species, that is, of the direct, not the representative kind. The Europeans have partly or wholly representative governments, but none at once wholly representative and wholly of the popular kind. It has remained for America to innovate the combination: governments wholly popular and wholly based upon the representative principle. The word "unmixed" must be read in its full force. The American states were not *mixed regimes;* as wholly popular states, they had no significant admixture of aristocratical or monarchical elements. And they were not small republics as that term had been traditionally understood; they were already *extensive* republics. All that is needed, Publius concludes, is to display the "full efficacy" of the representative principle in the unmixed and still more extensive republic proposed by the Constitution. But Publius' mild speech is deceptive; as we have seen, all that remains to be done is "the work most difficult to be executed."

Publius understandably treats gently the pride and affection of his readers for their state governments. The state governments are fine, he seems to say, and the Constitution will be even finer. He says that "the valuable improvements made by the American constitutions on the popular models, both ancient and modern, cannot certainly be too much admired." [18] This sentence can be read in two ways; the amount of praise it bestows is uncertain. How does Publius actually regard the "valuable improvements" in the state government? The state governments, for all their improvements, fail utterly to solve the problem of faction which is *the* problem of popular government. The state governments will founder on this rock as all previous democracies have foundered. They will founder because they do not have a sufficient "number of citizens and extent of territory." They are "extensive republics," but not extensive enough.

The ancient popular governments obscured the possibilities latent in republicanism, we were told, because "most" of them lacked the representative principle. But something else was lacking in antiquity. Publius therefore comes back to this very question many essays later. Now he warns "that the position concerning the ignorance of the ancient governments on the subject of representation, is by no means precisely true in the latitude commonly given to it." [19] He now gives a considerable list of ancient representative institutions. True, none of the ancient republics was based wholly on the representative principle as are the American states. And this was a defect. But it was a trivial defect; they suffered from a much worse ill. "It cannot be believed, that any form of representative government could have succeeded within the narrow limits occupied by the democracies of Greece." [20] The utility of the representative principle, then, which offers "the cure for which we are seeking," depends entirely upon the size of country. Even the relatively large American states will not suffice; only a union of the magnitude and character envisaged by the Constitution will solve the problem of popular government.

"The enlightened friends to liberty" would have had to abandon the cause of republican government as "indefensible" if this new solution had not been found. The solution rests upon the "science of politics," which "like most other sciences, has received great improvement. The efficacy of various principles is now well understood, which were either not known at all, or imperfectly known to the ancients."

The regular distribution of power into distinct departments; the introduction of legislative balances and checks; the institution of courts composed of judges holding their offices during good behavior; the representation of the people in the legislature by deputies of their own election: these are wholly new discoveries, or have made their principal progress towards perfection in modern times. They are means, and powerful means, by which the excellences of republican government may be retained and its imperfections lessened or avoided. To this catalogue of circumstances that tend to the amelioration of popular systems of civil government, I shall venture, however novel it may appear to some, to add one more, on a principle which has been made the foundation of an objection to the new Constitution; I mean the ENLARGEMENT of the ORBIT within which such systems are to revolve, either in respect to the dimensions of a single State, or to the consolidation of several smaller States into one great Confederacy.[21]

Publius is thus the spokesman for the new "science of politics," the previous teachers of which he does not name, who has himself made an important addition to the science, namely the possibility of a very large republic. Further, everything in that modern science of politics is seen now in a democratic light; if the earlier teachers of the new science only tended in a democratic direction, or suggested only partly democratic regimes, Publius takes the new science of politics and enlarges upon it and uses it for the amelioration of a "wholly popular" system of civil government. Finally, through Publius, the moment has come for the new science to cease being merely a teaching and to become a great political actuality.

Publius sees the problem of representative popular government as threefold. First, there is the possibility that the people will lose control of their government, that the representative rulers will subvert the regime. Second, there is the possibility that popular majorities, through compliant representatives, will rule oppressively. Third, there is the possibility that majorities, through compliant representatives, will rule not oppressively, but foolishly, failing to do the things necessary for the strength and stability of the government.

Protecting the people is the simplest task. "The whole power of the proposed government is to be in the hands of the representatives *of the people*."[22] The actual rulers will have no warrant ultimately save as they are "the objects of popular choice."[23] This guards against subversion by the representative rulers; making the representatives wholly dependent upon the people "is the essential, and, after all, only efficacious security for the rights and privileges of the people, which is attainable in civil society."[24] Although the regime is now to be wholly popular and wholly representative, there is nothing new thus far; democracy's oldest claim is that the right of suffrage guards the society against the oppression of its rulers. The new science of politics, however, offers an additional safeguard to the rights of the people. Separation of powers, "the regular distribution of power into distinct departments," lessens the threat that the rulers will be able to concert and execute schemes of oppression. The liberty of the people generally and the rights of individuals are secured by "the improbability of . . . a mercenary and perfidious combination of the several members of government, standing on as different foundations as republican principles will well admit, and at the same time accountable to the society over which they are placed." [25] This is what was sought in separation of powers by Jefferson, who feared above all oppression of the people by their rulers. How separation of powers will supply this protection can be better understood when we see how separation of powers mitigates the other evils Publius feared.

It is not enough, Publius argues, to guard society against the oppression of the representative rulers, it is necessary also "to guard one part of the society against the injustice of the other part." [26] In plain words, the problem is to guard against "overbearing" popular majorities. This is a far greater problem than the unconstitutional treachery of representatives because "the form of popular government" permits a popular majority "to execute and mask its violence under the forms of the Constitution." [27] In this sentence Publius boldly displays the democratic nature of the regime he expounds: the many rule and therefore can legally do oppressive things. Unlike Jefferson's "elective despotism," this evil occurs, not when the representatives are unfaithful to their constituents, but when they too faithfully heed the oppressive wishes of popular majorities. The great danger Publius sees is that popular majorities will demand oppressive measures and that their elected representatives will only too readily oblige. Publius seeks to solve the problem at both levels, among the people and among their representatives. "Multiplicity" of factions is his famous answer to the problem of the oppressive majority itself. But first we must consider how separation of powers solves the problem at the level of the representatives.

Publius is aware of two other respectable ways of preventing majorities from oppressing minorities. One is to create "a will in the community independent of the majority—that is, of the society itself." [28] But this is the monarchical solution which Publius rejects. The other is exemplified in the Roman republic where the legislative authority was divided into two "distinct and independent legislatures," [29] which enabled the patrician minority constitutionally to resist the plebeian majority. This may be taken to illustrate the traditional idea of the mixed republic which is excluded in Publius' "unmixed" republic, in which "all authority . . . will be derived from and dependent on the society." [30] The problem of oppressive majorities cannot be solved in a wholly popular regime by means belonging to the monarchical or mixed regimes. Publius finds in the new science of politics, which is not necessarily democratic, a solution which can be grafted onto democracy: separation of powers. Perhaps there is even a deeper kinship between separation of powers and democracy. In any event, Publius employs separation of powers, as he does all other things in the new science, so as "to preserve the spirit and the form of popular government."

Separation of powers mitigates the evil of oppressive majorities at the level of the government. In a republic without separation of powers, where a single body of representatives performs all the functions of government, there would be nothing in the machinery of government that could stay the will of an oppressive popular majority. But this is precisely what separation of powers is designed to do: to create a distance 'twixt the majority's cup and lip. Separation of powers takes the old distinction of the legislative, executive, and judicial functions of governing and makes it a distinction of the legislative, executive, and judicial personnel. This means, then, to create some representatives who will resist the wrong desires of the people to which other representatives are supinely yielding, or which they are even demagogically arousing. When the governing power is distributed into distinct departments, it is clear which are the representatives who may resist and which are those who will yield to popular demands. "In republican government, the legislative authority necessarily predominates." [31] "The legislative department" as the sad experience of the state governments had shown, "is everywhere extending the sphere of its activity, and drawing all power into its impetuous vortex." [32] As it were, it is against the legislature that the force of separation needs especially to be directed. "The great security against a gradual concentration of the several powers in the same department, consists in giving to those who administer each department the necessary constitutional means and personal motives to resist encroachment of the others." [33]

Publius had reason to speak blandly but his meaning is clear. The executive and the judiciary must have the means and personal motives to resist the legislature. For example, "when occasions present themselves, in which the interests of the people are at variance with their inclinations"; or when the legislators, who "commonly have the people on their side," are bent on oppression, then "the Executive should be in a situation to dare to act his own opinion with vigor and decision." [34] Separation of powers creates authorities who, despite their dependence upon the people and their lack of any independent title to rule, are yet likely to resist and stay the legislature when it is yielding to the wrong demands of the populace, the constitutional master of all three branches of government.

Publius shows quite easily how the executive and the judiciary will have the "means" to stave off oppressive legislation; the veto, the president's legislative initiative, his discretion in the enforcement of the laws, judicial review, and the judges' discretion in the adjudication of individual cases, all give to the other two branches the constitutional means temporarily to void or to moderate oppressive legislation. But it is more difficult to see why the executive and the judiciary will have the "personal motives" to resist the legislature. Why will they collaborate with the legislature in good actions, without which collaboration government would be reduced to the imbecility Publius despised, and collide with the legislature in its bad actions? Publius gives us two reasons. First, "ambition must be made to counteract ambition. The interest of the man must be connected with the constitutional rights of the place." [35] If the government is properly arranged, presidents and judges will defend their offices against the legislature because their pride, love of power or fame, even avarice, will lead them to identify their self-interest with the integrity of their offices. But there is a crucial assumption here. Publius assumes that oppressive legislation necessarily or at least ordinarily derogates from the dignity of the executive and judicial offices. Publius appears to assume that oppressive legislation requires servile execution and servile adjudication; and that servile executives and judges enjoy no dignity, no power, no fame, and ultimately not even pecuniary rewards. Hence Publius expects the executive and judiciary, for reasons of private interest and passion, to resist the legislature when it is oppressive. Separation of powers supplies democracy with governors who, without the traditional motives of family distinction or wealth, simply because of the jobs they hold and their self-regarding attachment to them, will tend to rule in the best interest of the democracy.

Publius' second reason for believing that the other branches will resist oppressive legislation desired by a popular majority is also based on his assumption that oppressive legislation ordinarily derogates from the integrity of the executive and judicial offices. But he appears further to assume that presidents and judges will resist oppressive legislation, not only because of interested attachment to their offices, but also out of a decent regard for the proper fulfillment of their duties. As reasonably decent men doing a job, they will have the motives, as it were the professional motives, to resist oppressive legislation because it tends to violate the arts they serve, and to subordinate the executive and judicial offices.

This last consideration leads to an understanding of how Publius expected separation of powers to help solve the third problem of popular government, not the oppressiveness but the ineptitude of popular rule. Again, Publius is confronting the traditional criticism of popular government which was that it gave over government into the hands

of the many, which is to say the unwise. The very principle of representation itself may be a step in the right direction. The effect of representation may be

to refine and enlarge the public views, by passing them through the medium
of a chosen body of citizens, whose wisdom may best discern the true interest
of their country, and whose patriotism and love of justice will be least likely
to sacrifice it to temporary or partial considerations. . . . It may well happen
that the public voice, pronounced by the representatives of the people, will be
more consonant to the public good than if pronounced by the people themselves, convened for the purpose.[36]

But we know that Publius does not count much on the wisdom and
courage of the legislature alone. It is those other representatives of the
people, the executive and the judiciary, who are crucial to elevating the
whole representation of the people. (It should be noted that much of
what is said here of separation of powers applies as well to "legislative
checks and balances," that is, those checks imposed by the existence of
the Senate.) The executive and judiciary are elected and appointed at
some remove from the immediate opinion of the people, but demo-
cratically, that is, not upon any authority outside the sovereignty of the
people. They serve for longer terms and serve larger constituencies; the
nature of their duties thrusts more forcefully upon them awareness of
what is necessary for the interest of the whole. They come to want to
do their jobs well. Separation of powers creates offices which of themselves tend to make the men who occupy them worthy of the offices.
      Moreover, separation of powers aids in securing for the executive
and judiciary the men most likely to acquit themselves well; that is,
it influences beneficially the majority choice. Separation of powers, one
can see, supplies a superb rhetorical mode to those who are concerned
with the ineptitude of popular rule. Publius has the courage—and it
says something about his audience that he felt he could dare—to ask
the many to select for their rulers men who are their superiors in wisdom and virtue. Every people ought "to obtain for rulers men who
possess most wisdom to discern, and most virtue to pursue, the common
good." [37] Separation of powers gives Publius a framework within which
to press the people to seek wisdom and virtue in their rulers. He can
present the executive and judiciary (and the Senate) as having, so to
speak, a list of job specifications, qualities which are necessary to the
performance of the functions and which approximate wisdom and
virtue. It is politically easier and more effective to ask the people to
select the right man for the specific job, especially a people with the
"commercial character of America." [38] More willing to vote for superior
men when superiority is presented in the guise of job qualifications, the

people are also instructed in how to choose the better men; the job specifications supply them with a kind of simple checklist to guide choice to better rather than poorer men.

Publius shows how separation of powers, legislative checks and balances, and numerous practical embellishments upon these make possible for the first time a sound popular regime, a system of popular rule which will be less oppressive and wiser in the art of government than any before. But we must now see that this achievement depends utterly upon the last item in Publius' science, the enlargement of the republican orbit.

Separation of powers is a refinement of the representative principle. It would have no place in a pure democracy. Separation guards against that "accumulation of all powers, legislative, executive, and judiciary, in the same hands, whether of one, a few, or many, and whether hereditary, self-appointed, or elective [which] may justly be pronounced the very definition of tyranny." [39] But a pure democracy, by Publius' definition, is precisely the accumulation of all powers in the hands of the many. Hence it is only in a representative democracy that the rulers can be separated into distinct departments. But just as it is not enough to have a representative democracy, so it is not enough even to have properly separated representatives. It must be remembered that Publius said that the small ancient democracies could not have been helped by "*any* form of representative government"; they fatally lacked the advantages of an extensive territory and a numerous population. The representative principle is meant to supply rulers who can govern the people better than the people can govern themselves directly. But in small republics, the representative rulers are so immediately under the scrutiny and influence of a compacted popular majority that the representatives constitute no independent presence in the regime, but are merely the tools of the majority. Hence the representative principle is useless in a small republic. [40] Nor can separation of powers save the small republic. The immediate influence there of popular majorities, sufficient to awe a single representative body, is sufficient also to make of separated departments the mere agents of popular will. Only when there is a distance between the people and their government will there be that difference between the ultimate authority of the people and the immediate authority of their representatives which is the decisive condition for the advantages supplied by the principle of both representation and separation of powers. Not even in those large republics, the states, but only in a very large republic, the union, will the representative principle and its corollary, separation of powers, work "to the amelioration of popular systems of civil government."

The representative principle, reinforced by separation of powers, is meant to deny the authority of the government to oppressive popular majorities *after* they have formed. But Publius was aware that this was not enough, even in large republics. If a majority comes to have the same oppressive passion or interest and holds to it for only four to six years, it will find the means to triumph over separation of powers, checks and balances, the not so difficult amending procedure, and all the contrivances of the Constitution. These devices were designed, and could be designed, only to stay the will of the majority. This is not to depreciate the importance of the legal barriers; they have enormous efficacy in tempering the force Publius feared. But that efficacy depends ultimately upon a prior weakening of the force applied against them, upon the majority having been deflected from its "schemes of oppression." This is why Publius calls the problem of the popular majority itself *the* problem of popular government.

Publius therefore seeks to solve the problem of the oppressive and unwise rule of popular systems by trying to deal with the popular majority itself. Again everything depends upon the novel conception of a very large republic and, as we shall see, a certain kind of very large republic. The problem is dealt with in the famous tenth essay on the problem of "violence of faction."

Publius is not concerned with the problem of faction generally; he devotes only two sentences in the whole essay to the dangers of minority factions. The real problem in popular government is majority faction, or, more precisely, *the* majority faction, *i.e.,* the great mass of the little propertied and the unpropertied. If the people is the sovereign, the many are the sovereign, and the many may desire to oppress the few; it is the many therefore from whom can come the greatest harm. Publius emphasizes one harm in particular, the harm which results from the struggle between the rich and the poor and which made the ancient democracies short-lived "spectacles of turbulence and contention." *The* problem for the friend of popular government is how to avoid the "domestic convulsion" which results when the rich and the poor, the few and the many, as is their wont, are at each others' throats. Always before in popular governments the many, armed with political power, precipitated such convulsions. The many can be diverted from this natural course, Publius says, by one of two means only.

Either the existence of the same passion or interest in a majority at the same time must be prevented, or the majority, having such co-existent passion or interest, must be rendered, by their number and local situation, unable to concert and carry into effect schemes of oppression.[41]

But "we well know that neither moral nor religious motives can be relied on" as a control if such a majority forms and concerts its action. The "circumstance principally" which will provide both defenses against oppressive majorities is the "greater number of citizens and extent of territory which may be brought within the compass" of very large republican governments.

The smaller the society, the fewer probably will be the distinct parties and interests composing it; the fewer the distinct parties and interests, the more frequently will a majority be found of the same party; and the smaller the number of individuals composing a majority, and the smaller the compass within which they are placed, the more easily will they concert and execute their plans of oppression. Extend the sphere and you take in a greater variety of parties and interests; you make it less probable that a majority of the whole will have a common motive to invade the rights of other citizens; or if such a common motive exists, it will be more difficult for all who feel it to discover their own strength, and to act in unison with each other.[42]

In a small republic the many poor come to see themselves as a single interest arrayed against the single interest of the few rich; accordingly, the politics of the small republic is the fatal politics of class struggle. That is what is important here about smallness. In the small republic, the many are divided into but a few trades and callings; further, it can be suggested, the smallness of the country makes instantly visible to anyone that these few differences among the many are trivial as compared with the massive difference between all the poor and all the rich. In a small republic, the divisions among the many are insufficient to prevent them from conceiving their lot in common and uniting in fatal struggle against the common enemy. In a large republic, however, distinctions arise among the many, sufficiently numerous and divisive to prevent the forming and concerting of such majorities. But clearly, largeness is not as such decisive; there can be large countries in which the poor are undifferentiated, poor only in a few ways. Only a certain kind of large republic holds out the prospect of the right kind of divisiveness. Publius tells us where this occurs. The properly divisive host of interests grows up "of necessity in civilized nations, and divide[s] them into different classes, actuated by different sentiments and views." Strikingly, as it does in Adam Smith, "civilized nations" means large nations devoted to the commercial life. The largeness of the large republic offers a remedy for the republican disease only if the large republic is also a modern commercial republic.

Publius' republican remedy depends entirely upon achieving the right kind of political divisions. Now Publius sees more than one source of division; for example, he clearly relies upon the presence of a "multiplicity of [religious] sects." [43] But he is well known to emphasize primarily the economic. "The possession of different *degrees* and *kinds* of property . . . [influences] the sentiments and views of the respective proprietors . . . [and produces the] division of the society into different interests and parties." Although other causes of division must not be overlooked, "the most common and durable source of factions has been the *various* and *unequal* distribution of property." (Italics supplied.) It is important to notice that in both statements Publius distinguishes two kinds of divisions which result from property: men differ according to the *amount* of property they hold, but also according to the *kind* of property they hold. The difference according to amount of property, between rich and poor, was the basis of the fatal class struggles of small republics. But Publius sees in the large commercial republic the possibility for the first time of subordinating the difference over amount of property to the difference over kind of property. In such a republic the hitherto fatal class struggle is replaced by the safe, even salutary struggle among different kinds of propertied interests. In such a republic, a man will regard it as more important to himself to further the immediate advantage of his specialized trade, or his specialized calling within a trade, than to advance the general cause of the poor or the rich. The struggle of the various interests veils the difference between the few and the many. In particular, the interest of the many as such can be fragmented into sundry narrower, more limited interests, each seeking immediate advantage. In such a republic and with such citizens, "you make it less probable that a majority of the whole will have a common motive to invade the rights of other citizens." In such a republic, popular majorities will still rule but now "among the great variety of interests, parties, and sects which it embraces, a coalition of a majority of the whole society could seldom take place on any other principles than those of justice and the general good." [44]


Publius is aware of what is involved in his novel teaching regarding the large commercial republic. His doctrine moves in directions which carry it beyond those manifestly political concerns with which we have dealt. Publius sees, as does Adam Smith, the connection between a very large area of trade and the possibility of division of labor, which in turn is so closely connected with the saving multiplicity of faction. This is why Publius so desperately seeks to preserve, render vastly more intimate, and strengthen the union. Publius also knows that his solution to the problem of popular majorities requires that the country be profoundly democratic, that is, that all men must be equally free and equally encouraged to seek their immediate gain and to associate with others in the process. There must be no rigid barriers which bar men from the pursuit of their immediate interest. Indeed, it is especially the lowly, from whom so much is to be feared, who must feel least barred from opportunity and most sanguine about their chances. Further, his solution requires a country that achieves commercial success, a wealthy country. That is, the limited and immediate gains must be real; the fragmented interests must achieve real gains from time to time, else the scheme ceases to beguile or mollify. Further, the laws, and especially the fundamental law, must look to the protection of the property of all, of the little propertied so that they may cleave to their little as their fundamental concern, and of the much propertied so as to make their property seem beyond the reach of envy. The fundamental law must also render difficult especially those most likely oppressive acts such as the states' tampering with the value of money or impairing the obligation of contracts.

And Publius is aware that his scheme involves an enormous reliance on the ceaseless striving after immediate private gains; the commercial life must be made honorable and universally practiced. Publius counts on a portion of patriotism and wisdom in the people and especially in their representative rulers. But precisely in his discussion of separation of powers, that device for securing enlightened rulers, he returns to his primary emphasis. Enlightened though they may be, it is primarily their private passions and interests that render them useful to the public. In perhaps the most remarkable and revealing single sentence of the book, Publius speaks of "this policy of supplying, by opposite and rival interests, the defect of better motives, [which] might be traced through the whole system of human affairs, private as well as public." [45] To understand fully how Publius understands "the defect of better motives," and how he seeks to make up for the defect by founding a regime in which the art of government is made commensurate with the capacity of men when their passions and interests are rightly arranged, is to understand Publius' contribution to the new "science of politics" and to understand the American republic he had so large a hand in framing.

# NOTES

1. The authorship of the 85 papers has long been disputed. According to the convincing attribution of Douglass Adair, Hamilton wrote 51 papers (1, 6– 9, 11–13, 15–17, 21–36, 59–61, 65–85), Madison 29 (10, 14, 18–20, 37–58, 62–63), and Jay 5 (2–5, 64).

2. See the fine essay by Douglass

Adair, "A Note on Certain of Hamilton's Pseudonyms," *William and Mary Quarterly,* third series, XII (April 1955).

3. *The Federalist,* ed. Henry Cabot Lodge, introduction by Edward Mead Earle (New York: Modern Library, 1941) 1, p. 6. Italics original.

4. *Federalist* 15, p. 89.

5. The organization of the essays is perfectly revealed in *Federalist* 39 which defends the Constitution on two grounds, that it is sufficiently republican and sufficiently federal. That is, in this essay, which links the two main divisions of the book and is in a sense the central essay, the issue is stripped to its essentials: union and republicanism.

6. *Federalist* 10, pp. 53–54.

7. *Federalist* 14, p. 84.

8. *Ibid.,* p. 85.

9. *Federalist* 49, p. 327.

10. *Federalist* 10, p. 57. *Federalist* 39, p. 244. See also *Federalist* 52, pp. 341–42: "The definition of the right of suffrage is very justly regarded as a fundamental article of republican government." It is "to be the same with those of the electors of the most numerous branch of the State legislatures." "It cannot be feared that the people of the States will alter this part of their constitutions in such a manner as to abridge the rights secured to them by the federal Constitution." The national suffrage is made as democratic as the very democratic suffrage in the states, and there is no likelihood that the suffrage will become less popular.

11. *Federalist* 39, p. 243.

12. *Federalist* 10, p. 58. Italics supplied.

13. Alexander Hamilton, *Writings,* ed. Henry Cabot Lodge (12 vols.; New York: Putnam, 1904), II, 92. Italics original.

14. *Federalist* 10, p. 58.

15. *Ibid.,* p. 59.

16. *Federalist* 14, p. 80.

17. *Ibid.,* p. 81. Italics supplied.

18. *Federalist* 10, p. 54.

19. *Federalist* 63, p. 412.

20. *Ibid.,* p. 413.

21. *Federalist* 9, pp. 48–49.

22. *Federalist* 28, p. 173. Italics supplied.

23. *Federalist* 57, p. 371.

24. *Federalist* 28, p. 173.

25. *Federalist* 55, p. 364.

26. *Federalist* 51, p. 339.

27. *Federalist* 10, p. 57.

28. *Federalist* 51, p. 339.

29. *Federalist* 34, pp. 203–4.

30. *Federalist* 51, p. 339.

31. *Ibid.,* p. 338.

32. *Federalist* 48, p. 322.

33. *Federalist* 51, p. 337.

34. *Federalist* 71, pp. 465–66.

35. *Federalist* 51, p. 337.

36. *Federalist* 10, p. 59.

37. *Federalist* 57, p. 370.

38. *Federalist* 11, p. 62.

39. *Federalist* 47, p. 313.

40. See also *Federalist* 10, p. 59, where Publius notes that the "effect" of representation "may be inverted."

41. *Federalist* 10, p. 58.

42. *Ibid.,* pp. 60–61.

43. *Federalist* 51, pp. 339–40.

44. *Ibid.,* p. 341.

45. *Ibid.,* p. 337.

# READINGS

A.  *The Federalist.* 1, 6, 9, 10, 14, 15, 23, 37–39, 47, 51, 63, 68, 70, 72, 78.
B.  *The Federalist.* All the remaining numbers.

# THOMAS PAINE

## 1737–1809

Thomas Paine was a brilliant pamphleteer in an age which gave full scope to his talents. Born and raised in England, he spent much of his life in America and France, where he took an active part, through his publications, in the great revolutions which swept over those countries in the late eighteenth century.

It was Paine's strength as a propagandist, though his weakness as a thinker, that he saw man and society entirely in black and white, with no shades of gray. The revolutions of his day were, for him, struggles between unmitigated good and evil. A typical child of the Enlightenment, he viewed the past as an almost unbroken reign of ignorance, superstition, and tyranny. But he felt that it was his privilege to live in "a morning of reason" when the native good will and common sense of the average man were beginning to assert themselves and would speedily make all things new.

There was a ground for Paine's confidence: "All the great laws of society are laws of nature." [1] Human reason, he believed, once freed from the impostures of political tradition and the absurdities of revealed religion, could easily apprehend the natural laws of society and government. As rational knowledge spread, governments would inevitably be reconstituted on natural principles. Then all major social problems could be solved without great difficulty. There was in Paine's thought more than a trace of what has been called "redemptive futurism" or "political messianism," the crusading faith that a revolution in the social and political order would uproot the tares of evil in man and create a new and sinless humanity. "The present age," he said, "will

594

hereafter merit to be called the Age of Reason, and the present generation will appear to the future as the Adam of a new world." [2]

The problem of social life, as Paine saw it, was essentially that of
founding government on right principles. Fortunately, it was a simple problem. "Notwithstanding the mystery with which the science
of government has been enveloped, for the purpose of enslaving, plun-
dering and imposing upon mankind, it is of all things the least mysterious and the most easy to be understood." [3] In regard to government,
"men have but to think and they will neither act wrong nor be misled." [4]

Underlying Paine's political philosophy was the doctrine of the
natural harmony of individual interests. "Society," he said, "is produced
by our wants and government by our wickedness." [5] Man is fitted by
Nature for society, because no man is capable of supplying his own
needs without the aid of society. These needs, and his natural social
affections, force man into society. Indeed, "man is so naturally a creature
of society, that it is almost impossible to put him out of it." [6] The
principle which forms society and holds it together, therefore, is common interest.

Common interest largely suffices for the purposes of social life.
Government correspondingly has a minimal role to play, because "society performs for itself almost every thing which is ascribed to government." All that government need do is "to supply the few cases to
which society and civilization are not conveniently competent." Social
progress therefore is in the direction of ever less government. "The more
perfect civilization is, the less occasion has it for government, because
the more does it regulate its own affairs, and govern itself." [7]

Government, as hitherto constituted, has been "the generating
cause" rather than the remedy of social disorder, of poverty and war.
The solution to the problem of government, however, is not its abolition
(an idea which Paine apparently never entertained), but its reconstitution on the right principles: "by the simple operation of constructing
government on the principles of society and the rights of man, every
difficulty retires...." The sum and substance of political philosophy, and
the one thing it is beneficial to know, is this: "*That government is
nothing more than a national association acting on the principles of
society.*" [8]

What then are the principles of society? As has already been said,
"All the great laws of society are laws of nature. ... They are followed
and obeyed, because it is the interest of the parties so to do. ..." [9]
Government's function is to enable men to follow their own interests.
"Every man wishes to pursue his occupation, and to enjoy the fruits of
his labors and the produce of his property in peace and safety, and with
the least possible expense. When these things are accomplished, all the

objects for which government ought to be established are answered." [10] In short, man's security in the pursuit of his own interest is "the true design and end of government."

This security is also man's right. Paine's theory of society and government is elaborated entirely in terms of rights. He speaks of duties, too, but they consist in guaranteeing to others the same rights one vindicates for oneself. All men deserve equal protection because they come into the world equally endowed with rights. These rights are the principles on which alone a just and legitimate political order can be built. This theory, of which Paine was an influential exponent though by no means the originator, furnished the intellectual ammunition for the great revolutionary movement of the eighteenth century.

The rights of man include both natural and civil rights. In *The Rights of Man,* Paine explains the distinction between them in these terms:

Natural rights are those which appertain to man in right of his existence. Of this kind are all the intellectual rights, or rights of the mind, and also all those rights of acting as an individual for his own comfort and happiness, which are not injurious to the natural rights of others. Civil rights are those which appertain to man in right of his being a member of society. Every civil right has for its foundation some natural right pre-existing in the individual, but to the enjoyment of which his individual power is not, in all cases, sufficiently competent. Of this kind are all those which relate to security and protection.[11]

That is to say, there are natural rights "in which the *power* to execute it is as perfect in the individual as the right itself." For example, "religion is one of those rights." In the exercise of these rights the individual is self-sufficient and has no need of government. But there are other rights, equally natural, "in which, though the right is perfect in the individual, the power to execute them is defective." These rights man "deposits in the common stock of society." [12] That is, he gives up the personal enforcement of some of his natural rights and exchanges them for civil rights, so that society may the more effectively protect him in exercising his rights.

Civil power is thus a sort of joint capital "made up of the aggregate of that class of the natural rights of man, which becomes defective in the individual in point of power." [13] Men pool their right to be judges in their own cause and establish a government to exercise judgment between their conflicting claims. But the power of government is only the collected power of individuals and cannot be used to infringe the natural rights which they retain for themselves. For natural rights are the rights with which God endowed man as man at his creation; they are consequently inviolable and imprescriptible.

Paine, it is obvious, belonged to the social-compact school of political thought. But he would not hear of a compact between the people and their rulers. There was only one contractual act, by which "the *individuals themselves,* each in his own personal and sovereign right, *entered into a compact with each other* to produce a government: and this is the only mode in which governments have a right to arise, and the only principle on which they have a right to exist." [14] This compact does not create a sovereign government but a sovereign community or nation. The title of king cannot make a man a sovereign. "Sovereignty, as a matter of right, appertains to the nation only, and not to any individual; and a nation has at all times an inherent indefeasible right to abolish any form of government it finds inconvenient, and establish such as accords with its interest, disposition, and happiness." [15]

Government is never more than an agent of the people who form the nation, and the only sovereignty which Paine will recognize is popular sovereignty. Just as the natural rights of the individual are imprescriptible, so, too, the inherent sovereignty of the nation is imprescriptible. No claim to authority by the holders of power stands against the right of the people to dispossess them and change the form of government. Paine showed no genuine understanding of the doctrine of prescription in government as expounded by Edmund Burke, but he left no doubt about the vehemence with which he rejected it.

All forms of government, at least in large states where direct democracy was impossible, could be classified under two headings: "government by election and representation" and "government by hereditary succession." Hereditary government included monarchy and aristocracy, or that combination of the two which prevailed almost everywhere in Europe in the eighteenth century. Paine's opinion of it can be stated succinctly: "All hereditary government is in its nature tyranny." [16]

It was impossible, Paine said, that hereditary governments, such as had hitherto existed, "could have commenced by any other means than a total violation of every principle, sacred and moral." [17] Not only the origin but the entire history of these governments was a monstrous record of crime. Their major purpose was plunder, called by the gentler name of taxation, and one of their chief means of raising taxes was to engage in continual warfare. Since they were systems of exploitation, they had to rely on fraud, mystification, and induced ignorance to maintain themselves. "Monarchy," said Paine, "is the popery of government; a thing kept up to amuse the ignorant, and quiet them into paying taxes." [18]

But the crimes of monarchical and aristocratic governments did
not constitute their radical fault. Rather it was that hereditary government was slavery by definition, because it deprived a nation of its inherent and imprescriptible right to govern itself through its chosen
representatives. Paine's conclusion was that "there is not a problem in
Euclid more mathematically true than that hereditary government has
not a right to exist." [19]

Representative government, on the other hand, was the only legitimate form of government, because it alone was founded on the inherent
right of the nation to govern itself. But since the nation was a collection
of originally independent individuals who had contracted among themselves to form a government, the ultimate right on which government
was founded was the natural right of every man to govern himself.
Paine drew the logical conclusion from this principle and objected to
the establishment of property qualifications on the right to vote for
representatives. "To take away this right," he said, "is to reduce a man to
slavery, for slavery consists in being subject to the will of another, and he
that has not a vote in the election of representatives is in this case." [20]
Representation must be accorded to everyone on the principle of one
man, one vote. In that way everyone's rights would be equally protected,
and that, after all, was the whole purpose of government.

If every citizen's equal right to representation were respected, Paine
professed to be indifferent about the particular form which the constitution assumed. The government would operate on the principle of majority rule, of course. The legislature, as the elected representative body,
would be supreme. The executive—a term which Paine disliked—would
have no function but to administer the laws made by the people through
their representatives; it certainly would not act as an independent force
in the state. But the best way of constructing and combining the several
organs of the government was a matter of opinion and in any case
was subject to revision in the light of experience.

What was essential was a republican government based upon a
large and equal representation. Under such a government men would
govern themselves in their own interest. Then there would be no com-
plaints about high taxes, for only such taxes would be levied as commended themselves to the reason of the nation. Nor would a republic
squander its treasure in wars, because its government would have no
interest distinct from the nation's interest. The people of the nation
would not of themselves be inclined to war. "Man is not the enemy of
man, but through the medium of a false system of government." [21] The
true system of government thus operated to reduce or abolish two major

social evils, war and the poverty caused by excessive taxation and exploitation.

Paine hoped that war could be abolished or at least sharply reduced as a feature of international relations. If England would accept the principles of the French Revolution, the two nations together could reform the rest of Europe. An end to the causes of war could then be reasonably expected. "When all the governments of Europe shall be established on the representative system, nations will become acquainted, and the animosities and prejudices fomented by the intrigues and artifices of courts will cease." [22] The combined English, French, and Dutch fleets would be able to enforce a general naval disarmament and reduce navies to perhaps a tenth of their present strength. An alliance of these three powers, which the United States would gladly join, could also force the end of Spanish rule in South America and put a stop to the Algerine piracy.

The other great social evil against which Paine inveighed was poverty, which he blamed on the high taxation and other unjust policies of monarchy and aristocracy. A son of the poor himself, Paine had a sincere and passionate hatred of the poverty he saw all about him in Europe. This hatred led him to propose a strong and positive governmental program for the abolition of poverty.

Paine assumed that if government were conducted without civil or military extravagance (as it would be in a representative republic), there would be a large surplus arising from taxation at the prevailing, or even at reduced, rates. Part of this surplus could be disposed of by abolishing the poor rates, namely the tax on householders for the relief of the poor. The rest of the surplus could be used to prevent the poverty that required relief. This would be accomplished by giving the poor what today would be called marriage, maternity, and funeral grants, family allowances, old-age pensions, and a crude form of unemployment relief. Accompanying this social security plan would be a progressive tax on the income of estates, designed to redistribute property by inducing families to break up estates instead of maintaining them through the law of primogeniture. A national fund would also be raised by an inheritance tax on estates, out of which all young people would be given a modest capital to start them in life on arriving at the age of twenty-one.

It is not necessary to accuse Paine of inconsistency with his fundamental principles in making these proposals. Government, on his principles, exists only to secure individual rights. But if one emphasizes the equality of the rights to be secured, then it follows that government has a positive function to perform. Still, it is striking that Paine, who proclaimed that government was "no farther necessary than to supply the few cases to which society and civilization are not conveniently competent," should almost in the same breath have revealed himself as a prophet of the modern welfare state.

Paine, of course, was not the first or the last to minimize and maximize the function of government at one and the same time. Behind such theories there is usually the doctrine of the natural harmony of interests and of a single, sovereign popular will which embodies and expresses that harmony. Government will have much to do until the popular will is executed, over the opposition of the wicked and the ignorant, but thereafter society will largely govern itself. As Paine said, the American and French revolutions had shown "that the greatest forces that can be brought into the field of revolutions, are reason and common interest. Where these can have the opportunity of acting, opposition dies with fear, or crumbles away by conviction." [23] In other words, democratic government, when it is truly democratic and completely responsive to the will of the people, really is not government at all.

## NOTES

1. *The Complete Writings of Thomas Paine*, ed. Philip S. Foner (2 vols.; New York: Citadel Press, 1945), I, 359.

2. *Ibid.*, I, 449.
3. *Ibid.*, II, 571.
4. *Ibid.*, I, 353.
5. *Ibid.*, p. 4.
6. *Ibid.*, p. 358.
7. *Ibid.*, pp. 357–58.
8. *Ibid.*, pp. 359–61. Italics original.
9. *Ibid.*, p. 359.
10. *Ibid.*, p. 388.

11. *Ibid.*, p. 275.
12. *Ibid.*, p. 276.
13. *Ibid.*
14. *Ibid.*, p. 278. Italics original.
15. *Ibid.*, p. 341.
16. *Ibid.*, p. 364.
17. *Ibid.*, p. 361.
18. *Ibid.*, p. 375.
19. *Ibid.*, II, 572.
20. *Ibid.*, p. 579.
21. *Ibid.*, I, 343.
22. *Ibid.*, p. 449.
23. *Ibid.*, p. 446.

## READINGS

A.   Paine, Thomas. *Rights of Man.*
B.   Paine, Thomas. *Common Sense.*
     Paine, Thomas. *Agrarian Justice.*
     Paine, Thomas. *Dissertation on First Principles of Government.*

# EDMUND BURKE

## 1729–1797

Edmund Burke was a member of the British House of Commons for
almost thirty years. Because of his occupation, and also because of his
native cast of mind, he did not present his political philosophy in an
organized way in any formal treatise. The student must pick Burke's
philosophy out of the large number of pamphlets, speeches, letters, and
polemical tracts which poured from the prolific pen of this unusually
gifted practicing politician. Almost everything Burke wrote on politics
refers to an immediate issue of his day. The American colonial crisis,
British rule in Ireland and in India, and the French Revolution were
among the principal ones. To summarize Burke's political thought in a
series of abstract propositions, therefore, is inevitably to distort the
perspective in which he originally expressed it. Brevity, however, requires the distortion.

Burke made his nearest approach to a formal political theory in
answer to the radical ideology associated with the French Revolution.
His opponents, of whom Thomas Paine was one and Rousseau another,
argued their case against the ancient and established order of Europe
on the basis of the natural and imprescriptible rights of men. But
Burke's defense of the old order did not entail a simple rejection of the
idea of nature as a norm for the social life of men. His position is more
subtle than a mere substitution of convention and history for nature as
the fundamental principle of political thought. Burke argued rather that
human nature can realize itself only in history and through conventional institutions. An explanation of this statement will develop into
an exposition of most of the characteristic features of Burke's political
philosophy.

The classical political tradition saw politics as an extension or subdivision of morals. Morals in turn were founded in nature. Burke remained within this tradition. "The principles of true politics," he said, "are those of morality enlarged." [1] To put it in other terms, politics for him were a means of satisfying the needs of human nature.

But for Burke human nature was the nature of men as they actually existed, and not the abstraction called "man in the state of nature" by the theorists of the social-compact school. "It is with man in the concrete;—it is with common human life, and human actions, you are to be concerned," as he once told a correspondent.[2] He felt that the needs of actually existing men were expressed originally and best through their spontaneous affections. He therefore had a deep faith in "natural sentiment" as the standard of sound judgment in morals and politics. In consequence, he habitually approached political problems with an attitude of mind which he once described as "so much trust in the inclinations and prejudices of mankind, and so little in any thing else." [3]

He did not believe, in the manner of Rousseau, that the first motions of nature are always right. Burke was quite aware of evil and perverted passion. But he did believe that human nature has a definite ontological structure, and that this structure is dynamic. Nature, that is, tends by its own inner orientation toward virtue. The moral virtues are not merely conventionally approved ways of acting. Neither are they habits imposed on men entirely from without by social conditioning. There are in men certain instinctive inclinations toward moral good which are the natural wellsprings of the virtues. And so "the wise legislators of all countries [have] aimed at improving instincts into morals, and at grafting the virtues on the stock of the natural affections." [4] Some examples of what Burke regarded as moral instincts are the religious sense, the love of kindred, and "the natural taste and relish of equity and justice."

But although Burke considered that the standards of right conduct are rooted in the affective and nonrational side of human nature, he did not take that part of man as by itself an adequate guide to moral action. Reason, too, has an essential role to play. "We are all of us made to shun disgrace, as we are made to shrink from pain, and poverty, and disease. It is an instinct; and under the direction of reason, instinct is always in the right." [5] The relation between natural feeling and reason may be stated in the following terms. The function of natural affection is to express and manifest the basic needs of human nature. But it is for reason to recognize the true structure of human values in and through the affective expression of needs. It is this structure which is then translated into the rational dictates of moral law.

Natural sentiment, moreover, is not the feeling of a nonexistent "natural man" abstracted from any historical and social context. Human nature always exists along with and by means of a "second nature" which situates men in time and space. "Man in his moral nature," Burke said, "becomes, in his progress through life, a creature of prejudice—a creature of opinions—a creature of habits, and of sentiments growing out of them. These form our second nature, as inhabitants of the country and members of the society in which Providence has placed us." [6] Prejudice and opinion, habit and acquired sentiment are, so to speak, the necessary vesture of man as a social being.

For society is held together by stronger bonds than laws and force. Governments are obeyed and laws observed in the long run because men think it right to submit to them. The true "cementing principle in the fabric of government" is opinion. Indeed, the whole system of institutions, manners, morals, and beliefs which was the Christian civilization of Europe was a structure of opinion, in Burke's sense of the term.

Opinion for him was a generic name for the habits of thought and feeling which sustain civilized society and its culture. Men are rational beings: Burke never denied that. But no one lives wholly on the rational convictions which he has worked out for himself. Most men indeed have comparatively few such convictions. Men live by and large on their prepossessions of mind and heart. A good society, such as Burke believed Europe, and Britain in particular, to be, is one which has a large fund of sound inherited opinion. In defiance of the philosophers of the Enlightenment, Burke chose to defend this traditional wisdom under the name of prejudice.

The issue between Burke and the Enlightenment was not, however, that between blind belief and reason. At least as Burke saw it, the issue was rather between intellectual individualism and social reason. He charged his opponents with contemning the accumulated wisdom of the past because of an overweening confidence in their own wisdom, which they dignified as "reason." But the British people, he said, took a contrary view. "We are afraid to put men to live and trade each on his own private stock of reason; because we suspect that the stock in each man is small, and that the individuals would do better to avail themselves of the general bank and capital of nations and of ages." [7]

Burke, in other words, brought the dimension of time into political thought. "The march of the human mind is slow," he said. The mind's constitution is such that it does not reason reliably about society and politics in the abstract. Time is needed for the achievement of political wisdom, time and the long experience of successive generations. "For man is a most unwise, and a most wise being. The individual is foolish.

The multitude, for the moment, is foolish, when they act without deliberation; but the species is wise, and when time is given to it, as a species it almost always acts right." [8]

Burke therefore found himself in the peculiar position of a political theorist who mistrusted political theory. He admitted that in certain moments of deep crisis in a society's history—1688 was one such in Great Britain—it was necessary to raise and answer theoretical questions about the constitutive principles of the state. But such questions should be avoided if possible. Criticism of specific social abuses accompanied by specific proposals for reform was useful, but needlessly to agitate fundamental questions of political theory had the effect of shaking popular faith in the wisdom and goodness of basic institutions. Such speculation was not a sign of a bold and praiseworthy freedom of thought. Rather it manifested "a certain intemperance of intellect" which was "the disease of the time, and the source of all its other diseases." [9]

Yet Burke felt himself obliged to advance a countertheory to the wave of radical ideology set in motion by the French Revolution. In his writings of the revolutionary period, rambling and rhetorical though they are, we find a fairly well developed theory of the nature and purpose of civil society.

Burke viewed civil society as an artificial or conventional structure which was man's natural milieu. He said:

The state of civil society . . . is a state of nature; and much more truly so than a savage and incoherent mode of life. For man is by nature reasonable; and he is never perfectly in his natural state, but when he is placed where reason may be best cultivated, and most predominates. Art is man's nature. We are as much, at least, in a state of nature in formed manhood, as in immature and helpless infancy.[10]

This passage clearly echoes the argument by which Aristotle sought to show that the state is natural. Man is intended by nature to develop into a completely rational animal, for reason is the specifically human attribute. But human reason can be brought to its proper development only in an organized political community. Civil society therefore is the natural state of man, because it is the condition in which "reason may be best cultivated and most predominates."

Burke's conception of the nature of man and society thus implies the notion of intellectual and moral perfection as a natural end or goal. Civil society, according to Burke, "is a partnership in all science; a partnership in all art; a partnership in every virtue; and in all perfection." [11] Society has a purpose, and that purpose is nothing less than

the natural perfection of man. This teleological way of thinking manifests itself throughout Burke's social and political thought.

Civil society, however, is natural only in the sense of being formed
in response to a natural need and for the attainment of a natural purpose. In that sense, too, it is willed by God: "He who gave our nature
to be perfected by our virtue, willed also the necessary means of its
perfection—He willed therefore the state." [12] But in itself civil society
is a product of convention. That is, it is a construct of human minds
and wills, a thing which men make for themselves. "In a state of *rude*
nature," Burke explained, "there is no such thing as a people. A number
of men in themselves have no collective capacity. It is wholly artificial;
and made like all other legal fictions by common agreement." [13]

Burke therefore denied that the natural rights of men, by themselves, furnish an adequate standard for determining the rights of men
in society. Since civil society is "wholly artificial," the rights of civil,
social man are a question of social utility as well as of abstract truth. The
correct answer to the question of the rights which men ought to enjoy
in society has to be worked out by experience and practical reasoning. It
is not enough to analyze the concept of the abstract individual in a prepolitical state of nature in order to know what rights properly belong to
men in historically existing societies.

The idea of the state of nature had been designed by the social
contract theorists in order to assert rights in the abstract and independently of the conventional framework of society. In this way it was hoped
to make certain basic claims sacrosanct and to protect them from impair-
ment by government. Burke's purpose in attacking "natural rights"
was not to deny that human beings have claims which even the most
powerful governments must respect. Nor did he deny that men once
had enjoyed original rights in a state of nature. He did insist, however,
that the abstract and absolute quality of original rights was necessarily
lost when men entered civil society.

"These metaphysic rights," he said, "entering into common life,
like rays of light which pierce into a dense medium, are, by the laws of
nature, refracted from their straight line." [14] Men did not cease to have
natural rights by submitting to civil authority. But their claims to
life, liberty, and property now have to be realized in artificial and conventional forms. Burke certainly did not believe, for example, that the
right to own property is a legal fiction which the state has created and
may destroy. But this original and natural right is meaningless and ineffective unless a conventional body of property law is established by
society. Yet the creation of a conventional form for men's rights neces-

sarily means that original rights must be divested of their absolute character and be subjected to modification by social authority.

The rights of men in society, therefore, are not properly the objects of the abstract and speculative sort of reasoning appropriate to metaphysics and mathematics. "The rights of men in governments are their advantages; and these are often in balances between differences of good; in compromises sometimes between good and evil, and sometimes between evil and evil. Political reason is a computing principle; adding, subtracting, multiplying, and dividing, morally and not metaphysically or mathematically, true moral denominations." [15]

Politics have their own proper kind of reasoning, which is concrete and practical. This is the true meaning of Burke's frequent denunciations of "theory," "metaphysics," and "speculation." He did not wish to imply that political problems can be intelligently handled "without the guide and light of sound well-understood principles." But although principles are necessary, they are not enough. They must be applied to concrete reality by a type of practical reasoning which Burke called prudence.

Burke saw clearly that the prudential judgments which are the substance of statesmanship are not concerned primarily with truth as such. The object of the statesman's thought is rather the *good* of his country. But the statesman is not concerned with the good in its abstract and necessary aspects, as is the philosopher. Political judgments aim at the good of an existing community as achievable in real situations, for the statesman does not take thought simply in order to *know,* but in order to *act.* Therefore he thinks only about situations and objectives in regard to which he *can* act.

The good which is the object of prudential consideration is therefore always a concrete good. It is conditioned by a nation's past and is highly contingent upon a multitude of present circumstances. Usually it is complex and related to many other goods which also contribute to the welfare of the community and must be the object of the statesman's solicitude. Finally, social and political good is inherently imperfect. The perfect and ideal state of human affairs is realizable only in utopia; and utopia, of course, means nowhere.

It follows that political reasoning seldom arrives at the certain and demonstrable conclusions which are sought for by the sciences. There are rules of political prudence, to be sure, but they "can rarely be exact; never universal." They are not the product either of precise scientific analysis or of strict logical deduction. The canons of practical political wisdom are derived from a knowledge of history and from long experience. But no amount of knowledge and experience provides infallible answers to practical questions. Sound decision demands a "constant vigilance and attention to the train of things as they successively emerge." The statesman must take into account all the factors relevant to a problem. To do this, he must be willing to consult with other men; and he must be willing to compromise. Even then he cannot be certain in advance that his decision will achieve its goal. For there is an "unavoidable uncertainty, as to the effect, which attends on every measure of human prudence."

Burke, it is evident, had a keen awareness of the relativity that affects all things human. Yet it would be wrong to assume that he was a relativist in the philosophical or moral sense. On the contrary, his political thought presupposed the doctrine of natural law which had come down through the Anglican tradition from the Middle Ages. This natural law, as Burke understood it, states an order of ends or goals, derived from human nature as created by God. The principles of natural law command the actions necessary to the attainment of those ends and forbid actions contrary to them. There are thus certain fundamental principles ruling the realm of political judgment and action. The function of "prudence" is not to waive but to apply the principles to the requirements of action in concrete situations.

The farther one goes into the field of social and political relations, the greater is the number of contingent factors that have to be taken into account in order to arrive at a sound decision. To grasp all these factors, to perceive their practical significance, to arrange them into a coherent and intelligent pattern of action: that is the work which prudence alone can do. It is prudence therefore which gives political reasoning its peculiar character and distinguishes it from abstract and speculative thought.

This conception of prudence and practical reason is the root of the peculiarly Burkean approach to politics. It was his understanding of the nature of the practical that led Burke to reject the proposition that the right order of society can be deduced from first principles. His awareness of the element of contingency in all concrete and existing reality made him insist that human values are realizable only in historically conditioned forms.

Burke conceived of men's rights and liberties as concrete parts of an actual social order on which their existence depended. Rights have meaning and effect only when they exist in a society structured by rank and property, ordered by law, and supported by long-standing sentiments and prejudices. In Burke's social philosophy, therefore, the idea of order is primary, while that of liberty is secondary and functional.

The social order evolves through history, but not aimlessly. If it

is a sound order, it conforms to a basic pattern which is set by the true
needs of human nature. Thus, for example, social inequality is natural
and necessary. Men divide naturally into various ranks and classes,
among which will be a ruling class. "In all societies, consisting of various
descriptions of citizens, some description must be uppermost." [16] Civil
society necessarily generates a "natural aristocracy" of men who by
native ability, education, wealth, and even inherited rank, are properly
qualified to rule. Egalitarianism, which would deny the presumption in
favor of rule by this class, is a crime, not so much against them as against
society.

The aristocracy is the bulwark of liberty, protecting society against
both monarchical despotism and popular tyranny. The possession of
large amounts of stable property enables the aristocracy to withstand
pressures that might upset the balance of the constitution and destroy
social, ordered freedom. Burke felt that gentle birth and entailed estates
normally ensured the sort of breeding and education which fitted men
to govern the state for the good of the community. But more than that,
the possession of that kind of property bred in a whole class of men a
temper which was the surest guarantee of a free, just, and stable social
order.

In like manner he upheld the institution of kingship for the sake
of "those principles of property, order, and regularity, for which alone
any rational man can wish monarchy to exist." Kings existed for the
established order, and not it for them. Their function was to defend the
people against the great, and the great against the people; to keep
things in their accustomed order and place; and to preserve in everything a due balance and equal justice.

The people, however, must not be left to the good will alone of
kings and aristocrats for their protection. Free citizens "in order to secure
their freedom . . . must enjoy some determinate portion of power."
Burke's idea of a sound social order was not that of a monolith, but of
a mixed and balanced constitution, in which the several parts of the
state checked and restrained each other. In expounding this idea he was,
of course, defending the British constitution as he knew it.

Of the British frame of government Burke said that it was "a prescriptive constitution; it is a constitution whose sole authority is, that it
has existed time out of mind." [17] He spoke these words in the course of
an attack on the natural-rights school. The basic issue between Burke
and that school of thought was the question of legitimacy. Whence came
the authority of the constitution and the right of government to rule?

The sole legitimate source of authority, said the partisans of natural
rights, was the free consent of the individual members of society.

Burke summarized their argument in these words: "they lay it down, that every man ought to govern himself, and that where he cannot go himself he must send his representative; that all other government is usurpation, and is so far from having a claim to our obedience, it is not only our right, but our duty, to resist it." [18] The only legitimate form of government, from this point of view, was direct democracy, or where that was not possible, representative government based on universal manhood suffrage.

On his part Burke simply denied that the original right of man in the state of nature to govern himself constituted a title to a share in the government of civil society. By the act of entering civil society and becoming part of an organized community, man "abdicates all right to be his own governour."

The necessary structure of a civil constitution therefore cannot be deduced from the original rights of men in the state of nature. "The moment you abate any thing from the full right of men, each to govern himself, from that moment the whole organization of government becomes a consideration of convenience." [19] A constitution is a convention, not the conclusion of a syllogism. The particular form taken by the constitution is not imposed by the natural order of society but is left to the community to determine according to its needs.

But as we have seen, Burke maintained that the British constitution rested on "prescription." This term, which he took from the law of real property, means ancient and unquestioned possession. He did not say that old institutions must be preserved merely because they are old. His argument rather was that, just as the undisputed possession of property over a long period of time is accepted in law as a valid title of ownership, so also with the possession of authority. That the constitution has been in existence for generations is sufficient proof of its legitimacy. No argument from the natural right of the individual to share in authority prevails against the valid claim of the established constitution on the obedience of British subjects.

Burke's meaning may perhaps be clarified by a parallel drawn with the American Constitution. Our Constitution is regarded in law as an act of the people. In 1789 it was in some meaningful sense an expression of the people's will. Yet the Constitution is binding on us today, who have never had the chance to vote on it. It may be said that we can change the Constitution, and that our failure to do so, except in certain details, is tantamount to an acceptance of the document as our supreme law. That is true. But it is also true that the American people of today can change the Constitution only through an amending process which is laid down in the Constitution itself. No other mode of change is valid, even for purposes clearly desired by a majority of the people. (In fact, amendments can easily be blocked by strategically located minorities.) We remain bound by the law established by our ancestors, even though not absolutely bound.

But why must we respect the will of past generations? Burke's answer was that prescription "is a part of the law of nature." The convention which is a society's constitution, once it is made, binds that society. It creates obligations which the members of the society are not free to throw off at will. Civil society is a public order created by men to satisfy their social needs. But because those needs spring from human nature, men's obligation to live by their constitution and to obey the government established under it is a natural moral obligation.

Furthermore, this obligation is passed on to succeeding generations without any formal act of consent on their part. A child is subject to his parents, although he did not ask to be born, because the natural order of the family (and his own needs) require his obedience to parental authority. In like manner, each new generation born into a civilized society finds a constitution and a government in possession. That possession passes for a title to obedience. If civil society is a necessity of human nature, so also is governmental authority. The existing constitution gives that authority concrete form. The law of human nature itself therefore prescribes that the constitution be obeyed until it is legitimately changed.

Yet the doctrine of prescription is not opposed to the principle of government by consent of the governed. As Burke said, prescription

is accompanied with another ground of authority in the constitution of the human mind, presumption. It is a presumption in favour of any settled scheme of government against any untried project, that a nation has long existed and flourished under it. It is a better presumption, even of the *choice* of a nation, far better than any sudden and temporary arrangement by actual election. Because a nation is not an idea only of local extent, and individual momentary aggregation, but it is an idea of continuity, which extends in time as well as in numbers, and in space. And this is a choice, not of one day, or one set of people, not a tumultuary and giddy choice; it is a deliberate election of ages and of generations; it is a constitution made by what is ten thousand times better than choice; it is made by the peculiar circumstances, occasions, tempers, dispositions, and moral, civil, and social habitudes of the people, which disclose themselves only in a long space of time.[20]

As authority is transmitted from generation to generation by prescription, so are rights passed on by inheritance. It was the "uniform policy" of the British constitution, according to Burke, to regard the liberties of the people "as an *entailed inheritance* derived to us from our forefathers, and to be transmitted to our posterity; as an estate specially belonging to the people of this kingdom, without any reference whatever to any other more general or prior right." [21]

These words should not be taken as a rejection of the proposition that men ought to enjoy certain rights in virtue of their nature as human beings. It is true that in this passage we encounter an important obscurity in Burke's thought. Here and in a few other places he seems to assert the independence of social tradition from considerations of natural right. But if we are to understand his words in the whole context of his thought, it is better to interpret them otherwise. Burke's meaning would seem to be that rights must be incorporated into a social framework to be practically effective, and that the "natural" way of preserving such socially embodied rights is to regard them as carried and guaranteed by tradition.

Burke touched here on a characteristic feature of the British legal system. The common law of England was formed by judges who applied their notions of natural justice to the decision of cases as they arose. In this manner a body of "case law" gradually came into being. Once this body of law was considered to be a complete system, adequate to the solution of any new problems that might arise, it became the policy of the constitution not to appeal directly to natural justice, but to precedents. Norms of natural justice still affected the decision of cases, as in any humane legal system they must. But these norms were now canons of interpretation of a formed body of law. By the evolution of the common law natural justice was not ignored, or abolished, or superseded. Rather it was embodied in a system of customary and judge-made law, which became the supreme law of the land. This embodiment of natural standards of justice in conventional forms is the inevitable effect of the development of a society in history. It is this notion which lies behind Burke's doctrine of prescriptive authority and inherited rights.

It is one thing, however, to look upon tradition as the vehicle of justice. It is another thing to take it for the ultimate standard of justice. Burke was aware of the latter view and considered it a fallacy. "*Precedents,*" he said, "merely as such cannot make Law—because then the very frequency of Crimes would become an argument of innocence." [22] In the last analysis, tradition must be subject to norms outside of and higher than itself.

What is the touchstone by which even the constitutional tradition can be tested? It is the welfare of the people, for this is the purpose of all government. Burke always maintained that "the freedom and safety of the subject" is "the origin and cause of all Laws." By the end of his life, as is well known, he had become most reluctant to say anything that might seem to justify revolutionary movements. Yet even in this, his most conservative period, he stated his position in these terms: "The sovereign's rights are undoubtedly sacred rights ... because exercised for the benefit of the people, and in subordination to that great end for which alone God has vested power in any man or set of men." [23]

Government therefore is a trust conferred by the people, for their own benefit, upon their rulers. For "although government certainly is an institution of divine authority, yet its forms, and the persons who administer it, all originate from the people." [24] It follows that all political power is by its nature limited power. Even despotism, "if it means any thing, that is at all defensible," is subject to "the primeval, indefeasible, unalterable law of nature, and of nations; and if no magistracies control its exertions, those exertions must derive their limitations and direction either from the equity and moderation of the ruler, or from down-right revolt on the part of the subject by rebellion, divested of all its criminal qualities." [25]

It is clear, then, that Burke recognized the ultimate right of the people to rebel against oppressive government. His position on this point underwent modification but not substantial change as he grew older. "Governments must be abused and deranged indeed," he wrote in 1790, "before [revolution] can be thought of; and the prospect of the future must be as bad as the experience of the past." [26] But to the end of his days Burke admitted that, given the proper circumstances, a government might rightfully be overthrown.

He was, after all, committed to the principle that governments derive their just powers from the consent of the governed. As he once put it, "in all forms of Government the people is the true Legislator; and whether the immediate and instrumental cause of the Law be a single person, or many, the remote and efficient cause is the consent of the people, either actual or implied; and such consent is absolutely essential to its validity." [27] The difference between Burke and the advocates of popular sovereignty thus was not over the question whether political power originated from the people and was to be exercised for their welfare. The point at issue rather was the meaning of "the people."

The people, for Burke, were not a collection of individuals, but an organized entity. There was, however, nothing totalitarian in this concept. Answering his own question, what is the standard of political expediency, Burke said: "Expedience is that which is good for the community, and good for every individual in it." [28] But although the welfare of the community is not something alien or opposed to the needs of individuals, the community itself is something more than a sum total of individuals. The idea of a people is that of a structured whole acting for its common good through differentiated organs.

The people as a political agent therefore are not either disparate individuals or the masses. It is the organized community which acts politically. Different phases of political action are performed by distinct organs of the state, according to their competence in relation to the communal good. Disregarding the argument that every man had, as such, the right to vote, Burke judged claims to share in the government of the state in the light of the claimant's ability to contribute to the proper solution of society's problems. By this standard he found most men wanting.

The great bulk of men, in Burke's opinion, were politically incapable. "God and nature never made them to think or act without guidance and direction." [29] Government was for their benefit, and therefore their grievances should be listened to and remedied. "But for the *real cause* [of their distress], or the appropriate remedy, they ought never to be called into council about the one or the other." [30] Sound public policy, such as would achieve the people's true good, must be framed "by those, who by their rank and fortune in the country, by the goodness of their characters, and their experience in their affairs, are their natural leaders." [31]

Yet Burke's theory of government was not one of unmitigated aristocracy. Although he assigned a passive role to the mass of the people, he recognized a "British public" which had an active part to play as the generator of public opinion. This class included "those of adult age, not declining in life, of tolerable leisure for [political] discussions, and of some means of information, more or less, and who are above menial dependence." Burke reckoned that there might be 400,000 such persons in England and Scotland together. Only they "in any political view, are to be called the people." [32] Under the haphazard system of representation in the unreformed (pre-1832) House of Commons, however, not all of the people, even in this restricted sense, composed the electorate.

The authority of the state was wielded by the king, lords, and commons. All three organs of state derived their power from the people and governed for the people, but in different ways. The king embodied the majesty of all the people collected to a center, and was that disinterested power in the constitution which was to arbitrate between the jarring interests of the parts. The lords personified the great hereditary masses of property. It was the duty of the commons to represent the people before the crown. This house alone therefore was an organ of public opinion.

The House of Commons nonetheless was not a mere sounding board for public opinion. The house was certainly to listen to the opinions and wishes of its constituents. But it could not be instructed by them "with absolute authority." For the house was a constitutional organ with a deliberative function, and its members were meant to exercise their judgment on public problems, not to be "canvassers at a perpetual election."

Even though positive law lacks validity without the consent of the people, in a representative form of government the people are not the immediate authors of law. Lawmaking is the proper function of the duly constituted legislature, whose enactments are understood to enjoy the consent of the people until the contrary is clearly established. "The people," Burke said, "are presumed to consent to whatever the Legislature ordains for their benefit; and they are to acquiesce in it, though they do not clearly see into the propriety of the means, by which they are conducted to that desirable end. This they owe as an act of homage and just deference to a reason, which the necessity of Government has made superior to their own." [33]

Furthermore, the individual members of a nation's legislature should not consider themselves primarily as delegates of their local constituents, but as representatives of the nation and the national interest. As Burke explained to his constituents in Bristol in 1774,

Parliament is not a *congress* of ambassadors from different and hostile interests; which interests each must maintain, as an agent and advocate, against other agents and advocates; but parliament is a *deliberative* assembly of *one* nation, with *one* interest, that of the whole; where, not local purposes, not local prejudices ought to guide, but the general good, resulting from the general reason of the whole. You choose a member indeed; but when you have chosen him, he is not a member of Bristol, but he is a member of *parliament*. If the local constituent should have an interest, or should form an hasty opinion, evidently opposite to the real good of the rest of the community, the member for that place ought to be as far, as any other, from any endeavour to give it effect. [34]

The primacy of the national interest determines the relationship that ought to exist between the representative and his constituents. In a clash between his personal interests and theirs, obviously theirs should prevail. But the constituents cannot bind their representative to subordinate his views to theirs on questions of national policy. He is present at the center where the problems of the nation are discussed in national terms. To require him to follow instructions from his constituents, who are less informed than he, would be a sin against reason. As Burke told the men who had elected him, their representative owed them "high respect," but "his unbiassed opinion, his mature judgment, his enlightened conscience, he ought not to sacrifice to you; to any man, or to any set of men living." [35]

The tone of this last statement did not mean that Burke proposed to maintain an Olympian aloofness from the views and interests of other men in Parliament. He had entered politics as the secretary of the Marquis of Rockingham, who was the leader of one of the Whig factions. In his service Burke evolved one of the earliest theories of parliamentary party politics and strove to rid the notion of party of its factional and unpatriotic connotations. In his famous definition, a party "is a body of men united, for promoting by their joint endeavours the national interest, upon some particular principle in which they are all agreed." [36]

The body of men which Burke had in mind was not the mass political party of today. It was instead a small group of noble lords and commoners who worked together in Parliament for the effectuation of certain policies and, of course, sought the power that was necessary to carry out the policies. Some degree of union, and some subordination of the led to the leaders, was manifestly required among them if they were to act as a group. To this Burke had no objection. He told Lord Rockingham's successor, Earl Fitzwilliam, "You ought never to recommend a Member for [election in] any place in which you have an influence who will not take your general Line, both as to persons and things." [37] Holding the views he did on prudence and the exigencies of practical politics, Burke found no great difficulty in being a party man.

He found cooperation in Parliament with the people's "natural leaders" all the more easy because, as we have seen, he did not consider it a representative's duty to do the will of his constituents. A member of Parliament represented the people and was bound to serve their interests. But the people whom he represented were not solely or even primarily those who had elected him, but the people of Great Britain. By far the greater part of the British people, to be sure, were not members of the electorate at all. But that made little difference, according to Burke, for they were represented in Parliament by what was called "virtual representation."

In Burke's theory of representative government, the franchise of voting could not be grounded on any abstract or "speculative" right. Nor was the denial of the franchise in itself a real, but only a speculative, grievance. The purpose of voting, he felt, was not the assertion of one's individual will but the remedy of real wrongs and the protection of real interests. Unless a group of men could point to concrete hardships which they suffered because they lacked the franchise, Burke conceded them no right to it. They were "virtually" represented in Parliament, and that was enough for them.

But what is virtual representation? "Virtual representation is that in which there is a communion of interests, and a sympathy in feelings and desires between those who act in the name of any description of people, and the people in whose name they act, though the trustees are not actually chosen by them." [38] It made no practical difference that not all the people of a constituency had the right to vote, if their member of Parliament had the interests of all of them at heart. Nor did it matter that some areas were much underrepresented in proportion to their population. "You have an equal representation," Burke told them, "because you have men equally interested in the prosperity of the whole, who are involved in the general interest and the general sympathy." [39]

Virtual representation, however, cannot exist "without a substratum in the actual. The members must have some relation to the constituent." [40] Burke's theory, in other words, supposed a community reasonably homogeneous in its interests. Given such a community, an electorate which was in effect a random sample of the population could choose a legislature which would adequately represent the interests of the whole. But where this condition did not exist, there could be no virtual representation. That is why in 1775 Burke laughed at the notion that the Americans were virtually represented at Westminister. The American colonies were too remote in distance to be in any real sense a part of the community represented by the British House of Commons. For a similar reason he insisted that the Irish Catholics could not be considered as represented in the Irish Parliament until they voted directly for some of its members.

Some of the people represented, then, must vote. How many of them? Enough of them to ensure that the real interests of all of them have a voice and are adequately cared for. Burke could say nothing more definite than that. Representation was a practical device for achieving certain practical goals and should be judged by no other standard. By this standard, in his opinion, "our representation has been found perfectly adequate to all the purposes for which a representation of the people can be desired or devised." [41] To the end of his life, therefore, he opposed all efforts to extend the franchise and equalize the representation in Britain. The system of representation which had come down with scarcely a change from the Middle Ages worked well enough for all practical purposes, and that was reason enough for keeping it just as it was.

Undoubtedly Burke's diehard opposition to parliamentary reform was influenced by the natural-rights ideology in terms of which reform was usually urged. If that ideology were accepted, he feared, much more would follow than that every Englishman had an equal right to be represented in the House of Commons. The whole prescriptive constitution of the kingdom, which the slowly evolving wisdom of generations had fashioned, would have to be abolished. As Thomas Paine made abundantly clear, the necessary consequence of a dogmatic belief in "natural rights" was a doctrinaire republicanism. The contempt for history revealed in this position so revolted Burke's soul that he became a root-and-branch opponent of even the most moderate parliamentary reform.

Yet Burke seems to have been betrayed by his fear of radicalism into a position inconsistent with his own principles. His parliamentary record was that of a supporter of various moderate reforms, so much so that he shocked most of his friends when he first came out against the French Revolution. Even when his opposition to that massive series of changes led him to develop his own counterrevolutionary theory, it was a conservative theory of reform which he proposed. It was not a doctrine of opposition to change as such.

Burke admitted, as an initial premise, that "we must all obey the great law of change." "A state without the means of some change is without the means of its conservation," he said.[42] Even the revered British constitution had "admitted innumerable improvements, either for the correction of the original scheme, or for removing corruptions, or for bringing its principles better to suit those changes, which have successively happened in the circumstances of the nation, or in the manners of the people." The country, he added, "has ever been bettered by such a revision."[43]

It was not change as such that Burke opposed, then, but sudden and, above all, radical change. That constitutions must be altered to remedy old injustices or to meet new situations, he conceded. But it is the part of wisdom "to provide that the change shall proceed by insensible degrees." The good must be preserved in the old as well as realized in the new.

Here again the issue as Burke saw it lay between the "speculative" and utopian ideals deduced from a purely abstract notion of man and the practical requirements of an existing society which sought to serve the needs of men in the concrete. The purpose of reform is to conserve and to extend the concrete advantages which a society has produced in the course of its historical development. To wipe the slate clean and to destroy the labors of ages in the hope of realizing an ideal order of society is not reform but criminal folly.

All true reform, therefore, must begin with an existing social and political order. This order by supposition is deficient and in need of improvement, else there would be no motive for change. Nonetheless the existing order is the indispensable foundation of all reform: "those who would reform a state ought to assume some actual constitution of government which is to be reformed." [44]

The problem of constitutional change, in Burke's eyes, was not simply that of replacing the old with something new and better. The new good must be developed out of the old. The sound parts of the constitution are the agency by which the defective parts are to be healed. Reform, in short, is not revolution. "There is something else than the mere alternative of absolute destruction, or unreformed existence," Burke insisted. "A man full of warm speculative benevolence may wish his society otherwise constituted than he finds it; but a good patriot, and a true politician, always considers how he shall make the most of the existing materials of his country. A disposition to preserve, and an ability to improve, taken together, would be my standard of a statesman." [45]

Sound reform therefore proceeds on "the principle of reference to antiquity." The reforming statesman looks back as well as forward. He strives to understand his society as it has evolved historically and to adjust the new institutions he is creating to the ancient pattern of which they must form a part. The social structure is in constant need of repair but, as Burke put it, "I would make the reparation as nearly as possible in the style of the building." [46] Or, to employ a more exact simile, as the common law develops from precedent to precedent by adapting old norms to new but analogous cases, so should the whole constitution grow and change by following "analogical precedent, authority, and example."

"The nature of man," moreover, "is intricate; the objects of society are of the greatest possible complexity; and therefore no simple disposition or direction of power can be suitable either to man's nature, or to the quality of his affairs." [47] It is consequently impossible to change one element of a vast social structure without affecting and altering many others. Caution therefore is dictated to the reformer. He must be restrained by a healthy awareness that a total reformation of a society's constitution is neither possible nor desirable. "There is," Burke warned, "by the essential fundamental constitution of things, a radical infirmity in all human contrivances; and the weakness is often so attached to the very perfection of our political mechanism, that some defect in it,—something that stops short of its principle,—something that controls, that mitigates, that moderates it,—becomes a necessary corrective to the evils that the theoretic perfection would produce." [48] The perfectionism characteristic of radical reformers is their most dangerous trait because it leads them to disregard the nature of man and society alike.

Burke's vision of man was that of a being "whose prerogative it is, to be in a great degree a creature of his own making." [49] On the other hand, Burke always thought of man as a creature of God "who gave our nature to be perfected by our virtue," and who in giving us our nature "impressed an invariable Law upon it." [50] In the harmony between these two notions, that of man the self-maker and that of man the creature of God, lies the essence of Burke's philosophy. Human nature, which is given by God, realizes itself and achieves its intended perfection through the slow, continuing construction of the vast network of conventions which is civil society.

Burke's philosophy, although it clearly affirms that man is ruled by natural norms, thus makes room for convention and historical evolution. The large part played in Burke's thought by custom, prejudice, prescription, and expediency complements, rather than cancels out, the fundamental notion of a structured human nature oriented by its Creator toward its own perfection. It was the tragedy both of Burke's radical contemporaries and of his historicist successors that where he saw continuity between nature and history, they saw contradiction.

## NOTES

1. Edmund Burke, *Correspondence,* ed. Fitzwilliam and Bourke (4 vols; London, 1844), I, 332. (A new and much more adequate edition of Burke's correspondence is being published by the University of Chicago Press, but since this work is not yet complete, we shall not refer to it here.)

2. *Corr.,* III, 114.

3. *Works,* Rivington Edition (16 vols; London, 1803–27), III, 194.

4. *Ibid.,* VIII, 173.

5. *Ibid.,* p. 47.

6. *Ibid.,* XVI, 117.

7. *Ibid.,* V, 168.

8. *Ibid.,* X, 97.

9. *Ibid.,* VI, 61.

10. *Ibid.,* p. 218.

11. *Ibid.,* V, 184.

12. *Ibid.,* p. 186.

13. *Ibid.,* VI, 210.

14. *Ibid.,* V, 125.

15. *Ibid.,* p. 126.

16. *Ibid.,* p. 104.

17. *Ibid.,* X, 96.

18. *Ibid.,* p. 95.

19. *Ibid.,* V, 123.

20. *Ibid.,* X, 97.

21. *Ibid.,* V, 78.

22. Unpublished MS, Wentworth-Woodhouse Muniments, Sheffield, England.

23. *Works,* XV, 99.

24. *Ibid.,* II, 288.

25. *Ibid.,* XIII, 169.

26. *Ibid.,* V, 73.

27. *Ibid.,* IX, 348.

28. *Ibid.,* X, 100.

29. *Corr.,* II, 72.

30. *Works,* VI, 346.

31. *Corr.,* II, 72.

32. *Works,* VIII, 140.

33. *Ibid.,* IX, 348.
34. *Ibid.,* III, 20.
35. *Ibid.,* p. 18.
36. *Ibid.,* p. 335.
37. Unpublished letter, Wentworth-Woodhouse Muniments, Sheffield, England.
38. *Works,* VI, 360.
39. *Ibid.,* X, 101.
40. *Ibid.,* VI, 360.
41. *Ibid.,* V, 116.
42. *Ibid.,* p. 59.
43. *Ibid.,* IX. 212.
44. *Ibid.,* Vi, 51.
45. *Ibid.,* V, 285.
46. *Ibid.,* p. 436.
47. *Ibid.,* p. 125.
48. *Corr.,* III, 117.
49. *Works,* V, 177.
50. *Ibid.,* IX, 349.

## READINGS

A. Burke, Edmund. *Reflections on the Revolution in France.*
   Burke, Edmund. *An Appeal from the New to the Old Whigs.*
B. Burke, Edmund. *Tracts on the Popery Laws in Ireland.*
   Burke, Edmund. *Thoughts on the Cause of the Present Discontents.*
   Burke, Edmund. *Speech to the Electors of Bristol* (Nov. 3, 1774).
   Burke, Edmund. *Speech on Conciliation with America.*
   Burke, Edmund. *Letter to the Sheriffs of Bristol.*
   Burke, Edmund. *Speech on Economical Reform.*
   Burke, Edmund. *Speech on the Reform of the Representation of the Commons in Parliament* (May 7, 1782).
   Burke, Edmund. *Letter to Sir Hercules Langrishe* (1792).
   Burke, Edmund. *Letter to a Noble Lord.*
   Burke, Edmund. *Four Letters on a Regicide Peace.*

# JEREMY BENTHAM

## 1748–1832

# JAMES MILL

## 1773–1836

Jeremy Bentham was a reformer of law and government rather than a political philosopher in the strict sense of the term. His philosophical views are partly to be gleaned from scattered discussions in works devoted to other subjects and partly to be inferred from his practical proposals. Starting as a critic of existing legal institutions and their philosophical foundations, he eventually turned to the devising of new institutions, both political and legal, based on what he thought was a more adequate philosophy. The implications of his view for the theory of government were worked out by his associate and disciple, James Mill.

## I. BENTHAM

"Nature has placed mankind under the governance of two sovereign masters, *pain* and *pleasure*." These, the opening words of the first chapter of Bentham's *An Introduction to the Principles of Morals and Legislation* (printed 1780), constitute the foundation on which the whole structure of utilitarian political theory is supposed to rest. This principle gives rise to a political theory that is psychologically oriented, placing its emphasis on what human nature is understood to be actually rather than potentially, and in every man everywhere rather than in the changing circumstances and conditions in which various groups of men find themselves. Pain and pleasure not only determine as psychological causes what men do, but also provide the basis on which men are to decide what they ought to do. Understanding happiness to be a life of pleasure and the absence of pain (as far as this is humanly achievable), and unhappiness as a life of pain with the absence of pleasure, Bentham is in a position to state the fundamental principle of moral and political science which he calls the Principle of Utility: "By the principle of utility is meant that principle which approves or disapproves of every action whatsoever, according to the tendency which it appears to have to augment or diminish the happiness of the party whose interest is in question. . . ."[1]

As a principle of moral science, this criterion has reference to the actions of individuals: Those actions are right which promote the happiness (pleasure) of those concerned, and wrong which promote their unhappiness. When applied to political science, it refers to measures of government: Those are right which further the happiness of the community and wrong which further its unhappiness. The community is a fictitious body composed of individuals; the interest of the community is the sum of the interests of the several members who compose it.[2] Since the end of government is the happiness of the community so conceived, this is the only end that legislators ought to have in view.

Bentham proceeds to classify the sources of pleasure and pain, which he finds to be four: physical (from nature, unmodified by human intervention), political (from particular persons chosen to act for the supreme ruling power in the state), moral or popular (from public opinion), and religious (from a superior invisible being).[3] The remaining component of Bentham's theory of morals and legislation that bears directly on his political theory is his calculus of pleasures and pains. According to this construction, pleasures and pains are all homogeneous and thus comparable, and measurable in terms of their intensity, duration, certainty or uncertainty, propinquity or remoteness, fecundity, purity, and extent (number of persons who are affected by them).

This system gives the legislator a technique for determining the utility-value of each of two or more alternative courses of action, that is, the effectiveness of each in promoting happiness. The legislator can then determine which is the correct course of action. This in substance is the philosophical basis of the utilitarian political theory on which Bentham was able to construct constitutions for newly formed states and reform measures for existing states, including his own. Bentham's psychological orientation thus made it possible for him to assume that his theory is valid for all men in all conditions at all times, because government rests simply on human psychology which is identical in all men under all conditions at all times. Circumstances, which for Burke were everything in politics, for Bentham were almost nothing.

In 1776 Bentham published his *A Fragment on Government,* an anonymous criticism of Sir William Blackstone's Introduction to his *Commentaries on the Laws of England.* This work of Bentham's was an effort to clear away the superstitions, errors, and confusions that prevailed in political thought in his time, most of which were found, he thought, in Blackstone's plausible and well-written Introduction.

Blackstone, while rejecting the concepts of a state of nature and a social contract as historical facts, had wished to preserve these notions as expressing the philosophical basis of government and law. Bentham attacks his views on two main grounds: first, he claims that Blackstone is confused in his understanding of natural society, the condition of mankind prior to the existence of civil society; and second, the social contract was an unnecessary and useless fiction.

On the first point, Bentham reformulated the distinction between political society and natural society as a psychological distinction rather than a legal or purely political one. Where there is a habit of obedience to a person or an assemblage of persons of known and certain description, we have a political society. The state of nature is the condition in which there is no such habit and is thus relative to the objects of obedience, *i.e.,* the state of nature exists where any group of adult individuals shows no habit of obedience to a particular individual or individuals. Blackstone had claimed that since the preservation of mankind was at one time the result of the fact that mankind consisted of families living in isolation, there could have been no historical social contract. Bentham sees this stage of social development as natural society which was succeeded by political society when once the required habit of obedience was established.

On the second point, Bentham sees the social contract as a fiction designed to explain the mutual obligations of governor and governed. He argues, however, that it fails in two respects. In the first place, fictions are no longer necessary as the basis for true rights and obligations. The social-contract theory claims that the rights and obligations of governors and governed derive from promises made, the former to govern so as to promote the happiness of their subjects, the latter to obey their governors. The obligation to keep promises is thus the basis of the social contract. If we ask why we must keep promises, Bentham rejects appeals to Right Reason, or Natural Law, or Justice, and says with Hume that the answer is furnished by the principle of utility. Once this is recognized, it can be seen that the social contract is superfluous: we can appeal directly to the principle of utility to justify the rights and obligations of king and subjects. Not only is the social contract an unnecessary addition to the theory in this respect, but it does not help us to solve practical problems, while the principle of utility, so Bentham thought, does.

## II. James Mill

While Bentham's *A Fragment on Government* contains suggestions for a political theory enunciated in the course of an attack on Blackstone, James Mill's *Essay on Government* (1820) is a brief and dogmatic statement of a theory of representative government explicitly based on the principle of utility. He accepts Bentham's psychology and ethics without discussion and applies them to the problem of government.

The end of government is the greatest happiness of the greatest number, and this is to be achieved by organizing and using the power that is found in the community. Since happiness is understood to mean the achievement of the maximum of pleasures and the minimum of pains, and since man labors to secure these ends, the aim of government is to secure "to every man the greatest possible quantity of the produce of his labor." [4] Men unite and "delegate to a small number the power necessary to protect them all. This is government." The problem of government is how to prevent those who are thus given power from abusing that power, *i.e.,* from using it to further their own interest rather than the common interest. Securities for good government are not to be found in any of the traditionally distinguished forms of government. Democracy, rule by the many, is incapable of carrying on the business of government. The "Aristocratical" form of government (rule by a few) and the "Monarchical" (rule by one) tend to develop an opposition between the interest of the government and the interest of the governed. Given human nature as it is (each man desires the maximum of happiness for himself), none of the traditional forms of government is satisfactory. Nor is the union of the three forms, as was proposed by the defenders of the idea of a mixed constitution, a satisfactory solution. Mill claims that the achievement of a balance is impossible in practice. In the long run one of the elements would be bound to predominate and eliminate the other two, and the subjects would be left with no security for good government.

Mill thus sees the problem of establishing good government in the following terms: The people themselves cannot govern. They cannot entrust the government to one man or to a group of men because their interests are only protected when they protect them themselves. Hence the possibility of good government depends on finding a way in which some may govern while the people can check the governors. Recognizing that the people themselves, just as they cannot govern, cannot check the governors, Mill claims to find the solution in having the people elect representatives who are to check the governors. He asserts that the system of representation is "the grand discovery of modern times" and "the solution of all the difficulties, both speculative and practical. . . ." [5]

Having established that on his terms good government is possible, Mill has still to show what conditions it must satisfy to achieve its purpose. He sees two further problems. First, how much power must the checking body possess? To this question he gives a merely tautological answer, namely, sufficient power to perform its function, *i.e.,* sufficient power to overcome the power of those who have an interest in abusing their power. If the House of Commons is the checking body, it must have enough power to overcome the combined power of the king and the House of Lords. This gives rise to the second problem. What is to prevent the checking body from developing a sinister interest of its own, or how is its interest to be kept identical with the interest of the community for which it is supposed to be acting? This latter problem, which for Mill is "the grand difficulty," is approached by recognizing that every representative has two capacities: as a representative he exercises power over others and hence has an interest in abusing it, while as a member of the community he has power exercised over him and hence an interest in preventing the abuse of power. A way must be found to make the latter interest predominate over the former, and Mill finds this way in granting power to representatives for only short periods of time. The shorter the duration during which a man possesses power over others, "the more difficult it will be to compensate the sacrifice of the interests of the longer period, by the profits of misgovernment during the shorter." [6] Yet Mill recognizes that the duration of the possession of power by the representatives must not be too short— it must be long enough to enable them to conduct their business, and he expresses the hope that good government will be rewarded with repeated re-election.

One final, but basic, point remains to be resolved. The system of checks on the government is designed to assure that the government governs in the interest of the community by having the checkers (the representatives) elected by the community. Which individuals constitute the community? Obviously all do. However, it is neither feasible nor necessary for all to vote. The interests of some are clearly, according to James Mill, included in the interests of others. The interests of children are included in those of their fathers, of wives in those of their husbands. (He makes no mention of orphans, unmarried women, or widows.) This point established, the electoral body is the adult male population. Is there any other basis for reducing the size of this body? Mill considers three possibilities: age, property, profession or mode of life. He supposes that raising the minimum age to forty would not seriously diminish the representativeness of the electoral body, since fathers have a strong interest in the welfare of their sons. Property qualifications above a certain minimum would produce an aristocracy with a sinister interest while a low property qualification would bring no benefit. Restricting voting to certain professions would also produce an aristocracy. Thus Mill comes out for universal adult male suffrage with some possibility of a higher minimum age than is customary.

To the objection that his system of representation would mean the end of the monarchy and the House of Lords, Mill replies that other agencies of government are required besides the representative body, and if the institutions mentioned are in the interest of the community they will be maintained.

To the more fundamental objection "that the people are not capable of acting agreeably to their interest," he gives a more detailed answer. He admits that those representatives who have an identity of interest with the community may be mistaken, but asks his readers to consider the alternative. The choice before the community is whether to be ruled by a minority which has an interest in abusing its power, or by one which has no such interest but which may by mistake so abuse it. To this first point is added one which is even more telling from Mill's point of view. The errors of the properly elected representative are due to defects of knowledge which are curable; the abuses of an aristocracy stem from human nature and are not curable. Finally, just as any group, aristocratic or democratic, is led by its best people, so the best people in England, the middle class, will provide the leadership for the masses, enabling them to elect representatives who will legislate and check on the government in the interest of the many.

## NOTES

1. Jeremy Bentham, *An Introduction to the Principles of Morals and Legislation* (New York: Macmillan, 1948), i.2.

2. *Ibid.*, 4.

3. *Ibid.*, iii. 2–6.

4. James Mill, *An Essay on Government* (Cambridge: Cambridge University Press, 1937), i.

5. *Ibid.*, vi.

6. *Ibid.*, vii.

# READINGS

A. Bentham, Jeremy. *A Fragment on Government.* Ed. with an introduction by Wilfrid Harrison. New York: Macmillan, 1948. Chaps i, ii.

Bentham, Jeremy. *An Introduction to the Principles of Morals and Legislation.* Ed. with an introduction by Wilfrid Harrison. New York: Macmillan, 1948. Chaps i–iv.

Mill, James. *An Essay on Government.* Cambridge: Cambridge University Press, 1937.

B. Bentham, Jeremy. *A Fragment on Government.* Chaps iii–v.

Bentham, Jeremy. *An Introduction to the Principles of Morals and Legislation.* Chaps v–xvii.

# GEORG W. F. HEGEL

## 1770–1831

The most important political writings of Hegel are his *Philosophy of Right* on the one hand and some essays like those on the German Constitution (1802) and on the British Reform Bill (1830) on the other. We shall limit ourselves here to a consideration of his political philosophy proper, notwithstanding the importance of his more practical works. His philosophy of right, or rather his philosophy of the state, is to an extraordinary degree inseparable from his philosophic teaching as a whole, for his doctrine is more "systematic" than are those of most other thinkers. This becomes clear in the bare outline of his presentation. The state that Hegel describes is the work of eternal Reason as it is presented in his *Science of Logic* and the *Encyclopedia of the Philosophic Sciences,* but it is also the result of universal history as Hegel traces it in his *Lectures on the Philosophy of History*. In the last analysis, Reason and History are not separable, according to Hegel. The unfolding of Reason parallels the process of universal history, or, the historical process is fundamentally rational. Hence, Hegel does not want to construct an ideal state but to rehabilitate the real state in showing that it is rational.[1] This rehabilitation is addressed to two kinds of opponents.

Against the attitude of a moral, religious, or intellectual consciousness which attempts to take refuge in the inner life and to reject the "sound and fury" of political realities, Hegel justifies political life as such. It is only in and by the state that the individual gains his true reality, for it is only in and by it that he comes to universality. Only the state can act universally by instituting laws. Morality, which seeks universality, can be actualized only by being incarnated in institutions and manners. Manners or morals (*Sittlichkeit*) are "the life of the state in the individuals." ² It is in his devotion to the state that the individual goes beyond his primitive spontaneous selfishness; it is the state's activity of instruction which gives him a training and an education. Hegel, with this in view, repeats the answer of a Pythagorean to a father who asked him about the best way to raise his son morally: "Make him a citizen of a state [which has] good laws." ³

In spite of what might be thought on the basis of certain Hegelian texts, this rehabilitation of the state should not be interpreted as a deification of it. It is true enough that according to Hegel the state constitutes a "final end" for the individual who finds in it the truth of his existence, his duty, and his satisfaction, and that the state constitutes the actualization or the appearance of the divine in the external world. Still, the state's relation with the individual is essentially reciprocal; it is only a final end for the individual to the extent to which its own end is his liberty and satisfaction. Moreover, an individual soul's morality or religion has an infinite value independent of the state. In the state, the individual goes beyond the level of his private, personal thoughts and wishes, his mere existence which Hegel calls the subjective mind. Through the state he has learned to universalize his wishes, to make them into laws and to live according to them. The state is a reality not a project; it can be lived and thought. It is only through the state that the individual takes his place in the world; it is as a citizen that he learns what is reasonable in his wishes. This is the stage of the objective mind. But the "appearance" or "realization" of the "divine," that is, of the absolute or the rational, is neither constituted nor exhausted by the state. The state only introduces and makes possible the absolute mind. It is the source of art, religion, and philosophy, which in a certain way transcend the state. When Hegel speaks of the state as divine, he is only insisting that it be respected in showing that it is fundamentally informed by rationality, that, in spite of its apparent faults and contingency, it is what it should be.

Therefore Hegel must defend the rationality of the real state against the romantics who turn away from politics simply, but equally against the utopians and reformers who turn away from the real state in favor of an ideal state. The function of philosophy is not to teach the state how it ought to be but to teach men how the state ought to be understood. Philosophy cannot go beyond the reality of its time but can only reconcile itself with it in recognizing reason "as the rose in the cross of the present." ⁴ Philosophy's function is neither to invent nor to criticize but to bring out the positive truth with which reality is already informed.

Thus Hegel wants to show the rational in the irrational. Not only does he want to discover the necessary essence of the state behind the contingent details, but he also wishes to show that what appears irrational in the state itself works unconsciously toward the triumph of the rational, that what appears contradictory will finally be brought into harmony, that the blind play of particular passions and actions necessarily ends in the advent of the universally just and fully developed political order. Hence the bad leads to the good, the passions to reason, contradiction and conflict to synthesis and peace.

It is the state understood as a harmonious and differentiated totality that makes this synthesis possible. To express the relation between the articulated whole which is nothing without its parts and the parts which are nothing without the whole, Hegel turns to the metaphor of the organism, in particular the human body, in which each organ has its true reality only in the particular function it fulfills within the whole, and also to the metaphor of an architectural structure like a Gothic cathedral. The paradox of such an articulation is that it is the result of the play of unconscious forces. The double Hegelian undertaking ends in this paradox, and to it corresponds the idea of the "cunning of reason." The state comes to light as both a final result and a precondition. It is a result of the action of individuals and of the play of the passions but, once constituted, its structure appears as first and primary while its genesis is interpreted as a merely empirical and external fact. "The state is a final result in which the fact that it finds its origin in the operation of individuals disappears." [5] That these individuals—whether one means by this the mass of men pursuing their particular interests or the great men who perform heroic actions—are unconsciously the instruments of a plan which transcends them and often directly contradicts their conscious objectives, that the action of irrational forces constructs an architectonic edifice which is the image of eternal reason, is what is meant by the "cunning of reason" [6] which demonstrates the rationality of history. This is what permits the philosophy of history to end in political philosophy and, conversely, what permits political philosophy to transform itself into a description of the final, fully developed state.

The state is born of conflict and is, in its turn, the theater and the origin of numerous potential conflicts. This is true of the state because it is true of man himself. Man does not raise himself to the level of humanity in isolation but in a battle to the death for "recognition." He exists for himself, is conscious of himself or of his own freedom only to the extent to which he is recognized, as consciousness or freedom, by another consciousness or another freedom. Each wishes to be recognized by the other without in turn recognizing him. Each establishes himself as free, and hence as human, only to the extent to which he is able to negate his natural being for the sake of recognition, risking his life for prestige. The struggle for recognition will thus be a life-and-death struggle. For that very reason it will end in an inequality. One of the two adversaries will prefer life to prestige or freedom. Moved by his fear of violent death, he will consent to recognize the other without insisting on being recognized by him. He will submit to the other. Thus man necessarily emerges from the fight for recognition as either a master or a slave. His reality is, then, essentially social and even political, since "the struggle for recognition and the submission to a mastery is the phenomenon from which men's social life emerged and it is the beginning of states." [7]

The conflict between master and slave is prior to the state. It has the same place in Hegel's formulation that the state of nature, the opposite of the civil state, has in Hobbes's. And, as in Hobbes, it leaves its imprint on the political reality which follows. For both, the state emerges from violence; the first relationship among men is one of conflict, which puts in play the two fundamental passions, vanity (or the desire for recognition) and the fear of violent death. But the relation of the master and the slave, far from stopping at the victory of the master, engenders a dialectic which will be the driving spring of human history. The master forces the slave to work for him. Essentially idle, the master's life is summed up in the quest for recognition, for prestige and glory, through war. He does not work, he is not in direct contact with things. The slave, on the other hand, who prepares the things to satisfy the master's needs, is the one who transforms nature and himself through work. He postpones the destruction of the thing (through consumption) in preparing it by work, and he postpones the satisfaction of his own needs in working to satisfy those of the master: "work is repressed desire." [8] He works in terms of an abstract idea, a project to be realized. He forms the external world which acquires a consistency of its own and bears his mark, and he forms himself by separating himself from his instincts and by becoming an apprentice in abstract general notions, language, and thought. Thus, through the slave's work, both the world of technique and society itself on the one hand, and the world of thought, art, and religion on the other are constituted. It is therefore the attitude of work and fear of violent death, the prosaic attitude, that of the slave and of the bourgeois as opposed to the heroic and aristocratic attitude, which, just as in Hobbes, is at the foundation of Hegel's society. Moreover, whereas for classical political philosophy leisure had a higher dignity than work because their opposition reflected that between theory and practice, for Hegel, thought and the universal are on the side of work, and leisure is conceived of as essentially warlike.

But this is not compensation enough for the slave, and he is still dissatisfied, just as is the master, for neither of them has obtained the recognition he hoped for, the recognition of another free consciousness. The conflict continues, and it is the function of the state to resolve it. The reconciliation which the state must effect is two-pronged. On the one hand, the state is founded on reciprocity: its citizens recognize one another; it is the ground of the reciprocal recognition at which the master and the slave aim in vain. On the other hand, the state finds within it both the moment (or element) of work and need and that of sacrifice and war. This tension appears in the form of the opposition between "civil society" and the state, between the "bourgeois" and the "citizen." The problem of the modern state will be precisely to tolerate the two moments and to reconcile them, i.e., to implement the synthesis of the aristocratic point of view and the bourgeois point of view, or, in the last analysis, of the master and the slave.

All the conflicts which are implicit in the relations of the individual, the family, the society, and the state ultimately refer back to a fundamental opposition which has its seat in the individual's will, a conflict the stakes of which are the individual's status in the state. At various levels the conflict stands forth as the opposition between the individual and the universal, the particular will and the general will, private interest and public interest, bourgeois and citizen, satisfaction of needs and sacrifice, rights and duties, passions and reason, negative inwardness and positiveness, critical consciousness and acceptance of the law, in sum, between what Hegel calls "subjective liberty" (as individual consciousness and will pursuing its particular goals) and "objective liberty" (i.e., "the substantial general will"). For Hegel, the state as "concrete freedom" is the union of these two elements in so far as the individual is satisfied in recognizing the universal as law and in taking the state as end. Hegel says that "the union of the particular and the universal in the state is that upon which every thing depends." [9] This "unity of its final universal end and the particular interests of the individuals" is expressed in the fact that "they have duties to the state in proportion as they have rights against it." [10] This reciprocity of rights and duties then permits the state to constitute a "serene totality." The right of subjective liberty should be recognized in two ways: as the right of the subject's particularity to be satisfied in its needs and its well-being, and as the right of consciousness to recognize nothing of which it does not approve rationally. But particularity should adapt itself to the universal and to collective life, and critical consciousness should not endanger the existence of an authority, of a government, of an organized state.

This condition is, of course, met only by the modern state. As for the past, historical examples abound to show the dangers which had to be surmounted in order to achieve the rational state. The imperfection and ruin of the Greek world, from the political point of view, are the consequences of its misunderstanding of the principle of particularity. "The right of the subject's particularity, his right to be satisfied, or in other words the right of subjective freedom, is the pivot and centre of the difference between ancient and modern times." [11] The Greeks lived naturally and immediately for the general or the substantial, for the fatherland. "Of the Greeks we may affirm that in the first and true form of their freedom they had no conscience. Among them there reigned the habit of living for their fatherland without further reflection." [12] Hence there is no place for subjectivity in any of its forms—as the right to the satisfaction of particular needs and to well-being (the quest for them belonging only to slaves), as the right to freedom in the choice of calling and in the determination of class position, or as the right of the critical consciousness which feels the need to found its attachment to the political regime and its moral action on reason. To the contrary, the independent development of particularity or subjective freedom appears in the Greek states as a hostile principle, as a destruction of the social order. Its emergence in the ancient states is coeval with the corruption of morals, and it is the supreme cause of their decadence.[13] In the Roman Empire, individuality is recognized, but abstractly and externally. The state as an organic whole is dissolved. "All the individuals are degraded to the level of private persons, equal with one another, possessed of formal rights and the only bond ... to hold them together is abstract insatiable self-will." [14] This is because a constitution and an organization of the concrete moral life in general, binding the master and the subjects together, were lacking.

In another form and in a very different context, the double reproach of abstractness and arbitrariness connected with the absence of organization is to be found in Hegel's allusions to France. The French Revolution represents an absolutely capital achievement, the decision to put thought or reason at the foundation of the state. It is the advent of the principle of subjective consciousness and, with it, of the principles of liberty, equality, and the rights of man and citizen. But these principles, which in themselves belong to the very essence of the modern state, are conceived in an abstract and individualistic fashion which leaves no place for organization and government, or for anything concrete. The fulfillment of this negative and destructive liberty, which wishes to suppress all differentiation and determinateness, is indefinite terror, "since any institution whatever is antagonistic to the abstract self-consciousness of equality." [15] Since the attempts at democracy in large, developed states can only lead to abstractness, and "since a government is always there," [16] revolutionary liberalism is condemned to being perpetually in opposition. After Napoleon, who had correctly understood the necessity of conciliating principles of the revolution with the authority of an organized state, French political life remained in the grip of the contradictions besetting a nation the life of which had been dominated by abstract categories: there was a perpetual opposition of statesmen to men of principle, and of government to the people.

So long as the people is not organized in and by the state, it is only a collection of particular wills and "does not know what it wills." [17] It can speak only arbitrarily, in a way harmful to all organization.

With this formalism of liberty, with this abstraction, no solid organization can be established. The particular dispositions taken by the government find themselves immediately opposed by freedom, for they are only manifestations of the particular will and hence arbitrary. The will of the many overturns the ministry and what was up to now the opposition comes on the stage as the new government. But it, inasmuch as it is now a government, has in its turn the many against it. In this way change and unrest are perpetuated.[18]

Hegel, therefore, denies that recognition of individual liberties and rights and juridical equality ought to lead to democracy.

To hold that every single person should share in deliberating and deciding on political matters of general concern on the ground that all individuals are members of the state, that its concerns are their concerns, and that it is right that what is done should be done with their knowledge and volition, is tantamount to a proposal to put the democratic element without any rational form into the organism of the state, although it is only in virtue of the possession of such a form that the state is an organism at all.[19]

The individual should be taken into political account only in so far as he occupies a definite place in that organism. The possibility for each to become a member of the governing class, juridical equality, ought not to be detrimental to social differentiation, nor ought public opinion, the possibility for each to make his voice heard by authority, do damage to the authority of the state and its competent representatives.

Thus Hegel desires a synthesis of "liberation and respect," of passion and morality, of revolutionary principles and the necessity of the political order. Historically the modern state should represent a synthesis of the *polis* (of which the unity, the citizens' mutual confidence and their attachment to the whole should be preserved) and the liberal society of political economy (of which the diversity and differentiation, the satisfaction of individual needs, the realization of the universal by the individual free will, should be preserved). Philosophically, Hegel wishes to effect a synthesis of classical (or substantial and concrete) morality and Christian-Kantian (or internal and abstract) morality, of the politics of Plato, founded on the primacy of reason and virtue, and the politics of Machiavelli, Bacon, Hobbes, and Locke, founded on the emancipation of the passions and their satisfaction.

The means of this synthesis is history. The subject and the end of history is the progressive revelation of freedom, or, what amounts to the same thing, the consciousness which the mind gains of itself through history. The mind grasps itself as being essentially constituted by its freedom, and its freedom is realized in this gaining of consciousness. Freedom is realized in the modern state because, on the one hand, the state has separated out and manifested freedom's different moments and aspects (objective liberty, subjective liberty, and so on); and, on the other, since freedom is now revealed as the essence of man, all men are in the state, and know that they are in it, as essentially free. The discovery of the true and complete essence of freedom coincides with the freedom of all. But then, if it is true that the end of history is only realized in and by the modern state, it is no less true, reciprocally, that the modern state can only be constituted when the principle on which it is founded has been revealed in its different aspects. Thus it is necessary that all men be recognized as free, that the principle of internal freedom, or of the infinite value of the individual, have made its appearance in religion, that the particularity of needs and the demand for their satisfaction have made their appearance in men's manners and morals. This revelation is only complete at the end of history, since the web of history is made of the progressive appearance of incomplete principles, each one of which manifests a new aspect of freedom but each one of which is doomed to disappear as a consequence of its very incompleteness. The developments of these particular principles are the spirits of peoples (*Volksgeiste*); they constitute concrete totalities within which the animating principle expresses itself comprehensively in religion, science, art, events, and destiny. Thus history is the history of religion, manners and morals, art, economics, and so on, at the same time as it is political history. The political constitution of a people is a result of its spirit (mind); thus it is dangerous to impose on a people a constitution constructed a priori. Political forms can only be spoken of historically; they can be judged only in relation to the extent of consciousness of freedom with which they are associated.

Fundamentally, universal history is arranged in three stages which are not three forms of government but three degrees of consciousness of freedom, ranked according to whether it is one, some, or all who know themselves to be free.

The Orientals do not know yet that mind or man as such are in themselves free; because they do not know it, they are not. They know only that one single man is free. That is why such a freedom is only caprice and barbarism. . . . This single one is hence only a despot and not a free man. It was with the Greeks that the consciousness of freedom first came to sight; that is why they were free; but they, as well as the Romans, knew only that some are free, not man as such. That even Plato and Aristotle did not know. This is why the Greeks not only had slaves, . . . but their own freedom was both closed up within narrow limits and at the same time a harsh servitude . . . of the human. Only the Germanic nations have in Christianity come to the consciousness that man as man is free, that spiritual freedom truly constitutes his nature. This consciousness appeared first in religion, in the most inward region of the mind; but to inform the world with this principle was a new task whose solution and execution exact a long and painful effort of education.[20]

It is "the application of the principle to the affairs of the world" which ultimately decides the fate of political regimes. The Greek city failed partly because it did not know the Christian principle, partly because its own principle was too simple to admit of sufficient development and diversity in society. In contrast, the modern state rests on the Protestant Christian religion and on an economically and socially differentiated society. It is only in the Christian religion that the principle of the individual's infinite worth makes its appearance.

But in order for the Christian principle to be realized in the world by means of the rational state, another spiritual revolution was required, the Reformation. It is only in the Protestant religion that Christian freedom is actualized and effects its reconciliation with the world and the state. The discovery of Christian inwardness engenders a series of oppositions: between the conscience and the world, the other world and this one, piety (which commands vows of chastity, poverty, and obedience) and terrestrial morality (which recommends marriage, work, and reasonable freedom), the clergy and the laity, the church and the state. In the Lutheran religion, however, "the reconciliation leads to the consciousness of the temporal world's capacity to contain the truth within itself." Marriage, work, industriousness, the crafts acquire a moral value. Above all, blind obedience is eliminated. In Protestantism there is no class of priests, but a universal priesthood; the individual conscience has the right to judge. This is eventually transformed into the right of the individual reason to judge. Thus the principle peculiar to Protestantism is that of the free mind: "that is the essential content of the Reformation; man decides by himself to be free." And in this way the rational state can be constituted, by leading subjective freedom to universality. But this is possible only because within religion itself truth resides henceforward in the subject as such to the exclusion of all external authority. There is no longer any difference between priests and laymen; the content of the truth is no longer exclusively reserved to a caste. "It is rather the heart, the sensitive spirituality of man, which can and ought to take possession of the truth, and this subjectivity is that of *all men*. Each must accomplish the work of reconciliation within himself." [21] This reconciliation, by abolishing the difference between the two worlds, leads to the result that, in a sense, religion is done away with while being fulfilled: Protestantism signifies both the Christianization of the *saeculum* and the secularization of Christianity. The modern state is Christian and Protestant to the extent that its principle has its source in religion. But, since that principle is nothing other than that of rational universality, it is accessible to all men as such, and the state which expresses it is secular. At all events, this state is inconceivable so long as the Reformation has not taught freedom to the peoples. If, in spite of Napoleon's activity, the modern principles have failed in the Latin countries, the reason is the Catholicism of those countries. Subjection to religion brings with it political servitude.

The other fundamental (which is, however, connected with the first) for the constitution of the rational state is economic and social differentiation founded on the liberation of individual wants and needs. The multiplication of individual circumstances and needs, competition, division of labor, make a regime founded simply on the wisdom and virtue of the rulers impossible. They make necessary the passage to the universality of law which characterizes the modern state. The rational state is far from being founded on a society without class or directed to homogeneity; rather, Hegel believes that the differences of class and wealth are not only inevitable but indispensable to the effectiveness of individual freedom and the activity of the state. There is, according to him, not yet a true state in North America because of the absence of economic and social tension.[22]

The modern state is characterized by its rational laws, but their introduction depends upon historical and social conditions in the absence of which those laws would be fragile or even pernicious. Hence Hegel exhibits a very prudent reserve in proposing concrete application of the universal principles. The manners or habits of the people must be prepared (this is the source of the importance of religion), and the transition to rationality must be made prudently in order to avoid a revolution. This is the task of governmental power, which must have a strong authority for the purpose. In his last article, devoted to the English Reform Bill of 1830 (aimed at doing away with the rotten boroughs and increasing the rationality of the English electoral system, thus promoting democratization), Hegel agrees with the theoretical inspiration of the project, which attempts to introduce in England the universal principles long since victorious on the continent, and he delivers a violent criticism of the political and social arbitrariness reigning in England as well as of its law, which is merely positive and reflects no thought. But, at the same time, Hegel criticizes the bill itself no less carefully and concurs in most of the fears of its adversaries. Although the article does not come to a conclusion, it leaves the impression that considerations of prudence led the author to decide against the Reform Bill in spite of his agreement with it in principle. The reason is that, besides the absence of a rational law, England's other great defect is the absence of a strong governmental power, the monarchy being weak and the aristocracy incompetent.

It was the action of the princes, aided by the civil servants, which permitted the introduction of rational principles in Prussia without the convulsions caused in France by the abstract spirit. In the absence of guidance and control by the firm hand of the government, in the absence of the preparation of a directing class founded on competence rather than money, tradition, or demagogy, the evolution runs the risk of being precipitate and engendering anarchy. The Prussian state is, for Hegel, the model most akin to the rational state because it represents, thanks both to the Protestant religion and the authority of the monarchy, a synthesis between the revolutionary exigencies of principles and the traditional exigencies of organization. The establishment of the modern state, then, requires three elements: rational laws, government, and sentiment or morals. Plato, according to Hegel, based his teaching on the second and third only, and neglected the first. The doctrinaire revolutionaries and liberals, on the other hand, recognize only rational laws, forgetting the importance of the government and the citizens' state of mind. The examples of France and England show, each in its own way, the dangers of the absence of a real government, just as the example of the Catholic countries, where the rational constitution is impossible, shows the political importance of religion and morals as bases for the individuals' "culture" (*Bildung*), their education to the universal, and their training as citizens of a free state.

The state is, in a sense, nothing less than the crown and the foundation of this labor of morals that raises the particular to the universal, teaching the individual to fulfill himself in giving himself to a whole. The stages of this education, or the moments of the concrete moral spirit (*Sittlichkeit*), are the family, civil society, and the state. We shall now discern the double movement already mentioned, the process by which the modern state fulfills that synthesis which is the result of the subordinate moments, founded on particularity, and of rational necessity, founded on the universal concept.

Both the family and the civil society are distinct from the state, that is, opposed to it, as particular to universal. But both have something in common with it, hence something by which they contribute to moral education in opening the individual to the universal. The family has a substantial unity: it constitutes a whole founded on the confidence of its members, an end in itself in which the individual is conscious of having his reality. It is thus the image of the state, with this difference: the unity that prevails in it is natural, immediate, felt, rather than thought or accepted rationally. Civil society, on the other hand, is an association of independent members in which the private person, as a totality of wants, is the first principle. Civil society thus represents the moment of separation and difference in which concrete morality (*Sittlichkeit*) seems to be dissolved in favor of particularity and egoism. But, at the same time, it is in civil society that thought makes its appearance in a form which is still abstract, that of understanding and formal universality. Although it represents the moment of particularity par excellence, the universal is present in it in several ways. In the first place, the reciprocal relations of individuals create a system of mutual dependence which produces a formal universality, one which is external and not willed by the individuals: the particular person, the first principle of civil society, "is essentially so related to other particular persons that each establishes himself and finds satisfaction by means of the others, and at the same time purely and simply by means of the form of universality, the second principle here." [23]

Political economy, a creation of modern times and a consequence of the liberation of individual needs, is precisely the science of this reciprocal dependency through which each, while following his particular interests, unwittingly obeys general laws. In the meantime, as a result of his relations with others, the individual, his needs, and his work undergo profound adaptation. Civil society engenders new needs which are created by it and are not natural. The necessity of orienting oneself according to others in a daily routine and in manners (clothing styles, hours of meals, and so on) raises the natural individuality of the members of civil society to the formal universality of culture. It is still a universality unconsciously obtained, but one which already transforms individuality itself. Beyond this, in civil society the universal has a direct presence, free and conscious, in the form of man's necessity to have recourse to law and administration. The property right, engendered by the system of needs and their reciprocal recognition, is itself recognized in its universality in so far as authority assures its protection. It is the sphere of the relative itself, culture, which gives birth to right.

Right means universality, willed and recognized as such; it is the ground of the only valid equality. "It is part of culture, of thought as consciousness of the individual in the form of universality, that I am apprehended as a *universal* person in which all are identical. A man counts because he is a man, not because he is Jewish, Catholic, Protestant, German, Italian, etc." [24] But this universality continues to have the character of merely abstract right. The actualization of its unity with the whole realm of the particular is the mission of the administration which insures that "first, . . . undisturbed safety of person and property be attained; and secondly, that the securing of every single person's livelihood and welfare be treated and actualized as a right . . . ." [25] Administrative foresight, *i.e.,* the action of the state, protects the universality in civil society's particularity in the form of external order and of institutions which maintain and support the mass of ends and interests in it. Hegel wishes to assure a balance between the freedom of industry and commerce and the necessity of foresight and direction by the state as a whole. Although the will and the interest of individuals are the springs of action of civil society and the function of the state is simply to "bring it back to the universal. . . . to diminish the danger of upheavals arising from clashing interests and to abbreviate the period in which their tension should be eased through the working of a necessity of which they themselves know nothing," [26] it is nevertheless still the case that the principle of their organization is the opposite of liberal. "Public social conditions are on the contrary to be regarded as all the more perfect the less (in comparison with what is arranged publicly) is left for an individual to do by himself as his private inclination directs." [27]

But, within the system of needs itself, there is an aspect through which the individual is connected to the universal in an immediate way and acquires a definite reality. This is in the division of classes or "general groups" (*Stände*). If the family is the first basis of the state, the *Stände* are the second. There are three classes, and their division is dialectic: the agricultural class, called substantial or immediate; the industrial class, called reflective or formal; and the class of civil servants, called the universal class. The agricultural class is the class of "security, consolidation, lasting satisfaction of needs" and these are "nothing but forms of universality. . . ." It has an immediate concrete morality resting on the family and good faith. [28] And "the universal class has in its very definition the universal for itself as goal, as ground, as end of its activity." [29] The civil servants are by nature oriented to the state and find in its service their *raison d'être* and their satisfaction.

Hence only the intermediary class, the industrial class, is essentially oriented to the particular. This is why it is enslaved to harshness, insecurity, the struggle of needs, their indefinite multiplication and the indefinite division of labor, and the contradiction of poverty and wealth. For this reason it requires the intervention of the state. On the other hand, since "for its means of subsistence it is thrown back on work, reflection and intelligence," [30] it is essentially this class which gives the individual culture, refinement, and intellectual formation. The individual in this class is awakened to freedom by being awakened to reflection. Freedom is born in the cities, while the country is traditionally more submissive because more passive. Above all, even in this class, particularity is led to take the universal as its goal: *Sittlichkeit* is thus reintegrated in civil society. To reintegrate it is the mission of the *corporation* (in the sense of guild rather than joint-stock, limited liability business firm), which limits the contradictions in civil society by making sure that there is a common ground for poverty and wealth, employees and employers, by giving a rational consecration to the diversity and rivalry of talents and aptitudes, by protecting individuals against particular accidents, in short, by surmounting the isolation and harshness of civil life in playing the role of a second family. The corporation introduces objective morality into civil society by means of the sentiments of professional honor, for which it provides a basis, and probity, which is truly recognized and honored in it. Thus, the corporation's role is central, for in modern society probity and professional honor are the only really living forms of virtue.

Since virtue in this case merely represents the individual's adaptation to the necessities of the situation in which he happens to find himself, it can only be called probity. Virtue itself, in the sense of subjective moral reflection or in the sense of virtue's determining a particular individual character, has a place in the daily life of modern societies founded on systematization and objective universality, only in extraordinary circumstances and conflicts of duties. In primitive and ancient states, heroic virtue had its place because there was room for the action of exceptional individuals. Today, once the modern state has been constituted, the rational system replaces them. What remains of virtue in society as such is the sanctity of marriage and professional honor. That is why "after the family, the corporation constitutes the second moral root of the state, that root which is implanted in civil society." [31] The corporation reunites within itself the moments of subjective particularity and objective universality which had previously been divided in civil society. But this work of union is merely a particular aspect of what the state sets as its goal. The sphere of civil society leads, therefore, to the state.

This movement can be understood if one reflects on the relation of *Sittlichkeit,* as it is expressed in the family and civil society, to patriotism. Family sentiment, professional honor, and probity seem in normal times to substitute themselves for political virtue and patriotism. But they lead to patriotism to the extent that the security and confidence they express are founded on the state, and those who possess these sentiments should, upon becoming conscious of this fact, take the state as their object. This conversion can be seen in the definition which Hegel gives of political sentiment or patriotism.

This sentiment is principally confidence . . . and the certitude that my particular interest and my substantial interest are preserved and maintained in the interest and the ends of another (here, the state) as a consequence of its relation to me as an individual. The result of this is that properly it is not an other for me and that in this state of consciousness I am free. . . . Under the name of patriotism, the disposition to sacrifice and extraordinary actions is understood, but it is essentially the disposition of consciousness which, in ordinary situations and circumstances, leads one to consider the collective life as the basis and the goal.[32]

In order to understand the content of this civic sentiment, we must now consider the state as a rational and necessary organization. "Civic sentiment receives its particular content from the different aspects of the state's organism. . . . This organism is the political constitution." [33]

This constitution "is rational to the extent to which the state inwardly differentiates and determines its activity in itself according to the nature of the concept," *i.e.,* in such a way "that each of the powers is in itself the totality of the constitution." [34] There must indeed be differentiation of powers, but it should be organic and not mechanical. The powers should be considered neither as entirely independent, nor as reciprocally limiting one another, nor still as mutually hostile; on the contrary, they should mutually reflect one another and be determined uniquely by the idea of the whole.

The whole forms a constitutional *monarchy* founded on a corps of professional *civil servants* and provided with certain *representative* institutions. "The completion of the state in a constitutional monarchy is the work of the modern world." The object of universal history is nothing but the history of its formation, which coincides with that of "the intimate deepening of the mind of the world." Only constitutional

monarchy corresponds to the fully developed idea of the state, which has
freed all its moments, and to a complicated society, which has freed the
powers of particularity. For example, the modern state cannot be
founded on virtue, as are republics according to Montesquieu: "in a
more complicated social state, when the powers of particularity are
developed and freed, the virtue of heads of state is insufficient. Another
form of rational law than that which manifests itself in subjective dispositions becomes necessary if the whole is to possess the force to maintain itself and accord to the developed particular forces their positive as
well as negative right." [35] Speaking generally, the classical typology—
monarchy, aristocracy, democracy—was only valid for a still undifferentiated society. These forms are found again as moments in constitutional monarchy: the monarch is one, a few participate in governmental
power, and the multitude in general participate in legislative power.
The true differentiation is not based on a quantitative distinction, however, but on the logical nature of the concept of the state. It distinguishes:

(*a*) the power to determine and establish the universal—the Legislature.
(*b*) the power to subsume the particular spheres and individual cases
under the universal—the Executive;
(*c*) the power of subjectivity as the will with the power of ultimate
decision—the Crown. In the Crown, the different powers are brought together in an individual unity which is thus at once the apex and the basis of
the whole, i.e. of constitutional monarchy.[36]

There must be a locus of supreme decision; the sovereignty and
unity of the state should be expressed in a will which determines finally.
The sovereignty of the state, as will, is personality; it should be incarnated in an individual, the monarch. Since he is "in essence characterized as this individual in abstraction from all his other characteristics," [37]
he should be designated in an immediately natural way: by birth. It is
only by the hereditary principle that the monarch's person, which sym-
bolizes the unity and continuity of the state, escapes from the struggles
of interest and opinion which necessarily dominate an elective empire.
But the prince's action itself has a certain symbolic and arbitrary character; it is, of course, he who declares war, signs laws, names his counselors, and settles their differences. But on each occasion it is the *fiat* of
decision which is incumbent on him rather than the actual task of governing, and most often the latter determines the former almost necessarily. That is why "with firmly established laws and a well defined
organization of the state, what has been reserved to the sole decision of
the monarch ought to be considered as slight with respect to what is
substantial. It must certainly be considered great good luck that a noble

monarch has fallen to the lot of a people. However, this is not of so
great an importance, for the force of this state is in its reason." [38]

Who, then, represents this reason and consequently exercises what
is essential in power? It is the government and, in general, the universal
class of civil servants, since "the government rests on the world of the
civil servants [*Beamtenwelt*]." [39] It is this government which both prepares and applies the sovereign's decisions. It affirms the general interest
even in the pursuit of particular ends. It is "in the actions of civil servants and in their training" that "one finds the point where the laws and
the decisions of government come into contact with individuals and are
actually made good." [40] It is in the situation of the civil servants themselves that the state's function, the synthesis of the particular and the
universal, is best realized, since it is only in the accomplishment of their
duty, in their service to the state, that they find the satisfaction of their
particular needs. They represent the type of man who incarnates the
spirit of the regime and serves as a model to the entire community. Each
member of the community can, by right, become a civil servant. The
universal class is open to all the citizens; this is the democratic aspect
of the rational state. But it is only open subject to an objective examination of their aptitudes and their intellectual and moral formation.

It is perhaps in this sort of examination, bearing on the sciences
directly related to administrative competence as well as on intellectual
training and general morality so that "a dispassionate, upright, and
polite demeanour becomes customary" [41] that the most important element of the Hegelian state is to be found, that state which is justly
characterized as the *Beamtenstaat* (bureaucracy) and is as such opposed
to the aristocracies of the old order founded on nobility, to the oligarchies founded on money, and to the modern democracies founded on
number, public opinion, and particular interests. In the article on the
English Reform Bill, Hegel deplores the absence, in both the bill and
the existing state of things, "of the conditions set in Germany, even on
those who have claims of birth, fortune or great property, requisite to
participation in government or affairs of state in either their general or
particular branches: theoretical studies, scientific training, and practical
exercises and experience." [42] In England, a man need only have a certain fortune to be able to enter Parliament, which holds the real power.
The result is that the rulers are a disparate collection of individuals instead of an assemblage of men competent and devoted to the state. "It
is those who know, *hoi aristoi,* who ought to reign and not ignorance
or vanity." [43] The government of civil servants is the modern form of
aristocracy. The "bureaucracy," a term which first appeared in the latter
half of the eighteenth century with the beginnings of the modern state

and which immediately acquired a pejorative sense, is rehabilitated in Hegel's thought. He sees in it the sytematized and rationalized form (in conformity with the spirit of modern times and the necessity of the concept of the state) of the government of the best. But, at the same time, Hegel is quite careful to avoid the reproach implicit in the pejorative sense of the term "bureaucracy": that it is a tyranny of civil servants, forming a caste, obedient to the *esprit de corps,* and constituting a state within the state. Not only does the hierarchy constitute an internal means of control against arbitrariness, but, above all, the institutions of sovereignty, from above, and the rights of the corporations, from below, keep the civil servants from taking the isolated position of an aristocracy and prevent culture and talent from becoming the means of arbitrariness and domination.

The legislative power brings into being not only the monarch and the government the moments of which we have just spoken, but also a new element, the "assemblies of the orders." The role of these latter is not precisely to legislate. They do not make any essential or definitive decisions. They give voice to the subjective freedom of individuals, to the opinions and the interests of the mass, and to civil society, to the extent that these are cut off from the government. Essentially, the assemblies mediate between the prince, the government, and the people. Thanks to this mediation, the prince's power does not seem to be isolated or, consequently, to be simple domination or willfulness; nor are the particular interests of communities, corporations, and individuals isolated from one another either. Everything is done to prevent the people, as an undifferentiated mass, from participating directly in power while giving it a relationship to the state. Thus there is no direct individual vote, which would give recognition to the existence and role of the isolated and abstract individual and would give authority to the weight of number. The individual should be represented in his concrete reality, as a man endowed with certain characteristics and interests which give him a place in the social organism. The vote is cast by orders (*Stände*). The orders in the political sense (assemblies of the orders) are founded on the orders in the social sense (classes); the economic and social groups, the groups with particular interests, must be represented as such. But here, too, there must be organs of mediation; there must, within the orders, be an element essentially oriented to the intermediary function which has been assigned to them.

This is the role of the substantial class of landed proprietors who are favored because of their stability and their great independence in relation to both the state and the uncertainties of economic life. The landed proprietors themselves sit directly in the assembly while

The second section of the Estates comprises the fluctuating element in civil society. This element can enter politics only through its deputies; the multiplicity of its members is an external reason for this, but the essential reason is the specific character of this element and its activity. Since these deputies are the deputies of civil society, it follows as a direct consequence that their appointment is made by the society as a society. That is to say, in making the appointment, society is not dispersed into atomic units, collected to perform only a single and temporary act, and kept together for a moment and no longer. On the contrary, it makes the appointment as a society, articulated into associations, communities and Corporations, which, although constituted already for other purposes, acquire in this way a connexion with politics.[44]

Thus the members of the industrial class are represented through the intermediacy of the corporations. The representatives themselves participate in the spheres of interest which they represent, and should, moreover, meet certain conditions of competence which correspond to the conditions of fortune exacted of the members of the first order. The two orders sit in two distinct assemblies; the role of the first chamber can be to conciliate the second and the government. Thus a series of intermediary bodies and mediating organs serve to set aside the specter of abstract democracy and to realize a state in which liberty coincides with organization.

To what extent do they succeed? More generally, what is the result of this enterprise of conciliation between modern abstract principles and the necessities of governmental organization, which constitutes the synthesis of the rational Hegelian state? It can be said that the institutions which we have discussed guarantee a free play of liberty, equality, and fraternity (or the universality of the human person), but within very strict limits imposed by this organization of the state. Thus there is freedom in the choice of calling, in the distribution of class membership (contrary to the rule in Plato's *Republic* where it is fixed by the government, or in the Indian caste system where it is determined by birth), and in the fact that the only demands the state makes in normal times are of money in the form of taxes. From all these points of view it is the free will which should be the intermediary through which the state obtains what it needs. As for public opinion, freedom of the press, and freedom of speech and writing in general, the situation is more ambiguous. "The formal subjective freedom of individuals consists in their having and expressing their own private judgments, opinions, and recommendations on affairs of state. This freedom is collectively manifested as what is called 'public opinion'. . . ."[45] It contains external principles of justice along with prejudices, profound tendencies of reality along with subjective and contingent particular opinion. In it truth and endless error are so immediately and closely united that the serious, or universal, element cannot be discerned by or on the basis of opinion itself.[46] It should, therefore, have the occasion to manifest itself but never to make the final judgment, since it is only justified in a general and confused way, not precisely and consciously. "Hence, to be independent of it (in science as well as in life) is the first formal condition of doing anything great or rational. Great achievement is assured, however, of subsequent recognition and grateful acceptance by public opinion, which in due course will make it one of its own prejudices." [47]

The liberty of public communication (and in particular of the press), "the satisfaction of this pressing instinct to say and have said one's opinion," is also recognized but limited because of its ambiguity. It is both the expression of the principle of the infinite freedom of critical consciousness and of the arbitrariness of subjective opinion and, ultimately, an inducement to disorder and crime. To define the freedom of the press as the freedom to say and write what one pleases belongs to "the ignorant barbarousness and superficiality of representation." [48] But the indeterminateness of the matter and the form in question (Where does opinion end and infraction begin?) makes the law which limits it always imprecise; the judgment against it always appears subjective. This subjectivity and contingency in repression, which are by nature inevitable, are still indispensable. Hegel nevertheless pleads for indulgence to the extent that the state is sufficiently healthy and strong to be able to bear the expression of irresponsible opinions because they are treated with contempt. But even here it is "those who know" who are judges of the extent to which public opinion, as it is expressed in the assemblies, should or should not be followed and freedom of expression, as it is found in the press and in speech, is helpful or dangerous and should be encouraged, ignored, or repressed.

In the same way *equality* is recognized, but only as abstract equality of persons before the law. It is politically and socially expressed in the possibility of each man's becoming a member of the universal and directing class. But equality must give way to the primacy of differentiation and articulation. There is no social equality. The equalization of fortunes is a dream produced by the abstract mind. The society based on the modern economy encourages social inequalities more significant than had been known previously, and the rational state presupposes great differentiation. From the political point of view, the power of number is carefully avoided. The viewpoint of the enlightened minority ought to win out over that of the mass (*hoi polloi*) which does not know what it wants. Finally, the universality of the human person is recognized, but only to the extent that it does not bring political cosmopolitanism with it. Just as the equality of persons does not signify a homogeneous state, so also the universality of human nature does not signify the universality of the state, which always remains a particular sovereign totality excluding, by its very individuality, other sovereignties. There is, indeed, the creation of a sort of world society from an economic point of view, but it does not do away with this essential individuality of states. Speaking generally, the Hegelian synthesis brings us back to the opposition between society and the state which was its point of departure. It is a largely liberal and decentralized society, but more from an economic and social than a political point of view. To make political decisions which concern the state, one must adapt oneself to its organization.

But it is in the relation between domestic and foreign policy, in the last analysis, between peace and war, that the problem of the relation between society and state, between the particular spheres and the universal good, is posed in all its intensity and breadth. From the state's point of view there is a community between war and peace. The state affirms itself through opposition. The sovereignty which is directed within brings with it a sovereignty directed outwards; in so far as the state is above all constituted by its independence and individuality, it necessarily comprises a negative and exclusive aspect which opposes it to other autonomous individualities. The state, therefore, cannot rightfully affirm its internal authority without thereby affirming its external independence. There is not only a necessary relation but a proportional relation: the more a country is unified within under the authority of the state, the more it is able to make its independence respected from without. ". . . peoples unwilling or afraid to tolerate sovereignty at home have been subjugated from abroad, and they have struggled for their independence with the less glory and success the less they have been able previously to organize the powers of the state in home affairs." Reciprocally, "successful wars prevent internal disturbances and consolidate the state's internal power." [49]

Only a great danger or a great external undertaking permits the achievement of the sacred union of the state by silencing divisions and particular interests. Thus it becomes evident that it is in and by war that the state best reveals itself and best fulfills its function. Normal times are characterized by the free activity of the particular spheres. Each individual lives for his family and his calling. The totality intrudes only indirectly in the form of tax levies, the sole requirement exacted by the state. There is a definite predominance of society, particularity, and diversity. On the other hand, it is crisis and especially war which bring the particular spheres together in the unity of the state; it is in crises that the true nature of the state and patriotism is seen affirming itself by exacting and obtaining from the individual the sacrifice of what in times of peace seemed to constitute the essence of his existence: his family, his property, his opinions, his life. Thus war, by showing the primacy of the state over civil society and the individual in its right to demand the supreme sacrifice in order to maintain independence, refutes the liberal contractual theories of the state proposed by Hobbes, Locke, or political economy. "An entirely distorted account of the demand for this sacrifice results from regarding the state as a mere civil society and from regarding its final end as only the security of individual life and property. This security cannot possibly be obtained by the sacrifice of what is to be secured—on the contrary." [50] And, what is more, "in peace civil life continually expands; all its departments wall themselves in, and in the long run men stagnate. Their idiosyncrasies become continually more fixed and ossified." [51]

Thus, although war brings with it insecurity of property and existence, it is a healthy insecurity, connected with life and movement. Insecurity and death are necessary naturally, but in the state they become moral in being freely chosen. Mortality becomes something willed, and the negativity at its root becomes that which constitutes the moral being in its essence.

War is the state of affairs which deals in earnest with the vanity of temporal goods and concerns. . . . War has the higher significance that by its agency . . . "the [moral] health of peoples is preserved in their indifference to the stabilization of finite institutions; just as the blowing of the winds preserves the sea from the foulness which would be the result of a prolonged calm, so also corruption in nations would be the product of prolonged, let alone 'perpetual' peace." [52]

Criticizing the Kantian idea of perpetual peace insured by an association of states, Hegel remarks that "even if a number of states make themselves into a family, this group as an individual must engender an opposite and create an enemy," [53] so true is it that true politics is foreign politics and that the latter is guided by the possibility of war.

As a result, international law is extremely precarious; it is *de facto* and even *de jure* incompetent to handle the possibility and the reality of war. "International law is the result of the relations between independent states. Its content has the form of the 'ought to be,' because its realization depends upon different sovereign wills." [54] Of course, states, like individuals, exist only to the extent to which they recognize one another; this leads to the possibility of contracts and treaties which ought to be respected. "But since the sovereignty of a state is the principle of its relations to others, states are to that extent in a state of nature in relation to each other. Their rights are actualized only in their particular wills and not in a universal will with constitutional powers over them." [55] When these particular wills cannot find a ground for agreement, their conflicts can be settled only by war. International law cannot prevent war by settling the conflicts, for there is no universal authority over the states imposing itself upon them; a league of the Kantian sort presupposes the adherence and obedience of the states, which are always contingent. Nor can international law distinguish between just and unjust wars according to the violation of treaties. For every state, its particular good is the supreme law; in the name of this good it can call into question all the engagements it has made whenever they no longer correspond to its interest. The conflict between morality and politics is resolved by the concrete existence of the state and not by the abstract demands of a universal justice. But to the extent to which the good of the state is the supreme law, war remains the supreme recourse by which this law is necessarily expressed.

However, the explanation based on the plurality of independent states does not exhaust the Hegelian theory of war any more than its justification by human negativity does ". . . real wars have need of still another justification. . . ." [56] This justification comes to them from their historic mission. During history, wars and revolutions are the instruments of the universal spirit. The rise of the people which bears the Idea and the diffusion of the principle in which the universal Spirit is incarnated are effectuated by wars. But the place which Hegel gives to this justification of wars by their historical role raises a difficult problem. If the sense of war is to be found primarily in the development and diffusion of civilization, what happens once this development and diffusion have been definitively realized? Politically, is it not the case that the end of history is defined by the disappearance of wars and violent revolutions? There would seem to be a tension, if not an opposition, between the two Hegelian ideas of the necessity of war and the end of history.

Both appear to be indispensable to the construction of the rational state. Without war the state would tend to be subordinated to society, the universal to the particular, and the whole moral and political life drawn from the classics which Hegel wants to reconstruct on the foundations of modernity—courage, patriotism, civic-mindedness—would collapse. The opposition of rich and poor and the multiplicity of states would seem to guarantee the permanence of crises and wars. But could they not give a new shape to things? Above all, in a world which would continue to be dominated by oppositions, would the end of history by the solution of all contradictions still make sense? On the other hand, without the end of history and without a total reconciliation, the whole Hegelian construction of the state would lose its definitive and necessary character. As we have seen, political philosophy can coincide with the philosophy of history because the final state replaces the best regime. Both Hegel's description of the historical development and that of the rational state imply that the final state represents a synthesis which reconciles all the human possibilities and leaves no room for the incompleteness and the dissatisfaction which would produce a further development of universal history.

Hegel's texts on this question of the end of history are remarkably ambiguous. On the one hand, the sun has set; the long day of the mind is ending; humanity has reached its old age which is also its flowering; history is finished because mind has found itself by knowing itself; liberty is realized in the coincidence of its form and its content.[57] On the other hand, Hegel speaks of the problems that history will have to resolve in the time to come; he cites America as "the land of the future where the burden of world history will reveal itself, perhaps in the antagonism between North and South America"[58]; he sees in Russia "a primitive solidity" which "may bear in itself an enormous possibility of development out of its intensive nature."[59] It is only by finding a solution to these apparent contradictions concerning the problem of the end of history itself that one can decide about its relation to the problem of war.

The way to a possible solution seems indicated by the texts in which Hegel distinguishes between the historical principles and their translation into reality, between their victory as such and their manifest victory. It is indeed concrete freedom which is the final principle; it is indeed the Reformation which is its definitive instrument; Europe is the terrain where universal history, begun in Asia, is completed. With regard to the Reformation Hegel writes: "Here the new, the last standard around which the peoples rally, the banner of the free mind, is unfurled.... This is the banner under which we serve and which we bear. Since then and up to our own days, time has had no other work to accomplish than to inform the world with this principle...."[60] But this introduction of the principle in the world is not completed, even though the principle is realized and the present world is the world of completion which has no further need of anything from without. The revolutions henceforward take place within.

The Christian world is the world of completion. The principle has been realized and thereby the end of days has come. The Idea can no longer see anything in Christianity which is unsatisfied.... Thus the Christian world has nothing external to it in an absolute sense but only relatively; it is an external which is, in itself, already overcome and which only needs to be shown that it has been overcome.[61]

Thus history is finished in the sense that the final principle has made its appearance. The world is virtually European or Western just as it is, in principle, Christian and Protestant. But just as there are still Catholic or non-Christian states, this spiritual victory of western Europe remains to be translated into the political reality. We have seen that, to the extent to which the Reformation represented the Christianization of the world, it also represented the secularization of Christianity. The universalization of the principle in a certain sense does away with the principle in realizing it. This is politically expressed by the fact that the true state should be founded on the Protestant religion but that citizenship in it should be open to Catholics, Jews, and others. Protestantism is the basis of the rational state and ceases to be its basis. In the same way, the Europeanization or Westernization of the world will signify the loss of western Europe's supremacy, or at least of its uniqueness as the privileged domain of the universal spirit. Hegel can, therefore, conceive that, within a world become definitively European, the rise of non-European powers like America or non-Western powers like Russia will, to the extent to which they become Europeanized, occupy the center of the historical stage without representing an original principle or introducing a new step.

We may now return to the problem of war. Hegel makes, it seems, a fundamental distinction between the peoples which have already reached the final stage of civilization and the others. Therefore, he considers wars of civilization to be legitimate, inevitable, and indispensable; this means the conquest by the civilized nations of those which have not reached the same level of development of the state. In virtue of this principle, "it is the necessary fate of the Asiatic empires to be submitted to the Europeans, and China too will some day have to adjust itself to this fate." [62] On the other hand, the fully developed states recognize each other as legitimate. They constitute a federation of states or at least a family within which the kinship or the community of manners makes possible a juridical tie that subsists during wars and that humanizes and limits them. What is more, this limitation, this transformation, ends with the withering away of war itself which, among European states, is no longer feasible. In his *Aesthetics* Hegel, with respect to the future of the epic, says:

If one wishes to get an idea of what future epics might be like compared to those of the past, one only needs to imagine living and universal American rationalism triumphing over imprisonment in an infinite process of bounding and particularization. In Europe today each people is limited by all the others and cannot alone undertake any war against the European peoples. If one wants to escape from Europe, it can only be in the direction of America.[63]

But, if Europe is the future of America, if America in its turn must come to know the rational organization of the developed state, then it too will go beyond the age of youth, of "nascent poetry," of heroism, and of war which is the age of epic. America, too, will come to "the form of general principles, duties, and laws, which are valid in themselves even without the living subjective particularity of individuals." It will go from epic poetry in which "the free individuality of the figures is given free rein," to "the simple rational prose of an ordered domestic and civil life." In short, the final state ought to conform to "a reality appropriate to prose" [64] in which abstract principles flower in the place of individual discovery, firearms in the place of heroes, the novel in the place of the epic. Europe in Hegel's time is the example of such a society. Like the epic, war in principle belongs to the past.

This, then, is the solution to which Hegel leads: war is indispensable to the rational state to the extent to which the state is distinguished from civil society. But the very realization of the fully developed state brings with it the withering away of war. Both indispensable and contrary to the developed state, it only subsists because of the existence of other states which are not yet developed. It is thanks to their relationship with the outside, with those peoples they do not recognize as states and which are not yet rationally organized and historically represent the past, that the developed modern states, which, like those nations of western Europe, can no longer fight among themselves, are able to insure their own unity and the political virtue of their citizens.

Such a solution obviously raises a great number of questions which Hegel does not answer, at least explicitly. In the first place, is it not essentially provisional? Is there in the peoples not yet converted to the rational state an "uncivilizable residue" which would make them the providential and permanent adversaries which the rational state needs? Would the Westernization of the world, the translation of the principle in reality, resemble that infinite progress which Hegel criticized in Kant? If, on the contrary, this process must be brought to its end, if the world, like Europe, must constitute "a prosaically organized society," will it not find an adversary, if necessary by forming one within itself, as Hegel insists would be the case for the society projected by Kant? Will war be reborn from the simple fact of the plurality of states and the absence of a sovereign authority? Or does this situation point toward the birth of a universal state? Or, finally, is the definitive situation that of a plurality of states among which war will have lost all normal and legitimate sense due to the reciprocal recognition of the similitude of their ways of life and manners and their community of principle, but among which it will always remain possible due to the contingency of their relations? In this last case, would not a war which was not an opposition of principles, which no longer represented historical progress, which no longer had this "other justification" which real wars need, a war which, in the extreme case, was only born of accident and, in any case, was the result of a contingency unredeemed by the necessity of history, a war contrary to the universal constitutive principle of the states which waged it, also lose the politically and morally educative function which it alone could fulfill? Even if the possibility of war continued to exist, would not civil society tend more and more to gain the advantage over the state? In short would not that decadence, that *Versumpfen des Menschen* which Hegel attributes to pacific civil society, continue and reach its end? Hegel refuses to answer; he refuses to make predictions. History has only to do with the past, and, as for philosophy, "the owl of Minerva flies only at dusk." [65]

Perhaps it is possible to say that, if Hegel wanted to make the synthesis of ancients and moderns, of pagan master and Christian slave, of ancient warrior and modern worker, of the *polis* founded on the devotion of the citizens and the society founded on the satisfaction of private persons, he ended up less with a true synthesis than with a tension between two poles or a precarious balance. It is perhaps possible to go even further and say that the balance reached tends, in the last analysis, in one direction. Taking the modern revolution and the emancipation of the passions as given, Hegel wanted on these bases to restore the political organization and the human excellence which he blames the moderns for endangering. But if it is true that his "state of civil servants" constitutes the formula which most rationally conforms to the essence of the modern state and the one which is most feasible, it is perhaps no less true to say that the reconciliation of ancients and moderns, as Hegel elaborates it in this formula and in his philosophy of history, represents in its essential elements a decisive consecration of modernity.

## NOTES

1. G. W. F. Hegel, *Philosophy of Right,* trans. T. M. Knox (Oxford: Clarendon, 1942), Preface, p. 11. Unless otherwise noted, citations refer to this translation.

2. G. W. F. Hegel, *Lectures on the Philosophy of History,* trans. J. Sibree (New York: Dover, 1956), Introduction, p. 52. All citations refer to this translation.

3. *Philosophy of Right,* par. 153 (trans. P.H. and A.B.).

4. *Ibid.*, Preface, p. 12. Reprinted by permission of the Clarendon Press, Oxford.

5. *Phenomenology of Mind,* ed. Hoffmeister ("Philosophisches Bibliothek" [Hamburg: F. Meiner, 1952]), chap. vi, B, a, p. 355 (trans. P.H. and A.B.).

6. *Philosophy of Right,* Preface, p. 6; cf. par. 275, pp. 174–75; *Philosophy of History,* Introduction, p. 33.

7. *Encyclopedia of Philosophic Sciences* ("Philosophisches Bibliothek" [Hamburg: F. Meiner, 1959]), par. 433, p. 352 (trans. P.H. and A.B.).

8. *Philosophy of Mind,* ed. Hoffmeister ("Philosophisches Bibliothek" [Hamburg: F. Meiner]), chap. iv, sec. A, p. 149 (trans. P.H. and A.B.).

9. *Philosophy of Right,* par. 261, addition (trans. P.H. and A.B.).

10. *Ibid.*, p. 161.

11. *Ibid.*, par. 124, p. 84.

12. *Philosophy of History,* p. 253.

13. *Philosophy of Right,* Preface, p. 10.

14. *Ibid.*, par. 357, pp. 221–22.

15. *Ibid.*, par. 5, addition, p. 228.

16. *Philosophy of History,* p. 450.

17. *Philosophy of Right,* par. 301, p. 196.

18. *Philosophy of History,* p. 452.

19. *Philosophy of Right,* par. 308, p. 200.

20. *Philosophy of History,* p. 18.

21. *Ibid.*, part IV, sec. III, chap. i, p. 416.

22. *Ibid.*, Introduction, p. 85.

23. *Philosophy of Right,* par. 182, pp. 122–23.

24. *Ibid.*, par. 209 (trans. P.H. and A.B.).

25. *Ibid.*, par. 230, p. 146.

26. *Ibid.*, par. 236, pp. 147–48.

27. *Ibid.*, par. 242, p. 149.

28. *Ibid.*, par. 203, p. 131.

29. *Ibid.*, par. 250 (trans. P.H. and A.B.).

30. *Ibid.*, par. 204 (trans. P.H. and A.B.).

31. *Ibid.*, par. 255 (trans. P.H. and A.B.).

32. *Ibid.*, par. 268 (trans. P.H. and A.B.).

33. *Ibid.*, par. 269 (trans. P.H. and A.B.).

34. *Ibid.*, par. 272 (trans. P.H. and A.B.).

35. *Ibid.*, par. 273 (trans. P.H. and A.B.).

36. *Ibid.*, p. 176.

37. *Ibid.*, par. 280 (trans. P.H. and A.B.).

38. *Philosophy of History,* part IV, sec. III, chap. iii, p. 456.

39. *Ibid.*

40. *Philosophy of Right,* par. 295 (trans. P.H. and A.B.).

41. *Ibid.*, par. 296, p. 193.

42. "On the English Reform Bill," in *Werke,* ed. G. Lasson (Leipzig: Meiner, 1921 ff.), VII, 304 (trans. P.H. and A.B.).

43. *Philosophy of History,* p. 456.

44. *Philosophy of Right,* par. 308, p. 200.

45. *Ibid.*, par. 316, p. 204.

46. *Ibid.*, par. 317, p. 205.

47. *Ibid.*, par. 318 (trans. P.H. and A.B.).

48. *Ibid.*, par. 319 (trans. P.H. and A.B.).

49. *Ibid.*, par. 324, p. 209.

50. *Ibid.*

51. *Ibid.*, addition, p. 295.

52. *Ibid.*, p. 210.

53. *Ibid.*, addition, p. 295.

54. *Ibid.*, par. 330 (trans. P.H. and A.B.).

55. *Ibid.*, par. 333, p. 213.

56. *Ibid.*, par. 324 (trans. P.H. and A.B.).

57. *Philosophy of History,* Introduction, pp. 78 and 109.

58. *Ibid.*, p. 86.

59. Letter to Baron von Uexküll, *Briefe von und an Hegel,* ed. Hoffmeister ("Philosophisches Bibliothek" [Hamburg: F. Meiner, 1952]), II, 298, No. 406 (trans. P.H. and A.B.).

60. *Philosophy of History,* part IV, sec. III, chap. i, p. 416.

61. *Ibid.*, p. 342.

62. *Ibid.*, part I, sec. II, p. 142.

63. *Aesthetics,* in *Hegels Sämtliche Werke,* ed. H. Glockner (Stuttgart: F. Frommann, 1927–41), III "System of Individual Arts," 3, A, a *Das Epische Allgemeine Weltzustand;* vol. III, pp. 354–55 (trans. P.H. and A.B.).

64. *Aesthetics,* p. 341 and c *Das Epos als Einheitsvolle Totalität,* p. 395 (trans. P.H. and A.B.).

65. *Philosophy of Right,* Preface (trans. P.H. and A.B.).

## READINGS

A.  Hegel, Georg W. F. *Philosophy of Right.* Trans. T. M. Knox. Oxford: Clarendon, 1942. Preface; Third Part.

Hegel, Georg W. F. *Philosophy of History.* Trans. J. Sibree. New York: Dover, 1956. Introduction; part II: "The Greek World"; part III, chap. ii: "Christianity"; part IV, sec. III, chap. i: "Reformation"; chap. iii: "Enlightenment and Revolution."

Hegel, Georg W. F. *Phenomenology of Mind.* Chap. iv, sec. A: "The Master and the Slave."

B.  Hegel, Georg W. F. *Philosophy of Right.*

Hegel, Georg W. F. *Philosophy of History.*

Hegel, Georg W. F. "On the English Reform Bill" and "On the German Constitution," excerpts in C. J. Friedrich, ed., *The Philosophy of Hegel.* New York: Modern Library, 1953.

# ALEXIS DE TOCQUEVILLE

## 1805–1859

The publication in 1835 of the first part of *Democracy in America* established Alexis de Tocqueville as one of the foremost analysts of the problem of democracy. Tocqueville was the first writer of modern times to undertake a comprehensive investigation of the way in which the democratic principle, equality, functions as a first cause, shaping or affecting every aspect of life within society.

Tocqueville's approach to the study of political things appears as a departure from the method of those political writers of the seventeenth and eighteenth centuries who began their inquiries with the study of man simply, irrespective of his citizenship in a particular regime. For Tocqueville, the study of politics begins with an inquiry into social condition.

Social condition is commonly the result of circumstances, sometimes of laws, oftener still of these two causes united; but when once established, it may justly be considered as itself the source of almost all the laws, the usages, and the ideas which regulate the conduct of nations; whatever it does not produce, it modifies.[1]

Tocqueville's *Democracy* is explicitly devoted to an exposition of the way in which a particular social condition, a condition of equality, has made itself felt in the political institutions of the nation, and in the customs, manners, and intellectual habits of the citizens. Social condition is the cause of a regime having its own particular characteristics. This is not to say that social condition explains everything about a society, for antecedent customs and geographical factors, among others, also play a role in shaping the regime. But in no enduring case will these secondary

657

factors conceal or frustrate the operation of the fundamental moving principle. Social condition forms opinions, modifies passions and feelings, determines the goals pursued, the type of man admired, the language in use, and, ultimately, the character of the men it encompasses.

That social condition which is the moving principle of democratic regimes is the condition of equality. For Tocqueville, this is the "fundamental fact from which all others seem to be derived." [2] Tocqueville's political thought originates with the recognition and acceptance of the inevitable triumph of the principle of equality. Not only has the course of the last eight hundred years been purposive (leading to the triumph of equality), but, also, in analyzing the record of man's deeds, Tocqueville sees an expression of divine will. The development of equality of conditions is a providential fact.

If the men of our time should be convinced, by attentive observation and sincere reflection, that the gradual and progressive development of social equality is at once the past and the future of their history, this discovery alone would confer upon the change the sacred character of a divine decree. To attempt to check democracy would be in that case to resist the will of God; and the nations would then be constrained to make the best of the social lot awarded to them by Providence.[3]

It is evident from these remarks that Tocqueville does not regard man as constrained within the grip of a complete determinism. "Providence," he tells us, "has not created mankind entirely independent or entirely free. It is true that around every man a fatal circle is traced beyond which he cannot pass; but within the wide verge of that circle he is powerful and free." [4] Tocqueville's work appears as an admonition to men to make the best of the lot awarded them by God—men cannot determine whether conditions will or will not be equal, but theirs is the responsibility whether equality will lead to wretchedness or to greatness, to slavery or to freedom. Indeed, it is a sobering reflection upon the providential march of history that the inevitable triumph of the democratic condition might eventuate as well in a condition of human slavery as in one of human freedom. A social condition has triumphed which man could not forestall, but it rests with man's art to grasp and to turn to advantage those potentialities of the democratic condition that are conducive to freedom. To accomplish this end, Tocqueville calls for a "new science of politics," one adequate to the novel conditions occasioned by the triumph of equality.

That equality can be understood to be the principle of democratic regimes may be seen in the language of the Declaration of Independence. "All men are created equal" is therein regarded as the primary proposition or self-evident truth; the rights of life, liberty, and the pursuit of happiness as universal rights are derivative from this fundamental truth. If all men are equal, no man has by nature a superior right to take another man's life, infringe his liberty, or determine for him his way of life. The equality in question does not extend to intellectual capacity. Tocqueville acknowledges that even with the advent of the most extreme equality of conditions the inequality of intellect will remain as one of the last irksome reminders of the old regime. But the passion for equality even where there can be none will lay to rest the practical force of the classical contention that the wise should rule. Men of democratic ages will brook no privileges, no matter what their foundation.

Tocqueville's purpose in the *Democracy* is to show men how they might be both equal and free, and by not equating democracy with any institutional form associated with it—government of the people, representative government, separation of powers—Tocqueville underscores his fear that the real driving force of democracy, the passion for equality, is compatible with tyranny as well as with liberty. Tyranny may very well coexist with what appear to be democratic institutions. Unlike some of his contemporaries who believed that the gradual development of equality went hand in hand with the final destruction of the possibility of tyranny on earth, Tocqueville understood that the democratic principle was prone, if left untutored, to a despotism never before experienced. We shall return to this theme below.

In his writings, Tocqueville turns to the American regime of the 1830's, not because it necessarily embodies the principles of the best regime, but because it marks the culmination of that historical progress toward ever increasing equality. The nature of democracy thus stands revealed in Jacksonian America; the visit to America is, for Tocqueville, a confrontation with democracy itself. In emphasizing equality of conditions rather than equality simply, Tocqueville calls attention to a state of society in which the concept of equality has become actualized. It is that state of society in which men confront each other when their equality in the abstract has been made manifest to them in equal opportunities for education, in a general levelling of wealth, in the uniform assurance of political rights. Tocqueville did not regard America, or any other society, as a state in which the principle of equality had become completely actualized, but America did approximate this ideal more closely than any other regime. Like all democratic states, it was characterized by the progressive diminution of the inequalities of the "old regime."

Equality of conditions is understood, of course, in contrast to inequality of conditions, the social state of the old regime, either of France or of feudal Europe generally. Within the *Democracy,* the characteristics of the old regime continually intrude upon the argument; it is through Tocqueville's awareness of democracy's grand and, at that time, still respectable alternative that he is able to inform and to chasten the democracy destined to be triumphant. In Tocqueville's characterization of the old regime—that standard against which he seemingly measures democracy and calls it to account—we may begin to grasp the meaning of his thought. It is as if we must say that no one can understand the democratic revolution who is insensitive to the qualities Tocqueville ascribes to an aristocratic state of society: a certain elevation of mind and scorn of worldly advantages, strong convictions and honorable devotedness, refined habits and embellished manners, the cultivation of the arts and of theoretical sciences, a love of poetry, beauty, and glory, the capacity to carry on great enterprises of enduring worth. An understanding of democratic things requires an awareness of the alternatives to democracy; this necessity is not obviated by the "march of history." With this awareness in mind we are ready to turn to Tocqueville's account of democracy.

## The Character of the Regime

The characteristic feature of democratic society is its atomism. The carefully prescribed codes which governed the relations of the three classes of society in aristocratic times have been overturned. The barriers separating the classes have been toppled; property has been divided and equalized; new avenues to social, intellectual, and political achievements have been opened to all. The concern of the ruling classes for those over whom they watched like shepherds over their flocks has been replaced by virtual indifference; the social and political bonds uniting men have been severed. Men confront each other as equals, each independent, each impotent. Individuals comprising such a society have, as citizens, no natural ties to one another; each being the equal of every other, no one is obliged to do the bidding of another. A major task of modern democratic society is the construction of artificial bonds to replace the ties of the Middle Ages.

According to Tocqueville, the key to the atomistic quality of democratic ages lies in the diffusion of "individualism," a disposition to reject as authoritative all obligations or articles of faith which have not been submitted to, or have not withstood the test of, personal inquiry. Each individual becomes the center of a tiny private universe consisting of himself and his immediate circle of family and friends. Wholly absorbed in the contemplation of this universe, the individual loses sight of that greater universe, society at large. The spiritual father of this "novel idea" or disposition is Descartes, whose philosophic method supplies the example and justification for submitting to the private judgment of each man all venerable objects of belief and attachment. Equality of conditions is responsible for the ready and widespread acceptance of the new disposition; in the fulfillment of its own attempts at overturning the social restraints of the Middle Ages, democracy finds a welcome ally in the Cartesian philosophy calling into question traditional beliefs. Around the issue of individualism will be seen to cluster certain propensities which together give rise to what we may call the problem of democracy. These are the passion for well-being and material comforts, a concern for one's private welfare to the exclusion of all consideration of public affairs, and an inevitable drift toward mediocrity. They make democratic man all too prone to accept or to drift into a soft despotism securing him in these pursuits and preferences. A resolution of the problem of democracy entails finding a place within democracy for liberty, for human excellence, for the re-emergence of public virtue, and for the possibility of greatness.

When individualism is linked with equality of conditions, an insatiable thirst develops for the material comforts of this world. In a society shorn of the traditional restraints and obligations—to country, to lords, to church—men strive eagerly to gratify their immediately felt and immediately intelligible desires to improve their conditions of life. Under the old regime, the disparity of wealth and material well-being was accepted as part of the natural scheme of things; moreover, the nobility of feudal Europe had managed to satisfy its desire for material comfort in such a way as to leave it free to cultivate the higher faculties. That is, the nobility were not apprehensive that such wealth as they enjoyed would momentarily be seized from them. This salutary peace of mind had been achieved through the legitimizing effect of long-standing usage and custom. With the overthrow of the feudal system, and with the dissemination of the individualistic doctrines, the need for the amelioration of the material conditions of life is seen as the legitimate expression of the natural rights of all men.

Democracy, then, must satisfy the desire for well-being, not of a few men, but of all men, and do it in such a way as to induce men to devote some part of their energies to other pursuits and to the needs of the nation at large. The problem is soluble either if there are enough material goods to satisfy everyone, so that no one need be apprehensive of not getting his share, or if democratic man can moderate his desires. Tocqueville appears to hold two conflicting views on the likelihood of effecting a resolution of the problem. On the one hand, he appears confident that the taste for physical gratifications will be kept within modest bounds. Democratic man will seek out the little comforts of life: the means of rendering existence less arduous, the purchase and planting of a few more acres of land, the enlargement of his dwelling. Tocqueville's reproach to the principle of equality is not that it encourages men in the pursuit of unlawful or excessive gratifications, "but that it absorbs [men] wholly in quest of those which are allowed. By these means a kind of virtuous materialism may ultimately be established in the world, which would not corrupt, but enervate, the soul and noiselessly unbend its springs of action."[5] The sudden, dramatic, and violent upheaval against religion, morality, and property which erupted in 1789 was but a transient reaction, characteristic only of a revolutionary period; it should not be looked upon as a permanent penchant of democratic eras. Democratic man's taste for well-being is not only compatible with morality and public order, but may not even be satisfied without them. It may even be combined with "a species of religious morality." Thus, although democracy may be accompanied by the neglect of what is highest in man, at least it will solve the problem of a modest well-being for the greatest number. This is the virtue of democracy that Tocqueville celebrates in his famous conclusion to the second part of the *Democracy*.

There is, however, another and less sanguine facet of the pursuit of material comfort. All avenues to the satisfaction of the desire for well-being have been opened, but opened equally to all—the competition is overpowering. However much one may have, he thinks continually of the vast store of goods which constantly eludes him; this thought "fills him with anxiety, fear, and regret and keeps his mind in ceaseless trepidation."[6] If this is so, there can be no technological solution to the problem of well-being—the desires of men increase with what they feed upon; there can never be enough for all.

This unexpected shift from a decent materialism to a more or less thoroughgoing pursuit of material comforts is concomitant with the rise of a commercial spirit—commerce is seen as the most fruitful way of facilitating the satisfaction of the taste for well-being. Commerce readily transforms the simple desire for modest comforts into a caricature of its former self. It comes to be regarded as itself the noblest pursuit, and beguiles the faculties of the men of most competence in society. Men of superior intellect are diverted from politics to business, from public life to private affairs. In commerce, these men find adequate outlets for their distinctive talents, as well as freedom from the conformity and vulgarity of political life. In fact, these men threaten to form the nucleus of a new aristocracy: Tocqueville warns the "friends of democracy" to be wary, "for if ever a permanent inequality of conditions and aristocracy again penetrates into the world, it may be predicted that this is the gate by which they will enter." [7]

Individualism and materialism, divisive features of democracy, are offset to a degree by a general softening of manners and the growth of a spirit of compassion or human fellow-feeling. The classes of the Middle Ages had looked upon each other as beings belonging to different species, such was the difference in their manners, pursuits, and tastes. Society had been cool, uncompromising, severe. The democratic revolution succeeds in dissolving social or political obligations while bringing to the fore natural human ties. As conditions become equal, men become cognizant of their likeness to each other; this awareness evokes feelings of genuine sympathy, and an act of the imagination suffices to enable one to experience the sufferings of another. The democratic revolution discloses the natural goodness of man; he would not needlessly hurt another. We may recognize here the parallelism between Tocqueville's "democratic" man and Rousseau's "natural" man.

There is, moreover, a link between the consequences of individualism and the growth of compassion. Contrary to what might have been expected, the freedom to rely wholly upon oneself, along with emancipation from traditional restraints, does not make democratic man altogether confident and proud. His gravity reflects the seriousness of the enterprise upon which he is engaged, but his confidence is undermined by the "anxiety, fear, and regret" which accompany his condition. Confronted as he is on all sides by those who, like himself, are restlessly striving for unattainable goods, "each citizen is habitually engaged in the contemplation of a very puny object: namely himself." [8] He has no alternative but to seek the assistance of others, something he is obliged to do the more equal social conditions become.

It might appear that compassion and self-interest could combine to serve as the foundation of a social or political bond in democratic times, thus overcoming the divisive forces of individualism and the pursuit of well-being. Yet compassion and self-interest, while not necessarily opposed, are not always compatible. Tocqueville, like Rousseau before him, suggests that compassion, although a natural instinct in man, is weakened by calculation. Inasmuch as men are not disinterested, they will consult their own self-interest before looking to the welfare of others; democracy encourages this by throwing each man upon his own resources. Democratic men will come to the aid of one another if it involves no loss or injury to themselves. For the spirit of compassion to become fully effective, society would require not only a condition of equality, but also a condition of plenty, one in which there were enough material goods for all. We have already alluded to the forces at work within democracy thwarting such a possibility.

Moreover, the spirit of compassion transcends national boundaries, and, as such, operates to weaken political ties; men become indifferent to those arbitrary usages which distinguish men as citizens. Compassion is a natural instinct tending to undermine ties which are merely conventional; for Tocqueville, political society itself has just such a conventional character. The gentleness, softening of manners, and air of humanity which characterize democratic societies are apt to be felt most strongly within the family unit rather than between citizens. "Democracy," Tocqueville tells us, "loosens social ties, but tightens natural ones; it brings kindred more closely together, while it throws citizens more apart." [9]

### THE PROBLEM OF DEMOCRACY

These characteristics—materialism, mediocrity, compassion, domesticity, and isolation—arising, or gathering their strength from, equality of conditions and individualism, constitute the core of Tocqueville's teaching about democracy. A regime in which their effects were not somehow mitigated, a regime in which there would be no encouragement offered for the exercise of higher human faculties, in which society itself would seem to stand still and public virtues languish—such a regime might well cause one to call into question the goodness of the Providence that promotes it.

Nor is this all. The fundamental paradox of democracy, as Tocqueville understands it, is that equality of conditions is compatible with tyranny as well as with freedom. A species of equality, at least, can coexist with the greatest inequality. Left to its own devices, democracy is actually prone to the establishment of tyranny, whether of one over all, of the many over the few, or even of all over all. To the elaboration of this paradox we must now turn.

The ruling passion of democratic ages is love of equality. This passion is itself generated out of the prevailing social condition which, as we have seen, is the fundamental source of all the passions, ideas, and manners of society. But the love of democratic man for equality overpowers every other feeling, even that for liberty. Liberty requires effort and vigilance; it is difficult to attain, and easily lost; its excesses are apparent to all, while its benefits may easily escape detection. The advantages and pleasures of equality, on the other hand, are immediately felt and require no exertion. They are accessible to all, even to those of the meanest capacity, and, "in order to taste them, nothing is required but to live." [10] But if this is true of the pleasures of equality, its shortcomings may not be evident at all except perhaps to those who have not been benumbed by its delights. Equality of conditions, then, has unleashed a passion which will not be put down; every government of the future must acknowledge its roots in this omnipotent drive. The passion of men of democratic communities for equality is "ardent, insatiable, incessant, invincible; they call for equality in freedom, and if they cannot obtain that, they still call for equality in slavery." [11]

Love for equality may express itself in either of two forms, a "manly and lawful passion for equality" which seeks to raise all to the level of the great, or a "depraved taste for equality" which strives to reduce all to the lowest common denominator. Obviously, if the former passion for equality were to prevail, the power of the objections to democracy would be appreciably reduced. But the forces at work under conditions of equality offer little hope that the manly passion for equality will triumph. Men are driven to desire goods they cannot obtain. Equality raises in everyone hopes for the attainment of these goods, but the competition is such that each has little likelihood of realizing his ambitions. Moreover, the race to satisfy these desires is not an equal one; the victory inevitably goes to those of superior ability. All cannot be raised to the level of the great, for differences of ability originate from God, or from nature. Democracy thus awakens a consciousness of the equal right of all to the advantages of this world, but it frustrates men in the attainment of them. This frustration breeds envy and displaces respect. Man's soul is thus constantly excited, forever battered, and hopelessly wearied in the struggle; he cannot long endure such a condition. He seeks a solution which will satisfy his most intense desire while relieving him of the anguish to which it gives rise. Equality thus prepares man to surrender his freedom to safeguard equality itself.

To Tocqueville, this surrender of man's liberty might be made to a despot of the time-honored description, but more than likely the character of the despot would assume a form entirely novel. In fact, terms like "despotism" and "tyranny" become almost inadequate to express Tocqueville's thought, and he seeks to describe rather than name the new despotism. In a society in which all are equal, independent, and impotent, one agency alone, the state, is specially prepared to accept and to supervise the surrender of freedom. Tocqueville calls attention to the increasing centralization of governments—the growth of immense tutelary powers which willingly assume the burden of providing for the comfort and well-being of their citizens. Democratic men will abandon their freedom to these mighty authorities in exchange for a "soft" despotism, one which "provides for their security, foresees and supplies their necessities, facilitates their pleasures, manages their principal concerns, directs their industry," and, ultimately, "spare[s] them all the care of thinking and all the trouble of living." [12] Tocqueville foresaw that such a government was not inconsistent with popular sovereignty, or at least with the forms of popular sovereignty. The people as a whole might very well console themselves with the knowledge that they themselves had chosen their own masters. Democracy originates a new form of despotism, society tyrannizing over itself.

No statement of the problem of democracy would be complete without an account of Tocqueville's description of the tyranny of the majority, of the many over the few. Tocqueville is not unaware of the pleadings of special interest groups or of the fact that the composition of a majority in a democracy frequently fluctuates. But such fluctuation takes place within the context of a settled conviction upon certain principles which are themselves unchanging—in this sense one can speak of a permanent majority within a democracy. Moreover, the apparent homogeneity of democratic society conceals from view two ineradicable sources of heterogeneity: intellect and wealth. Intellectual capacity is distributed unequally, and Tocqueville affirms that the majority of mankind lack the capacity to arrive at rational convictions. Beyond the question of capacity, the requirements of knowledge are such that men under democratic conditions will rarely have either the time, the patience, or the interest to pursue it. Tocqueville envisages no revolutionary breakthrough in the means of education, no "profusion of easy methods and cheap science" sufficient to overcome the want of time and talent. As long as the people remain the people, *i.e.,* the many, they will be obliged to earn their bread and hence lack the leisure indispensable for the cultivation of knowledge. The many, if they acknowledge these facts at all, dispute the significance of them. For the intellectual superiority of the few, they substitute a superiority derived from considerations of quantity: "The moral authority of the majority is partly based upon the notion that there is more intelligence and wisdom in a number of men united than in a single individual, and that the number of the legislators is more important than their quality." [13] The authority of the majority is such that even the minority at last assent to this assault upon the intellect. This, Tocqueville observes, marks a new phenomenon in the history of mankind. The majority not only demand conduct that conforms but strive also to make it impossible for individuals to conceive of nonconformity. To hold an opinion on an important matter contrary to that of the majority is not merely imprudent or unavailing but even dehumanizing. "The power of the majority is so absolute and irresistible that one must give up one's rights as a citizen and almost abjure one's qualities as a man if one intends to stray from the track which it prescribes." [14] The tyranny of the majority over the minds of those who are its intellectual superiors absolutizes the disposition of democracy toward mediocrity.

The tyranny of the majority over the wealthy, the propertied few, is less clear. Tocqueville certainly tries to overcome the fear of those critics of democracy who saw in the rule of the many the inevitable destruction of all property rights; in his Preface he takes care to point out that in the most advanced democratic country in the world property rights have enjoyed greater guarantees than anywhere else. Still, Tocqueville is not sanguine that the eternal struggle between the rich and the poor has been resolved by the democratic revolution—neither have all been reduced or elevated to the same level of wealth, nor has the envy of the poor toward those in better circumstances been assuaged by whatever levelling has occurred. How secure, then, are the rights of property?

According to Tocqueville, the division between the few and the many, the rich and the poor, is a permanent feature of all societies, destined to remain despite the progressive realization of equality of conditions. This is a "fixed rule" to which all communities are subject. On the other hand, the proportion of individuals within a society making up each of the three great orders—the wealthy, those of moderate means, and the poor—may vary from one society to another. Though these proportions may change, Tocqueville rejects the idea that the wealthy or the moderately wealthy may ever constitute a majority. "Universal suffrage, therefore, in point of fact does invest the poor with the government of society." [15] Moreover, he declares that it is inescapable that the ruling class be the oppressor: "It is certain that democracy annoys one part of the community and that aristocracy oppresses another." [16] Finally, Tocqueville despairs of instructing the poor to realize that it is against their own interest to impoverish the rich. He sees, then, no reason to believe that the traditional conflict between rich and poor will cease under democratic conditions, or that the one will lack the will or the opportunity to oppress the other. Since the majority are poor, and since it is they who will be sovereign, the fears of the critics of democracy are justified after all.

Yet how are we to reconcile this with statements apparently quite to the contrary in other portions of the *Democracy*? In the second part, for example, Tocqueville declares that in democratic communities the poor, instead of comprising the great majority of a nation, as they have always done hitherto, will be comparatively few in number, their place being taken by those of the new middle classes. Not only do the middle classes now constitute the majority, but they possess property, and, in fact, are the foremost defenders of the rights of property. What, then, have the rich to fear from a majority whose passions and interests are so similar to their own?

We may suggest a link between the tyranny of the majority and the new despotism. The men who surrender to this soft, comfortable tyranny are the men of the new majority who have tasted and enjoyed the first fruit of the universal pursuit of well-being. But their desires have outrun their opportunities: frightened at the prospect of losing what they have to those more able than themselves, the majority turn to the government as the only power capable of protecting their rights and goods and of restraining the ambitions of the few. The new despotism is one form the tyranny of the majority may assume. At the expense of the few, the wealthy, it secures to the many a modest enjoyment of the good things of this life; in this sense, it is not incompatible with protection of the rights of property on a limited scale.

## THE RESOLUTION OF THE PROBLEM

If the problem of democracy is to be resolved, the resolution must take place on the level of democracy, that is to say, the resolution must be consonant with the principle of democracy, which is equality. Any attempt to temper democracy with principles or practices from a regime alien to it is doomed to failure; not even a despot can rule under the democratic principle without making his obeisance to equality. Thus Tocqueville warns his contemporaries that the task is not one of reconstructing aristocratic society, but of making liberty proceed out of the democratic state of society and of working out "that species of greatness and happiness" appropriate to equality of conditions.

The irony of the democratic predicament is that democracy encourages men to surrender their liberty, the one thing essential to their deliverance. If individualism is responsible for the atomism of democratic society, it is freedom which, paradoxically, can re-establish a sense of political interdependence by fostering an awareness of the dependence of each individual upon every other. What is the likelihood that liberty will issue from a democratic state of society? Tocqueville's reply discloses an essential optimism at the foundation of his political thought:

Far from finding fault with equality because it inspires a spirit of independence, I praise it primarily for that very reason. I admire it because it lodges in the very depths of each man's mind and heart that indefinable feeling, the instinctive inclination for political independence, and thus prepares the remedy for the ill which it engenders.[17]

The passion for equality at any cost is confronted by a similarly engendered passion for equality in freedom. Nevertheless, these passions are of unequal strength, as we have already seen. Moreover, the passion which induces a man to turn over to government the concern for his own welfare is augmented in its effect by the omnipresent tendencies toward centralization of government. Governments grow more powerful; individuals appear more helpless than ever. Consequently, the natural passion for freedom must be supplemented by the political art, an art which Tocqueville finds has been practiced in an exemplary way by America. The American experience suggests for the resolution of the democratic problem certain "democratic expedients," such as local selfgovernment, the separation of church and state, a free press, indirect elections, an independent judiciary, and the encouragement of associations of all descriptions. It must be recognized that Tocqueville does not simply recommend the adoption of each and every American practice. Although he admires the federal system, for example, he argues that such a complicated mechanism is wholly unsuited to the temperament and realities of European political life. More than anything else, America provides the principles, such as the principle of self-interest rightly understood, upon which a respectable democratic order might be constructed. Before turning to consider the doctrine of self-interest, the heart of Tocqueville's resolution of the problem of democracy, we must examine some aspects of the democratic expedients we have just named.

To counteract the effects of centralization, Tocqueville acknowledges the value of local freedom at the township and community level. Within the confines of this smaller whole, each citizen receives his initial training in the use of freedom. By learning to care for and to cooperate in matters within his own purview, the citizen imbibes the rudiments of public responsibility. The township is the locus of the transformation of self-interest into patriotism, at least into a species of patriotism. According to Tocqueville, free institutions, particularly those at the local level, transform essentially selfish individuals into citizens whose first consideration is the public good. Still, the importance or perhaps the relevance Tocqueville attaches to local self-government may easily be overstated. It should be noted that he nowhere gives a simple or a comprehensive formula for the determination of the affairs which properly belong to local as distinct from national authorities. Moreover, he suggests that the more complex and civilized a nation grows, the less likely it is to establish local freedom, or to tolerate the stumbling efforts of a community with no tradition of freedom.

The jury system is another of the democratic expedients Tocqueville recommends to preserve freedom and counter the individualistic tendencies of democracy. Like local freedom, it, too, impresses upon citizens a consciousness of the needs of others. Critics have remarked that Tocqueville's expectations from this source have scarcely been fulfilled, but they have generally failed to recognize that Tocqueville pinned his hopes for its success upon the availability of a body of superior judges, and that he was aware that the quality of judges as a class would diminish in proportion to the increase in their number. It is upon the qualities of such men that Tocqueville relies in his belief that the jury system will form the judgment of the people and instill in them an awareness of the requirements of justice. Tocqueville's characteristic procedure is to attempt to discover those means by which the tastes and passions of the many may be tempered and instructed; the jury system is one such means, and, in this regard, serves as a particular instance of the general and pervasive role Tocqueville expected judges and others associated with the legal profession to play in a democracy. The training lawyers, in particular, receive gives them certain tastes for order, for legal and political forms, and for the connection of ideas—tastes which distinguish them from the multitude and give an aristocratic turn to their thinking and preferences. Their spirit tends to be conservative and antidemocratic; to the extent that they come to play a prominent role in society (as they are bound to do in a society where almost every political question is transformed sooner or later into a legal issue), they will act to restrain the impulses of the many. We may note that the role of lawyers in resolving the problem of democracy is an apparent breach of the principle that such a resolution must take place on the level of democracy, but it is, after all, only a partial breach. While lawyers are marked by aristocratic tastes and habits, they retain their fundamental tie to the people by birth and interest; thus they do not constitute a distinct class.

Of all the democratic expedients, freedom of association is the foremost. Tocqueville looked upon associations as artificial substitutes for the nobility of former ages which, in virtue of its wealth and position, served as a bulwark against the encroachments of the sovereign upon the liberties of the people. Similarly, Tocqueville argues, associations protect the rights of the minority in a democracy against the tyranny of the majority. Since each individual in a democracy is independent but also impotent, it is only by associating himself with others that he may oppose his views to those of the majority. This is one "political" function of the right of association, a right which has its origin in nature. Tocqueville attaches to the proliferation of associations a dignity which is perhaps novel in political thought. Whereas earlier writers had looked upon the encouragement of parties, factions, or associations as a divisive measure in society, Tocqueville thought it absolutely essential to the

well-being of democratic society. Far from contributing to the destruction of the unity of society, associations overcome the divisive propensities of democracy: in the acts accompanying the organization and
operation of an association, individuals learn the art of adapting themselves to a common purpose. But the utility of associations goes far beyond any merely political considerations. Participation in political groupings engenders a taste for, and reveals the advantages of, associations for
other purposes as well—educational, scientific, commercial. According
to Tocqueville, learning to associate is the prerequisite for the preservation of civilization itself: "A people among whom individuals lost the
power of achieving great things single-handed, without acquiring the
means of producing them by united exertions, would soon relapse into
barbarism." [18] Tocqueville saw in associations a means not only of mitigating the tyranny of the majority, but also of overcoming that mediocrity to which democracy was prone.

Democracy places the responsibility for government in the hands
of those who, in Tocqueville's view, "will either believe they know not
wherefore, or will not know what to believe." [19] Nevertheless, a democratic regime may achieve viability if a certain enlargement of view
does occur; the free institutions Tocqueville recommends are designed
to facilitate this. Men are to be transformed into morally conscious citizens through the operation of these democratic expedients. Individuals
will cease to think only of themselves; their capacities will be enlarged
through contact with great judges; their sympathy for their fellows will
grow through jury service; their minds will be broadened by participation in associations. Tocqueville thought it impossible to devise a
system of institutions which would ensure good government through
the actions and reactions of citizens who were wholly thoughtless or
driven by base motives.

The evolution of a sense of public morality out of the spirit of extreme individualism characterizing democratic ages is the theme not
only of the institutions we have been discussing but of Tocqueville's
work as a whole. Men will be made citizens through the operation of
the principle of self-interest rightly understood. In his Introduction to
the *Democracy,* Tocqueville tells us that the poor man "has adopted
the doctrine of self-interest as the rule of his actions without understanding the science that puts it to use; and his selfishness is no less
blind than was formerly his devotion to others." [20] Tocqueville's call for
a "new science of politics" to meet the novel conditions of equality is a
call for a science which would establish the principle of self-interest on
a firm foundation. Of course, it is the "poor" man who is to be taught
the principles of the new science, for it is he who, as a member of the

majority, will govern the new society; by the same token, the principles of the new science must be commensurate with the level of his understanding.

Whatever may be the ultimate shortcomings of the doctrine of self-interest rightly understood, Tocqueville insists it is "the best suited of all philosophical theories to the wants of the men of our time," [21] and that all moralists and educators must bend every effort to impart its principles. The possibility of motivating the many by appeals to self-sacrifice or to the inherent attractiveness of virtue vanishes with the destruction of the feudal system and, with it, of the belief in authority and of the dignity of nonmaterial ends. Under conditions of equality, private interest becomes the principal if not the only spring of human action. Private interest, Tocqueville affirms, is "the only immutable point in the human heart." [22]

Tocqueville contrasts the doctrine of self-interest rightly understood with the view that man serves his fellow creatures best in serving himself. Both views appeal, ultimately, to the self-regarding instincts of man, but the latter makes no provision for the emergence of political virtues: it would only intensify the tendency toward individualism. If men are not to withdraw entirely into their own domestic circles, if public spiritedness is not to disappear altogether, men must be taught that out of an enlightened regard for themselves they need constantly assist one another and sacrifice some portion of their time and wealth to the welfare of the state or community. Men must come to see the desirability of postponing the immediate gratification of their desires in the expectation of a more certain or greater degree of satisfaction at a later time, an expectation arising from the contribution of the common welfare to their own well-being. The foundation of the public or social order rests upon enlightened selfishness: each individual accepts the view that "man serves himself in serving his fellow creatures and that his private interest is to do good." [23] Faithful to the requirements of equality, Tocqueville appeals to the self-regarding instincts of man and strives to erect upon this basis a species of public morality and of patriotism: he would make men virtuous by teaching them that what is right is also useful.

The doctrine of self-interest is one that may be thoroughly relied upon:

The principle of self-interest rightly understood is not a lofty one, but it is clear and sure. It does not aim at mighty objects, but attains without exertion all those at which it aims. As it lies within the reach of all capacities, everyone can without difficulty learn and retain it. By its admirable conformity to human weaknesses it easily obtains great dominion; nor is that dominion precarious, since the principle checks one personal interest by another, and uses, to direct the passions, the very same instrument that excites them.[24]

This succinct statement reveals Tocqueville's fundamental agreement with the presuppositions of modern political thought; despite apparent departures, Tocqueville follows in the tradition originating with Machiavelli and continued in the natural right teaching of Hobbes. The political problem of man is solved by lowering one's standards— the doctrine of self-interest rightly understood does not aim at lofty objects. The realization of such standards as are adopted is insured through the reliance upon a doctrine within the reach of the meanest capacity, hence within the reach of all. The doctrine has its roots in what is considered to be man's most powerful passion, here, the concern for individual well-being. The success of the doctrine is still further guaranteed by the device of playing one interest against another while turning over to reason the office of insuring the satisfaction of the passions. In common with most of the typically modern political philosophers, Tocqueville strives to erect his system upon what is operative in most men most of the time and, not unexpectedly, this turns out to be what is lowest rather than what is highest in man. As in Machiavelli, we take our bearings from what men are, not from what they may become. Tocqueville is no Philistine; he is not insensitive to what is highest in man. Nevertheless, we are confronted with his acquiescence in, and encouragement of, a principle of political morality whose effect is to settle a middling standard upon mankind:

If the principle of interest rightly understood were to sway the whole moral world, extraordinary virtues would doubtless be more rare; but I think that gross depravity would then also be less common. The principle of interest rightly understood perhaps prevents men from rising far above the level of mankind, but a great number of other men, who were falling far below it, are caught and restrained by it. Observe some few individuals, they are lowered by it; survey mankind, they are raised.[25]

We noted earlier that the resolution of the problem of democracy must, according to Tocqueville, take place on the level of democracy. Tocqueville accepts equality and, with it, the individualism which is its inevitable accompaniment. Equality undermines the deference given to those in other ages whose responsibility it was to care for the common good; individualism turns men away from a concern for the common welfare. The problem of democracy is to re-create a sense of public morality on the basis of equality and individualism. The doctrine of

self-interest rightly understood constitutes Tocqueville's attempt to resolve the problem upon this basis. To rely upon self-interest rightly
understood necessitates, of course, that self-interest be *rightly* understood. Within the context of the *Democracy,* self-interest is understood
primarily in an economic sense—it is a concern with the most immediate, tangible, material signs of a man's well-being. Out of an
enlightened regard for one's own material welfare, a good other than
an economic one will emerge: patriotism or public spiritedness is the
by-product arising from the intelligent pursuit of one's own interest.

   We have so far omitted any mention of the role of religion in
mitigating the problem of democracy. At first sight, Tocqueville's
insistence upon the indispensability of religion seems to point to a
radical deficiency in the doctrine of self-interest rightly understood.
There are certain sacrifices which individuals are called upon to make
for which they cannot reasonably expect a reward in this life; moreover, whatever ingenuity may be employed to prove that virtue is useful, there are individuals upon whom such arguments fail to make any
impression. Virtue, then, must have an otherworldly support. The
solution lies in a simple extension of the principle of self-interest to
include the rewards of a future life. Tocqueville contends that the
founders of almost all religions have used the same language in advancing their cause as have moral philosophers in setting forth the
principle of self-interest: the track is the same, "only the goal is more
remote." [26] He does not deny that some religious individuals may have
been motivated by nothing other than the love of God, but he insists
that "self-interest is the principal means that religions themselves employ to govern men, and . . . that in this way they strike the multitude
and become popular." [27] Not only may self-interest be supplemented by
religion, but a species of religious feeling may itself be grounded in a
spirit of calculation.

   Tocqueville's treatment of religion is "popular" throughout. Religion is invoked not only to justify the supreme sacrifice, but also to
combat both the individualism and materialism of democratic ages.
Religion cannot but show men that there are goods and aspirations
which transcend the experience of their senses; it thus combats the
materialist teaching that everything is reducible to matter and perishes
with the body. It awakens the use of man's "sublimest faculties." Religion, moreover, serves to remind men of their obligations to one
another and, by so doing, withdraws men from their exclusive preoccupation with themselves. Tocqueville affirms that freedom is impossible without morality, and morality impossible without religion.
Religion supplies those "dogmatic beliefs" which are the cement of
society, beliefs about the nature of God, the soul, and of men's obli-

gations to each other and to that greater whole, the state, of which they are a part. This is especially necessary in times of extreme individualism, when men are free to form and to hold their own opinions but lack the confidence to do so. In this situation, when all is in doubt and all opinions ill-defended and easily abandoned, men are prone to submit to the first demagogue who lulls their sensibilities with false promises of order and stability. General ideas about God and the human soul are therefore preservers of human freedom. But if individuals cannot determine for themselves the answers to the eternal questions; if philosophers, as Tocqueville declares, cannot supply unequivocal answers; if it is nevertheless essential to the freedom and well-being of society that there be a common core of such beliefs, then society must have recourse to religion to supply the defect. Although Tocqueville alludes to "false and very absurd" religions, he does not insist on truth or consistency in the religion which is to serve this political function; he is virtually indifferent to the particular tenets of the religion professed by this or that democratic society.[28] His recommendations thus amount to little more than the justification of simple beliefs designed to satisfy (and to keep within proper bounds) the instinctive demand of the human soul for some answer to the question of immortality.

Tocqueville's defense of the utility of religion does not lead him to advocate a state religion; on the contrary, he draws from political considerations the necessity of the separation of church and state. But unlike those who sought to sever the two in order to strengthen the political while weakening the religious order, Tocqueville argues that only by separation will the religious influence remain strong enough to exert its beneficent effects upon civil society. The salutary effect of the spirit of religion upon society in democratic ages would be jeopardized were religion, by its entry into the political realm, to implant the suggestion that its tenets were subject to majority determination. Only by relying upon the natural passion for religion which belongs to man as man, and by eschewing alliance with any particular party or state, can religion maintain its hold upon men in democratic times. Religion must remain strong, and hence separate, in order to fulfill its political function. The settlers of New England had transmitted to their descendants this precious bequest: the knowledge of the manner in which the spirit of liberty and the spirit of religion could be combined. In the political realm, all was malleable and subject to change; but

having reached the limits of the political world, the human spirit stops of itself; in fear it relinquishes the need of exploration; it even abstains from lifting the veil of the sanctuary; it bows with respect before truths which it accepts without discussion.[29]

Democracy, it seems, is impossible without such a sanctuary above and beyond democratic inquiry.

Tocqueville is acutely aware that conditions of equality impose their own limitations upon religion. If religion is to remain faithful to its political function, it must accept these limitations; it, too, must be consonant with the principle of the democratic regime and with the passions unleased by equality. It cannot hope, for example, to persuade men that the passion for self-gratification is immoral, but it may try to regulate and to moderate the drive for well-being. Religion must defer without surrendering to democratic passions. While holding fast to its essential beliefs, religion must not excite the hostility of the majority by needlessly running counter "to the ideas that generally prevail or to the permanent interests that exist in the mass of the people." [30] Tocqueville's efforts are devoted to preserving the religious sanctuary from the impious and destructive inquiry of the many.

## THE JUSTIFICATION OF DEMOCRACY

Tocqueville's work has been celebrated for its objectivity, and to suggest that he undertakes to provide a justification for democracy seems contrary both to the spirit and to the letter of his work. Tocqueville attempts to grasp the propensities of democracy and turn them to advantage, but he studiously avoids stating a preference either for democracy (even in its perfected state) or for aristocracy, the regime it had succeeded or was in the process of succeeding. In the Introduction to his *Democracy,* he warns that he has not written to praise democracy or to advocate any particular form of government, nor will he even hazard a judgment whether the irresistible movement toward equality is detrimental or advantageous to mankind. And, at the conclusion of his great work, he says of aristocracy and democracy that they are like two different kinds of human beings, not susceptible of any just comparison. In this same conclusion, however, Tocqueville declares,

We may naturally believe that it is not the singular prosperity of the few, but the greater well-being of all that is most pleasing in the sight of the Creator and Preserver of men. What appears to me to be man's decline is, to His eye, advancement; what afflicts me is acceptable to Him. A state of equality is perhaps less elevated, but it is more just: and its justice constitutes its greatness and its beauty.[31]

Tocqueville rejects the classical contention that justice has as its theme the pursuit of human excellence. In common with modern political philosophers, he holds that justice is derivative from natural rights;

the idea of natural rights, he tells us, is "simply that of virtue introduced into the political world." [32] The natural rights of all are, in turn, derivative from the natural equality of all men, a conclusion which escaped the greatest minds of antiquity and had to await the Christian revelation before its truth could be grasped. The inequalities characterizing the Middle Ages were founded not upon nature but upon positive law. Aristocracy itself, according to Tocqueville, is contrary to "natural equity," and cannot be established without recourse to violence. Even the rule of aristocracy is oppressive to the greatest number of people in the state, the virtue and the talents of the aristocrats notwithstanding; the aristocrats constitute a distinct group having interests typically adverse to the interests of the many. On the contrary, through the operation of a "secret tendency," the majority, though they be ignorant, can hardly help ruling in the interests of the greatest number.

Tocqueville argues, furthermore, that moral obligation derives from two sources—either from the wants and interests common to all men, or from the particular needs of a specific nation or ruling group. General notions of justice have, in every previous state of society, been overlaid with systems of morality reflecting or supporting the particular needs of that society, or of the particular ruling groups within that society, as, for example, the principles of inequality which allegedly justified the rule of the feudal aristocracy. These secondary moral codes were thus tied to special circumstances or issued from those individuals enjoying distinct privileges at certain periods of history. With the disappearance of these privileges, the moral codes to which they gave rise also disappear, and only that simple and uniform code of justice remains which is based upon the wants and the interests common to all men as men. In other words, as conditions become equal, conventional moral codes wither away, to be replaced by that natural code of morality corresponding to the natural condition of man, equality. The democratic condition is thus the only condition which does not give rise to a conventional moral code, and, in this, we may infer from Tocqueville's thought, democracy receives its justification. In its foundations, at least, democracy is in accordance with nature.

Those to whom Tocqueville's *Democracy in America* was primarily or immediately addressed were both the partisans and the critics of democracy. Tocqueville sought to moderate the passions of the former and temper the fears of the latter. The result was a statesmanlike work in which both factions could find some solace and neither too much offense, while the cause of a moderate democracy was itself advanced. Tocqueville accepted the democratic revolution, divined its weaknesses, and sought to remedy them by wholly democratic means.

## NOTES

1. Alexis de Tocqueville, *Democracy in America*, the Henry Reeve text, rev. Francis Bowen, ed., with a historical essay by Phillips Bradley (2 vols.; New York: Vintage Books [Knopf], 1958), I, 48.
2. *Ibid.*, p. 3.
3. *Ibid.*, p. 7.
4. *Ibid.*, II, 352.
5. *Ibid.*, p. 141.
6. *Ibid.*, p. 145.
7. *Ibid.*, p. 171.
8. *Ibid.*, p. 82.
9. *Ibid.*, p. 208.
10. *Ibid.*, p. 102.
11. *Ibid.*
12. *Ibid.*, p. 336.
13. *Ibid.*, I, 265.
14. *Ibid.*, p. 277.
15. *Ibid.*, p. 222.
16. *Ibid.*, p. 197.
17. *Ibid.*, II, 305.
18. *Ibid.*, pp. 115–16.
19. *Ibid.*, I, 196.
20. *Ibid.*, p. 11.
21. *Ibid.*, II, 131.
22. *Ibid.*, I, 255.
23. *Ibid.*, II, 129.
24. *Ibid.*, p. 131.
25. *Ibid.*
26. *Ibid.*, p. 133.
27. *Ibid.*, p. 134.
28. See, *e.g., ibid.*, pp. 22, 154–55; I, 314.
29. *Ibid.*, I, 45.
30. *Ibid.*, II, 28.
31. *Ibid.*, p. 351.
32. *Ibid.*, I, 254.

## READINGS

A.  Tocqueville, Alexis de. *Democracy in America*. Vol. I, Preface, Introduction, chaps ii, iii, iv, v (61–71, 89–101), vi (102–7), viii (165–80), ix, x (181–86), xiii (206–9, 240–45), xiv, xv, xvi (281–90), xvii, xviii (433–47, 452); vol. II, bk I, chaps i, ii, v, viii, xx; bk II, chaps i, ii, iv, v, vii, viii, ix, x, xi, xiii, xiv, xix, xx; bk III, chaps i, xvii, xviii, xix, xxi; bk IV, chaps i, ii, vi, vii, viii.

B.  Tocqueville, Alexis de. *The Old Régime and The French Revolution*. Trans. Stuart Gilbert. Garden City: Doubleday Anchor Books, 1955.

Tocqueville, Alexis de. *The European Revolution and Correspondence with Gobineau*. Ed. and trans. John Lukacs. Garden City: Doubleday Anchor Books, 1959.

Tocqueville, Alexis de. *The Recollections of Alexis de Tocqueville*. Trans. Alexander de Mattos. New York: Meridian Books, 1959.

# JOHN STUART MILL

## 1806–1873

### I. Method in Political Philosophy

John Stuart Mill was plunged into the problem of determining the proper method for the study of politics by the appearance of Macaulay's criticism of *Essay on Government* by his father, James Mill. Up to that time, J. S. Mill, along with other Utilitarians (or Philosophical Radicals as they called themselves), had accepted the deductive method of Bentham and James Mill as the proper one for political science. According to their conception of deductive method, the principles of political philosophy and the practical rules of political action were to be deduced from a few simple laws of human nature, *i.e.,* psychological axioms. Bentham enunciated these principles, and James Mill worked out the theory of government based on them.

Thomas Macaulay presented a brief but devastating criticism of this approach to politics.[1] He argued that the theory of human nature on which it was based was incorrect: men were guided in their action by more than the desire for their own pleasure. He thus showed that even as a deductive theory, James Mill's view was too narrow. More important, he questioned the possibility of developing a theory which would have relevance to practice from a priori first principles. What we know about politics we learn from observation and from the study of history. With observed and recorded historical events and sequences of events as our data, the fruitful procedure, Macaulay thought, was to classify and generalize in the manner advocated by Francis Bacon. These generalizations, continually tested by comparison with new facts, would constitute political knowledge, both theoretical and practical, and would lead to a science of politics far superior to the barren a priori theories of the Philosophical Radicals.

J. S. Mill was much impressed by these and other criticisms made by Macaulay.[2] However, he believed that the Utilitarians were correct in the essentials of their theory, and that the error of his father was one of form and not of content. He held the *Essay on Government* to be a polemic for parliamentary reform rather than a systematic treatise and regretted that his father did not admit this. Thus, while the essay was correct in its major conclusions, it was inadequate in its method. In his own thinking he tried to formulate a method which would do justice both to the insights of utilitarianism and to the strictures of Macaulay.

His own conclusions concerning method rest on distinguishing three kinds of deduction: direct, concrete, and inverse.[3] Thus he recognized four methods, all scientific, but applicable to different subject matters. Induction proper, or, as he called it, the "Chemical Method," establishes causal laws by comparing specifically observed cases using the canons of induction: the methods of Agreement, Difference, Concomitant Variations, and Residues. While applicable to chemistry and useful to some extent in the study of history, this approach is inapplicable to the science of politics. The direct deductive or "Geometric" method, that used by James Mill, argues by syllogistic reasoning from first principles to less general laws. This method is applicable only in those areas where there are no other causes to impede the operation of the cause being studied. It can therefore be used in mathematics, but not in mechanics or politics. The concrete deductive or "Physical" method infers the laws of effects not from one causal law, but from a number of them taken together, considering all the causes which influence the effect and compounding their laws with one another. The aggregation of causes is possible because the effect which is produced is the sum of the effects which would be produced by the causes taken singly. Simple aggregation is not operative in chemistry but is in mechanics and social science, since men remain men even when they act on or in conjunction with other men. Thus the concrete deductive method is proper for that part of social science which is concerned with determining the effect of a given cause, *e.g.,* a new law, in a given condition of society.

On the other hand, to ascertain how conditions, or states of society, themselves are determined, we must invoke the inverse deductive, or "Historical" method. The procedure here is to develop empirical laws of society on the basis of induction and then to "verify" those laws by deducing them from the a priori laws of human nature. The inductive approach in itself is not sufficient because we have too few cases to use as data. Any generalization we develop gains plausibility only by its deductive connection with a general theory. It was from Comte that Mill drew the general theory he believed to be necessary for bringing human progress itself within the scope of science. Usually, and for practical purposes, the physical method is serviceable. It breaks down when progress becomes a factor in political action, that is, when the circumstances which are the background for an action cannot be assumed to remain constant. Thus there are two branches of social science, one which supposes that conditions remain the same but that new or different factors or agencies are introduced (*e.g.,* political economy), and one which attempts to determine how it is that conditions themselves change (*i.e.,* philosophy of history). In Mill's view, no social science is complete without both branches, and the latter historical branch is basic. As will appear, both are directly applicable to political studies, the physical when considering the value of a specific legislative proposal in a particular stage of society, the historical when considering the effects of particular proposals on the progress of society to the next stage.

## II. PHILOSOPHY OF HISTORY

The content of Mill's philosophy of history was strongly influenced by eighteenth-century French thought, by the movement for reform in England to which he contributed, and by his study of nineteenth-century French philosophies of reform, especially those of the Saint-Simonians and Comte.[4] He believed in the possibility and desirability of social progress, but not in its inevitability. Mankind, we know from history, is capable of moving from barbarism to civilization, and this forward movement takes different forms and occurs at various paces in different societies, although, he admits, there is a certain order of human progress. By the use of the proper historical method we can determine the stages through which any people must pass in its progress, and this understanding of the pattern of historical change provides the coordinates within which it is possible to determine what steps must be taken to advance to the next stage. Thus the philosophy of history, understood as the philosophy of the progress of society, is basic for the practical science of politics and gives that science an added dimension. It is not merely necessary to know what must be done in the present situation to achieve the ends of the presently existing government in the present society. It is also necessary to know how that should be done so as to enable mankind to move to the next higher stage of civilization. Even this must be done in such a way as to pave the way for the stage of civilization beyond the next. Such a theory, it may be pointed out, is satisfactory as long as we are looking at less advanced societies from the point of view of the more advanced. We ask, What do such societies require to achieve the level of civilization that we have already reached? This is the kind of question that Mill raises about primitive societies. It is more difficult to determine what our society, a highly civilized one, requires to move on to its next stages of which we at present have no example and no clear conception. The gap in the philosophy of history is filled by the ideal derived in a deductive fashion from a theory of human nature and a theory of ethics.

When he was still a young man, Mill formulated a suggestive approach to this problem.[5] He distinguished two basic states of society: the natural and the transitional. The natural state of society was that in which those best fitted to govern were actually the governors. In the transitional state, on the other hand, individuals other than those best fitted were in power. Natural states tend to be undermined by the rise of new leaders; the struggle between them and the old leaders produces the state of transition which is eventually replaced by a new natural state. While Mill later seems to have abandoned this type of analysis, there remained a residue of it in his thinking, namely, that no state of society is satisfactory unless those who are best fitted to rule exercise the major authority in society.

Mill was also impressed by the three-stage analysis of Comte. That the intellectual development of mankind has had a theological and a metaphysical stage, and is now in a positive (or as Mill would prefer to call it experimental) stage, he thought quite correct, and his acceptance of this doctrine survived his disillusionment with Comte's later social philosophy.

If we ask Mill what is the efficient cause of social progress, we find that he has no simple answer. At each stage of civilization certain conditions may be produced which make possible the next stage; e.g., he points out that the first lesson that must be learned before any social progress is possible is the lesson of obedience. Yet the existence of the conditions of progress does not guarantee that progress will occur. The forward movement of society is actually produced by the ideas, example, and moral and intellectual leadership of superior individuals. Superior individuals have flourished chiefly under conditions of liberty, so that liberty becomes a necessary condition for progress. The argument is fairly simple: Progress depends on the emergence of new ideas; new ideas emerge only as challenges to old and accepted ideas, and then only if there is freedom to challenge the existing beliefs and to suggest alternatives. That the existing beliefs provide a basis for the stability of society Mill recognized. That the challenging of those beliefs was a threat to society he also recognized. The implicit tension between the demands of stability and the demands for reform is considered at length by Mill in his *Representative Government* (to be discussed below).

Another question that must be considered by any philosophy of history if it wishes to contribute to the study of politics is the place of the existing society in the pattern of history. Mill had no doubt that the societies of western Europe and the United States were civilized. There were also areas in the world which were uncivilized, and others at various stages of civilization below the levels achieved in western Europe. The signs of civilization are the existence of responsible government and the emergence of scientific knowledge. Mill seems to believe that the measure of a society's advance is the state of the intellect, and he seems to have little doubt that the future progress of mankind is tied to the continued development of scientific knowledge, especially in the area of social science (since he believed that the physical sciences were on the verge of becoming complete). That further progress remains to be achieved is a foundation stone of his whole system of political thinking, and that it can only be achieved deliberately through a science of society is a corollary for which he is indebted to Comte and the French Socialists.

To understand Mill's philosophy of history in its relation to his political science, one must appreciate the influence upon him of Tocqueville.[6] Mill accepted Tocqueville's thesis that the movement toward more and more democracy, that is, toward greater and greater equality of status, was almost inevitable. Like Tocqueville he felt not that this movement was in itself progress, but rather that it indicated the problem to be faced by those who wished to promote progress. Equality carried too far interferes with justice and can undermine both the liberty and the respect for intellectual and moral excellence that is the condition for further progress. It is from this analysis that Mill was led to qualify in his own theory the faith in radical democracy of the earlier Utilitarians.

### III. MORAL CONSIDERATIONS

The philosophy of history adopted by Mill required a revision of the ethical theory of utilitarianism in so far as it was applied to politics.[7] The end of the state, for the earlier Utilitarians, was the good of the individuals who composed the state, and that good was defined in hedonistic terms as the maximum of pleasure attainable with the minimum of pain. Thus government was looked upon as an agency for increasing pleasure and decreasing pain. That Mill accepted this view in principle is true without a doubt, but he found it inadequate, both in neglecting one aspect of human nature and in misunderstanding the aspects it included. The burden of Mill's argument in "Utilitarianism" is directed against the intuitionists who, he believed, claimed that the distinction between right acts and wrong acts, or between correct moral principles and incorrect ones, could be known a priori. He rejected this view and claimed that the fundamental principle of morality is known by experience, and he even goes so far as to offer a sort of inductive proof for the greatest happiness principle.

Mill revises the theory of Bentham in the course of his attempt to answer specific objections to the earlier version of utilitarianism. The objection that seemed to concern him most was that utilitarianism took a low view of human life, not distinguishing a life fit for animals from what is fit for men. In reply to this, Mill introduced a qualitative distinction among pleasures to supplement the merely quantitative distinctions of Bentham, and he traces this qualitative distinction back to ancient Epicureanism. Some pleasures, specifically the mental and spiritual ones, are in themselves superior to the bodily pleasures, regardless of quantitative or circumstantial considerations. Thus happiness would require not only a life of pleasure without pain, but the achievement of the superior pleasures even at the cost of pain and the sacrifice of the inferior pleasures.

This point is significant for Mill's political philosophy in three ways. First, it is connected with his theory of human progress. A society in which people pursue the superior pleasures is more advanced in civilization than one in which they do not. Thus the promotion of the pursuit of the higher pleasures is at the same time the promotion of the advancement of society. In the second place, the cultivation of the higher pleasures requires social freedom, so that only a free society can be truly civilized in Mill's sense. Finally, men can live together more justly and with higher human achievements to the extent that they pursue the higher pleasures rather than the lower. Thus the problem of government is partly solved by the pursuit of the higher pleasures, because those traits of character which are developed from that pursuit are the very traits of character which are necessary to achieve the best form of political organization. Science, the highest achievement of the intellectual life, requires just that objectivity and disinterestedness that man requires to be a truly moral being, and hence to be a citizen in the best type of state.

Thus, while the core of utilitarianism is present in Mill's assertion that those actions, individual or social, are right which produce the greatest happiness of the greatest number, that core has been so modified and expanded that the resultant theory has a cast different from that of original utilitarianism. Government does not exist merely to produce the maximum of that kind of pleasure which the citizens happen to prefer. Rather some types of pleasure are better than others, and the government has the responsibility for having its citizens educated to pursue the higher pleasures in place of the lower pleasures. Moral education, whether it is actually carried on by the government or by private individuals (and Mill seems to prefer the latter), is thus one of the responsibilities of the good society; and moral education must be directed at man not simply as a pleasure-seeking animal, but as "a progressive being."

Some further distinctions are important for the politically relevant portion of Mill's ethical theory. For Mill the individual is prior to the state, but not the individual as he is, rather the individual as he may become with proper education in a well-organized society. This does not mean that Mill conceives of one pattern of human life which should serve as a model for all men, but rather that there is a great variety of potentials in men, and society should provide the conditions in which each man can develop his special talents and make them available to the community. He can do this best by having the opportunity actively to use his talents. Mill sees the active life as morally superior to one of passive obedience at almost all levels of human achievement. From this it follows that the government which encourages active participation in its operation by all its citizens is better, in spite of the problems which may arise as a consequence, than one which is more orderly but encourages its citizens to be passively obedient to the commands of a ruling group, whatever the morality and justice of those commands.

## IV. THE END OF THE STATE

Mill commences his most extended single treatment of political philosophy, *Considerations on Representative Government*,[8] with a reworking of the old question as to whether governments exist by nature or by convention. He takes this as a question concerning the range of choice as regards forms of government. If government is entirely a matter of convention, then choice is unlimited. If governments exist entirely by nature, then no choice is possible. He rejects both positions and tries to show the element of truth in each by pointing to three conditions that any people must satisfy in order that a particular system of government may succeed among them: They must be willing to accept it, willing to do what is necessary to keep it standing, and willing to do what is necessary to enable it to fulfill its purpose. The conditions favorable to the establishing and maintaining of particular systems of government may be to some extent the result of the education of the people; and within the limits set by these conditions, the specific form of government is a matter of choice.

The choice of one form of government from among the ones whose conditions are present should be guided by an understanding of the purpose or purposes of government. After canvassing some current views on the subject, Mill finds that the most widely held view, even among the Utilitarians, is that governments exist to preserve order and to achieve progress in society. He finds this redundant since the achievement of progress presupposes order, *i.e.,* security in what has been achieved. Mill would thus be willing to say that progress is the whole end of government, but somewhat reluctantly, since saying this does not place sufficient emphasis on the equally important need to guard against the danger of retrogression. A more appropriate way to get at the requisites of a form of government is to recognize that the supposed antithesis between order and progress is merely a reflection of a deeper psychological antithesis between two types of human character, the type in which caution predominates and that in which boldness is dominant. Good government, that which achieves progress on a basis of order, requires men of both types to provide a balance, though no special provision in the constitution is necessary to assure this. All that is necessary is to be sure that neither type is systematically eliminated. What is fundamental is the qualities of the human beings over whom the government is exercised, and this is seen in two perspectives. One test of good government is the extent to which the virtue and intelligence of the people themselves are promoted. The other is the extent to which the machinery of government takes advantage of the good qualities of the populace. Thus, the end of government is to make the people better, and the means are to educate the people and to put to use the highest qualities which they have achieved.

Thus Mill's moral theory provides the basis for his political theory, and both of these are supported by his account of the stages of social progress. While Mill recognizes that the government must take care of the affairs of the community, its responsibility for developing the people is more important. The criterion of its effectiveness in the former is its efficiency, and the standards of efficiency are the same for all forms of government. The criteria of its effectiveness in the education of the people are more complicated and depend on the stage of development in which the people find themselves. Just as there is a natural order in the education of an individual, so there is a natural order in the education of a people. Easiest lessons are learned first; those which presuppose others cannot be learned until those others have been mastered.

If the precivilized condition is barbarism, obedience is the first lesson, labor is the next, and self-government is the final step. Mill sees a continuous line of development from slavery to self-government, with each stage prepared by the learning of a specific lesson, that is, by the acquiring of a new character trait on the part of the population as a whole. Apart from the business side of government, the criterion of the best form of government for any particular people is that it provide what is necessary to teach them the lesson they must learn in order to move to the next more advanced state of society, and that it not hinder them from moving on, after suitable training, to the step beyond. It is in this context that we can understand Mill's view that despotism is "a legitimate mode" of government for barbarians, if "the end be their improvement." [9] For Mill this sequence of steps implies a culmination in the best form of government altogether, one which, if the necessary conditions existed, would promote more than any other, not one form of human improvement, but all forms and degrees of it. This he says is some variety of the representative system.

## V. The Argument for Representative Government

Representative government has only one rival for its place as the ideally best polity, and that is benevolent despotism.[10] After considering carefully the benefits to be derived by the absolute rule of an intellectually and morally superior individual, Mill finds several arguments decisive against its claim. One, which comes from the earlier Benthamite theory, rests on the principle that the "rights and interests of any person are only secure from being disregarded when he is able and disposed to stand up for them." In a benevolent despotism, however, the rights of individuals, those limitations on the power of others to interfere with a man's actions which can be justified on the principle of utility, are not secure because they depend on the guarantee of the despot. While specific despots may in some cases protect these rights, human nature being what it is, despotism is not reliable in that respect. Historical evidence, which shows that free people have prospered more than those under despotisms, supports this argument. The other argument goes to the root of what is distinctive in Mill's theory. Despotism requires obedience on the part of the citizen body, that is, passivity. Intellectual, practical, and moral excellence, the highest aims which the state ought to strive to cultivate among its citizens, are all the products of an active character. Thus while despotism may be suitable where a people has to learn obedience to progress to higher stages of civilization, once it has learned that lesson, it ought to be encouraged to active participation, which is possible only in a popular government. Popular government therefore appears to be the ideal polity for two reasons: It protects the rights of individuals, and it promotes their highest moral and intellectual development. However, Mill has one more step in his argument: The highest development of individuals rests also on an advanced civilization, which is only possible in a large state. Popular government is only possible in small states. The closest approximation to popular government which is feasible in large states is representative government, *i.e.,* representative democracy.

Representative government is not only the ideally best polity, all things considered, but is also a form of government that can be established in the modern world. Its existence depends on the three conditions already mentioned, together with a degree of maturity which makes possible this form of self-government. Where the people have some lesson still to learn, some other form of government will be more suitable for them, *e.g.,* they may learn obedience more easily from a military leader, or a king may teach them to overcome that spirit of locality which prevents them from joining with other localities to set up the central authority which representative government presupposes. Barring such defects as these, and they were certainly, Mill felt, not problems in the England of his time, a properly constituted representative government could do most to aid the people to achieve progress to the next stage of society.

## VI. THE ANALYSIS OF REPRESENTATIVE GOVERNMENT

The proper constitution of a representative democracy is not a simple matter, however, and no government of Mill's time exhibited it, chiefly because the role of the representative in government had not been understood correctly. The usual error in conceiving of representative government, Mill believed, was in holding that the representatives of the people should actually govern. The functions of government, executive, legislative, and judicial, are highly skilled activities which require experienced, well-trained individuals whom the populace is not qualified to select. Thus it may be said that Mill believes in government by experts. However, every constitution has "an ultimate controlling power," and this power must in a democracy reside in the people themselves. Not being able to exercise this power themselves, the people exercise it in effect, can control the operations of government in the public interest, through periodically elected deputies. Thus, for Mill, the representatives are not the government, but act for the people to control the government.

A parliament of elected representatives would serve as the controller of the government in the interest of the people. Mill sees this parliament as chiefly a deliberative body, at once a "Committee on Grievances" and a "Congress of Opinions." Containing "a fair sample of every grade of intellect which is at all entitled to a voice in public affairs," its function would be "to indicate wants, to be an organ for popular demands, and a place of adverse discussion for all opinions relating to public matters. . . ." [11]

The point of interest here is that Mill's "Representative Democracy" is two stages removed from democracy in the literal sense of the term, rule by the people. Rule by the representatives of the people is one stage removed, and rule by experts controlled by the representatives of the people is another stage removed. Mill comes to this view not only on the basis of considerations of practicality, but on the basis of his belief that while justice requires democracy, an uncontrolled democracy can be just as much a tyranny as absolute monarchy.

The effective operation of representative democracy requires the presence of conditions not required of other systems of government. A nice balance must be preserved between the representative body and the actually governing bodies. Too strong a representative body will hinder the government from carrying out its functions. One that is too weak will be unable to control the government. The representative body might not have the mental qualifications needed for its work. Sinister interests, interests not identical with the interest of the community as a whole, may gain predominance. These latter defects tend to be present in all constitutions. They are inherent in the nature of monarchy and aristocracy, but by suitable institutions their danger may be reduced to a minimum in a representative system. Mill devoted considerable attention to designing specific arrangements for the representative democracy he favors, to enable it to overcome its possible defects.

The technique of the better monarchies and aristocracies for securing talents of a sufficiently high order for governmental functions is the establishment of a bureaucracy. But bureaucracy relapses into routine, which represses the individuality of its members and becomes a system governed by trained mediocrity. Only popular government (and Mill considers his system of representative democracy the most feasible type of popular government) keeps alive antagonistic interests in the community, and thus stimulates individual thought and initiative, enabling the man of original genius to pierce the barrier of trained mediocrity. However, the freedom produced by the representative system must be combined with trained skill. The distinction between governing and controlling, which is at the basis of Mill's system, produces the combination. The experts govern, but they are controlled by the representatives of the people.

Mill's specific proposals for the reform of existing representative government can be understood as attempts to secure the establishment of a skilled democracy. Without skill the complex problems of the government of a free society cannot be solved. Without democracy there is no security for good government, that is, for the protection of the rights of citizens. Mill finds that the current conception of democracy is based on an inadequate understanding of majority rule. If democracy means government of the whole by a majority which alone has representation, the ends of democracy are bound to be frustrated, for the minority, having no representatives, has no assurance that its rights will be protected, and the majority will be in a position to pursue its sinister interest. Mill fears, for example, that a representative body representing the interests of the working class will jeopardize the property rights of the wealthy, and thus undermine the economy of the nation. Rule by the majority in its own interest is as much a government of inequality and privilege as rule by a privileged minority in its interest. True democracy on the other hand is government of the whole by the whole equally represented. The existing system of false democracy involves both misrepresentation (of those of the majority party who opposed the candidate chosen) and nonrepresentation (of those who vote for the party which loses). The absence of an effective voice in opposition to the majority in the representative body tends to produce a mediocre and incompetent ruling group.[12]

Mill believed that Thomas Hare's scheme for personal representation provided means for giving representation to each voter. In Hare's variant of proportional representation, each voter votes for a series of candidates, marking them as his first choice, his second choice, his third choice, etc. When a sufficient number of ballots to elect is credited to a candidate, the remainder for him go to second, third, and subsequent choices so that each vote counts for someone who is elected. Every voter has at least one candidate who may be said to represent him. Mill believed that in the existing system in which a majority in a geographic district determines the representation for that district, the voters for the losing candidates are disenfranchised. Under Hare's system every vote counts. On Mill's theory of representation the elected representative had the responsibility of thinking and discussing public issues in the interest of the whole, not merely reflecting the views of his constituency. He argued against pledges on the part of candidates for office and refused to give any when he himself stood for Parliament in 1865.

While the earlier Utilitarians had assumed that the extension of the suffrage alone would guarantee that the interests of all would be defended, Mill felt that without personal representation universal suffrage would lead to the tyranny of the majority. The earlier reformers also assumed that the lower classes would choose their betters to represent them. Mill was by no means as sanguine. He believed that special measures had to be taken to prevent the views of the instructed classes from being drowned in a flood of votes from the uninstructed classes. The system of personal representation would obviate the rule of the uninstructed by enabling the instructed from all parts of the nation to pool their votes to secure the election of the candidates they preferred. But this was not enough for Mill. To give the instructed an even greater weight than their mere numbers would merit, he advocated plural voting for the professional and other classes that carried greater responsibility in the community. While personal representation has an ambiguous effect on democracy (being democratic in the sense that it gives everyone a voice, and contrary to democracy in that it increases the strength of the minorities in relation to the majority), the system of plural voting is definitely a curb on democracy and indicates the strength of Mill's conviction of the dangers of unlimited democracy. He placed his reliance on a representative body in which the interests of the two major classes in society, the working class and the upper class, were evenly balanced, on the expectation that most of the representatives would vote in accordance with their class interest, while a minority of each group, carrying the balance of power, would vote in the public interest.

## VII. Theory of Liberty

The essay *On Liberty* was held by Mill to be his most carefully composed work and the one which was most likely to be of enduring value. We can appreciate why Mill felt this way and judge more adequately of the significance of the book if we consider it in the context of his philosophy of history and his theory of the state.

Believing in the progress of society from lower to higher stages of civilization, Mill saw the political culmination of this development as the emergence of a system of representative democracy. Thus he judged representative democracy to be the ideally best polity, *i.e.,* that form of government toward which mankind was progressing. Nevertheless Mill did not see the emergence of representative democracy as the emergence of utopia. Not only was there an ever-present tendency toward retrogression which society had continually to struggle against, but equally dangerous was the tendency of the most idealistic and high-minded

reform movements to harden into dogmatic systems which forced conformity and thereby inhibited future progress. Just as obedience and
work were the main conditions of human progress at earlier stages of
man's development, so in the civilized period, obedience and industriousness having been engrained, liberty becomes the condition for subsequent progress.

Evidently Mill's theory of liberty is far from a universal doctrine
which applies to all peoples at all times. Rather it is practically relevant
only when society becomes more important than the state. As long as
there is a recognized opposition of interest between the governors and
the governed, the progress of mankind requires that men work to
achieve the conditions of representative government. Once these conditions are achieved, a representative democracy can emerge in which the
opposition between governors and governed disappears, for the governors then represent the interests of the governed. This condition,
which makes possible the liberty of the individual, does not guarantee
it. The very emancipation of society from the constraint of a government in the interests of a few creates in society itself, in the great mass
of the people, a new and more dangerous threat to the liberty of the individual. In dealing with this newly emerging problem, Mill believes
that he is thinking for the future. The problem of subsequent stages of
progress is to prevent the individual from being oppressed by the ever
more powerful and confident mass of mankind. Progress toward civilization requires curbs on individual liberty; progress in civilization requires the emancipation of the individual from those restrictions.

What is required, Mill believes, is a practical principle which will
so define the area of individual liberty as not to prevent government
from meeting its obligation to promote the progress of society. Mill
grounds this principle in his moral theory: The only thing of ultimate
value is the happiness of individuals, and individuals can best achieve
their happiness in a civilized society when they are left free to pursue
their own interests with their own talents as these have come to be
understood and developed by them under an adequate system of education. Underlying all this is the assumption of the ultimate value of
individuality, of individual development, both for the individual himself and for the future progress of society—for the individual, once the
conditions of free development, namely, civilization and representative
government, are achieved; for the society because the progress of civilization depends on the contributions that can be made only by individuals who think for themselves. The civilized man, for Mill, is the one
who acts on what he understands, and who exerts every effort to understand. This Socratic model is not meant for the few who have the philo-

sophic bent, but is intended as a model for all men in so far as they are capable of achieving it.

The question then arises as to the conditions under which society can progress toward this goal. The principal condition is self-restraint on the part of the individuals in society, and Mill's theory of liberty is an attempt to spell out in practical terms what that self-restraint requires. It requires as a foundation that each individual, groups of individuals, the government, and the mass of the people refrain from interfering with the thought, expression, and action of any individual. This is the basic principle of liberty.

Radical noninterference with individuals, applied abstractly and absolutely, would of course make government and an orderly society impossible. It is in effect an anarchistic principle. Mill qualifies it in its practical application by recognizing that while thought must be absolutely free, the freedom of action of individuals must be limited for the safety of society. Mill argues that the individual belongs to himself and is subject to social control only for the purpose of preventing him from harming others. The individual is sovereign over himself, and the society is sovereign over the acts of the individual that impinge on others. The thoughts of the individual are part of himself, and therefore the principle requires that society exert no control over them. (Here we must bear in mind that Mill is not talking about any collection of individuals anywhere, but about a mature body of citizens who have been educated to a sense of public responsibility. He explicitly excludes children and savages.)

The public expression of one's private thoughts might be supposed to fall into a different category, that of action. Mill admits that it does so, in some isolated cases, but generally speaking he believes that expression requires the same absolute liberty as thought for the following reasons: First, expression is so closely related to thought that the control of expression would become in effect a control on thought. Second, he asserts that the claim to the right to limit freedom of expression, that is, the claim to the right to silence the expression of opinions in society, presupposes infallibility on the part of those who make the claim. Mill's belief is that no one can legitimately claim infallibility, and hence no one can legitimately claim the right to suppress any opinion. On the contrary, society has everything to gain and nothing to lose by absolute freedom of discussion. An unpopular opinion may be true, in which case the rest of mankind can learn something from the dissident view. This would hold even if it were partly true and partly false. Even if the dissident opinion were entirely false, society would be the gainer by allowing it to be expressed. Society would be kept alert as to the grounds of its own (true) view, which would become a dead dogma if it went forever unchallenged; and the instruction of the mistaken dissident would always remain as a possibility.

Mill's approach to the problem of the limits, if any, to freedom of public discussion in society assumes, it must be recalled, a mature public carrying on its discussion in a restrained and civilized way. Those who do not live up to the rules of the game have no such rights; they must be restrained in the same way as those whose actions harm others in society. The implicit principle here is that as long as discussion remains discussion, it ought to be permitted absolute freedom; but once it passes beyond discussion to action, it ought to be treated as action. The illustrations that Mill gives of the latter, *e.g.,* telling an excited mob that corn dealers are starvers of the poor in front of the house of a corn dealer, suggest that it is not the opinion alone which determines to which category, thought or action, expressing the opinion belongs, but rather the circumstances in which the opinion is expressed.

It is generally agreed that actions cannot be as free as opinions. Actions must be limited to the extent that they result in harm to others. Mill is very careful to make sure that this rule is not made the basis for a general restriction of liberty of action. When men consent to the action by which they are harmed, that action is of no concern to society. In general, the burden of proof is on society to show that the individual's action is harmful, rather than on the individual to prove that it is harmless. Danger of harm to oneself, once one is a mature individual, is no ground for interference by government. Under that circumstance the individual may be remonstrated with, but not coerced.

The ultimate aim of social action should be "to secure to all persons complete independence and freedom of action." This includes especially freedom to gratify tastes and engage in pursuits, as well as freedom of association, all to the extent that other individuals are not harmed. By education in the self-regarding virtues the individuals in society should be encouraged to use their freedom to advance themselves morally and intellectually; if they succeed, they become suitable objects of admiration and emulation; if they fail, they become objects of distaste and perhaps even contempt. However, they are not to be interfered with by society or by government unless they fail in some social obligation which is ultimately grounded in the utilitarian principle of the greatest happiness of the greatest number. To the objection that it is difficult, if not impossible, to distinguish between that part of a person's life which concerns only himself and that part which concerns society, Mill offers a partial answer in practical terms. If the basis of the objection is that many apparently self-regarding actions do harm to others, Mill replies that to the extent that they do harm to others they should be punished. Definite damage or harm to others should be punished, but merely contingent injury (that which does not violate a specific duty) ought to be tolerated for the sake of greater freedom. In these terms Mill discusses spending income, drinking fermented beverages, sale of poisons, polygamy, gambling, and other acts which have been objects of legal restriction. He admits that there is no mechanical application of his basic principles, but insists that they are the only proper guides to correct social policy.[13]

He concludes by restating the arguments for individual initiative in preference to social control: Most things tend to be done better when done by individuals than when done by the government; individual action promotes the mental education of the individual, which governmental action does not; and increased governmental action is a threat to liberty.

While Mill does not rule out the interference of government in the economic life of the community as either impossible or undesirable in principle, he would restrict those interferences to the area of the distribution of goods, exempting the area of the production of goods as being governed by laws of nature. Though in later life he came to consider himself something of a Socialist, he also expressed fears of the extension of social control over economic life. Using individuality, liberty, and the progress of society as his standards, he recognized the advantage of "non-authoritative" governmental interference in the form of supplying advice and information and in competing with private enterprise where there was danger of monopoly. Recognizing that the organization of society on a communistic basis might raise the standard of living of the laboring classes, he did not believe that the increased standard of living would be worth the price of restrictions on liberty if these should be the outcome.[14]

## NOTES

1. "Mill on Government," *Edinburgh Review,* vol. X (March, 1829). Reprinted in *The Miscellaneous Writings of Lord Macaulay* (London: Longman, Green, Longman, and Roberts, 1860), I, 282–322.

2. J. S. Mill, *Autobiography* (New York: Columbia University Press, 1924), pp. 110–13.

3. J. S. Mill, *A System of Logic* (1843), III and VI.

4. *Ibid.,* esp. VI.

5. J. S. Mill, *The Spirit of the Age* (Chicago: University of Chicago Press, 1942). These essays were originally published in 1831.

6. J. S. Mill, "M. de Tocqueville on Democracy in America," in *Dissertations and Discussions* (New York: Henry Holt, 1874), II, 79–161. See also *Autobiography,* pp. 134, 141.

7. J. S. Mill, "Utilitarianism," *Fraser's Magazine* (1861). Reprinted in many editions.

8. J. S. Mill, *Considerations on Representative Government* (London, 1861). Reprinted in many editions.

9. J. S. Mill, *On Liberty* (London, 1859), i.

10. *Considerations on Representative Government,* iii.

11. *Ibid.,* v.

12. *Ibid.,* vii.

13. *On Liberty,* iii–v.

14. J. S. Mill, *Principles of Political Economy* (2 vols; London, 1848), V.

## READINGS

A.  Mill, John Stuart. *On Liberty,* in *Utilitarianism, Liberty, and Representative Government.* New York: Dutton, 1951.
Mill, John Stuart. *Representative Government,* in *ibid.* Chaps i–vii.
B.  Mill, John Stuart. *Utilitarianism,* in *ibid.*
Mill, John Stuart. *Representative Government,* in *ibid.* Chaps viii–xviii.
Mill, John Stuart. *A System of Logic.* New York: Longmans, 1949. Bk VI.
Mill, John Stuart. *Principles of Political Economy.* Ed. W. J. Ashley. New York: Longmans, various dates. Bk V.

# KARL MARX

## 1818–1883

Marxism presents itself as a comprehensive account of human life, and not only of human life but of nature as well. It offers an account of man's present, and of his past and future, educing its teaching from the premise that a full and final account of things is impossible except as an account of the transitoriness or endless flux of things. The definitive description of the present is given in Marx's economic writings, *i.e.,* in his critical analysis of capitalism. The account of past and future, or of the evolution of society, is given in Marx's writings on the theory of history and the relation of history to a certain notion of metaphysics. Marx's political philosophy consists of his teaching on economics and his teaching on history and metaphysics—on the present society and on the coming into being and passing away of all societies including the present.

The reader might wonder whether an economic analysis of capitalism is the same as a full account of the modern time (ignoring for the present the existence of communist countries). It is Marx's contention that the economy is the living kernel of the society, and therefore to grasp the truth about the modern economy is to understand the most potent facts about modern society. But the reader might also wonder whether a full account of society is equivalent to a full account of human life. Marxism takes the two, if society is rightly understood, to be equivalent. Marxism can thus present itself as a comprehensive explanation of the past, present, and future of man. It claims to have discovered that the economy is the true ground of society and therewith of human life. Marx's analysis of the present, *i.e.,* of capitalistic economy, is based upon his labor theory of value. His account of the transition from past to future, *i.e.,* of history, depends on his doctrine of dialectical materialism. Our description of Marx's political philosophy will therefore have this outline: (1) Dialectical materialism, or Marx's theory of history and of the priority of the economic conditions; (2) the labor theory of value and Marx's account of the capitalistic present; (3) the convergence of dialectical materialism and the labor theory of value.

In what follows we shall speak of "Marxism" and the doctrines of Marx. It should be understood that from 1844 on, Marx had as his collaborator Friedrich Engels, who gracefully and without doubt justly declared that Marx's was the genius of the movement, although he, Engels, had made his contributions to it. We shall not try in every case, even were it possible, to distinguish Engels' work from Marx's.

Marx repeatedly asserts that the study of man must concern itself with "real" men, not with men as imagined or hoped for or believed to be. Marx means by this that the foundation of social science is not a notion of some wished-for human good, or some reconstruction of pristine "natural" man, but rather empirical man as anyone could at any time observe him. Empirical man is primarily a living organism consuming food, clothing, shelter, fuel, and so on, and compelled to find or to produce those things. Men might once upon a time have survived by using materials which they simply found and gathered, but the increase in population at some point forced them to produce their necessities and thereby to become distinguished from the beasts. The singular sign of humanity is conscious production—not rationality, or political life, or the power of laughter, for example, as some have maintained. There is, to be sure, an element of unclarity in Marx's teaching on this point, since he concedes that human production differs from "production" by beasts in that the human being plans or conceives in advance the completed object of his labor while the bee or insect toils by mere instinct. In other words, only human production is characterized by rational intention, and human production could thus be said to be unique because it is the doing of the rational animal. Then, however, it would be more exact to assert that man's singular characteristic is rationality rather than productiveness; but Marx is prevented from saying so because the implications of that assertion would interfere with his materialism, which argues that man's rationality or rather "consciousness" is not fundamental but derivative. The Marxist doctrine of the primacy of production in human life rests upon the belief that it was the pressure of his needs that first forced man upward into his humanity and then continues to press him onward and upward; and that the content of his reason must be determined by conditions external to his reason, conditions which are strictly material.

In what ways, more exactly, do the material conditions determine life and thought, according to Marx? He begins by observing that, in every epoch, men have access to certain productive forces, which they apply by making use of the objects—animals, tools, machines, and so on —in which those forces are embodied. But the forces of production— say, roughly, the bare technology—compel men to adapt themselves and their institutions to the requirements of the technology. Nomads, for example, who suddenly gained access to steam power and mechanically drawn agricultural implements would be forced to give up their nomadism and to adopt instead the sedentary habits, division of labor, trading practices, and property institutions which are determined by factory production, and also to take up the practices and institutions correlate to agriculture. That this is true in a general sense is self-evident; it surely was well understood in Greek antiquity. As stated above, however, it is insufficiently comprehensive to express Marx's meaning. Marx asserts repeatedly that to a given set of forces of production there corresponds a certain "mode of production," such as the Asiatic, the ancient, the feudal, and the modern bourgeois or capitalist. According to the feudal mode of production, for example, the possessors of the means of production and the men who labored with or upon those means were connected by a personal relation of mutual responsibility; under the capitalist mode, employers and employees are, as the terms imply, users and used, free of duty to each other, with only the payment of money connecting them. With each such mode of production, there goes, as an effect, one form of social organization. A compact formulation of this view is given by Marx in his letter to P. V. Annenkov, December 28, 1846: "What is society, whatever its form may be? The product of men's reciprocal action. Are men free to choose this or that form of society for themselves? By no means. Assume a particular state of development in the productive forces of man and you will get a particular form of commerce and consumption. Assume particular stages of development in production, commerce and consumption and you will have a corresponding social structure, a corresponding organization of the family, of orders or of classes, in a word, a corresponding civil society. Presuppose a particular civil society and you will get particular political conditions which are only the official expression of civil society." This he compresses further, in *The Poverty of Philosophy* in the remark, "The hand-mill gives you society with the feudal lord; the steam-mill, society with the industrial capitalist." [1]

The conditions of production determine the prevailing property relations, meaning by the latter not the abstract definition of property, but rather who in the particular situation has access to property and who is prevented from acquiring it. Under feudalism, there were lords who possessed land and had rights to other property, and serfs who could accumulate no property. Similarly under the other social circumstances: under capitalism, employers own and accumulate, employees struggle along on the verge of destitution, owning nothing, separated from the means of production. This doctrine is directly connected with the Marxian belief that the conditions of production control distribution of income and consumption of output. They also govern exchange: if production is organized around a commonly occupied arable, for example, there will not even be exchange of the produce of the soil, only sharing. It follows also that money will be in use or not depending on the mode of production: money is not, in its present meaning or use, intrinsic to every economic situation or to economic life as such.

Marx asserts, therefore, that it is a mistake to treat consumption, distribution, exchange, money, and so on as eternal categories having an abstract, permanent content, relevance, or validity. It is one of the defects of the science of political economy, "bourgeois" economics, that it views these purely historical phenomena as fixed categories, having an objective, essential, "natural" character—things that can be understood once and for all because they exist once and for all. Not only are the "categories" historical products, but the science of those categories, namely economics, proves itself to be merely historical or transitory by mistaking the transitory for the eternally true, i.e., by believing itself to consist of laws founded in a changeless nature. Marx denounces Edmund Burke, but through Burke all economists, for his assertion that "the laws of commerce . . . are the laws of Nature, and consequently the laws of God." [2] Actually, according to Marx, the economic science of the capitalist period is given its "categories" (wages, interest, exchange, profit, and so on) by the practices prevalent under capitalistic production, and it takes up these categories without recognizing their genesis in the historical conditions. Failing to treat its material as historical and bound to pass away, it of course condemns itself to pass away when its material does so.

Marx's doctrine of the dependence of theories on the historic conditions of production takes in far more than economic theory. He asserts that all morality, philosophy, religion, and politics are the result of the conditioning of men by their environment—their manmade environment which is the expression of the mode of production. The opposite view, that man has an independent intelligence by the light of which he fashions his institutions and forms his convictions, is rejected as ideology, the Marxist term for the doctrine that thought has an independent status.[3]

Marx's materialism has been presented thus far as asserting simply that the conditions of production determine the concrete character of human life, which exists as a "superstructure" on the foundation of the more truly real material conditions. Nothing has been said, however, about the goodness or badness of the actual superstructures that have in fact arisen on the hitherto existing material foundations. Such a judgment is intrinsic to Marx's materialism, however, and to it we now turn.

All historic modes of production have had one feature in common, and that feature has in turn affected all the corresponding societies: control of the means of production has not been shared by all men, but in each age some have been owners or possessors while many more have had to give of themselves, *i.e.,* of their capacity for work (having nothing else to give), in order to have access to the instruments of production, to gain a livelihood. Thus in all previous history the act of production has brought many men into dependence upon the few. The masses have been deprived of the opportunity to become free and self-respecting men because they have always been forced into the position of cringing dependents—slaves, serfs, or proletarians—subject to men who, although private citizens or subjects like themselves, could yet arbitrarily deprive them of their living by cutting off their connection with the means of production. The dehumanization inevitably resulting from such servile dependence has been compounded by the poverty imposed upon the many by their exploiters.

Furthermore, the process of production, from its inception, had a character that Marx calls "natural" in the sense that certain natural differences among men (of physique, talent, and so on) determined the allotment of special tasks to individuals, and the relations of production were therefore determined, imposed, or involuntary, thus natural in the sense of not resulting from human choice. The prototype of all such allotments is the division of function between male and female in continuing the race. This grew into the more general form of division of labor incorporated in the family. As the forces of production were developed, the division of labor became increasingly elaborated, and the particular occupations became correspondingly restricted. As men are compelled by the conditions of production to become shepherds, plumbers, or violinists, they are deprived of the opportunity to develop to the full their human capacities by turning their minds freely in all directions. They are made into fragments of men, prevented by the stultifying division of labor from growing into whole men for whom labor would become a source of satisfaction rather than pain.

While this parcellation is going on within each man, the same process is being repeated among the men. The community comes to be composed of weavers who are set in opposition to bakers, farmers pitted against merchants, townsfolk versus country people, hand workers against brain workers—a war of all against all, fought on the field of material interest, the terms of struggle dictated by the mode of production. Finally, the fracture of society is completed by the coalescence into a class or group of classes of the few who control the means of production, and the parallel coalescence of the many dispossessed into the class or classes that work at the means of production.

The fracturing of social life may be epitomized in the existence of civil society or bourgeois society. (The German term used by Marx is *bürgerliche Gesellschaft,* which may be translated as either civil or bourgeois society.) The breakdown of the integrity of human life is symptomatized and presupposed by the split in our common existence between the political and the economic and social: "Where the political state has attained its true development, the individual leads not only in thought, in consciousness, but in reality, a double life, a heavenly and an earthly life, a life in the political community, wherein he counts as a member of the community, and a life in bourgeois society, wherein he is active as a private person, regarding other men as a means, degrading himself into a means and becoming a plaything of alien powers."[4] Civil society means for Marx an individualistic enclave in society, the realm of privacy as against community, with the understanding that community finds its corrupt expression in political society under now-prevailing conditions. Civil society, far from being synonymous with political society for Marx, is the infrapolitical cognate of political society that is an inevitable part of the capitalistic order. A simple equivalent of "civil society" in this sense is "the economy" of a capitalistic state, or even "the market." Civil society is the stratum of common life that is given its essential character by the self-assertiveness of men, one against the other, in the name of their inalienable, irreducible rights. The sanctity of those rights, thought by writers like Locke to be the ground for guaranteeing the freedom and thus the humanity of men, is rejected by Marx because he views the assertion of those rights as the source of, surely the expression of man's dehumanization. The war of Marxism against the ruling principles of Western constitutionalism must never be mistaken for a mere skirmish.

It is evident, according to Marx, that the many-sided factual negation of all community of interest under capitalism results from the private ownership of the productive resources. Production, a social act in the sense of being by and for all men, cannot be carried on humanely and rationally if the institutions of production are private, particular, and hence antisocial.

The modes of production and institutions of property that have existed hitherto have caused fragmentation and conflict within and among men. What has kept the fragments of society from flying apart? Or, more pertinently, what has prevented the many from summarily ridding themselves of the impositions of the few? According to Marx, the state power is precisely the agency devised by the oppressive few to keep the many in order. The state is the organ of class coercion, made necessary by the dividedness of society that is engendered in turn by the private control of the means of production. It goes without saying that the government does not appear in this light to the multitude of men. Marx allows that all classes collaborate in sustaining government by respecting it and its power of coercion; but this means no more than that men, because of the imperfection of their material conditions, are prepared and compelled to erect over themselves their own tyrant, their own creature that must, as it does, assert itself against them.

It was Marx's belief that while men remain in the state of constraint, of subjection to want and to one another via the process of production, they will be unable to lead fully human lives; for full humanity would require perfect emancipation from bonds of every sort. If Marx had ever used the term "state of nature" in his own name, he would have meant by it the state of man's incomplete domination of nature, the alternative to the state of freedom. While men are in bonds, as they have been under government and "civil society," they experience as part of their bondage a constraint that compels them to contribute to their own dehumanization through institutions of their own devising.

We may conclude this summary of Marx's materialism by explaining the foregoing remark, and at the same time showing how Marx conceives the state of need and the state of political society to coexist as the state of human bondage or what he calls man's alienation. Without a grasp of this element of Marxism it would be impossible to form a sufficient judgment of Marx's political philosophy as a whole.

Returning to our point of departure, we note Marx's primary observation that man is a needing being. Each man is condemned to dependence upon external things, say nature, and upon other men to help supply his needs. But in addition to being essentially needy, man is what Marx calls a species being or a social being, which does not mean simply that man must live and act in common with other men, but that man cannot realize his human possibilities except by acting upon and being acted upon by other human beings. That man knows his fellow-men to constitute a whole of which he is a part, and that he therefore associates himself with them in thought in a way which is ruled out for all subhuman animals, is part also of Marx's rather diffuse notion of man as a species-being. At any rate, it was Marx's belief that man's essential activity, production, has in all previous societies been carried on under institutions that compel men to look upon each other and upon nature itself as alien things, objects, mere means to the end of satisfying the individual's needs. Productive labor itself has always been regarded as a painful necessity because of the conditions under which it has been performed. Thus men's environment and their fellow-men have been objects of predation, and the acting men themselves, and their very own essential life-activities, have been merely instrumental, means to ends without the intrinsic worth they must have if man is to be fully human, to be at one with himself, or to overcome his "estrangement" from nature, from himself, and from the fruits of his labor. Marx's contention is no less sweeping than this: until every man simply merges himself in the whole of humanity, producing only because production is the release and cultivation of human energy, and not because production is a way of obtaining subsistence directly or through exchange by exploiting other men's neediness—not until then will men be perfectly free and the perfect, final articulation of man, society, and nature be achieved. Until that time, men will distort each other's natures by treating each other as objects, each being made thus to grow up as at odds with his species, even regarding nature itself, incidentally, not in its beauty and splendor but as a source of gain. The arrangement of the process of production within the institution of common ownership of productive resources, under the formula "From each according to his ability, to each according to his needs," is thought by Marx to be the condition for causing the absolute translation of human life onto a basis which is in the most literal sense unprecedented. Men have lived hitherto in civil society, *i.e.,* under institutions that have presupposed or positively cultivated self-interest as the principle of productive life and life itself. Marxian materialism leads up to the supersession of all civil society and its replacement by the human species as a universal brotherhood. Marxian materialism, which begins by insisting upon the need to consider empirical man, paradoxically ends in a social prescription with no empirical foundation or precedent.

It was stated above that, from the point of view of Marxism, economics or political economy is defective in that it gives an account of economic life in terms of prices, wages, costs, profit, capital, and so on as if these were transhistoric "categories," or eternal elements intrinsic to economic life under all circumstances. The now common definition of economics as the science of the allocation of scarce resources among alternative uses is a better example of what Marx objected to than most economic notions that existed in his own day. This definition implies that there is something that can be called the economic problem for all men in all stages of civilization and technology, and that the rational solution of that problem requires either genuine or simulated markets to produce certain equilibria between commodity and discommodity— a universal law resembling the generalizations of physics. Marx's denial of the truth of political economy was not only a denial that the economists had given an accurate description of free enterprise. It was a denial that the description of a particular economic arrangement was a timelessly true description of the essence of economic life. This in turn is part of Marx's broad doctrine that in general there are no timeless essences and therefore no eternal truths which are not either trivial or purely formal. Marx's political philosophy is mingled with a theory about the nature of all things; indeed his political philosophy is to a certain extent governed by a universal scheme or "system," a doctrine that things neither have essences nor do they, as fixed things, have existences, but they have histories or careers. Becoming, according to the formula, takes the place of being.

Marx followed Hegel in fact, if not in expression, in rejecting as "metaphysical" the view that there are finished "things" or "objects" which have a fixed, given, straightforward constitution. He asserted on the contrary that everything is affected by both change and relation. Thus the various species are forever evolving and the individuals come into being, grow, and then decline. The inanimate things are thrown up by natural processes and then erode, oxidize, or otherwise decay, while internally, they are, like the living beings, constantly in motion. Moreover, each thing is affected, indeed constituted, by the relation in which it stands to other things. For example, a man who is a servant is a servant only in virtue of his relation to another being who is the opposite of a servant, namely a master. The nature of a servant is not intelligible by exclusive reference to the servant himself, just as one could not understand "employee" if there were not "employers." In addition, there is an element of contradictoriness that is introduced into the constitution of perfectly motionless, unchanging things independently of their relations with other things: a curved line, everywhere curved, is nevertheless straight between two points infinitesimally separated. The best example of this paradox is given not by Marx and Engels but by Democritus: "If a cone were cut by a plane parallel to the base, what ought one to think of the surfaces resulting from the section: are they equal or unequal?" [5] The easy answer is "both."

Further, the lines of distinction between classes of things are not sharp, for there are individuals at the margins that are as much of one class as of another ("plant-animals" and "sensitive plants"); and even life itself is not simply distinguishable from nonlife. The transition from life to death is not instantaneous (*e.g.,* the nails and hair continue to grow after "death"), and life proper consists of a process by which the living thing continually dies and renews itself through excretion and nutrition, so that life is inseparable from a continuous dying. It goes without saying that if life and death were in no way distinguishable, it would be impossible to distinguish living from dead material, or to say of life that it implied or presupposed or even required death; yet the Marxist position is that life as a process is not simply life, but it is also necessarily and at the same time death. Life exists as a process in virtue of a contradiction: life is both life and death. And so it is with the other "things."

All things are in flux, as Marxism asserts following Heraclitus, and all flux is motion. To understand the character of all things, it is necessary to grasp the universal law of motion, the law governing nature, human history, and thought. That law is derived from the Marxist doctrine of the essential contradictoriness of motion itself. Since the time of Zeno the Eleatic, a "proof" has existed that motion is impossible: every moving body is at each instant in one and only one place—which is the definition of being at rest. To be in motion is thus to be at rest and also not to be at rest. Each thing is, therefore, by analogy with a body in motion, equally what it "is" instantaneously and what it "is" historically, not in spite of, but in virtue of the fact that the two are contradictory.

Contradiction is fundamental to development, *i.e.,* to historical change, when change is assimilated to physical motion. Change is generated by contradiction through the mutual opposition of the two contradictory elements present in the thing in question. Consider an example given by Engels: a grain of cereal is planted, and it is annihilated as a grain while the plant grows up. As the plant develops to its own extinction, it produces many grains like the one from which it sprang. The grain is the affirmation (or "thesis"), the plant the negation (or "antithesis"), and the many grains the negation of the negation (or "synthesis"). Let us consider one more example: select any algebraic quantity, $a$, as the affirmation. Negate it by multiplying it by $-1$, to form $-a$. Negate the negation by multiplying it by itself, and the product is $a^2$, the affirmation on a higher level. The sequence of affirmation, negation, and negation of the negation is called the dialectic, and it is this that Marxism believes to be the universal law of nature, history, and thought. All development occurs on this pattern.

In the special case of human history and thought, a cause is assigned to the unfolding of the dialectical process. That cause is the mode of production and its mutations. Because the primary phenomenon is the material conditions of production, the Marxist doctrine of history is called dialectical materialism, to distinguish it from the idealist dialectic of Hegel which asserted the primary phenomenon to be self-dependent reason as the source of historical change. As a theory of human life, dialectical materialism asserts that the ground of all development in society and understanding is contradiction in the order of production. The most massive of such contradictions is the conflict between classes in society. By subsuming the opposition of class interests under the apparatus of the dialectic, Marxism seeks to show that the conflict cannot be resolved through compromises or mutual accommodations but only by a "negation of the negation," *i.e.,* by revolutionary changes in which the existing classes are annihilated and replaced by a synthesis "on a higher level."

An important element of Marx's political philosophy is his reconstruction of history for the purpose of showing that history has in fact been governed by the materialist dialectic. According to that reconstruction, each epoch inherits a mode of production and a complex of relations among men that is peculiarly fitted to that mode of production. Eventually a change takes place in the mode of production, brought on perhaps by a change in needs that could have been engendered by that very mode of production, and, more immediately, brought on by a fundamental discovery or invention stimulated by those needs. The new mode of production comes into being while the relations among the human beings are still those generated by the previous mode of production. The contradiction between existent social relations and the emergent mode of production, *i.e.,* the clash between the established and the embryonic dominant classes, is the source of "all collisions in history."

Marx and Engels cite a number of historical developments as evidence of this hypothesis, the most amply treated being the transition from feudal to capitalistic society, and the evolution toward postcapitalism. The former is explained by recurring to the rise of machine manufacture in the Middle Ages, first in the textile industry and then more generally. The spread of machine production broke down the structure of guildmasters with journeyman and apprentice labor, replacing it by a relation of bourgeois employers and wage-earning employees between whom no ties existed but that of the wage payment. The manufacturing mode of production was the vehicle by which the most fortunate and most active escaped serfs rose to displace the guild-masters as the owners of the new means of production, and to become the progenitors of a new class, the bourgeoisie. Opposed to them, and at the same time indispensable to them, were the proletarian laborers having nothing to live by but the wages from the sale of their labor power. As industry and commerce expanded, the scale of production increased enormously, and as it did, the relations between the owning and non-owning classes underwent a further change, an aggravation. The clash of interests between capitalists and wage-earners inevitably sharpened, for the proletarians' condition had to deteriorate because of the contradictions that are intrinsic to capitalism, contradictions that will appear when we consider Marx's critique of capitalist production. For the present it suffices to say that, according to Marx, the full development of machine production (under private ownership) requires the absolute pauperization and dehumanization of the wage-earners because of the pressures of capitalist competition. At last the wretchedness of the masses will become unbearable, and the conflict of the classes will break forth into a decisive combat—decisive because the victory of the proletariat will usher in a new age of man.

The proletarians have neither the wealth nor the wish to become the owners of the means of production *as a class*. Unlike every other insurgent class in the past, their purpose is not to take the place of their oppressors but to put an end to oppression. The means of achieving this end is to abolish the private ownership of the means of production and thus to abolish the distinction between owners and nonowners thereof, the distinction which is the condition for the division of human society into classes. Upon the dissolution of classes will necessarily ensue the end of the class struggle and the beginning of strictly human history. When that has occurred, the relations among men will have caught up with the latest great development in the mode of production; the conditions of oppression disappearing, the need for coercion will disappear as well, and the state will wither away to be replaced by the universal brotherhood of man.


Marx was well aware that his prognosis for mankind was necessarily linked to a diagnosis of prevailing conditions. He realized that he must investigate the contemporary (European) world in its essentials, which is to say in its economic character, in order to satisfy himself and others that the dialectic of materialism is actually operative in the decisive period, namely the present. It was necessary for him to demonstrate that the law of the nature of capitalism is the law of the transformation of capitalism into something radically different. His enterprise incidentally required him to show that no explanation of capitalism other than his own had grasped the essential character of capitalism, and therefore no other account, at least no other then known, could be made the basis of a prognosis for mankind. This means that ordinary political economy, which did not come to the conclusion that capitalism is self-vitiating, is in various respects unsatisfactory even as a description of how capitalism works. Marx's own economics is almost wholly "critical," devoted not to the explanation of how a socialist economy should or would be constituted but to a detailed representation of the self-contradictoriness and transitoriness of capitalist institutions, and to the inadequacy of political economy as known. The inseparability of the two criticisms is implicit in the subtitle of *Capital: A Critique of Political Economy.*

Marx's general criticism of political economy has already been mentioned. We must take up here his critical analysis of capitalism proper, and with it his more specific reflections on political economy. The title of his major economic work, *Capital,* indicates what seemed to him to be the central economic problem. Capital, according to Marx, does not mean simply the artificial means of production—equally a stone axe in the hand of a primitive, a bow in the hand of a Grecian hunter, or a power loom in nineteenth-century England. Capital is productive wealth in the peculiar form that generates profit. The prevailing system is called capitalism because the means of production, privately owned, are a source of profit to their owners the capitalists. It is very important to understand the nature of profit with perfect precision, for profit is at the heart of the prevailing social and economic order. Profit is not simply any economic surplus, such as might arise in primitive or feudal economies, any more than capital is simply productive wealth. Profit and capital are uniquely, mutually complementary.

Profit appears directly as a part of the price of a commodity, a part which the owner of the means of production, the capitalist (as Marx was not the first to call him) is able to claim. What exactly does his share consist of? How does it originate and by what right does the capitalist lay claim to it? Classical political economy had provided a certain answer, which was the point of departure for Marx's own analysis. Classical political economy had begun with the assertion that labor is the source of value, that the amount of labor embodied in a good is thus related to the amount of value in the good, and that the relative values of two goods must be in proportion to the relative amounts of labor embodied in them. The accompanying presumption is that the one who has created the value by pouring his labor into the object has the right to be the owner of his product. The classical economists agreed that, when production was carried on by individuals for themselves, using their own hands and the implements fashioned by them or owned by them, each man could claim for himself whatever he produced. But that condition ceased when, in order to carry on production, men required access to land and instruments belonging to others. Thereafter, those others had a right to share in the product. Evidently, profit (to leave aside the problem of rent) is coeval with the accumulation of productive property by some members of society.

There was, according to the classic view, a period of human life when every man could "produce" independently; and then there was—and still is—a period in which land was made subject to appropriation, and the accumulation of durable property was made feasible. In the earlier period of human life, the labor theory of value applied in its simple and direct form. In the latter period, the product of labor is shared with capitalists and landlords. Readers of the doctrines of Hobbes and Locke, but especially the latter, will be reminded of the division of all human history between a period in the state of nature and a period in the state of civil society. We are now prepared to understand more fully Marx's asseveration that classical political economy assigns to the institutions of capitalism the status of prospectively timeless, natural conditions. Classical political economy and the political philosophy to which it was linked regarded as absolutely epochal the progress of man from the prepolitical to the political condition. That same crucial change was perfected or consummated with the replacement of absolute monarchy by constitutional government, for between a subject and an arbitrary master there is only the law of nature. That crucial change in the human state was connected by classical political economy with the accumulation and protection of property in the means of production. The institutions of property thus come to parallel, and to have the same status as, civil society or civilization—political life—itself. Neither Hobbes and Locke nor the classical political economists looked beyond civil society for a further radical melioration of man's estate. It was left for Rousseau to raise the broad question of the goodness of both civil society and property, and thus to open the way for his successors to search for a horizon beyond that of civil society. Marx, in rejecting the view that property and civil society, or say political life, were the absolute condition for decent human existence in peace and prosperity, denied the natural and permanent status of "the laws of commerce." He rejected the implication of classical political economy that profit and the private ownership of the means of production are here to stay, as much as and for the same reasons that political society is here to stay.

Surely Marx did not concede that the transition from the state of nature to the state of political society was the absolutely epochal change in human life. Neither did he concede that the parallel change from the pure to the diluted application of the labor theory of value was epochal or even that it provided a valid ground for understanding the prevailing economic institutions. That a difficulty indeed existed in that mode of explanation was noticed by Ricardo as he examined Adam Smith's theory of value and wages. Ricardo pointed out that if it were true in a simple sense that a commodity which required a day's labor for its production should be said to contain a day's-labor-worth of value, then when that commodity is exchanged for labor, it should purchase its equal in value, namely a day's labor. The brief formulation would be, labor embodied equals labor commanded, for any commodity.[6] In other words there would be no profit: a workman could be hired for a week only if his product for the week (or the full value of it) were paid him as his wage. The fact that the wage is not equal to the whole product compelled Ricardo (and Smith, incidentally) to find an alternative formulation, one that ascribed value-productivity to capital as congealed labor. Marx rejected the Ricardian and other classical explanations of profit, wages, and value because those explanations, in accounting for the difference between the labor embodied in and the labor commanded by a commodity, did not lead up to a condemnation of profit as resting upon exploitation, which Marx believed it to do. We must now consider his alternative explanation.

Marx begins by noting a problem that arises out of the exchange of goods: when one commodity is exchanged for another, a common ground is indicated between two things which appear to have nothing at all in common. Suppose a pair of shoes to be exchanged for three shirts. The shoes and the shirts are so perfectly unlike as to be incommensurable. How can the ratio of three for one, or any other ratio, ever be arrived at? To deal with the problem of commensurability, Marx recurs to, but modifies, a distinction which was traditional in political economy, the distinction between value in use and value in exchange. For the distinction use value–exchange value, regarded by political economy as fundamental, Marx substitutes use value–value. The reason for this is that he does not regard exchange as a permanent, natural institution but rather as a historic and transitory one. But exchange value is derivative from value proper, and in order to understand capitalism it is necessary to understand exchange value and therefore value simply. Returning now to the two commodities, we notice that they are absolutely unlike so far as we consider their value in use or their qualitative character, each good being designed for a certain purpose that the other could not serve. Now a shoe comes to be a shoe in virtue of having been produced by the peculiar labor of a shoemaker. A shirt is a shirt because it is the product of shirtmaking labor. The difference between shoe-making and shirtmaking labor is the source of the qualitative difference between shoes and shirts. Marx goes on to assert that, just as the two commodities can, indeed must, be looked at as if they are not only dis-similar but also have commensurable values, so the labor that produced them must be capable of being looked at not only as qualitatively differ-entiated labor. It must also be seen as homogeneous or undifferentiated human labor, as the generation of a certain amount of motion in a cer-tain mass by a certain expenditure of human energy. As skills, there-fore, the kinds of human labor are simply different; but as toil, all labor is the same, and is measurable in units of time, according to the length of its duration. Upon this latter fact depends the mensurability and commensurability of values. The summary formula would be, differen-tiated human labor produces use values and qualitative differences among commodities, while undifferentiated human labor produces value simply and quantitative commensurability among the commodities. Thus it is in their character as products of undifferentiated human labor, not as products of specific labor aimed at satisfying specific wants, that commodities have commensurable values and can enter into exchange.

It should be pointed out that the assignment of labor alone as the source of value is not demonstrated by Marx, but is asserted by him as something self-evident.[7]

The foregoing account of value provides support for Marx's defi-nition and elaboration of the notion of a commodity. By a commodity Marx means a good which is privately produced for the sake of ex-change (or sale, *i.e.,* exchange against money.) Capitalism could thus be described as a system of commodity production and, as such, based upon confusion and distortion. Rationally, the sum of all the individual labor-powers in the community is the aggregate of labor-power avail-able to the society for the satisfaction of all its wants. If men were to live without distortion in their affairs, their labor-power would be directly applied to the satisfaction of their wants rather than to produc-tion for exchange. Because the means of production are privately owned, however, production is carried on not directly for its true purpose—the satisfaction of wants—but for the special advantage of the owners of the means of production. The social character of labor is thus mediated and distorted by the mode of production. What Adam Smith regarded as a peculiar virtue of private enterprise, namely, the voluntary performance of a social function under the influence of a desire for private advantage, is regarded by Marx as the ground of the iniquity and instability in the prevailing system. Why he did so conclude can be understood if we look further at the capitalistic mode of production as Marx interpreted it.

Indispensable to capitalism are the private ownership of the means of production and the existence of a body of men who both do not own any means of production and are perfectly free, in the sense of being unbound to the owners of the means of production by any personal ties of duty or rights. In order to live, the unpropertied must therefore engage themselves to labor at the machines and on the land of the propertied. The propertyless in effect sell to the propertied a commodity called labor-power—not labor. Labor-power means the ability to labor for a given period; labor means the actual duration of the labor. For Marx the distinction is crucial. Labor-power is a commodity, under capitalism, and that means that it is something produced for sale and having a value determined by the amount of labor congealed or incorporated in it. But what could be meant by the amount of labor incorporated in the capacity of a laborer to work for eight hours? The answer is, that amount of labor that was required to produce the necessities that must be available to the man furnishing the labor-power in question. Somewhat more broadly, the value of a day's labor-power is determined by the amount of labor necessary to produce the subsistence for the laborer and his family in order to maintain the supply of labor-power at its level, not only from day to day but from generation to generation.

Let us suppose that in order to provide all the materials of subsistence necessary to support a labor-power of eight hours, six hours of labor must be performed. Then the value of a labor-power of eight hours would be equal to the value of six hours' output. One would then obtain the output of eight hours by giving for it the output of six hours. The value generated by the employed labor-power during the two hours of its application while it is "not paid for" is called by Marx "surplus value"; it is the basis of profit. Profit exists only because a portion of the workingman's labor-power results in an output for which he is not paid. Yet he is not being cheated, in a certain sense. Marx is at pains to point out that the labor-power is bought at its full value, its value understood as being rigidly subject to the labor theory of the value of all commodities including labor-power itself. Thus the man is paid in full for his labor-power but not for his labor. By this formulation Marx believed he had solved the problem that classical political economy had failed to clarify with consistency, the problem caused by the inequality of the labor embodied in a product and the labor commanded by it. His solution depends on the distinction between labor and labor-power. By this radicalization of the labor theory of value that applies it to labor-power itself, Marx was enabled to argue that a serious hidden contradiction of capitalism was brought to light: the relation between employer and employee is at one and the same time both cheating and not cheating. In the sense that it is not cheating, no one can individually be blamed: the buying and selling of labor-power are done at full value according to the rules of the market. So far as it is cheating, however, it requires rectification. Marx's conclusion is that the abuse demands the abolition of the system rather than a change of the rules within the system: "reform" could never suffice, because no mere reform could terminate the buying and selling of labor-power.

This contradiction is but the ground for many more. For example, from the proposition that profit originates in the consumption of labor-power by the capitalist, it follows that profit can be made to increase either by consuming more labor-power or by increasing the amount of labor that is produced by a given labor-power (say, approximately, increasing the output per working day). But the increase in output per day (increase in productivity) is achieved by increasing the use of machinery. Increasing the use of machinery opposes the increase in consumption of labor-power. In order to prevent the introduction of machinery from suppressing the profitable consumption of labor-power, the working day must be lengthened. Marx thus arrives at the conclusion that the introduction of machinery leads and will lead to the lengthening of the working day and to the formation of a large population of the chronically, technologically unemployed.[8] Here and elsewhere, Marx's economic analysis led him to make certain grossly incorrect predictions as to conditions in a matured capitalistic economy. Not because his power of prediction is in itself of great interest, but because so much of his revolutionary animus is vindicated by the horrors he professes to foresee in the flowering of capitalism, his mistakes of prediction come to have a singular effect on the credibility of the analysis on which they rest.

To continue. The restless struggle for profit causes the capitalistic economy and society to be in a state of endless flux. Under the lash of competition, which tends to reduce profits, capitalists must constantly revolutionize the process of production in order to cheapen it. Old skills are rendered obsolete and the average level of skill required in the work force is reduced as the motions of the artisan's hands are analyzed and copied in machinery. Since the fundamental condition of capitalist economic life is a free, propertyless work force toward which the propertied have no duty, the whole burden of technological change falls upon the wage-earners in the form of unemployment and poverty. But technological change as such is not peculiar to capitalism; only under capitalism does it become a source of misery. In a dialectical manner, Marx argues that in its abuses, capitalism serves to expose a transcapitalistic human problem that can be resolved only by the transcending of capitalism:

. . . Modern Industry . . . through its catastrophes imposes the necessity of recognizing, as a fundamental law of production, variation of work, consequently fitness of the labourer for varied work, consequently the greatest possible development of his varied aptitudes. It becomes a question of life and death for society to adapt the mode of production to the normal functioning of this law, Modern Industry, indeed, compels society, under penalty of death, to replace the detail-worker of to-day, crippled by lifelong repetition of one and the same trivial operation, and thus reduced to the mere fragment of a man, by the fully developed individual, fit for a variety of labours, ready to face any change of production, and to whom the different social functions he performs are but so many modes of giving free scope to his own natural and acquired powers.[9]

It must be pointed out that the tendency of technological change has not in fact been to reduce the average level of skill in the work force or to lead to falling real wages and a growing "industrial reserve army of the unemployed." Nor is there any evidence anywhere in the world that modern technology can be made compatible with institutionalized jack-of-all-tradeism.

Marx takes up many more aspects of capitalistic economic life than we can deal with here. His single-minded purpose throughout is to show that in virtue of what capitalism is, in virtue of its being intrinsically contradictory, its development must be its dissolution: the more it fulfills itself and approaches its peak, the more it destroys itself and approaches its fall. He provides a remarkable summary of his understanding of the case, late in Volume I of *Capital*:

We saw in Part IV., when analysing the production of relative surplus-value: within the capitalist system all methods for raising the social productiveness of labour are brought about at the cost of the individual labourer; all means for the development of production transform themselves into means of domination over, and exploitation of, the producers; they mutilate the labourer into a fragment of a man, degrade him to the level of an appendage of a machine, destroy every remnant of charm in his work and turn it into a hated toil; they estrange him from the intellectual potentialities of the labour-process in the same proportion as science is incorporated in it as an independent power; they distort the conditions under which he works, subject him during the labour-process to a despotism the more hateful for its meanness; they transform his life-time into working-time, and drag his wife and child beneath the wheels of the Juggernaut of capital. But all methods for the production of surplus value are at the same time methods of accumulation; and every extension of accumulation becomes again a means for the development of those methods. It follows therefore that in proportion as capital accumulates, the lot of the labourer, be his payment high or low, must grow worse. The law, finally, that always equilibrates the relative surplus-population, or industrial reserve army, to the extent and energy of accumulation, this law rivets the labourer to capital more firmly than the wedges of Vulcan did Prometheus to the rock. It establishes an accumulation of misery, corresponding with accumulation of capital. Accumulation of wealth at one pole is, therefore, at the same time accumulation of misery, agony of toil, slavery, ignorance, brutality, mental degradation, at the opposite pole, *i.e.,* on the side of the class that produces its own product in the form of capital.[10]

Marx believed that when, at last, the bourgeoisie had been reduced for the most part to proletarianism by savage competition, and the proletariat had been reduced to stark poverty by the laws of accumulation and profiteering, then the uprising would occur and mankind would stand on the eve of history.[11] It is not going too far to assert that Marx's economics consists of the attempt to show how that fateful transformation is implicit in the labor theory of value as concretized in the practices of capitalism.

Whether or how far these doctrines of Marx are sound is a question of more than ordinary interest to the world. It arises in two parts: whether what Marx regarded as inevitable is so; and whether the premises of his system are acceptable. These questions we must now take up.

Marx's predictions are on two subjects—the fate of capitalism and the character of socialist society. On the former he is at great length, as we have seen, and to a large extent he predicts incorrectly. A century after he came to his conclusions, it is fair to deny that the introduction of machinery must lead to lengthening of the working day, that there must be massive, growing, technological unemployment, that the bourgeoisie must be proletarianized and the proletariat pauperized, and that socialism is the culmination of capitalism. Marx's predictions were based upon the belief that an economic order has a life and being of its own, that it resembles the articulation of inert parts, and that when it is somehow or other launched on its way, it functions mechanically, as little subject to change of direction as a bullet shot from a gun. Marx had a certain loathing for utilitarianism, but he was as prone as any utilitarian doctrinaire to liken social life to a syllogism. Logic is supremely universal, everywhere and at all times the same. It is expressive of reason, but it has nothing to learn from prudence. Marx made concessions, but absolutely insufficient ones, to such simple and undialectical influences as laws—laws to limit the length of the working day, laws to encourage or compel collective bargaining, to enact workmen's compensation, progressive income taxation, unemployment insurance, old-age benefits, laws to regulate securities exchanges, to promote full employment, to protect competition, to control the money supply, to support agriculture, to relieve the sick, to suppress the adulteration of food, to compel the young to submit to be educated, to insure savings, and a thousand other laws, not the least of which is the law that puts lawmaking under the influence of the reigning multitudes that he mistook for a pauperized proletariat. Marx was an astute journalistic observer of political things, but in his teaching he conceded nothing significant to politics, *i.e.,* to discretion, which he discounted as mere "reform." He postulated the economic man with as much narrow assurance as any political economist, if with a more brilliant rhetoric.

Marx's predictions are not only of the baleful kind. Occasionally he alludes to the character of life in the postcapitalistic epoch and gives brief sketches of the communist world. There is no way to test empirically his visions of socialism, because all existing socialist societies claim to be in a state of transition toward communism proper, and every disparity between the expectation and the reality is explained as temporary. Whether all such disparities are in truth temporary, or how many could be temporary, depends upon the soundness of the ground upon which Marx's expectations rested. We turn to that question in conclusion.

The ruling principle of Marxian socialist society is, "From each according to his ability, to each according to his needs." This is a maxim fit to serve as the fundamental law among loyal, wise, and incorruptible friends, devoted to one another with an absolutely unselfish benevolence. Among such friends, not only would no individual seek his advantage at the expense of others, but the thought of doing so would never occur to him. In this sense, duty as duty would be transcended: what the mere sense of duty dictates to a man capable of selfishness would be the most spontaneous desire of a man as member of the friendly society. His duty would not appear to him as duty. Marxian society would be a society of billions of friends warmly joined in the rarest and most sensitive union of amity.

It is imaginable that there would be a great concourse of men living together without any threat of coercion to restrain them from offending each other, but that their uncoerced sociality would reflect not goodness but utter indifference, the extinction of every animating impulse. Marx

emphatically does not have this in mind: his socialists would be alive at
the peak of all their powers, each abundantly active. His vision of life
for the generality of mankind is what the ancient thinkers conceived
as the highest possibility open to the wisest and the best—the mutual
love of a few noble spirits, elevated above every petty desire, free from
every trace of envy or worldly ambition, willingly sharing that invalu-
able good which does not pass away from its possessor when he bestows
it upon another and which is multiplied when it is divided, that good
being wisdom. The notion of the quintessence of justice materializing
among the wise is intelligible, for wisdom excites the admiration that
generates love, and wisdom is a good for which men cannot contend
invidiously but only harmoniously. The conditions for rational benevolence would be fully met among the few who desire a good the pursuit
of which cannot corrupt. The perfect society is the society, then, in
which philosophy as the rule of life would become indistinguishable
from justice, which also is the rule of life. In the perfect society, justice
would administer itself, and it would therefore be perfectly pure because untainted by the need to coerce, to punish, or to deceive. The disappearance of justice into philosophy might be said to be equivalent to
the disappearance of the political in the philosophic.

The perfect society could not be described except on the premise
that there is such a thing as philosophy, that a few men take it to be the
greatest good, that more than a few never can or will take it to be so,
and that therefore it is in the nature of things that justice and political
society or government will not dissolve into philosophy. Marxism
dreams of the disappearance of justice and political society—not in
philosophy, it goes without saying, but in rational economics, and
therefore for the mass of humanity, not merely for the infinitesimal few.

The economic system that would be approved as rational by Marx
would of course not be the liberal economy in which the "economic
man" finds free scope for his "rationality." That rationality, which is
in fact only self-interested calculation, is thought by Marx to be infected
with contradiction. A self-contradicting rationality would appropriately
serve as the spring of action in a system that seeks prosperity through
poverty, freedom through subordination, and the common good through
the emancipation of self-preference.

Pre-Marxian, or at any rate pre-Hegelian, political philosophy, both
ancient and modern, was characterized by a certain moderation that
allowed it to approve regimes which achieve reason through myth,
freedom through coercion, or sociality through selfishness. Wayward
and unreflective as men are, they may still be made amenable to social

life if they can be brought under the guidance either of well-disposed men or of cunning institutions that play men's lower motives off against each other to a salutary outcome. In either case the end or outcome was conceived to be of utmost importance, apart from such considerations as whether the end is given by nature, or whether it justifies the means. How far Marx was affected by the tendency of Kant to depreciate the mere ends we cannot here consider; but it is certain that Marx repudiated the willingness of the ancient and the eagerness of the modern traditions to make peace with, though not to surrender to the weaknesses of human nature, and to be content with society consisting of men as they are. Marx dreamed of that human condition in which good ends would be sought by good men using only good means and responding to (because possessing) only good motives. The basis or presupposition of his dream was the generation of a new man, or the regeneration of man—and the instrument of regeneration would be the rational economy rightly understood.

Unexpectedly, we now see coming into view a ground of agreement between ancients and pre-Marxian moderns on this most important point: political life rests upon the imperfection of man and continues to exist because human nature rules out the elevation of all men to the level of excellence. The connection between civil government and man's imperfection is expressed by Rousseau, for example, in the form of the distinction between state and society: men can be social while uncorrupted, but in political community they prey and are preyed upon by one another.[12] At the beginning of *Common Sense,* Thomas Paine wrote, "Society is produced by our wants, and government by our wickedness; the former promotes our happiness *positively* by uniting our affections, the latter *negatively* by restraining our vices. . . . The first is a patron, the last a punisher."

Rousseau may be said to have suggested, via the doctrine of the perfectibility of man, that government may be more and more replaced by society: in the perfect freedom of self-government, coercion loses most of its sting. But Rousseau did not at all suppose the utter collapse of government into society, for he did not suppose that all men would become philosophic, nor that there is any perfect substitute for the full rationality of men that would render coercion and rhetoric of all kinds, *i.e.,* political life, dispensable. He did not, in brief, expect ordinary selfishness simply to disappear from among the generality of men.

What in Rousseau was a limited suggestion, although an emphatic one, came to be the dogmatic core of a confident prognosis, a strident propaganda, and a revolutionary incitation in Marx: the state or political order will wholly wither away, and homogeneous mankind will live socially under the rule of absolute benevolence—from each according to his ability, to each according to his needs. No longer will duty be performed incidentally to the pursuit of selfish interest. The link between duty and interest, which is to say the subordination of duty to interest, will be broken for once and all by the abolition of the categories "duty" and "interest." They will be abolished by the revision of the property relations, by the inauguration of a new economics which will bring on the full perfection of human nature via the transcendence of production for exchange.

In barest outline, Marx's radicalization of Rousseau can be said to rest upon the supersession of philosophic reason by historic reason. Philosophic reason, the intelligence of individual human beings, being unequally present among men, political society with coercion and rhetoric cannot be dispensed with if calamity is to be avoided. So the philosophic tradition believed. Marx's teaching is that there is a reason inherent in the course of history: History abhors a contradiction as profoundly as nature was ever thought to abhor a vacuum. Whether a contradiction means more than a clash of interests, we are not told. In any case, the unviability of every individual contradiction is transformed by the philosophy of history into the unviability of contradiction simply. The philosophy of history tries to communicate its confidence that contradiction must wipe itself out, working through the discontents of men afflicted with the symptoms of the contradictions that exist in society. The progressive resolution of contradictions, and the movement of man toward the condition free of contradiction deserves to be called the expression of historic reason. It supersedes or overcomes the philosophic reason, or the intelligence of individual men, not only in the obvious sense that, through the historic evolution of human nature, the unequal distribution of intelligence will cease to have political relevance. When the new breed of man is generated by the common ownership of the means of production, all the old (natural) categories of right will fall before the logic of history, and subphilosophic men will live in uncoerced and myth-free (*i.e.,* perfectly rational) society, as only the rarest of men were thought to be able to do, but even more emancipatedly than the rarest, who never had the benefit of the perfect environment. The multitudes of men will be conditioned to reach the heights by abundance of goods produced and distributed without any opposition of interest. Marx appears to believe that, if men are divided by scarcity, they would be united by abundance. We would be readier to be convinced of this if there were reason to believe that men will some day be indistinguishable from the grazing herbivores.

Marxism is famous for looking forward to the end not only of political life but also of religion. Religion is the belief in the existence of a realm of the whole where there is a rectification for every defect in the terrestrial world. Here there is death, there life. Here iniquity goes unseen or unpunished, there it is recorded and retributed; or if it is beyond human punishment, it receives divine punishment even here below. The goodness that is ignored or mocked on earth is accounted and honored in heaven. The belief that the whole is or tends to be good can be maintained even if the visible part of the whole is imperfect, by arguing that the invisible part perfectly makes up the deficiencies present to our view. We would be led far out of our way if we attempted to compare the teachings of the theological and the philosophic traditions with respect to this question; but we may observe that the ancient philosophic tradition also taught that nature as a whole is good. Yet it is not so unequivocally good as to render superfluous the coercion and rhetoric that support political life; thus the goodness of nature as a whole does not permeate all of human life. On this fundamental point there is a ground of agreement between ancient philosophy and revealed religion: for all practical purposes, the goodness of the whole, whether the whole is the sum of the natural and the supernatural, or the complex of form and matter in nature itself, cannot be translated or transformed into the goodness of man's common life. In the case of modern political philosophy, the goodness of nature as a whole was characteristically not asserted; teleology was of course rejected, and the wretchedness of the state of nature strongly argued. Nature required to be rectified, or rather to be governed; and the clue to the government of nature was to be found in the laws of nature—the laws of science and the laws of politics and economics. The belief in the possibility of conquering or governing nature perhaps opened the way to the Marxian notion that the perfection of human life is possible, and not only possible but foreseeable, in the classless society. But as has been seen, that consummation was not explicit in the teaching of pre-Marxian modern political philosophy. Not before Marx asserted the historicity of nature itself,[13] the absolute perfectibility of human nature under the influence of economic conditions, was it supposed that political life and religion must vanish and be replaced by uncoerced, rational society.

We are led, through the doctrines of Marxism, to reconsider some commonly held views. One is that there is a deep hostility between philosophy and political society because philosophy, by its unconfined questioning, eventually exposes the polity itself to the blasts of skepticism; while the body politic, suspicious of theories and prone to Philistinism, always threatens the thinking sort of men with contempt or worse.

But however well-founded the mutual suspicions might be, we observe that philosophy, certainly classical political philosophy, argues that man is by his nature political and that political society is the truly human society taking into view the characteristics of men generally. Philosophy has been thought to threaten politics; we see that in fact it defended politics, and that the anticipation of the end of political life had to await the supersession of philosophy by history—that is, by the doctrine of the emendation of Nature.

Another opinion brought under revision is that between philosophy and religion there is in principle war to the death, the one asserting the supremacy of reason, the other of faith. We have seen that philosophy can have, and did for ages have, a certain common ground with religion; both had views of nature that did not lead to the expectation of perfect society within the natural order. The theoretical discountenancing of religion in the name of an aspiration toward perfect society had to await the supersession of philosophy by history.

We might summarize by saying that the replacement of philosophy by history was the condition for the replacement of politics and religion by society and economics. This is the kernel of Marxism.

Marxism is not simply another political system, or one more ideology. It proposes nothing less than the end of the West—of political life, philosophy, and religion—as the foregoing summary indicates. Perhaps we should look forward with eager anticipation to the end of the West—but we cannot know whether we should without rationally examining the project for strangling philosophy. That rational examination is part of the philosophic quest itself. We cannot free ourselves of philosophy, if only because we must philosophize to pass judgment on philosophy. We begin to suspect the soundness of the antiphilosophic historicism of Marx. Observing its weakness prepares us to concede that history can make room for spiritually impoverished societies: the viability of Marxist nations is a sign not of the soundness of Marx's prophecy but of the unsoundness of the sanguine historicism on which he based it. We have every right to conclude that history is the opiate of the masses.

## NOTES

1. Karl Marx, *The Poverty of Philosophy,* ii. 1. 2nd observation.

2. *Capital* (New York: Modern Library, n.d.), I, 834, n.l. Copyright by the Modern Library. Pagination is the same in the edition published by Charles H. Kerr & Co. The reference is to Burke's "Thoughts and Details on Scarcity."

3. Cf. Engels' *Herr Eugen Dühr-*

ing's *Revolution in Science* [*Anti-Dühring*], x. 1: ". . . ideology, the deduction of reality not from itself but from its mental image." Also Engels' *Ludwig Feuerbach,* iv. 7th par. from the end: ". . . ideology, that is, occupation with thoughts as with independent entities."

4. "On the Jewish Question," in *Selected Essays by Karl Marx,* trans. H. J. Stenning (New York: International Publishers, 1926), pp. 55–56.

5. From K. Freeman, *Ancilla to the Pre-Socratic Philosophers* (Cambridge: Harvard University Press, 1957).

6. David Ricardo, *Principles of Political Economy and Taxation,* i. 1.

7. See, for example, *Capital,* i (p. 45).

8. *Ibid.,* IV. xv. 3 (p. 445).

9. *Ibid.,* 9 (p. 534). .

10. *Ibid.,* xv. 4 (pp. 708–9).

11. See *ibid.,* xxxii.

12. Cf. the sentence with which Montesquieu begins I. iii of *The Spirit of the Laws.*

13. See above, p. 705.

# READINGS

A. Marx, Karl, and Engels, Friedrich. *The Communist Manifesto.*
   Marx, Karl, and Engels, Friedrich. *The German Ideology.* Ed. R. Pascal. New York: International Publishers, 1939. Part I.
   Marx, Karl. *Theses on Feuerbach.*
   Marx, Karl. *Capital.* New York: Modern Library, n. d. Bk I, part I, chap. i, secs 1, 2, 4.
B. Engels, Friedrich. *Ludwig Feuerbach and the Outcome of German Classical Philosophy.* Ed. C. P. Dutt. New York: International Publishers, n.d. Chap. iv "Dialectical Materialism."
   Engels, Friedrich. *Herr Eugen Dühring's Revolution in Science (Anti-Dühring).* Trans. E. Burns. Ed. C. P. Dutt. New York: International Publishers, 1935. Part I "Philosophy."

# FRIEDRICH NIETZSCHE

## 1844–1900

The young Nietzsche thought of the philosopher as a physician of culture. His own philosophy is both a diagnosis of the sickness or crisis of his time, the nineteenth century, and the search for a cure. In his first published book, *The Birth of Tragedy* (1872), Nietzsche placed his hope in a revival of German culture through the music of Richard Wagner. His second book, *Untimely Considerations,* known in English as *Thoughts Out of Season,* consists of four essays published separately between 1873 and 1876. One of these is again a tribute to Wagner. Nietzsche soon ceased to believe in the cure he had suggested, repudiating Wagner and losing faith in the possibility of a German cultural revival. He thus entered into the second stage of his development, a stage characterized by disillusionment and a turning to Western positivism. Symbolic of this is the dedication of his third book, *Human, All-too-Human* (1879) to Voltaire.[1] Nietzsche's final position is articulated in *Thus Spoke Zarathustra* (its four parts were written and published between 1883 and 1885) and the books following it. Nietzsche, however, never repudiated but only deepened the view of his time as sick and critical, a view which is to be found in the writings of his first stage of development; and the problems he raised at this stage are problems with which he never ceased to wrestle. One is, therefore, justified in beginning an exposition of Nietzsche's political philosophy with a discussion of one of his earlier writings, the second essay of *Thoughts Out of Season.*

The title of the essay, which was published in 1874, may be translated as "Of the Use and Disadvantage of History for Life"; in English it is known as *The Use and Abuse of History.*[2] Nietzsche's thoughts are out of season because they are meant to be contrary to his time and yet with an influence upon it for the benefit of a coming time. The essay is a critique of a specific "fault and defect" of the time, historicism, which Nietzsche calls the historical movement, the historical trend, or the historical sense. He believes his time to be suffering from a "malignant historical fever." [3]

Nietzsche's critique of historicism is also his confrontation with, and criticism of, Hegel. In the latter part of the essay Nietzsche refers to a "very celebrated philosophy" and continues, "I believe there has been no dangerous turning point in the progress of German culture in this century that has not been made more dangerous by the enormous and still living influence of this Hegelian philosophy." Hegel regards contemporary man as the perfection of world history; Hegelianism establishes the sovereignty of history over other spiritual powers such as art or religion; for Hegel "the highest and final stage of the world process came together in his own Berlin existence." [4] Against Hegel's doctrine that the historical process is a rational process which in Hegel's time has ended in an absolute moment at the zenith, Nietzsche asserts that the historical process neither is nor can be finished, that the completion of history is not merely impossible but undesirable because it would lead to a degeneration of man, and that history is not a rational process but is full of blindness, madness and injustice.

It might thus appear that Nietzsche simply effects a return to a pre-Hegelian viewpoint which considers history a realm of chance rather than a dimension of meaning. However, Nietzsche's critique of historicism does not deny the validity of the essential premises of historicism, and his criticism of Hegel is based on a crucial area of agreement with Hegel, as a closer analysis of *The Use and Abuse of History* will show.

The essay begins with a consideration of the life of animals. Animals forget each moment as soon as it passes. To live entirely in the present, without memory of the past, means to live unhistorically. Man remembers the past and cannot escape from it; man lives historically. He also suffers from the awareness of the past and the passing of time, if only because it brings with it an awareness that man is an imperfectible imperfection. Happiness depends on the ability to forget and to surrender completely to the present. A man who could forget nothing would be a totally unhappy man, for he would see only flux and change and would have no fixed points by which to take his bearings.

On the other hand, man would not be man without a memory of the past. Moreover, it is only by developing his historical sense and by virtue of his power of turning the past to the uses of the present that man rises above other animals and becomes man. Man's problem is therefore to find that balance between remembering and forgetting which is most conducive to his life as man. The degree and limits of man's memory of the past must be fixed by the extent to which man can incorporate or absorb the past. A healthy organism is one which instinctively assimilates only as much of the past as it can digest; the rest it simply does not see. The dividing line between the historical and the unhistorical is the organism's horizon. According to Nietzsche, "This is a universal law: a living thing can only be healthy, strong and productive within a certain horizon. . . ." [5]

Man's horizon is constituted by his fundamental set of assumptions about all things, by what he considers the absolute truth which he cannot question. His historical knowledge must be surrounded by an unhistorical atmosphere of darkness which limits the historical sense of man.

The proper sphere of history lies within and under the unhistorical atmosphere which must envelop man if he is to endure. Nietzsche admits that there are uses as well as abuses of history. He speaks of three kinds of history which can serve life. *Monumental* history provides the man of action with models of greatness by its depiction of the great men and events of the past. *Antiquarian* history addresses itself to the preserving and revering element in man, imbuing him with a salutary love for tradition. It is of special benefit to less gifted peoples and races because it keeps them safe from a restless and unproductive cosmopolitanism. *Critical* history places obsolete aspects of the past before the bar of judgment and condemns them; it brings to light injustices surviving from the past so that they can be abolished in the interest of the present.

Nietzsche is, however, more concerned with the abuses than with the uses of history. He is quick to point out how easy it is to misuse each of the above-mentioned kinds of history. Monumental history's models of past greatness can be erected to hinder the emergence of present greatness. The reverence for the past which antiquarian history fosters can act to stultify the present. There is always the danger that critical history will uproot more of the past than deserves to be uprooted. Moreover, Nietzsche links the efficacy of each kind of history to its blindness to the whole truth. By paying insufficient attention to the conditions needed for the emergence of greatness, monumental history deludes one into thinking that, because greatness was possible, it is still possible, which need not be the case. Critical history fails to realize the extent to which men are the results of the past they seek to condemn.

In cultivating a general reverence for the past, antiquarian history is necessarily indiscriminate and praises aspects of the past which do not deserve praise. The uses of the past for the present depend on a violation of the truth about the past: useful history cannot be scientific history.

Science and the demand that history become a science disrupt the proper relation between history and life. Historical science is motivated by the desire to know rather than the desire to serve life, and it forces on the attention of man more historical knowledge than he can properly absorb or digest. At this point history no longer serves life; it disrupts life.

Nietzsche presents the reader with a catalogue of calamities resulting from an excess of history. One of these calamities is that men, confronted with a spectacle of history so vast that it becomes meaningless for them, will come to think of themselves as *epigoni,* late arrivals on the scene for whom there is nothing whatever to do. If Hegel were right, if history were finished, modern men would indeed be *epigoni.* Hegel is wrong, but the belief that he is right makes men act as if they were *epigoni.* Men who have no further task to accomplish or men who believe there is nothing more to be done are bound to degenerate, for what is best in man is his aspiration.

But neither the assertion that the historical process is finished nor the assertion that the historical process is rational is the most fundamental assertion of historicism. Historicism asserts the overwhelming importance of history, the determination of man's life and thought by history, and the impossibility of transcending the historical process. Nietzsche accepts this assertion of the omnipotence of history, and his acceptance constitutes a crucial area of agreement with Hegel. The calamities which Nietzsche attributes to an excess of historical knowledge can be summarized by saying that an excess of historical knowledge destroys man's horizon. There is, however, no permanent horizon of man as man. Men's fundamental assumptions about things are unevident, unsupported, historically variable and historically determined. There are neither eternal things nor eternal truths; there is only flux and change, which Nietzsche calls the finality of becoming.[6] While doctrines asserting the finality of becoming are true they are also fatal. History as the science of universal becoming is true but deadly.

If human life can only thrive within a certain horizon which men believe to be the absolute truth, but which in reality is merely one of many possible horizons, then life is in need of illusions, and the truth which exposes the horizon as a *mere* horizon is deadly. There is, then, a conflict between truth and life, or between life and wisdom.

In such a conflict, according to Nietzsche, one must choose the side of life. There can be life without wisdom, but there can be no wisdom without life.

It is, however, impossible to accept the illusions which life demands if they are known to be illusions. Myths are useful only so long as they are mistaken for the truth. A man's horizon is his most comprehensive myth, and it enables him to live because he thinks of it as the truth. To see a horizon as horizon is to be beyond that horizon. At the very least the continued acceptance of a discredited horizon would involve man in a degrading self-deception, but Nietzsche is concerned with the ennoblement of man. If there is a tension between wisdom and life, it cannot be resolved by the preference for life. An impasse has been reached.

Yet *The Use and Abuse of History* ends on a note of hope, asserting a harmony between life and wisdom. After historicism's exposure of the arbitrary character of all human horizons, man is subjected to "the hopeless waves of an infinite skepticism"; but Nietzsche professes to sight land: man can recover from "the malady of history." [7] Such a recovery is only possible if historicism is proved to be untrue or at least not completely true. Tentatively in *The Use and Abuse of History,* and more comprehensively in his later writings, Nietzsche attempts to overcome and transcend the historicist insight; what begins as the questioning of the objective truth of historicism ends as a questioning of the very possibility of objective truth.

The kind of history which culminates in historicism is history which understands itself as scientific and objective. Historicism is a theoretical assertion based upon an examination of historical phenomena. Nietzsche questions whether the historical phenomena can be understood by objective and scientific history and historians; he questions whether history will yield its secrets to disinterested inquiry. History is made by historical actors, by great men. History-making men are dedicated men having a commitment to a cause. They act within a horizon of commitment, unhistorically believing the absolute validity of their attempt. The great men of history were the great creators, facing the future and devoting themselves to that which was to be. The greatest creators are those who create horizons within which future men will live. They create these horizons unconsciously and under the illusion that they are merely discovering truth. All previous horizons enveloped a belief in an absolute truth which cannot be created but which may be discovered.

Objective history stands or falls by its fidelity to its object, by its ability to present the past as it really was. Nietzsche quotes with approval the old maxim that like can only be understood by like. Only committed men facing the future and only creative men can understand the creations of future-directed and committed men of the past. "The language of the past is always oracular. You will only understand it as builders of the future who know the present." [8] The objective historian is not a creative man, and he does not face the future. He may establish the date of Michelangelo's birth, but only an artist can really understand Michelangelo.

The objective historian deludes himself into thinking that he does not interpret the past but only describes it. There is, however, an illusion which lurks in the very word "objectivity." Any statement about facts is an interpretation of facts. The very selection of data from an infinity of data is already an interpretation. Ultimately there is not a choice between objective and subjective history but only a choice between a noble, rich interpretation of the past and a base, impoverished interpretation of the past.

Thus Nietzsche does not deny the validity of the insight that horizons are the creations of men; he attacks historicism as a particular interpretation of that insight. He attempts to transcend the apparent deadliness of the historicist insight by interpreting it nobly. If it is a fact that the values by which men have lived have been their own creations or fictions, it is an ambiguous fact. Nietzsche moves in the direction of viewing this insight as a revelation of man's creativity and therefore of his power. Man is revealed as the animal who is able to create horizons. For the first time he can create his horizon consciously: could not a consciously created horizon be the most glorious horizon yet created by man?

Nietzsche only hints at the possibility of such a solution in *The Use and Abuse of History,* and the questions raised by those hints are not resolved in that essay. If horizons are the creations of men, can there in principle not be as many different horizons as there are men? If horizons are free projects, how is one to choose between different horizons? When these questions arise, one must turn from *The Use and Abuse of History* to the main body of his work, but with an appreciation of the importance which the historical process has for Nietzsche. In *Human, All-too-Human,* Nietzsche criticizes traditional philosophy for its lack of the historical sense.[9] The importance of the historical process is such that Nietzsche's own political philosophy can almost be said to be couched in terms of a historical analysis. Nietzsche tries to create man's horizon of the future. His creation cannot, of course, be derived, or merely derived, from history, for it is a free project. But the historicist insight into horizons as horizons, for instance, is necessarily a post-

Christian insight, as will be seen. And Nietzsche's own project is in some respects meant to be a synthesis of the best projections of the future which have occurred in history. With these considerations in mind, one may turn to Nietzsche's interpretation of man's history, which has led men to the total crisis of Nietzsche's time.

The peak of man's history was reached near the beginning of recorded history; the highest culture hitherto was that of the Greeks. To Nietzsche culture is the perfection of nature, and every culture is characterized by a unity of style which pervades all its activities. A great culture is one which abounds with great, creative men and which elevates men. In *Beyond Good and Evil* Nietzsche writes:

Every elevation of the type "man" has hitherto been the work of an aristocratic society and so it will always be—a society believing in a long scale of gradations of rank . . . and requiring slavery in some form or another. Without the *pathos of distance,* such as grows out of the incarnated difference of classes, out of the constant outlooking and downlooking of the ruling caste on subordinates and instruments, and out of their equally constant practice of obeying and commanding, of keeping down and keeping at a distance— that other more mysterious pathos could never have arisen, the longing for an ever new widening of distance within the soul itself, the formation of ever higher, rarer, further, more extended, more comprehensive states, in short, just the elevation of the type "man". . . .[10]

The pathos of distance existed in Greek society, which was a master-slave society. Nietzsche also notes with approval that the Greeks made a virtue of combat and contests; even the poets contested each other.

If Greece is the peak of recorded history, Greek tragedy is the peak of that peak. Man's fundamental experience is abysmal: he is confronted with an abyss of meaninglessness in a world that is a chaos and not a cosmos; man is a suffering animal. Optimism is a shallow reaction to man's condition, a self-deception. Pessimism may be a mere weakness of the will, but it can be a courageous confrontation of the abyss. Greek tragedy is a pessimism of strength, an affirmation and therewith a transfiguration of man's suffering.

The Greek culture Nietzsche admires is primarily pre-Socratic, just as the Greek philosophers he praises are mainly pre-Socratics, especially Heraclitus. Socrates is, to Nietzsche, the destroyer of Greek tragedy. A healthy culture is one in which men's creative instincts are maximized. Socrates is the enemy of the instinctive life, a theoretical man who is critical rather than creative, who bizarrely equates both happiness and virtue with reason, who withers nobility and the noble virtues by subjecting them to a ruthless dialectical inquiry they cannot withstand, who imposes his will on posterity so successfully that, since Socrates, rationalism has been the fate of Western man.

Socrates and Plato are an anticipation of an even greater calamity for mankind: the appearance of Christianity. Nietzsche labels Christianity as "Platonism for the people."[11] Christianity's triumph over Rome is the triumph of slave-morality over master-morality.

For Nietzsche moralities are creations, but the first creators were not individuals but herds. Herd-morality is the first form of morality, from which both slave- and master-morality derive. However, there were always strong herds and weak herds. Strong herds impose their will on weak herds and enslave them. Master-morality is the affirmation of strength by the strong, a celebration of the vigorous and active life by those who are possessed of vigor and capable of action. The strong do not repress their instincts but glorify them. Masters are cruel but they are innocently cruel. They identify the good with the powerful, and they dismiss the weak with contempt, calling it bad.

Conversely, slave-morality is the rejection of strength by the weak. Whereas masters distinguish between good and bad, slaves distinguish between good and evil; what the master affirms as good the slave rejects as evil. Slave-morality is essentially negative, being a reaction against, and a revenge upon, the rulers and their values. Its primary concern is with evil. Good becomes a label attached to various kinds of weakness, such as humility and passivity. Eagles cannot help being eagles, and lambs cannot help being lambs, but lambs pretend—and must pretend —that their weakness is voluntary, just as the strength of the eagles is voluntary and can therefore be condemned.

Nietzsche tends to use the terms slave-morality and priest-morality interchangeably. Slave-morality is formulated by priests who are members of the ruling herd, but weak and decadent members. They make common cause with the herd: the sick minister to the sick. They develop ascetic ideals which are the revenge which weak life attempts to take on life, but this attempted revenge serves life by keeping the herd from destroying itself. *The* priestly people are the Jews, who are the inventors of Christianity. Through Christianity they connive to effect a transvaluation of all values. They succeed: humility becomes a virtue and pride a vice; master-morality is stood on its head. Christianity makes life soft by sapping its vigor. The instincts are denied their free play and forced to turn back upon themselves.

The worst effect of this transvaluation of all values is to preserve what Nietzsche calls a surplus of "defective, diseased, degenerating forms of life"; in the economy of life this preservation is necessarily at the expense of higher forms of life. It has made man a "sublime abortion" who is too tame for his own good.[12]

Nietzsche conceived of his own labors as an attempt at a transvaluation of all values, but it would be a mistake to assume that he merely attempted to restore a pre-Christian master-morality. Such a restoration would be impossible because of the changes in Western man which Christianity has produced, and it would be undesirable because the changes have not all been for the worse. Nietzsche thinks of the abortion as sublime in a very serious way. Christianity has deepened man. Slave-morality spiritualizes man by sublimating his instincts until there is a possibility of their expression in ever more delicate forms. The spiritualization of man has produced, among other things, science, which has widened the scope of man's possible future. Furthermore, Christianity has universalized man and has made any restoration of limited goals for peoples or races obsolete. Christianity has superseded the Greeks. Nietzsche's transvaluation of values will replace the false universalism of Christianity with a true universal goal for mankind; it will transcend Christianity rather than merely destroy it.

When Nietzsche compares his own time with the great age of the Greeks or even with the eras in which Christianity produced in European man a magnificent tension of the spirit, he finds it wanting in all decisive respects. There are almost no true individuals in the nineteenth century; even the rare true selves that do occur in such a paltry time are stunted by the time. The rule of low forms of life at the expense of higher forms is for Nietzsche the meaning of democracy. Democracy is mediocrity. There is no significant difference between democracy and socialism. Both democracy and socialism preach egalitarianism and both are the true heirs of Christianity and its slave-morality. Christianity prepares the way for egalitarianism by holding all men to be equal in decisive respects: they have, in God, a common father; and they are all sinners.

Nietzsche finds that all the governments of his day are inherently democratic. Even states which consider themselves to be monarchies take their bearings by the many and cater to them. All modern states yield to public opinion; Nietzsche equates public opinion with private laziness. The rule of public opinion is the rule of sloth and laziness, breeding conformity. Modern societies are all mass societies which not only mold all men into one shape but also into a very degraded shape. The morning paper replaces the morning prayer. The time prides itself on its pacificism: the truth is that men no longer believe in anything strongly enough to fight for it.

Nietzsche condemns both the modern state and modern society. The state is a powerful, new idol, whereas Nietzsche is concerned with the destruction of idols. The state is a mere superstructure based on the unique quality of a people, but it warps that uniqueness: the state preaches universal doctrines like the rights of man. Its shallow universalism destroys the genius of particular people; its impersonal machinery depersonalizes man.

A false quality pervades society. Success in the market place is a sign of worthlessness. One must be an actor, the opposite of a genuine self, to succeed.

Modern education no longer molds true individuals but turns out specialists. The corruption of education necessarily produces a corruption of the general level of taste. Symptomatic of this is the debasement of literary style. People cease to speak well and to write well, for excellence as such tends to be rejected.

Philosophy, too, has been affected by the total crisis of Nietzsche's time. It is tolerated only because of its impotence. It is no longer sovereign over other disciplines. It is in such a bad state that it almost deserves the disrepute in which it is held. All varieties of philosophy which Nietzsche examines he finds deficient. To begin with, they all tend to be dogmatic. Philosophies turn into philosophic systems; the will to a system is a lack of integrity. Certain varieties of philosophy continue to be instructive. One can learn from cynics the "seamy" underside of values and to appreciate the animal qualities in man; one can learn from skeptics a necessary kind of detachment, and from pessimists the necessarily great role of suffering and pain in life. In themselves, however, these philosophies offer no solution for the crisis of the time, being themselves symptoms of the crisis. Nor does science offer a solution. It possesses the rare virtue of integrity, but it is involved in the crisis: science is the last form assumed by the ascetic ideals of slave-morality. Science turns against life in the interest of truth. Its very truthfulness, however, disarms it. Science has taken to discrediting itself by revealing its own limitations.

Nietzsche has a short saying to express what is at the root of the total crisis of his time, a crisis reflected in thought and in deed, in individuals and in institutions. That saying is, "God is dead."

With Nietzsche's saying that God is dead one arrives at the core of his philosophical endeavors. In Nietzsche's greatest book, *Thus Spoke Zarathustra,* Zarathustra, who to some extent is the self-idealization of Nietzsche, asserts the death of God near the very beginning of the work.[13] He does not at first prove that God is dead but makes it, as it were, a matter of personal honor that God be dead. The belief in God

has become an indecency for all men except those who have had no
opportunity to hear of the death of God. Later on the meanings of the
saying, its basis and its consequences, are articulated.

Nietzsche is obviously not the inventor of atheism, but his atheism
is nevertheless unique and significant in various ways. First of all,
Nietzsche makes no attempt to conceal his atheism but proclaims it
again and again with all the eloquence at his command; many previous
atheists had tended to be more reticent about their atheism. Secondly,
atheism had been in the nineteenth century chiefly a preserve of the
political left. Nietzsche, who abhorred the politics of the left and who
envisioned a new aristocracy, may be said to have invented the atheism
of the political right. Aristocracy has traditionally been associated with
the preservation of religion; Nietzsche's aristocrats are to be candid
atheists. Thirdly, Nietzsche's atheism is historical atheism. The saying
that God is dead implies that God once existed. God existed while one
could believe in God; God is dead because belief in God has become
impossible.

Since Nietzsche is concerned with an analysis of *his* particular
time, his teaching of the death of God refers primarily, but not exclusively, to the death of the Christian God. The speeches in Part I of *Thus
Spoke Zarathustra* are to a large extent concerned with Christianity and
its effects. It is part of the intention of the whole book to be an imitation
and parody of the Bible. Zarathustra wants to create a true universal
goal for humanity and must therefore overcome the false universal goals
which already exist. Christianity and Buddhism are false universal
goals, but since only Christianity is a significant force in Europe,
Nietzsche devotes more attention to it. The death of the Christian God
leaves European man without a universal goal but at the same time so
universalized by the influence of Christianity that he is beyond any
national or ethnic goal.

The death of God is the last event in the history of Christianity,
but with the death of the Christian God all other gods die also. With
the exposure of man's most universal horizon as mere horizon, all belief in eternal truths and beings becomes impossible. At the end of
Part I of *Thus Spoke Zarathustra,* Zarathustra proclaims the death of
all gods.[14] The death of God is also the death of the Platonic ideas and
of metaphysics. Traditional philosophies and traditional religions have
shared a belief in a true world which they distinguished from the
world known by man through his senses, the apparent world. Both
philosophy and religion have been other-worldly. The impossibility of
the belief in God is also the impossibility of the belief in a true world,
but the abolition of the true world is also the abolition of the apparent

world: the world known by man through his senses and feelings and through his whole being is now the only world and not the apparent world. Or, one could say that with the death of God the apparent world becomes the true and real world.

The death of God comes about when men realize that God is their own creation. The descendants of the men who created God, men who have been radically changed by the belief in God, now murder God. The Christian God is the anchor of Christian morality. Christian morality, by making man conscious of his weakness, also made him strive to overcome that weakness. Christianity deepened and heightened man's spiritual powers. Christian morality emphasizes the desirability of truthfulness. It not only makes man a tamer but a more subtle and clever animal. The devotion to God evolves into a devotion to truth which may be called science. The strict and tender conscience which the belief in the Christian God creates finally turns against God. The Christian God is killed by intellectual probity, which is the consummation of Christian morality.

But with the death of the Christian God at the hands of Christian morality, Christian morality renders itself baseless. Christian morality cannot survive the death of God. Devotion to the truth or devotion to anything now becomes problematical: all visions and aspirations are exposed as arbitrary and unsupported. The death of God is the death not only of Christian morality but also of all traditional moralities.

In *Thus Spoke Zarathustra,* Christianity is considered as a metamorphosis of man's spirit, which by the acceptance of Christianity becomes a camel. It burdens itself with moral obligations which say to the spirit, "Thou shalt." Man "burdens" himself with the mortification of his pride, with the denigration of his own wisdom, with devotion to lost causes, and with the search for truth. The camel goes into the wilderness but there a second metamorphosis occurs: the spirit of man becomes a lion. It rebels against its burdens. It slays the dragon of obligation; instead of listening to the dragon's "thou shalt" it now says, "I will." But while the lion may slay the dragon of values which precede the will of man, he cannot create new values; he is left in a desert.[15]

With the death of God man finds himself in a desert which is the total crisis of Nietzsche's time. It is obviously more than a crisis in the history of ideas. Christian morality may continue to be observed for a while, perhaps out of habit, but such a situation cannot endure. Men are progressively less able to believe in anything. There is no longer a horizon to give life meaning: the crisis is total.

The politics of the left are to Nietzsche a symptom of the total crisis and an aggravation of it, so they obviously are not a solution. What about conservatism, or the politics of the political right? Nietzsche rejects the possibility of a conservative solution on various grounds, criticizing both the specific form which German conservatism took under Bismarck and the general assumptions of conservatism.

First of all, nineteenth-century conservatism is forced to make overwhelming concessions to the democratic movement of modern times. Bismarck attempts to preserve a monarchy but at the same time is forced to introduce universal suffrage and extensive welfare legislation and thus to advance the democratic movement. The king is no longer considered the ruler but merely the first servant.

Secondly, conservatism embraces the ideals of nationalism. Nationalism is inherently a democratic phenomenon, as is shown by its outgrowth from the French Revolution. It is also an anachronism. The very concessions which all European states must make to democracy and the increasing likeness of all European cultures show that there is already a hidden European unity which cannot be denied: Nietzsche calls himself a good European. The few true individuals of the nineteenth century, like Napoleon and Goethe, were not national but European events. The superficial conflicts of European nation-states can no longer be tolerated, if only because of the threat to Europe from the sleeping giant Russia.

Thirdly, conservatism relies on the old nobility, which is decrepit. What is needed is a new nobility and a new idea of nobility.

Finally, conservatism is allied with Christianity, but, as has been seen, Nietzsche advocates a candid atheism.

One may summarize Nietzsche's view of conservatism by quoting from an aphorism in one of his late works, *The Twilight of the Idols:*

*Whispered to Conservatives.* What was not known formerly, what is known, or might be known, today: a reversion, a return in any sense or degree is simply not possible. . . . Today there are still parties whose dream it is that all things might walk backwards like crabs. But no one is free to be a crab. Nothing avails: one *must* go forward—step by step further into decadence (that is *my* definition of modern "progress"). One can *check* this development and thus dam up degeneration, gather it and make it more vehement and *sudden:* one can do no more.[16]

Nietzsche rejects both the politics of the right and the left as petty politics, opposing to them his rather vague concept of great politics, the politics of the future. The transvaluation of all values is also the transvaluation of all politics; Nietzsche equates the moral with the political.

The total crisis of the time must be resolved but there is absolutely no necessity for it to be resolved for the benefit of man. With the death of God man is exposed to the greatest danger: man may become utterly degraded. Both the belief in God and the fight against God improved man; with the death of God man has no more opportunity to love or to hate God. The death of God may result in man's abandonment of all striving, all aspirations, and all ideals. Such a man, motivated only by the desire for comfortable self-preservation, is called by Nietzsche the last man. The last man is the most despicable man because he is no longer able to despise himself. He neither wants to rule nor be ruled, to become rich or poor; he wants everyone to do and be the same. " 'We have invented happiness' say the last men, and they blink." [17] When Zarathustra describes the last man in order to warn men, his listeners are enthralled by the picture he draws: contemporary man is not yet the last man but his ideal is the last man.

Nihilism is a protest against the approach of the last man. The formula for nihilism is: nothing is true, everything is permitted. Since all aspirations and ideals have proved meaningless, men cannot devote themselves to a cause: they have no future to will. Nihilists will nothingness rather than to desist from willing. The ascetic ideals of Christianity, being a denial of life, can be seen as an unconscious form of nihilism. Furthermore, nihilism is a necessary consequence of modern science which destroys the validity of values. Nietzsche at times thinks of nihilism as the inescapable future of Europe; at other times he calls himself a nihilist. The creator of new values must be a destroyer of old values.

However, the death of God is not only the time of man's greatest danger but of his greatest possibility, because it makes possible the supreme creation of the values of the future. The death of God is the liberation of man from God. Previous horizons have kept man in chains; they have prevented him from being at home in this world which is the only world. Man can now be loyal to the earth, as Zarathustra admonishes him to be. The heart of the earth is gold: there is no hell. The death of God is the liberation of man from guilt: the productive innocence of the blond beast, the finest specimen of prehistoric man, can be recovered on a higher level.

The death of God is the discovery of man's creativity. Knowing that horizons are his creations, he also is more aware of his own power; if nothing is true, everything is possible. Man has become man by unconsciously projecting horizons; with the conscious projection of horizons man can become more than man.

At this point it becomes evident that Nietzsche needs a philosophical doctrine to explain man and the situation of man. Previous doctrines are discredited with the dissolution of previous horizons. The new doctrine must explain how man has become man without recourse to teleological principles; the new doctrine must be in harmony with the knowledge of the sovereignty of becoming, of man's animal origins, and of the inherent meaninglessness of all givens. Nietzsche calls this doctrine the doctrine of the will to power.

Nietzsche maintains that the will to power is the basic characteristic of all reality. The doctrine of the will to power is a wholly new philosophical doctrine. In *Thus Spoke Zarathustra* and in *Beyond Good and Evil* the presentation of the doctrine is coupled with a rejection of all previous philosophical doctrines. These share the belief in an objective truth; that belief is, according to Nietzsche, a mere prejudice. Philosophers have spoken of a will to truth and have assumed that there is a truth which can be discovered by thinking. In reality, according to Nietzsche, they have merely and unconsciously sought to imprint their interpretation on the world. The thought or reason of philosophers is inseparable from the philosopher's personality. The will to truth is only a form of something more basic, a will to overcome and to master everything, the will to power.

In *Thus Spoke Zarathustra,* the fullest exposition of the doctrine of the will to power is given in Zarathustra's speech on "Self-Overcoming." [18] Zarathustra has observed living things and has found that wherever there is life there is obedience. But obedience is always obedience to something, it is relative to commanding. This commanding must not be sought outside of life. The urge to overcome, to command, to master is not a mere characteristic of life but the core of life.

Life is will to power. A living thing is one which tries to *overcome;* it "seeks above all to *discharge* its strength." However, it does not try to overcome and discharge with any view to a given end. Nietzsche denies that the instinct of self-preservation is the cardinal instinct of an organic being. Self-preservation is merely a result of the will to power, not the purpose of life; the instinct of self-preservation is a superfluous teleological principle.

The will to power is not peculiar to human beings, though it explains how man has become man: life consists in overcoming, and some beasts have overcome their beastliness, just as some men may overcome their humanity. The beast's preying in the jungle and the artist's painting of a picture are both forms of the will to power. Finally, the doctrine of the will to power is a cosmological doctrine, explaining the character of all reality. There are no inanimate things: the doctrine refutes not only all idealistic but also all materialistic philosophies.

Nietzsche's primary emphasis, however, remains on *man's* will to power. Man is the horizon-creating animal. For Nietzsche, man has no

determined nature or function; man is the animal which has not yet
been defined (*festgestellt*). Man is a rope over an abyss, an interlude
between what is less than man and what is more than man. The will
to power explains all of man's activity, from his lowest cravings to his
highest creations. Philosophy is the highest and most spiritualized form
of the will to power.

Reason can then no longer be understood as being of man's essence,
as traditionally it had been. Man is not primarily a thinking being.
Reason and consciousness are mere surface phenomena. Man's ego is
created; it is part of the total organism which is the source of reason
and which reason cannot fathom. The highest things are neither accessible to reason nor communicable by reason. Beneath the ego is the
self, the ground of the ego, the seat of the will to power, the source of
all possible meaning. Nietzsche's concept of the self has some relation
to Freud's concept of the id, and Nietzsche once called the self an "it."
But Nietzsche's self, in contradistinction to Freud's id, is meant to be
radically mysterious and itself a creation.

Zarathustra calls the self the body. The traditional dualism of mind
and matter, of body and soul, is thus abolished; the self is also called
the soul. The result is not only a less exalted notion of what had previously been thought to pertain to the soul, but a more spiritualized
notion of things previously thought to pertain to the body; for instance,
Zarathustra refers to blood as spirit.

The doctrine of the will to power necessarily leads to a revision of
traditional notions of virtue. To Nietzsche, virtues are sublimated and
transfigured passions, dedicated passions. Nietzsche compares traditional virtues with sleep because they were thought to lead to happiness
understood as a state of peace and rest, and because traditionally the
highest virtue is a wisdom conceived of as the contemplation of the
eternal and uncreated. For Nietzsche virtue is creativity; wisdom is
self-conscious creation. With Nietzsche's emphasis on the self comes an
increased emphasis on self-realization and on such virtues as sincerity
and integrity. Since every self is, however, unique and mysterious, there
can be no comprehensive doctrine of virtues for Nietzsche: one man's
virtue may be another man's vice. It may also be maintained that
Nietzsche attempts to reduce notions of virtue and vice to notions of the
sickness and health of the self which is the body, and these notions in
turn to notions of strength and weakness.

Nietzsche is aware that the doctrine of the will to power raises difficulties. Is the doctrine of the will to power merely the expression
of Nietzsche's will to power or is it an objectively true doctrine?
Nietzsche can neither maintain that it is simply true nor that it is

-in no way more plausible than the man on the street's opinion about the character of reality. Nietzsche wrestles with this problem in various ways. Previous philosophy had understood itself as simply true. Nietzsche characterizes traditional philosophy as dogmatic philosophy. He therefore takes pains to present his own philosophy differently. The doctrine of the will to power differs from previous doctrines not only in content but in mode. Nietzsche thinks there can be no objective knowledge of reality but only perspectives of reality. At times he therefore not only admits but asserts that the doctrine of the will to power is a perspectivistic interpretation of reality, characterizing it as a hypothesis to be tested. He thinks of his own philosophy and of the philosophy of the future to which his own philosophy is a prelude as an experiment, an attempt which is also a temptation. Even is there can be only perspectives of reality, there can be more and less comprehensive perspectives. Nietzsche's perspective is the highest perspective yet attained because it embodies the insights of all previous perspectives, and because it is the first perspective aware of the law of perspectivity. Nietzsche's doctrine of the will to power, similarly, represents the first self-consciousness of the will to power; Nietzsche's philosophy is the first creative interpretation of creativity; Nietzsche has reached a peak where there is no difference between creation and contemplation. But this still means that some kind of finality has been reached. Nietzsche is both compelled to affirm and compelled to deny the objective truth of the doctrine of the will to power; the doctrine of the will to power must somehow be both an insight into the truth of things and the creation of Nietzsche's unique, created self. The arguments for the will to power in *Beyond Good and Evil* are also only Nietzsche's most private thoughts. *Thus Spoke Zarathustra* is, as its subtitle indicates, "A Book for All and No One." It is both a new Bible for all mankind and Nietzsche's most personal expression. Nietzsche can only hint to others of what he means. At best he can only demand that others become true, creative selves. Zarathustra wants no disciples. Nietzsche's teaching is a creative call to creativity and can only be understood by creative men.

There is a second difficulty. What are the limits of the will to power? Can everything be overcome? If everything can be overcome, then man will finally overcome even the conditions of inequality which, according to Nietzsche, are indispensable for the elevation of man. Finally men will indeed become *epigoni;* there will be nothing left to overcome. Nietzsche believes in a hierarchical society, in the superiority of men over women, and in the necessity for suffering. But if the will to power is all, and if all is in principle possible, why should not and why will not the difference between the sexes or the rank differences

between men be abolished? Traditional political philosophy does not
need to face these problems because it takes its bearings by nature. For
Nietzsche man has no determined nature. There can be nature in the
sense of the outside world but this nature is valueless and consists of
meaningless data. One cannot live according to nature because nature
dictates no course of action. To Nietzsche nature is a problem, but he
cannot do without some concept of nature and a natural principle of
ruling and being ruled which would guarantee hierarchy.

The gravest question of the limits of the will to power concerns the
past. In principle everything can and must be willed, but can the past
be willed? Nietzsche's own project of the future is based, if only negatively, on the past. His project is the creation of the self, but the self is
also a creation of the past. Do not the passing of time and the past frustrate the will? Nietzsche thinks of previous philosophies as the will's
*reaction* to its own impotence before the passing of time, the revenge
of the will to power on time by the creation of fictitious eternal beings.
But his own philosophy is not negative but a liberation from the spirit
of revenge. It is to be a total affirmation, even of the past. The past
could only be willed and affirmed if it were shown to be also the future.
If there were an eternal return of all things, then the past would also
be the future. Nietzsche's doctrine of the eternal return asserts that all
things have already happened an infinite number of times before and
will happen an infinite number of times again, exactly as before. The
doctrine of the eternal return is a moral as well as a cosmological doctrine. If there is an eternal return, man will be aware of the awful gravity of all his actions, since they *will recur* an infinite number of times.
Furthermore, by willing the eternal return of all things, man wills and
affirms a future that will become his past; he can, so to speak, become
the cause of himself. Finally, the return of all things guarantees the
existence of low things and therefore of things which cannot be overcome by the will to power. By willing the eternal return the will
reaches its highest peak: it overcomes itself but survives in the total
affirmation of all things. Through the total affirmation of all things man
can cease to be man and become superman.

The superman is Nietzsche's project of man's future. He is meant
to be a fulfillment and a transcendence of the highest ideals of man
which have been previously conceived. He is part poet, part philosopher,
part saint. He is a poet because he is creative, but he is more than the
poets of today, whom Nietzsche criticizes for lying (they falsify the
meaningless given) and for failing to create new values but rather
acting as the servants of traditional morality. The superman will create
new values and in this respect will resemble the traditional philosopher,

but his creations will be self-conscious creations. Finally, the superman will resemble the saint because his soul will contain all the depth which Christianity has given to man. The superman will be Caesar with the soul of Christ. Ultimately the Christianity which Nietzsche curses plays a larger part in the noble future of man than does the classical antiquity he praises. Zarathustra is the most pious man who never believed in God.

The superman must be willed. There is no necessity for him to emerge; he is merely a possibility of the future, as is the last man. The total crisis means only that man can no longer be man; he must rise to the superhuman or sink to the subhuman.

The superman is Nietzsche's *free* project of man's future, but its roots in the past ideals of man which it transcends save the project from being arbitrary. The superman will recapture the innocence of the blond beast on an infinitely higher, post-Christian level. The superman represents the third metamorphosis of the spirit. The nihilistic lion who can only say "I will" and who destroys old values without being able to create new ones is replaced by the child who says "I am," who affirms all, and whose creativity resembles the innocence of a child at play.

The superman as a type cannot be fully described because he will be above all a true self. Every superman will be unique. One cannot describe the values by which he will live, because each superman will give his own law unto himself. One can, however, say he will be a man who suffers much and who creates much, and that he will be a man of infinite pride and infinite delicacy. For instance, he will not turn his cheek to his enemies, not because he is brutish, but because he does not want to shame his enemies. But the exact forms his delicacy and pride will assume are necessarily undetermined.

Nietzsche's concept of the superman is thus necessarily vague and ambiguous. It is not even certain whether the superman will be a ruler. Nietzsche does speak of the planetary rule of a new nobility, and the superman is Nietzsche's new idea of nobility. At other times he speaks of the coexistence of last men and supermen: last men will live in communities that resemble ant heaps and supermen will roam the earth, but the supermen will not rule the last men and will try to avoid having any contact with them.

Nor can Nietzsche recommend a way of political action which will make the possibility of the superman a reality. There is a strong strain of radical individualism in Nietzsche. He counsels men to become true selves. He advises men to seek solitude, to flee from public life, to reject established modes of conduct and thought. From this point of view it might be maintained that the superman represents an apolitical solution to the total crisis of modernity. Nietzsche's creative call to creativity accounts in part for the predominant interpretation of Nietzsche which sees in him a teacher of true individualism. Such an interpretation, however, fails to understand the serious political consequences of a suggested apolitical solution. There is an underside to Nietzsche's advocacy of radical individualism. He teaches men to abdicate their public responsibility, to despise the pettiness of day-to-day politics, and to abstain from the ordinary duties of the citizen. There is always the danger, even from his point of view, that the worst men and not the best men will listen to this advice. Even if only the best men were to heed the advice, there would be the danger of withdrawing from the political arena the men most needed in it.

The predominant interpretation of Nietzsche is compelled also to overlook another strain in Nietzsche's writing, a strain which is overtly political. Nietzsche foresees a time of apocalyptic politics. What is more, he sees a necessity for an apocalypse and welcomes it. He looks forward to a time of great wars which will be an important part of the great politics of the future. He speaks approvingly of the need for a eugenics program; he anticipates a time when whole sectors of the earth will be devoted to man's experimentation on man; and he is in favor of the merciless extinction of inferior people and races. Nietzsche thinks of nihilism as knocking on the door of Europe. In his hatred for the degradation of man which is the last man, he advises that the door be opened to nihilism.

Part of the significance of Nietzsche's political philosophy lies in the fact that it is an implicit critique of Marxism. Nietzsche never refers to either Marx or Engels, but he was familiar with various forms of nineteenth-century socialism. Furthermore, Nietzsche, like Marx, was influenced by Hegel. One may summarize the relationship of Marxism to Nietzsche's political philosophy as follows: the Marxist realm of freedom which is to be secured by the revolution is for Nietzsche the realm of the last man, the utter degradation of man. Nietzsche thought more philosophically, more profoundly, than Marx did about what was to follow the revolution.

If Marx is inseparably linked to the growth of communism, it must be admitted that Nietzsche is linked to the emergence of fascism in the twentieth century. The relation of fascism to Nietzsche recalls the relation of the French Revolution to Rousseau. The problem of Nietzsche's connection with fascism is unfortunately not resolved by claiming, as many interpreters of Nietzsche are prone to do, that Nietzsche was no fascist, that he was a violent critic of German nationalism, and that he would have loathed Hitler. These things are undoubtedly true, and uttering them shows the absurdity of a crude identification of Nietzsche's doctrines with Hitler's ravings. Nietzsche was a man with a noble vision of man's future. His own delicacy, integrity, and courage shine through his writing. He was also free of the crude racism which was to be an important element of fascism, and he had only contempt for political anti-Semitism. But the fact remains that in various ways Nietzsche influenced fascism. Fascism may have abused the words of Nietzsche, but his words are singularly easy to abuse. Nietzsche was an extremist, and no man was more gifted than he in making an extreme view seem appealing by presenting it with great audacity and eloquence. A man who counsels men to live dangerously must expect to have dangerous men like Mussolini heed his counsel; a man who teaches that a good war justifies any cause must expect to have this teaching, which is presented half in jest but only *half* in jest, to be abused. Nietzsche praises cruelty and condemns pity without reflecting sufficiently on whether man must really be advised to be more cruel than he is, or what the effect of such a view will be on cruel men. Nietzsche was not a racist, but his writings abound with reflections on race and the possibilities of a biological rejuvenation of man. Nietzsche not only fails to advocate or teach prudence and public responsibility; he slanders prudence and public responsibility. Finally, it must again be repeated that Nietzsche is the inventor of an atheism of the political right.

Any exposition of Nietzsche's political philosophy must not only reveal the deep ambiguities, but must point to the grave consequences, of that political philosophy. Neither the revelation of ambiguity, however, nor a demonstration of grave consequences constitutes a refutation. Even if one could prove Nietzsche to be in error, one might still ponder what Nietzsche himself wrote about Schopenhauer: ". . . the errors of great men are venerable because they are more fruitful than the truths of little men. . . ." [19]

# NOTES

1. The dedication appears in the first edition of the first volume of this work (Chemnitz: E. Schmeitzner, 1878). It does not appear in the English translation in *The Complete Works of Friedrich Nietzsche*, ed. Oscar Levy (Edinburgh and London: T. N. Foulis, 1910), vol. VI.

2. Trans. Adrian Collins (New York: The Liberal Arts Press, 1949).

3. *Ibid.*, pp. 3–4.
4. *Ibid.*, pp. 51–52.
5. *Ibid.*, p. 7.
6. *Ibid.*, p. 61.
7. *Ibid.*, pp. 65, 69, 73.
8. *Ibid.*, p. 41.
9. Levy, *op. cit.*, aphorism 2, pp. 14–15.
10. Aphorism 257; translation from *The Philosophy of Nietzsche* (New

York: Modern Library, 1927), p. 575. Reproduced by permission of George Allen & Unwin, Ltd.

11. *Ibid.*, Preface, p. 378.

12. *Ibid.*, aphorism 62, pp. 448–50.

13. See secs 2 and 3 of "Zarathustra's Prologue," *Thus Spoke Zarathustra,* in Walter Kaufmann, ed., *The Portable Nietzsche* (New York, 1954), pp. 122–26. Copyright 1954 by the Viking Press and reprinted by their permission.

14. *Ibid.*, p. 191.

15. *Ibid.*, pp. 137–40.

16. *The Portable Nietzsche*, pp. 546–47.

17. *Thus Spoke Zarathustra,* Prologue, sec. 5, in *The Portable Nietzsche,* pp. 128–31.

18. *Ibid.*, pp. 225–28.

19. *Ibid.*, p. 30.

## READINGS

A. Nietzsche, Friedrich. *The Use and Abuse of History.* New York: The Liberal Arts Press, 1949.

B. Nietzsche, Friedrich. *Beyond Good and Evil,* in *The Philosophy of Nietzsche.* New York: Modern Library, 1927. 5. "The Natural History of Morals," p. 473; 8. "Peoples and Countries," p. 548; 9. "What is Noble," p. 575.

# JOHN DEWEY

## 1859–1952

John Dewey has been widely recognized as the foremost American philosopher of democracy of the twentieth century. His guiding intention throughout an extraordinarily long and influential career may be summarized as the attempt to further the realization of democracy in every sphere of life. Accordingly, he sought an all-embracing conception of democracy, a comprehensive formulation which he opposed to the understanding of democracy held by all preceding philosophers. Prior political philosophy, he contended, had tended to restrict its attention to such narrowly political concerns as "the state" and the various institutions of government. Dewey's fundamental objective was rather the development of a democratic philosophy designed not merely to encompass the traditional concerns of politics, but, more importantly, to provide a democratic understanding of ethics, education, logic, esthetics, and the many other fields of thought and activity with which he was concerned. Every element of his work as a whole was affected decisively by his political intention.

Dewey's philosophy is politically programmatic, which is to say that it addresses itself to what it regards as the true end of philosophy, social progress, and it concentrates its attention on the contemporary state of things rather than on any supposedly eternal, fixed conditions. Thus Dewey's rejection of traditional political philosophy springs partly from his belief that it led to little more than a sterile "consideration of the logical relationship of various ideas to one another, and away from the facts of human activity,"[1] as if those logical or rational relations were self-sufficient and themselves important. His rejection of traditional political philosophy is also partly inspired by his conviction

746

that its approach and content, governed as they were by historical conditions that no longer existed, required to be modernized.

Nevertheless, Dewey consistently refused to join the ranks of those "positivists" who rejected philosophy as simply meaningless or who insisted that man cannot deal rationally with questions of "value," but only with matters of "fact." Dewey sought to achieve fresh meaning for philosophy by making it relevant to the solution of the most pressing problems of life. He sought this goal through a thoroughgoing *Reconstruction in Philosophy,* an objective expressed most clearly in his well-known work by that title and reiterated in one form or another in virtually all of his major writings. Dewey's democratic political teaching, the primary concern of this essay, must be understood as but one aspect of this reconstruction of philosophy in the interest of democracy. We must, therefore, concern ourselves initially with certain of the fundamental objectives of this reconstruction: (1) Dewey's attempt to make philosophic investigation relevant to the solution of contemporary social problems, (2) his development of "the method of intelligence" as the chief tool for the solution of these problems, and (3) his development of a political theory based on an evolutionary understanding of man and society, an understanding which is at the root of Dewey's concept of "growth" as the ultimate human good and true measure of social justice.

1. The beginning of Dewey's reconstruction in philosophy is his contention that the genuine "problems and subjectmatter of philosophy grow out of stresses and strains in the community life in which a given form of philosophy arises." [2] It follows, in Dewey's view, that the initial task of the genuine philosopher is the identification of the most fundamental and pressing problems of *his* society. Dewey has endeavored to do just this. The subject matter of Dewey's social philosophy is decisively shaped by the observation, forcefully expressed in *Human Nature and Conduct,* that "one class of the community" has consistently attempted "to secure *its* future at the expense of another class." [3] Class divisions are understood by Dewey as symptomatic of a deeper derangement in society, the derangement between production and consumption, which persistently leads to the undermining of sound human relationships. The fervor and scope of Dewey's indictment of this aspect of modern society can be appropriately conveyed only in his own words, when he writes that mere production has been

grossly and intensely attended to. Making things is frantically accelerated; and every mechanical device used to swell the senseless bulk. As a result most

workers find no replenishment, no renewal and growth of mind, no fulfillment in work. . . . The fatuity of severing production from consumption,
from present enriching of life, is made evident by economic crises, by periods
of unemployment alternating with periods of exercise, work or "over-produc-
tion." . . . Leisure is not the nourishment of mind in work, nor a recreation;
it is a feverish hurry for diversion, excitement, display, otherwise there is no
leisure except a sodden torpor. Fatigue due for some to monotony and for
others to overstrain in maintaining the pace is inevitable. Socially, the separation of production and consumption, means and ends, is the root of the most
profound division of classes. Those who fix the "ends" for production are in
control, those who engage in isolated productive activity are the subject-class.
But if the latter are oppressed the former are not truly free.[4]

One may better understand Dewey's criticism of contemporary,
capitalist society by contrasting it, as he himself frequently does, with
the Marxist critique. He credits Marxism for its attempts to address
itself to many of the dominant problems of modern capitalist society.
He notes also that, given the debased conditions of modern society, the
"materialistic conception of history" or "economic determinism" is of
considerable pertinence. Indeed, "we are in for some kind of socialism,
call it by whatever name we please, and no matter what it will be called
when it is realized. Economic determinism is now a fact, not a theory."[5]
While granting the usefulness of particular aspects of the socialist diagnosis of the ills of capitalism, Dewey nevertheless vigorously criticizes
the Marxist prescription for a cure. Marxism's most pernicious, as well
as most revealing, error he holds to be its promulgation of "the monstrous belief that class-struggle civil war is a means of social progress,
instead of a register of the barriers to its attainment."[6] In Dewey's view,
social progress must be achieved by application of "the method of intelligence," not through Marxism's reliance on increasing tension and
strife. What Dewey regards as the underlying reason for the failure of
Marxism, and of the other twentieth-century "isms" as well, becomes
clear through consideration of the second major objective of his reconstruction in philosophy, the development of "the method of intelligence" as the chief tool for the solution of social problems.

2. Mankind's failure to achieve social justice, while understandable in past ages, is now tragically unnecessary, according to Dewey.
An instrument is now available for the effective solution of the problems which have perennially plagued mankind. This instrument is "the
method of intelligence," or "scientific method," as Dewey frequently
terms it. It is defined in *Reconstruction in Philosophy* as but "a short-
hand designation for great and ever-growing methods of observation,
experiment and reflective reasoning," or again, as the threefold tech-

nique of observation of facts, construction of hypotheses, and testing of consequences.

Dewey gives chief credit for the discovery of scientific method to Francis Bacon, whom he describes as "the real founder of modern thought." The "method of intelligence," which Bacon sought to usher in, is distinguished in part from non-Baconian science by its resort to active *experimentation,* in contrast to the passive *contemplation* of nature. The traditional, contemplative approach is inadequate because "scientific principles and laws do not lie on the surface of nature. They are hidden, and must be wrested from nature by an active and elaborate technique of inquiry. . . ." Paraphrasing Bacon, Dewey contends that the true scientist "must force the apparent facts of nature into forms different to those in which they familiarly present themselves; and thus make them tell the truth about themselves, as torture may compel an unwilling witness to reveal what he has been concealing." [7] Through such *subjugation* of nature, mankind has "opened up marvelous possibilities in industry and commerce, and new social conditions conducive to invention, ingenuity, enterprise. . . ." [8] Accordingly, enormous advances have been made possible in the industrial, agricultural, and medical arts. A far happier and more abundant life has become possible for all mankind.

Why then, he is led to ask, have these seemingly boundless goods made possible by "the method of intelligence" remained largely unrealized? Why has the greater part of mankind fallen victim to new evils? How has it come to pass that the new science "has played its part in generating enslavement of men, women and children in factories. . . ." Why has it "maintained sordid slums . . . grinding poverty and luxurious wealth, brutal exploitation of nature and man in times of peace and high explosives and noxious gases in times of war"? [9]

Dewey believes that the cause for the tragic frustration of "the method of intelligence" can be traced to defects in the practice of politics. Obsolete and unjust political institutions whose origins antedate the development of Baconian science are found to have been chiefly responsible for the abortion of the benefits promised by the conquest of nature. Archaic social institutions unsuited to an epoch of scientific technology and production have persisted, a phenomenon which Dewey summarizes by the term "cultural lag." He concludes that "the new industrialism was largely the old feudalism, living in a bank instead of a castle and brandishing the check of credit instead of the sword." [10] These outmoded institutions are perpetuated and controlled by the manifestly unjust rulers of mankind: kings, aristocrats, the "possessing and acquisitive" classes of modern society, who have consistently misappropriated the benefits of science for "pecuniary ends to the profit of a few." That is, the benefits of science largely serve the interests of "a possessing and acquisitive class," whereas a *democratic* dissemination of the benefits of science "would signify that science was absorbed and distributed." [11] In short, it is only within a genuinely democratic social order that the benefits promised by the Baconian understanding of science can be effectively applied to " 'the relief of man's estate.' " [12]

Realization of the benefits of the new science requires democracy, but the requisite development of democracy depends, in turn, on application of "the method of intelligence" to social problems, on its application to human relations—political, economic, and moral. Dewey's plea for such application of scientific method is reiterated through his entire work. He is convinced that the acknowledged triumph of the natural sciences in the physical realm can and must be extended to every sphere of human existence. This hope is strongly expressed in his 1946 introduction to *The Public and its Problems:*

science bears exactly the same relation to the progress of culture as do the affairs acknowledged to be technological (like the state of invention in the case, say, of tools and machinery, or the progress reached in the arts, say, the medical) .... a considerable part of the remediable evils of present life are due to the state of imbalance of scientific method with respect to its application to physical facts on one side and to specifically human facts on the other side; ... the most direct and effective way out of these evils is steady and systematic effort to develop that effective intelligence named scientific method in the case of human transactions.[13]

There are, then, according to Dewey, no insuperable difficulties involved in applying to "human and moral" problems the method "by which understanding of physical nature has been brought to its present pitch." [14] The scientific method of observation, hypothesis construction, and evaluation of consequences is applicable to the social as well as the natural sciences. Dewey does, however, take note of a complicating factor in the application of scientific method to the solution of social problems. His point, simply put, is this. The evaluation or testing of consequences in the natural sciences is facilitated by the existence of general agreement regarding objectives. For example, there is usually little disagreement about at least the immediate goals "of invention in the case ... of tools and machinery," [15] or in the medical art. Consensus as to the goals facilitates the measurement and thus the evaluation of the consequences of introducing newly invented tools or machines. A similar argument may be made as regards the medical art, the agreed purpose of which is the maintenance or restoration of health. Consider, for example, a number of medical scientists engaged in cancer research in a large clinic. Observation of the same patients, analysis of roughly the same data, may give rise to diverse hypotheses regarding the nature and treatment of cancer. Yet the testing of the consequences of these various hypotheses presents no insuperable difficulty since there is consensus on the goals of research, namely, prevention of cancer or reduction of its incidence and ravages.

Dewey acknowledges that testing consequences proves to be considerably more difficult when one attempts to apply "the method of intelligence" to human relations, to political, economic, and moral problems, because consensus for judging consequences is notably lacking in these spheres. As he grants, "every serious political dispute turns upon the question whether a given political act is socially beneficial or harmful." [16] We are therefore forced to consider the question of how the application of scientific method to human concerns can overcome the difficulty which results from the fact that parties to human disputes have sharply divergent opinions as to what *is* socially beneficial or harmful. An example suggested by Dewey may illuminate this problem. Suppose that in a hitherto "unorganized" steel mill certain workers initiate measures to form a labor union. Their action may be motivated by certain evident facts on which there is no disagreement, *e.g.,* wage rates, hours of work, lack of worker participation in controlling conditions of labor. The very facts which lead workers to the hypothesis that union organization will prove beneficial often lead management to the opposed hypothesis. How then will application of "the method of intelligence" assist management and workers in resolving this disagreement?

Dewey's answer appears to take the following form. He calls, first of all, for a detailed statement of the specific consequences which would ensue from unionization, as well as those consequences which would follow from maintenance of the *status quo.* Unquestionably, strikingly different consequences would stem from the failure or the success of the union movement. In the event of success, there would probably be general increases in wages, changes in hours and other conditions of labor, and some reduction in the autonomy of management. In similar fashion, the consequences associated with maintenance of the *status quo* could be traced out at considerable length and in great detail. The next step required by "the method of intelligence," Dewey says, is to contrast and evaluate these differing consequences. Still, it is at precisely this point that the crucial difficulty in applying "the method of intelligence" again presents itself. Would not workers and management insist on applying different standards in evaluating consequences? Would not this disagreement, in turn, stem from sharply divergent understandings of what will contribute to their well-being or self-interest? Not necessarily, Dewey contends. Genuine application of "the method of intelligence" makes possible the evaluation of consequences by a standard which transcends the selfish interests or limited perspectives of such disputants. This higher standard he terms "growth."

The meaning of "growth" and its place in Dewey's political teaching can be understood only through consideration of his evolutionary understanding of man and society, the last aspect of his reconstruction in philosophy with which we must be concerned.

3. It was Charles Darwin who "freed the new logic" which had produced such revolutionary effects in the natural sciences "for application to mind and morals and life." [17] In an essay entitled *The Influence of Darwin on Philosophy* Dewey delineates the consequences of his understanding of evolution for his social philosophy, thereby further distinguishing it from traditional political philosophy. The latter is understood by Dewey to have been engaged in a misguided search for "fixed species and essences" within "a closed world"—a world consisting "of a limited number of fixed forms." Following Darwin, Dewey decries the notion of fixed species, especially in its application to "the nature of man." Such an understanding, he argues, reduces human life to "the monotonous traversing of a previously plotted cycle of change," a principle and prospect as little challenging as that "in virtue of which the acorn becomes the oak." [18] In opposition to this drab vision of traditional philosophy, Dewey offers the bright promise of an evolutionary understanding of human potentialities, a view which presents boundless possibilities for development, for "novel and radical deviation." From an evolutionary perspective, "change becomes significant of new possibilities and ends to be attained; it becomes prophetic of a better future." [19] Change should be "associated with progress" rather than with lapse and decline, the position he ascribes to traditional political philosophy.

Dewey further argues that general acceptance of the evolutionary perspective has been impeded by yet another of the deficiencies of traditional philosophy, its postulation of a rigid hierarchy of "fixed ends." While Dewey grants that the ethical standards that exist side by side with those ends may have been compatible with a static conception of social justice and human nature, an evolutionary understanding of man demands that they be replaced by a standard of the human good which provides for progressive change. This standard he terms "growth."

The concept of "growth" provides Dewey with a criterion of the good which is universal and at the same time compatible with an evolutionary understanding of man and society. It permits Dewey to reject the alleged absolutism and inflexibility of traditional philosophy without embracing that radical relativism which points to nihilism. Human "growth" is understood by Dewey as the progressive realization of human possibilities produced by a complex interaction between "habit" and "impulse," a formulation which he develops exhaustively in *Human Nature and Conduct,* his treatise on social psychology. The crux of his teaching on this point is that "the direction of native activity depends upon acquired habits, and yet acquired habits can be modified only by redirection of impulses." [20] Since the content of neither "habit" nor "impulse" is understood by Dewey to be determined by the fixed "nature of man," the outcome of this interaction may produce infinite human variation. Whatever the substantive content of the "habits" or "impulses," Dewey asks only that the outcome of their interaction produce "growth"—hence "growth itself is the only moral 'end.' " [21] Since Dewey eschews any substantive definitions of "growth," the standard remains always formal, thus providing a relativistic understanding of human development within a universalistic framework. For example, "growth" is said to signify the realization of an organism's full potential, the "full release," as Dewey frequently terms it, of its latent capacities. Indeed, "reality *is* the growth-process itself .... real existence is the history in its entirety." [22] With respect to man, Dewey calls for "all-around growth," by which he explains that he means "growth, or growing as developing, not only physically but intellectually and morally" as well.[23] The scope and significance of this standard is well summarized in *Reconstruction in Philosophy,* where Dewey concludes that

government, business, art, religion, all social institutions have a meaning, a purpose. That purpose is to set free and to develop the capacities of human individuals without respect to race, sex, class or economic status. . . . Democracy has many meanings, but if it has a moral meaning, it is found in resolving that the supreme test of all political institutions and industrial arrangements shall be the contribution they make to the all-around growth of every member of society.[24]

"Growth" serves as the capstone of Dewey's reconstruction in philosophy. As such, it subsumes and makes more intelligible the other aspects of this reconstruction. Thus, it is the concept of "growth" which guides philosophic investigation to those contemporary problems that require solution, for it is precisely "growth"-retarding "stresses and strains" in community life which must be eliminated through application of "the method of intelligence." Since the sweeping social reconstruction required for the sake of "growth" must be carried out to a certain extent through political means, Dewey has concerned himself primarily with those aspects of political theory which appear to bear on this objective.

Dewey's democratic political theory may, for present purposes, best be considered under two headings. In his terms, they are: (1) a modified pluralistic conception of society, and (2) the "indirect consequence" test for defining the legitimate scope of state authority.

1. *The Public and its Problems* emphasizes that human "growth" takes place primarily within associations. Man's very existence depends on associated activity, inasmuch as "each human being is born an infant. . . . immature, helpless, dependent upon the activities of others. That many of these dependent beings survive is proof that others in some measure look out for them. . . ." Human beings are associated, then, in virtue of their very structure. "They are made that way; it is 'the nature of the beast.' " [25]

Among the many associations contributing to human "growth," Dewey takes special note of the family, clan, and neighborhood, as well as schools, trade unions, business and industrial corporations, and a variety of groups and clubs designed for scientific, artistic, and athletic pursuits. These associations may be divided into two categories for purposes of investigation.

The first category includes those groupings which are characterized by relatively permanent, "face to face relationships": the family, clan, neighborhood, and even the small village. These groupings "have always been the chief agencies of nurture," or "growth," since "there is something deep within human nature itself which pulls toward settled relationships." Such "vital, steady, and deep" ties can be developed "only in an immediate community." It is here that the basic, human "dispositions are stably formed" and ideas acquired which form the very "roots of character." Dewey is led to conclude that "the local is the ultimate universal, and as near an absolute as exists." [26] It is important to note that Dewey initially excludes these immediate associations from the realm of political concerns since the "face to face relationships, have consequences which generate a community of interests, a sharing of values, too direct and vital to occasion a need for political organization." [27] Informally established customs and special measures improvised to meet emergencies as they arise are said to suffice for such regulation as may be needed within the "local community."

Those groupings which transcend the local community give rise to the need for political regulation for two reasons. First, certain associations may find themselves working at cross-purposes or locked in conflict, as in the case of the labor-management dispute cited previously. Such conflicts abound, in one form or another, in all complex societies: school and church dispute their respective spheres of influence; organizations intent on securing equal treatment for downtrodden minorities are opposed by associations seeking to preserve the *status quo*. Such conflicts lead frequently to civil strife, and, in any event, they consume energy and resources which might otherwise contribute to the "growth" of the members of the associations involved. "The method of intelligence," we will recall, demands the peaceful resolution of conflict, a "reordering," as Dewey says, of the contending associations for the common good. Since "this supervision and regulation cannot be effected by the primary groupings themselves," [28] a special agency must be created for this purpose. This agency Dewey terms the "state." Thus understood, the state is a "secondary" form of association chiefly empowered to facilitate the smooth and effective functioning of all other associations. Dewey compares this function of the state with that "of the conductor of an orchestra, who makes no music himself but who harmonizes the activities of those who in producing it are doing the things intrinsically worthwhile." [29]

It is in the necessity for harmonizing the relations of other associations that Dewey has found the initial justification for the state. He grants that the figure of the orchestra conductor "has obvious points of contact with what is known as the pluralistic conception of the state," and he finds much to recommend that position. Pluralism appears to provide a safeguard against the "totalitarianism" allegedly inherent in the dominant formulations of traditional political philosophy which are said to permit "the monopolistic absorption of all associations into The State . . . of all social values into political value." The strict pluralistic conception, by contrast, permits the state to act only "to fix conditions under which *any* form of association operates . . ." thus preventing the glorification of the state and magnification of its power. For that matter it often happens "that the state, instead of being all absorbing and inclusive, is under some circumstances the most idle and empty of social arrangements." [30] The locus of "growth" continues to be found in other associations, and this is as it should be, he concludes.

Although pluralism provides the foundations for Dewey's formal political theory, he nevertheless finds conventional pluralistic theory insufficient. Strict pluralism limits political action "to settling conflicts among other groups," thereby tending to restrict the state to the role of a mere umpire. Dewey is anxious to retain this aspect of the theory as a safeguard against totalitarianism; at the same time, he has an extremely important and interesting reason for wanting to go beyond strict plural-istic theory. He is determined to transcend the umpire conception of the state in order to realize the *positive* contribution which the state may make in fostering "growth." This potential contribution of the state is unduly restricted, Dewey argues, if the state may do no more than fix the rules "under which *any* form of association" operates. To be sure, there would be no difficulty if, in fact, all associations contrib-uted to "growth," but Dewey acknowledges that such is not always the case. The state must therefore be empowered to evaluate, even to look behind the avowed objectives of associations in order to determine their real intent, the factual consequences of their operation, and to under-take appropriate action.

Dewey illustrates this aspect of his theory in *Democracy and Edu-cation,* where he discusses certain characteristics of some of the less desirable associations found in society. There are, unfortunately, associa-tions of "men banded together in a criminal conspiracy, business aggre-gations that prey upon the public while serving it, political machines held together by the interest of plunder. . . ." [31] Now, the problem posed by the criminal conspiracy may indeed be adequately met by conven-tional pluralistic theory, for it may be argued that upon the perpetration of crime, the criminal association violates agreed conditions or breaks "rules of the game." The "umpire-state" may accordingly suppress such criminal activities and the associations from which they stem.

On the other hand, those "business aggregations that prey upon the public while serving it," and "political machines" intent on selfish gain present conventional pluralistic theory with a more serious diffi-culty. As long as the activities of such businessmen and politicians re-main within the framework of the law, the "umpire-state" has no legiti-mate grounds for interference with their operations. Yet these are the very associations which, in Dewey's view, require the most thorough-going, even radical, reconstruction. We may recall his reiterated casti-gation of the disastrous effects on men of the malpractices of modern capitalistic industrial enterprises. It is pertinent also to take note of his further contention that these destructive practices are sustained and abetted by the "machine politicians," the "bosses," as he often terms them, who have formed an alliance with business interests. Together, they dominate contemporary public life and misdirect the activities of the state. Characterizing this relationship in *The Public and its Prob-lems,* Dewey finds that "the forms of associated action characteristic of the present economic order are so massive and extensive that they deter-mine the most significant constituents of the public and the residence of power." Furthermore, they inevitably "reach out to grasp the agencies of government; they are controlling factors in legislation and administration." Dewey is unwilling to permit the tenets of conventional pluralistic theory, which provide for only the "umpire" function of the state, to stand in the way of the reformation of the rapacious business associations and political machines, for they seriously interfere with the "growth" of the multitude of ordinary citizens. "Growth," the universal nurturing of "growth," is always Dewey's ultimate standard for political action. He therefore insists that the state must not confine itself simply to fixing the conditions "under which *all* associations" may operate. The good state, therefore

renders the desirable associations solider and more coherent; indirectly it clarifies their aims and purges their activities. It places a discount upon injurious groupings and renders their tenure of life precarious. In performing these services, it gives the individual members of valued associations greater liberty and security. It relieves them of hampering conditions which if they had to cope with personally would absorb their energies in mere negative struggle against evils.[32]

Dewey provides two standards by which the state may determine whether the activities of a particular association should be fostered or discouraged. They are precisely summarized in *Democracy and Education* as follows: "How numerous and varied are the interests which are consciously shared? How full and free is the interplay with other forms of association?" Dewey clarifies these standards by applying them to such destructive associations as the criminal band, the rapacious corporation, the self-seeking political machine. Each of these associations he finds restrictive of "growth" in that the ties which bind its members are few. This is most apparent in the case of the criminal band, membership in which is based on "a common interest in plunder." By the same token, the tie that binds entrepreneurs in a rapacious business aggregation is limited chiefly to an interest in pecuniary profit. It is the narrow quest for "spoils," rather than a broad concern with the common good which characterizes membership in a political machine. It follows that participation in such associations tends to isolate its members "from other groups with respect to give and take of the values of life." [33] By contrast, Dewey speaks glowingly of the possibilities of "growth" which stem from membership in associations devoted to scientific and artistic pursuits, education, social service, and the like.

The full measure and meaning of democracy cannot be realized, Dewey adds, until a second qualification is made to conventional pluralistic theory and practice. The material conditions of life have generally been such as to handicap severely the "growth" of a substantial part of the citizenry, even in a country as rich as the United States. Concentrated economic power "has consistently and persistently denied effective freedom to the economically underpowered and underprivileged," [34] thereby depriving many of an opportunity for sound development. Such deprivations, as Dewey argues in *The Public and its Problems,* tend to perpetuate themselves, since the "underprivileged" have often been unable to provide their children with adequate education and the other essentials for full "growth." When such primary associations as the family are unable to provide adequate conditions for "growth," the state must accept the responsibility. Thus Dewey welcomes the "steady tendency for the education of children to be regarded as properly a state charge in spite of the fact that children are primarily the care of a family." The cooperation of the state in such matters is indispensable, since "the period in which education is possible to an effective degree is that of childhood; if this time is not taken advantage of the consequences are irreparable. The neglect can rarely be made up later." Of course, "those who are not parents are taxed" to make possible sound education for all, since it is the responsibility of the state to provide sound conditions for the maximum "growth" of everyone, regardless of economic or other handicaps.

The principle underlying this argument is elucidated by Dewey's further contention that "other dependents (such as the insane, the permanently helpless) are peculiarly" the wards of the state, for "when the parties involved in any transaction are unequal in status, the relationship is likely to be one-sided, and the interests of one party to suffer. If the consequences appear serious, especially if they seem to be irretrievable, the public brings to bear a weight that will equalize conditions." [35] The full application of this principle would obviously require extensive taxation of the wealthy in order to equalize opportunities for all citizens. It would also result in an increase in the power and complexity of state machinery as administrative agencies were created to collect such taxes and to carry out or supervise state-supported programs. The human wants and needs which require something like the democratic welfare state for their satisfaction are not to be denied by the limitations of conventional pluralistic theory, so far as Dewey is concerned.

It is in the light of this conclusion that one may better understand Dewey's insistence that the precise size and character of the state cannot be determined in any universal or a priori fashion, but must be discovered anew within the context of particular circumstances through application of "the method of intelligence." The standard for guidance must be the empirical determination of which consequences of private activity are sufficiently "serious" or "irretrievable" to warrant political intervention. This argument points to two further questions: Who, precisely, is to make this determination, and What are the criteria by which it may be determined whether the activities of a given association are conducive to sound "growth" and thereby to be fostered—or the opposite? The very great breadth, if not to say vagueness, of such criteria as "growth" or "seriousness" makes all the more relevant the question of who is to define and apply them. These questions assume even greater significance when one considers the fact that Dewey's progressive modification of pluralistic theory has extended the sphere of legitimate state activities even to those "face to face" associations which were initially said to lie outside of the political realm. In order to provide compulsory public education, protect the weak and dependent, and equalize opportunities for the "growth" of all, political authority would necessarily intrude into the affairs of even "the family, clan, neighborhood." It would seem that if such pervasive political authority were to fall into unjust hands, the threat would arise of that very "totalitarianism" which Dewey is so intent on avoiding. Dewey's awareness of this threat leads to his formulation of the "indirect-consequence" test of the legitimacy of any exercise of state authority. The test is the second major element of his formal political theory which must be considered.

2. The application of Dewey's "indirect-consequence" test may be most easily understood through an illustration. Suppose that the workers in a steel mill are attempting to organize a union. At its inception, the union movement may be limited to a few workers, who might utilize a portion of their lunch hour to "talk shop," *i.e.,* to discuss the problems which they encounter in their work. Such discussions, even if regularized, are characterized by Dewey as "private" according to the rule that an action is private so long as its consequences "are confined, or are thought to be confined, mainly to the persons directly engaged in it. . . ." [36] As such, the discussions are of no concern to the state and may suffer no interference.

Suppose, however, that the participants in these initially private discussions decide to form a union and then take action to implement their decision. In order to achieve their goal they may bring other workers into their meetings, outside organizers may be introduced into the plant to help the cause, a strike may be precipitated in order to force recognition of the union. Should the union movement succeed, there will be extensive indirect consequences that will affect the lives of many. Increases in the cost of steel may have important effects on the operation of associated industries, rising labor costs may induce management to introduce automatic equipment, an action which would give rise to further, indirect consequences. The ramifications of all these consequences will, in one form or another, finally reach the consumers, the buying public.

Those who are seriously affected by such indirect consequences form a "public," as Dewey defines it. The "public's" welfare requires that such indirect consequences be controlled. It is for this purpose that the members of the "public" must select representatives who, in turn, will exercise political power. Dewey is little interested in the institutional details of the state. He contends that "the only statement which can be made is a purely formal one: the state is the organization of the public effected through officials for the protection of the interests shared by its members." [37]

It is apparent to Dewey that the complex, industrial society of the twentieth century gives rise to many such "publics," "for conjoint actions which have indirect, serious and enduring consequences are multitudinous beyond comparison, and each one of them crosses the others and generates its own group of persons especially affected. . . ." Given this diversity of "publics" with overlapping membership, Dewey is necessarily led to wonder whether there is any way in which "these different publics [can be brought] together in an integrated whole." [38] This question is of fundamental importance, since the terms of Dewey's theory authorize the members of each "public" to elect representatives to deal with the indirect consequences generated by particular private activities, as in the example above. This would appear to require the election of an enormous number of representatives, or the devising of a system by which one individual would be elected to represent many "publics."

Dewey does not, unfortunately, develop his doctrine of representation much beyond this point. Such further guidance as he provides is largely negative, as, for example, his argument against the idea of functional representation on the grounds that such a system affords political expression to interest groups rather than to those affected by their operation. Dewey is insistent that "political democracy" requires some system of representation, but he willingly leaves to others the task of working out the institutional forms and details of his political teaching. He does so for two reasons. First of all, he argues that political institutions must be subject to constant modification in order to give prompt expression to the endlessly changing conditions of associated life. Consequently, any attempt to fix their shape would prove to be dangerously restrictive. Second and far more fundamental is Dewey's view that it is the character of the citizen body which is virtually all-important for the achievement of the good polity. Throughout his political writings, Dewey deliberately minimizes the importance of institutional and constitutional arrangements. He thereby places almost full dependence for the achievement of the good, democratic regime upon the existence of an educated, enlightened, public-spirited, and active citizenry. Such a citizenry, he proclaims throughout his work, could bring into being a new era in democratic living, an era which, for the first time in human history, would make possible the realization of the rich and abundant potentialities of life.

A citizenry which, by contrast, is predominantly ignorant, selfish, and apathetic promises a different outcome. Dewey's "indirect-consequence" test of the limits of state authority, as well as his theory of association, have been seen to place in the hands of the "publics" and their representatives complete responsibility for determining the limits of political power and its mode of implementation. It is they who must determine whether indirect consequences are sufficiently "serious" or "extensive" to warrant political control. The misunderstanding or misapplication of such standards by "publics" swayed by passion or misguided by demagogues might obliterate the sphere of the private. Tyranny of the majority presents itself as a distinct possibility.

The only sound protection against misgovernment now and in the future lies in the development of a citizenry which is fully democratic in every respect. One of the most important instruments for producing democratic men, Dewey has consistently argued from virtually the beginning of his work, is a school system designed for the purpose. In the schools, the future citizens must be so formed that the society they will create as adults will be somewhat better than their parents' society, and each generation in its turn will repeat the process, thus engendering endless "growth." The task of the schools therefore is not simply to link the minds of the generations but to form "personalities" by the organization or method as well as by the content of instruction, and so doing to prepare and safeguard the progress of the society.

What democracy requires is men whose natures have been so democratized that they can tolerate, not to say benefit from democracy, as purified of the institutions that now contaminate it. Uncooperative men would threaten the democracy of Dewey's dream, as would men inclined to grasp coldly for wealth or power and men who do not wish to grow in every direction. Therefore, in their impressionable years children should be conditioned by life in their classrooms to strive without "competing," to study and work cooperatively in groups, and to acquire the expansive habits of self-expression that will fit them for life in ever more perfect democracy. It is well-known that the influence of Dewey upon the theory of education has been considerable.

Dewey's efforts in the field of education were consistent with his belief that all theory should be brought into the service of democracy and that all aspects of life must be democratized in practice if democracy is to be secure and progressive. From the latter it might be thought that Dewey had recurred to the traditional view of a comprehensive political order, the all-embracing political community in which there were no institutionalized strongholds of resistance against the legitimate ruling principle, but every citizen's life was guided by the laws toward the good. How far this was from being in fact Dewey's position may be seen by recalling his own judgments on traditional political philosophy. He denied the existence of a fixed, substantive good for man and asserted instead that the good is a process of "growth" and change. Moreover, he did not conceive the community as primarily political, *i.e.,* a unity determined in the fundamental respects by the "constitution." He believed rather that the influence of psychological and economic factors was decisive in forming the dispositions and thus the behavior of men. The measure of Dewey's depreciation of the political is his refusal to treat democracy as primarily a form of government; instead it is a way of life, and political or legal democracy is more in the nature of an effect, though a very important effect, than a cause of psychological and economic democratization.

Political democracy, then, stands firm only as it rests on foundations secured through a democratic reconstruction in philosophy and in every aspect of life. Dewey's awareness of the enormousness of this task was relieved by his unquestioning faith in the capacity of men everywhere to achieve the "growth" which is the indispensable concomitant of democracy. Always hopeful, he did not permit the calamities of the twentieth century to destroy his sanguine expectations for the future of mankind. His work rests always on the assurance that with the progress of the democratic reconstruction for which he calls,

we have every reason to think that whatever changes may take place in existing democratic machinery, they will be of a sort to make the interest of the public a more supreme guide and criterion of governmental activity, and to enable the public to form and manifest its purposes still more authoritatively. In this sense the cure for the ailments of democracy is more democracy.[39]

## NOTES

1. John Dewey, *The Public and its Problems* (Chicago: Gateway Books, 1946), p. 9. Reprinted by permission of Holt, Rinehart and Winston, copyright 1927 by John Dewey. This work was originally published by Henry Holt and

Company in 1927. The 1946 edition, to which exclusive reference is made in this essay, is distinguished by an extensive, new introduction of considerable importance.

2. John Dewey, *Reconstruction in Philosophy* (New York: New American Library, 1950), p. 8. Reprinted by permission of the Beacon Press, copyright 1958 by Beacon Press. This work was originally published by Henry Holt and Company in 1920. An enlarged edition was published in 1948 by Beacon Press, with an important, new introduction written by Dewey. References in this chapter are to the New American Library (Mentor) edition of 1950.

3. John Dewey, *Human Nature and Conduct* (New York: Henry Holt and Company, 1944), p. 270. Reprinted by permission of Holt, Rinehart and Winston, copyright by Henry Holt and Company. No important changes appear to have been made in this work since it was published initially in 1921. References in this essay are taken from the paperback edition of 1944.

4. *Ibid.*, pp. 271–72.

5. John Dewey, *Individualism Old and New* (New York: Minton, Balch and Company, 1930), p. 119.

6. *Human Nature and Conduct*, p. 273.

7. *Reconstruction in Philosophy*, pp. 10, 46, 48.

8. *Human Nature and Conduct*, pp. 212–13.

9. *The Public and its Problems*, p. 175.

10. *Human Nature and Conduct*, p. 213.

11. *The Public and its Problems*, p. 174.

12. *Reconstruction in Philosophy*, p. 52.

13. *The Public and its Problems*, p. x.

14. *Reconstruction in Philosophy*, p. 10.

15. *The Public and its Problems*, p. x.

16. *Ibid.*, p. 15.

17. John Dewey, *The Influence of Darwin on Philosophy* (New York: Henry Holt and Company, 1910), pp. 8–9.

18. *Reconstruction in Philosophy*, pp. 62, 65.

19. *Ibid.*, p. 102; cf. *Human Nature and Conduct*, p. 284.

20. *Human Nature and Conduct*, p. 126.

21. *Reconstruction in Philosophy*, p. 141.

22. *Experience and Nature* (Urbana, Ill.: The Open Court Publishing Company, 1925), p. 275.

23. John Dewey, *Experience and Education* (New York: The Macmillan Company, 1938), p. 28.

24. *Reconstruction in Philosophy*, p. 147.

25. *The Public and its Problems*, pp. 24, 11.

26. *Ibid.*, pp. 211, 213, 214, 211, 215.

27. *Ibid.*, p. 39.

28. *Ibid.*, p. 27.

29. *Reconstruction in Philosophy*, pp. 158–59.

30. *The Public and its Problems*, pp. 73, 72, 28.

31. John Dewey, *Democracy and Education* (New York: The Macmillan Company, 1916), p. 95.

32. *The Public and its Problems*, pp. 107, 71–72.

33. *Democracy and Education*, p. 96.

34. "Authority and Social Change," printed in the Harvard tercentenary publication *Authority and the Individual* (1937), p. 178, and more readily available in *Intelligence and the Modern World, John Dewey's Philosophy*, ed. J. Ratner (New York: Modern Library, 1939), pp. 351–52.

35. *The Public and its Problems*, pp. 63, 62.

36. *Ibid.*, p. 12.

37. *Ibid.*, p. 33.

38. *Ibid.*, p. 137.

39. *Ibid.*, p. 146.

## READINGS

A.  Dewey, John. *The Public and Its Problems.* Chicago: Gateway Books, 1946.
     Chap. i, pp. 3–36; chap. ii, pp. 37–74; chap. vi, pp. 208–19.
     Dewey, John. *Reconstruction in Philosophy.* New York: New American
     Library, 1950. Introduction, pp. 8–28.
B.  Dewey, John. *Human Nature and Conduct.* New York: Holt, 1944. Chap. iv,
     pp. 125–30; chap. vi, pp. 223–37.
     Dewey, John. *Experience and Education.* New York: Macmillan, 1938.
     Chap. iii, pp. 23–32.
     Dewey, John. *Liberalism and Social Action.* New York: Putnam, 1935. Pp.
     74–85.
     Dewey, John. *Democracy and Education.* New York: Macmillan, 1916.
     Chap. vii, pp. 94–102.

# INDEX

of interest, 702–3; Marx's critique of, 708–16; laws of nature of, 709; timeless status of institutions of, 710–11; as system of commodity production, 712; mode of production of, 713–16; and burden of technological change, 714–15

Captivity, 375

Carlstadt, Andreas, 301

Carlyle, Thomas, 310

Carneades, 143, 263, 245

Carthage, 92–93, 474, 475

Cartwright, Thomas, 315, 320

Catholicism: and failure of modern principles of freedom, 637

Catholics: toleration of, 301

"Catilinarian existences," 36

Catilinian conspiracy, 235

Cato, 140, 262–63

Cause and effect: Hume's discussion of, 493–96, 504

Cave, 31, 42, 43

Celestial law, 317

Censorship: as power of Hobbes's sovereign, 365

Chaldeans, 309

Chance: in Aristotle, 122; in Machiavelli, 267, 274; in Bacon, 338, 342 n. 19; in Spinoza, 414–15; in Montesquieu, 484; in Hume, 511; as gap between intent and effect of virtuous acts, 557

Change: as factor affecting all things, 705, 706

Charles I, king of England, 399

Checks and balances: under the Roman constitution, 139; Calvin's discussion of, 296; as feature of free government, 508–9; English system of, 540; Blackstone's mention of, 542; mentioned, 480, 582, 587, 588, 589, 608, 625

"Chemical method": of J. S. Mill, 680

Children of Israel, 194

China: Hegel's prediction for, 652

Christ, Jesus, 239, 241, 304, 316

Christian Aristotelians, 329

Christian morality: Nietzsche's discussion of, 735

Christian priesthood: Marsilius' view of, 227, 228, 230

Christian scholasticism: and development of Jewish philosophy, 182; influence on Abravanel, 194

Christian theology: of Hobbes, 374–77

Christianity: "world view" of, 151; philosophy of society, 151–52; conflict between spiritual and temporal governments, 230–31; Machiavelli's analysis of effects of, 259–61;

Spinoza's treatment of, 431; Montesquieu's criticism of, 489; principle of infinite worth of individual, 636; completion of Christianization of world, 651–52; Nietzsche's denunciation of, 731–32, 734–35; as metamorphosis of man's spirit, 735

Church: St. Augustine's concept of, 153, 155; effect on politics and political philosophy, 201–2, 221; intervention in civil affairs, 206–7; deposition of heretical rulers, 207–8; Marsilius' view of priesthood, 227–28; as oligarchy rather than aristocracy, 237; as realm without boundary, 259; universalist requirement of, 259–60; effect of rule on Italy, 261–62; Machiavelli's opposition to, 263–66; Bible as basis of authority of, 264–65; growth of temporal powers, 265–66; indulgence system, 279; "Invisible," 286; "Visible," 286–87; end of temporal powers, 567–68. See also Church and State

Church and State: Aquinas' view of, 201–8; Luther and Calvin's view of, 286–89; Hooker's discussion of, 320–21; Milton's desire to reform relations between, 406–7; necessity for separation of, 675

Church Fathers, 258, 316

Churchill, Sir Winston, 562

Church of England, 330

Cicero: the best regime, 136–43; mixed regime, 139–43; active versus contemplative life, 133–36, 148–49; on justice, 143–46, 147, 148; on natural law, 146, 147–48; definition of an organized people, 157; and law of nature, 347; on peace and war, 350; mentioned, 41, 160, 235, 290, 345, 354, 368, 372, 502

Cities: ancient and modern meanings of, 6; founding of in Plato's *Republic*, 16–19, 22–23; the healthy city, 17; the purified city, 17–19; unwillingness of philosophers to rule, 29–32; parallelism with soul, 35–36; impossibility of just city, 41; potential effect of skepticism on, 131–32

Citizens: defined by Aristotle, 96–97; virtues of good men and good citizens, 98–100; classes of in virtuous regime, 164–65; inalienable rights of, 365–66

Citizenship: defined by Aristotle, 96

City-state: in classical political philosophy, 5–6

Civil disobedience: justification for, 366; sinfulness of, 372–73

Civil government: Reformers' discussion of, 293–94; and new science of politics, 583, 584–85

Civil injuries: redress of, 538

231–32, 233–35, 238; Publius' view of, 580–81; proposed by U. S. Constitution, 583–91; ineptitude of, 586–87; oppression by majority, 583, 584–85, 589–90

Popular majorities: oppression by, 583, 584–85, 589–90

Popular sovereignty: Marsilius' statement and retraction of, 233–36, 238, 242; Lutheran and Calvinist view of, 286, 294, 296; as espoused by followers of Calvin, 315; Milton's view of, 399–400; Paine's belief in, 597; and increasing centralization of government, 666

Positive law: consent and possibility as intrinsic limits on, 208, 219–22; Aristotle's definition of, 219; Luther's contempt for, 306–7; and eternal law, 470; relations preceding, 471; and regulation of natural personal rights, 538; judge's duty to maintain, 543–44; as foundation of inequalities of Middle Ages, 677

Possibility and consent: as intrinsic limits on positive law, 208, 219–22; as elements of middle-class government, 216

Poverty: Paine's proposals for abolition of, 599

Power: transfer of in formation of political society, 453; limited nature of, 454

Power, will to, 738–40

Powers of government: Aristotle's analysis of, 479

Prejudice: as traditional wisdom of society, 603

Prescription in government: Burke's doctrine of, 597, 609–10, 611

President: veto and other powers, 586

Pride: as cause of quarrels among men, 357–58, 359, 361

Priesthood: Aristotle's teachings regarding, 228–30; Marsilius' rational concept of, 229–30; power of multitude to elect and remove from office, 232–33; sovereign as source of authority for, 375

Priest-morality, 731

Primitive man: Rousseau's investigation of, 518–19

Primitive society: Montesquieu's description of, 483

Princes: Machiavelli's models of, 268–70; God's judgments on, 309–10; in state of nature, 435; scope of discretion of, 459–60; loss of political power, 463–64; godlike, 464–65

Printing, licensing of: Milton's attack on, 397, 399

Probity: as form of virtue in modern society, 641

Probus, 351

Production: primacy of, 698; Marx's modes of, 699; means of, 699, 700, 701, 702, 708, 712, 713; rearrangement as condition for translation of human life, 704; ills resulting from severance from consumption, 747–48

Production, conditions of: effect on distribution of income and consumption of output, 700; dependence of theories on, 700–701

Professional honor: as form of virtue in modern society, 641, 642

Profit: Marx's explanation of, 709–10, 713

Progress: idea of, 394–95; as decadence, 736. See also Social progress

Proletarians: growth and triumph of, 708

Promises: invention of, 505–6

Property: Socrates' mention of abolition of, 9; Aristotle's view of, 84–85; inequality of as cause of civil disturbance, 85–86; defects in Spartan system of ownership, 91; stabilizing effect on polity, 215; Grotius' discussion of origin and types of, 351; acquisition in state of nature, 443–44, 453; Locke's discussion of, 443–52; origin of, 445–50; transfer by consent, 505; cause of formation of civil society, 520; as root of power in civil society, 532; divisions resulting from, 591; protection of, 592, 667–68; as cause of fragmentation and conflict among men, 703

Property, right of: origin of, 545; as absolute right of individuals, 537–38; universality of, 640; determination by conditions of production, 700

Prophecy: nature of, 169; in supreme ruler of virtuous regime, 172–73; of Moses and other Hebrew prophets, 185–86; Jewish view of, 187–92; definition of, 188; preconditions for, 188, 189; political function of, 190–91; Abravanel's view of, 194

Prophet: as highest kind of man, 188, 189; function of, 189–91, 193

Prophet-legislator: and philosopher-king, 166–70

Propriety: as ground of moral virtue, 551, 552, 556, 557

Protestantism: Hegel's view of, 636–37, 638

"Provisional morality," 329

Provisional political philosophy: of Bacon, 329–30

Prudence: Burke's meaning of, 605–6, 606–7

Prussia: introduction of rational principles, 638

Public morality: evolution from individual self-interest, 671–74

Public opinion: limits on, 634; Hegel's de-

Soderini, Piero, 271
Solomon, 193, 232, 265
Solomon's House: in Bacon's *New Atlantis,* 335ff.
Solon, 266, 334, 474
Sophocles, 19
Soul: proof of immortality of, 40–41; Descartes' view of, 388–89
Sovereign: distinction between sovereign and government, 231, 234; right to wield police power, 364; and legislative power, 364; and judicial power, 364–65; absolute power of, 365–67; pursuit of private advantage, 367–68; and social contract, 369, 524–25, 526; as supreme interpreter of law, 371; failure to claim sufficient power, 371–72; sinfulness of disobedience to, 372–73; duty to educate citizens, 373; as source of authority for priests and prophets, 375; determination of general interest, 422–23; indivisibility of, 526
Sovereignty: Marsilius' doctrine of human legislator, 231–32, 233–35; in church affairs, 321; and liberties of a subject, 368; Paine's view of, 597; locus in Hegel's state, 643–44
Sparta: defects of laws, 52–54, 127; destruction of, 55; as mixed regime, 57; use of property in common, 85; Aristotle's discussion of, 89–91; as Rousseau's model republic, 516, 525; mentioned, 59, 121, 351, 382, 474
"Speculation": Burke's denunciation of, 606
Speculative intellect: likeness to God, 202; and attainment of perfect happiness, 203–4
Spinoza, Benedict: defense of democracy, 413, 415, 417, 423–24, 429, 431; and Machiavelli, 413, 414, 415; definition of freedom, 414; scientific metaphysics, 414–15; and Hobbes, 415–16, 417; view of natural differences in men, 417; and Substance, 418; on religion, 420, 421, 427–28; on freedom of speech, 426–27; regulation of democracy, 429–30
Spiritedness, 21–22
"Spiritual use" of law, 304
Spoiling: as major limitation on property in state of nature, 446–48
State: concept of, 5–6; as species of contract, 66; St. Augustine's concept of, 153, 154–55; and cultivation of wisdom in citizens, 202–3, 206; Machiavelli's analysis of beginnings of, 266–71; as servant of God, 293–94; law of, 306–7; desire for self-preservation as basic principle of, 421; philosophy as end of, 423; withering away of, 529–30, 555, 708, 720; Hegel's rehabilitation of,

628–29, 634–35, 638; as fully developed totality, 630; as child of conflict, 630–32; function of reconciliation between master and slave, 632; as union of "subjective" and "objective" liberty, 632; as basis and goal of individual interest, 642; primacy over civil society, 649; J. S. Mill's view of end of, 685–87; as organ of class coercion, 703; Dewey's concept of, 755–56; umpire conception of, 755–56, 757; standards for regulation of associations, 757–59; responsibility for providing conditions for growth, 758; "indirect consequence" test for legitimacy of state authority, 759–61
State governments: and problems of factionalism, 581–82; and growth of legislative power, 585
State of nature: Hobbes's theory of, 356–63, 372, 415; transition to political society, 416, 443–52; rationalization by democratic regimes, 423–24; and wrongdoing, 428; differences in views of Hobbes and Locke, 434–35, 442; Locke's view of, 434, 436, 462; and state of war, 437, 438–39; acquisition of property in, 443–44; reasons for penury of, 445–46; limitations of property by spoiling, 446–48; and lack of cultivation of land, 448; invention of money, 448–49; difficulties in preservation of property, 453; natural powers of man in, 453–54; Montesquieu's description of, 483; Hume's opinion of, 504; and Rousseau's concept of man, 517–20, 533; and absolute rights of individuals, 537; state of civil society as, 604–5; man's original rights, 605–6, 609; Bentham's view of, 623; and relations between states, 650
States, association of: for establishment of perpetual peace, 649
*Statesman* (Plato), 42–51
Statesman: divine calling of, 308–9
Statesmanship: Plato's discussion of, 43, 44–45; concern with practical good, 606
Stevin, 394
Stoicism, 144–45, 145–46, 147, 345, 414, 416
Stoics, 2, 381, 382, 489, 490
Struggle for recognition: as beginning of states, 631
Suárez, Francisco, 344
Subjective consciousness: advent of in French Revolution, 633–34
Subjective freedom: progress to universality, 637
"Subjective liberty": Hegel's meaning of, 632, 635
Subjective mind: Hegel's concept of, 629
Subjective rights, 346